Reinventing Ourselves

Reinventing Ourselves

Interdisciplinary Education, Collaborative Learning, and Experimentation in Higher Education

Barbara Leigh Smith
John McCann

Editors

The Evergreen State College

Anker Publishing Company, Inc.
Bolton, Massachusetts

Reinventing Ourselves

Interdisciplinary Education, Collaborative Learning, and Experimentation in Higher Education

ISBN 1-882982-35-5

Composition by Keller & Keller *Designs in Print*
Cover design by Deerfoot Studios

Anker Publishing Company, Inc.
176 Ballville Road
P. O. Box 249
Bolton, MA 01740-0249

www.ankerpub.com

CONTENTS

ABOUT THE EDITORS

BARBARA LEIGH SMITH is Provost at The Evergreen State College. She founded the Washington Center for Improving the Quality of Undergraduate Education and has longstanding interests in learning communities, interdisciplinary education, collaborative learning, and institutional change. She thinks longevity matters in creating sustainable long-term change and has been at Evergreen since 1978.

JOHN MCCANN received his undergraduate and MPA degrees from The Evergreen State College and his PhD in US history from the University of Oregon. He taught for several years in the evening part-time studies at Evergreen, where he founded the half-time labor studies program. He has published a history of the machinists' union at the Boeing Company, and has been active in labor education in the Pacific Northwest. He currently works as Academic Grants Manager in the provost's office at Evergreen.

ACKNOWLEDGEMENTS

We gratefully acknowledge a grant from the American Council of Learned Societies (ACLS) and the John D. and Catherine T. MacArthur Foundation, which helped fund the 1997 Evergreen Conference on Interdisciplinary Education from which this book grew. We thank Doug Bennett (then vice president of ACLS, now president of Earlham College) and Maureen Grolnick (ACLS program officer for education) for their support and encouragement.

We thank our colleagues who contributed to this book. It was a great pleasure working with you. We learned a lot.

We are grateful to staff members at The Evergreen State College who helped us with the often complex logistics of producing this book. We especially thank Sandra Abrams, former administrative secretary to the provost, and Audrey Streeter, grants coordinator. We also thank Esmé Ryan for her work in helping us compile the index to this book.

Finally, we are grateful to the efficient and highly professional staff of Anker Publishing Company.

About the Contributors

Les K. Adler is Professor of History and Interdisciplinary Studies in the Hutchins School of Liberal Arts at Sonoma State University. A former provost of the Hutchins School, he is currently Director of the Hutchins Center for Interdisciplinary Learning. He received his PhD in American history from the University of California, Berkeley in 1970.

Charles W. Anderson is Professor Emeritus of Political Science and Integrated Liberal Studies at the University of Wisconsin, Madison. He is the author of many books, including *Pragmatic Liberalism* and *Prescribing the Life of the Mind.* He is currently writing and consulting in the area of liberal education reform.

Robert Benedetti is Dean of the College, University of the Pacific, in Stockton, California. He was 19 years at New College of the University of South Florida, the last six as provost. A political scientist by training, he has served as chair of both the Florida Endowment for the Humanities and the California Council for the Humanities. Currently, he is exploring issues of governance in higher education.

Gary L. Bornzin received his PhD in mathematical physics from the University of Colorado in 1972. From his background in systems modeling, his areas of interest and research evolved into determining means by which a graceful transition could be made to a more healthy, sustainable society. He is currently teaching at Fairhaven College, an interdisciplinary alternative college within Western Washington University in Bellingham, Washington. His courses include "Feminist Perspectives in Science," "Green Politics and Values," "Visioning Sustainable Futures," and "Bioregionalism, and Applied Human Ecology."

James R. Chen served as vice president for academic affairs at the State University of New York/Empire State College from 1996 to 1999. He is the past president of the SUNY-wide Faculty Senate and was professor of physics at SUNY/Geneseo. He has been active in setting policy directions for distance learning and interdisciplinary studies.

Steven R. Coleman received his BA from Goddard College, a Masters in Education from Antioch University, and a PhD from Colombia University.

Joseph J. Comprone is currently Associate Vice Chancellor and Campus Director at the University of Connecticut, Avery Point, where he oversees the development of interdisciplinary degree programs in maritime sciences and maritime studies. Interdisciplinarity has followed him throughout his career, first as a researcher, writer, and teacher within cross-disciplinary composition and rhetoric programs, and later as an administrator and program developer within an interdisciplinary arts and sciences program. Avery Point offers him the opportunity to work with colleagues in developing programs within a context free of departmental encumbrances.

Grant H. Cornwell is Associate Professor and Chair, Department of Philosophy, St. Lawrence University. He received his PhD in philosophy from the University of Chicago in 1989. In addition to articles exploring epistemological issues within postcolonial studies, multiculturalism, and critical pedagogy, in 1997 he published, with Richard Guarasci, *Democratic Education in an Age of Difference* (Jossey-Bass). Cornwell's most recent publications, coauthored with Eve Stoddard, include "Cosmopolitan or Mongrel? Reading *Creolité* and Hybridity via 'Douglarisation' in Trinidad," in the *European Journal of Cultural Studies*, and *Globalizing Knowledge: Connecting International and Intercultural Studies*, a monograph published as part of the Association of American Colleges and Universities' series *The Academy in Transition.* Cornwell and Stoddard are currently editing a volume of essays, *Cultural Cartographies: Comparative Studies in Global Multiculturalism,* and doing research for a book on the semiotics of sugar mill ruins in the Caribbean.

Magda Costantino, a native of the former Czechoslovakia (currently Slovakia), is the Director of the Evergreen Center for Educational Improvement at The Evergreen State College. The primary focus of her work is education reform in the state of Washington, particularly in the areas of curriculum integration, performance-based assessment, and educating diverse learners. She holds an MA in English and Spanish, MEd in Spanish, and PhD in curriculum and instruction.

Emily Decker is the Associate Director of the Washington Center for Improving Undergraduate Education, a public service center of The Evergreen State College. She helps to design and implement professional development workshops and conferences focusing on collaborative, pluralistic, and interdisciplinary learning. Her doctorate is in American literature from the University of Michigan.

Jeanine L. Elliott is Director of the Washington Center for Improving the Quality of Undergraduate Education at The Evergreen State College. The Washington Center, a consortium of 48 two-year and four-year colleges and universities in Washington state, focuses on learning communities, collaborative learning, cultural pluralism, academic success of students of color, reform calculus, interdisciplinary science, and technology on a human scale. Elliott's educational background includes an undergraduate degree in English literature from the University of Illinois, theological training at Chicago Theological Seminary and the University of Chicago, and a PhD from the Union Institute in women's studies and higher education.

Celestino Fernández has served as a professor and senior-level administrator at the University of Arizona since he completed his doctorate at Stanford University in 1976. He presently serves as Professor of Sociology, and he teaches and conducts research in the areas of popular culture, Mexican culture, and ethnicity in the United States. Until 1998, Dr. Fernández served in various administrative positions, including vice president for undergraduate education, vice president for academic outreach and international affairs, and executive vice president and provost of Arizona International College, a new liberal arts college he founded in Arizona.

Susan Fiksdal teaches linguistics and French at The Evergreen State College. A student of conversation analysis, her research focuses on cross-cultural interactions and seminar discussions in college settings. She has published a book, *The Right Time and Pace: A Microanalysis of Gatekeeping Interviews,* and several articles and book chapters.

Donald L. Finkel lived in Olympia, Washington for the past 23 years with his wife and four children and taught at The Evergreen State College. In addition to a number of articles, he published two books: *Teaching with Your Mouth Shut,* published by Heinemann Publishers in February 2000, and *Education for Freedom: The Paradox of Pedagogy* (1995) with William Ray Arney, published by Rutgers University Press. He was educated at both Yale University (AB Philosophy, 1965) and at Harvard University (PhD in Social Relations, 1970). His interests included music (jazz, classical, and opera), literature and reading, puzzles of all kinds, chess, poker, and spending time with his family. Don became ill with nonHodgkins lymphoma in the summer of 1998 and, after extensive treatments, died of the disease in September 1999.

Michael V. Fortunato earned his BA in economics from Columbia College of Columbia University, and his MA and PhD in economics from the Graduate School of Arts and Sciences of Harvard University. He has taught on the faculties of Williams College, Boston University, and the State University of New York/Empire State College, where, at the time of the writing of this paper, he was the director of a management education program. Dr. Fortunato, now a Visiting Professor of Economics at Williams College, has written extensively on the economics and strategies of corporations and the development of judgment and competence in managers and others.

Laura Gaither received her MA in American studies from the University of Maryland and her BA in history from the College of Wooster, Ohio. In 1994 she joined the administrative faculty at George Mason University, Virginia. From 1996-1999 she was the director of service-learning at the Center for Service and Leadership. She has served as a board member for the Virginia Campus Outreach Opportunity League (VA COOL) and has presented papers at regional and national conferences, including the National Society for Experiential Education (NSEE), American College Personnel Association (ACPA), and the Forum on Volunteerism, Service, and Learning in Higher Education. Currently she is combining her interest in sustainable "green" design and therapeutic design as a home consultant for Argonauta Interiors in Washington, DC.

Julie Thompson Klein is Professor of Humanities at Wayne State University. She is past president of the Association for Integrative Studies and former editor of *Issues in Integrative Studies.* Her major works include *Interdisciplinarity: History, Theory, and Practice* (Wayne State University Press, 1990), *Interdisciplinary Studies Today* (New Directions in Teaching and Learning, Jossey-Bass, 1994), *Crossing Boundries: Knowledge, Disciplinarities, and Interdisciplinarities* (University Press of Virginia, 1996), and *Mapping Interdisciplinary Studies* (AACU, 1999). She has held visiting posts in Japan, Nepal, New Zealand, and Canada, and was senior fellow at the Association of American Colleges and Universities.

Joy Rosenzweig Kliewer is Program Director of the College of Education and Assistant Professor at the University of Sarasota-California campus. Previously, she was wellness promotion associate for the health education outreach office of The Claremont Colleges, and program coordinator for the Howard R. Bowen Institute for Policy Research in Higher Education at the Center for Educational Studies, Claremont Graduate University. She is author of the book, *The Innovative Campus: Nurturing the Distinctive Learning Environment* (Onyx Press/American Council on Education, 1999), a comparative national study of the history and endurance of innovative institutions. She has given numerous presentations on the topic of distinctive college and university programs around the country and has served as a research consultant for Claremont University Center, the American Assembly of Collegiate Schools of Business, the Center for the Study of Community Colleges, and the Spencer and Ford Foundations academic labor market project.

Robert H. Knapp, Jr. has a BA in physics from Harvard and a PhD in theoretical physics from Oxford. Of equal importance in his education have been the years since 1972 when he joined the faculty at The Evergreen State College and began working in Evergreen's team-taught, full-time, interdisciplinary format. He has received the Burlington Northern Award for innovation in teaching and served twice as one of Evergreen's deans. Presently he alternates between undergraduate physics and integrative sciences/arts/humanities teaching, with a special involvement in ecological design.

Tina Kuckkahn is the Director of The Evergreen State College Longhouse Education and Cultural Center, and is an enrolled member of the Lac du Flambeau Band of Lake Superior Chippewa. She received her BA from the University of Wisconsin, Madison in 1988, graduating summa cum laude and as a recipient of the "Outstanding Graduating Senior" Award from the School of Education. In June of 1991, she received a Juris Doctorate from the University of Wisconsin Law School, and was admitted to the State Bar of Wisconsin. Since April 1996, she had administered the Native Economic Development Arts Initiative through the Longhouse, serving as project director. The mission of the arts initiative is to promote education, cultural preservation, and economic development for Native artists in the Pacific Northwest.

Helen Lee is the Director of The Evergreen State College Labor Education and Research Center. She has a masters degree in public policy and labor economics from Empire State College, and is the immediate past president of the Thurston/Lewis County Labor Council.

Alan Mandell is Director of the Mentoring Institute of the State University of New York/Empire State College, and Professor at ESC in New York City. He has been a mentor and administrator for 25 years, and has regularly written on adult learning, including *Portfolio Development and Adult Learning* (with Elana Michelson) and many essays with colleague Lee Herman.

Ann P. McNeal is Professor of Physiology at Hampshire College in Amherst, Massachusetts. She has a BA from Swarthmore College and a

PhD from the University of Washington. She has developed and taught numerous innovative courses in human health, including interdisciplinary courses on third world health and women's health. She especially loves teaching courses in which students learn to carry out original research projects. She served as a program director in the division of undergraduate education at the National Science Foundation in 1993-1994.

WILLIAM H. NEWELL is Professor of Interdisciplinary Studies, Director of the Institute in Integrative Studies at Miami University in Oxford, Ohio, and serves as Executive Director of the Association for Integrative Studies. He has published widely on interdisciplinary higher education, most recently editing *Interdisciplinarity: Essays from the Literature.* He has served as a consultant or external evaluator on the application of interdisciplinary studies and complexity theory to business, public administration, and engineering, as well as education at all levels at over 85 colleges and universities in the United States, Canada, and New Zealand. He was a faculty member at St. Olaf College's Paracollege during its formative years, and then a founding faculty member at Miami University's School of Interdisciplinay Studies (the Western College Program).

SUSAN OAKS is a faculty mentor at the State University of New York/ Empire State College. She coordinates courses in communications, arts, and humanities for ESC's Center for Distance Learning and also coordinates a program with AARP. She has written on the teaching of writing and on the creation of electronic environments, and has recently been developing web materials and courses.

KAREN KASHMANIAN OATES is Professor of Integrative Studies at George Mason University's New Century College and is currently serving as the Senior Science Fellow at the Association of American Colleges and Universities. She was instrumental in integrating the Center for Student Leadership and Service-Learning into the college, and initiating an experiential learning graduation requirement for all New Century College students. Her accomplishments also include a continuous improvements assessment process for the Center for Student Leadership and Service-Learning.

JANET F. OTT was trained as a neurophysiologist at the University of Southern California and continued in that vein during her postdoctoral work at the University of Florida College of Medicine. Since that time she has been a faculty member at The Evergreen State College and has studied and taught alternative medicine and the history of science, particularly focusing on the issues in the Middle Ages that led to the building of the Gothic cathedrals.

MARK PEDELTY holds a faculty position in the General College of the University of Minnesota, where he teaches and conducts research on intersecting issues of anthropology, communication, performance, interdisciplinary education, and developmental education. Much of his work focuses on Mexico and Central America. He is the author of *War Stories: The Culture of Foreign Correspondents* (Routledge, 1995), an ethnographic study of journalists in El Salvador, as well as various articles and book chapters. Current areas of research and writing include team teaching as a means of modeling debate in first-year seminars, the influence of media environments on college learning, performance as a means of teaching cultural anthropology, and Mexican music as public pedagogy.

DUNCAN RYANMANN is Faculty Director of the FORUM program at the State University of New York/Empire State College. He has taught on the faculties of the University of Pennsylvania, Rutgers University, and Williams College. He has also worked in managing health programs for Washington state, and has published in the areas of industrial organization, health economics, and higher education.

SANDRA J. SARKELA is Assistant Professor of English and Communication at the State University of New York/College at Potsdam. From 1996-1999, she served as interim associate provost at SUNY Potsdam. Her responsibilities included supervision of learning communities, the interdisciplinary general education program and interdisciplinary degree programs in women's studies, Native American studies, and African studies.

KARL L. SCHILLING holds a PhD in clinical psychology from the University of Florida (1975). He worked at Earlham College for three years before coming to the Western College Program at Miami University where he served as assistant/associate dean and assistant/associate professor of interdisciplinary studies from 1978-1998. During his time at Western, he developed a number of assessment projects designed to capture the characteristics of the powerful learning environment which Western created for its students and faculty. From 1992-1994 he served as director of the AAHE Assessment Forum. He currently is serving as Deputy Director of Policy for the State Council of Higher Education in Richmond, Virginia.

ANNE G. SCOTT received her PhD in psychology at the University of Arizona, where she was the director of the Center for Research on Undergraduate Education. She is currently on a one-year leave from Arizona International College of The University of Arizona where she serves as Professor and Director of Institutional Research, Evaluation, and Assessment. She is currently working for a large educational management company as the Senior Director of Academic Affairs.

Eve W. Stoddard is Director of the Center for International and Intercultural Studies, and Associate Professor of English at St. Lawrence University, Canton, New York. Her PhD is from the University of California, Los Angeles. Having studied the history and literary representations of slavery in eighteenth and nineteenth century Britain, she is currently researching tensions between civic and ethnic identities in the English-speaking Caribbean. Stoddard's most recent publications, coauthored with Grant Cornwell, include "Cosmopolitan or Mongrel? Reading *Creolité* and Hybridity via 'Douglarisation' in Trinidad," in the *European Journal of Cultural Studies,* and *Globalizing Knowledge: Connecting International and Intercultural Studies,* a monograph published as part of the Association of American Colleges and Universities' series *The Academy in Transition.* Stoddard and Cornwell are currently editing a volume of essays, *Cultural Cartographies: Comparative Studies in Global Multiculturalism,* and doing research for a book on the semiotics of sugar mill ruins in the Caribbean.

Peter Tommerup has long been an advocate of interdisciplinarity and student-centered teaching and learning, having enjoyed them greatly as an undergraduate at New College (of San Jose State University) and Pitzer College. His interdisciplinary doctoral work at UCLA was grounded in folkloristics, but also drew substantially from organizational studies and symbolic anthropology. He serves as Assistant Professor at the California School of Professional Psychology in Alameda, California, where he teaches in a doctoral program in organizational psychology.

Frederick Stirton Weaver is Professor of Economics and History at Hampshire College, where he has also done several shifts of deaning, institutional research, and other odd jobs. He is the author of several works on higher education, including *Liberal Education: Professions, Pedagogy, and Structure* (New York, 1991), which was awarded the F. W. Ness Book Award by the Association of American Colleges and Universities, and *Presencia de la Mujer en los Programas de Ingenieia, Clencia y Tecnologia,* with Ing. Estela Altuna (Quito, 1994). His principal teaching and research focuses on Latin America. His most recent work is *Tribute, Trade and Debt: Latin America in the International Economy since 1500* (Boulder, CO, 2000).

PREFACE

Reinventing Ourselves: Interdisciplinary Education, Collaborative Learning, and Experimentation in Higher Education examines the experiences and lessons from a variety of institutions which have pioneered new approaches for organizing for more effective teaching and learning. Included here are freestanding interdisciplinary institutions as well as alternative interdisciplinary programs within traditional institutions. Many of these colleges began as both educational and social experiments, representing new ways of thinking about educational goals, curricular organization, institutional governance, and faculty roles and rewards. These institutions have been bellwethers for much of the education reform efforts across the nation. While many of the alternative colleges disappeared or turned conventional, the work of some longer-established alternative institutions has sustained and deepened over time, with new work emerging. A new generation of experimenting institutions is being born in the 1990s, with new calls for rethinking our approaches to teaching and learning as well as the traditional boundaries within institutions and between disciplines. These institutions represent striking alternatives in terms of organizing for learning that foreshadow more recent reform efforts.

To facilitate a better understanding of the evolution of these alternative types of teaching and learning, the book has been divided into three sections:

- Section I: Historical Perspectives and Institutional Examples
- Section II: Powerful Pedagogies
  - Part One: Learning Communities
  - Part Two: Rethinking Teaching and Learning
- Section III: Taking Stock and Looking Ahead

SECTION I: HISTORICAL PERSPECTIVES AND INSTITUTIONAL EXAMPLES

The 1920s and early 1930s were a period of robust experimentation in higher education, through institutions like Goddard, Bard, Sarah Lawrence, Antioch, and others. The 1960s saw a revival of experimentation with a new generation of institutions specifically designed to support teaching and learning. Section I explores the history and lessons of these two important periods of educational experimentation, the significant colleges and programs, and the factors that influenced their development.

SECTION II: POWERFUL PEDAGOGIES

Section II discusses various ways in which organizational structure, culture, and pedagogy are being changed to support new approaches to teaching and learning. Topics range from realpolitik matters such as promotion, tenure, funding, and faculty roles and rewards, to issues like professional identity, collective versus individual responsibility, and long-term sustainability. These chapters provide concrete examples of the impediments to institutional change as well as visions of what a coherent organizational structure and culture might look like.

SECTION III: TAKING STOCK AND LOOKING AHEAD

Innovative programs and institutions carry a special burden to demonstrate their effectiveness, and yet they are often established with different goals and yardsticks. This section addresses critical questions about assessing the effectiveness of these efforts to reorganize around new approaches to teaching and learning. Have they been effective? What is known about the impact of interdisciplinary education on student learning? How is interdisciplinary understanding being assessed? Student voices as well as quantitative and qualitative reports on these efforts are contained here.

Additionally, this concluding section provides an overview of the lessons from previous attempts to reinvent the academy around new cultures, structures, and practices. It also examines the similarities and differences between the climate of reform now and in the past, and explores new directions for alternative education in the future.

The section concludes with a philosophical argument for the need for a coherent theory of knowledge to underpin contemporary interdisciplinary education and makes the case for pragmatic idealism.

FOREWORD

Although the United States is generally regarded as having the finest higher education system in the world, most American colleges and universities have been slow to embrace real innovations in curriculum and pedagogy. What is particularly vexing about mainstream higher education's reluctance to embrace many of the innovative approaches that are so well presented and discussed in this book is that there is a large and growing body of hard research evidence suggesting that the quality of the undergraduate experience could be substantially improved if more of these practices were to be adopted. The importance of student involvement and the value of student-faculty contact, interdisciplinary studies, and collaborative learning, for example, has been known for several decades, and during the past decade the power of the student peer group and the efficacy both of service-learning and of learning communities has been convincingly demonstrated.

One obvious problem is that we really do not have a very good understanding of why mainstream institutions are so slow, if not downright resistant, to adopting needed reforms. Do we need tastier carrots, bigger sticks, or a little of both? On the stick side, politicians and policymakers are not of much help because they focus on things like accountability rather than good practice. On the carrot side, administrators have not been able to get very far with teacher of the year awards or by tinkering with the faculty reward system. One problem that needs much more attention is faculty belief systems: Most college teachers seem to believe in what I like to call the "banking" theory of teaching, whereby 1) the learning process consists of withdrawing information from the head of the professor and depositing it in the head of the student, and 2) the most efficient and effective banking technologies are lecturing (perhaps combined with a bit of Q and A between students and the lecturer or TA), reading textbooks, and preparing for tests. The banking theory also assumes that most learning takes place in the classroom and, to the extent that students are able to learn something on their own, it is assumed to be a solitary process. And when reformers try to get such colleagues to consider some of the innovations described in this book, they are often confronted with still another set of closely related beliefs: that interdisciplinary studies are either too costly or too time-consuming, that students are not capable of designing their own courses of study, that problem-centered learning (what I like to call inductive learning) dilutes the course subject matter, and that such things as narrative evaluations, collaborative learning, and service-learning run the risk of compromising academic standards because they lack rigor.

If I am at least partially correct in assuming that such collective beliefs—which in many respects describe part of what we might call "traditional faculty culture"—lie at the heart of institutional resistance to pedagogical and curricular innovation, then we can at least partially account for the dilemma so well documented in the opening sections of this book: that the most successful attempts at innovation have been largely confined to institutions that have been deliberately designed to accommodate innovation, and that similar innovations have a hard time surviving in mainstream institutions. In the case of many new institutions, faculty are recruited in part because they reject traditional views about teaching and learning and because they believe in the innovative approaches that characterize these new institutions. In fact, it would be interesting to determine if the innovative colleges that have failed tend to be those where the faculty recruitment process relied more on traditional criteria.

Where do faculty acquire such beliefs? And how do we go about changing them? While these questions are much too difficult and complex to discuss here, one thing seems certain: The adoption by traditional institutions of innovations like those described in this book is going to be a challenging educational task, where reformers will have to contend with deeply entrenched beliefs about what constitutes a normal curriculum and proper pedagogy. At the same time, the reformers will need to supply their student colleagues with valid curricular content about what these innovations are, why they are generally superior to traditional approaches, the conditions under which they are likely to be most effective, and how to acquire the expertise to be an effective practitioner. Clearly, this book should be must reading for any reform-minded college professor or administrator who is seriously interested in preparing such a curriculum for the reeducation of more tradition-bound colleagues.

Alexander W. Astin
University of California, Los Angeles

SECTION I

Historical Perspectives and Institutional Examples

The 1920s and early 1930s were a period of robust experimentation in higher education through institutions like Goddard, Bard, Sarah Lawrence, Reed, Bennington, St John's, Antioch, Black Mountain, and others. Within traditional institutions, much experimentation also occurred. At the University of Wisconsin, for example, Alexander Meiklejohn established the Experimental College, a coherent two-year general education program. Despite its brief lifespan, the Experimental College, like many of the other early experiments, planted seeds that would later take root in new innovative institutions. Coming on the heels of the Progressive Movement, the educational reform effort was fueled by new thinking about the role of the academy and the ways in which students learn. Seminal thinkers such as John Dewey, Alexander Meiklejohn, W. E. B. Du Bois, Charles Elliot, Stringfellow Barr, and Scott Buchanan were influential in articulating new visions for higher education and in establishing new institutions to put these theories into practice.

The 1960s saw a revival of experimentation in higher education with a new generation of institutions specifically designed to support teaching and learning, new notions of faculty roles, and new visions of the relationships between the academy and the larger society. Many new institutions were founded including Hampshire College, New College, Empire State College, The Evergreen State College, Ramapo College, Pitzer College, University of Wisconsin-Green Bay, Sangamon State University, the University of California, Santa Cruz, Franconia College, and many others. Within large traditional institutions, hundreds of cluster colleges and experimental programs were also established. Many were living/learning programs designed holistically to bring together the student's curricular and cocurricular life. Some of these cluster colleges included Fairhaven College at Western Washington University, Western College at Miami University, the residential college at the University of Michigan, the College of the Pacific, Centennial College at the University of Nebraska, and the Goodrich Program at the University of Nebraska, Omaha, to mention just a few.

In their classic book, *The Perpetual Dream: Reform and Experiment in the American College* (1978), Gerald Grant and David Reisman examined a number of the significant experiments of the 1970s, classifying some as fundamental reform efforts—"telic reforms"—and others as "popular reform efforts." Unlike the telic reform efforts, the popular reform efforts did not fundamentally challenge the goals of the research university. Stockton College and Ramapo College, most of the cluster colleges at Santa Cruz, and New College of Florida all represent popular reform efforts in their scheme. Grant and Reisman contend that the popular reform efforts were partially a response to the "discontents that came to characterize student life in the most selective colleges and universities . . . (where) students sought relief in a wide range of popular reforms that gave them . . . greater autonomy and resulted in dramatic changes in their relationships with teachers" (p. 16). Many of the colleges characterized as popular reform efforts became more traditional over time, facing many internal compatibility challenges since most of their organizational structures were hybrids. Nonetheless, many of the educational ideas of the popular reform efforts were widely adopted. Telic reform efforts, such as St John's College, the College for Human Services, and the early Kresge College at the University of California, Santa Cruz, represented radically different notions of higher education. St John's College and the College for Human Services, later renamed Audrey Cohen College, remained intact as telic reform efforts with St John's representing a revival of the neoclassical vision of higher education and Audrey Cohen representing the activist-radical impulse.

While Grant and Reisman did not study The Evergreen State College or the earlier Meiklejohn Experimental College at the University of Wisconsin, these have been described by others as "telic reform efforts" (Cadwallader, 1981). Alexander Meiklejohn's early Experimental College (1927–1932) at the University of Wisconsin and its later successors at Berkeley (1965–1969), San Jose (1965–1969), SUNY-Old Westbury, and The Evergreen State College (established in 1971), represented a revisioning of general and liberal education.

In the early 1920s vigorous debates were already taking place about the role of education in preparing citizens for democracy. Writers such as

John Dewey and Alexander Meiklejohn argued that the schools must prepare students for citizenship. Many years later at the University of California, Joseph Tussman would eloquently describe general education as most appropriately vocational education for citizenship while critiquing most current general education programs as incoherent and without purpose.

In the past twenty-five years the dialog about educational purpose has continued in the face of increasing academic specialization and fragmentation within higher education. Growing diversity in the classroom has also been an important influence. Recent endeavors to reinvent the academy reflect a certain continuity with the past as well as new directions. There is a new awareness of the importance of structure and holistic reform efforts, and growing sophistication about what long-term change requires. On the other hand, many of the new reform efforts stress pedagogical approaches and principles that are distinctly Deweyian. In fact, there is a renaissance of interest in the work of John Dewey, who had little impact on higher education in his lifetime. Growing interest in connecting with the community through the service-learning movement resonates with earlier themes in the progressive era and in the work of Jane Addams and others active in social reform in the 1920s and 1930s. Issues about the role of the academy in building citizenship are also arising with new urgency through both the cultural pluralism and the service-learning movements.

This section explores the history and lessons of two of the most important periods of educational experimentation, several of the significant colleges and programs, and the factors that influenced their development.

In "Dangerous Outposts: Progressive Experiments in Higher Education in the 1920s and 1930s," Steven R. Coleman argues that the progressive educators in the 1920s and 1930s saw liberal arts colleges as more than preparation for careers in business and the professions. They saw liberal arts colleges as institutions for individual growth and social change. The pedagogy was designed to draw students into the community. Through extensive use of field study, the project method, participation in college governance, and off-campus work, students experienced the interdependence of self and community. Although these experimental programs were not widely emulated at the time, they have been important progenitors of campus innovation and offer a potent legacy of the role of the college in American society.

Joy Rosenzweig Kliewer's chapter, "The Innovative Colleges and Universities of the 1960s and 1970s: Lessons from Six Alternative Institutions," presents the results of a comprehensive study of the history and endurance of educational reform at six colleges and universities that were founded in the 1960s and early 1970s as alternatives to the mainstream of American higher education. The goal of the project was to understand how and why innovative institutions preserve their founding missions or dreams in a changing social, political, and economic climate. Her findings corroborate earlier research documenting the influence of external pressures upon public, nontraditional institutions, in particular. Kleiwer argues that smaller institutions were generally more successful in preserving their distinctiveness. Key factors included an appropriate organizational structure, academic reward systems that value innovation, recruitment strategies that support ongoing innovation, administrative support, and a nondepartmental organizational structure.

Since its founding as one of the major alternative colleges in the 1960s, Hampshire College has continued to evolve as an interdisciplinary institution. While the planners envisioned interdisciplinary faculty units, courses, and study programs, they did not foresee the unusual dynamics that would be created by the interactions of students and faculty. In "Interdisciplinary Education at Hampshire College: Bringing People Together Around Ideas," Ann P. McNeal and Frederick Stirton Weaver describe the evolution of a unique institution and the structure and culture that supports and extends the commitment to interdisciplinary education. The chapter provides important lessons for other institutions pursuing interdisciplinary education.

Barbara Leigh Smith's chapter, "Evergreen at Twenty-Five: Sustaining Long-Term Innovation," traces the history of The Evergreen State College, one of the principal innovative colleges established in the late 1960s. This college has widely influenced higher education through its integrated learning community curricular structure, but, like many nontraditional institutions, its founding years were inwardly focused. The chapter argues that innovative institutions go through a developmental process of establishing their identity and addressing compatibility challenges with the external environment. Smith contends that external pressures actually helped the college survive by pushing the institution to continually expand its vision. Now more than twenty-five years old, Evergreen has matured into an institution with a broader vision of its role in higher education and a new set of challenges as scores of founding faculty members retire and many of its innovations have become mainstream in traditional institutions.

In "Bridging Theory and Practice: Public Service at The Evergreen State College," the authors describe The Evergreen State College's active commitment to public service and outreach. The authors, directors of the college public service centers, discuss the institution's ongoing efforts to promote links with the Native American community, the K-12 system, and higher education throughout Washington state and the nation.

References

Cadwallader, M. (1984). Experiment at San Jose. In R. Jones & B. L. Smith (Eds.), *Against the current: Reform and experimentation in higher education* (pp. 343–366). Cambridge, MA: Schenkman.

Dewey, J. (1916). *Democracy and education.* New York, NY: Macmillan.

Grant, G., & Riesman, D. (1978). *The perpetual dream: Reform and experiment in the American college.* Chicago, IL: University of Chicago Press.

Meiklejohn, A. (1932). *The experimental college.* New York, NY: Harper & Row.

Tussman, J. (1969). *Experiment at Berkeley.* New York, NY: Oxford University Press.

1

Dangerous Outposts: Progressive Experiments in Higher Education in the 1920s and 1930s

Steven R. Coleman
Columbia University

Never before have so many colleges endeavored to initiate programs leading to sound learning or have so many of them earnestly sought information and guidance for their efforts. (National Society for the Study of Education, 1932, p. 157)

So concluded a survey of 128 colleges and universities by the American Association of University Women (AAUW) in 1930. At that time, educators throughout the nation were attempting to end "a chaotic period, when the wide-open elective system ran riotously into utter confusion" (p. 17) across American campuses (National Society for the Study of Education, 1932).[1] Most institutions surveyed by the AAUW moved cautiously, introduced tentative reforms, or offered innovations to a portion of their students. Leaders of a dozen experimental, progressive colleges, however, designed their programs around new approaches, and expected their entire faculty, staff, and student body to participate in them. Brainchildren of visionary educators, these institutions were supported by maverick industrialists and politicians. They attracted a cadre of faculty and generations of students to create what they hoped would be a new paradigm of higher education. Inspired by progressive schools, settlement houses, Danish folkschools, English universities, and each other, they developed strategies such as experiential learning (on- and off-campus), participation in college governance, and a combination of academic and nonacademic work, to achieve what Dewey (1916) had earlier termed "conjoint communicated experience" (p. 87). They created programs, in short, to engage students in many levels of education. Their aim was to enable graduates to be full participants in the various overlapping communities they would belong to in their lives. The founders of these colleges, in effect, developed ways to initiate the transition from schooling to lifelong learning.

Moreover, these institutions advocated learning for a purpose that went beyond individual enlightenment or advancement. In a period of remarkable economic growth (that nevertheless left a third of the nation below and another third just above the poverty level), enrollments on most campuses swelled with aspiring high school graduates eager to take their places in the expansion of big business and corporate America. Leaders of these experimental programs, however, deeply influenced by the preceding era of progressive reform, were guided by alternative social philosophies and values. These aims were strengthened with the onset of the Great Depression. Acknowledging the career goals of students, they sought to further those ambitions by providing them with experiences of the world they would be inheriting. Again it was Dewey (1916) who articulated their highest ideals.

> The present industrial constitution of society is, like every society which has ever existed, full of inequities. It is the aim of progressive education to take part in correcting unfair privilege and unfair deprivation, not to perpetuate them. (p. 119)

What distinguished this movement, then, from other contemporary reform efforts, was that, at a time when colleges and universities first became the gatekeepers to the power structures of the nation, it attempted to wed social responsibility to individual ambition in the future leaders of the country.

These progressive experiments were not widely emulated. They were viewed as idiosyncratic by contemporaries and largely ignored or misinterpreted by historians. Some of the reasons for the limited impact of these programs on mainstream higher education will be outlined below. The ideals, however, have persisted, emerging when the role of the college in American society has been scrutinized. Current campus reformers, including those who advocate a greater interdisciplinary approach, are among the inheritors of this movement that saw the college as a potential platform for social change.

This chapter will trace the development of this early attempt to integrate self and community and bridge the gap between schooling and lifelong learning, by examining aspects of the programs at several of the progressive colleges formed or reorganized during the 1920s and 1930s. It will consider the histories at Antioch, Sarah Lawrence, Bennington, Bard, and Goddard colleges, because these, among the dozen experiments of that period, have, for better or worse, survived for nearly three quarters of a century. Distinctive as they were, all of these institutions sought to extend education beyond the campus. Students at each college utilized the institutions themselves and the communities around them as laboratories for learning. Programs were structured in different ways, and succeeded when they integrated the students' intellectual and experiential learning.

The first college to draw heavily on nonacademic learning experiences was developed at Antioch, in Yellow Springs, Ohio. Founded in 1852 and led for a few brief years by Horace Mann, by 1919 Antioch was in desperate financial straits and was described as "having been a derelict on the educational ocean for a generation."[2] Arthur E. Morgan, a flood control engineer based in nearby Dayton, who provided housing, health clinics, and night classes for workers on his projects, submitted a plan to completely reorganize the failing college. His proposal addressed both fiscal and curricular problems and first placed the Co-op Plan at the center of a liberal arts education, in which students alternated work on jobs with study at the college. Every student spent half of the five-year program at a series of job placements in business, industry, and public or private agencies. This addressed the fiscal needs of both the college and the students by allowing Antioch to enroll twice the number of students it could house, and giving students the opportunity to earn a substantial portion of their tuition. In addition, it introduced students to career opportunities, and their education was enhanced by learning experiences beyond the college walls.

To launch his experiment, Morgan secured the financial backing of Charles Kettering, whose invention of the electric starter for the motorcar contributed to the rapid development of the automobile into the nation's primary mode of transportation, with far-reaching social and economic consequences for American society. When Kettering invested part of his fortune in Morgan's vision, he expected nothing less than a similar transformation of American higher education. A vice president and member of the board of directors of General Motors, Kettering was not a utopian. Like many of his peers, he was simply appalled at the job colleges were doing preparing young people to find a place in, and assume the responsibilities of, a democratic society.

Morgan and Kettering were among a group of educational reformers who learned from the experiences of Alexander Meiklejohn at Amherst

College who struggled, with limited success, to change existing institutions. They concluded that entrenched interests on campus, notably faculty and alumni, posed obstacles too large to overcome. Really to "change the formula" of education, as Kettering[3] put it, new colleges would have to be established, with radically different programs.

Morgan (who was not a college graduate) hand-picked the faculty, a few from outside academe, based on their expertise and their "unity of purpose" in pursuit of what he called "symmetry" in education: a preparation for leadership achieved through a trinity of academics, co-op work, and community service. More than six hundred highly qualified students came from across the country to participate in this new program. And the business community, both regionally and nationally, supported the Co-op Plan by employing Antioch students in a wide variety of occupations. And yet, ten years after the reorganization, Morgan expressed his disappointment in the college. His hope that Antioch would be the beginning of a new learning experience had not been realized. Had something gone wrong? The entire community plunged into what was later called the "Whither Antioch" period of self-examination.

Faculty members discovered that they held widely differing opinions about the college's educational plan. They were uniformly in favor of students combining class and co-op work. Most were skeptical, however, about the value of autonomous (independent) course work, and of taking a more interdisciplinary approach in their classes. Morgan suspected many instructors of intellectual and social complacency, but it is also true that they simply had not the training or skills to effectively oversee independent studies or extend the boundaries of their fields of expertise. Ultimately, they rejected Morgan's, and some of his more progressively-minded colleagues' attempts to steer the college on to paths taken by other experimental colleges that were formed later in the 1920s. Students continued to split their time between fairly traditional class work and employment off campus, on an alternating semester basis. Although their co-op experiences were for many the most profound and educational of their college careers, these experiences were usually poorly integrated into the academic curriculum. Morgan believed this lack of integration hampered the symmetrical development of the students, and contributed to his biggest disappointment—the failure to awaken in Antioch students the desire to change their world. He left Yellow Springs when appointed by FDR to launch the Tennessee Valley Authority, a much larger project that changed the way of life for a whole region of the United States.

The Antioch experiment generated a tremendous amount of national publicity, and the notion that colleges could be organized around different principles encouraged others. Particularly interested were educators who recognized a need for a more modern college program for women. William Van Duzer Lawrence, a New York manufacturer, real estate developer, and philanthropist who shared Charles Kettering's low opinion of college graduates, was convinced by Henry Noble McCracken, the president of Vassar, to establish a new, progressive college for women. He named it after his late wife, Sarah Lawrence.

After clashes with the faculty over some modest reform on his campus, it was clear to McCracken that Vassar was not the institution that was going to introduce, in a meaningful way, the innovative ideas that were percolating up from the progressive grammar and secondary schools that had captured the imagination of many of the nation's educators. But he saw an opportunity in Lawrence's desire to turn his Bronxville estate into a school of some sort, to create such an experiment. Under the umbrella of Vassar College, then, for its first five years beginning in 1928, Sarah Lawrence College introduced a program described by its most prominent faculty member as "individual education . . . rooted in the conviction that community responsibility and individual development are essential to each other" (Lynd, 1945, p. viii).

The key innovation in the Sarah Lawrence program was the "don" system. Modeled after the English university tutors, dons served as academic and personal advisors, and interpreters of school objectives. Each faculty member (and most administrators) acted as don to a handful of students, met with each of them every week, and had the responsibility of overseeing their education and growth at the college. Another innovation was the widespread and sophisticated use of field work as part of the curriculum. Although not required of all students, most participated, in varying degrees, in broadly conceived courses designed to offer field experience for students concentrating in various disciplines, including the social sciences, psychology, education, creative writing, and the arts. The benefits of the field work extended to the surrounding communities. A survey conducted by Sarah Lawrence students, for example, was used by the city of Yonkers to obtain a $325,000 federal grant to erect low-income housing. Looking back in 1945, sociology professor Helen Lynd believed Sarah Lawrence had done a better job integrating the field work experience with its academic courses than had Antioch's Co-op Plan, or Bennington College's winter work term. This was supported by the dons, who tried to help students see the connection between their schooling and off-campus experiences, and reinforce the ideal of personal growth through social commitment.

At the time Henry McCracken and William Lawrence were making plans for a progressive women's college in Westchester County, New York, a group of wealthy women who summered in Bennington, Vermont, were pursuing a similar project in that New England town. They turned for guidance to William Heard Kilpatrick of Teachers College, Columbia University, widely known as an interpreter of John Dewey's educational theories and the author of "The Project Method"

(1918). Kilpatrick envisioned a college that would fit education to each individual student; that would not rely on books only, but would stress living experiences, with the goal of developing creative, self-motivated young women.

Although he served as chairman of the college's board of trustees for eight years, Bennington didn't turn out as Kilpatrick had hoped it would. This was partly because his more radical notions were mitigated by experiences Robert Leigh, the first president of the college, brought with him from Reed College. More importantly, though, one senses that the living experiences Kilpatrick hoped would shape the educational program were somewhat different than those brought to the campus by the daughters of wealthy patrician families. The Great Depression had foiled the plans of the founding trustees to open the school with an endowment, and, as at Sarah Lawrence, tuition alone had to support the expense of a personalized curriculum with a very low student-faculty ratio. Both colleges provided an alternative to wealthy families whose daughters could not, or chose not to, attend the so-called Seven Sisters colleges. Many of these young women's lives were changed by their off-campus experiences and the roles they played in the structure of their education and the governance of their communities. But the impact of these experimental programs on mainstream higher education was limited, primarily because they were only available to students who could afford to pay what were, and what remained for about five decades, the highest college costs in the nation. In addition, admissions criteria based more on ability to pay than a proper fit with the educational program, adversely affected the achievement of the goals of the progressive colleges.

There were few opportunities until 1931 for those experimenting with liberal arts programs to directly exchange experiences with each other. In that year, Arthur Morgan and Constance Warren, president of Sarah Lawrence, were among the 17 participants at a curriculum conference chaired by John Dewey and hosted by Hamilton Holt at Rollins College in Winter Park, Florida (Lane, 1984). Impressed by Warren's experiences at Sarah Lawrence, Morgan tried, without success, to initiate at Antioch some of the curricular reforms that Warren had put forward. It was also an opportunity for these young leaders to benefit from the experience and observations of such luminaries as Dewey, James Harvey Robinson, Max McConn, Joseph K. Hart, Alexander Caswell Ellis, and Henry Turner Bailey.

In this growing spirit of innovation on college campuses, several universities spun off experimental colleges, the most radical among them being Alexander Meiklejohn's Experimental College of the University of Wisconsin, and the New College of Teachers College, Columbia University (Meiklejohn, 1932; Mix, 1968). These institutional stepchildren of large universities were shut down within a few years, however, owing to financial and other considerations. Two more small, independent college experiments were launched during the 1930s, however, and remain, with Antioch, Sarah Lawrence, and Bennington, the survivors of the first wave of progressive reform of higher education: Bard College in Annandale-On-Hudson, New York, and Goddard College in Plainfield, Vermont.

Like Antioch, both Bard and Goddard were reincarnations of 19th century institutions that had fallen on hard times. Both had sectarian affiliations—Bard was formerly the Episcopalian St. Stephen's College, founded in 1860, and Goddard had been the Universalist Goddard Seminary since 1863. By the 1930s, decreased enrollments and mounting debts were forcing both of them into bankruptcy. St. Stephen's was rescued by affiliation with Columbia University, as part of President Nicholas Murray Butler's expansive vision of his urban university as a centerpiece of a network of small, quasi-independent, "country" campuses. Butler appointed Donald Tewksbury dean of the college.

Tewksbury, a professor at Teachers College (which had by then launched its experimental New College) and visiting professor at Sarah Lawrence, drew on both of these experiments in his vision of what was renamed Bard College in 1934. Tewksbury's inspiration was to stand the accepted approach to liberal education on its head. Instead of starting with survey courses and annually narrowing the scope of one's studies, he proposed that freshmen first concentrate on subjects they were deeply interested in, and had already acquired skills in, such as music, mathematics, or a foreign language. Pursuit of these areas would lead students to branch out to include other fields, and finally, "general survey courses organized as interdepartmental seminars . . . would thus serve as the natural culmination of a student's program of studies" (Tewksbury, 1934, p. 5). His metaphor for this process was that of a tree that first roots itself, "develops in time a trunk of stable and living proportions, and finally reaches out through its branches towards the fulfillment of its life purpose" (Tewksbury, 1934, p. 5). Looking beyond college, the graduating student is equipped for the lifelong task of pursuing multiple interests and integrating them into his life.

From his experience at Sarah Lawrence, Tewksbury realized that students should be primarily responsible for their own education but that they would need some direction in order to take full advantage of this course of study. He adopted a form of the don system, assigning a general advisor to each student. He also integrated Sarah Lawrence's tutorial conference into each course, and stressed that students be given opportunities that would allow for contact with the outside world. But while Bard became a much more interesting campus than St. Stephen's had been—the college newspaper turned from sports to national events, political editorials, and creative writing pieces, and the Bard Theater became a lively and important regional cultural institution—Tewksbury's educational innovations met with limited success.

Not all students were ready, willing, or able to assume the level of responsibility that the college program demanded. Likewise, not all faculty were up to the challenge of being guides and mentors, in addition to their roles as professors or instructors. They certainly were not prepared for it, either in their graduate schooling or their prior experiences at other colleges or universities. Financial instability exacerbated the situation. Some of the best faculty left for more secure, better paying jobs that offered greater opportunity for professional advancement. The admissions staff had to accept any student able to pay the fees, resulting in a student body that ran the gamut from the worst to the best of their high school graduating classes.

These points were articulated a few years later, when Robert Leigh, still president of Bennington College, was asked to spend his semester-long sabbatical as acting dean of Bard and submit a report to the Trustees regarding the future of the college. The key finding in Leigh's 148-page evaluation was that "Bard needs neither a new program nor new direction" (1940, p. 57). It needed financial support from Columbia to be more selective in admissions, and increased guidance and counseling to bring up the level of quality and distinction of the students. He recognized the great difficulty of full-time faculty providing such intense support to students, and recommended that

> the Bard teacher should be . . . judged increasingly by the Dean for retention and promotion on the basis of his skill and effectiveness in guiding a student in his general intellectual development. (p. 65)

Tewksbury, too, may have been part of the problem. Having less of the charisma of a Morgan or the finesse of a Warren, he was still required to lead a necessarily strong-spirited faculty and student body. He resigned in 1937, and returned to Teachers College as director of New College. To its credit, Columbia did support the college financially for four more years, at which time Bard ended its affiliation with the university and became an independent coeducational institution. But it was the influence of Bennington College, in the persons of Leigh and Harold Gray, who moved from the faculty of Bennington to become the next dean of Bard, that was crucial in transforming Tewksbury's blueprint into a functioning and distinctive college.

Strength of leadership cannot be said to have been lacking in the founding of Goddard College. Royce Pitkin converted the failing seminary into a college in 1938, and for the next three decades cajoled and bullied succeeding generations of faculty and students into a learning community that integrated academic studies, physical work, and democratic governance. Inspired by Danish folkschools that brought working people together for weeks or months at a time to mutually solve their problems, Pitkin hoped local Vermont families would enroll their sons and daughters in his "Vermont school for living."[4] It turned out that even without high tuition fees, students from New York, Massachusetts, and beyond far outnumbered rural New Englanders. But they did not remain apart—the program, centered on experiential learning and the project method, immersed them thoroughly in their new environs.

Courses called simply "Psychology" or "Modern Economic Problems" entailed interviews with local residents, businesses, and agencies as part of surveys of regional health care, nursery school programs, and unemployment. Projects developed into federally funded studies of local school systems, juvenile delinquency, and mental health needs, and resulted in the creation of several independent political councils and lobbying groups.

Physical work was an important part of Goddard's educational program. Each student worked for the college one hour per day, which reduced maintenance, service, and clerical staff. Goddard students prepared meals, washed dishes, planted trees, and worked in the library. In the early years of the college, students helped to convert barns into dormitories and classroom buildings, dug ditches to connect the college to the town sewage system, and laid pipe to enhance the water capacity. As in the other progressive colleges, Goddard students also worked at other jobs during the two-month winter break between semesters.

The third and final component of the college program was its governance structure. Patterned after the Vermont town meeting, each person—administrator, faculty, staff, and student—had one vote at Goddard's weekly community meeting, therefore giving most weight to the students. Although Pitkin reserved authority in areas he believed critical to the success of the institution, students spent many long hours debating issues that vitally affected their daily lives. Not satisfied with their own governance system (they never would be), in 1941 the student president and secretary of the Community Council invited representatives from five other progressive colleges to a conference on community government. Seventeen delegates from Antioch, Bard, Bennington, Black Mountain, Goddard, and Sarah Lawrence met for two days at Teachers College in New York. The students compared their governance structures and discussed limitations and applications of community councils. They concluded, in part, that "to learn to live as a member of a cooperative community, without sacrificing individuality, is an important part of the educational experience offered by the college."[5]

Conclusion

In 1922, John Dewey wrote that to revitalize a complacent American public, schools would have to become "the dangerous outposts of a humane civilization" and "begin to be supremely interesting places" (Boydston, 1976, p. 334). The founders of the progressive colleges of the 1920s and 1930s believed such a humane civilization could only be achieved by individuals working cooperatively, and designed programs to foster that as a lifelong pursuit.

Antioch introduced the notion that cooperative work was an essential part of a liberal education. Sarah Lawrence made field work an important part of class curricula, and recognized the need for students to get individual, ongoing guidance to make sense of their college experience. Bard tried to invert the undergraduate process from one of specialization to an expanding awareness of the interrelationship of all things. Goddard's extensive use of the project method in classes, and reliance on student work on campus, pushed the boundaries of experiential learning. At all these colleges, students, and faculty, too, played a much larger role in the governance of their communities than was typical of the rest of academe.

But these institutions remained outposts, on the frontier or the periphery of the educational landscape. They did not change the paradigm of higher education. True, they, and others that came after them, have proven there is a place in American higher education for programs that embrace the principles that learning cannot be confined within departments, or separated from one's experience outside academe, or formulated without the direct participation of faculty and students. Their innovative success for five decades no doubt inspired the establishment of a second wave of campus experimentation in the 1960s and 1970s (Grant & Riesman, 1978). These campuses will continue to attract those most frustrated with the shortcomings of our mainstream institutions, the renegades and misfits, and the seekers and visionaries. At their best moments, these colleges germinate conceptual seeds that find fruition at many other places. Arthur Chickering (1984) has outlined how ideas tested and proven at just one of these experiments (Goddard, in the 1950s) inspired further research and innovation and influenced the founding of several other nontraditional institutions. The progressives, then, were important progenitors of a nearly century-long process of developing schools into more effective and engaging learning communities.

But what of the their greater social goals? The visionary educators who created the experimental programs of the 1920s and 1930s were clear about their aspirations for their students.

> We must trust these individuals to meet issues as they arise, and to remake the social conditions they face into something worthier of man and of life. (Dewey, 1930, p. 282)

There is no doubt that a number of the students that emerged from these programs continued throughout their lives to seek personal fulfillment through commitment to social change. They have been among those whose have championed ideals of creativity, community, and compassion in a society that has exalted competition, status, and acquisition. But in truth, the impact of these progressive institutions on the academy, much less the nation's political, economic, and cultural landscape, was far less than the founders had hoped. To a large degree, it was a matter of accessibility. An educational model characterized by highly personalized curricula, tutorial classes, and frequent meetings with faculty and advisors proved too expensive for all but the wealthy or most determined students.

We have, of course, made tremendous progress in terms of accessibility in the last few decades, notably assisted by federal financial aid programs and advancements in technology. Distance learning, interdisciplinary approaches, and other innovations have made inroads at large, affordable, state-supported universities. These programs must be broadened to include larger segments of the population at these and other institutions. But the social legacy of the progressives must be a vital component. As contemporary educational reformers search for ways to enhance the learning experience of a more diverse population, they must articulate social goals beyond the academy. In doing so they will continue the effort to help students lead meaningful lives and create a saner, more humane world.

References

Boydston, J. (Ed.). (1976). *John Dewey: The middle works, 1899–1924.* Carbondale, IL: Southern Illinois University Press.

Chickering, A. (1984). Alternatives for the 80's: The Goddard-Pitkin legacy. In R. Jones & B. L. Smith (Eds.), *Against the current: Reform and experimentation in higher education* (pp. 303–319). Cambridge, MA: Schenckman.

Dewey, J. (1916). *Democracy and education.* New York, NY: Macmillan.

Dewey, J. (1930). Philosophy and education. In P. A. Schilpp (Ed.), *Higher education faces the future* (pp. 273–283). New York, NY: Horace Liveright.

Grant, G., & Riesman, D. (1978). *The perpetual dream: Reform and experiment in the American college.* Chicago, IL: University of Chicago Press.

Kilpatrick, W. H. (1918). The project method: The use of the purposeful act in the educative process. *Teachers College Bulletin*. New York, NY: Teachers College, Columbia University.

Lane, J. C. (1984). The Rollins Conference, 1931 and the search for a progressive liberal education: Mirror or prism? *Liberal Education, 70,* 297–305.

Leigh, R. D. (1940, March 10). *Final report to the president and board of trustees of Bard College.* Unpublished report, Bard College, Annandale-On-Hudson, NY.

Lynd, H. M. (1945). *Field work in college education.* New York, NY: Columbia University Press.

Meiklejohn, A. (1932). *The experimental college.* New York, NY: Harper & Row.

Mix, M. D. (1968). *New College of Teachers College: A history 1932–1939.* (Doctoral dissertation, Teachers College, Columbia University, 1968).

National Society for the Study of Education. (1932). *Yearbook 31, Part II: Changes and experiments in liberal arts education.* Bloomington, IN: Public School Publishing.

Rosenzweig, J. S. (1997, October 30). *The innovative colleges and universities of the 1960s and 1970s: What keeps the dreams of experimentation alive?* Paper presented at the Evergreen Conference on Interdisciplinary Education, The Evergreen State College, Olympia, WA.

Tewksbury, D. G. (1934). *An educational program for St. Stephen's College: A preliminary statement submitted for the consideration of the board of trustees of the college, by Donald G. Tewksbury, acting dean, approved March 1, 1934.* Annandale-On-Hudson, NY: Bard College.

Endnotes

1. Only relatively recently have historians of higher education acknowledged the turmoil on liberal arts campuses during this period. See Levine, D. O. (1986). *The American college and the culture of aspiration, 1915–1940.* Ithaca, NY: Cornell University Press.

2. Arthur E. Morgan to Willard Johnson, 24 March 1965, recounting a rejection of a grant application by the General Education Board in the early 1920s.

3. "Dinner at Engineer's Club, Dayton, Ohio," Wednesday, January 19, 1921, Antiochiana Collection, Olive Kettering Memorial Library, Antioch University, Yellow Springs, Ohio.

4. Ralph Flanders suggested that Pitkin call the college a "school for Vermont living" (Flanders to Pitkin, January 27, 1938, Pitkin Papers, Vermont Historical Society, Montpelier, Vermont). Pitkin changed the wording and used it in numerous publications such as the "Program for the First Meeting of the Vermont Committee for the Development of Goddard College, A Vermont School for Living, Plainfield, August 17, 1938" (Goddard College Archives, Eliot Pratt Learning Center, Goddard College, Plainfield, Vermont).

5. "Community Government Conference, October 27-28, 1941," Pitkin Papers, Vermont Historical Society, Box 10.

2

The Innovative Colleges and Universities of the 1960s and 1970s: Lessons from Six Alternative Institutions

Joy Rosenzweig Kliewer[1]
Western University of Health Sciences

There are places I'll remember
All my life, though some have changed
Some forever, not for better,
Some have gone and some remain
All these places had their moments
With lovers and friends I still can recall . . .
In my life, I've loved them all . . .[2]

—John Lennon & Paul McCartney, 1965

Background and Overview

In the 1960s and early 1970s, academic planners, reformers, countercultural gurus, faculty members, and students converged upon mountaintops, held retreats in the woods, occupied classrooms and board rooms for days at a time, to give life to new and radically different institutions of higher education. Scores of innovative or experimental colleges and subcolleges burst onto the scene against a backdrop of social and political turbulence, heated and passionate student demonstration, rapid enrollment growth, economic upswings, and countercultural lifestyle exploration.

Witness the birth of the Alternative One College at Keene State in New Hampshire; the Aquarian University, built on a "spiritual commune" in Baltimore; the Student Center College in Mendocino, California; the College Within at Tufts; and the College of the Person in Washington, D.C. There was the College of the Atlantic in Bar Harbor, Maine, founded "in part to help the island's economy and in part to make a difference in the world" (Hall, 1994, p. 52); the Campus Free College in Arlington, Massachusetts; the Colleges Within The College at the University of Kansas; free-spirited Franconia College in the "round green mountains of New Hampshire;" and the Experimental College at Fresno State—here students enrolled in courses on "Love and Violence," "Basic Mountaineering," and the "Practice of Yoga." There was the student-run Experimental College at San Francisco State; the neoclassical experiments at Berkeley and San Jose State; the encounter group college (Johnston) of the University of Redlands (now Johnston Center for Integrative Studies); New College in Florida; Hampshire College in Massachusetts; The Evergreen State College, a public experimental college in Olympia, Washington; and the University of California (UC) Santa Cruz, an innovative university that was built in the middle of a redwood forest (Coyne & Hebert, 1972; Gaff, 1970a, 1970b; Grant & Riesman, 1978; Hall, 1991; McDonald & O'Neill, 1988; Tussman, 1969).

Most of these dazzling departures thrived in the 1960s and early 1970s, many of them attracting renowned faculty, top-notch applicants, and anti-establishment attendees. But by the mid-1970s, the years of prosperity and high hopes gave way to stagnation and decline. Friends and founders began to flee. Faculty and students ran for cover. Severe economic hardships, decreases in the rate of enrollment growth, and shifting student values (materialistic or careerist student goals and aspirations) brought an end to the age of experimentation (Cheit, 1971; Hall, 1991; Levine, 1980a, 1980b). UC Santa Cruz began the "long, mutinous march back to the familiar lines of academic responsibility" (Adams, 1984, p. 24); Johnston College was absorbed into the University of Redlands; the phone lines were cut, the learning "huts" taken away, the office doors padlocked at the Experimental College at San Francisco State (Grand & Bebout, 1981). One by one, the bold new campuses began to close their doors or to abandon their visions of educational innovation.

When the storm cleared and the enrollments stabilized, only a few beautiful little experiments were intact or operational (e.g., College of the Atlantic, Hampshire College, The Evergreen State College). What kept these imaginative ventures healthy and strong? What are some of the keys to the survival or longevity of academic innovations?

While previous researchers have tried their hands at explaining or accounting for why the innovative higher education movement lost its momentum, and why some distinctive campuses abandoned their early visions or simply collapsed while others endured or succeeded, there have been no recent empirical investigations that have examined these phenomena across institutions. With few exceptions (e.g., Grant & Riesman, 1978; Levine & Weingart, 1973), the bulk of the writings in this creative corner of the higher education literature are nonempirical pieces (memoirs, personal thoughts, and reflections) usually based on a single campus experience (e.g., Anzulovic, 1976; Coyne, 1972; Grand & Bebout, 1981; Kahn, 1981; Ruopp & Jerome, 1973). Systematic investigations that contemplate the question of how and why innovative colleges and universities sustain or transform their distinctive founding missions are few and far between.

This study attempted to fill this void in the research literature. In order to gain insight into the history and endurance of institutional innovations in higher education, I conducted four- to five-day site visits to six distinctive colleges and universities across the United States in the 1995–1996 academic year. The six institutions were Pitzer College in Claremont, California; New College of the University of South Florida in Sarasota; Hampshire College in Amherst, Massachusetts; the University of Wisconsin-Green Bay (UW-Green Bay); University of California, Santa Cruz; and The Evergreen State College in Olympia, Washington.

This chapter provides an overview of the investigation and presents the results of the case studies. It begins with a definition of innovation and innovative colleges and universities. Next, it reviews the research questions that guided the study. The following section describes the methodological design: the institutional selection process and data gathering and analysis techniques. The next section presents a profile of the six innovative campuses and summarizes the findings of the institutional studies. Then, the cross-campus findings are reviewed, including the factors that have been found to either facilitate or inhibit long-lasting innovation. The chapter concludes with a discussion of the implications of the research for distinctive institutions and the higher education community and suggestions for future studies of alternative colleges and universities.

Definition: What is an Innovative College or University?

It is a challenge to grasp, put your fingers around, touch, and feel the idea of innovation in higher education (Townsend, Newell, & Wiese, 1992). Different authors conceptualize reform in different ways, and there are "a cornucopia of typologies to choose from" (Levine, 1980b, p. 4). There are those who single out alternative campuses for their out-of-the-ordinary programs, their "wacky," "handmade," "one-of-a-kind" designs—e.g., the mountain hiking classes, the Zen and You workshops (Gehret, 1972; Levine, 1980b; Townsend et al., 1992). Friends and foes conjure up images of caterpillars about to become butterflies; educational paradises or Gardens of Eden; classical Greek societies; and "hairy," "messy" homes for the radically inclined (Childs, 1981; Coyne & Hebert, 1972; Greening, 1981b; Martin, 1982; Von der Muhll, 1984).

In one of the more well-known conceptions, Gerald Grant and David Riesman (1978) divide experimental institutions into the "telic" (the counterrevolutionary, that is, reforms in the underlying purpose or philosophy of undergraduate education) and the "popular" (reforms in the processes, the means or delivery of higher education). James W. Hall (1991) categorizes innovative colleges along curricular lines (i.e., integrated or interdisciplinary, human development, and cluster models). Arthur Levine (1980b) offers a typology based on structural reform: new experimenting organizations; innovative enclaves within existing organizations; holistic and piecemeal changes; and peripheral, environmental reforms. And L. Jackson Newell and Katherine C. Reynolds (1993) place experimental or "maverick colleges" into a four-quadrant schema based on student selection (who should attend, arrayed on a continuum ranging from open to elite institutions) and educational methods (how best to integrate theoretical and practical knowledge, on a continuum ranging from campuses that connect theory to practice at "immediate times and locations" [inside the classroom] to those that prefer to keep experiential practice distant from the classroom setting or entirely separate from the college or university program).

For the purposes of this study, "innovation" has been operationally defined as any significant departure from traditional practices in American higher education (Levine, 1980b). Therefore, "innovative," "experimental," or "distinctive" colleges and universities refer to those campuses that were founded amidst the social, political, economic, and demographic transformations of the 1960s and early 1970s as alternatives to the mainstream American college or university. How do these campuses depart from the mainstream? Drawing on the literature, there appear to be five dimensions that "mark out the territory" of innovative institutions of higher education:

1) *Interdisciplinary teaching and learning.* Cross-disciplinary study and collaboration in curricular and cocurricular activity (Grant & Riesman, 1978; Newell, 1984).

2) *Student-centered education.* Students engineer or take charge of their academic programs (e.g., students invent their own academic majors, design courses, and assist in curricular planning and development) (Adams, 1993; Grand & Bebout, 1981; Newell, 1984).

3) *Egalitarianism.* Participatory governance structures—town meetings, general assemblies, and/or community forums where administrators, faculty, and students share equal voice in decision-making; an absence of status symbols, such as titles and ranks; close-knit relations between faculty and students; narrative evaluations as opposed to letter grades; and cooperation and collaboration rather than competition in teaching and learning (Grant & Riesman, 1978; Hall, 1994; Kuh et al., 1991; Townsend et al., 1992).

4) *Experiential learning.* Out-of-classroom projects, theses, and/or internships are integral to the academic program (Adams, 1993; Newell, 1984).

5) *An institutional focus on teaching* rather than research and/or publication. There is an intensity, a spirit of vocation about teaching that "permeates these communities" (Grant & Riesman, 1978, p. 33).

While some colleges and universities today may refer to themselves as distinctive or innovative, this investigation focuses specifically on those campuses that came into being as part of the educational reform movement of the 1960s and early 1970s, and that typically embodied these distinctive characteristics at the time of their inception.

Research Questions

This study asks how and why do innovative colleges and universities maintain their distinctive founding missions? What keeps the dream, the spirit of reform, alive (or leads to its compromise or demise)? What do these colleges and universities, their life cycles, stories, and experiences, have to teach us about the processes of innovation and the preservation of reform efforts in higher education?

Methodology

In order to answer these questions, I conducted field visits to innovative colleges and universities across the United States. Institutional selection included a comprehensive review of previously published guides on alternative campuses and interdisciplinary programs in higher education (e.g., Bear, 1980; Coyne & Hebert, 1972; Heiss, 1973; Lichtman, 1972; Newell, 1986), and the readings and research on distinctive colleges and universities. Campus "nominations" were also sought through consultation with 28 nationally recognized experts on reform in higher education. Drawing on the literature review and information provided by the expert panel, a "master list" of 316 innovative institutions was generated. In order to limit the size of the master inventory, nontraditional campuses for adults, innovative colleges and universities that offered primarily external degree programs, and distance learning institutions that came into being during the 1960s and 1970s, were excluded from the list. The master list also excluded the small number of innovative community colleges, upper division colleges, and graduate schools (and free-standing graduate institutions) that grew out of the 1960s and 1970s reform movement.

Next, a "candidate list" of possible research sites was compiled from the master inventory. In order to narrow down the number of potential sites, subcolleges and free universities were excluded from this list. For ease of research and accessibility to participants in the campus communities, the list was also confined to those colleges and universities that remained open in the 1990s. The result was a list of 22 free-standing innovative institutions from which the final sample of case study sites would be drawn.

The final list of institutions included two small private liberal arts colleges (Pitzer and Hampshire), two small public liberal arts colleges (New College and Evergreen), and two public universities (University of California, Santa Cruz and the University of Wisconsin-Green Bay). Three alternate sites were also selected in the event that the proposal to participate in the research project was declined by one or more of the campuses (see Table 2.1).

Altogether, 151 interviews were conducted with 164 faculty, administrators, students, trustees, and alumnae/i during the six campus visits (approximately 25 interviews were held at each case study site). Key informants were drawn from the ranks of the veteran and charter faculty and administrators, the forward-thinking planners and leaders who gave "life" to these institutions (and who remained on campus or in the vicinity). Interview participants were encouraged to reflect upon the unique nature of the college or university today and, where possible, to look back to the early days or start-up years, to think about how the institution had transformed (and/or recreated) itself.

The interviews were supplemented with extensive archival research and institutional document analysis, along with observations of campus activities, programs, and meetings. All interviews were tape recorded and nearly all 151 interviews were transcribed verbatim. Data were analyzed inductively both within and across case study sites.

Case Study Results

The following paragraphs present the results of the case studies, drawing on the data gathered in the campus interviews, document analyses, and observations. Each profile describes the evolution and endurance of the innovative ideals that shaped the guiding visions of the founders of the institutions.

TABLE 2.1 Final List of Innovative Institutions and Alternate Sites

Institution	Founding Year	Carnegie Classification[a]	Control	Location (State)	Enroll-ment	Writings/ Reports[b]	Presumed Status[c]
Selected Sites							
1. The Evergreen State College	1967	BA II	Public	WA	3,477	X	M
2. Hampshire College	1965	BA I	Private	MA	1,050	X	M
3. New College of the University of South Florida	1960	not listed*	Public	FL	526	X	M
4. Pitzer College	1963	BA I	Private	CA	890		NM
5. University of California, Santa Cruz	1962	Res II	Public	CA	10,173	X	NM
6. University of Wisconsin-Green Bay	1965	MA II	Public	WI	5,205		NM
Alternate Sites							
1. College of the Atlantic	1969	BA I	Private	ME	217		M
2. Ramapo College of New Jersey	1969	BA II	Public	NJ	4,683		NM
3. The Richard Stockton College of New Jersey (formerly Stockton State College)	1969	BA I	Public	NJ	5,619		NM

Note: The data in column 3 (Carnegie Classification) are from *A Classification of Institutions of Higher Education 1994 Edition.* (1994). Princeton, NJ: The Carnegie Foundation for the Advancement of Teaching. The data in columns 2, 4, 5, and 6 are from Rodenhouse, M. P. (Ed.). (1995). *1995 Higher Education Directory.* Falls Church, VA: Higher Education Publications.

a) BA I = Baccalaureate I institutions, BA II = Baccalaureate II institutions, MA II = Master's II institutions, Res II = Research II institutions (*A Classification of Institutions of Higher Education, 1994*).

b) X = The institution has been the subject of six or more journal articles, books, chapters in edited volumes, and/or scholarly reports.

c) M = Presumption that the institution maintained its founding principles, NM = Presumption that the institution did not maintain its founding principles. (Based on a review of the literature and current campus catalogs, and consultation with a panel of experts on innovation in American higher education.)

*The Carnegie classification for the University of South Florida is Res II.

Pitzer College

Pitzer College opened in 1964 as an undergraduate residential liberal arts college with a curricular emphasis on the social and behavioral sciences. The campus started as a women's college, but became coeducational in 1970 as enrollments grew and planners "came to envisage Pitzer as an institution with a broader impact and appeal" (Bernard, 1982, p. 622).

Pitzer is one of six institutions of The Claremont Colleges, a distinguished consortium of private liberal arts colleges in Southern California that includes Pomona College, Scripps College, Claremont McKenna College, Harvey Mudd College, and Claremont Graduate University. Modeled after the Oxford University plan of clusters of small residential colleges, each of the colleges in the Claremont group has a life and a character of its own—a distinct curricular mission; a president, faculty, and board of trustees; independent legal status; and institutional guidelines—while sharing in the resources of the other colleges (e.g., joint academic programs, research opportunities, cross registration) and the central programs and services of the Claremont consortium (the library, health services, counseling center, bookstore, etc.).

The founders of Pitzer College dedicated themselves to creating a campus that would embrace the ideals of participatory governance and individualized education in a close-knit, egalitarian teaching and learning community. According to interviewees, there was a concerted effort to begin the college with as few rules as possible. Every student, every faculty member, and every staff person would have a voice in campus decision-making. There was a spirit of adventure and creativity in faculty teaching and scholarship, and interdisciplinarity was a hallmark of the Pitzer College curricular offerings and research activities.

In the start-up years, the Pitzer faculty formed "field groups" (groupings of faculty with similar disciplinary interests) rather than traditional academic departments. The field groups had "conveners" as opposed to department chairs, and the academic budget was centrally coordinated, rather than being administered through individual field groups or disciplines (Bernard, 1982; Clary, 1970; Pitzer College, 1963).

Today, the early spirit and involvement in open, participatory governance has diminished to some extent, but the ideals of the small, student-centered community and of creative, interdisciplinary education remain in place at the institution. Pitzer undergraduates continue to take part in college-wide governance, offering input into policy making and even faculty appointment, promotion, and tenure decisions. The campus remains free of traditional, budgeted disciplinary departments and the academic budget is centrally coordinated through the office of the academic dean (Kliewer, 1999; Pitzer College, 1996).

Why has Pitzer been able to largely preserve its innovative founding ideals? Interviewees single out the college's unusual "institutional arrangements," its "light" hierarchical organization. They emphasize, over and over again, the importance of the campus' nondepartmentalized structure and the fact that professors are rewarded for interdisciplinary teaching. People are a "thread" at this institution, long-time faculty and staff observe, and it is the continuing presence of founding professors (and incoming cohorts who share the visions of the pioneers) that sustains the early innovative ideals. At the same time, Pitzer's connection with The Claremont Colleges, the cross-campus resource sharing and curricular opportunities, has enabled this campus to survive and to carry on as a distinctive institution.

In the words of an administrator at the college, "I think one of the reasons [that Pitzer remains innovative] is the fact that [we're] a part of a consortium in which there's the opposite or the complement . . . . [W]e sit next to *much* more traditional institutions, share their resources, are in the dialog with them all the time so that we're not out there all by ourselves."

A professor of 28 years explained that Pitzer has always been regarded by the other Claremont Colleges as the "experimental" school. It has been protected in some ways by the fact that there are more traditional schools in the system, allowing Pitzer the freedom to do experimental things that maybe the other schools don't do.

Where there have been changes in the founding innovative philosophies of Pitzer College, interviewees point to the natural processes of institutional aging—campus growth, increasing bureaucratization. At the same time, the social environment has changed. The radicalism out of which this campus was born in the 1960s is no longer, and so the kindred spirit and intensity of pioneering a brand new venture has faded. In the end, Pitzer College has moved from the 1960s to the 1990s with a few compromises, but with a sense of style and grace. The heritage of the pioneers, the spirit of small, participatory, student–centered community; of interdisciplinary education; and creative, nourishing academic pursuits, lives on in many ways in Claremont today.

New College of the University of South Florida

New College of the University of South Florida opened in 1964 as a distinctive private liberal arts college in Sarasota, Florida. In 1975, the college merged with the University of South Florida (USF), becoming an innovative branch campus of USF. (USF is a comprehensive public research university in Tampa, with branch campuses in Fort Myers, Sarasota, Lakeland, and St. Petersburg.)

Since its dynamic start-up years, New College has been offering a unique educational program with an emphasis on student-centered learning—students negotiate "educational contracts" each term with a faculty member to design an individualized course of study. There are no disciplinary departments, no academic deans, no academic credits or units, and no letter grades at New College; all students receive written evaluations of their coursework. Faculty enjoy a tremendous amount of freedom in designing new and creative courses, and students are encouraged to work side by side with their professors as "colleagues" in the learning process (Arthur, 1995; Burns, 1994; Kliewer, 1999; New College of the University of South Florida, 1994).

Over the past 31 years, the institution has sustained its pioneering missions in the face of financial crisis, near closure, a merger, and a changing social, political, and economic climate. What are the factors that have enabled this campus to preserve its distinctive heritage? First, as in the case of Pitzer College, interviewees single out the continuing commitment of the original or veteran faculty members. The incoming cohorts of academics who share the visions of the pioneers also keep the spirit and spark of innovation alive. Then there are the students who come to New College year after year in search of unorthodox and individualized educational experiences and whose energy and resourcefulness renew the founding visions.

All of this occurs in the context of an open and decentralized academic and administrative organizational structure (e.g., there are no departments, curriculum committees, or complex hierarchies at New College). Despite the red tape and rules imposed by the state university system, interviewees believe that the affiliation with the state has been essential for the institution's survival. "In 1975, we were probably two hours from closing the institution and firing everybody," a charter professor explains. President Arland Christ-Janer convinced the State of Florida that a merger between USF and New College would result in "the world's best real estate deal" and a "jewel in the crown of the state university system." What's more, the state has essentially kept its hands off the New College academic program. Written into the merger agreement, Furman C. Arthur (1995) notes in his compelling history of the college, was a proviso "that the educational programs of the private college would be continued 'at no cost to the state' while preserving the 'identity and the unique concepts and quality' of the college" (p. 128).

Another integral factor to the college's survival has been the New College Foundation, a private organization that raises funds so that the institution can maintain its distinctive educational programs and low student-to-faculty ratio (and a low tuition). The Foundation funds the differential between the amount that the state provides to the college and the actual costs of the New College program. Without the support of the Foundation, interviewees say, New College would never have been able to carry on as a distinctive campus within a large state university. The fact that New College exists today, Arthur (1995) points out, is a testimonial to the success of the campus' partnership with the State of Florida and the fundraising achievements of the New College Foundation.

Hampshire College

Hampshire College opened its doors in 1970 as an innovative private liberal arts college in the Pioneer Valley of Massachusetts. The Pioneer Valley is home to the famed Five College Consortium of institutions, which includes Hampshire College, Amherst College, Mount Holyoke College, Smith College, and the University of Massachusetts Amherst. These five neighboring institutions carry out cooperative programs, share resources and library facilities, and offer intercollegiate faculty exchanges and cross-campus enrollment opportunities.

Since its inception, Hampshire College has departed from the norms of traditional higher education. The founders of the college set out to create a campus that would embrace student-initiated or self-directed learning. Rather than traditional, credit-based requirements, students would proceed through a series of individualized "divisions" to complete their baccalaureate work: Division 1, basic studies, introduces students to the conceptual ideas and methodological tools ("modes of inquiry") of the college's four interdisciplinary schools; in Division II, the student completes a "concentration," which is similar to a college "major"; and in Division III, the student enrolls in advanced, integrative seminars and undertakes an intensive independent project or thesis (Astin, Milem, Astin, Ries, & Heath, 1991; Hampshire College, 1995).

Hampshire College encourages active student participation in campus governance and, like New College, views undergraduates as "teachers" or colleagues with the faculty in the classroom arena. There are no grades and no academic departments at Hampshire, and there is no tenure system for faculty. Teaching is prized at the institution and there is a tremendous amount of freedom for faculty to engage in curricular experimentation and team teaching. Interdisciplinary education remains a hallmark of the Hampshire education and students are encouraged to pursue cross-disciplinary projects and divisional work (Alpert, 1980; Astin et al., 1991; Birney, 1993; Kliewer, 1999; Patterson & Longsworth, 1966).

What are the factors that have enabled Hampshire to sustain its unorthodox educational principles? First, interviewees, here again, single out the dedication of the founding and long-time faculty. These faculty pioneers pass along the Hampshire vision to latter generations of academics and students who keep alive the early missions of the founders. The decentralized organization of the campus, with its multidisciplinary schools and absence of academic departments, has also paved the way for long-lasting interdisciplinary innovation and spirited teaching and learning.

Above all, it may be Hampshire's association with the Five College Consortium that has enabled this one-of-a-kind campus to carry on as an innovative institution. Hampshire students can enroll in more than 5,000 classes, study with some 2,000 faculty members, and enjoy the facilities and library resources of three highly regarded liberal arts colleges and a research university. As is the case with Pitzer College, location and affiliation have been key.

University of Wisconsin-Green Bay

The University of Wisconsin-Green Bay opened in 1969 with an emphasis on the environment and interdisciplinary, problem-focused education. The founders of the university believed that conventional disciplinary fields should be subordinate to interdisciplinary areas of study and inquiry. Undergraduates at the early university would major in an interdisciplinary concentration, although they could "co-major" in a disciplinary field (Weidner & Kuepper, 1993).

Experiential learning and outreach to the community were integral to the original academic program of the University of Wisconsin-Green Bay. There was a strong emphasis on student-initiated education or students actively shaping or taking charge of their own learning processes. Undergraduate teaching was the faculty member's primary activity, and the campus fostered close-knit relationships between professors and students (Kliewer, 1999; Lane et al., 1968; Weidner, 1977; 1994).

Today, while much of the original, distinctive mission of the campus has faded (gone, for example, is the environmental focus, gone is the emphasis on individualized learning, and gone is the experiential education component), the University of Wisconsin-Green Bay continues, at least in part, to honor its roots of experimentation. The central organizing academic units on campus continue to be the interdisciplinary departments, which have authority over academic budgets, curricular policy, and faculty appointments (Brown, 1974; Kliewer, 1999; Rice & Bremer, 1994; Weidner & Kuepper, 1993).

What are the factors that have enabled UW-Green Bay to preserve its interdisciplinary organization and principles? Interviewees emphasize over and over again the importance of the campus' budgeted interdisciplinary departments as the key to the endurance of the cross-disciplinary educational mission. At the same time, here again, they cite the presence of a critical mass or core group of founding faculty and administrators who have remained at the institution and who have kept the founding spirit of interdisciplinarity and educational innovation alive in their creative leadership, scholarship, and teaching.

When it comes to the changes or transformations in the founding distinctive philosophies, interviewees point to shifts in the attitudes and interests of the student generations, increasing student-to-faculty ratios, and institutional efforts to accommodate the disciplinary and professional needs of the local community. They also make reference to the budgetary cutbacks imposed by the State of Wisconsin, and University of

Wisconsin System-wide pressures to conventionalize programs, academic reward structures, and curriculum (Kliewer, 1999).

Perhaps the most transformational event in the institution's history occurred in 1974 when the University of Wisconsin merged with the then Wisconsin State University System, incorporating the nine former public comprehensive universities in the state. "As I reflect on our history," a charter professor and former UW-Green Bay administrator remarks, "one of the reasons that we were not able to protect [the distinctive missions] was because of the dramatic change that took place in Wisconsin higher education in the '70s with merger." Prior to the merger, he says, there was a "strong sentiment that . . . innovation was necessary" and that "Green Bay should be sort of the innovating, cutting edge institution [of the University of Wisconsin]."

During the merger, budget cuts were instituted at all of the former UW System institutions in order to bring the costs of the UW campuses closer to those of the old Wisconsin State University institutions (Weidner & Kuepper, 1993). Soon, UW-Green Bay lost its preferential funding as the interdisciplinary, environmental campus of the University of Wisconsin.

In the end, although UW-Green Bay has witnessed much of the early visions of the pioneers fade away, the innovative heritage of the university is kept alive by the long-time faculty, the new leadership on campus, and in the continuing interdisciplinary organization of the institution today.

University of California, Santa Cruz

University of California, Santa Cruz opened in the fall of 1965 in the foothills of Santa Cruz overlooking Monterey Bay and the Pacific Ocean. The founders sought to create a "collegiate university," one that would run counter to the isolation and impersonality of the large, monolithic "multiversity." In order to foster a sense of belonging and close-knit community among students and faculty, the planners established a series of small residential cluster colleges. These colleges would function as personal, interdisciplinary, teaching communities that would coexist along with the university's research-oriented disciplinary "departments" or boards of studies (Grant & Riesman, 1978; McHenry, 1977; Von der Muhll, 1984).

Early students at the Santa Cruz campus were encouraged to take charge of their learning, to pursue individualized majors, and to design their own courses and independent studies projects (University of California, Santa Cruz, 1965). Instead of conventional letter grades, students would receive written evaluations of their coursework. There was a firm commitment to interdisciplinary teaching and learning in college-based courses and faculty coteaching (McHenry, 1977).

While the residential, collegial organization of the university remains an integral feature of the institution today, and while UC Santa Cruz continues to offer narrative evaluations (along with a letter grade option) for students, the early interdisciplinary teaching and student-centered ethos has, for the most part, disappeared. The campus was radically reorganized in the late 1970s to embrace disciplinary research and the conventional standards and practices of the University of California system (Adams, 1984; Grant & Riesman, 1978; Kliewer, 1999; McHenry, 1977; Von der Muhll, 1984).

In discussing the reasons for the changes at the university, nearly all interviewees point to the shifts in the economy, severe budgetary cutbacks, a faculty reward structure that emphasizes academic research, and shifts in the attitudes and interests of students and faculty. The tensions implicit in the dual organization of the early colleges and boards of studies, the enrollment downturns of the 1970s, and pressures and standards imposed by the UC system, all resulted in the radical restructuring of the university. Santa Cruz today is an institution of excellence and high standing, according to long-time faculty, staff, and alumnae/i, but it is not the campus of which its founders dreamed.

The Evergreen State College

The Evergreen State College opened in 1971 as an innovative public liberal arts college in Washington. The cornerstone of the Evergreen curriculum was and continues to be the Coordinated Studies program. Coordinated Studies are full-time, team-taught, multidisciplinary programs involving about four to five faculty members and 80 to 100 students. The curriculum is constantly changing or being "reinvented" in order to ensure a continuing sense of vitality and excitement in teaching (Kuh et al., 1991; Youtz, 1984).

Individualized learning is a cherished and long-lasting ideal of the Evergreen community. Students are placed at the center of the educational process and are considered to be colearners with the faculty in the teaching experience. There are no required courses, no majors, no faculty ranks, no academic departments, and no grades at Evergreen. Experiential, out-of-classroom learning is integral to the educational philosophy of the institution and teaching remains at the heart of faculty life. Academics at Evergreen are evaluated on the basis of a portfolio of cumulative teaching experiences. The portfolio includes self-evaluations and evaluations from students and colleagues in team-taught programs (The Evergreen State College, 1997b; Kliewer, 1999).

Campus governance processes are flexible and participatory at Evergreen. In order to prevent power-wielding structures from "penetrating" the college, Evergreen's founders created temporary ad-hoc committees (called Disappearing Task Forces or DTFs) that involved students, faculty, and staff in consensus decision-making. The DTFs, which continue to function as the primary vehicle for campus governance today, address a single problem or task, and when the work of the group is completed, disband or disappear (Clemens, 1987; The Evergreen State College, 1989; Kliewer, 1999; The Evergreen State College, 1972; Youtz, 1984).

What are the factors that have enabled this maverick college to sustain its pioneering principles in a rapidly changing sociopolitical and economic environment? What has kept the innovative educational philosophies alive at Evergreen? Like their counterparts at the other institutions, interviewees at Evergreen single out the continuing presence and dedication of early faculty. A remarkable number of the founders have remained on the faculty of the college. In 1995–1996, at the time of the field visit, 30 of the 58 original faculty members and academic deans (more than 50% of the charter faculty) continued to teach at Evergreen. Forty-one percent of all regular, full-time faculty in 1995–1996 had been employed at Evergreen for at least 25 years. The founding president of the college, Charles J. McCann, also continued to serve as an emeritus member of the faculty (The Evergreen State College, 1996).

Interviewees report that the new faculty cohorts at Evergreen are recruited for their interest in collaborative, interdisciplinary teaching. The students who elect to attend the college and the campus' visionary administrators also sustain the institution's cooperative, interdisciplinary learning missions. In addition, Evergreen, like many of the other campuses, remains free of rigid and hierarchical organizational structures, which allows for a continuing sense of vitality in teaching, an openness and freedom to experiment.

The college has also been fortunate in having its own board of trustees. Unlike many of the other state-supported innovative institutions of the era (e.g., UC Santa Cruz, the University of Wisconsin-Green Bay), Evergreen has been granted relative independence and its own built-in system of support through its board of trustees. Although there is now a Higher Education Coordinating Board in the State of Washington, there is no central governing board of trustees in Washington whose interests represent the norms of a large conventional public university system. This has been a key factor in Evergreen's longevity.

Cross-Campus Results

Looking across the results of the campus case studies, the longevity of innovation among institutions is striking. All campuses that started without course requirements, academic units, and faculty ranks, for example, have remained free of these conventional structures. All sites that resisted departmental organization in the beginning (including the University of Wisconsin-Green Bay) continue to exist without traditional disciplinary departments. All campuses that offered individualized learning contracts and personalized educational programs in the early years have successfully retained these distinctive features. And all campuses that started with a narrative or nongraded evaluation system have resisted the establishment of a traditional grading approach (including UC Santa Cruz).

On the whole, the cross-campus portrait of innovation in this study reveals a remarkable pattern of stability, especially among the smaller colleges (Pitzer, New College, Hampshire, and Evergreen). In general, it seems that the smaller liberal arts colleges (whether they be private or public) are more likely to keep hold of their distinctive founding heritage than the larger public universities.

These findings confirm and extend the results of previous studies of experimental colleges and universities (e.g., Grant & Riesman, 1978; Townsend et al., 1992), which indicate that public institutions are more vulnerable to external pressures and are less successful in maintaining their distinctiveness over time. The present study adds to the research literature by suggesting that certain types of public institutions—small public liberal arts colleges (like Evergreen or New College)—are more successful in sustaining their innovative founding missions than are the larger public universities (University of Wisconsin-Green Bay, UC Santa Cruz). Autonomy or independence from a centralized state governing board or university system seems to be an important factor in this success. New College has, again, benefited from its autonomy and geographical distance from the University of South Florida, and by having its own independent fundraising foundation. Evergreen has been supported by having its own board of trustees as opposed to a system-wide or statewide coordinating system of regents.

Factors that Facilitate the Endurance of Innovation Across Campus Sites

What are the factors that enable a distinctive institution to maintain its original unorthodox values in a changing sociopolitical and economic environment? Based on the results of the case studies, there appear to be five key variables that facilitate the endurance of distinctive educational approaches at innovative colleges and universities. These are the presence and support of founding faculty members; faculty recruitment strategies; an academic reward system that values innovation; free-flowing, nondepartmental organizational structures; and administrative support for innovation.

The Presence and Support of Founding Faculty Members

Across all campuses, interviewees single out the presence and the dedication of charter faculty members as integral to the success and longevity of innovation. The veteran scholars are often hailed as the faithful supporters and advocates of the original distinctive missions of the institutions. At Pitzer College, the charter academics are viewed as the creators and innovators who fuel the visions and who keep alive the spirit and processes of participatory governance. At New College, the veteran faculty are considered to be the "conscience of the place," in the words of one administrator, "a constant poke in the back to remind everybody why we got together up there in the first place." The charter (and newer cohorts of) faculty sustain the rich traditions of individualism and active and egalitarian classroom environments.

The presence of a large number of original faculty members at Hampshire has also been fundamental to the preservation of the student–centered educational missions and the long-standing dedication to participatory governance. At Evergreen, the traditions of interdisciplinarity, individualized education, experiential learning, and students serving as "teachers" or "colearners" with the faculty, and are all kept alive, in part, by a dedicated core group of veteran academics who continue to teach at the campus and who champion the ideals and visions of the early days.

Even at those institutions that have, for the most part, abandoned their innovative principles, it is, again, the commitment of the founding faculty that has sustained the innovations that do remain in place. At the University of Wisconsin-Green Bay, for example, an institution that has in many ways succumbed to external pressures to conventionalize, the founding faculty and administrators are the guiding forces in preserving the campus' interdisciplinary organization. At UC Santa Cruz, a university that has embraced traditionalism since its free-wheeling start-up era, there is still a sense that the veteran faculty (only a handful of whom remain at the institution) keep alive the early spirit and ideals, especially with regard to the narrative evaluation system.

In the end, the long-time faculty at innovative colleges and universities serve as models and mentors for other academics and voices for the preservation of the founding missions. In their lively and creative teaching, in their dynamic approaches to curriculum development and campus governance, and in their fond memories and storytelling about the cherished start-up years, they are the keepers of the dreams.

Faculty Recruitment Strategies: Passing the Torch

The distinctive heritage of an institution is also perpetuated by the incoming cohorts of faculty who share the founders' passion and spirit for innovation and who have been drawn to the college or university because of its alternative mission. At Evergreen, for example, the campus' cooperative educational philosophies are perpetuated and passed down to new faculty members who value the interdisciplinary approaches of the institution. There is an "Evergreen way" that pervades the campus, and new faculty, working in close collaboration with veteran academics, come to appreciate and adopt the multidisciplinary, team teaching approaches of the institution.

At Pitzer, professors refer to a process of "like hiring like," or bringing in new faculty members who share the college's basic commitment to cross-disciplinary perspectives. Likewise at New College, incoming cohorts of academics who share the values of the pioneers sustain the campus' distinctive heritage of individualized education, faculty creativity, and cooperative learning activities. And at Hampshire College, academic recruitment has been key to the preservation of the interdisciplinary mission and the emphasis on undergraduate teaching and faculty freedom. Hampshire has been described as having "an infectious vision."

An Academic Reward System That Values Innovation

Next, academic reward structures that value distinctive or creative approaches in teaching or scholarly activity are critical for innovation to endure. Those campuses that have been most successful in sustaining their early interdisciplinary teaching approaches promote faculty for engaging in cross-disciplinary or creative teaching endeavors. At Pitzer, for example, one of the most important criteria in academic advancement and tenure decisions is successful joint teaching. At Evergreen, creative, team-taught seminars and interdisciplinary approaches are perpetuated by a faculty reappointment system that values excellence in teaching and interdisciplinary education.

At those campuses that have, for the most part, sacrificed their distinctive pedagogical approaches or teaching missions, it is often the case that faculty were not being rewarded for innovative teaching or curriculum development. At UC Santa Cruz, for instance, the original interdisciplinary, student-centered teaching in the colleges was abandoned, in large part, because academics were being evaluated on the basis of the conventional, disciplinary research and publication standards established by the University of California. At the University of Wisconsin-Green Bay, the early teaching mission of the institution was also sacrificed to some extent as the campus increasingly began to emphasize research and publication criteria in faculty promotion decisions.

Free-Flowing, Nondepartmental Organizational Structures

In addition, open or flexible organizational structures have been essential for ensuring long-lasting innovation. Antihierarchical, nondepartmental arrangements allow for curricular experimentation and pedagogic risk-taking. At Pitzer College, for example, professors are free to engage in creative approaches in teaching and research activity and to cross disciplinary boundaries without the constraints of traditional academic departments or a complex administrative hierarchy. At New College, an absence of departments, curriculum committees, academic deanships, and rigid bureaucratic structures has sustained a continuing sense of experimentation in teaching and learning. At Hampshire College, too, the freedom from departments, course credits, and grades has helped to keep alive the campus' imaginative interdisciplinary approaches and educational programs. Evergreen has also resisted the establishment of departments, curriculum committees, course requirements, faculty rank, and competitive grading systems. The faculty and students at the college enjoy a tremendous amount of freedom in collaborative teaching and learning activities. The University of Wisconsin-Green Bay has also been able to preserve its early interdisciplinary organization by resisting the establishment of conventional budgeted disciplinary departments.

Administrative Support for Innovation

Next, the commitment, vision, and dedication of campus administrators and trustees has been essential to the longevity of the innovative missions at a number of these alternative colleges and universities. At Pitzer, for example, interviewees praise the college's leadership for its longstanding support of innovation and its openness and willingness to encourage faculty to engage in creative, unexplored areas of scholarship and curriculum building. "For the most part, we've had very strong administrative support for innovation, for creativity," a professor who has been at Pitzer for 26 years explains. "We've been blessed with wonderful presidents," an early alumna and trustee agrees, "who have understood what Pitzer was supposed to be and what the faculty were committed to have Pitzer be." A top-level administrator affirms that it has been critical that the campus leadership has "not forc[ed] faculty" into narrowly defined areas of "intellectual thought." We try "to respect and let people go where their energies [lie]." It is all about appreciating differences, a former faculty member explains, a certain openness to creative expression.

At Hampshire, too, the dedication of institutional leaders and the board of trustees is singled out as an integral factor in the preservation of the campus' distinctive interdisciplinary ethos. And at Evergreen, where the academic deans are drawn from the faculty of the college, there is a continuing level of administrative support for and commitment to the campus' collaborative teaching and learning communities. Evergreen's presidents, including former Washington State Governor Dan Evans, have remained strong advocates of the college's unique brand of higher education.

Factors that Inhibit the Endurance of Innovation Across Campus Sites

While there are a number of factors or circumstances that tend to promote the longevity of innovations, there are also variables that seem to inhibit the endurance of alternative ideals or practices. Drawing on the findings of the campus studies, there appear to be three major variables that limit or constrain long-lasting innovation in distinctive colleges and universities: 1) pressures imposed by a large public university system, 2) shifts in enrollments and changes in the student generations, and 3) increasing student-to-faculty ratios.

Standards and Pressures Imposed by a Large Public University System

First, as indicated earlier, innovation may be ill-fated in a large public university. While all of the public experimental ventures in this investigation have come up against budgetary cutbacks and pressures to dissolve their distinctive practices, public universities have been particularly constrained by the policies and rules imposed by a large bureaucratic higher education system.

UC Santa Cruz, for example, has faced enormous pressures to standardize its unique curricular approaches and teaching philosophies as an institution of the University of California. The campus has gone from being a highly unorthodox interdisciplinary, teaching-centered institution, to a fairly traditional research-oriented university.

At the University of Wisconsin-Green Bay, the merger and the pressures and standards imposed by a state-supported higher education system also limited the campus' ability to maintain its free-spirited interdisciplinary programs and student-initiated educational activities. As professor Sydney H. Bremer remarked in a 1994 address to the Association of American Colleges, the merger of the University of Wisconsin and the Wisconsin State University "in the mid-70s, just a few years after UWGB opened, set in motion forces toward centralization, bureaucratic regularization, and even curricular homogenization" (Rice & Bremer, p. 11).

Shifts in Enrollments and Changes in the Student Generations

Second, enrollment downturns and changes in the attitudes and values of the student generations may jeopardize long-lasting innovation. Many distinctive colleges and universities experienced enrollment downturns in the 1970s and had to sacrifice some of their innovative approaches in order to attract the more career-oriented students of the decade. UC Santa Cruz in the mid- to late 1970s, for example, was suffering from its reputation as a "hippie campus" that offered "weird" and unusual interdisciplinary degrees. When the institution began to lose students, the interdisciplinary courses in Santa Cruz's residential colleges were abandoned as the university embraced traditional disciplinary departments and majors. At the University of Wisconsin-Green Bay, the campus' early interdisciplinary mission was also jeopardized by severe enrollment problems in the 1970s. The institution moved to establish traditional disciplinary majors in the early 1980s in order to accommodate the career ambitions and interests of local students. At New College, an institution that has been remarkably successful in preserving its distinctive heritage, some interviewees indicate that New College students have changed since the early days, and that over the years more students have been pursuing standardized (or course-based) learning contracts as opposed to the more creative, field-based contracts that were undertaken in the start-up years.

Increasing Student-to-Faculty Ratios

Third, increasing student-to-faculty ratios may limit innovation. When an institution grows and if student-faculty ratios increase, there is often a sense of loss of the intimate, personalized feeling and engagement in the learner-centered ideals of the distinctive college or university. At the University of Wisconsin-Green Bay, for example, according to interviewees, the early individualized curriculum and the opportunities for close-knit interactions between faculty and students have largely disappeared as the proportion of students to faculty on campus has risen in recent decades. At UC Santa Cruz, the founding spirit of undergraduate teaching in a face-to-face learning community has also been sacrificed since the 1970s as enrollments have grown and the student-to-faculty ratios have increased. Those institutions that have been more successful in preserving their individualized programs are those that have been able to maintain a relatively low student-to-faculty ratio (e.g., New College, Evergreen).

Implications and Recommendations

Each of the campuses in this study has at some point in its history dared to be different, to be a maverick, a rebel. Three decades since the dawn of the alternative higher education movement, some of these institutions are still rebelling, while others have settled into a more traditional or conventional pattern of being. Looking back over the results of the campus case studies, what are the overall lessons to be learned for the new millennium? What are the implications of the findings for future innovators and leaders of distinctive colleges and universities? What are the general implications of the results for the larger higher education community? These questions are addressed in the two sections that follow.

Implications for Innovative Institutions of Higher Education

Linking together the cross-campus themes and analyses, I offer the following guidelines and strategies for ensuring long-lasting innovation at distinctive institutions of higher education.

Retain Founding Faculty

First, in order to ensure that innovative ideals are passed down from one generation to the next, distinctive campuses should follow the lead of the institutions in this study and seek to retain a significant number of founding faculty members until the time of their retirements. Campuses should provide opportunities for interaction among charter professors and other academic cohorts (e.g., team teaching, educational workshops, or round-table discussions).

Recruit New Faculty and Administrators Who are Committed to Innovation

One of the most serious and widespread concerns among innovative colleges and universities today is the forthcoming retirements of charter faculty members. At all case study sites, long-time professors and administrators fear that the early dreams and innovative ideals of the institutions will be lost when the last of the pioneers retires over the next decade or two. If innovative campuses are to maintain their imaginative principles or philosophies, it is critical that they recruit new faculty members and administrators who value the distinctive ideals of the institutions and who will carry forward the visions of the founders.

Establish Reward Systems that Value Innovation

Third, academic reappointment, promotion, and tenure systems that reward innovative approaches to teaching and curriculum development are critical to sustaining innovation. If creative, interdisciplinary teaching and learning approaches are to flourish at distinctive institutions, then faculty members must be actively supported and rewarded for innovative teaching and program development.

Provide Open and Flexible Structures

Fourth, open or flexible organizational structures are essential to the success of distinctive educational approaches and decision-making. Institutions should strive to keep administrative hierarchies, academic committees, and disciplinary departments to a minimum. Governance structures should remain open and participatory. Faculty members should be given the freedom to experiment, to engage in creative approaches to teaching and scholarship. Students should be granted the space to design their own curricular pathways, to invent their own courses, majors, and/or independent study projects.

Affiliate with a Consortium of Institutions

Fifth, innovative campuses should seek out opportunities for affiliation with a consortium of institutions or neighboring colleges and universities. Opportunities will vary, of course, from one setting to another, but this kind of interinstitutional collaboration and exchange offers the small distinctive campus access to a wealth of information, resources, and shared facilities at other, more traditional or established institutions. Pitzer has, again, benefited from its association with five other solidly established liberal arts colleges and a graduate university in the Claremont Consortium. Hampshire has persevered because of its ties to a renowned consortium of institutions in the Pioneer Valley of Massachusetts. In both cases, the surrounding campuses have served as a kind of buffer of support for the innovative college, and students and faculty have access to other academics, students, and a wide variety of courses and programs. The surrounding campuses, in turn, benefit from the creative approaches, interdisciplinary teaching, and curricular activities of the innovative institution. It is a healthy partnership for all.

General Implications for the Higher Education Community

Now having considered the implications of the research findings for innovative colleges and universities, what are the general implications of the results for the wider higher education community?

Recognizing the Need for Alternatives in Higher Education

First, this study turns our attention to the importance of providing alternatives, creative and nourishing educational places and spaces for students and scholars who are seeking unique, person-centered classrooms and programs in American higher education. The six campuses in this investigation are six islands of educational difference, each having evolved over the decades with at least some important elements of its original distinctive principles intact.

One of the major lessons to be learned from this investigation is that traditional methods of higher education are not the sole means of educating all students, and are not the most effective or appropriate strategies for all learners. Innovative colleges and universities fill a distinct niche in the higher education community, offering refuges for those who are dissatisfied with the mainstream practices and approaches of conventional higher education. They produce graduates who are successful entrepreneurs and leaders with an imaginative heart and spirit. Higher education would do wise to recognize and reward innovative campuses for their genius. Philanthropical foundations and agencies should follow the lead of the John D. and Catherine T. MacArthur Foundation, which recently awarded grants of $750,000 apiece to six innovative liberal arts campuses (Alverno College, Antioch College, College of the Atlantic, Hampshire College, Johnson C. Smith University, and Marlboro College). These one-time grants were offered as part of a $5.9 million initiative to show support for distinctive institutions of higher education. In the words of Woodward A. Wickham, Director of the MacArthur Foundation general grants program, "Parents are increasingly asking whether this kind of education is worth it. With these grants we wanted to say that it is absolutely worth it, and to help insure that liberal arts and these innovative colleges and others like them flourish" (Arenson, 1996, p. B9).

Promotion

In visiting distinctive campuses, you get the sense that you are uncovering a hidden jewel or undiscovered treasure in American higher education. Nation-wide promotional strategies are needed to raise awareness about these unique teaching and learning communities. Educational organizations and professional associations should sponsor conferences and institutes on the topic of innovative higher education, where teams of participants from distinctive campuses across the country can gather to present their teaching and learning approaches. Joint research reports and local or regional workshops are also essential for building connections and providing networking opportunities across this family of creative institutions. National respect, recognition, and appreciation for the innovative sector of higher education is critical for combating stereotypes and for ensuring the survival of alternative colleges and universities.

Models and Practices

Many higher education institutions today are searching for creative strategies to improve or revitalize their teaching and learning environments. In these difficult budgetary times, when it may be impossible to develop new programs or campuses, mainstream colleges and universities should look to the practices of innovative colleges and universities and consider the merits of their unique approaches—for example, narrative evaluation systems, portfolio assessment for faculty. Evergreen's Washington Center for Improving the Quality of Undergraduate Education has made excellent strides in transmitting the Coordinated Studies model to colleges and universities throughout the State of Washington. There are currently 46 colleges and universities participating in Washington Center programs, including all of Washington state's public four-year institutions and community colleges, ten independent colleges, and one tribal college (The Evergreen State College, 1997a). Similar centers or offshoots could be founded across the nation to guide or assist traditional institutions in incorporating alternative, student-centered teaching and learning techniques.

Suggestions for Future Research

The study of innovative colleges and universities is an important and relatively undeveloped area of contemporary research. There are a number of ways in which future investigators could expand upon the findings of the present investigation by exploring additional issues or aspects of these very unusual and interesting institutions.

First, in order to broaden the findings of this investigation, qualitative research studies of the history and persistence of innovation should be conducted at other four-year distinctive institutions of the 1960s and 1970s. Investigators should examine the experiences of distinctive community colleges, nontraditional institutions for adults, and experimental subcolleges to understand how these campuses have evolved in a changing social, political, and economic climate. Further research could also be conducted at public innovative campuses to determine how issues of affiliation or control impact the life and longevity of other state-supported distinctive colleges and universities.

A scholarly comparison of the experiences of the six distinctive campuses in this study with those of the older experimental colleges of the late 19th and early 20th century (e.g., Antioch College, Reed College, Deep Springs College) could yield important insights. What are the lessons to be learned about the history and transformation of innovation from the older and progressive-era innovative campuses, and how do these results compare and contrast with findings of the current investigation? These are important questions for future researchers.

There are a host of other topics and concerns that deserve consideration in the writings about institutional reform in higher education. Future studies are needed to examine subjects such as student and faculty life at the distinctive campus, alumnae/i outcomes and success, issues of student attrition and retention, faculty burnout, and faculty mobility. One important area for further investigation is the topic of institutional maturity. Future research is needed to determine how the aging or maturation of an innovative college or university (the lifecycle of the campus from its newborn phase to its "adolescent" and "adult" years) impacts the endurance of distinctive missions.

Researchers should also turn their attention to the study of financial concerns and leadership issues, as well as multiculturalism and diversity in the innovative college or university. Future investigators should conduct in-depth studies of the governance processes, the nongraded or narrative evaluation systems, and the student-centered curricular models at these creative campuses to understand how these approaches could be applied or utilized in other college or university settings. There is much to be learned from the imaginative practices and programs of the innovative colleges and universities. The research pathways are open and this investigator invites others to join the journey.

References

Adams, E. A. (1993). Prescott: From Parsons to parsimony. In L. J. Newell & K. C. Reynolds (Eds.), *Maverick colleges: Ten notable experiments in American undergraduate education* (pp. 89–103). Salt Lake City, UT: The University of Utah, Utah Education Policy Center, Graduate School of Education.

Adams, W. (1984, May/June). Getting real: Santa Cruz and the crisis of liberal education. *Change,* 19–27.

Alpert, R. M. (1980). Professionalism and educational reform: The case of Hampshire College. *Journal of Higher Education, 51* (5), 497–518.

Anzulovic, B. (1976). The rise and fall of Prescott College. *The University Bookman, XVI* (3), 51–57.

Arenson, K. W. (1996, June 26). Six colleges with 'genius' given $750,000 rewards. *The New York Times,* p. B9.

Arthur, F. C. (1995). *New College: The first three decades.* Sarasota, FL: The New College Foundation.

Astin, H. S., Milem, J. F., Astin, A. W., Ries, P., & Heath, T. (1991). *The courage and vision to experiment: Hampshire College, 1970–1990.* Los Angeles, CA: Higher Education Research Institute, Graduate School of Education, University of California, Los Angeles.

Bear, J. (1980). *The alternative guide to college degrees & non-traditional higher education.* New York, NY: Stonesong.

Bernard, R. J. (1982). *An unfinished dream: A chronicle of the Group Plan of The Claremont Colleges.* Claremont, CA: Claremont University Center.

Birney, R. C. (1993, Summer). Hampshire College. In V. R. Cardozier (Ed.), *Important lessons from innovative colleges and universities* (pp. 9–22). New Directions for Higher Education, No. 82. San Francisco, CA: Jossey-Bass.

Brown, B. (1974). *The founding of the University of Wisconsin–Green Bay.* Green Bay, WI: University of Wisconsin-Green Bay.

Burns, S. (1994, October). The New College chronicles: Marketing, miracles and mindpower underlie the smashing success of this 30–year-old Sarasota institution. Sarasota, 4647; 118120; 122123.

The Carnegie Foundation for the Advancement of Teaching. (1994). *A classification of institutions of higher education 1994 edition.* Princeton, NJ: Author.

Cheit, E. F. (1971). *The new depression in higher education: A study of financial conditions at 41 colleges and universities.* New York, NY: McGraw-Hill.

Childs, B. (1981). The obligatory inspirational commencement address (Johnston College graduation, May 1980). *Journal of Humanistic Psychology, 21* (2), 143–146.

Clary, W. W. (1970). *The Claremont Colleges: A history of the development of the Claremont Group Plan.* Claremont, CA: Claremont University Center.

Clemens, M. (Ed.). (1987). *Twenty years of making a difference: The Evergreen State College 1967–1987.* Olympia, WA: The Evergreen State College.

Coyne, J. (1972, October). Bensalem: When the dream died. *Change,* 39–44.

Coyne, J., & Hebert, T. (1972). *This way out: A guide to alternatives to traditional college education in the United States, Europe and the Third World.* New York, NY: E. P. Dutton.

The Evergreen State College. (1972). *The Evergreen State College bulletin 1972–73.* Olympia, WA: Author.

The Evergreen State College. (1989, August). *Constancy and change: A self-study report.* A report prepared by The Evergreen State College for the Northwest Association of Schools and Colleges Commission on Colleges. Olympia, WA: Author

The Evergreen State College. (1996). *The Evergreen State College 1996–97 catalog.* Olympia, WA: The Evergreen State College, Admissions Office.

The Evergreen State College. (1997a). *The Evergreen State College 1997–98 catalog.* Olympia, WA: The Evergreen State College, Admissions Office.

The Evergreen State College. (1997b). *Faculty handbook* [Prepublication copy]. Olympia, WA: The Evergreen State College.

Gaff, J. G. (1970a). The cluster college concept. In J. G. Gaff & Associates, *The cluster college* (pp. 3–32). San Francisco, CA: Jossey-Bass.

Gaff, J. G. (1970b). Organizing learning experiences. In J. G. Gaff & Associates, *The cluster college* (pp. 33–62). San Francisco, CA: Jossey-Bass.

Gehret, K. G. (1972, May). Reports: Washington's Evergreen College. *Change,* 17–19.

Grand, I. J., & Bebout, J. (1981). Passionate discourse: The experimental college at San Francisco State. *Journal of Humanistic Psychology, 21* (2), 79–95.

Grant, G., & Riesman, D. (1978). *The perpetual dream: Reform and experiment in the American college.* Chicago, IL: The University of Chicago Press.

Greening, T. (1981a). The first days of Johnston College. *Journal of Humanistic Psychology, 21* (2), 3–15.

Greening, T. (1981b). Power, decision making, and coercion in experimental colleges. *Journal of Humanistic Psychology, 21* (2), 97–109.

Hall, J. W. (1991). *Access through innovation: New colleges for new students.* New York, NY: The National University Continuing Education Association, American Council on Education, and Macmillan.

Hall, M. (1994, November-December). A distaste for walls. *Harvard Magazine,* 52–57.

Hampshire College. (1995). *1995–96 catalog and course guide.* Amherst, MA: Author.

Heiss, A. (1973). *An inventory of academic innovation and reform.* Berkeley, CA: The Carnegie Commission on Higher Education.

Kahn, M. (1981). The Kresge experiment. *Journal of Humanistic Psychology, 21* (2), 63–69.

Kliewer, J. R. (1999). *The innovative campus: Nurturing the distinctive learning environment.* Phoenix, AZ: Oryx Press/ACE.

Kuh, G. D., Schuh, J. H., Whitt, E. J., Andreas, R. E., Lyons, J. W., Strange, C. C., Krehbiel, L. E., & MacKay, K. A. (1991). *Involving colleges: Successful approaches to fostering student learning and development outside the classroom.* San Francisco, CA: Jossey-Bass.

Lane, C. D., Nugent, F. T., Tulos, D. J., Hess, J. D., Ruiz, J. E., & Snyder, D. I. (1968, November). *Comprehensive development plan: The University of Wisconsin-Green Bay.* Green Bay, WI and Grand Rapids, MI: University of Wisconsin Green Bay Campus; The State of Wisconsin Department of Administration Bureau of Engineering; and Daverman Associates, Inc., Architects-Engineers-Planners.

Lennon, J., & McCartney, P. (1965). In my life [The Beatles]. On *Imagine: John Lennon* [cassette]. Hollywood, CA: EMI Records. (1988)

Levine, A. (1980a). *When dreams and heroes died: A portrait of today's college student.* San Francisco, CA: Jossey-Bass.

Levine, A. (1980b). *Why innovation fails.* Albany, NY: State University of New York Press.

Levine, A., & Weingart, J. (1973). *Reform of undergraduate education.* San Francisco, CA: Jossey-Bass.

Lichtman, J. (1972). *Free university directory.* Washington, DC: American Association for Higher Education.

Martin, W. B. (1982, March). The legacy of the sixties: Innovation—bloodied but unbowed. *Change,* 35–38.

McDonald, W., & O'Neill, K. (1988). *"As long as you're havin' a good time." A history of Johnston College 1969–1979.* San Francisco and Redlands, CA: Forum Books.

McHenry, D. E. (1977). Academic organizational matrix at the University of California, Santa Cruz. In D. E. McHenry and Associates, *Academic departments: Problems, variations, and alternatives* (pp. 86–116). San Francisco, CA: Jossey-Bass.

New College of the University of South Florida. (1994). *New College of the University of South Florida: A brief history.* Sarasota, FL: Author.

Newell, L. J., & Reynolds, K. C. (1993). Introduction. In L. J. Newell & K. C. Reynolds (Eds.), *Maverick colleges: Ten notable experiments in American undergraduate education* (pp. ii–vii). Salt Lake City: The University of Utah, Utah Education Policy Center, Graduate School of Education.

Newell, W. H. (1984). Interdisciplinary curriculum development in the 1970's: The Paracollege at St. Olaf and the Western College Program at Miami University. In R. M. Jones & B. L. Smith (Eds.), *Against the current: Reform and experiment in higher education* (pp. 127–147). Cambridge, MA: Schenkman.

Newell, W. H. (1986). *Interdisciplinary undergraduate programs: A directory.* Oxford, OH: Association for Integrative Studies.

Patterson, F., & Longsworth, C. (1966). *The making of a college.* Cambridge, MA: MIT Press.

Pitzer College. (1963, September). *Pitzer College bulletin.* Volume I, Number 1. Claremont, CA: Author.

Pitzer College. (1996). *Pitzer College catalogue 1996–97.* Claremont, CA: Author.

Rice, E., & Bremer, S. H. (1994, January 22). *Institutional environments for innovation: Comparing the Antioch and UW-Green Bay experiences.* Paper presented at the Association of American Colleges Conference, Washington, DC.

Rodenhouse, M. P. (Ed.). (1995). *1995 higher education directory.* Falls Church, VA: Higher Education Publications.

Ruopp, R. R., & Jerome, J. (1973). Realities: Death in a small college. In G. B. MacDonald (Ed.), *Five experimental colleges: Bensalem, Antioch-Putney, Franconia, Old Westbury, Fairhaven* (pp. 114–156). New York, NY: Harper & Row.

Townsend, B. K., Newell, L. J., & Wiese, M. D. (1992). *Creating distinctiveness: Lessons from uncommon colleges and universities.* ASHE-ERIC Higher Education Report No. 6. Washington, DC: The George Washington University, School of Education and Human Development.

Tussman, J. (1969). *Experiment at Berkeley.* New York, NY: Oxford University Press.

University of California, Santa Cruz. (1965). *Undergraduate program* [UC Santa Cruz catalog]. Santa Cruz, CA: Author.

Von der Muhll, G. (1984). The University of California at Santa Cruz: Institutionalizing Eden in a changing world. In R. M. Jones & B. L. Smith (Eds.), *Against the current: Reform and experimentation in higher education* (pp. 51–92). Cambridge, MA: Schenkman.

Weidner, E. W. (1977). Problem-based departments at the University of Wisconsin-Green Bay. In D. E. McHenry & Associates, *Academic departments: Problems, variations, and alternatives* (pp. 63–85). San Francisco, CA: Jossey-Bass.

Weidner, E. W. (1994). Inventing a university: The University of Wisconsin-Green Bay, 1965–1969: Up against the clock and entrenched rivals. *Voyageur,* 23–33, 36–37.

Weidner, E. W., & Kuepper, W. G. (1993, Summer). University of Wisconsin-Green Bay. In V. R. Cardozier (Ed.), *Important lessons from innovative colleges and universities* (pp. 23–35). New Directions for Higher Education, No. 82. San Francisco, CA: Jossey-Bass.

Youtz, B. L. (1984). The Evergreen State College: An experiment maturing. In R. M. Jones & B. L. Smith (Eds.), *Against the current: Reform and experimentation in higher education* (pp. 93–118). Cambridge, MA: Schenkman.

Endnotes

1. Portions of this chapter appear in *The Innovative Campus: Nurturing the Distinctive Learning Environment* (1999) by Joy Rosenzweig

Kliewer, published by Oryx Press and the American Council on Education.

2. I owe the musical reference to Jim Bebout and Tom Greening, editors of the *Journal of Humanistic Psychology* (Volume 21, Spring 1981), who wove John Lennon's lyrics throughout the writings of this special issue on "humanistic" colleges. This particular excerpt appears in Greening (1981a), page 3.

3

INTERDISCIPLINARY EDUCATION AT HAMPSHIRE COLLEGE: BRINGING PEOPLE TOGETHER AROUND IDEAS

Ann P. McNeal and Frederick Stirton Weaver
Hampshire College

Since its founding in 1970, Hampshire College has continued to develop an evolving and thoroughly interdisciplinary education program.[1] While the planners envisioned interdisciplinary faculty units, courses, and study programs (Patterson & Longsworth, 1966), they did not foresee the unusual dynamics that would be created by the interactions of students and faculty. In presenting the nature of interdisciplinary work at Hampshire College, this chapter aims not only to describe a unique institution but to do so in terms that might be useful for others.

Three themes kept emerging as we examined our institution's embodiment of interdisciplinary education. First is that critical inquiry—actively challenging ideas and interpretations—is central to the institution's ethos. There is a local joke in our Five College Consortium about the professor who walks into the classroom and says "Good morning, class." The Amherst College student replies, "Oh yes, sir. It is indeed a very good morning!" The University of Massachusetts student asks, "Will that be on the exam?" and so on, until the Hampshire student demands, "How do you know that?"[2]

The second theme is that the educational organization of the college requires collaboration by people from diverse fields, and a collaboration that is frequent and of changing patterns. Faculty and students interact a lot, and they interact by raising questions (in courses, in student-faculty research, and in student projects) that involve several fields or disciplines. Third, students are actively involved in the intellectual and academic process. For example, by convening of faculty committees to oversee their work in the examination system, students draw faculty from seemingly disparate fields into working relationships.

All three of these features are necessary for the very operation of the college's academic program and are solidly embedded in the organization of the college. We will briefly describe four central aspects of how the college functions with particular attention to how these features and their interplay sustain college-wide support for interdisciplinary education. The four are:

- the divisional examination system, in which students design much of their educational program
- the organization of the faculty in interdisciplinary schools
- the nature of courses
- opportunities for the faculty to develop as teachers and scholars

The Examination System: Students' Indivualized Programs of Study

The inclusion of students as idea-generators injects considerable energy into the system and keeps it flexible, and the examination[3] system is central to that student participation. After completing a set of breadth requirements (Division I), all students at Hampshire College design their own programs of focused study, or Division II Concentrations. Each student's concentration is negotiated with a committee formed by the student who fashions a formal contract that spells out the study program. While perhaps a third of the students choose programs that closely resemble conventional majors in history, biology, writing, etc., the vast majority express their interests by designing more imaginative combinations, which are substantively defined around a set of questions and themes. Even the concentrations that do look more like disciplinary majors contain the student's rationale for the particular design, and it is a rationale that explicitly relates each element of the concentration to the student's educational goals and includes courses outside a particular discipline.

Students start with some ideas for programs of study at the end of their first year or beginning of their second year of college, talk over the ideas with academic advisors and often with friends, and then begin to draw up plans for a contract. This concentration comprises 10–15 courses plus other activities such as independent studies, field studies, lab or performance work, annotated bibliographies, internships, and so on. The student usually consults several faculty members for advice. After negotiating the various parts of the concentration (for example, courses, other educational activities, a Third World Expectation, and community service), the student draws up a formal contract signed by at least two Hampshire faculty members. This contract, which is usually revised at least once, covers about two years of work, during which the student is expected to demonstrate growth in both knowledge base and analytical sophistication.

This process of student-designed programs of study is often portrayed by the college's promotional literature and understood by the students themselves in terms of student freedom. And in a sense, this idea is accurate, but as students soon find out, the need to define a significant study area, justify the appropriateness of its components, and defend its coherence at every stage is hard work. This freedom is an academic requirement that is unusually demanding for undergraduates.

At the end of the contract period, the committee convenes a final meeting to evaluate the student's portfolio of work, which includes:

- a retrospective statement tying together the intellectual threads of the concentration
- evaluations and grades from courses (Hampshire courses are ungraded, but most students will take some courses at the other four colleges in the Five-College Consortium for grades)
- evaluations, retrospectives, or other evidence from field studies and internships
- a series of research papers (or art works or other productions) from the concentration
- evidence of completion of the Third World Expectation and community service

In the final meeting, the faculty committee members and the student discuss the student's progress, the quality of the work, and the ideas arising from the student's work. If the faculty judge the endeavor to have been successful, the committee composes a written assessment of the entirety of the concentration, an evaluation that forms a major part of the student's transcript.

The final stage of students' work at Hampshire, the Division III or extended senior thesis, also provides ways for the students to bring faculty together. At this stage, there is more variety in the way in which examination committee's work. The faculty members often function as a committee of the whole, meeting weekly or biweekly with the student to go over drafts of the project, or the chair provides the main guidance, while other faculty serve as consultants on different aspects (e.g., a health scientist serving as science consultant on a educational film project) or serve to balance the student's interests (a psychologist serving on a project on dance education).

Campus wisdom from student peer advising and faculty advisors counsels students how to get Division II and Division III committees that reflect their interests, and it is common for a student to have faculty from different disciplines and schools on both Division II and Division III committees. On the faculty side, these student committees at both the Division II and Division III levels provide a forum for the interchange of ideas and often lead to new combinations of faculty undertaking team-taught courses or research projects. This is crucially important at a college where faculty can be too busy to rely on spontaneous conversations for intellectual exchanges.

These student-designed concentrations and Division III projects play a strong role in drawing together faculty into novel and frequently long-standing collaborations. Students carry out combinations such as writing and history, dance and the science of human movement, video documentary production and psychology, law and ethics, linguistics and animal behavior, ecology and economics, anthropology and media production, education and science, gender studies and literature, and so on. For example, as a physiologist, I (Ann) have been drawn into student examination committees with faculty in dance, visual arts, psychology, African history, literature, mathematics, and outdoor education, to name a few, and I (Fred) as an economist and historian, have served on student examination committees with faculty in all social science disciplines as well as in literature, biology, media, mathematics, philosophy, and creative writing.

Organization by Schools Instead of by Disciplinary Departments

Interdisciplinary schools of about 20–30 faculty are the basic administrative units of the faculty. Despite the schools' interdisciplinary nature, all but a very few faculty have disciplinary titles (for example, assistant professor of biology; associate professor of economics). These titles reflect graduate training, and all but a few faculty did their graduate work in traditionally organized disciplinary departments. While faculty titles do have some meaning within the college, their major use is for external audiences, such as letters of recommendation, submissions of articles to academic journals, and applications for grants.

Schools perform some of the functions of departments at other colleges, including serving as the primary locus of decisions about faculty appointments, reappointments, and promotions. As a consequence, each faculty member needs to be respected and credible as a teacher, intellectual/artist, and colleague to a large number of people in his or her school. But unlike traditional departmental structures, faculty with a common disciplinary background are always a minority within a school. It is not uncommon for a disciplinary faculty's recommendations to be outvoted by their school colleagues and student school members, although it is not done lightly.

On the other hand, faculty trained in several disciplines (for example, history, psychology, and anthropology) are located in more than one school. In any case, so many disciplinary categories are incoherent ensembles of diverse subject matters, approaches, and even epistemologies that colleagues frequently have more intellectual affinity with colleagues from disciplines other than their own.

Intellectually and pedagogically creative work across Hampshire's schools is also encouraged, because there are no restrictions on cross-listing courses and team teaching by faculty in different schools. In addition, Division II concentrations and Division III projects, unlike the Division I breadth requirement, have only a loose relationship with schools.

Schools also operate like departments in that they are the principal curriculum-sponsoring units of the college. But unlike departments, they neither set requirements for majors nor ordain set formulas of course offerings. School curricula are not coherent, because the responsibility for the coherence of individual students' programs of study lies with the individual students' Division II committees. Nevertheless, the schools do monitor the balance of upper- and lower-division courses, persuade faculty to offer popular courses, and note gaps and attempt to fill them. In most schools, these general decisions are made by the full body of faculty and student members.

The real curriculum-setting authority at Hampshire lies with individual faculty members, who may work individually or in small groups relatively independent of school membership. Some faculty groups may assume responsibility for the regular appearance of certain service courses, usually introductory courses and intermediate courses necessary for constructing a wide range of concentrations. Sometimes needs for regular courses are defined by discipline (e.g., chemistry, economics, mathematics, drawing) but at least as often by interdisciplinary theme (environmental studies, cognitive science, feminist studies, the Third World, legal studies). The arts—theatre, dance, visual arts, film and photography, and writing—are exceptional in having become more departmental in the ways that they oversee curriculum.

Over the years, groups of faculty have proposed the establishment of a new school, sometimes in addition to the existing four schools and sometimes to supplant one. None of the proposals convinced many faculty, however, and the four schools along with a slowly changing cast of informally organized intellectual and political interest groups (variously called programs, clusters, and centers) persisted for well over twenty years. Nevertheless, this organization was not immutable, and there have been some recent changes in the number and configuration of the schools. The increasing difficulties of combining cognitive science and cultural studies into a workable school triggered an extended faculty-wide discussion of school organization. While grace and good will were notable by their absence in the process, the outcome seems so far to have been productive, and it contains the potential for enabling the heavily over-subscribed arts faculty to participate more fully in interdisciplinary teaching.[4]

COURSES: INTERDISCIPLINARITY IN TEAMS AND INDIVIDUALLY

About 15% of Hampshire's course offerings are team-taught. The faculty reward structure encourages such courses, and faculty reappointment and promotion files frequently contain assessments from colleagues about the teacher's collaborations with other faculty. The culture of coteaching has progressed to the point where a faculty member who does not team-teach is at somewhat a disadvantage.

Most team-taught courses at Hampshire focus on an interdisciplinary problem such as gender expression in city planning, land use in New England, etc. (Table 3.1). That is, interdisciplinary courses are created when faculty desire to explore a question, theme, or problem in conjunction with one another and a set of students rather than from a perceived need to cover a body of material contained in a preset, codified intellectual category (discipline). The varied approaches from different fields may be explicitly contrasted, as in "Women's Bodies, Women's Lives" (cotaught by a biologist, a sociologist, and a literature professor) in order to help students realize that there are multiple ways to do scholarly inquiry, more than one approach is valid, and while some approaches are complementary, others are not. To develop these contrasts, different faculty members may expressly elaborate their methods of inquiry. In other courses, the model is more of a collaborative, seamless interweaving of approaches, with all faculty using their expertise to work on the problem, without an explicit contrasting. In almost all cases, Hampshire team teaching requires all faculty to be present in the classroom at the same time, rather than taking a "tag team" approach in which one person hands off the class to the next and disappears. The logistics of curricular offerings means that team-taught courses are expected to accommodate larger numbers of students.

In addition, many individually taught courses are effectively interdisciplinary. As increasingly happens at other colleges and universities,

TABLE 3.1 Examples of Recent Team-Taught Interdisciplinary Courses at Hampshire College

Women's Bodies, Women's Lives	literature, sociology, and biology
Art and Revolution	art history and European history
Poetry and Playwriting: A Workshop	theater and writing
Research in Nutrition and Pollution	chemistry and biological anthropology
When Machines Talk	computer science and linguistics
Culture/Gender/Self	anthropology and social psychology
World Food Crisis	biology and international politics
The American West	history, ecology, and literature
Cruising the Net: Interchanges, Rest Stops, and Traffic Cops on the Information Superhighway	computer science and media studies
Children and Their Environments: Messages from Space	urban geography, sociology, history, and psychology
Ecology and Politics of Land Use in New England	ecology, history, and politics
Race in the US: Under Color of Law	US History and legal studies
Global Capitalism and the Changing Political Economies of Africa and Latin America	politics, economics, history, sociology, and anthropology

faculty at Hampshire often construct courses around topics or questions that are of interest to them rather than from putatively universal categories. Examples from Hampshire include fiction as history; sound, music, and mind; AIDS and the law; a cultural history of Christianity; Third World, second sex; how people move; pollution and our environment.

In exploring these questions, faculty are not limited by particular disciplines, but they are highly disciplined. For example, Ali Mirsepassi, whose degree is in sociology, teaches a course entitled "Societies and Cultures of the Middle East" in which he uses an anthropology monograph and three personal narratives as the main texts. This course, while transgressing disciplinary boundaries, was disciplined in its intellectual approach: The texts were subjected to intense scrutiny rather than merely being accepted as factual narratives or authoritative expositions, and students had to develop and apply critical analyses in class and in extensive writing assignments.

The Changing Role of Courses at Hampshire

Much of what is distinctive about a Hampshire education resides in the character of the examination system, and courses are important only as they serve students' educational purposes that are expressed through the divisional examination system. In this sense, the early aspiration of the college's planners—to dethrone the course—has been realized.

Nevertheless, courses at Hampshire have not been displaced by other formats; they remain a centrally important mode of instruction. Most students' completion of Division I breadth requirements depends directly or indirectly on courses; the vast majority of the academic accomplishments recorded in students' Division II Concentration portfolios have their origins in courses; and even Division III students, who are deeply involved in their theses must take at least one advanced seminar.

Courses are certainly not the exclusive format for teaching, but there are at least three interlocking reasons for the survival and even expansion of the role of courses. First, there is a definite efficiency in exploring interesting ideas or examining an analytical tool with, say, fifteen or twenty students at a time. This efficiency is particularly appealing to faculty members, who have substantial examination, advising, and governance responsibilities. Second, the faculty have primary responsibility for designing and conducting courses, which therefore offer dedicated teachers an opportunity for systematically testing their ideas about issues and pedagogy.

The third and probably most important reason for the prominence of courses at Hampshire is that they have proven to work extremely well for students. While the examination system itself contributes to the particular spirit of the courses, there is more to it. Courses are collaborative enterprises in a highly individualized academic program, and faculty members and students enjoy and are stimulated and educated by participating with others in grappling with new types of understanding. The idealized model of teaching exclusively through individual tutorials (Rudolph, 1956) represents a limited, even tepid, pedagogy when compared to the excitement of a Hampshire seminar that works for an active and committed group. In good measure, learning is a social enterprise.

No discussion of courses at Hampshire College is complete without some mention of the nearby four institutions of the Five College consortium (Amherst, Hampshire, Mt. Holyoke, and Smith Colleges and the University of Massachusetts, Amherst). The students of the consortium circulate quite easily among the five institutions on the free bus service, and the cooperative arrangement enables Hampshire students to include Five College disciplinary courses in their interdisciplinary concentrations and Five College students to enroll in our classes. For Hampshire's interdisciplinary curriculum, however, it is particularly important, because we do not have to cover many of the areas that are included in standard disciplinary curricula. Moreover, our students' ability to experience "real" disciplinary courses complete with grades is of great value to both Hampshire students and faculty, because it helps us maintain confidence in and a better perspective on what we are doing and on how well we are doing it.

Faculty Development in an Interdisciplinary Setting

We have emphasized the contributions that our students make to the durability and success of our interdisciplinary curricula. Nevertheless, it is the faculty who are the mainstay of the institution and whose work, year in and year out, sustains the interdisciplinary program. Faculty commitment is important for the success of any college's academic program, but there are notable differences of degree. On a continuum ranging from institutions with relatively fixed curricula to institutions whose curricula are more fluidly determined by faculty and faculty-student relationships, it is clear that Hampshire College is located at or very near the latter end. This puts a premium on the importance of the faculty's dedication and intellectual creativity in sustaining its program of interdisciplinary inquiry education. Hampshire's parallel tracks of courses and the divisional examination system encourage faculty vitality and investment, and enable teachers to deliver a demanding program year after year.

The openness and flexibility of the Hampshire academic program, the commitment to teaching around substantive questions not governed by disciplinary prescription, and the frequency of team teaching contribute to a curriculum that continues to be intellectually exciting and educational for teachers as well as for students. One of the most important aspects of Hampshire's academic program, and especially of its divisional examination side, is the way in which it promotes better teaching.

The divisional examination system requires each student to pursue a unique program of study, but for the faculty, divisional examination committees are collaborative enterprises, thus inverting the conventional pattern of collective student programs and individual modes of faculty teaching. Divisional examination committees require faculty to talk extensively with one another and with individual students about teaching and patterns of student progress. The conversations take place in settings that for faculty are informal and nonthreatening.

Through patterns of examination committee memberships, faculty members quickly find that they belong to several faculty groups defined by particular fields of intellectual interest within and among schools, and the individual's own discipline may be one of those fields. And as already mentioned, students' efforts to form divisional examination committees are an important source of information for faculty about other faculty members' interests. In courses, conversations, the Advising Center, and other institutional channels, students learn of mutual intellectual interests among faculty members who may not be aware of such links. It is not unusual for jointly taught courses and even cooperative research ventures to result from a student's acting as broker in setting up his or her divisional examination committee. The frequency with which particular sets of faculty see each other on divisional examination committees also works as a market survey device, indicating patterns of student interest and alerting faculty to the need for new courses, and even new faculty, in particular areas of study.

Another positive feature of the Hampshire curriculum is the way in which it supports faculty scholarship. The flexibility of teaching assignments allows faculty to teach in areas of current research, and the organization of student work by projects rather than by short assignments and exercises enables faculty and students to collaborate on and even to coauthor research. The frequency of coteaching within and among schools is a third means by which faculty integrate their teaching and scholarship. In addition, the faculty sabbatical leave policy, revised in 1990 to a paid semester every seven semesters, was in good part to compensate for so little success in raising salaries, but it has contributed to the ability of the faculty to engage in active scholarship.

In the same way that Hampshire students are not constrained by the need to fit into conventional modes of disciplinary professionalism, neither is the faculty's research. Unusual patterns of cross-school collegial encouragement have led many faculty into exciting research and publishing projects that are innovative both in terms of subject matter and approach. Twenty or thirty years ago, it would have been more difficult to find good outlets for publishing such work, but this has changed. The creation and expansion of specialized journals and interdisciplinary associations that focus on feminist issues, the Third World, race and ethnicity, cultural studies, the environment, AIDS, cognitive science, college teaching and whatever have provided forums for many Hampshire faculty to go public with critical, heterodox scholarship and thus to engage in national debates significant to their intellectual lives. At Hampshire, this scholarship is judged by its intellectual vitality rather than by its adherence to academic conventions.

All together, the faculty continue to be active learners in their own rights. This has led several faculty to develop entirely new teaching and research fields, a process that makes long-range curricular planning difficult but that retards faculty burnout and encourages continued intellectual growth and innovation that keeps even the most senior faculty engaged in both intellectual and institutional issues.

As important as are the fostering of colleagueship and intellectual vitality, probably the primary reason that faculty continue to support the demanding interdisciplinary educational system is that it appears to work for students, and to work in ways clearly discernible to teachers. The Hampshire divisional examination system requires faculty to observe individual students' academic progress over an extended period of time, and to observe it closely. As a result, faculty are able to see the tangible (and often very impressive) intellectual growth by students over two- and three-year periods, and of course they attribute that growth to their teaching. Although the system has obvious built-in stresses for faculty, it also has significant rewards.

But one cannot run on too blithely about teaching and research without explicitly acknowledging how labor-intensive the Hampshire academic program is; it requires a prodigious amount of faculty resourcefulness, patience, self-confidence, and time to negotiate and renegotiate each student's academic program and assess students' work through narrative evaluations. The earliest planning documents seriously underestimated this, an error that seems to have stemmed from a hydraulic conception of educational effort in which more academic responsibility for students was taken to mean less for faculty. Moreover, the enthusiasm of the faculty and students led, in the first three years of the college, to the creation of an academic program that was more ambitious than that envisioned by the college's planners (Patterson & Longsworth, 1966). Apart from some minor modifications, the academic program has changed little in its essentials since it was developed. Two changes are noteworthy. First, the college made the teaching load a bit more feasible by changing from an original 16:1 student/faculty ratio to a 13:1 ratio in about 1980. Second, the faculty instituted clear guidelines (and increasingly firm enforcement) regarding a timetable for completion of the different Divisions. "In the old days," it was common for students to be working on their Division I distributional requirements up to the last semester of college. Certainly there has been some loss of flexibility, but students generally progress more steadily under the guidelines for academic progress.

In addition, the interdisciplinary inquiry goal of Hampshire's education is inherently demanding. Although the educational goal does include students' retaining some facts and learning how to apply techniques, it also includes convincing students that certainties are at best elusive, that analytical techniques embody important assumptions affecting results, that critical questioning is necessary for learning, and that artistic impulse has to be brought into a relationship with intellectual history.

Integral to this form of interdisciplinary education, then, students have to take intellectual risks, and making mistakes is a necessary and productive part of academic progress. Therefore, each piece of student work has to be evaluated with the thoroughness that faculty, under ordinary circumstances, might reserve only for professional colleagues' efforts. But a significant part of the process is students' learning to revise their work, not once but many times, and learning also to resolve sometimes contradictory faculty feedback. The difficulty of defining closure on a faculty member's responsibility to student work, together with narrative rather than numerical evaluative measurements of student academic progress and an institutional ideology of innovation and participation, often leaves faculty, especially new faculty, without a clear idea of how much effort is enough.

Advising first- and second-year students is also a time-consuming responsibility. Faculty are responsible for socializing first-year students and transfer students in particular to the culture of Hampshire: Advisors have to convey to students how to initiate committee meetings, call faculty and make appointments, get forms filled out on time, navigate the Five-College system, and become comfortable in one-on-one meetings with faculty; these are all survival skills that a new student needs from an advisor. And in common with students in all colleges, many students find dormitory life away from their families for the first time to be daunting, and they need a variety of supports for their Hampshire experience to work for them. Advising first- and second-year students is a demanding responsibility for faculty, and although retention rates suggest that we may have been doing it a little better recently, this is an area of faculty work that calls for substantial improvement and will probably require some type of imaginative institutional reform to make it work better.

From an institutional perspective, the principal danger of workload pressure is its potential for eroding the faculty's ability to maintain high academic standards. To some extent, the divisional examination system functions as a monitor, protecting standards of faculty as well as student work. As already mentioned, the same divisional examination system designed to individualize student work requires cooperative work among faculty through the divisional examination committees. The public nature of the divisional examination system for faculty means that every decision a faculty member makes about a Division II student's academic progress is available to faculty colleagues on the student's Division II concentration committee. The Division II committee reads the student's concentration portfolio, which includes all of the student's work and the various instructors' responses to that work, whether or not the course instructor is a member of that student's concentration committee. Finally, at a more formal and immediate level, a faculty committee in each school is designated to read all divisional contracts and reports.

The best safeguard of standards, of course, is consistently responsible action by all faculty members. That this has generally been the case at Hampshire does not alter the reasons to emphasize the effect of the college's general structures. An institutional ethos that encourages responsibility and shared commitment must be nurtured and reproduced by the framework in which teaching is done. And Hampshire's unusual interdisciplinary set of arrangements appears to be quite effective in doing so.

Hampshire will soon face an interesting challenge. Like Evergreen, it was founded in the early 1970s with a young and idealistic faculty. Over the next ten to fifteen years, most of the faculty will come to retirement age and will be replaced, while the next generation of faculty, those who are now in the 30s and 40s, will become the college's leadership. We wonder what trends will develop in several areas: scholarship, curriculum, and the divisional system. Formal measures of scholarly productivity have become more important at Hampshire, as elsewhere in the country; we hope that there will remain a healthy balance in emphasis on teaching and scholarship. In some areas of the college, faculty feel an urge to set curriculum in ways that emphasize faculty control and diminish students' choices; we hope this current will be resisted, as the interplay of student and faculty interests is a vital force for innovation. Finally, this curricular hardening and other moves to make Hampshire more conventional could impinge upon the divisional system with its unique opportunities for student to design their own curricula. On the bright side, we feel confident that faculty and students will firmly retain the tradition of faculty teaching from their current interests.[5]

Support for Interdisciplinary Inquiry: Structures and Culture

An intellectual enterprise will succeed in the long run only if it draws people together into combinations that are professionally productive and personally nourishing. In reflecting on our experience in sustaining interdisciplinary teaching and research for nearly three decades, we have emphasized how four aspects of the Hampshire educational program contribute to those necessary conditions.

The divisional examination system requires students to propose their own educational programs, and as a consequence, the definition of student study programs at Hampshire is in the hands of those who have little or no regard for the disciplinary categories of faculty professionalization. The interdisciplinary organization of schools prevents the reification of disciplines through administrative units and fosters nondisciplinary connections among faculty. The role of classes in student programs, along with the Five College connection, has produced a flexible formal curriculum of courses. This flexibility is a headache for those who prefer stability, academic planning, and predictability, but on the other hand, it infuses a continuing interest and excitement into classroom teaching. This last point is one of the elements of faculty commitment and renewal.

The interdisciplinary environment appears to have included a sufficient mix of opportunities, incentives, stimulation, support, and encouragement for the faculty to create rewarding professional lives as teachers at Hampshire as well as scholars in broader arenas.

These components have created an institutional dynamics that support and extend our commitment to interdisciplinary education. Although this statement in true, it is also misleading because it leaves out a crucial step: These components have actually created institutional dynamics that support and extend our commitment to providing a rigorous and exciting education based on principles of critical inquiry. This commitment in turn requires interdisciplinary education, because a reliance on academic disciplines would impede achieving our educational goal.

Well-developed disciplines supposedly have solved basic conceptual problems. It is all too easy, then, for disciplinary curricula to point students in directions already set by those solutions and to discourage questioning the intellectual grounds for those directions. Since disciplinary curricula seldom include examination of the implications of disciplinary categories, they expose students to the results of analyses rather than involving them as active, self-aware participants in constructing the bases for analysis.

Hampshire remains a changing, evolving interdisciplinary institution, and an indication of how smoothly and naturally the organization of our teaching works for faculty and students is that interdisciplinary education, in and of itself, does not appear to be especially interesting to most of us. Administrators on occasion do talk about interdisciplinary this and that, and it is a deliberate and explicit part of Hampshire's self-representation to outside audiences. Nevertheless, one seldom hears faculty and students discussing it; what one does hear most often between and among faculty and students in the hallways are discussions, and often heated arguments, about ideas. As we have described, these arguments make use of various disciplines and their methods in the service of the discipline of inquiry. The instrumental character of our commitment to interdisciplinary education means that it would probably be better to characterize Hampshire's education as **a**disciplinary rather than interdisciplinary.

References

Patterson, F., & Longsworth, C. R. (1966). *The making of a college: A new departure in higher education.* Cambridge, MA: The MIT Press.

Rudolph, F. (1956). *Mark Hopkins and the log: Williams College, 1836–1872.* New Haven, CT: Yale University Press.

ENDNOTES

1. Hampshire is a private liberal arts college with about 1,200 students and ninety-some faculty.

2. As you might suspect, the joke varies significantly institution by institution.

3. "Examinations" at Hampshire mark the formal passing of Divisional requirements (Divisions I, II, and III). They are not examinations in the conventional sense but may be the satisfactory completion of projects (as in Divisions I and III) or the fulfillment of contracts for a program of courses and activities (Division II).

4. Until recently, there were four schools—Humanities and Arts, Social Science, Natural Science, and Cognitive Science and Cultural Studies—each consisting of 15–35 faculty members. After the reorganization, we now have three "core schools" (Humanities and Arts, Social Science, and Natural Science) and two "clusters" (Cognitive Science, and InterArts).

5. The retirements so far have been paced gradually enough to enable us to replace them by using usual decision-making procedures without having to employ extraordinary planning. This may change by the end of the next decade, and at the same time, our current, rather casual practice of socializing new faculty through team teaching and shared memberships on student divisional committees may have to become more structured.

4

Evergreen at Twenty-Five: Sustaining Long-Term Innovation

Barbara Leigh Smith
The Evergreen State College

In 1971, The Evergreen State College (TESC) opened its doors to an entering class of 1,100 students, becoming the first new public four-year college in Washington in 75 years. Twelve years later, Evergreen was lauded in the popular press for its high-quality education and exceptional value; but meanwhile, closer to home, bills were being introduced in the state legislature to close the college.

Evergreen occupies an unusual place in the history of American higher education. Not only is it one of the few surviving nontraditional colleges[1] established in the late 1960s, but it also became the seedbed for a burgeoning national reform effort to restructure traditional curricula and pedagogy through learning communities (Gabelnick, Matthews, MacGregor, & Smith, 1990).[2] Evergreen also became part of a rising sector in higher education—sometimes referred to as the public liberal arts colleges or the public ivies. This emerging sector came to some prominence in the late 1980s when a group of public liberal arts colleges organized to argue for the value of their distinctive contribution to higher education.[3] What these public liberal arts colleges have in common is relatively small size (at least by the standards of four year public institutions), and a learning-centered identity that attempts to combine access, quality, and innovation. They strive to provide students at public institutions with the quality liberal arts education previously only available at private colleges.

Evergreen's dual identity as a nontraditional institution and a public liberal arts college created both stresses and opportunities for the college as it developed. This chapter explores the college's development and the lessons that it holds for other institutions attempting to organize for learning in new ways.

Decades of Transformation

Evergreen is one of a number of nontraditional institutions established in the late 1960s, a period of enormous expansion and innovation in American higher education. Clark Kerr (1990) characterized the 1960s and 1970s as decades of fundamental transformation. Enrollment in higher education increased 140%. The nation's faculty went from 235,000 in 1960 to 685,000 in 1980, and the number of colleges expanded from 2,000 to 3,200 (Kerr, 1990).

The 1970s and 1980s were also a period of establishing new hierarchies and sorting roles and relationships in higher education. Differential funding made investment in less costly two-year institutions an economical way to increase access. The community college system was largely created in this period. Enrollment in two-year colleges went from fewer than half a million students in 1960 to four million by 1980 (Kerr, 1990). In the State of Washington, as elsewhere, the fates of the two- and four-year colleges would become increasingly intertwined. By the 1990s, fully half of the students in Washington (and increasingly in the nation as a whole) would enter college through a two-year institution.

In many ways, the nontraditional colleges and the new public liberal arts colleges were caught in the middle, in the crosswinds between the different missions of the existing traditional four-year institutions and the new teaching and community-centered two-year colleges. But the full implications of this didn't become apparent until the 1980s, when the public liberal arts colleges would argue for a distinctive role and mission.

Evergreen faced many challenges as a nontraditional college, but it was also aided by three critical early factors. First, it had the luxury of a fully funded planning year in which a core of 18 planning faculty and administrators designed the campus and the program. Second, although the temper of the time was profoundly ahistorical, Evergreen learned from the mistakes of the earlier alternatives. It was founded toward the end of the era of expansion in nontraditional higher education, and Evergreen hired a number of faculty from those earlier experiments.[4] Finally, Evergreen was a more holistic alternative than many of the earlier experimental institutions, less riddled by the dualisms and contradictions that would eventually drive many of them back to traditional structures and practices.

The Founding: Seizing the Mandate to Experiment

What immediately strikes any close observer of a new alternative college is the long arm of the founding and the self-absorption of these communities with their beginning moments. Founding a new institution is, quite literally, an unforgettable experience. For many of the early participants the founding represents a crucial and singular turning point, the unsullied and rare opportunity to innovate and create something completely new—however many different versions there may be of that vision. This unique opening also enabled institutions like Evergreen to attract unusual faculty who were not interested in business as usual. The commitment to innovation and reaching out to the community in new ways was especially important in attracting a number of social activists and faculty of color to the college in its first years.[5]

Evergreen's founders had broad latitude to experiment, latitude they quickly translated into a mandate to experiment. The college was, in fact, chartered with a threefold mission: to serve as a nontraditional institution; to maintain a special relationship with state government, and to provide service to southwestern Washington. Senator Sandison, then chair of the Senate Higher Education Committee, is credited with creating the mandate to be experimental in a brief comment he made at an August 1967 meeting with the newly appointed Board of Trustees. He advised the board to study innovations around the country and called for "a college that can be as modern fifty years from now as at the present."[6]

As Peter Tommerup (1993) notes in his ethnographic study of Evergreen,

> working to create a new kind of college within this flexible though ambiguous environment had a discernible impact on the founders. On the one hand, they enjoyed the freedom afforded them by this flexibility and the opportunity to create a new world. The flip side of this inspirational high, however, was frustration due to the large amount of ambiguity involved in the project. It was difficult at times for the group to determine whether they were still on track due to the lack of a pre-existing model for this sort of school. Additional burdens included pressure from interested outsiders as well as the participants internal desire to create something truly special, something that reflected their ideal image of what teaching and learning should be about. (pp. 46–47)

Two figures loom large in Evergreen's early history: the founding president Charles McCann and one of the founding deans, Mervyn Cadwallader. McCann came to Evergreen from a deanship at Central Washington University. An unassuming humanist devoted to the liberal arts, McCann didn't think he had a chance of winning the presidency against a national pool of candidates, but the opportunity was unprecedented so he stood for the position anyway. He was candid with the Board of Trustees about his views that the new college should be different. He saw no reason to replicate traditional colleges, especially when they were so obviously flawed and ill-suited to the needs at the end of the 20th century. McCann's earliest comments indicate a special interest in decentralizing education by placing responsibility in the hands of faculty and students rather than committees, departments, or faculty senates. Narrative evaluations and integrating the world of work into the curriculum were also two of his passions.

While McCann had certain notions about the new college, he did not have a detailed curricular design or organizational structure in mind when he assumed office. He came, however, firmly convinced that he had a mandate to design a distinctive institution that was not a carbon copy of the other state colleges.[7]

The three founding deans represented the traditional academic divisions—Don Humphrey (sciences), Charles Teske (humanities and arts), and Mervyn Cadwallader (social sciences). They were chosen for their previous experience with innovation in undergraduate education, but they came—some said simply as a way to get on the faculty—with rather traditional notions about their roles, thinking they would be divisional deans. But the academic organization changed radically as a result of early discussions about the curriculum.

One of the most influential founding deans, Mervyn Cadwallader recounted the early discussion at Evergreen:

> We met for the first time in a trailer. The conversation was absolutely formless. Nothing happened. We were talking about lectures and courses. We looked at floor plans . . . Lecture halls . . . big lecture halls, little lecture halls . . . Finally, to get things moving I described my previous coordinated studies program at San Jose, and I said I'd like to have an opportunity to do that with 100 of the thousand students we admitted. And then, as I recall, 'Don said if it's good for 100, it's good for a thousand' . . . and that's how Evergreen got committed to coordinated studies. (White, 1974)

Cadwallader also recalled being astonished at this turn of events:

> The moment Don said if it's good for 100 it's good for a 1000, I was really appalled and shocked and scared. I started to back pedal and emphasize the difficulty of finding faculty who could teach cooperatively and across disciplinary lines in coordinated studies. When I came to Evergreen, the most I was hoping for was two coordinated studies programs, one starting each year and 100–200 students, counting for the work of 10–12 faculty. I was completely bowled over when in a matter of hours we found

ourselves committed not to one coordinated studies but to 12 on opening day. (White, 1974)

The planning faculty were a diverse group with many different—sometimes contradictory—views about education, but they were all taken by the notion of establishing a team-taught, theme-based curriculum in which students and faculty would work together in year-long programs rather than discrete three or four credit courses. After reading Joseph Tussman's account of the Experimental College at the University of Wisconsin and his replication at Berkeley, they agreed to resurrect the structural and pedagogical features of the Experimental College established briefly at the University of Wisconsin from 1927–1932 by Alexander Meiklejohn.[8] As a group, they did not chose to emulate the basic content of the Meiklejohn curricula, the so-called "moral curriculum" organized around the history of western and American civilization topics, though Cadwallader continued to lobby for this emphasis. But that too had a place. One of his favorite programs, "Democracy and Tyranny," was loosely based on the content of the Meiklejohn curriculum. It continues to be offered periodically. The decision to adopt the structure of coordinated studies provided everyone with considerable latitude to experiment with content and pedagogy in their own ways. And they did.

Cadwallader doubted whether the entire institution should be organized around full-time coordinated studies programs. He argued instead for a more hybrid type of institution in which the lower division was organized around thematic interdisciplinary programs but the upper division curricula was more conventionally structured. Debates among the faculty about the desirable curricular structure continued to revisit this point of view which was dubbed "the two college approach," especially in times of enrollment shortfall, but there was never a serious attempt to alter the basic structure established in the early years. While full-time programs created certain rigidities in the college's curriculum, the wholesale commitment to coordinated studies at this early date was probably critical in preserving the college's distinctiveness in the tough times that followed.[9]

Many of the founding faculty brought previous experience that proved invaluable in designing a new institution. They came from diverse institutions—from elite private colleges such as Reed, Harvard and Oberlin; from the new "alternative colleges" such as New College in Florida, SUNY-Old Westbury, and the University of California, Santa Cruz; and still others from innovative cluster colleges within traditional institutions, such as San Jose's.[10] A half dozen of the founding faculty were familiar with other Meiklejohn-like programs. They brought a variety of progressive education ideas with them—narrative evaluations, interdisciplinary study, collaborative learning, team teaching, internships, self-paced learning, individualized study, community-based education, and hands-on experience in the sciences.

The founding faculty also brought a litany of lessons from their mistakes. Many had concerns about the nonacademic turn many alternative colleges had taken and the endless haggling about governance. When Byron Youtz was at Old Westbury, where he served as the academic vice president (he had previously served as acting president at Reed College as well), it had become embroiled in a variety of disputes. Old Westbury subsequently closed and reopened with a new identity. At San Jose, where a Meiklejohn-type integrated studies program had been briefly established, some of the faculty participants described it as "a disaster."

While the founding faculty may have been wiser for their hindsight, their enthusiasm for educational reform was undiminished. Much to their surprise, the more experienced "veterans" found themselves in the awkward position of being the conservatives, the "cassandras" as one put it, as they cautioned their more inexperienced colleagues about the perils of interdisciplinary studies and team teaching.

Richard Alexander came to Evergreen from San Jose State University where he had participated in a Meiklejohn-type program. He, like a number of others, was particularly drawn to Evergreen's avowed agenda of applying an honors-type education based on book seminars to a nonselective student body. He was cautious but optimistic that it could succeed:

> I was convinced this would take an enormous amount of creative elaboration and that we would make many mistakes and would have to learn from them, but I was also enthusiastic about applying this model that had previously only been tried with elite honors students and applying that to the ordinary student body of a state college. I wanted that student body. For my money that is the crucial ongoing experiment of this place . . . one that we haven't satisfactorily resolved . . . but we've done it better than the most optimistic of us believed we would. (The Evergreen State College, 1987)

Other founding faculty came with quite different visions, but the basically permissive curricular structure allowed nearly all of the various agendas to be accommodated. Ultimately, student demand decided which curricular visions prevailed, but student demand had a slightly different meaning at Evergreen since choices were severely constrained by the limited number of full-time programs.

Evergreen's main features emerged in the first year and changed little over the next twenty-five years: a stress on collaboration and avoidance of hierarchy (no faculty rank or tenure, a uniform salary scale based upon years of experience, rotating academic administrators, use of narrative evaluations rather than grades), interdisciplinary study in the context of structural innovation through year-long programs, and a strong commitment to a diverse faculty. Organizationally, the college was decentralized and firmly based on the assumption that faculty teams could be trusted to develop strong academic programs. Decentralization was seen as a key element in maintaining an innovative climate at the college. Dozens of new practices—such as student portfolios, teaching team covenants, narrative evaluations, required weekly faculty and student seminars, collaborative learning, and a reappointment policy based upon faculty teaching portfolios—gave life and structure to these new values, resulting in a largely holistic environment devoted to interdisciplinary and collaborative teaching and learning. Many of these practices later became part of the reform efforts in the 1980s and 1990s in higher education as a whole. In the process, Evergreen developed new forms and languages which would become part of its identity and also part of its problem in relating to the outside world.

Playing by the Numbers

The issue of how large Evergreen could and should be is a recurrent theme in its history. For many, this question is intertwined with concerns about the college's mission, cost, and responsiveness. The original forecasts assumed that Evergreen would grow rapidly to more than 12,000 students by the early 1980s, and the physical plant and administrative structure were planned accordingly.

The college did grow rapidly in its first two years, adding 1,000 students each year. But then the economy slipped, fueled by ongoing recession and huge layoffs at the Boeing Company, which dominated the Washington economy. As a result, higher education enrollments throughout the state were cut back. Even so, by 1973 it had become clear that the original demographic projections for the college were way off base, and the decision was made to rescale the college to 4,200 students.[11] The local newspaper, long unfriendly to the college, was filled with stories of layoffs. This led to an early feeling of failure and contributed directly to the problems the college would later face in justifying its cost per student in the face of large diseconomies of scale.

This basic demographic error created all sorts of problems for the college in the succeeding years. Especially in times of economic downturn, critics would argue that Evergreen was too small, too expensive, or too specialized. For some, Evergreen was unaffordable in times of austerity, and the Washington economy suffered substantial swings over the next twenty-five years. But cost wasn't the only source of criticism. Some felt the institution had arrogantly chosen to emphasize only one part of its mission—the mission to serve as an alternative college. But in many cases, the bottom line was Evergreen's nontraditional nature: Many critics simply didn't like the political, educational, and cultural milieu. Evergreen was tarred with the criticisms that all the nontraditional colleges faced: they were too soft, too radical, too impractical, and too much of a challenge to the way the rest of "us" were educated.

Most in the Evergreen community were relieved when the decision came to downsize the institution. The campus was designed largely around small teaching spaces organized to support a seminar-based form of instruction. Most faculty saw the small residential college as the ideal campus environment. But the debate about size and mission continued well into the late 1980s when the college's mission was officially changed. By the mid-1990s the college would be asked to grow even further to accommodate the growing number of students seeking higher education in the state.

Mid-Course Corrections

By 1974, internal issues developed about the way the college operated, and the students began to demand more predictability in the curriculum. Three critical inquiries focused attention on the future direction of the college: the 1974 accreditation report, a 1975 Long Range Curriculum Review, and the report from a 1976 review panel established by the Evergreen Board of Trustees. All three reports made essentially the same recommendations, some of which would be repeated, again, in the 1978 report of the Council on Postsecondary Education.

Evergreen's first accreditation visit took place in 1974. The visiting team was strongly supportive of the new college but also suggested ways in which it could improve. The accreditation team recognized the power of the coordinated studies programs and saw this as the strongest part of Evergreen's educational program. But they also found considerable variation in quality among programs, and felt there was a need for better overall balance in the curriculum. The committee also suggested that the college needed to face some essential questions about boundaries in light of the wide variations in the different modes of study, in student advisement, in the integration of the program themes, and in the level of challenge in the curriculum.

Many of the issues raised by the accreditation report were addressed by the 1975 Long Range Curriculum DTF (Disappearing Task Force, Evergreen's name for committees). It recommended that a portion of the curriculum be repeated and that the overall curriculum be organized around interdisciplinary specialty areas to create more sequence, coherence, and predictability. In addition, several more career-oriented areas were established, such as a specialty in management and the public interest and an evening program for state workers.[12] At the same time, an upper division program was established in Vancouver, Washington, a community that many considered a logical alternative site for the original campus. Limited part-time studies were also established in Olympia. All of these moves had the consequence of diversifying the student body and the faculty, but within the framework of coordinated studies programs and the essential values with which the college had begun.

Some faculty remained committed to a completely zero-based curriculum planning process, contending that the creativity, vitality, and timeliness of the curriculum came from creating it anew each year. To others, this perspective represented an overly rationalized justification for faculty autonomy at the expense of students. Over the next fifteen years the specialty area framework stayed in place. More regularity was established in areas that needed significant equipment and staff support such as the performing and visual arts and the sciences. Nonetheless, specialty areas (later called planning units) bore little resemblance to the structure of traditional departments or divisions. Faculty had only a loose attachment to their areas, and movement between areas was freely allowed, indeed encouraged. Specialty areas remained largely powerless curriculum planning units with no budgetary authority and minimal leadership. Institutional values continued to emphasize "re-forming" the curriculum and rotating the faculty. At the same time, the college became more explicit about expectations for team teaching and rotating through the curriculum.[13]

In 1976, a review panel was appointed by the Board of Trustees. Acting like an accreditation team, they sought to augment the accreditation evaluation committee's view, particularly emphasizing the extent to which the college was benefiting citizens of the state. This phenomena of outside reviews assisting internal change processes would be repeated throughout the college's history.

At the same time, the academic administration of the college was reorganized in 1976 by the Board of Trustees in the interests of greater continuity. A system of two nationally chosen long-term deans (four-year terms, twice renewable) and two (nonrenewable) rotating deans from the faculty was established.[14] This approach was designed to give continuity to long-term functions while still providing the faculty perspective and vitality that comes from having academic administrators more recently in the classroom. This system was again changed in mid-1980s by the faculty in the interests of equalizing status relationships and attracting internal deans.

Despite the turn toward internal candidates, academic deans have tended to serve for longer periods of time in recent years and a variety of approaches have developed to produce more continuity. The deans continue to organize their work by desk assignments and operate as a collaborative team on all major issues. This has been important in maintaining interdisciplinary perspectives. Instead of organizing around departmental or divisional subject area principles, the deans' responsibilities are larger functions. With five current deans, one dean is charged with budget, space, and equipment. Another has overall responsibility for faculty hiring and faculty development. Lead responsibility for a third major desk resides with a part time studies dean while another has responsibility for freshmen core programs. The so-called "curriculum dean" has overall responsibility for the undergraduate, full-time curriculum. Developing administrative structures that promoted interdisciplinary perspectives has been important in maintaining Evergreen's founding values. The college continues to struggle with the tension between structures that might better promote efficiency and a desire to remain nimble and nondepartmental.[15]

THE EVANS ERA

A crucial turning point in Evergreen's history came in June 1977 when popular three-term Republican former governor Daniel J. Evans assumed the presidency of Evergreen, causing raised eyebrows among many and second thoughts about Evergreen on the part of more than a few. While some criticized the appointment, arguing that he had created the college as a retirement spot, most observers respected the former governor, and his appointment brought a new level of respect to the college. While Evan's political reputation cut both ways, it is difficult to imagine what might have happened had he not assumed Evergreen's presidency when he did. In close collaboration with a much-respected provost and founding faculty member, Byron Youtz, Evans played a key role in stabilizing the college and creating an improved image in the state.

During the first two years of Evan's term, the college experienced absolute enrollment declines, nearly dipping (precipitously, many thought) below that crucial 2000 mark in 1978. Student retention also reached a low of 55%. In 1977, the legislature asked the Council for Postsecondary Education (CPE), the oversight agency for higher education, to conduct a study of Evergreen to "determine the actions necessary to increase enrollment and reduce the average cost of educating an Evergreen student" (Chance & Curry, 1979). The CPE responded with a detailed study of the college's programs; its enrollment patterns and process; its cost; and the college's image among current Evergreen students, area high school students, alumni, and employers. There was particular concern that the college was not attracting a proportionate number of local high school and community college students. Surveys were conducted to ascertain why this was happening.

Surprisingly, the surveys indicated that Evergreen provided many of the features that the high school students said they valued, but the students did not associate these features with Evergreen. The areas in which the college was perceived to fall short were areas in which the college excelled, such as the ability of graduates to get jobs, teaching as the most important mission, faculty expecting students to work hard, students committed to learning, small classes, faculty are accessible to students, and low tuition. Clearly, Evergreen was not communicating well. The CPE surveys questioned whether Evergreen's problem was one of communication or genuinely being unattractively different and not offering the right campus environment or curricular options.[16] Ultimately, the authors of the CPE report sat on the fence, assuming it was probably some of each, but banking on the college's ability to better communicate. It also recommended that the college institute some new activities and programs to broaden its appeal.

The study concluded with twenty recommendations, the most important one being that the college be given a four year breathing period to implement changes and reverse declining enrollment trends. The CPE report estimated that the college would need to grow to 4,250 FTE to reach cost parity with its sister institutions, and it recommended that it do so. Previous studies had indicated that the direct costs of instruction at Evergreen were only slightly higher than the other regional public colleges ($1,325 vs. $1,219), but the gap was much larger in terms of the overall support costs. Most of the differences were attributable to size.

Issues about cost were recurrent, though the grounds would shift in later years. Studies in the early 1990s indicated that Evergreen remained number three in cost per student behind the two research universities, though the gap between Evergreen and the other regional institutions closed considerably. The main areas in which TESC's costs remained higher at this time were in public service, library, and administration, and not instruction. Evergreen was funded at the same student faculty ratios as the other regional public colleges, though it deployed its faculty in markedly different ways. In the mid-1980s Evergreen established four distinctive public service centers that would set it apart from its regional sisters. Throughout its history Evergreen would continue to be buffeted by the crosswinds that encouraged it to be distinctive, on the one hand, and comparable, on the other.

With very specific directions from the state, Evans and Youtz had considerable leverage to engage the community in serious self-analysis and corrective actions. Over the next several years, Evergreen reexamined many of its processes and implemented most of the CPE recommendations including simplifying the application process, adding the bachelor of science degree, offering additional graduate programs, contracting with another institution to provide a teacher education program, sponsoring state training programs, establishing interinstitutional programs to share resources, simplifying the college's narrative transcripts, assessing entering students' skills, establishing career pathways through the curriculum, establishing more predictability and continuity in the curriculum; increasing part-time curricular options, establishing programs to ease the transition to Evergreen, establishing a limited program of intercollegiate athletics, tightening up internship and individual contract programs, exploring the establishment of off-campus programs in other parts of Southwest Washington, improving student advising, and aggressively working to improve the college's image and communicate the college's strengths to the community and to the state's high schools and community colleges.

Though the fundamental approach and values of the institution did not change as a result of the CPE recommendations, the college created a variety of ways of translating what it did to make it more intelligible to outsiders. These included recruiting brochures translating Evergreen programs into disciplinary equivalencies, and transcript face sheets summarizing traditional course equivalencies. The college also established a highly professionalized, intensive program of student recruitment, and engaged in an aggressive program of institutional research and assessment of its efforts. The college already had a strong base on which to build in describing itself since the career planning office had tracked graduates from the outset and Evergreen's strong internship program provided ample evidence of the student's skill in the workplace.

Though the college responded decisively, political opposition continued under Evan's adversary Democratic Governor Dixie Lee Ray who called for closing Evergreen and Central Washington University as cost cutting measures in 1981. Until 1983, bills to close TESC continued to surface, but the local community rallied on the college's behalf. This was a turning point for the college which had by this time established local and national credibility.

Meanwhile, the Washington economy started to recover, and declining enrollment trends throughout the state reversed. At the same time, a long parade of stories began to appear in the national media about Evergreen. Later in the year, Evans resigned to take the United States Senate seat of Henry Jackson, and after a period of interim leadership in 1984, Joseph Olander was appointed president. [17]

Extending the Reach of the Innovation

Evergreen's most recent decade is characterized by rapid growth and increasing diversity in the student body and faculty, a growing climate of respect in the state and the nation, and an aggressive effort to extend the reach of its innovations.

By the late 1980s Evergreen enrolled more than 3,200 students. The number of students enrolling directly from high school increased 174%

between 1983 and 1988. Community college enrollment also grew substantially. National interest in Evergreen continued to grow, and the college was the focus of a number of prominent studies of effective institutions.[18] But Evergreen, like most of the colleges in the state, had to deal with the problems of over-enrollment. At the same time, retention reached new highs with 80% of the freshman returning in 1989, a 15% increase over the retention low in 1982.

With newfound confidence, the college significantly lowered its boundaries and started to extend itself in new relationships with the community and other colleges and universities. Strategic partnerships became a key element in Evergreen's attempts to extend the reach of its innovations. Four public service centers were established to reach out and support innovation and collaboration with key communities, including labor, Native American tribes, the K-12 system, and the rest of the higher education system. A variety of creative efforts were also undertaken to diversify its student body and broaden curricular options. While some of the partnerships changed over time and a few were terminated (such as the closing of the Vancouver campus), the new relationships are perhaps most remarkable for the ways in which they evidenced an institutional willingness to reach out and make long-term commitments. At the same time, these new ventures reflect a consistent effort to maximize compatibility with institutional values, undoubtedly a key element in Evergreen's long-term success.

In *Why Innovation Fails* (1980), Arthur Levine argues that compatibility and profitability are the key variables in explaining why innovations flourish or fail. Wholesale nontraditional institutions like Evergreen probably have some natural advantages since they are not constantly facing compatibility challenges from the rest of the institution. Citing Burton Clark's study of Swarthmore, Antioch, and Reed (*The Distinctive College,* 1970), Levine argues that distinctive institutions often need to maintain relatively rigid boundaries (especially in their early years) to maintain their uniqueness. "In the case of Clark's three colleges, this meant a small, little-changing core of personnel; a little changing program; clearly articulated clientele and financial support groups; a student subculture for socializing entering students to appropriate norms, values, and goals; and a true ideology. In combination, these elements preserved the three experiments. At the same time, they ruled out other types of innovations" (p. 170). This was certainly true of Evergreen as well.

Evergreen extended the reach of its innovations gradually, slowly building on past success. Some of the following efforts are especially notable.

- *Serving multicultural communities.* The Evergreen Tacoma campus, which started in 1972 with two students in founding director Maxine

Mimm's kitchen, grew to 120 upper division students and was formally recognized as an off-campus center by the state Higher Education Coordinating Board in 1983. Increasingly assertive about its sense of obligation to the local community, the campus moved into the heart of the economically troubled Hilltop area of Tacoma to help rebuild the multicultural community. In 1985, an innovative lower-division bridge program was added in collaboration with Tacoma Community College to serve an additional 50 students who needed the lower division program to enter Evergreen's upper division curriculum. The bridge program is taught by a team of faculty from the two colleges and located on the site of Evergreen's upper division program. This partnership represents a radical vision of intercollege articulation, the type that may be increasingly required to expand the baccalaureate completion rate as more and more students—especially students of color—begin their college career in a two-year institution.

- *Teacher education.* As the college reached out in new directions, it also became increasingly assertive about doing programs its own way, i.e., through team-taught coordinated studies programs. Evergreen had been more or less forced into offering a teacher education program in the late 1970s as a result of the CPE study which suggested it contract with another institution. This turned out to be the University of Puget Sound. While the program was quite successful, it never had high compatibility with Evergreen's institutional culture and approach to teaching. In 1985, Evergreen switched from the six year contracted partnership with the University of Puget Sound to a more integrated collaborative program with Western Washington University. This too had limits in terms of institutional compatibility and in 1990 Evergreen established its own master in teaching program.[19]

- *Leveraging innovation statewide.* In 1985, with support from the Exxon Foundation and the Ford Foundation, Evergreen established the Washington Center for Improving the Quality of Undergraduate Education, a unique statewide public service initiative. With the establishment of the Washington Center, Evergreen assumed an explicit statewide leadership role in reforming undergraduate education. A primary focus has been supporting adaptations of Evergreen's curricula, commonly referred to as structural reform through purposefully created learning communities.[20] The effort has been remarkably successful. Hundreds of colleges and universities throughout the US now have learning communities. More than 34 Washington colleges now offer learning community curricula, and 46 Washington colleges are affiliated with the Washington Center. The

Washington Center has also attracted major funding for statewide projects in such areas as calculus reform, cultural pluralism, and interdisciplinary approaches to the sciences. The center acts as a statewide support system for educational reform and sponsors a variety of activities including faculty exchanges, conferences and retreats, assessment initiatives, and technical resources.

The success of the Washington Center suggests that a third party organization can expand institutional boundaries to create and nurture a larger community committed to educational reform. Diffuse boundaries, complex styles and sources of leadership, and continual revisiting of the mission were key elements in the center's success. The work of the Washington Center has demonstrated that many aspects of the Evergreen experience are transferable, and that learning communities and collaborative learning are successful in diverse institutional settings.[21]

Constancy and Change

In 1987, the State Master Plan for Higher Education was reexamined, and Evergreen's role and mission was formally changed from being a regional state college to a statewide public liberal arts college based upon interdisciplinary study and collaborative teaching and learning. This change in mission was a capstone to Evergreen's seventeen-year struggle to establish its credibility and distinctive identity as an alternative public liberal arts college. The mission change put to rest one of the critical tensions that had plagued the college—the tension between being a statewide and national alternative college and the obligation to serve southwest Washington. Two years later Evergreen was reaccredited.

The 1989 reaccreditation team was particularly impressed with the self-study which eloquently articulated the college's core educational values in terms of the five principles of interdisciplinary study, personal engagement in learning, linking theory and practice, collaborative work, and teaching across significant differences. This was an important turning point for the college which had now successfully learned to describe itself in terms of what is was rather that what is was not (no departments, etc.). The reaccreditation report, entitled "Constancy and Change," described an institution that had continued to grow and evolve while remaining true to its fundamental values. The visiting team asserted that the college had "moved from an experimental college often operating on the defensive to a nationally recognized and robust enterprise willing to continue experimentation in the context of a more mature alternative college" (The Evergreen State College Reaccreditation Report, 1989, pp. 14–15). The team concluded that they were "not able to gauge the importance of any one element of the curriculum or pedagogy to the total outcome, but the fusion of all elements results in a powerful learning experience" (37). They encouraged the college to take its new official designation as an alternative liberal arts college with the utmost seriousness, noting, in particular, its obligation to educate students "who would be better educated outside the conventional college" (37) and in term of "its continuing responsibility to experiment, to increase its educational power, and to test the validity and relative merit of its own settled arrangements" (37).

The reaccreditation team also recognized the structural tensions inherent in the design of the college, such as the dual demand for both flexibility and predictability in the curriculum, dilemmas about student choice versus educational quality in terms of balance, and issues about the effectiveness of year-long programs versus the rigidity this structure imposed. These were recurring tensions within the college, dating back to its founding, but nonetheless, critical tensions that needed periodic revisiting. The reaccreditation team left Evergreen with a variety of queries about these tensions while also reassuring the institution that some tensions were both necessary and desirable. The title of Evergreen's 1989 reaccreditation self-study was a fitting description of its twenty-five year evolution. Evergreen has matured into a widely respected alternative institution. It has held to its founding values and fundamental character. Its structures and processes have proven adaptable to changing times and circumstances.

In its founding period, Evergreen, like many new institutions, was focused inward, preoccupied with the challenges of creating an identity and surviving the turbulent waters and changing expectations of state government and a fickle public.

As Evergreen matured, it came to recognize the dangers of this insularity as well as its wider responsibility. The college lowered its boundaries and reached out to a wider public, connecting with the larger higher education community and its own local communities in a variety of creative ways. This recent era in the college's history suggests many new ways in which alternative public liberal arts colleges can forge their identities and relationships.

Looking Ahead

As a public institution, Evergreen must remain responsive to state policy issues. In the past decade, state policy has often been reactive, ad hoc, and highly dependent upon the economic circumstances of the state. Higher education has usually been treated as a budgetary balancer after taking care of other essential state obligations of which health care, corrections, and K-12 education consume an increasingly large portion. As a result, higher education is never high on the state policy agenda. A period of exploring institutional distinctiveness in which the state encouraged institutions to develop centers of excellence is followed by a period of concern about comparability and program duplication, and a period of promoting quality by mandating a certain level of expenditures for instruction is followed by a period of budget cuts. While some legislators remain interested in higher education as a populist issue, they tend to define and support access in terms of low tuition, open admissions, and geographic convenience. Legislative attitudes towards Evergreen have improved over time, but there are still pockets of mistrust and misunderstanding that surface periodically. In most situations, Evergreen is treated as one of the pack (like its regional sister institutions)—a position that often protects but sometimes exacerbates institutional interests.

In 1993, a state initiative to control the state budget and limit tax increases passed, and in 1999, additional tax limitations were imposed. These initiatives put increasing pressure on higher education budgets, especially since they came at a time of substantial increases in K-12 enrollments. Evergreen is projected to grow to 5,000 students to help accommodate the large number of students in the K-12 system. The debate about access and quality is deepening in Washington, and questions are being asked about productivity and how to get more for less from the education system. In the K-12 system as well as higher education, there is a robust statewide conversation about improving student learning outcomes as well.

Washington is one of a handful of states that made a considerable long-term investment in assessment, with few strings attached, beginning in the late 1980s. As a result, there is a well-developed history of assessment in Washington state and at Evergreen. The confluence of the work of Evergreen's Washington Center and statewide investments in assessment was fortunate: they reenforced each other, creating a long-term tradition of innovation and working together across institutions.

Calls for greater institutional accountability are also accelerating. Increasingly joined with the more recent accountability movement, calls for institutional assessment are being turned to narrower and more fundamental questions about institutional efficiency and faculty productivity. Evergreen is in a perplexing situation with respect to calls for greater efficiency and productivity since it already leads all of the other institutions on most measures. The college continues to argue for accountability measures specific to each institution's mission but has found it difficult to get recognition for its effectiveness on statewide measures without an accompanying demand for even greater efficiency in terms of student contact hours and class size.

The increasingly tight fiscal climate in Washington is only one of the critical challenges facing Evergreen. The college is entering a period of substantial enrollment growth and turnover in the faculty as large numbers of the founding faculty retire. Recognizing that new faculty are not necessarily trained for the kind of educational practices at Evergreen, the college has developed careful hiring and socialization practices. While there is presently high alignment between faculty values and practices and institutional goals, there is recognition that this can never be taken for granted. Investing in many different forms of faculty development is an institutional priority. The college has developed many avenues for bringing the faculty together, including an extensive array of summer institutes, an extensive new faculty orientation and buddy system, and an array of one-on-one approaches to address issues among the faculty.

At the same time, many of Evergreen's reform efforts have now come full circle as colleges across the nation are adopting traditional Evergreen practices such as integrated curriculum design, collaborative learning, teaching portfolios, narrative evaluations, service-learning, and student self-assessment. There is talk at Evergreen about this being a period of refounding. As dozens of new faculty join TESC and new students enter, the academic practices that had vitality in earlier times need to be reborn and revitalized or they will atrophy or become tiresome bureaucratic requirements. The challenge of constancy and change remains: to maintain continuity with core values, and to maintain a sense of rooted identity and vitality in the face of critical transitions.

References

Astin, A. (1993). *What matters in college: Four critical years revisited.* San Francisco, CA: Jossey-Bass.

Bopegedera, D. (1997). Atoms, molecules and research: A learning community in upper division chemistry. In A. McNeal & C. D'Avanzo (Eds.), *Student-active science: Methods of innovation in college science teaching* (pp. 321–336). Fort Worth, TX: Harcourt Brace.

Brown, C. S. (1981). *Alexander Meiklejohn: Teacher of freedom.* Cabin John, MD: Meiklejohn Institute.

Casey, B. (1990). The administration of interdisciplinary programs: Creating climates for change. *Issues in Integrative Studies, 8,* 97–100.

Chance, W., & Curry, D. (1979). *The Evergreen study: Report and recommendations on The Evergreen State College.* Olympia, WA: The Washington State Council for Postsecondary Education.

Clark, B. (1970). *The distinctive college: Antioch, Reed and Swarthmore.* New Brunswick, NJ: Aldine Press.

Diffendal, E. (1986). *Significant difference: An ethnographic study of women and minority faculty in the development of an innovative liberal arts college.* Unpublished doctoral dissertation, The Union for Experimenting Colleges and Universities.

Dressel, P. (Ed.). (1971). *The new colleges: Towards an appraisal.* Iowa City, IA: The American College Testing Program and the American Association for Higher Education.

Elbow, P. (1986). *Embracing contraries: Explorations of learning and teaching.* New York, NY: Oxford University Press.

The Evergreen State College. (1987, March 2). Founding faculty discussion. *Founding festival series* [videotape]. Olympia, WA: Author.

Fiske, E. (1999). *The Fiske guide to colleges.* New York, NY: Random House.

Gabelnick, F., Matthews, R., MacGregor, J., & Smith, B. (1990). *Learning communities: Creating connections among students, faculty and disciplines.* San Francisco, CA: Jossey-Bass.

Gabelnick, F., Matthews, R., MacGregor, J., & Smith, B. (1992, Fall). Learning communities and general education. *Perspectives, 22* (1), 104–121.

Goodsell, A., Maher, M., Tinto, V., Smith, B. L., & MacGregor, J. (1992). *Collaborative learning: A sourcebook.* University Park, PA: Penn State University, National Center on Teaching, Learning, and Assessment.

Grant, G., & Reisman, D. (1978). *The perpetual dream: Reform and experiment in the American college.* Chicago, IL: University of Chicago Press.

Jones, R. (1981). *Experiment at Evergreen.* Cambridge, MA: Schenkman.

Kerr, C. (1990). Higher education cannot escape history: The 1990s. In L. Jones & F. Nowothy (Eds.), *An agenda for the new decade* (pp. 5–17). San Francisco, CA: Jossey-Bass.

Knapp, R. (1997). Scaffolding for dreams at Evergreen State College. In A. McNeal & C. D'Avanzo (Eds.), *Student-active science: Methods of innovation in college science teaching* (pp. 95–107). Fort Worth, TX: Harcourt Brace.

Kuh, G. D., Schuh, J. H., Whitt, E. J., Andreas, R. E., Lyons, J. W., Strange, C. C., Krehbiel, L. E., & MacKay, K. A. (1991). *Involving colleges: Successful approaches to fostering student learning and development outside the classroom.* San Francisco, CA: Jossey-Bass.

Levine, A. (1980). *Why innovation fails.* Albany, NY: State University of New York Press.

MacDonald, G. (Ed.). (1973). *Five experimental colleges.* New York, NY: Harper & Row.

MacGregor, J. (1987). *Intellectual development of students in learning community programs, 1986–1987.* Unpublished manuscript, the Washington Center, The Evergreen State College, Olympia, WA.

MacGregor, J. (1991). What differences do learning communities make? *Washington Center News, 6*, 4–9.

Mayhew, L. (1978). *Legacy of the seventies.* San Francisco, CA: Jossey-Bass.

McHenry, D., & Associates. (1977). *Academic departments.* San Francisco, CA: Jossey-Bass.

Moll, R. (1986). *The public ivys: A guide to America's best state colleges and universities.* New York, NY: Penguin-Vintage.

Ott, J. (1977). Science and society: A case study of a science-based coordinated studies program for freshmen at The Evergreen State College. In A. McNeal & C. D'Avanzo (Eds.), *Student-active science: Methods of innovation in college science teaching* (pp. 241–251). Fort Worth, TX: Harcourt Brace.

Powell, J. W. (Ed.). (1981). *The experimental college.* Arlington, VA: Seven Locks Press.

Smith, B. L. (1988, October). The Washington center: A grassroots approach to faculty development and curricular reform. *To Improve the Academy, 7*, 165–177.

Smith, B. L. (1991, March/April). Taking structure seriously. *Liberal Education, 77* (1), 42.

Smith, B. L. (1993). Creating learning communities. *Liberal Education, 79* (4), 32.

Smith, B. L. (1994). Team teaching methods. In K. Prichard & R. M. Sawyer (Eds.), *Handbook of college teaching* (pp. 127–137). Westport, CT: Greenwood Press.

Smith, B. L., & Smith, M. (1994, January). Revitalizing senior faculty through statewide initiatives. In M. Finkelstein & M. LaCelle-Peterson (Eds.), *Developing senior faculty as teachers* (pp. 81–93). San Francisco, CA: Jossey-Bass.

Smith, B. L. with MacGregor, J. (1991, Fall). Reflective interviews with learning community teaching teams: Strengthening dialogue about teaching and learning. *Washington Center News, 6* (2), 26.

Smith, B. L. with MacGregor, J. (1992). What is collaborative learning? In A. Goodsell, M. Maher, V. Tinto, B. L. Smith, & J. MacGregor, (Eds.), *Collaborative learning: A sourcebook.* University Park, PA: Penn State University, National Center on Teaching, Learning, and Assessment.

Tinto, V. (1987). *Leaving college: Rethinking the causes and cures of student attrition.* Chicago, IL: University of Chicago Press.

Tinto, V. (1997, November/December). Classrooms as communities. *Journal of Higher Education, 68* (6), 599–623.

Tinto, V., & Goodsell, A. (1993). Freshman interest groups and the first year experience: Constructing student communities in a large university. *The Journal of the Freshman Year Experience, 6* (1), 7–28.

Tinto, V., Russo, P., & Kadel, S. (1994). Constructing educational communities: Increasing retention in challenging circumstances. *Community College Journal, 64* (4), 26–29.

Townsend, B. K., Newell, L. J., & Wiese, M. D. (1992). *Creating distinctiveness: Lessons from uncommon colleges and universities.* ASHE-ERIC Higher Education Report No. 6. Washington, DC: The George Washington University, School of Education and Human Development.

Tussman, J. (1969). *Experiment at Berkeley.* New York, NY: Oxford University Press.

Tussman, J. (1997). *The beleaguered college: Essays on educational reform.* Berkeley, CA: University of California, Institute for Government Studies.

White, S. (1974). Planning deans, 1974. *Dreams and goals: Early visions of Evergreen series* [videotape]. Olympia, WA: Public Information and Minority Affairs Group Contract, The Evergreen State College.

Youtz, B. (1984). The Evergreen State College: An experiment maturing. In R. Jones & B. L. Smith (Eds.), *Against the current: Reform and experimentation in higher education* (pp. 93–118). Cambridge, MA: Schenkman.

Useful Unpublished Documents

Fiksdal, S. (1990). *Seminar talk.* Unpublished manuscript, The Evergreen State College, Olympia, WA.

Fiksdal, S. (1992). *Getting the floor.* Unpublished manuscript, The Evergreen State College, Olympia, WA.

The Evergreen State College Reaccreditation Report. (1989, August). *Constancy and change: A self-study report for the Northwest Association of Schools and Colleges.* Unpublished manuscript, The Evergreen State College, Olympia, WA.

Mott, P., & Hunter, S. (1991). *Greeners at work.* Unpublished manuscript, The Evergreen State College, Olympia, WA.

Thompson, K. (1991). *Learning at Evergreen: An assessment of cognitive development.* Unpublished manuscript, Washington Center for Improving the Quality of Undergraduate Education, Olympia, WA.

Thompson, K. (1992). *Learning at Evergreen II: Writing and thinking at The Evergreen State College.* Unpublished manuscript, The Evergreen State College, Olympia, WA.

Tinto, V., & Goodsell, A. (1993). *A longitudinal study of freshman interest groups at the University of Washington.* Unpublished manuscript, National Center for Postsecondary Teaching, Learning, and Assessment, Syracuse University.

Tinto, V., Goodsell, A., & Russo, P. (1994). *Building learning communities for new college students: A summary of research findings of the collaborative learning project.* Unpublished manuscript, National Center on Postsecondary Teaching, Learning, and Assessment, Syracuse University.

Tinto, V., & Russo, P. (1993). *A longitudinal study of the coordinated studies program at Seattle Central Community College.* Unpublished manuscript, National Center for Postsecondary Teaching, Learning, and Assessment, Syracuse University.

Tommerup, P. (1993). *Teaching and learning at Evergreen: An ethnographic study.* Unpublished doctoral dissertation, University of California at Los Angeles.

Trow, K. (1987). *The experimental college in retrospect: An exploratory study.* Unpublished report produced under a grant from the Fund for the Improvement of Postsecondary Education.

Tussman, J. (1988). *A venture in educational reform: A partial view.* Unpublished manuscript, Center for Studies in Higher Education, University of California, Berkeley.

Endnotes

1. The early history of this era of nontraditional education is described in David Reisman and Gerald Grant, *The Perpetual Dream: Reform and Experiment in the American College* (University of Chicago, 1978) and Lewis Mayhew, *Legacy of the Seventies* (Jossey-Bass, 1978). The story of these institutions is continued in Jones and Smith (Schenkman, 1985).

2. There are perhaps as many as five hundred colleges and universities doing integrated curriculum through learning communities today. See Gabelnick, et al. (1990), and MacGregor, Smith, Matthews, & Gabelnick (forthcoming) for a summary of this approach.

3. Richard Moll's book *The Public Ivys: A Guide to America's Best State Colleges and Universities* (Penguin-Vintage, 1986) popularized the concept of the "public ivys." Other college guides such as *The Fiske Guide to Colleges* (Random House) later set aside special sections on the public liberal arts colleges. Which institutions are best described as public liberal arts colleges is an ongoing question, and one they debate among themselves. In the late 1980s a group of these colleges formed an association called the Council of the Public Liberal Arts Colleges. The presidents at Evergreen, the University of North Carolina, Asheville, and Ramapo College of New Jersey started this association. Later, a number of these institutions would gain formal recognition as public liberal arts colleges in their mission statements.

4. There is a relatively large literature on the development and failures of the nontraditional colleges, from which Evergreen is, for the most part, conspicuously absent. See, for example, Grant and Reisman (1978), Mayhew (1978), Dressel (1971), Levine (1980), and MacDonald (1973).

5. The story of the "founding mothers" and the contribution of women and people of color is told in a 1997 video titled "Telling Our Stories," edited by M. Brown and in a doctoral thesis by Elizabeth Diffendal, "Significant Differences: An Ethnographic Study of Women and Minority Faculty in the Development of an Innovative Liberal Arts College," 1986, Union for Experimenting Colleges and Universities.

6. *Daily Olympian.* August 31, 1967.

7. The founding president Charles McCann's job description actually included a charge to ensure that Evergreen would not be "just another four-year college."

8. The book they read was *Experiment at Berkeley.* The Meiklejohn curriculum and history is also described in Tussman (1969, 1997); Jones (1981); Powell (1981); Brown (1981); Jones & Smith (1984); and Trow (1987).

9. These rigidities were most evident in terms of serving part-time students and providing options for students to pursue more sequenced, stand-alone courses in such areas as music, foreign language, and mathematics.

10. Founding faculty Will Humphrey came from New College in Florida, Alexander and Brian from San Jose State where a Meiklejohn type program had been established. Cadwallader had started the program at San Jose and then moved to SUNY-Old Westbury. Jones had been involved in an experimental program at Harvard. Byron Youtz came from Reed and Old Westbury along with Eickstaedt and Sluss.

Charles Teske, another of the founding deans, came from Oberlin. A large cadre came from Oregon State including Don Humphrey, Beryl Crowe, Bill Aldridge, and Sid White. Mountaineer Willi Unsoeld brought a history working with Outward Bound and other forms of experiential education. The number of individuals hired in clumps is noteworthy. Many were preachers' sons, bringing a spiritual cast to their commitment. All of the founding faculty were men, but in the second year of the college, the faculty profile was dramatically diversified. By the end of the second year, 23% of the faculty were female, and the college quickly established a record of attracting an ethnically diverse faculty as well.

11. This demographic miscalculation also happened at a number of other new institutions such as Ramapo College in New Jersey, the University of California, Santa Cruz, and Southwestern State University in Minnesota. While many, such as the University of California, Santa Cruz, later grew substantially, early enrollments often critically shape institutions' futures. Evergreen was fortunate to start with robust entering classes. At other institutions, low enrollment often became a primary reason for changing nontraditional colleges back into traditional curricula and organizational structures.

12. While some faculty were unhappy about what they saw as a turn toward vocational education, the management program was clearly a liberal arts program and never very large. It never exceeded 5% of the college's overall enrollment. This was markedly different from the enrollment trends at other previously nontraditional colleges such as Ramapo College, where 50% of the students majored in business.

13. In the 1988 revision to the Faculty Reappointment Policy, faculty rotation and team teaching were explicitly written in as requirements for reappointment. Team teaching was required in at least half of the years under contract. Continuing faculty on eight-year contracts were required to teach with at least eight different people. New faculty were required to teach with at least four different colleagues over a three year period. Since most faculty prefer team teaching, these requirements were not difficult to meet. Nearly all faculty also rotate into the freshman core curriculum periodically. Many regard the freshman core curriculum as the most interesting place to teach since the curriculum is the most open and the teaching teams the most interdisciplinary.

14. Only two long-term external deans were ever recruited from a national pool under these guidelines: Barbara Leigh Smith, who served the full twelve-year maximum term, and John Perkins, who served for six years.

15. The story of the early academic organization at Evergreen is told in C. McCann. (1977). Academic administration without departments at The Evergreen State College. In D. McHenry & Associates (Ed.), *Academic departments.* San Francisco, CA: Jossey-Bass. Joseph Comprone's article in this volume on departments offers an interesting counterpoint to this discussion.

16. In *Legacy of the Seventies,* Lewis Mayhew argues that many large-scale changes were implemented in higher education in the late 1960s that challenged traditional ways of doing things. These new approaches, unfortunately, came precisely at a time when higher education started to encounter serious financial difficulty. As a result, many of the original nontraditional institutions were underfunded and forced to become conventional and/or to lower standards to survive. Mayhew contends that many of the nontraditional education efforts were of low quality and more motivated by survival needs than genuine educational objectives. They gave the nontraditional colleges in general a bad name. Both of the major studies of this era by Mayhew and Grant and Riesman contend that Evergreen did not fit this overall pattern. They saw Evergreen as a genuine educational alternative that was high quality and well funded. In this instance, being a state institution may have made the critical difference. Mayhew questions whether nontraditional education, in general, is affordable when it is done right. Evergreen's later experience exporting its learning community curricular approach suggests that nontraditional education can be affordable, even to institutions less well endowed.

17. Olander's presidency was stormy, ultimately ending in his resignation in 1989 after a prolonged period of conflict. His departure, along with the vacancy created by his forcing the resignation of the provost Patrick Hill (who joined the teaching faculty), led to a long period of interim leadership in the institution.

18. Evergreen was one of the colleges in such studies as George Kuh's *Involving Colleges and Alexander Astin's What Matters in College?: Four Critical Years Revisited.*

19. Graduate education remains somewhat contested territory at Evergreen. Some faculty would clearly prefer to have the institution remain exclusively focused on undergraduate education. Teacher education is a particularly hard case of compatibility with the norm of maximal faculty autonomy and recreating the curriculum because of the extensive state requirements that accompany this program. Staffing repeating programs remains a critical issue at Evergreen in the face of the attractive alternative faculty have of creating new programs.

20. Many different learning community models have been developed though Evergreen's coordinated studies model. The learning community approach is described in Gabelnick, Matthews, MacGregor, & Smith (1990, 1992, 1996, 1999); MacGregor (1987, 1991); Smith & MacGregor (1992); Smith (*Liberal Education,* 1991, 1994). The Washington Center history is described in Smith (1988, 1994).

21. The work by Vincent Tinto and his colleagues at the National Center on Postsecondary Teaching, Learning, and Assessment is especially noteworthy. Tinto's work on collaborative learning included in-depth studies of learning communities at the University of Washington and Seattle Central Community College. Tinto's approach included both quantitative and qualitative assessments of collaborative teaching and learning.

5

BRIDGING THEORY AND PRACTICE: PUBLIC SERVICE AT THE EVERGREEN STATE COLLEGE

Madga Costantino, Emily Decker, Jeanine L. Elliott, Tina Kuckkahn, and Helen Lee
The Evergreen State College

The purpose of The Evergreen State College's public service centers is to provide leadership in building relationships and forming networks that enhance and promote Evergreen's integrative and collaborative approach to learning, in a variety of settings among a variety of groups. The public service centers create a reciprocal relationship between the wider community and Evergreen, providing a forum to enrich and broaden the exchange of knowledge in an ever-widening circle.

—Mission Statement for the Public Service Centers

Current conversations within higher education reflect widespread agreement that civic engagement is an important outcome of college. Effective civic or public engagement requires the capacity to see that particular problems and issues are part of larger biological and sociological systems. Consequently, a critical task for alternative liberal arts colleges is to help students and faculty alike to explicitly practice dual thinking—to see figure and ground, forest and trees, particular and general, concrete and abstract, local and universal—at the same time. Students need opportunities to practice this dual vision: what it means to be a good citizen, and what it means to be a good citizen inhabiting a particular place with a particular group of people. Historically, liberal arts colleges have been more effective at addressing the first issue. Unlike community colleges, the mission of liberal arts colleges is to educate citizens of the world rather than citizens of a particular place. Service-learning programs create opportunities for students to get involved in communities. At The Evergreen State College (TESC), the four public service centers are evolving as a kind of institutional service-learning.

The public service centers at The Evergreen State College put into practice a necessary dimension of alternative liberal arts education by grounding the college in its particular geographical place. If the interdisciplinary academic programs at the college are the trunk of a tree, the public service centers are evolving as the roots. As a young tree, Evergreen was tended like other young nursery trees—special efforts were made to water it and help it take root. As the college enters its second quarter century, however, it needs a strong root system to sustain it. The public service centers provide much of this system, because they reach out to four critical communities of people within the state of Washington.

The Evergreen Center for Educational Improvement collaborates with K-12 teachers and administrators within the state to facilitate the development of integrated curriculum and classroom assessment. The Washington Center for Improving the Quality of Undergraduate Education collaborates with faculty and administrators from two- and four-year public and private colleges across the state to create more and better opportunities for students to experience interdisciplinary, collaborative, and pluralistic learning. The Evergreen State College Labor Education offers labor studies to students and collaborates with workers across the state to provide educational forums in which working people discuss their working environments, analyze the political economy, and devise strategies for positive social change. The Longhouse Education and Cultural Center, in addition to being a multipurpose facility used to house classes, conferences, and cultural events, administers the Native American Economic Development Arts Initiative. The Arts Initiative is a regionally-based endeavor that promotes Native artists of the Pacific Northwest. In providing hospitality and service for students, the college, and surrounding Native communities, the Longhouse becomes a place where bridges of understanding between the regions' tribes and visitors of all cultures can be created.

Public education, higher education, workers, and Native communities—these groups define four of The Evergreen State College's critical neighboring communities. Through the work of the public service centers, the college's relationships with these constituent groups are evolving. Making sure that these relationships evolve in ways that benefit both the college and the constituent group is the primary work of the public service center staff. A critical resource which staff have to draw upon in that work are the learning principles central to the college itself: 1) interdisciplinary study, 2) personal engagement, 3) linking theory to practice, 4) collaborative/cooperative work, and 5) teaching across significant differences. The following scenarios illustrate how each of the centers work within this framework to establish and enhance relationships which promote situated learning.

The Evergreen Center for Educational Improvement

The Evergreen Center for Educational Improvement was created to help K-12 educational communities in their efforts to improve. Our work takes us into many spheres of schooling. We are engaged in professional development training and group facilitation on curriculum, instruction, and assessment issues. We also facilitate organizational improvement and planning efforts, and provide various types of research. Much of this work brings together groups of teachers and whole school communities striving to achieve higher educational standards, although we also, at times, provide individualized support and engage in state-wide efforts.

Our center allows the college to provide resources and expertise, as well as share its educational philosophy and values with the state's K-12 community. In return, we learn about best practices and innovations in the public schools and share those with faculty, staff, and students at the college. We bring to our work with school communities the values of the college as well as specific knowledge and skills to assist schools.

In workshops and planning meetings, we incorporate the values of collaborative learning communities, as we support teachers struggling through figuring out for themselves what they will do and how to make it work best. We break the traditional mold of the higher education institution, which sees itself as the holder of great wisdom, with the role of the distribution of knowledge to the unknowing teacher practitioner. We respect and value the knowledge, ideas, and real world experience that teachers bring. Together with the knowledge and ideas we bring, we engage in collaborative design.

Virtual Science Classroom Project

The Virtual Science Classroom Project is an example of a project we supported which typifies how many aspects of our mission and values are carried out in practice. The Evergreen Center was invited to be a partner in a grant funded year-long K-12 science project. The project aimed to integrate technology and communication skills into the ninth grade science curriculum, at five high schools in two school districts. Students were expected to integrate the use of computers into learning and communicating about science.

We began under less than ideal conditions. For this project, state technology grant funds were not awarded until just prior to the beginning of the school year in which the project was to take place. As is often the case for teachers, our nine participants were required to plan and implement a new curriculum, while continuing to teach the current curriculum full-time.

Fortunately, we arranged to set aside three days prior to the start of the school year for our first planning meetings. Our center served as the main facilitator for the direction and goal setting and the curriculum and assessment development. One district, which housed four of the five schools, organized the project and their technology director and a science teacher, on special assignment, ensured the smooth initial administration of the program. Later, a director of a local environmental nonprofit group coordinated the remainder of the project on a half-time basis.

During the initial planning meetings, we helped the teachers come to some common agreement on what they wanted their project to look like. We facilitated a goal setting meeting where teachers determined what a successful project would look like, what their students and even what they themselves would attain from this experience. They determined that the project would be successful if they could develop a meaningful, hands-on, performance based integrated course, although they later decided to start with a two to three week unit. They envisioned a course where students communicate their knowledge in a variety of forums and produce products with relevant human data and analysis. Right from the start, their goals of integrated curriculum, student engagement, and ties to real world problems directly dovetailed with three of Evergreen's five foci. We had definitely found a good match.

In this planning meeting, teachers determined those things they wanted to gain for themselves. They wanted decision-making ability and freedom, the chance to network and plan with peers (collaborative inquiry is another of Evergreen's foci), to use technology in sophisticated ways, to bring resources into their schools, to increase their learning and receive technical training. And of course, the teachers considered student benefits. They felt students would benefit from the hands-on field based science tied to real world problems, which would be a better learning opportunity than the current curriculum. Visits from environmental experts were expected to result in increased student learning, and teachers expected the students would have a fun experience.

The grant application laid out some of the specifics of the project. This was to be an integrated interdisciplinary, conceptually-based curriculum. Once the goals for the project were formulated by the teachers, we were ready to begin the planning process. None of the teachers had ever written such a curriculum before, neither had they any experience in collaborative curriculum design. The anxiety and expectations were written all over their faces.

There were other challenges as well. The teachers all came from different subject matter backgrounds. Their fields included physics, chemistry, biology, and earth sciences. None felt very comfortable outside of their own specialty area. They were also concerned that in an integrated curriculum unit, they might not have the opportunity to cover their subject in depth. A final challenge was getting the teachers to take risks in front of their peers. It was our goal to get them to participate in a colearning process and take the necessary risks to develop a high quality curriculum.

We began curriculum development by introducing concepts necessary for the design process. We introduced outcome-based education, student learning outcomes, the Washington State standards; all the tools necessary to start the discussion. The participants were then given an opportunity to begin molding what they wanted the project to be. They started with the questions: What is a concept? What is a theme? What is the difference between them? What do we want the concept to be?

After the group discussed these issues and came to a shared understanding, they examined a list of science concepts and another long discussion evolved. What would be the most appropriate concept for this project? Should it be systems or change? Should it be interdependence or force? The group decided upon the concept of systems and to develop an integrated curriculum unit around a study of watersheds.

To begin to figure out what the unit would look like, we illustrated the process of concept mapping and asked each teacher to draw a concept map of what the unit should contain. Through the lenses of their particular disciplines the teachers drew concept maps of the watershed's biological, chemical, and earth science characteristics. They did not know each others' subject areas in any depth. We were at another critical juncture, the apprehension again apparent in their faces. How would we pull all of this together into a coherent unit and how will I ever be able to teach it all?

After some struggle and several attempts to come up with the right essential questions to facilitate the systems unit, a small miracle occurred. One of the teachers suggested a question that everyone could agree upon. Then, not long after, a second was adopted. After a couple of hours, the group had decided upon four essential questions to guide the unit. Over the course of several additional planning meetings the curriculum took shape.

One of the greatest barriers to professional development among teachers is isolation in the classroom and a lack of opportunity to collaborate with other teachers. The Virtual Science Project's professional development model brought teachers into close working relationships with their colleagues. Teachers learned to rely on each other's subject matter expertise to guide them in those portions of the project that were unfamiliar to them. The teachers grew together as a group and grew in their individual skills and confidence. An external evaluation of the project, conducted by researchers at the University of Washington, found greater enthusiasm for collaboration among teachers, despite the challenges.

The point of any curriculum change, however, is student learning. According to the research findings, students were the greatest beneficiaries of the project. Teachers reported that students who took part in the project were better able to make connections between what they learned in school and what was happening in the real world and that student motivation was increased. Students reported:

- increased learning and more interesting curriculum in Virtual Science than in other science classes
- enthusiasm about integrated science
- positive responses to the integrated use of computers helpingthem to learn and increasing their motivation, while distinguishing the limited value of busy work on the computer
- a connection between what they were learning and the real world
- a belief they would take those lessons into their own lives

Virtual Science stands out as a shinning success of the collaboration between Evergreen and public schools. Accounts from everyone involved attest to the value of the experience for teachers and students and the research from the University of Washington supports it.

The Evergreen State College Labor Education Center

Integrating and reflecting The Evergreen State College's core learning foci were not on the minds of the original organizers of the Labor Center. Rather, in 1985, the founders were seeking a safe place to discuss the often devastating consequences of a worldwide recession and free market strategies on the lives of workers and communities. After years of program development and experimentation, the linkages to TESC's core foci became very clear. In the course of seeking our theoretical framework, the Labor Center recognized its own unique role in reflecting and enhancing Evergreen's core principles.

Evergreen's foci of interdisciplinary study provided both a rationale and a context for TESC Labor Education Center to move beyond a training model of education. This training model dominated labor education. It had three pervasive assumptions, which conflicted with the emerging vision of the center. First, it assumed political neutrality. This political neutrality permeated conventional curriculum and pedagogy. Information put forth was relayed as truth without an analysis of history, economic systems, or government structures. Secondly, this neutrality assumed a person, once trained, could internalize knowledge and become an expert in a given subject. It assumed the receivers of information were without the capacity to critically analyze information and come to their own conclusions. Third, it implied equal opportunity in power relations once a person had the facts.

The context of interdisciplinary studies opened the door for the TESC Labor Center to explore a variety of disciplines within the labor education curriculum and then integrate them. This integration had the potential of challenging union and community members to move beyond the simple truths and seek a variety of perspectives relating to labor movement.

The first opportunity to test these perspectives came in 1987, with the first union sponsored project which called for a revamping of the steward program for the Machinists union, which represents Boeing workers. The original discussions with leadership framed the project narrowly. The steward manual was outdated, and union stewards needed to be trained in the specifics of grievance handling. Following extensive interviews, however, the project team came up with an educational program that included labor history and economic education.[1]

This was also the first opportunity the TESC Labor Education Center had to experiment with oral historians. These historians were retired machinists union activists who participated in the steward education programs. They told stories and shared experiences and lessons from the past. The student evaluations of this pilot program showed this aspect of the program was the most rewarding to the stewards.[2] The historians brought in a variety of perspectives. Union stewards had little or no knowledge of their union beyond issues of wages, hours, and working conditions. By integrating discussions about labor history and the economy, union stewards were able to reach a much more sophisticated analysis about their work lives, their community, and the relationship with management.

The Evergreen foci of personal engagement was critical given the state of the labor movement. Because of corporate restructuring, working people could no longer depend upon their labor organizations to maintain benefits and decent working conditions. This loss had grave implications. First and foremost it meant that union members in particular could not take negotiated wages and benefits for granted. If they did, all working people would lose, including those without the benefit of union membership. Second, it meant an organizational crisis within the house of labor.

Evidence of this crisis was reflected in the AFL-CIO's 1985 report, *The Changing Situation of Labor,* which documented organized labor's decline and loss of power.[3] This report identified an organizational crisis that demanded a response by its membership. This response depended upon workers to "develop their capacity to judge, speak and act on the basis of reasoned beliefs understanding and commitments." It would take a new level of responsibility on the part of workers to be active participants in the discussions about their future.

TESC Labor Center's use of surveys and committees reflect the importance of the principle of personal engagement. The surveys used go far beyond needs assessment by asking questions that would lead to an in-depth knowledge of where people were at and how labor education might provide an avenue to help them get where they wanted to go.[4]

Planning committees are also used extensively. They are made up of committed rank and file union members and students and Labor Center staff. These committees were like mini think tanks. Beyond the goal of creating and promoting labor education programs, the committees are a forum to discuss the economy, social justice, and strategies for change.

This has been especially evident in labor center initiated programs. One example of these programs included Camp Solidarity, a residential school. Its goal was for union members to discuss how to respond to global restructuring. In order for Camp Solidarity planners to create this discussion, they analyzed the political economy and possible strategic responses by union members.

The format of the first Camp Solidarity was inspired by the struggle of the mineworkers in south west Virginia against the Pittston Coal Company. Planners learned that this struggle reflected a trend that was taking place throughout the country, which put corporate profits before worker's safety and health. The school used cultural events, international solidarity, and community coalition discussions in order to understand the implications of the struggles of the mineworkers. A strategy role-play exercise was used to facilitate a practice of possible solutions.[5] The first Camp Solidarity program was attended by seventy union members including representation from the United Mine Workers from south west Virginia and United Auto Workers from Mexico City. Based on the success of this school, the Labor Center organized a second Camp Solidarity in the summer of 1991.

Linking theoretical perspectives with practice was a natural role for TESC Labor Center. The notion of connecting workers to the community has been at the foundation of the labor movement. This notion, however, had been lost over a period of years. This loss was due to the increasingly narrow agenda of organized labor that focused primarily on wages, hours, and working conditions on the job. In the past, a union member's role had been integrated with the community. By the 1980s a member's role became somewhat limited to voting for contract ratification.

It would be up to TESC Labor Center to utilize this principle of linking the theoretical perspective with the practical to reconnect labor with the community. In the initial year of the center, the lack of this connection showed up in the original surveys. When asked about building alliances with the community, 90% of the union members surveyed indicated that this was of primary importance.[6]

The Labor Environment and Social Justice conference and The New School for Union Organizers are two examples which reflect this principle. In 1993, we began the effort to bring organized labor, environmental activists, and social justice activists to the table to discuss common ground and possible coalition work. We worked closing with the TESC masters in environmental science program. This partnership was a key to its success. Along with MES, we organized a planning committee reflective of possible participants. We raised sufficient funds to invite major speakers in the various fields. Most importantly, we structured the conference to stimulate dialog amongst the diverse participants. Each area of concern such as forest, urban development, labor rights, and poverty had three facilitators. These facilitators represented labor, environment, or social justice work. The outcome created open communication about past differences, new trust, and a commitment to work together on future projects.

The New School for Union Organizers was developed to offer a forum for discussion of community/labor issues. Reflective of the mission of the center, the new school, which is a mix of undergraduate students and full-time workers, concentrates on labor history, a strategic study of the political economy, and models of positive social change. Students have an opportunity to explore how racism, sexism, and homophobia have divided people historically while examining strategic models of social change and alternative approaches to coalition building. The New School also offers students an opportunity to intern with organizations which match their interests.

The principle of collaborative/cooperative work has deep roots in the values that have driven the labor movement. Without these values, the labor movement's struggles would have been relegated to individual actions and outcomes. The ability to act collectively has put organized labor at the reins of achievement for most social progress in the US.

Because these achievements were under threat in the late 1970s to mid-1980s, collective thinking had to be reintroduced and reinforced. Because this group thinking was part of Evergreen's success, the TESC Labor Center naturally integrated it into its programs. This notion of group work would run counter to labor leadership's need to stand in front of the room and issue orders and direction.

Joanne McCaughlan, a student intern at TESC Labor Center in 1986–1987, thought the idea of group work was an essential ingredient of the center. "I worked with Jan Frost during the planning of the first

Women's Summer School. I had worked as a laborer through the 1970s and had my fill of issues of sexual harassment. We needed a place to discuss these issues. Evergreen's model of education which focused on group discussion was a perfect place."[7]

This idea of group work was discussed in Pat Holm's master's thesis study of theater artists and unions. Pat wrote, "Creating theater together can allow people to think about the work they do and in the process of making theater, experience working together in nonhierarchical ways." She goes on to quote a passage in *We are Strong: A Guide to the Work of Popular Theaters Across Americas.*

To build a humane society will necessitate practicing democracy, and not just talking about it. Within cultural groups, people can be free to choose their own tasks, to give and take and to think together and decide for themselves the messages they want to carry—and to whom.[8]

Pat Holm had a strong influence on the staff to use theater as a medium for working as a group. Because of her influence, the center embarked on an ambitious project of bringing Rob Rothensals's Rock Opera 1919 general strike in Seattle to the live stage. His master's thesis on the same subject inspired his work. It was recorded in a studio and produced a record album, but had never been played live. TESC Labor Center raised funds, sold tickets, and worked with the Local American Federation of Teachers. The end result was a week-long symposium on labor history and the strike. The president of Seattle Central Community College responded by designating the week before the concert, "labor history Week." The performance was played to a sold out crowd at the Broadway Performance hall in Seattle, Washington.[9]

Evergreen's core foci of teaching across significant differences posed the greatest challenge and in many ways became TESC Labor Center's greatest strength. The challenge was reflected in the knowledge by the original organizers that the labor movement had a complicated history with issues of diversity. The foundation of this knowledge was the understanding that issues of diversity had to be looked at within the context of the economic system of capitalism. This understanding led to the initial investigation, which highlighted the labor movement's historical role as a leader in social equality. It also exposed the labor movement's responsibility for tolerating, and in some case initiating, racist and sexist practices.

The culmination of this knowledge led the founders to a commitment to raising issues of diversity as integral part of TESC Labor Education Center. This commitment would become the center's greatest strength because the people most affected by racism and sexism were highly motivated to create a safe place to discuss these issues.

Since 1985, center staff have committed themselves to integrating the discussion of racism and sexism into the basic curriculum. This was played out by first raising the issue in the planning process of union as well as center sponsored programs. As the staff and advisory committee learned more, they integrated homophobia discussions. These discussions were not counseling sessions, but rather were political discussions based on an economic analysis of the economy. That analysis helped facilitate a pathway beyond historical divisions so those workers could strategize positive solutions.

The five core foci of The Evergreen State College provided the links necessary for the early success of TESC Labor Center. They also helped solidify what would become a driving force of The Evergreen State College Labor Center.

The Longhouse Education and Cultural Center

Nearly twenty years ago, TESC founding faculty member and Lummi elder Mary Ellen Hillaire articulated a need for a gathering place which would provide a locus for cross cultural exchange and education at The Evergreen State College. This desire garnered widespread support and guided The Evergreen State College in its 15-year quest to build a longhouse on its Olympia campus. Mary Ellen Hillaire's philosophy is embodied in her statement of the Longhouse Code of Ethics (1981):

> There exist between people, significant differences which require alternative education, an internal and external environment designed in consideration of providing culturally referenced opportunity, and academic skills to cope with the demands of a plural society.[10]

The facility will be designed to take the best advantage of traditional Native American hospitality in a contemporary architectural expression which will define an open educational opportunity developed in individual, group, and community activities which revitalize important human relationships to land, to others, to work, and to the unknown. The relationship of the educational partnership of student/college/community, will be guided by an understanding of the potential (talents and interests) of each student as this relates and interacts with the total educational resources of the student/community/college.

Thanks to major legislative support and contributions from both Native and non-Native communities, the Longhouse Education and Cultural Center opened its doors in the fall of 1995.

Mission

As a public service center of The Evergreen State College, the Longhouse exists to provide service and hospitality to students, the college, and the surrounding Native communities. With a design based in the Northwest Indigenous Nations' philosophy of hospitality, the Longhouse is a gathering place for cultural ceremonies, classes, conferences, performances, art exhibits, and community events.

The Longhouse provides the opportunity to build a bridge of understanding between the regions' tribes and visitors of all cultures. It is a resource for nonNatives interested in the dynamics of cultural exchange and alternative learning styles. For learners from a Native background, the Longhouse provides a hospitable environment and a source of support honoring the cultures of the first peoples of this land.

Relationship to TESC Mission

The Longhouse as a public service center builds upon a history of TESC involvement with the Native American community. In 1996, TESC was named by the American Indian Science and Engineering Society as one of the most successful colleges in the United States in working with American Indian students. The college has an active Native Student Alliance. TESC has had an on-campus Native American Studies Program for twenty-five years. For those students who choose not to participate in an on-campus program, the college offers a community-determined, reservation-based degree program, often referred to as the Tribal Program at five reservations. The most recent Native American initiative is the Native Economic Development Arts Initiative, a partnership between the Longhouse and six local tribes. The arts initiative promotes education, cultural preservation, and economic development among Native artists and tribes of the Pacific Northwest.

The Longhouse embodies the college's commitment "to create a rich mix in the composition of its student body, staff, and faculty, and to give serious consideration to issues of social class, age, race, ethnicity, gender, and sexual orientation."[11] By providing cultural events, Native art exhibits, Native student recruitment/retention, and classroom space for academic programs such as Native American Studies, the Reservation-based Tribal Program and MIT 2000: Teachers of Native American Learners, the Longhouse contributes to the principles that guide Evergreen's educational programs.

By bringing the Native Economic Development Arts Initiative into the surrounding Native communities, the Longhouse supports the college's mission to "serve diverse place-bound populations."[12] Conversely, the Arts Initiative programs that take place on campus, such as the storytelling apprenticeship and traditional arts classes, enhance and enrich the opportunities for students, faculty, and staff at the college.

Description

The Longhouse Education and Cultural Center is a multipurpose facility able to serve a variety of educational and cultural functions. Strategically located close to campus resources, the center is able to accommodate up to 500 people for academic program lectures, conferences, and cultural events. The 10,020 square foot Longhouse Center is the first public college building based on Native American tradition and infused with modern teaching technology on a public campus in the United States. In keeping with a Pacific Northwest Native tradition of naming significant buildings, the Longhouse received the name "The House of Welcome" during a ceremony conducted by local tribal elders and spiritual leaders in May of 1997.

Native Economic Development Arts Initiative

The primary public service program of the Longhouse is the Native Economic Development Arts Initiative (NEDAI). The initiative seeks to promote education, cultural preservation, and economic development for Native artists and tribes residing in the Pacific Northwest.

NEDAI components include a Native arts marketing service, semiannual Native art sales, a tribal minigrant program, business management and marketing workshops, and an artist in residence program. The components of the Arts Initiative illustrate how the public service work of the Longhouse furthers the principal elements of the college's unique approach to learning: 1) interdisciplinary study, 2) personal engagement, 3) linking theoretical perspective with practice, 4) collaborative/cooperative work, and 5) teaching across significant differences.

One example of a Longhouse program furthering the Evergreen approach to learning is a bent wood box apprenticeship that took place under the artist in residence program of the Arts Initiative. This section will examine comments from the bent wood box apprentices that demonstrate how the apprenticeship provided an opportunity to engage in Evergreen's unique style of learning.

The model for the artist in residence program is to bring established Native artists to work, teach and provide technical assistance and training for emerging artists at Evergreen and reservation sites. During the fall/winter quarter of 1998, Pete Peterson, Sr. led an apprenticeship in the art of bent wood box making. Pete Peterson is a master carver and member of the Skokomish Tribe. He instructed twelve apprentices in an ancient traditional technique in which cedar planks are steamed and bent into boxes. The apprentices then learned how to carve and paint the boxes using Pacific Northwest design imagery. The boxes are then used for a variety of purposes, such as for storage, to give as gift items, etc.

Interdisciplinary Study

The apprentices learned about tribal history regarding the meanings of the designs that were used, they learned about natural resource issues (in particular the scarcity and difficulty of obtaining cedar), and they learned the technical skill of bent wood box making.

> I wanted to learn the techniques involved in box bending to bring it back to my family and community and pass it on to others. Hanford McCloud (Nisqually)

> In the near future, I hope to accompany Pete Peterson to collect cedar in the forest. As a basket maker, my grandmother, uncles, and aunts have taught me the basket is a gift from the earth and Creator. Basket making begins at the time of gathering. If you do not collect your materials, you aren't really making a basket. Therefore, I feel I must experience the gathering of cedar from the forest in order to really craft a bent wood box. Chris Richardson (Chehalis)

> In addition to learning the skill of bending a cedar box, I learned a new way to tell a story. Traditionally, Karuk stories and values can be told through and expressed through the art of the storyteller. In this case, the story of the contemporary Karuk woman and her spouse is told using their power animals (a continuation of Karuk values and traditions), bear and otter, in a circular design which represents infinity and love and marriage. Bari Talley (Karuk/Yurok)

Personal Engagement

Each student was responsible for creating an individual design that would decorate the box. Under the guidance of the master carver, each student worked to produce his or her own box and lid.

> Karuk art, culture, and language was not passed on in my immediate family because of racism and enforced schooling. In my quest to learn the culture from relatives outside my immediate family, through schooling and this workshop, I will be able to pass Karuk culture on to my children, and at last, with my mother and siblings. Bari Talley (Karuk/Yurok)

> I'm a three dimensional artist, yet I never carved cedar. This opportunity opened up a huge world of possibility for my creative spirit. Learning the technology of bent wood box carving as well as the techniques of design application gave me skills that I can use; new applications plus complementary skills to use in my usual work. It is the most meaningful learning time I have had in years. What a discovery! Lois Chichinoff-thadei (Aleut)

Linking Theoretical Perspective to Practice

After discussing the history and origin of bent wood box making as a traditional art form, each student created his or her own box representing the individual's unique personal and tribal background.

> Working with cedar has been quite an education. I have learned a lot more about Northwest Coast Native Art and it has motivated me to do more research. This has truly been an educational opportunity. Laura Wong (Colville)

Collaborative/Cooperative Work

Native American communities have long engaged in collaborative/cooperative work. It was natural, then, that an atmosphere of collaborative learning and sharing was fostered among the group.

> It was a real treat to share and network with other artists from other tribal communities. I had never met many of them before this class. Max Engle (Squaxin Island/Skokomish)

> Lastly, I thank the Creator for giving me this class: especially the other Native American artists, for the time, skill, patience, and good health to reexplore the art of the bent wood cedar box with them. Chris Richardson (Chehalis)

Teaching Across Significant Differences

The apprentices and instructor represented nine tribes from around the United States; as a result there was a tremendous amount of cross-cultural sharing. Additionally, participants spanned the age generations, with several Native youth and tribal elders participating. The level of experience in the field of art also ranged considerably.

> I never thought of myself as an artist before this class; that potential seems to be there now if I do more with what I have learned. I also learned cultural skills that I had never learned before. Gary Peterson (Skokomish)

> As a single parent with a teenage son, this was absolutely one of the best classes we could have participated in together. It kept his interest throughout the entire process. Trudy Marcellay (Chehalis)

> I am the oldest male member of the Skokomish tribe. I am glad to see this work passed on. It is important to the heritage of our people. Andrew Peterson (Skokomish elder)

The bent wood box apprenticeship of the Artist in Residence Program is just one example of how the public service work of the Longhouse exemplifies The Evergreen State College's mission and approach to learning. Conversely, the campus is enriched by having diverse groups of people come to the college to colearn and share. The effects of programs like artist in residence are continuous—an apprenticeship leads to new technical skill building and networking among artists, exhibits of the apprentices' work educate the public about Native American culture, history and art, and relationships between the college and the surrounding Native communities grow. As these relationships build, more Native students are likely to see the college as a hospitable place to learn and they, in turn, will send their children, who will continue to enrich the campus environment with their diverse backgrounds and experiences. Public service at The Evergreen State College makes sense; it forms a mutually beneficial relationship between the college and the diverse communities that are served by the various public service centers.

The Washington Center for Improving Undergraduate Education

The Washington Center for Improving the Quality of Undergraduate Education works to improve undergraduate teaching and student learning by building grassroots partnerships among faculty, staff, and administrators across disciplines, departments, and higher education institutions of Washington state. It is the oldest of the public service centers, and was initiated when faculty from Seattle Central Community College hopped in a van and drove south to Olympia to see what the Evergreen faculty were up to with their approach to curriculum design. In its first year, the Washington Center focused almost exclusively on introducing faculty and staff to the practice of developing curricular learning communities by bringing faculty from several disciplines together to plan a program around critical questions. Restructuring curricula to give students a deeper and more coherent learning experience leads to an examination of pedagogy, and the Washington Center was also an early leader in disseminating information about active and collaborative learning. In addition to a focus on designing curricula, the center has also focused attention on the diverse students who are in those classes. For over ten years, the center has convened groups around issues of diversity and around learning community development.

In its practice, the Washington Center builds upon the educational principles embodied in the Evergreen community, but implemented within the context of colleges and universities with differing missions, cultures, faculties, and students. Through interactions with colleagues in different types of colleges and universities, new learnings are developed which are carried back to the home institutions. For Evergreen, this means that faculty and administrators have an opportunity to be in an ongoing dialog about evolving innovative practice across the state and beyond.

The Washington Center has an in-state network which includes the forty-six institutions that are members of the consortium and nearly 1,700 faculty, administrators, staff, educational agency personnel, and interested community members who have some involvement with one or more strands of the work of the center. A thirty member planning committee which serves as an advisory board includes representatives from public and independent colleges and universities; two-year and four-year institutions; faculty, administrators, and staff involved with the various strands of work with the center; and state education organizations. Evergreen's provost serves on this committee, along with a dean for faculty development and a faculty member, and participation in the three annual meetings is itself an opportunity for significant professional development. Everyone on the planning committee is committed to providing more and better opportunities for students in Washington state to experience interdisciplinary, collaborative, and pluralistic learning, but they come from a range of institutions so strategies for accomplishing this end vary widely. When asked how involvement with the Washington Center has shaped institutional practice, one committee member wrote this:

> My institution is remote from Olympia and probably one of the last to get involved in Washington Center activities. Nevertheless, it has played a significant role in the life of the institution since the early 1990s at least. The center has provided important impetus for general education reform, for learning communities, for classroom assessment, and, more recently, for engaging issues of diversity in the classroom. The center has influenced my institution in many ways—as a facilitator of campus discussions, a channel by which initiatives and new ideas reached our campus, a provider of significant faculty development (i.e., the Ford Foundation team on diversity), and a source of external validation for people and programs on campus trying to enliven the campus academic culture. The center is known and respected by all levels of the institution; as a result, reforms on campus which seem in accord with center initiatives draw power and prestige from that fact. It needs to be said that the center's reputation is derived from the vision and the values the center has championed.

While the work of the Washington Center has evolved over its fifteen year history, learning community development remains a foundational piece. Every year, the center holds two curriculum planning retreats, one on the eastern side of the state and one on the west. Brochures go out to everyone on the mailing list well in advance of the event, and each year draws a mix of alums and new people. These retreats offer an encapsulated version of the Washington Center's practice.

The retreats are held off campus, in quiet settings. Participants are encouraged to spend the night, and most do. That facilitates informal sharing and the development of friendships, which are a critical ingredient in sustaining innovative work. Those who return to the retreats frequently cite the luxury of being with like-minded educators as one of the strongest benefits. Participants sign up to come as a curriculum planning team, and often report that the two days away from campus allow them to have the extended, reflective conversations crucial in developing good programs which are all but impossible to manage on campus. The agenda is structured to accommodate a range of learners, from novices to experts. Structured workshops are offered, which are arranged sequentially to move from "why a learning community," to who are the students, to how do we teach it, to how do we assess what's being learned. At every point in the agenda, teams are free to participate in the workshop, or to go off on their own and plan. Faculty consultants, affectionately called "kibitzers," are on hand to work with teams on an as-needed basis, so the learning environment for faculty is one that supports all learners with a range of expertise. Support is available in several forms, depending on the needs and the learning style of the participants. Theory and practice get blended as people talk about their intentions, their hopes, and their experiences. Conversations with colleagues from across the state is the norm, so collaboration is a central part of what makes the retreats effective. Comments from retreat evaluations illustrate these principles in practice:

> The setting and social dynamics are consistent with learning community philosophy, energizing, and enabling.
>
> The open structure of the agenda was ideal in that it gave me and my team member large chunks of time to brainstorm, plan, and develop a structure. The quietness of the location was perfect.
>
> I like the unstructured part of the retreat to work on a project with support and help available. There are too few opportunities for faculty to have quality planning time.
>
> Having a very good space for developing and planning. This has been the perfect occasion for working on our project, a step we would not have been able to take otherwise, and yet it will be essential to our success.
>
> This retreat space gives me a chance to slow down, unplug, and think about my goals. Last year I had a chance to directly become oriented to what I could do in collaboration in the community college setting. This year I valued the talking I did with individuals more than acquisition of new information. I also valued time to think.

When faculty participate in these curriculum planning retreats, they realize two important things. First, they are not alone in trying to bring innovative practices to higher education. They have colleagues in other colleges, particularly the community colleges, who are exploring similar pedagogical territory, and the opportunity to share ideas is very invigorating. Second, in a more abstract way, they discover again that there is a wide network of people committed to similar values, who believe in the power of education to shape society. Too often, people engaged in innovative work get caught up in the work required to make the innovation happen and lose sight of the wider social network that could sustain them. The goal of the Washington Center is to help weave that network together.

Conclusions

In its first decade, The Evergreen State College struggled to develop an organizational structure and a pattern for its curriculum—its focus was primarily on getting started. By the mid-1980s, the notion of public service as a way to connect the college with surrounding communities lead to the creation of the centers. From their inception, the public service centers are designed to bridge theory and practice by making authentic links between the world inside the college and the communities outside. In that process, the centers' evolution echoes that of the college: initially, each center focused on getting started and establishing connections between the college and a particular community. In the next decade, the challenge will be to connect the public service centers with the core of the college. Unlike a tree whose roots and trunk are organically connected, on the surface, the public service centers and the academic program at the college have no intrinsic connection. But it is through these connections that Evergreen will metamorphose once again, putting into practice an even richer version of what it means to be an alternative liberal arts college.

Endnotes

1. Machinist 751 Steward Education Project. Team John McCann, Sue Moyer, Virginia Roberts, and Dan Leahy, 1986.
2. Evaluations, Pilot Steward Program, Machinists DC Lodge 751, 1987.
3. *The Changing Situation of Workers and Their Unions*, Washington AFL-CIO, 1985.
4. TESC LERC Annual Report, September 1987–July 1988, Submitted September 19, 1988, 10.
5. Program Agenda, Camp Solidarity, 1990.
6. Survey conducted by TESC LERC, September, 1985.
7. Phone Interview, Joanne McCaughlan, 5/28/97.

8. *Union and Roses: Alliances Between Theater Artists and Union Activists 1913 to the Present* (TESC Masters thesis, May, 1987), 4–5.
9. Notes from Seattle 1919 Rock Opera. May 1, 1989.
10. The Longhouse Code of Ethics, Mary Ellen Hillaire, 1981.
11. The Evergreen State College Mission Statement, Self-Study, 1998, p. 34.
12. The Evergreen State College Mission Statement, Self-Study, 1998, p. 34.

SECTION II

Powerful Pedagogies

This section discusses various ways in which organizational structure, culture, and pedagogy are being changed to support new approaches to teaching and learning. Neither remaking institutional cultures in traditional institutional environments nor forging new cultures in new institutions is an easy task. There is much to be learned from these rich case studies. Topics range from realpolitik matters like tenure, promotion, funding, and faculty roles and rewards to issues like professional identity, collective versus individual responsibility, and long-term sustainability. These institutional stories provide concrete examples of the impediments to institutional change as well as visions of what a coherent organizational structure and culture might look like.

Powerful new pedagogies are key elements in these new approaches to learning. Service-learning, collaborative learning, team teaching, and interdisciplinary approaches are some of the powerful pedagogies. These approaches have much in common in terms of their assumptions about the nature of the learning process and the goals of education. They recognize the social nature of the learning process and the need to actively involve the learner. We are now beginning to understand the differences and the commonalities between these approaches and their potential when they are combined.

Many of these new pedagogies reflect an attempt to transform the curriculum in fundamental ways. One of the distinctive features of the "new" alternative institutions and programs is their penchant to reach out and collaborate in marked contrast to the earlier experimental colleges. This reflects a new and expanded notion of institutional role and mission with new visions of community involvement, faculty role, public service, and leadership in higher education.

Learning communities represent one of the most comprehensive approaches to educational reform. While they can take many different shapes and forms, learning communities as we define the term are a purposeful restructuring of the curriculum and linking courses together to produce a greater sense of community, more coherence in the learning environment, and more active learning. Some of the most effective and comprehensive forms of learning communities are found in the institutions discussed in this book. As the learning community movement has spread, the term learning community has been widely appropriated to cover many curricular restructuring efforts that go little beyond cohorting of students into a block of classes. This type of learning community is little more than a registration device. Truly effective learning communities necessarily involve a rethinking of educational goals, faculty and student roles, and pedagogy.

Part One: Learning Communities

Part One of this Powerful Pedagogies section examines various aspects of learning communities, perhaps the most profound and widespread effort at reform in higher education over the past three decades. At the center of the learning community is the functional reality of the student as colearner with fellow students and faculty, and, depending on the structure of the program, the community at large. Colearning means that students are active constructors of their education, not merely receptacles for faculty-provided knowledge, or mere synthesizers of received information. The learning community is a problem or theme-centered inquiry which makes all participants—faculty and students alike—full and equal partners in the construction of meaning. The learning community focuses on a theme or problem from interdisciplinary perspectives, replicating or approximating the way we learn outside of the academy. Real problems are not neatly arranged in disciplinary clusters. We bring a variety of disciplines and methods of inquiry to the themes of our lives. So, effective learning communities are interdisciplinary in approach and often team-taught by faculty from different disciplines focusing on a common idea.

Nor do we learn in isolation. So the learning community is in fact a community, with community members focused together on the process of inquiry. Faculty, instead of providers of knowledge, become facilitators of the learning process. Students, rather than silent receivers of faculty lectures, become active voices in their own learning. The seminar is an important part of the learning community, because here the community cooperatively and actively participates in discussion of a text, working together to wrest meaning, understand complexities, and support one another in the difficult and joyful process of analysis, synthesis, and vocalization of ideas. Team teaching is an important part of the learning community because here faculty model a cooperative and interdisciplinary process of inquiry for students. Time is an important part of the learning community, because we do not learn best in fifty-minute segments, but need time for effective conversation and time to build relationships. So, programs which are learning communities cluster multiple courses for a quarter or sometimes up to a year.

Learning communities are profoundly different in their philosophy and practice from traditional higher education. Here, respect for the student as a colearner is essential. Pedagogies which encourage active cooperative learning are central. The traditional separation of faculty and student roles blur when faculty see themselves as equal to students in the community of learners, and as facilitators of critical thinking.

The learning community movement has grown from its beginnings in Washington state, as an initiative of the member schools of the Washington Center for Improving the Quality of Undergraduate Education, to national prominence. In "Learning Communities: A Convergence Zone for Statewide Educational Reform," Barbara Leigh Smith describes the development of learning communities in Washington state, where the national movement began and where learning communities are most pervasive. The chapter argues that they represent one of the most vibrant and practical attempts to institutionalize interdisciplinary education. They have become powerful and widespread because they provide a practical response to deeply felt issues in contemporary society—issues of community, personal engagement, life-long learning, diversity, and institutional change. The author describes how learning communities have become a powerful convergence zone for a variety of mutually reenforcing educational reforms in Washington. The chapter suggests that a statewide climate of innovation can be fostered through learning communities while also addressing critical statewide issues relating to student retention, transfer, diversity, and educational innovation.

Service-learning, when incorporated into learning communities, provides a powerful means of enhancing student learning and of integrating campus and community. In "Integration and Assessment of Service-Learning in Learning Communities," Karen Kashmanian Oates and Laura Gaither argue that at a time when many university campuses are undergoing a shift from a teacher-centered hierarchy to a student-centered community, the learning community/service-learning model invites expansion of one's ways of knowing. Learning communities and service-learning share many elements of cognitive development and learning processes which strengthen and inform each other synergistically. This chapter explores these commonalities and provides examples of integration, assessment, and best practices.

In its interdisciplinary approach and conscious construction of community, learning communities, argues Les K. Adler in "Uncommon Sense: Liberal Education, Learning Communities, and the Transformative Quest," offer both students and faculty an antidote to the fragmentation characteristic of much of modern social and intellectual life. Adler explores the theory and practice of learning community development at the Hutchins School of Liberal Studies at Sonoma State University and outlines the conditions which promote a truly transformative and holistic liberal education in a university setting.

Learning communities are catalysts for change in traditionally organized institutions. The very nature of interdisciplinary work runs counter to established disciplinary departments and reward systems. In "Toward an Interdisciplinary Epistemology: Faculty Culture and Institutional Change," Grant H. Cornwell and Eve W. Stoddard discuss the perils and rewards of interdisciplinary work at traditional institutions, chronicling a recent ten-year period of intense interdisciplinary faculty and curriculum development at St. Lawrence University. They argue that interdisciplinary team teaching and collective scholarship have at least partially transformed an institutional culture formerly organized by the disciplines. To maintain institutional change, however, systems of faculty roles and rewards—particularly hiring and tenure—must be reformed.

The student-active seminar is crucial to learning communities at many institutions. Defining the seminar as "a space to discuss a text (in its largest sense of written piece, a moving image, or a common experience) in order to work collaboratively towards a better understanding of it than an individual perspective can provide," Susan Fiksdal, in "Voices in Seminar: Ideologies and Identities," examines the sociolinguistic aspects of seminar and offers advice on pedagogical strategies, choice of text, preparation, goals, facilitation, and assessment.

Part Two: Rethinking Teaching and Learning

Part two of the Powerful Pedagogies section, "Rethinking Teaching and Learning," poses the question, "How do we reorganize ourselves to pursue innovative interdisciplinary, student-centered teaching and learning?" Part of the answer lies in how we think of and organize the learning process itself. What pedagogies do we employ? How do we conceive of the teacher's role in the way we approach teaching and learning? How do we organize a truly student-active inquiry? How do we incorporate students' different methods of communication into programs?

Evidence suggests that the effect of several pedagogies when employed together in an interdisciplinary inquiry is cumulative. In "Powerful Pedagogies," William H. Newell argues that collaborative learning, experiential learning, learning communities, living/learning, multicultural learning, service-learning, and study abroad can all be considered integrative in the sense that they involve drawing on diverse perspectives and integrating their insights. Newell advances the thesis that these pedagogies are mutually reinforcing; indeed, the transformative education of experimental colleges is rooted in the multiplicative effect of integrated pedagogies.

Donald L. Finkel, in "Should the Teacher Know the Answer? Two Ways to Organize Interdisciplinary Study Around Inquiry," discusses two different ways to organize interdisciplinary study around inquiry—one in which the teacher is guided by his own answer to the question directing the inquiry, and the other in which he starts by assuming he doesn't know the answer to the inquiry around which the course is organized. As a prelude to this discussion, Finkel contrasts four different ways that faculty and administrators conceive of interdisciplinary education, and argues that one of them—inquiry-centered teaching—is the most powerful.

In "Jenny's Painting: Multiple Forms of Communication in the Classroom," Mark Pedelty examines the use of oral, aural, and kinesthetic forms of expression and exposition in the interdisciplinary curriculum. He argues that today's students learn less effectively through traditional literacy-based approaches, and that the mass mediated world our students inhabit and will eventually work in requires us to reconsider traditional modes of classroom communication.

Janet F. Ott, in "Student-Active Science in Interdisciplinary Studies: Problems and Solutions," focuses on hands-on, student-active teaching and learning of science in an interdisciplinary setting. She discusses the issue of coverage, addresses objections to departures from traditional instruction, and presents a comprehensive rationale for active, interdisciplinary approaches to science.

Gary L. Bornzin takes a different approach to science in "Increasing Access in the Sciences Through Interdisciplinary Feminist Perspectives." This chapter recounts the author's experiences using a framework of feminism to enable students to approach science from various disciplinary perspectives. His approach respects the fears and resentments which many students feel toward science by showing them comparable feelings among feminist writers who see the ills of society intertwined with the conception, practice, and teaching of science. The chapter presents a summary of the attributes of "a feminist perspective" as defined by students and numerous resources and ideas which can be incorporated into more traditional courses in science or women's studies.

An equally important part of the answer to the question "How do we reorganize ourselves to pursue innovative interdisciplinary teaching and learning?" deals with the structure of our institutions. Can disciplinary departments accommodate interdisciplinary modes of study? How do we reward teaching in institutions which traditionally value research? Can innovative interdisciplinary colleges survive as islands in larger research universities? How do we reconceive of faculty roles and rewards as we move away from the traditional values of higher education?

Who hasn't dreamed of the opportunity to build a new college? Anne G. Scott and Celestino Fernández recount such an adventure in "Building an Organization that Reflects Interdisciplinarity," an examination of the birth and difficult first years of Arizona International College. They focus on the excitement and difficulties of founding an interdisciplinary, innovative institution within a traditional university structure, addressing conflicts which grew from divergence from practices of the host university: interdisciplinary study in a disciplinary tradition, nontenured faculty in a system anchored by tenure, and team teaching valued above research in a research university.

Joseph J. Comprone addresses a similar problem in "The Academic Department in a Multidisciplinary Context: An Argument for the Administrative Holding Company Amidst Communities of Learners," arguing that a major cause of low faculty morale, high political tension, and an unwillingness to cooperate among faculty in the early years at Arizona State University West derived from one structural difficulty. The College of Arts and Sciences, while it struggled to support intellectual and curricular cross-disciplinary work, attempted to build programs within a traditional departmental structure. The author acknowledges the institution's growing pains and concludes that despite the apparent contradiction of departments and interdisciplinary teaching and learning, faculty and adminstrators can intentionally craft effective learning communities within a departmentally organized college.

In "Alternative Ways of Organizing: The Importance of Organizational Culture," Sandra J. Sarkela reviews two periods of curricular innovation and interdisciplinary study in the history of SUNY Potsdam, arguing that reference to an organization's traditional values can support change and innovation. Despite the territorial imperatives of disciplinary units and budget cuts that drained resources from one initiative after another, Potsdam's cultural traditions continue to support interdisciplinary approaches to teaching and learning.

The concluding chapter in this section, "Reconceptualizing the Faculty Role: Alternative Models," by James R. Chen, Michael V. Fortunato, Alan Mandell, Susan Oaks, and Duncan RyanMann, all of SUNY Empire State College, explains how the college's approach to teaching and learning has transformed the faculty role from the traditional lecturer to encompass views of faculty as mentors, resource creators, entrepreneurs, and program developers.

SECTION II

Part One
Learning Communities

6

LEARNING COMMUNITIES: A CONVERGENCE ZONE FOR STATEWIDE EDUCATIONAL REFORM

Barbara Leigh Smith
The Evergreen State College

Learning communities have become a widespread and robust national curricular reform effort in the last fifteen years. Current estimates suggest that more than four hundred colleges and universities are experimenting with learning communities. They are now situated in both two- and four-year colleges, and are found in research universities as well as liberal arts colleges all across the United States. The term learning communities has been broadly appropriated, and, we think, too loosely applied. We are limiting our usage to the following: A purposeful restructuring of the curriculum by linking courses together so that students enroll in a more coherent curriculum with opportunities for active learning and greater interaction between students and faculty members (Gabelnick, Matthews, MacGregor, & Smith, 1990).

This chapter explores educational reform in Washington state where the national learning community movement began and where they are the most pervasive. The Washington experience demonstrates new ways of promoting innovation in higher education when there is a convergence between state policy initiatives and holistic grassroots faculty-based efforts. We argue that learning communities have become a kind of convergence zone and a support system for ongoing education reform in Washington. Washington provides a good example of how state mandates for education improvement can flourish if they are accompanied by systematic, long-term grassroots efforts.

Learning communities became powerful and widespread in Washington because they responded to a felt need. They provided a practical response to deeply felt issues in contemporary society—issues of community, personal engagement and empowerment, life-long learning for students and faculty, and curricular coherence. But they have also prospered because they built upon and were complementary to a variety of other state reform efforts. They became a vehicle for addressing statewide issues such as promoting collaboration between two- and four-year colleges, enhancing quality and innovation in undergraduate education, and increasing student retention. Learning communities continue to play a crucial role as a kind of skunkworks or innovation center for educational experimentation and improvement, but they face challenges as they reach a new stage of development.

The Beginning

The learning community effort began in Washington in 1983 almost serendipitously with a simple, but unusual, boundary crossing request. Looking for ways to revitalize his institution, a dean at Seattle Central Community College arranged a visit to The Evergreen State College, a nontraditional four-year institution, organized around team-taught, year-long interdisciplinary coordinated studies programs rather than traditional four credit courses.

As the dean later recounted the story:

> Ten of us went to Evergreen to observe their program in action. We spent the morning observing classes, visiting seminars, and talking with students and faculty. In the afternoon, we stayed to discuss the philosophy behind the educational program. The high energy and intellectual engagement of the community was palpable and contagious. One visit was enough to convince us that we should try to import the model to our community college. The decision was simple, but its accomplishment was complex and difficult. Not really knowing what we were getting ourselves into, but trusting that it would be worthwhile, both colleges stepped up to the challenge. Two of our faculty were transferred to Evergreen on two weeks notice to spend spring quarter learning the approach firsthand by team teaching with Evergreen faculty. These two Seattle Central pioneers and two other Evergreen faculty began the first Seattle Central interdisciplinary studies program in Fall 1984. We've been doing learning communities on a large scale ever since. They did literally transform significant aspects of this institution. (Hamberg & Smith, undated)

Word about the Seattle Central experience spread quickly. Who would have thought it possible for two- and four-year colleges to exchange faculty members who would create new programs and teach together! With growing interest and enthusiasm, other colleges began developing learning communities.

The learning community effort began as a pedagogical innovation but grew as a statewide faculty development effort. It quickly became apparent that learning communities worked powerfully for students, faculty, and institutions and that we had discovered a low-cost, community-building approach to improving our colleges and universities. In 1985, with seed money from the Exxon Foundation and then the Ford Foundation, The Evergreen State College established a public service center, The Washington Center for Improving the Quality of Undergraduate Education, to support the budding reform effort. Jean MacGregor and I created the new enterprise. (For an early history of the Washington Center see Smith, 1988.) Each of us brought different strengths to the enterprise. MacGregor had years of experience with grassroots community organizing. I was in a key administrative position as senior academic dean, which gave us access to important academic administrators at Evergreen and in other institutions. By 1987, seventeen institutions were affiliated with the Washington Center, and ten institutions were offering learning communities. With growing statewide interest, the Washington Center won legislative support to become a state funded public service center with a small and predictable annual budget of approximately $200,000. This stable funding allowed the center to sharply focus on its mission rather than expending all its energy writing grants to survive.

Learning Communities Proliferate

Between 1984 and the mid-1990s learning communities proliferated across the state of Washington. With modest assistance from the Washington Center, the network came together periodically through faculty exchanges, conferences, curriculum planning retreats, and collaborative writing projects. The common interest in improving undergraduate education and learning from one another grew and was nurtured by these periodic gatherings of people who came to gradually see themselves, individually and collectively, as change agents, and good friends.

The community colleges led the way. The small faculty exchange between Evergreen and Seattle Central was quickly followed by other exchanges between various colleges and, with them, the establishment of more learning community programs. A North Seattle Community College historian went to Seattle Central. A sociologist from Central went to North. Bellevue Community College, Centralia, Whatcom, Lower

Columbia, Peninsula, and Spokane Falls all participated in the faculty exchanges. The four-year colleges participated as well. More than a half dozen community colleges exchanged with Evergreen. Seattle University, University of Washington, and Western Washington University all exchanged faculty with one another and with the community colleges. With each exchange came new points of view, new relationships, and new possibilities.

In all cases, the goal was to use the faculty exchanges for team teaching to build the learning community effort rather than simply conceiving of the exchanges as an individual faculty development opportunity. Interinstitutional faculty exchanges became the human equivalent of a technology transfer/dissemination system throughout the state. By the mid-1990s more than four hundred faculty had been involved in doing a faculty exchange or team teaching with an exchange faculty. Most of these were done on a no-cost basis. Each home institution simply kept their faculty on their home institution's payroll. Working out the details fell to creative administrators willing to develop new procedures and make the extra effort to recruit the right people for the exchanges.

The exchanges heightened everyone's sense of what was possible. They signaled a lowering of the status boundaries between the two- and four-year colleges, a new seamlessness in the higher education system for both students and faculty. Seattle Central and Evergreen hoped the exchanges would increase the transfer rate through a personal connection that went considerably beyond signing articulation agreements. Students at Seattle Central Community College might be taught by Evergreen faculty members, creating a human connection that would make transfer to a four-year institution seem more possible to students previously not considering it.

It worked. In one case, the interinstitutional exchange worked so well it became permanent when Tacoma Community College and Evergreen agreed to jointly teach a lower division bridge program that would lead into Evergreen's upper division program in Tacoma. This bridge program turned out to be extraordinarily successful in terms of the number of students completing their four-year degrees. Located on the site of the upper division campus, the bridge program builds in many joint meetings and times for the lower and upper division students to mingle, inspiring an informal mentoring process as well as a community of aspiration.

More flexible in organizational structure, more centralized in their decision-making, and less rigidly organized into departments, the community colleges had missions and reward systems largely focused on teaching and learning. As a result, many quickly saw the advantages of the learning community approach. Strong communication networks among the two-year colleges promoted the rapid dissemination of the ideas through colleague networks. The five-credit course system in place at most community colleges facilitated blocking of the curriculum into relatively large chunks of credit and time, including fifteen credit team-taught programs, making teaching and learning more focused and coherent. The general education program, encapsulated in the associate of arts degree requirement, and sometimes described as "marching orders from the University of Washington," was suddenly liberated by new visions of integrated interdisciplinary programs.

In fact, the transfer system in Washington had always encouraged innovation. The associate of arts degree requirements were quite general and easily accommodated interdisciplinary programs. A statewide committee, the Inter-College Relations Committee, had been in existence for a number of years to work on transfer issues. This committee played a key role in supporting the learning community effort from the outset. It included a number of faculty and administrators with experience teaching in learning communities who established a climate supportive of innovation. Person-to-person connections between people in key offices at the University of Washington and the community colleges facilitated communication and bridge building, making critical transfer of credit issues quickly resolvable.

A receptive and largely stable cadre of community college administrators supported the endeavor and one another in the beginning stages of the learning community movement. This was especially important when key organizational changes needed to be made to put learning communities in place. The Washington Center's annual gatherings increased the rate of learning among institutions as the innovation spread. The Washington Center planning committee's initial composition was important in creating a collaborative context from the outset. Institutions sent members in pairs: a key academic administrator and a faculty member. Much time in these meetings was spent sharing learning community experiences and reading and discussing the literature that informed its theory and practice. As a result, there was considerable alignment about the purposes of learning communities among both faculty and administrative leaders. When this leadership cadre began to change as key individuals retired or moved to other institutions, the learning community effort faced significant transition problems on a number of campuses.

It is significant that the most integrated form of learning community—team-taught coordinated studies programs—was common in the beginning years throughout the community college system. Through team teaching faculty developed new models for teaching and learning while reinventing colleague relationships at the same time. Teams also produced a multiplier effect for the effort as large teaching teams quickly spread innovation through peer networks. At many colleges, well-established senior faculty led the way, giving the movement credibility, reliable leadership, and well-honed skills in collaborative teaching and learning. On some campuses, the initiators were highly inclusive and worked hard to recruit others to teaching in learning communities. On others, the teams became inbred and experienced little turnover, often prompting jealous reactions on the part of outsiders. The critical issue of who joins a movement defines the effort in many ways and can become a real limit on its expansion, and this is certainly true of the learning community effort in Washington. (For a provocative article on the writing across the curriculum as a movement see Walvoord, 1996.)

Meanwhile, new ways of thinking about learning communities were always encouraged, and new approaches were transmitted through Washington Center events and activities. The adaptability of the learning community idea proved to be an asset, building naturally on the creativity of the grassroots. All sorts of learning community models were possible, and people could contribute to the statewide effort in various ways. The University of Washington became known for its excellent training and evaluation program for Freshmen Interest Groups, while Edmonds Community College led the effort on learning outcomes. Yakima Valley became known for excellent work in collaborative learning in the sciences. The simple model of linking two courses together (often a skill course and a content course) became especially common, proving to be a flexible and practical model in many institutional settings. Most institutions began offering a variety of different models, but continued with the team-taught coordinated studies as well, feeling that this approach was unsurpassed in promoting faculty creativity and faculty development. As the effort matured, institutions began thinking more strategically about learning community program goals, seeing a variety of purposes beyond faculty development. Some institutions chose to develop learning communities primarily for students in developmental education while others focused on students pursuing the associate of arts degree. Many emphasized the first quarter of college, thinking it essentially set the expectations for the students about the new college environment. Because English composition courses were often included, the learning community effort revived interest in writing across the curriculum, which had swept the state some years earlier and then somewhat lost momentum. In a number of institutions, vocational and professional programs were a natural site for learning communities. Transfer interest groups at the University of Washington—a new type of learning community—became a means of facilitating transfer between two- and four-year institutions.

An early relationship between the Washington Center and the State Board for Community and Technical Colleges was a key factor in the expansion of learning communities throughout the community college system. Washington's thirty-two technical and community colleges are organized under a state board, while the four-year institutions are more loosely coordinated by a state higher education coordinating board. The Washington Center and the State Board for Community and Technical Colleges began working together soon after the learning community effort began. The State Board made a key early decision to try to improve quality through an educational rather than a regulatory approach. Collaborating with the Washington Center around joint initiatives effectively joined grassroots work with state policy initiatives.

At the four-year colleges and universities, learning communities emerged more slowly. The University of Washington was one of the first four-year institutions to start learning communities after hearing about the University of Oregon's freshman interest group model at a Washington Center conference. A dean at the University of Washington often describes the beginning of their freshmen interest group (FIG) program (a simple learning community model in which a cohort of students enroll in three classes in common and take a one-credit seminar led by a peer advisor) as a modest effort to ease the transition to college (see Goodsell, 1993; Tinto et al., 1994; Tokuno, 1993; Tokuno & Campbell, 1992). They expected little more from the effort which started with four sets of clustered courses, but they established conditions which would allow the innovation to scale-up with quality. The results turned out to be more substantial and long lasting. In follow-up studies years later, many senior students pointed to the FIG program as one of the highlights of their undergraduate experience.

The University of Washington now has nearly one hundred freshmen interest groups each fall and conceives of the program in a much broader way. In addition to the advantages it has for the students enrolled in the FIG's, the program is a highly competitive student leadership opportunity for senior students who act as peer advisors. The program has also become a platform for all kinds of other reforms in undergraduate education at the university. As the dean put it,

> When we wanted to infuse technology in the curriculum we established the U-WIRED project and put an emphasis on connecting this to the FIG program. Now we are doing the same thing with service-learning. FIGS are a powerful platform for all sorts of educational reforms. Learning communities are like a lego set: you can take them apart, put them together in different ways, and attach all sorts of innovations to them. (F. Campbell, personal communication, February 1999)

Other four-year institutions came into the learning community effort much later, mostly through first year initiatives. The freshmen interest group model, linking existing classes through enrolling a common cohort of students, was the most common since it easily adapted to the large freshmen classes typical of four-year universities. Since many of these classes were taught by teaching assistants and part-time faculty, it also limited the reach of the learning community effort into the full-time faculty. Nonetheless, state efforts to improve institutional performance made learning communities look attractive, especially after research began to suggest that students in learning communities had higher retention rates and more rapidly completed their degrees. As pressure increased as a result of state performance measures, learning communities seem to be one promising solution.

By 1998, learning communities were present on the campuses of nearly all of the public two- and four-year colleges in the state. While the bandwagon effect did not appeal to everyone, there was a sense of healthy competition among the institutions not to be left behind in the statewide innovations. This sense of competition was buttressed by a supportive climate for self-improvement with structures of collaboration for sharing and learning from one another. On many campuses, learning communities have now become a regular part of the curriculum. Some colleges have come so far as to make interest in teaching in learning communities a hiring criteria.

Nonetheless, it must be acknowledged that the reach of the learning community effort and the level of institutionalization varies greatly. On many campuses, the effort has reached a plateau and it has been institutionalized at what seems like an appropriate scale. On other campuses, even where the effort initially appeared to be strong, administrative turnover and an underlying lack of broad faculty involvement has left the effort vulnerable. Across the board, institutions are facing classic second stage reform issues. The innovators and early adopters who initially led the effort are starting to retire and move on to other things. The level of volunteerism that first fueled the effort has ebbed. The institutions are not typically investing enough in ongoing faculty development to replenish the learning community effort and to continue to build broader faculty interest. A myriad of other, new agendas have pushed the learning community effort off central stage. At the same time, many of the institutions are in a critical period of high turnover among the faculty. If new generations of faculty and administrators are not brought into these efforts to improve undergraduate education, they will not last. As a result, the statewide and the campus level efforts are still very fragile. Interestingly, many of the same second stage issues are also confronting the related enterprises that played such an important role in the first decade of learning community development in Washington.

Relationship to Other Reforms

The state diversity and assessment initiatives have been especially important companions to the learning community effort. At their best, there has been powerful synergy among the efforts. The association between learning communities and other reform efforts has deepened the learning community movement in a variety of ways and kept the concept open and growing. The relationships among these initiatives and the people involved are complex and multifaceted.

Assessment

The learning community movement embraced assessment before it became a statewide issue. In 1986, the Washington Center established an assessment and evaluation committee drawn from nine campuses. The committee immediately decided to embrace assessment for its own sake, not simply as a means of responding to the requirements of the Ford Foundation grant under which it was then operating. The committee began reviewing the national literature on assessment and started collecting information about learning community results. It established working groups that eventually produced a number of publications on assessing learning communities: a book of case studies, another on student self-evaluation, and an assessment handbook that could be used in any classes organized around collaborative learning. Washington faculty and administrators became active in national assessment conversations as well. The state was always well represented at the early AAHE assessment conferences. The Washington Center also organized training on promising approaches such as Alverno College's work on learning outcomes (Mentkowski, 2000) and Pat Cross and Tom Angelo's (1993) classroom assessment work. The Alverno approach was particularly embraced by a number of the community colleges. As a result of these efforts, faculty were more aware of the language of learning outcomes when this became a state initiative some years later.

When a state assessment initiative surfaced in 1989 at the Higher Education Coordinating Board, there was an energetic and well-placed group of people familiar with the assessment literature and cognizant of the need for assessment both to prove what works and to improve practice. After a brief foray into toying with statewide standardized tests, Washington entered a long period of amply funded local experimentation with assessment. Colleges across the state established offices of institutional research and assessment, and faculty did pilot assessment projects in many different areas. Again, the community colleges tended to emphasize grassroots experimentation which empowered large numbers of faculty, and the four-year colleges also became increasingly active, especially after they established their own annual colloquy retreat to discuss assessment issues and approaches. At the same time, annual reports to the state around minimal common measures brought a certain amount of ongoing visibility and accountability to the effort. An annual statewide assessment conference became a rich gathering place for two and four-year college faculty interested in assessment. The conference regularly draws three hundred people from across the state and has become a regional resource for faculty in nearby Oregon and British Columbia as well. Participants come back year after year. As a consequence, the learning is cumulative and of increasing depth and sophistication.

The State Board for Community and Technical Colleges made a critical early decision to appoint Bill Moore as director of the statewide community college assessment effort. He was committed to using assessment to improve student learning and to doing grassroots work with teaching faculty. The State Board simultaneously followed a top-down and bottom-up strategy of promoting change. In addition to seeding campus level change through local funds to experiment, the board reserved some assessment money for statewide work. This allowed them to convene events to bring the campuses together to continue to learn and be challenged by one another. Under Moore's leadership, the assessment effort flourished and was continually renewed with new activities and approaches. He brought a community organizing perspective to his efforts to build a culture of assessment. He convened retreats to discuss various topics (learning outcomes, developmental education, diversity, writing, and quantitative reasoning), published a newsletter that drew heavily upon the voices of the faculty participants, and was continually on the road doing workshops with, by, and for the campuses. Most important, he and his colleagues at the State Board continued to think about how assessment could be usefully linked to other issues about improving undergraduate education, never allowing the assessment agenda to become too technical, narrow, and fragmented. A culture of assessment was being nurtured on a broad scale, and a vibrant community of people interested in assessment was carefully cultivated. As it turned out, there was considerable overlap between the faculty interested in assessment and learning communities, and the approaches used to mobilize interested people were very similar.

In 1996, the assessment movement in Washington, like many other states, took a sharp political turn. Performance based accountability measures were introduced in the state legislature around relatively narrow notions of institutional performance, largely based upon efficiency. Despite the long experience with assessment, many felt caught off-guard and unprepared for the new emphasis on accountability goals. For most of the previous ten years the assessment effort and the accountability initiatives had been sharply differentiated. This was seen as crucial in getting faculty interested and keeping the efforts directed at classroom improvement. As the efforts became more sophisticated the distinctions became more difficult to maintain, and attention focused on what was happening in the aggregate, beyond individual classrooms. At the same time, both the accountability and the assessment initiatives were moving in the same direction—toward student learning outcomes, especially when this became a key focus in reaccreditation as well.

The tension between local innovation and the larger state mandate remains unresolved in terms of the assessment issue. At the state level, the most significant debates are around how to move the institutions ahead on long-term state goals, whether all institutions should be held to the same standards, what's measurable, and whether to use an incentive based system or a punitive approach to motivate the institutions. At the institutional level, critical questions are being raised about how to assess student learning, how to promote change, how to define success, and how to communicate attainment of significant educational goals, especially in a highly charged political environment.

Diversity

Diversity was the second statewide issue that emerged at approximately the same time. As with the assessment issue, grassroots statewide work significantly shaped and was shaped by the state mandates in this area. In the late 1980s academic administrators at the two- and four-year colleges met to discuss the growing student diversity in the state and the implications for higher education. As a result of these meetings, the two- and four-year colleges and universities developed action plans and approached the legislature about funding robust diversity initiatives that included early awareness programs in K-12, student support initiatives, and related programs. They were not funded. State interest in diversity did continue to grow at the policy level, however, culminating in the passage in 1991 of a Minority Participation Policy which set higher education goals in the areas of minority employment, recruitment, retention, and graduation, and set expectations about curriculum change and institutional climate.

The community colleges decided to focus on diversity despite the lack of special legislative funding, and instead earmarked part of their general quality enhancement funds for this purpose. They approached the Washington Center about a joint project, believing that this alliance might give them greater access to the grassroots faculty. Together, they designed a three-year project that came to be called the Minority Student Success project. State Board staff leaders Jan Yoshiwara and Rhonda Coats were both grassroots oriented in the same way that Moore was. The project was based upon what became a typical approach for most of the center's statewide efforts: build institutional teams appointed by the president that include staff, faculty, and key administrators, commit to a multistep, multiyear project that requires increasing institutional commitment, build in opportunities to learn from state-of-the art literature and experts, have the campus teams develop concrete action plans, and build in a process of monitoring, encouragement, and feedback from the center staff. A key component was always a multiday off-site retreat where teams would have the opportunity for sustained focus in the company of friendly consultants (kibitzers) and other schools also interested in diversity.

The Washington Center's view of effective change projects was based upon assumptions that fragmentation in the organizational structure and lack of focus were obstacles that needed to be addressed in a more holistic manner. The structural analysis was strikingly similar to the structural case for learning communities. The solutions were also similar: build teams, work on clarifying and planning for longer term goals, and set up optimal learning conditions. Twenty-three of the twenty-seven community colleges participated in the Minority Student Success project. More than half made significant progress in defining and beginning to work on their institutional issues. In many cases, working on the curriculum was defined as a critical need. It was notable that many of the original learning communities did not enroll significant numbers of students of color, even at Seattle Central which is a highly diverse community college. This need drove the next phase of the work and provided an ideal opportunity to bring the learning community work and the diversity initiatives together.

In 1992, the Ford Foundation gave major funding to the Washington Center as part of its national diversity initiative. Working in collaboration with the University of Washington's American Ethnic Studies Department and then chair Johnnella Butler, the Washington Center developed the Cultural Pluralism project which focused on the curriculum and faculty development. In many ways, the project was an ideal blend of the different resources of the Washington Center and the University of Washington. The University of Washington brought faculty with solid expertise in American ethnic studies to the project while the Washington Center contributed its network of people broadly committed to educational improvement and its extensive experience with organizational change and alternative pedagogies.

The challenge of curriculum transformation was seen as a multifaceted issue. First and foremost, there was a content gap: The faculty needed to be broadly educated about the literature relevant to American ethnic studies, a new and blossoming interdisciplinary field. Second, there was significant learning that needed to take place about new pedagogical approaches that would reach an increasingly diverse student population. Third, and most related to the previous Minority Student Success project, institutional planning and the organizational structure needed to support the change initiative.

Twenty-six of the state's colleges and universities joined the Ford-funded opportunity, committing themselves to a comprehensive diversity project. The Cultural Pluralism project followed a design similar to previous Washington Centers projects, and added a seven to ten day intensive institute for teams of faculty and administrators. Heavily focused on content, the institute took a comparative perspective on the five major ethnic groups: African American, American Indian, Chicano-Latino, Asian-Pacific Islander, and Euro-American.

The Ford project succeeded in bringing diversity into the curriculum in many institutions across the state, and brought many of the four-year colleges and universities into the statewide work. Learning communities were a significant arena for developing this new emphasis, especially in the community colleges. A number of institutions passed multicultural curriculum requirements, but the usual thrust was to address diversity throughout the curriculum. Again, team teaching contributed to rapid dissemination of the new learning. The effort had broad spillover effects in terms of faculty recruitment and hiring, faculty development, and relationships between units such as student affairs and academic affairs. Many institutions made a commitment to hire a more diverse faculty and were successful in doing so. This was the right direction at the right time since the student demographics were already shifting dramatically. All of this work left the state's higher education system in a healthier position in terms of its commitment to diversity when Initiative 200 was passed in 1998 eliminating affirmative action.

When the amply funded Ford three-year project ended in 1995, soundings were again taken by the Washington Center and the State Board about what was needed next that could be done on the modest base of existing resources. The result was a new project, the Multicultural Efforts project, which revisited some of the same strategic planning and organizational issues of the very first Minority Student Success project. A critical priority at this point was to build the capacity of the institutions to make planning more data driven after it became clear that there was far more information available to guide institutional planning than was being used. With support from the State Board's data experts, institutional teams identified critical questions about where students of color were located and lost in the curriculum, what their success rates were, and which courses seemed to be particularly troublesome. Armed with this information, more careful and strategic interventions became possible. Several other smaller scale efforts to study retention and transfer also continue to work on the structural issues arising from a two-tiered educational system in which students of color are disproportionately located in two-year colleges.

A Different Kind of Reform Effort

The notable thing about both the diversity and assessment initiatives is how they both influenced and broadened the learning community effort and vice versa. Some of the same people were involved in all these efforts, of course. One of the major challenges, especially in small institutions, is to work on so many initiatives with so few people. By merging these initiatives they become more complex, more holistic, and, in some ways, more manageable. But these cross connections also tend to bring in people with different interests and talents. Learning community proponents become interested in assessment and diversity, and faculty with a primary interest in diversity find new arenas and colleagues in the learning community network. When this occurs, it strengthens all of the initiatives at once. This results in a more holistic way of conceptualizing the work and a much broader base of potential support, both in terms of the people who might be involved and the financial resources that might be available. It also often involves rethinking the organizational structure and practices of the institution.

There are many features of the Washington story that may be idiosyncratic: An education system with comparatively low status boundaries between two- and four-year colleges and a fairly long history of working together, a nontraditional four-year institution playing a statewide leadership role in networking the various colleges and universities, key individuals like Bill Moore, Jan Yoshiwara, and Rhonda Coats at the State Board for Community and Technical Colleges, and Jean MacGregor, Jeanine Elliott, and Emily Decker at the Washington Center. So the question is, what are the larger lessons in this story? Can the Washington experience inform others interested in promoting interinstitutional change?

Our answer is yes. There are many lessons from this story. One lesson is, of course, that individuals do matter. Champions, innovators, and early adopters are necessary, especially in the beginning stages of an innovation. Structures also matter. They can facilitate or impede the innovation process. Clearly, the actions of Evergreen's Washington Center, the State Board for Community and Technical Colleges, and even the Inter-College Committee on College Relations helped establish structures for collaboration and ongoing innovation. These approaches certainly suggest different ways for bureaucracies to operate as they pursue change initiatives.

It is significant that the approach to all of these endeavors has been long term, and not project-based. Projects are, to be sure, vehicles for moving the long-term goals, but the work in all three arenas—learning communities, assessment, and diversity—continues with or without substantial resources. It's also important to recognize the significant synergy between the campus level efforts and the state mandates. It's doubtful that the diversity effort, in particular, would have been as rich and far reaching if it had not been focused on the grassroots. Although there was a state diversity policy, there was no state support to implement the mandates. But there was more to it than that. Reaching the grassroots is necessary. For things to change, teachers must recognize and use their own power to reenvision how and what they teach. State mandates only take root when this happens on a large scale. As Moore later put it, "I could rely on the campus energy to help catalyze state efforts" (personal communication, Summer 1999).

Unlike many educational innovations, the learning community effort began as a partnership between institutions and between faculty and administration. At the same time, it began with faculty at the course level, rethinking what is important for students from their own field and how it relates to what other faculty in other fields think is important. In this sense the learning community effort came directly from faculty interests and needs. It is centered in the basic core of the academy— learning. It is built on a model of intellectual discourse and exchange and fosters an interactive community of learners. It is based on the ongoing study and research, growth and development of faculty. It opens up new fields of study for faculty, and fosters a rethinking of old ideas in the context of new ones, new perspectives, new fields of learning and methodologies. It provides for ongoing faculty learning in writing-across the curriculum, new pedagogical approaches, and new discipline intersections. Team-taught learning communities, in particular, foster depth and spontaneous interactions among colleagues in a manner that rarely ever happens. The learning community effort is, in fact, a holistic response to many issues and many people in different roles at once. It addresses important needs and issues of students, faculty, and administrators. It provides a way for many perspectives to come together. It is not a narrowly based effort.

It is important that these were ongoing conversations across institutional boundaries. To be healthy growing places, colleges need to think globally and act locally. They need windows on the outside world that broaden their perspectives while finding fertile ground at home to plant the new seeds. Many colleges and universities could benefit by rethinking the balance in this regard, asking themselves, in what ways is our college a community? How is this sense of community nurtured? How do we support growth and a more cosmopolitan perspective? In some institutions, there is little sense of local community. For some, the scholarly communities are national and disciplinary and the current institution is a stopping place on a career. But this is actually not true of most people's relationships which tend to be longer lasting. Community colleges, in particular, are relatively small communities. Establishing a broader set of colleagues opens new windows. Finding and affirming the common ground that all educators share—a love of learning, a deep regard for students, and the betterment of society—is renewing.

The learning community movement has had a support structure through the Washington Center for Improving the Quality of Undergraduate Education. It acts as an ongoing support system, cheerleader, and dissemination system for a variety of new innovations, most frequently through the vehicle of the learning community curricular structure.

Finally, it is important that the learning community effort is not a canned program, but a philosophy, a value system with guiding principles and structure for rethinking the curriculum, in manageable, authentic experimental modules, rather than through hours and years of procedural committee work. Ultimately the learning community effort is about relationships. They have enabled faculty and staff to come together to create new ways for students to succeed.

References

Angelo, T., & Cross, P. (1993). *Classroom assessment techniques.* San Francisco, CA: Jossey-Bass.

Gabelnick, F., Matthews, R., MacGregor, J., & Smith, B. L. (1990). Learning communities: Building connections among disciplines, students and faculty. *New Directions in Teaching and Learning, No. 41.* San Francisco, CA: Jossey-Bass.

Goodsell, A. (1993). *Freshman interest groups: Linking social and academic experiences of first-year students.* Unpublished doctoral dissertation, Syracuse University.

Hamberg, R., & Smith, B. L. *Making our colleges learning organizations.* Unpublished, undated manuscript, The Evergreen State College, Olympia, WA.

Mentkowski, M., & Associates. (2000). *Learning that lasts.* San Francisco, CA: Jossey-Bass.

Smith, B. L. (1988). The Washington Center: A grassroots approach to faculty development and curricular reform. *To Improve the Academy, 7,* 165–177.

Tinto, V., Goodsell, A., & Russo, P. (1994). *Building learning communities for new college students: A summary of research findings of the collaborative learning project.* Syracuse, NY: Syracuse University, National Center on Postsecondary Teaching, Learning and Assessment.

Tokuno, K. (1993). Long term and recent student outcomes of the freshmen interest groups. *Journal of the Freshman Year Experience, 5* (2), 7–28.

Tokuno, K., & Campbell, F. (1992). Freshmen interest groups at the University of Washington: Effects on retention and scholarship. *Journal of the Freshman Year Experience, 4* (1), 7–22.

Walvoord, B. (1996, January). The future of WAC. *College English, 58* (1).

Acknowledgement

I want to thank the following people who read early drafts of this chapter and gave me valuable suggestions for improvement: Emily Decker, Jim Harnish, Jean MacGregor, and Bill Moore.

7

Integration and Assessment of Service-Learning in Learning Communities

Karen Kashmanian Oates and Laura Gaither
George Mason University
New Century College

The contemporary learning community movement in higher education is now over 25 years old. Like many other sustained innovative programs, the learning community movement has taken the lead in providing examples of what can be done on both a local and national level to change how knowledge is constructed, connected, and disseminated. At the heart of learning communities, whether they be in the form of linked classes, federated learning communities, freshman living/learning environments, or coordinated studies, is the active participation of students. Another successful method to increase active participation of students is service-learning. Service-learning, as defined by Jacoby, is "a form of experiential education in which students engage in activities that address human and community needs [combined] with structured opportunities intentionally designed to promote student learning and development" (1996, p. 5) and by Howard as "a pedagogical model that intentionally integrates academic learning and relevant community service" (1998, p. 22).

Service-learning, community-based learning, or the variety of permutations involving serve and learn initiatives can be found housed in either the student service or academic arm of the university. Benefits of association with either are significant. However, it is our experience that truly successful service-learning initiatives take advantage of the teaching experience of expert faculty and the student development expertise of student affairs professionals. Initiatives of this nature encourage participation of faculty with student affairs professionals to integrate service-learning in learning communities as well as in a variety of traditional discipline-based courses. Transforming a passive lecture style classroom into a learning community which integrates academic based service-learning is a formidable task and one which should not be timidly entered into. The transformation is not immediate nor without a clearly defined faculty and professional staff development plan. Workshops, seminars, and best practice discussions amongst faculty and professional staff not only result in a significant transformation in the classroom but contribute significantly to building community amongst student services and academic faculty. In our institution as well as others, transformation (or change) is often faced with challenge. Inevitably, the following questions are asked: What does the process of integration take away from the academic task? Is rigor maintained? To answer these questions we first must ask: How do we define our course objectives? How are the objectives best accomplished and in what context do our objectives impact the learner? If our goal is to impart as much information as possible regardless of whether learning takes place, or for that matter is connected to authentic life problems, then the integration of service-learning takes away from the information delivery model. If, however, the goals are to connect information to practice and application, and to internalize understanding and develop abilities, then the integration model meets the course objectives. The question of rigor can also be addressed.

In a recent address, Palmer Parker (1998) asserted that students, as they approach their academic course of study, fear failure and it is fear which often prevents learning. Parker has observed that we must first establish an open and supportive climate in our learning environments and then, and only then, can we move forward to rigor. Rigor, he contends, arises from a willingness to disagree, to engage in honest questioning, to challenge current thought and in acknowledgment of what one does not know. Rigor can only come when students feel the environment is hospitable to such dynamics. Through the combination of the learning community (providing the supportive climate for academic content) and service-learning (providing context and process), rigor can be achieved. The following diagram expresses the interrelationship between content, context, and process (Figure 7.1). Service-learning results from the integration of content, traditionally consisting of lectures, readings, speakers, exams and quizzes, and an experiential context to explore real world applications of content which meets a human or community need. Service-learning pushes us to reconsider the multiple origins of the knowledge base (what), the dissemination of information (how), and

FIGURE 7.1 Complexities of an Integrated Service-Learning Community

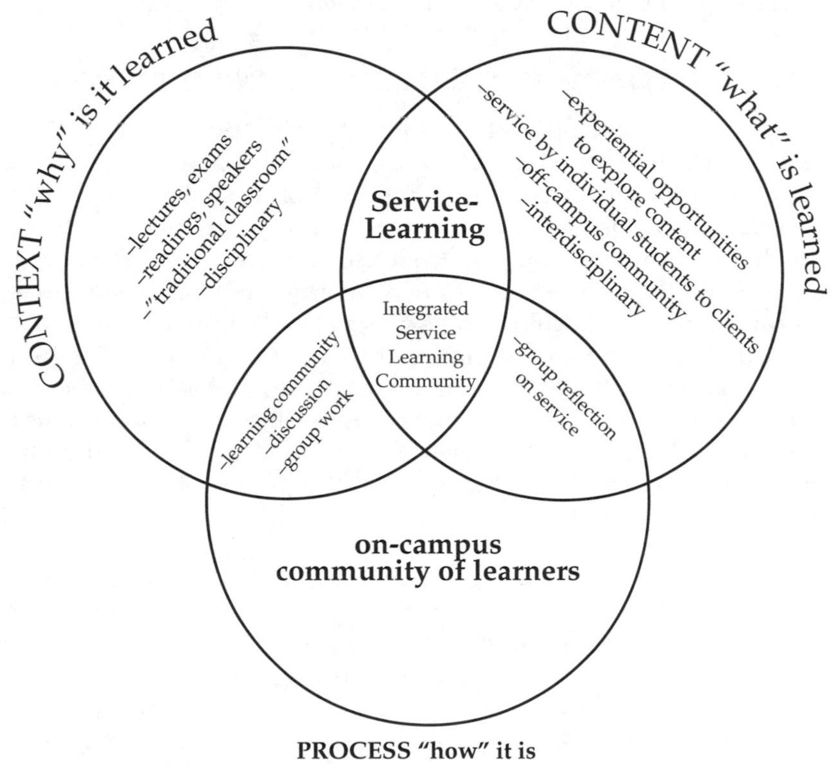

raises questions as to which perspectives are included or excluded (who). We must also reconsider the process by which the integration occurs. By considering the organic nature of learning and the renegotiation of content because of context, the integrated learning community environment provides an excellent structure to synergistically foster authentic, connected learning over the semester.

Clearly, over the last five years, national initiatives to combine both the service-learning and the learning communities movements have met with enthusiasm for a shared pedagogy as well as recognition of the synergy between the movements to provide supportive and rigorous collaborative learning environments. The movement has also been met with apprehension for how meaningful models of incorporation and assessments can be developed and implemented. In this chapter we will explore the context, content, and process of learning shared by both learning communities and the service-learning movement, the developmental influences on learning, models of integration as well as the tools used to assess and disseminate service-learning initiatives into the traditional (nonlearning community) classroom experience.

Shared Developmental Influences on Learning

The intellectual development theories of Kolb (1984), Dewey (1916), Lewin (1951), and Perry (1970) are recognized in the practical application of service-learning in learning communities. Kolb describes the process of intellectual development as a cycle in which the learner passes through four distinct learning abilities: Concrete Experience (CE), Reflective Observation (RO), Abstract Conceptualization (AC), and Active Experimentation (AE). Kolb summarizes the cycle as an immediate concrete (affective) experience which is then used as the basis for future observation and reflection. An individual uses these observations to build an idea, generalization, or 'theory' from which new implications for action can be deduced and rendered. These implications and actions then serve as guides to create new experiences. This process of recognition and deduction is commonly encountered in integrated service-learning in learning communities.

Dewey and Lewin describe the process needed to break the traditional model of passive solitary learner to active participant while the Perry scheme for intellectual development parallels the engagement of inquiry-based interdisciplinary problem solving. As students make connections between the classroom and the world, between right and wrong to relativism (appreciation of multiple points of view), they move through the positions of the Perry Scale. An integrated service-learning approach facilitates the development from dualistic thinking to the construction of knowledge in an environment where ambiguity is acknowledged and accepted as a reality. When a concept is experienced, discussed, and dissected, authentic learning occurs by everyone who has participated. The material is no longer distant or foreign to the participants but is owned by members of the discussion group. These discussions are guided or facilitated by the more experienced faculty. This is exactly why the traditional disciplines and professional schools have had their own form of learning analogous to that of integrative service-learning experience. Traditionally, nursing students have clinical rotations; social workers, practicums; scientists, research; education majors, student teaching; and art majors, studio.

Integration of service-learning and learning communities fosters the opportunity for active application of our current cognitive development/student development theory. One could argue successfully that experiential education, such as service-learning, internships, co-op and adventure learning, completes the learning community structure.

TABLE 7.1 Learning Community/Service-Learning Models Contrasted With Traditional Models of Teaching

Coordinated Learning Communities	Service-Learning	Traditional
Learner-centered	Community-centered	Teacher-centered
Active participation	Active participation	Passive absorption
Team learning (students)	Team learning (students and community mentors)	Individual learners
Teacher as guide	Community as expert	Teacher as expert
Curriculum is continuously negotiated and discovered in process	Curriculum is derived from experience	Curriculum is set
Learning to learn and create knowledge	Learning from the realities of others	Prescribed learning
Interdisciplinary	Interdisciplinary	Based on a discipline
Learning occurs in both classroom and community	Learning occurs in community	Learning occurs in classroom

Furthermore, without experiential education, the learning community remains untransformed in any meaningful way. Instead, an integrated structure allows the progression through a process in which the learner constructs knowledge, skills, and values from direct experiences. Learning community and service-learning pedagogy is strengthened by the influences of the other, and is contrasted to the traditional models of classroom learning above (Table 7.1).

From the above comparisons, the synergy of service-learning integration within learning communities becomes evident. Synergies take the form of:

- Mixed individual and team projects related to academic study and service to the community.
- Connections between what is taught in the classroom and what is experienced on the street.
- Breaking the traditional course based (3 credit hour) delivery mode based on seat time in a classroom.
- An interdisciplinary view of problems and possible solutions rather than a rigid discipline-based response.
- Focusing on the future, rather than emphasizing tradition.

MODELS OF INTEGRATION

There are multiple models to integrate service-learning into learning communities. The first is the add-on variable credit model (Figure 7.2). In this model, an additional course experience (service-learning) is offered to students who select this option. It is not required of all the students of the course, but is an optional activity. This model may relieve faculty of large numbers of students selecting the option, resulting in fewer placements to monitor, reduce risk/liability issues (since it is not a required activity), and can create a dynamic dialog between students doing the service and those who are not. It can also introduce faculty to service-learning in a concrete, yet low-risk, less involved way (Koliba, 1995). However, in this model, the service-learning experience is not considered a vital part of the learning community, but an option for those electing the experience. As a result, students opting for a service-learning experience may feel isolated and proceed without adequate supervision, recognition, and structured reflection. Students may not have a vehicle to discuss their experience with other students or faculty.

The linked model provides more input from faculty by linking specific service-learning requirements to the course material. Reflections on the required service-learning experience are treated as an independent but linked activity. For example, faculty include readings on subjects which explore the service, require journals, and may choose to dedicate one or two specific class periods for discussion in which students are encouraged to reflect on their experiences. However, the structure of the classroom environment may still be controlled solely by the faculty. The curriculum remains predetermined and nonnegotiated and students' experiences both at the service site and in class remain highly individualistic. The classroom environment remains essentially unaltered with the addition of service-learning, although individual students may have profound learning experiences.

In contrast to the add-on and linked model, the integrative model is required and integrated within the learning community. Service and community learning acts as a central text to the course and as a catalyst for transforming the classroom environment. Depending on the course credit structure, our experience indicates service-learning could range between 25 to 135 hours of direct experience per semester. In an integrated model, the initial content is set by faculty through a syllabus, texts, and discussion topics. Yet as students engage in the materials, new topics emerge for exploration. Members start with a knowledge of basic functions and hypothesis and then begin their interdisciplinary inquiry and exploration as learning proceeds. As a result of contact at the community learning site, faculty, students, community supervisors, and clients drive discussion, research and analysis, and renegotiate content. The curriculum is

FIGURE 7.2 Models of Service-Learning

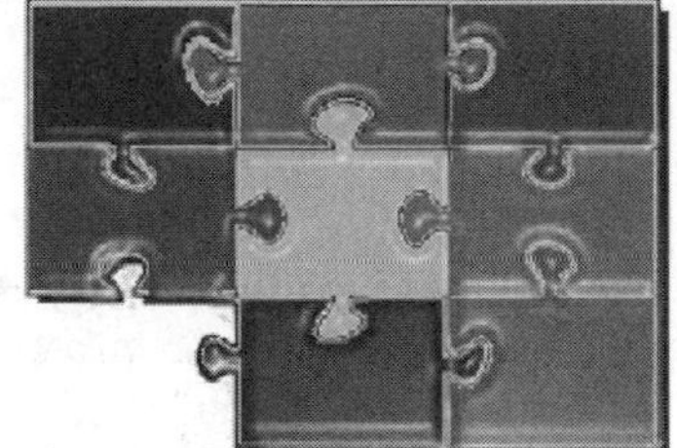

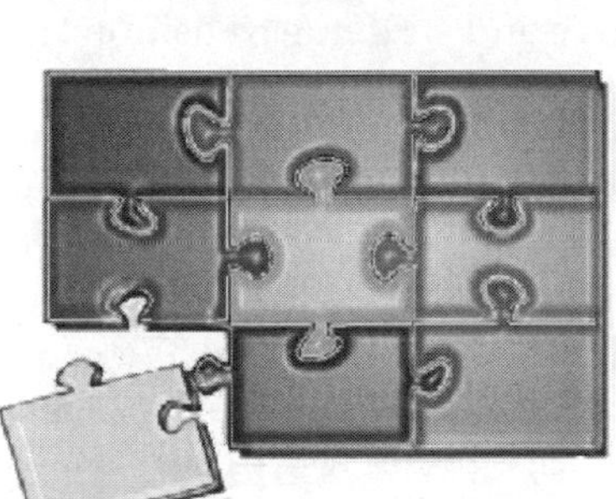

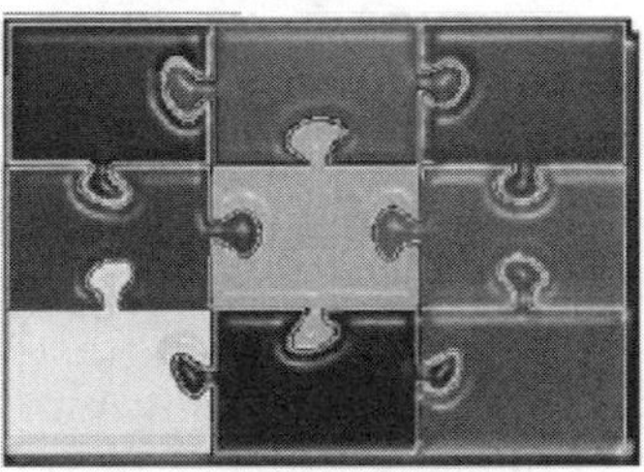

constantly evolving as an organic entity throughout the semester. Students and community members contribute to the content. The context is used as a mirror to reflect into the classroom the multiple perspectives and interdisciplinary applications (or lack of applications) of classroom materials in the field. Students in the integrative model are required to participate in service-learning. Reflective exercises and discussions are based on what is observed at the community site as it relates to the class readings and text. The advantages of this model are that all students in the learning community share a common experience that informs their contribution to the learning community. Since the learning community values contributions from all members, each student's historical experience and interpretation of current service can be brought to the table as vignettes shaping the content and driving discussion. Everyone has experience, everyone has participated, and everyone is able to contribute to and better understand the issue. Learning in this model is connected and personal.

Howard (1998) clearly defines the difference between an academic service-learning experience which is integrated within the learning community and one in which the addition of a community service option or requirement is in lieu of another assignment. He confronts the issues that arise when context begins to subvert traditional methods of conveying content. Howard's synergistic classroom model depicts the stages through which faculty and students progress, as faculty choose to be less directive and more facilitative and students transition from passive recipients to active learners.

Howard (1998) discusses the phases through which students pass in order achieve the synergistic classroom, the fourth phase. The first stage is the traditional classroom, or norm stage, typified by a directive instructor and passive students. In the second renorming stage, the instructor desocializes and resocializes their behavior to be facilitative. In the third stage, students respond to the new environment as their behavior desocializes and resocializes. In the fourth and final stage, the synergistic classroom, instructors are facilitative and students active. As students and faculty adjust to the contributions of service-learning and to the meaning/knowledge base of the course, the group transitions together through the desocialization and resocialization process in which the learning community environment is intentionally designed. Both students and faculty move through the stages as the faculty member creates an environment for students to be more active and the teacher more facilitative. Howard's model is instructive: he maps out the process of service-learning interfacing with a course to become a learning community. However, at New Century College, students pass through the four phases very quickly; most by the completion of the freshman fall semester. Stage one, the traditional classroom, does not exist in New Century College.

Dissemination Practices

We find that as the learning community model emerges on more and more university campuses throughout the country, many take the form of small-scale initiatives for specific populations (honors programs and first year experiences). With the additional complexity of an integrative model with service-learning, special attention needs to be given to how dissemination of this pedagogy can be made available for more students as an option to the traditional passive classroom experience. Without a concerted campaign to link integrated service-learning/learning community movements to the university mission, student retention and satisfaction, and faculty development as part of the equation in promotion and tenure, the efforts can easily fail. Some common steps for dissemination are listed below.

- Link the integrated service-learning initiative directly to the mission of the university.
- Devote university-wide faculty development seminars to the topic (this is often done through the university's faculty development program board or teaching excellence centers).
- Bring in a dynamic speaker from a prestigious institution to present best practices derived at their institution.
- Be political—talk with your faculty senators, curriculum committee, provost, and head of university life to get their support.
- Apply for small seed grants to establish a dissemination program.
- Work with both academic and student affairs offices to provide professional staff to research and make contacts with community agencies. If your institution does not have a center for service-learning (or equivalent) work to establish one. With a modest outlay of resources a center can make a big difference. Once established, highlight the center as a partnership.
- Find success stories and tell these stories over and over again.
- Read faculty testimonials as well as student journals describing the difference the integrated service-learning experiences has made in their learning.
- Fund release time for faculty interested in learning more about integrated service-learning who will develop a new integrated service-learning offering as a result. The release time should come in the form of a competitive grant (to attend to promotion and tenure issues).

We have been active in the dissemination of an integrated service-learning initiative at George Mason University. Our success has been linked to the right combination of a supportive provost, several committed deans, senior faculty, and the professional staff of our center for service and leadership. Without this combination, dissemination efforts become even more difficult.

Assessment

Traditional classroom assessments primarily rely on three elements: 1) the written curriculum, 2) classroom instruction, and 3) results of student test scores. Clearly these elements do not form the majority of the relevant foundation needed to assess a coordinated learning community nor an integrated service-learning/learning community. When one combines the active collaborative and experiential pedagogy of learning communities with the nontraditional environment of service-learning, the assessment process becomes more complex. The decentralization of learning, student contributions, to curriculum and out-of-class service experiences contribute to the complexity of assessment. Here the foundations for assessment rely on content, context, and process as it relates to both learning within and outside of the classroom with the additional complexity of how content, context, and process relate and are informed by the integrated service-learning model (see Figure 7.3).

Goals for assessment include the development of a student (developed and designed), portfolio which captures and documents the elements of content. By design, the construction of a student portfolio is in and of itself a service-learning reflective learning experience. Evaluation of content for integrated in learning communities models reside with the faculty designed assignments. A presentation (oral, written, electronic) negotiated with the student to represent their unique learning experience as well as tests, case studies, poster sessions, and papers and reports form the basis of assessing content learning. Content, however, is not isolated from both process and context in the integrated model.

In the integrated service-learning community model, context may range from passive to active. Faculty may still dominate the assessment process. However, because the learning also occurs in contexts outside of the classroom, assessment can extend into the community. In context learning, a third partner joining student and faculty assessment is the community sponsor/mentor, who may contribute evaluations to the faculty. Students are asked in the reflection process to evaluate themselves as learners in the experiential learning process itself.

Process is often assessed through critical reflection on a specific individual assignment, activity, or experience in the form of journals, stories, and logs. In the integrative model, metalearning is a central theme for a process which allows more than a sequence of single events to be assessed as performed in more traditional programs. Through writing and dialog, students build understanding and awareness of their own learning. Engagement in the process facilitates the learning experience.

A central theme feature of Kolb's model for experiential education is the key role of reflection in the learning process. In order to draw out meaning from content and connect the meaning to the service experience, reflection is integrated at all stages of the course. Giles, Eyler, and Schmiede (1996) point out four principles of critical reflection. First, reflection must be continuous in time. It occurs before the experience in the form of goal setting, during the experience via problem solving, and

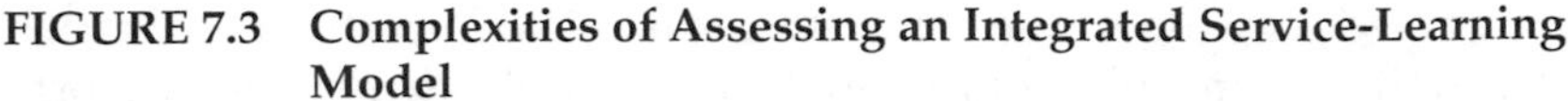

FIGURE 7.3 Complexities of Assessing an Integrated Service-Learning Model

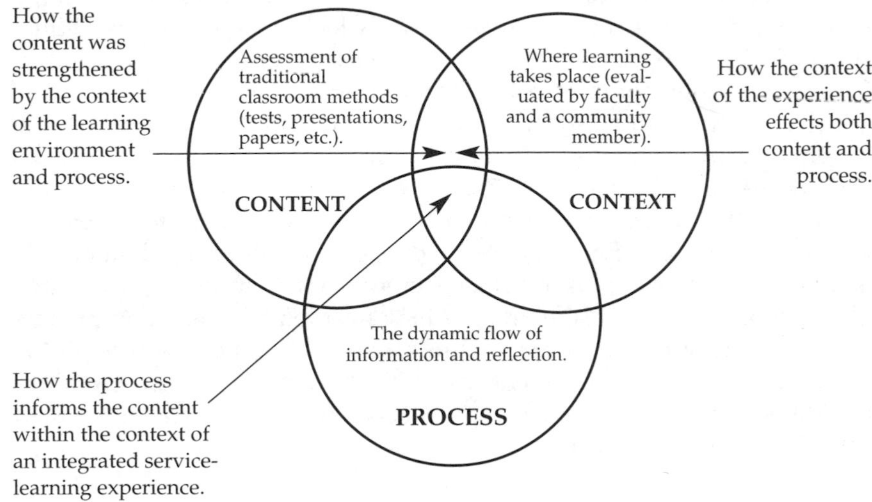
How the content was strengthened by the context of the learning environment and process.
Assessment of traditional classroom methods (tests, presentations, papers, etc.).
Where learning takes place (evaluated by faculty and a community member).
How the context of the experience effects both content and process.
CONTENT
CONTEXT
The dynamic flow of information and reflection.
PROCESS
How the process informs the content within the context of an integrated service-learning experience.

after the experience as the meaning of the service is evaluated. Secondly, reflection on the service is connected to the goals and vision of the learning community. Assignments and experiences relate to and build upon one another. Students are asked to use theories and models to apply to their field experience. We are especially fond of the following remarks by Giles, Eyler, and Schmiede:

> Service experiences illustrate theories and concepts, bringing statistics to life and making academics real and vivid. Through classroom work, in turn, students begin to develop conceptual frameworks that explain service experiences. . . . Academic pursuits add a "big picture" content to the personal encounters of each isolated service experience and help students to search for causes and solutions to social problems. (1996, p. 18)

Thirdly, the reflection must challenge assumptions and complacency. By playing devil's advocate or probing students' initial conclusions about social issues, client behavior, or community needs/responses, instructors can push students to consider alternative questions and solutions, discover root causes, and explore the complexities associated with our society. Without challenging students to think in new ways, students' growth will stagnate and rigor will never be achieved. Finally, reflection must be in itself contextualized to the design and scope of the service. Giles, Eyler, and Schmiede explain further, "the environment and method of reflection corresponds in a meaningful way to the topics and experiences that form the material for reflection" (1996, p. 17). For example, how formal will the reflection activity be? In some cases, a lively learning community discussion is more appropriate; in other cases, a research paper is more suitable. Often it is possible for reflection to occur in close proximity to the service, with clients and community organization supervisors facilitating the experience. In other cases, it may be more appropriate to return to campus for the reflective activities.

With the described complexities of an integrative service-learning/learning community model, the development of student portfolios have become a means to tell a coherent story of students as learners. The portfolio is a purposeful integration of content, context, and process as it relates to students' effort, progress, and achievement. Although the portfolio communicates content, context, and process, it also identifies the intersection of them for a comprehensive evaluation of the integrated service-learning experience.

Best Practices

Over the course of four years implementing the integrated model, faculty have found the following best practices for guiding learning communities.

- **Plan in advance.** Successful learning community faculty meet with the center for service and leadership usually three to six months before the course is offered to identify clear learning and service goals in the core curriculum and discuss possible community organizations with which to partner.
- **Complete learning contracts.** Learning contracts spell out the responsibilities of the student, faculty, and community organization. Students answer questions about the service activity including what the project is, supervisory information, and method of evaluating the project. Students list specific learning goals, discuss how the project relates to course themes, and method of evaluation (Stanton, 1982).
- **Create a shared vision statement.** Faculty prepare their goals in advance. Share them with students, allowing the learning community members to come to consensus about a statement that articulates what they are going to learn, in what way, and with what results.
- **Establish group ground rules.** Generate a list of agreed-upon behaviors which promote learning in a collective, safe environment. Sample ground rules include the need for confidentiality, use of "I feel" statements, and classroom etiquette (policies on lateness, cell phones, side conversations, etc.).

- **Establish community service ground rules.** Discuss expectations of attendance, number of service hours, confidentiality, risk management, etc.
- **Discuss rights and responsibilities.** What does the service site expect of students? What can students expect of supervisors? What does the campus service-learning center expect of students? What can students expect of the campus service-learning center?
- **Clarify roles.** What are students responsible for during the semester? Faculty? Community Supervisors? Clients?
- **Set standards for group work.** Promote contracts for group work in which group members collectively establish consensus for attendance, distribution of group grades, expected member contribution and consequences for slackers.
- **Know campus resources.** The service site can potentially generate difficult and challenging emotions and thoughts for students. Gabelnick (1990) points out that with a whole-student orientation, issues may rise to the surface of the students' emotional and psychological lives. Provide information on campus resources, such as counseling services, sexual assault services, etc. Discuss norms for self-disclosure.

It is the classroom at George Mason University which constitutes the primary point of contact between student and faculty. The learning community model at George Mason University's New Century College is one of integration because it is not merely the addition of service to classroom learning but the integration of service within the context of an active coordinated learning community. The integrated service-learning/learning community initiatives have the additional benefit of increasing student involvement through class-related experiences resulting in a higher level of student performance and persistence in college (Lewin, 1951).

"Connecting the Classroom to the World" is George Mason University's New Century College's motto, which recognizes that education is in part connecting students to ideas, resources, activities, and experience from which the rigor of learning grows.

References

Dewey, J. (1916). *Democracy and education,* New York, NY: Macmillan.

Gabelnick, F., & Associates. (1990, Spring). Students in learning communities. In F. Gabelnick, R. Matthews, J. MacGregor, & B. L. Smith, *Learning communities: Creating connections among students, faculty and disciplines.* New Directions for Teaching and Learning, No. 41. San Francisco, CA: Jossey-Bass.

Giles, D., Eyler, J., & Schmiede, A. (1996). *A practitioners guide to reflection in service-learning.* Nashville, TN: Vanderbilt University, Corporation for National Service.

Howard, J. F. (1998, Spring). *Academic service learning: A counternormative pedagogy.* New Directions for Teaching and Learning, No. 73. San Francisco, CA: Jossey-Bass.

Jacoby, B. (Ed.). (1996). *Service-learning in higher education,* San Francisco, CA: Jossey-Bass.

Kolb, D. (1984). *Experiential learning: Experience as the source of learning and development.* Englewood Cliffs, NJ: Prentice Hall.

Koliba, C. (1995, February 13). *Fourth credit option* [On-line]. Available: www.csf.colorado.edu/sl.cu/cu.html

Lewin, K. (1951). *Field theory in social sciences.* New York, NY: Harper and Row.

Palmer, P. J. (1998, March). Reclaiming spirituality in student affairs work. *Proceedings of the ACPA Convention, USA, 25* (3).

Perry, W. (1970). *Forms of intellectual and ethical development in the college years.* New York, NY: Holt, Rinehart, and Winston.

Stanton, T. (1982). *The experienced hand: A student manual for making the most out of an internship.* Cranston, RI: Carroll Press.

8

Uncommon Sense: Liberal Education, Learning Communities, and the Transformative Quest

Les K. Adler
Sonoma State University

Midway this way of life we're bound upon
I woke to find myself in a dark wood,
Where the right road was wholly lost and gone.

—Dante

We must always follow somebody looking for truth, and we must always run away from anyone who finds it.

—Andre Gide

Defining the elusive quality of a liberal education has challenged educators since the modern university began its slow rise to prominence nearly 800 years ago. Where once mastery of a particular body of knowledge and the possession of certain moral and intellectual traits were the recognized hallmarks of a liberally educated person, modern educational systems now offer only statistical variations of what might be called the mass educated being (MEB).

For all practical purposes, the MEB is basically defined as one who has collected a specified number of units across a Whitman's Sampler of introductory classes ranging from sociology to statistics, along with a specialized major where, presumably, she or he would have acquired the real tools necessary for a successful life and career. What is happily avoided in such a scenario, of course, is any discussion of what a liberal education actually consists of or what the liberally educated student has or should have become in his or her four or more years at college. To paraphrase Descartes, I count therefore I am!

Recognizing that modern universities must serve a variety of socially useful purposes, including preparing students for careers and advancing the cutting edge of knowledge through basic research— purposes which at the moment need no advocates—I want to address, however, the institution's most ancient and basic purpose which in far too many cases is reflected all-too-often in name only. Rooted in the Greek *holon,* or whole, or its Latin translation *universum,* the university was originally organized as a society of teachers and students where the whole, or the meaning of the whole, could be studied.

Certainly, we are long past believing either that there is a single nameable whole to be grasped, or that anyone can seriously claim to achieve the necessary breadth of knowledge to do so in one or more lifetimes, or even that there is a specific methodology for doing so. Yet in fact, Western societies have maintained the university as the principle institution devoted to teaching and learning on the highest level, entrusting, and even requiring, in most cases, that its leaders in virtually every field of endeavor gain its mark of approval. Whatever its limitations, society evidently agrees there is no better place than the university for the educating process to take place. Perhaps the question to pose at this point is: What is it that we believe goes on in a university to warrant this trust?

Does society merely want the assurance that our graduated artists and architects will be able to draw, our accountants count, our engineers build, and our doctors heal? For these skills, and most others, high-level trade or professional schools might—and often do—suffice. Obviously there is some more basic quality or transformation of mind we deem vital, especially in our experts and leaders, but more and more inherently in a democracy, in our people themselves. Granted that the meaning of the whole may never be entirely understood, the foundation stone of modern thought is that through the gradual application of human reason, important connections and relationships within that whole can be known and brought to benefit humankind. Indeed, the entire premise of democratic government rests on the assumption that self-governing individuals can grasp the complex dimensions of the vital issues of their times in order to make essential judgments as citizens.

The role of higher education in this process appears to be two-fold. To act responsibly, individuals must first be capable of making accurate judgments about the islands of purported truth constantly being discovered, claimed and mapped by others in the vast, oceanic unknown surrounding them. Critical thinking skills and a highly developed "crap detector," coupled with breadth of knowledge and exposure to the wide variety and elasticity of the human experience are essential ingredients here. Educated in such a fashion, a citizen, presumably, is less likely to be swept up in the passions of the moment and more likely to substitute reason for prejudice in making essential judgments.

A second level of educational achievement rests on the attainment of that harder-to-define attribute of mind which we call wisdom. Building on that solid base of knowledge and mastery of critical reasoning skills, wisdom also implies a high degree of self knowledge coupled with a greatly enhanced ability to evaluate complex issues and determine courses of action based on the application of the deepest perceptions and highest ideals of the individual or group involved.

Important as these achievements are, there is yet an even more basic transformative task for liberal education to perform, one which is certainly the hardest of all both to articulate and achieve in the academy as it is presently structured. Like all of us, students are invariably shaped by the increasing fragmentation characteristic of our world on virtually every level. It is hardly a new idea that the anguished, often frantic search for belonging, meaning, and belief in our powerfully individualistic and rapidly changing society contributes to many of its most destructive excesses.

Conditioned to the separateness of existence, prey to the reflexive divisions of psyche and self, mind/body, good/evil, us/them, male/female, human and animal, and myriad consequent subdistinctions, including the specialization and fragmentation of knowledge, our students come to us at a time of fundamental challenge to most of these rigid lines. A new universum of knowledge is emerging in which the rule appears to be wholeness and integration, interconnection and relatedness, rather than separation. It is here, in the service of healing the divisive and limiting breaches within and between ourselves, as well as between the human and natural worlds, that the contribution of a contemporary liberal education is potentially the greatest. For this to happen, however, a substantial rethinking of both the methods and goals of the educational process itself may be required. Whether a fragmented system of education can in any effective way produce integrated beings is perhaps the most significant question confronting practitioners of liberal education today.

In order to discuss what an alternative holistic model of education might look like, it is useful to define the term itself. More than 25 years ago, the late Arthur Koestler (1967, 1979) proposed the word *holon,* combining the Greek word for whole with the suffix which suggests a particle or part. A holon, as Koestler defined it, thus has the two seemingly contradictory properties of being both a whole and a part of larger wholes. A holon exists as a self-contained functional unit, independent and self-regulating within its environment; yet it simultaneously exists as a subordinated part of larger holons which themselves exist as part of a larger holarchy or hierarchy of self-regulating holons. Theorists such as Ken Wilbur (1996) have since applied the concept to an enormous range of phenomena from biological organisms, to mental processes to the organization of knowledge.

To make sense of this conception within an education setting, one might think of the university holon itself. Within it, individual students take individual courses in individual departments which are themselves parts of individual schools or divisions within the campus structure. Autonomous, self-regulating holons (students, courses, departments, divisions, campuses) clearly exist at each level within the larger system. Yet each unit simultaneously exists in supra-ordination to its own parts, and as a dependent part in subordination to controls on a higher level—that is, each holon is at all times both independent and relational. Finally, it is essential to recognize that each holon in this system exists, as well, as an information-carrying or cognitive representative of numerous other systems (students as parts of families, social and cultural groups, departments as representatives of disciplines and subdisciplines and made up of individual faculty members, universities as parts of larger public or private political, economic, and social structures, etc.)

Looked at closely, the dominant educational model as practiced from public schools to colleges and universities, rests on several basic assumptions. First among these is that exposure to introductory level, discipline-based courses followed by a graduated exposure to a specific discipline, will produce the liberally educated individual who is capable of making the critical and decisive judgments required of an educated citizen and a future societal leader in this day and age. While this is a model which has grown up under the guidance of the modern university, whose rules and boundaries it reflects, I suggest that it is based on the confusion of the powerful research tools of the disciplines, of which faculty are justifiably proud and to which they are deeply attached, with those best designed to bring about the personal and intellectual transformation which is actually at the heart of a liberal education.

In addition, the model most often rests on the beguilingly efficient and seemingly cost-effective method of a one-pointed system of information transmission which may actually work directly against the desired personal transformation discussed above by reinforcing both individual fragmentation and the habit of intellectual passivity while further confusing the act of absorbing information with the essence of education.

Finally, the model's deepest and most rarely challenged message is that specialized learning is somehow higher and of greater value than more generalized education, which for most students is perceived as something to get through as quickly as possible. The act of integrating and relating disparate bits of knowledge—making sense of it—for the most part, is left entirely to the individual student, busy as she or he is competing for grades, collecting units, and preparing for the job market. It is a task analogous to expecting each assembly line worker to collect and assemble enough individual parts to create a functioning automobile, while simultaneously installing spark plugs as the line speeds by.

It is hardly surprising that from somewhat different perspectives, major national reviews of higher education in America beginning in the 1980s all concluded that undergraduate education was suffering from a serious malaise brought on by just such factors as over-specialization and professionalization. David Kennedy, then president of Stanford University, publicly called for serious reconsideration of the relative place of research and teaching on his own prestigious campus, admitting that undergraduates, at what have been considered the best universities, were being cheated of an essential part of their education because of an increasing imbalance in favor of research. Despite strong criticism of the existing model, however, neither Kennedy's report nor other critical studies went very far in specifying either the viable alternatives available or the underlying educational or philosophical rationale necessary to support a liberal education outside of the framework that has traditionally existed. While suggesting that the answers may lie in smaller classes and closer contact between faculty and students, most critics stopped short of confronting two of the most basic issues of all: whether discipline-based, highly specialized education may itself be a barrier to the stated goals of a truly liberal education; and whether the almost universally-practiced methods of transmitting knowledge are adequate to the task at hand.

It is here, I would suggest, that the theory and practice of learning communities—as they have been evolving at campuses across the nation—can best contribute to educational reform efforts. Let me draw on two sources to illustrate the point: 1) the educational implications of Koestler's concept of the holon, and 2) nearly thirty years of learning community experience in the Hutchins School of Liberal Studies at Sonoma State University.

Koestler's nested conception offers a radically different educational vision largely because it shifts the focus to the hierarchical multiplicity of relationships implicit at each holarchic level and point-of-intersection of knowledge. The process of education is conceived of less as a narrowing, two dimensional ladder than as an expanding three dimensional web where the learner's growing mastery of an area of knowledge depends on his/her ability to integrate, connect, and define both the area's own patterns and relationships as well as its reciprocal and relational meaning relative to the larger patterns of which it is a part. Significantly, the model reconceives of the student as the active pattern maker at the center of the web, making and applying connections, rather than as the mountaineer scaling the peak of one specific body of knowledge.

The holarchic model recognizes that students at every educational level are involved in what my colleague, Nelson Kellogg, has called the cocreation of wisdom, a necessarily collective and interactive process which requires profound engagement with questions, ideas, and problems, as well as effective personal and intellectual interaction with others engaged in similar processes.

Most importantly, the holarchic model suggests that just as the transformative vision of Earth from space has changed forever our perspectives on our home planet, an aerial view of knowledge, looking across, beyond, and through the disciplines to discover and explore the fundamental questions and deepest connections underlying them, may similarly alter our vision of education.

It is within this framework that the experiment carried out in the Hutchins School can best be understood.

Despite its choice of name, the Hutchins School is, in fact, more a spiritual than a direct descendant of the undergraduate college created by Robert Hutchins and Mortimer Adler at the established and well-endowed University of Chicago in the 1930s. Created by a small group of interdisciplinary-minded faculty at a young, rural, and highly innovative branch of the California State University in northern California, the Hutchins School first opened its doors to a freshman class of 100 in the fall of 1969. Of the four founding faculty drawn from existing departments, only two survived the turmoil of the school's first year.

As was the case in numerous other experimental programs at the time, bitter differences rapidly surfaced over the program's philosophy and structure. In the Hutchins case, the structuralists won, establishing the principle that at the bare minimum, college classes—even experimental ones—required reading lists, regular meeting times, and recourse to traditional academic requirements and standards. One has to recall the extremely radical anti-establishment feeling pervading much of higher education (as well as most other aspects of national life) in the late 1960s and early 1970s to appreciate the utter sincerity and passion of those on both sides of such arguments. Any number of well-meaning experimental programs at universities and colleges across the nation foundered on just such disputes.

In outlining the principle features of the Hutchins School, two in particular seem significant for this discussion: the process of curriculum building and the undergraduate seminar. In contrast to the top-down evolution of courses and programs in every academic discipline, in which undergraduate education is conceived of as a series of graduated introductions to specialized fields, the Hutchins program evolved, as it were, from below. No specialized graduate-level liberal studies curriculum existed to drive undergraduate preparation. The surviving faculty, joined over the next two years by eleven new recruits hired directly into the Hutchins School, were in the enviable position of being charged with creating a meaningful undergraduate education from the ground up, and in the process with rethinking virtually all standard educational beliefs and formulas.

As in similar innovative programs, the evolution of the curriculum in large part reflected the growth and evolving interests of the faculty members themselves as they expanded outward from their original areas of specialization to address the issues central to interdisciplinary, liberal education. Initially sharing a common commitment to little more than the ideal of interdisciplinarity and the belief in education as a community process, the faculty eventually self-organized into teams, or what in those more radical days we called cadres, to work out the large thematic units that gradually allowed us to overcome the gravitational force of our own academic disciplines as well as the temptation to fall back upon an established canon of great books at the core of the curriculum. Keeping the larger focus on questions and issues we took to be essential for educated individuals to ask and encounter in the modern age, we gradually developed a sequence of integrated courses: "The Human Enigma," "In Search of Self," "Exploring the Unknown," and "Challenge and Response in the Modern World" as the program's fundamental building blocks—though with constantly evolving content and changing faculty.

At the risk of imposing the artificial harmony of theory on what was experienced most often as an organic, evolutionary, and at times highly contentious human process, I would propose, however, that the evolution of both the structure and content of the Hutchins Learning Community can be best understood as the emergence of a new and more comprehensive holistic form of learning. Using Koestler's formula once again, the act of stepping back from the sharp edge of discipline-based structures of knowledge in order to permit the emergence of less differentiated but more highly integrated holarchic forms—a paradoxical regression in order to progress—effectively opened the way for the evolution of new and more comprehensive ways of organizing learning and teaching.

Beyond the nature of the curriculum, the most distinctive feature of the Hutchins School itself has been its undergraduate seminar. Typically consisting of 12 to 14 students and a faculty member, the seminar has been the crucible in which the variety of ingredients available in the Hutchins Learning Community have been mixed. Unlike research-oriented seminars familiar to many who have attended graduate school, or presentation seminars common in the sciences in which experts share their specialized work, or highly directive seminars in which the more or less Socratic instructor asks and the students answer the relevant questions which move the discussion from predetermined point to point, the Hutchins seminar involves students from freshmen to seniors in a highly interactive process in which both instructors and students conduct a joint exploration of the topics and materials at hand.

While in almost all cases an individual faculty member or a faculty cadre will have planned the course, selected the readings, and designed the basic topics and issues of study, the open-ended nature of the Hutchins seminar mandates active student participation in shaping the interior structure of the course. As one senior described her learning experience, "we were given basic requirements and encouraged to fly. There is something elemental about being behind the wheel of your own education; it is liberating, empowering, and inspiring." Within the seminar, the issues raised by students are explored as seriously as those raised by the instructor, and in the process all participants are challenged to question their own personal and intellectual assumptions on every level. The seminar's very nature as a deliberately collective and noncompetitive exploration of truth provides a relatively safe testing ground in which students are encouraged to try out ideas and risk asking their own questions rather than continually relying on or responding to those of others. Refining their thoughts and judgments while confronting respectfully those of both other seminar members and accepted authorities, students gain an enormously empowering sense of their own intellectual power and responsibility. In the process they encounter a stimulating and evolving mixture of the best of classical and current thought, all of which is to be discussed, analyzed, written about, and employed in the context of many of the major issues and problems facing both the students and the contemporary world.

What is unique is less the specific curricular material, much if not all of which is used in a variety of combinations in other higher educational institutions, than the way in which it is used within the seminar itself. As a form of a learning community, the seminar's goal is decidedly not to showcase the brilliance and knowledge of either individual faculty or individual students. Instead, moving toward the more elemental meaning of the term community of scholars, its aim is to involve all participants in a common process of active inquiry and shared insight leading to intellectual growth and personal transformation. Coming from a traditionally competitive educational background, a student spoke of her dawning realization that "being a 'good' seminar participant required more than preparing my own analysis of the text," adding that, "a 'good' seminar is one where each person is both participant and facilitator. The responsibility of the seminar is shared and becomes a truly rich experience."

Faculty and students become colearners in a process which vastly revises the traditional relationship between the two, requiring an often ego-threatening abandonment by the faculty member of the protective barriers provided by his or her professional expertise and status. The seminar format itself removes the physical support of podium and lectern. Wide-ranging and often unpredictable discussions render obsolete carefully crafted notes and a planned coverage schedule of material. Excursions outside the faculty member's syllabus or even original areas of specialization demand a constant process of reading, thinking, and exploring, akin to, but more advanced than that being undergone by the students themselves. This does not mean, however, that the instructor's hard-earned expertise is useless or abandoned, only that it is used in a very different fashion and for significantly different goals. One newer faculty member likens the facilitator's role in a Hutchins seminar to that of an artist whose trained viewfinder and carefully refined sensibilities are most powerfully employed in enabling others to see reality in new ways and aiding them in framing the gems of their own visions more effectively.

Essential to any faculty member's transformation from purveyor of specialized knowledge to facilitator of interdisciplinary learning is his or her active participation in faculty cadres where courses and themes are formulated and through which the process of continuing interdisciplinary faculty education occurs. Ideally, providing faculty members with a learning community of their own in which pedagogical strategies, knowledge, and insight are shared, the cadre serves likewise as a primary vehicle for the creation of new and unique course syntheses.

For the student, the format poses a series of immediate challenges. Since virtually all of his or her previous education occurred within the context of individual competition (for grades, attention, standardized test scores, etc.) effectively depicted by Paolo Freire's (1970) "banking" model of knowledge accumulation, the collective model of the seminar initiates a serious process of unlearning deeply entrenched behavioral patterns and assumptions. Reflecting back at the end of her Hutchins experience, one student admitted frankly that "I did not enter the program to become educated. I entered it to become an educator." Yet the seminar experience of being part of a team of "twelve to fourteen students and one professor working together to solve a problem . . ." raising and attempting to answer "some of the truly puzzling questions of our time . . ." gradually led to her recognition "that my education has now just begun."

Functioning in the seminar likewise requires a combination of both active and interactive learning skills which often are neither taught nor tolerated in the traditional classroom. Though critical thought and rigorous analysis of texts and ideas are required, it is equally essential that the seminar become what one proponent calls "a hospitable environment" in which "every attempt at truth, no matter how off the mark, is a contribution to the larger search for corporate and consensual truth" (Palmer, 1989, p. 25). This does not imply absence of conflict and disagreement, only that these exciting and inevitable differences in individual perception and levels of understanding be treated as part of a larger process of personal and intellectual community-building. Assessing the workings of the seminar process itself, one student described the task as one of developing, "a vocabulary to give voice to the intricate processes which constitute the keystone of meaningful dialog." Her recognition that the seminar's goal of increasing understanding rather than winning a game of intellectual hand-to-hand combat is of critical importance in defining the meaning of both a true learning community and a holistic liberal education today.

Underlying this model of learning is indeed an alternative epistemology, one in which, as Parker J. Palmer (1989) has written, "the relational nature of reality" (p. 24) supersedes a previously held vision of separation, fragmentation, individualism, and simple objectivism. Here we move to "juxtapose analysis with synthesis, integration, and the creative act" (p. 24). For this to occur effectively in the classroom, a radical shift in emphasis is essential. What may be appropriate training for specialized research in the disciplines should be recognized as counterproductive in creating the conditions for liberal learning, particularly when we are faced with questions which fall outside the boundaries of any single field or collection of disciplines.

We are increasingly being confronted with the fact that the important issues regarding human life, our coexistence with nature and the planet, the proper allocation of natural, social, and human resources, and our judgments about the uses of our immensely powerful technological tools cannot and should not be left to specialists alone. While we necessarily concern ourselves with the seemingly mundane requirements and activities of our individual lives, we are now inevitably faced with the larger consequences and broader relational web of those actions.

In many ways, the seminar models for students an alternative method of dealing with the complex issues which face all of us. A learning community which supports the individual in exploring both his or her own ignorance and knowledge enhances not only external but internal learning. The variety of perspectives, observations, and experiences readily available on any topic provide a healthy antidote to the typical isolation of traditional learning experiences, contributing to a deep understanding of alternative ways of seeing reality. The fact that the "right road" alluded to in Dante's classic lines has always been "wholly lost and gone" (1960, p. 71) can serve symbolically as a starting point for the collective search which has always been central to a liberal education. Gide's warning that our greatest enemy may be the persistent human tendency to accept answers—our own or those of others—and to stop asking questions is the paradoxical meat and drink of the seminar process.

If the real value of the liberal education process is that through it students will learn how to live successfully in the vast middle ground between attachment to absolute truths and surrender to powerlessness and personal despair, and to make accurate, creative, and wise judgments about the important issues confronting them as individuals who are also part of a social community, then a serious reconsideration of current educational structures is essential. Just as the eternal questions of good, evil, beauty, truth, love, justice, and meaning cannot be answered on a scantron sheet, so the academy cannot pretend to confront them adequately without providing an interactive, relational, and assessable structure in which students and teachers can search for their own answers together.

Wholeness will not be found either in isolation or absolutes, but by individuals who have confronted and challenged their own definitions and limitations, using all the tools universities have to offer, and who have also developed their own identities within true learning communities.

References

Dante, A. (1960). *The divine comedy, canto I* (D. L. Sayers, Trans.). New York, NY: Penguin.

Freire, P. (1970). *Pedagogy of the oppressed.* New York, NY: Seabury.

Koestler, A. (1967). *The ghost in the machine.* London, England: Hutchinson.

Koestler, A. (1979). *Janus: A summing up.* New York, NY: Vintage.

Palmer, P. J. (1989, September/October). Community, conflict, and ways of knowing: Ways to deepen our educational agenda. *Change, 21* (5), 25.

Wilbur, K. (1996). *A brief history of everything.* Boston: MA: Shambala.

9

Toward an Interdisciplinary Epistemology: Faculty Culture and Institutional Change

Grant H. Cornwell and Eve W. Stoddard
St. Lawrence University

Much like larger societies, campus communities have dominant cultures, stratification, alternative, resistant, and emerging cultures (Williams, 1976). Traditional faculties have both horizontal stratification in the form of ranks and tenure and vertical stratification in the form of disciplines. This chapter will use St. Lawrence University (SLU), a small liberal arts college in northern New York, as a case study to analyze the perils and rewards of interdisciplinary work at traditional institutions. We are specifically interested in analyzing how interdisciplinary teaching and collective interdisciplinary scholarship have, tentatively and partially, transformed institutional culture. As we focus on the word "interdisciplinary," it is instructive to pause over the sedimented meanings of the word discipline, along the lines Foucault (1997) pursued in *Discipline and Punish.* A discipline is a reified set of practices and beliefs to which one apprentices oneself. To be disciplined (adjective) is to be bound strictly to the proper rules and practices of the discipline. One can be self-disciplined: having internalized the rules of practice, one enforces them on oneself, with no need of external authority. The earning of a PhD, and subsequently, of tenure, signifies that one has achieved this level of self-discipline. Thus, the horizontal stratification system both depends on and enforces the vertical stratification of separate academic disciplines.

On the other hand, to be disciplined (verb) by authorities is to be punished, to have the boundaries of the discipline imprinted on one's body so that one can incorporate them into a regime of self-discipline. Once one achieves sufficient self-discipline and mastery of the discipline, one becomes an authority who can both teach the discipline and discipline those who fail in its performance. Hence, traditional disciplines are fields of power/knowledge bounded with invisible electric fences. Those who cross those boundaries wearing their academic degrees get punished like dogs who fail to heed the beeps on their electronic collars. Those who perform their discipline well, developing it further, but within bounds, receive rewards like publication, promotion, and tenure. They also receive the less tangible but potent reward of comfort with and approval from their peers, both at their home campus and in the larger academic community.

Nonetheless, despite the strict methods and bounds of traditional disciplinary inquiry, academic culture is founded on the possibility of resistance and subversion. The essential value of academic research is, after all, the expansion and reevaluation of knowledge. Traditional disciplines encourage these goals, but they assume that they can only be achieved through the bounded and legitimated methods and materials of inquiry. Thus, specialized research looks deeply at a small patch of ground well within the boundaries of the fence. When one goes so far as to challenge the sufficiency of the discipline itself, punishment kicks in. It is the senior peers of the discipline who judge the legitimacy of the methods, and these are people who have been thoroughly disciplined to stay within bounds. At a traditional college or university, the weight of power, structure, and practice is vested in these well-disciplined senior peers. Because of vertical stratification throughout graduate school and the probationary period of teaching, individuals rarely encounter peers who question the foundational assumptions of the discipline. Interdisciplinary teaching and learning offer exactly such questions.

Interdisciplinary inquiry turns off the electric fence and opens up worlds of new questions, practices, and horizons. These questions can be as unsettling to the willing explorer who has incorporated the rules of the discipline as they are to the disapproving senior peers guarding the gateway. The philosopher is asked to think about emotions, and the literary critic is asked to think about evolutionary hypotheses about aesthetics. An economist is asked to think about the aesthetic or social quality of life for those calculated in the GDP. Scientists are asked to consider that Africans have a science of their own that does not depend on universal cause and effect. Anyone who has earned a PhD in a discipline has internalized rigid notions of what counts and what does not count as legitimate scholarship. She or he may be willing to concede that a criterion counts for another discipline, but that is quite different from agreeing to count it as part of his or her own research or teaching.

It is no accident that the language in the preceding sentences echoes the language of multi- or intercultural encounter. The first step in interdisciplinary collaboration, whether in teaching or research, is accepting the different practices and beliefs of others. This stage parallels the evolution of cultural relativism, both historically through voyages of exploration, and developmentally in the individual. Disciplines are like separate cultures and the work of interdisciplinary inquiry parallels the work of intercultural knowledge. What is more, learning to listen and talk to colleagues trained in other disciplines has many of the same complexities and pitfalls as intercultural communication. In short, disciplines are discourse communities, bounded cultures, and interdisciplinary teaching and scholarship calls for and teaches earnest listening, patience to stay in conversation through struggle, and a disposition to see differences as productive. But the second phase of interdisciplinary collaboration transcends the comparison or juxtaposition of two ways of knowing two cultures. The next phase is radically revaluing one's own inquiry to incorporate the questions, methods, and perspectives of others, to perceive the partiality of disciplinary practices.

If one persists long enough in an interdisciplinary project or program, ultimately a kind of Creole language and culture emerges, a new set of discourses and practices which draws on the original ones but is not reducible to them. It is able to see new and different questions and issues, and to draw on multiple methods and the knowledge to address them. In Williams' terms, such Creolized disciplines can be alternative, resistant, or emergent. For example, women's studies can be seen as an emergent discipline with its own canons, methods, and issues, but it can also be alternative or resistant to the traditional discursive practices of disciplines. It would be alternative if it were content to coexist peacefully with traditional structures, offering a different mode of learning and knowing to its faculty and students. Insofar as it sought to challenge and undermine the authority and hierarchies of the university as a whole, to reconfigure them along feminist lines, it would be resistant.

This chapter chronicles a recent ten-year period of intense interdisciplinary faculty and curriculum development at St. Lawrence University, focusing on two different initiatives, the First-Year Program and the Cultural Encounters Program. Begun in 1987, the First-Year Program is a required year-long, living/learning program in which students take a multidisciplinary course taught by faculty from three different disciplines. Started in 1992, Cultural Encounters was initially an externally funded faculty seminar aimed at significantly reeducating faculty and creating an internationally based general education curriculum. Whereas the faculty development in the First-Year Program comes primarily through the practice of team teaching, in Cultural Encounters it is primarily through group reading, discussion, and field study. We will discuss the programs, their goals, their political history, and we will argue that participation in these programs has indelibly changed the professional identity of many, in some cases at high cost.

Beginning with the planning for the pilot First-Year Program in 1986–1987, through its evaluation and revision in 1990–1992, and moving onto the Cultural Encounters initiative, we look at major areas of cross-disciplinary development as well as incidents of backlash, ever mindful that the departmental power structure remains with us. The structural outcome has been a substantially transformed curriculum and faculty culture, though the jury is out on whether the revolution will survive. The most certain outcome is that at least a third of the faculty has experienced transformative developments in pedagogy and/or epistemology, developments wrought through tremendous releases of creativity as disciplinary walls eroded or crumbled under the pressure of interdisciplinary team teaching and collective reading seminars.[1]

The First-Year Program created a kind of institutional ferment and destabilization which allowed for a dramatic shift in faculty culture. In the early 1980s, SLU had a traditional, upper-middle class, predominantly male and WASP faculty. For those in the majority it was a comfortable, friendly small community. Departments reigned supreme as self-reproducing fiefdoms which were held in fealty to the dean and president. What was good for the department was held to be good for the students, the institution, and the individual faculty member. In 1986–1987, under a new dean, the faculty voted in a pilot version of the First-Year Program. The votes came from segments of the faculty with widely differing motives and goals. Some thought they were voting in a fairly traditional core curriculum which would ground students in the essential texts and ideas of high western culture. Others thought they were voting for an enhanced set of courses in writing and speaking skills. Others thought they were revolutionizing instruction by mandating multidisciplinary team-taught courses. Others were focused on changing a student culture oriented around the Greek system and partying by implementing a living/learning program.

Almost overnight, a faculty which had been used to departmental autonomy and automatic reproduction was faced with a university core curriculum which demanded that faculty team-teach interdisciplinary material, that all participating faculty teach writing, speaking, and researching skills, and that all participants cross the boundary between academic and student affairs. Furthermore, staffing decisions would heretofore take into account not only departmental needs, but also university-wide needs. No longer could the English department assume that a Shakespearean would be replaced by another Shakespearean. By 1988–1989, the first year that the First-Year Program served all first-year students, there was a huge gulf of engagement and experience between those in the First-Year Program and those outside, which is not to say that political support for the program divided along that fault line, but rather that a fault line had emerged between those practicing teaching in an alternative culture and those continuing to teach within departmental bounds, often within a traditional lecture format.

In other words, the First-Year Program developed first into an alternative faculty culture at St. Lawrence, but then into a resistant and finally into an emergent one. Interdisciplinary team teaching in a living/learning structure became transformative faculty development, and both individuals and institutional culture were transformed. The program is a learning community composed of learning communities; the 36 faculty who mount the program each year, and the hundred or so who have cycled through it, participate in a discourse about teaching and learning which now has a history, epic tales of success and failure, communal norms and practices, even annual rituals. When the program was young, it occupied the space of a rebellious subculture; it was implicitly and explicitly critical of the dominant institutional culture. Both its curriculum and pedagogy were subversive of institutional norms of teaching and learning. Interdisciplinary team teaching challenged the accepted domains of professorial authority. Since all faculty in the First-Year Program teach writing, speaking, and research, previously comfortable distinctions between content inquiry and skill development came under scrutiny. Collaborative learning pedagogy suggested that knowledge was communal rather than private property. And most subversively, the living/learning structure of the First-Year Program bridged deeply entrenched boundaries between faculty and student development staff, especially with regard to who has responsibility for what.

Ultimately, a program can only assume the position of a critical upstart for so long. Programs (and persons) who occupy that position typically exhaust themselves. Either they disappear in failure, and are looked back on as quaint, idealistic, ineffectual experiments, the dominant culture reasserting its hegemony, or they succeed in some measure in transforming the dominant culture. The First-Year Program is securely institutionalized. Perhaps the best evidence of this is that its long-standing critics now complain that its norms and values have themselves become hegemonic. There is much lost and much gained through this incremental shift in positionality. One gain is that St. Lawrence has a program which engages its faculty in sustained and critical reflection on teaching.

It is ironic that one of the most important outcomes of the First-Year Program, faculty development, is an epiphenomenon. An external evaluator, Patrick Hill, brought this to our attention: "For many or most of them [SLU faculty], the FYP experience has been a rich and rewarding faculty development experience. Yet the enabling legislation of the FYP and the literature of FYP does not speak of faculty development as a purpose of the program" (1991, p. 18). We have since sought to become more intentional about this dimension of the program. We now offer many more in-service workshops and seminars on teaching; we have added a series of training sessions for faculty entering the program; and we take care to read and discuss as a program new literature that bears upon our work. Still, we would argue, that for all our efforts, the most powerful location of faculty development within the First-Year Program remains where it has always been, in the dynamics of interdisciplinary team teaching.

Since its inception, the program has been a laboratory for innovative pedagogy. Part of this was by design; one of the original mandates of the First-Year Program was to help entering students become more active, engaged, and critical learners. Part of this is also due to the fact that teaching in the First-Year Program is voluntary, and those who are drawn to it tend to be those who enjoy being creative and self-reflexive with their teaching. But pedagogical innovation is also what is bound to occur when three faculty from different disciplines together work out how to teach a course. Assignment designs and college research projects tend to be elaborate and varied. Since we share our work with one another, in an atmosphere which is sometimes playfully boastful, there is a pedagogical lore that has developed about what works and what doesn't. Successes are impressive, failures legendary.

Three faculty make up a First-Year Program team; ideally, through a delicate and organic process of team formation, a person in the natural sciences, a person in the social sciences, and a person in the arts or humanities find that there are topical or thematic interests that they share in common. Ideally, they also find one another's company sufficiently delightful that they can imagine spending the hours, the years, together that it takes to create and implement a successful First-Year Program college. The first growth spurt is when the team sets about in earnest to define collaboratively the thematic focus of the college. For example, it may happen that a biologist, a historian, and a philosopher agree that they have a shared interest in how humans construct their relationships with the natural world, and they think this area would be rich and appropriate for first-year students. The intercultural communication, which is essentially what is called for in interdisciplinary team teaching, begins when each tries to explain to the others how she would conceptualize such a course. What are the central questions? What would a coherent organization of the inquiry look like?

There have been cases in the First-Year Program where a team which appeared perfectly matched broke down in this early stage. As scholars trained in disciplines, this conversation is for many the first time the point of view and basic assumptions of the disciplines come under scrutiny. Sometimes the scrutiny can be hostile, intolerant, and dismissive. Even when good will prevails between the interlocutors, people have bailed out at this point because they correctly grasp the commitment interdisciplinary team teaching requires to listening, to explaining one's fundamental beliefs without defensiveness, and in this way to making oneself intellectually vulnerable. Of course, when teams do hang together through this early process, a lot has already happened that can make one a better teacher and scholar. The goal is not to persuade or agree, but to listen and talk across basic differences, and then build collaboratively a vision for a course which can accommodate the differences in creative tension. By the time teams get to the point of writing the paragraph description required for the First-Year Program catalog, they have a basis for understanding one another that will undergird the course building process in the subsequent stages.

Constructing a syllabus with an interdisciplinary team tends to be an exercise in reigning in enthusiasms. As faculty liberate themselves from the discipline of disciplines there emerges a collective, creative energy, the products of which are a joy for the faculty, though typically excessive. At this stage teams are fully revved-up; the excesses which are born of this collaboration are evidence of the constraints faculty work under, alone, in their disciplines. In our ten-year history with the First-Year Program, it is predictable that the first time a team offers a course they will try to do too much, and that with each subsequent year course become more successful with less material.

The faculty development at this stage lies in encountering questions, methods, and texts from other disciplinary cultures. Most faculty report that this process, which amounts to an interdisciplinary miniseminar in one's area, is one of the most energizing and intellectually rewarding dimensions of working in the First-Year Program. This does not mean, of course, that negotiations are not vigorous when it comes time actually to agree upon what will be included and excluded from a syllabus. But at this point the groundwork has been laid, and the talks have much more the tenor of building with than fighting for.

The First-Year Program has ambitious skill development goals, and every college is expected to devote serious attention to working with students on writing, speaking, and research. Here again, interdisciplinary team teaching develops faculty by first asking them to become articulate about their standards, goals, and methods, and then by asking them to consider those of their teammates trained in different disciplines. Typically, the second growth spurt for a faculty team comes when they have to translate the interdisciplinary ideas and texts they have been discovering into elaborate writing, speaking, and research projects for their students. This can seem like an overwhelming challenge, but it ends up producing collaborative projects that students will never forget, such as mosaic tile structures in which each student designs a group of tiles to represent his or her identities, or a theatrical production of personal narratives about women's development, or a health fair for the whole campus.

There are two remaining dimensions of faculty development in the First-Year Program that merit discussion, and both occur during the actual unfolding of the course over the year. Team teaching in the program does not, when it's working up to its ideals, mean serial teaching. While it is true that some teams resort simply to taking turns teaching texts or even whole units, this often signals a team dynamic which is less than mutual, creative, and collaborative. What is more common is that someone will present to the team a plan for how to teach a certain text or unit, work it out collaboratively with them, and then take primary responsibility for its implementation. Also common for more experienced teams is something that would be the pedagogical equivalent of improvisational jazz; here all three faculty share the front of the classroom, teaching a text by building on one another's comments and working with the students in ways that have the spontaneity (and risk) of trading riffs. This way of working calls for a good deal of clarity about goals and process before each class, and it also means that after each class there is an opportunity for critical reflection. Many faculty say that it is the regular debriefing sessions, sometimes formally part of the team's schedule, often less formal but no less intense, that makes teaching in the First-Year Program so productive of growth as a teacher. To see one's colleagues teach, day in and day out, to discuss their teaching and one's own with them over the course of a year, is, in the end, the most powerful vehicle of faculty development in the First-Year Program.

Thus far we have emphasized the effects of interdisciplinary team teaching for faculty development. But St. Lawrence's First-Year Program asks more of faculty than crossing the boundaries of academic disciplines; it asks them more radically to cross the line that divides students' social lives from their course work.[2] A First-Year Program team is composed of more than simply the faculty; it includes as well three upper-class students selected and trained as college assistants, who live in the colleges, an upper-class student who is, ideally, an alumnus/ae of the First-Year college who is trained as a writing and research tutor, and a masters level, student development professional, who helps work with issues of student and community development. Working in a living/learning program, faculty must attend to the development of the whole student, and we have learned that this means both attending to the individuals in one's college and to the dynamics and vitality of the college itself, as a community. This is complicated, risky business, which faculty are neither trained for, nor typically well-suited to attempt on their own. While there is some division of labor, and faculty do not have to negotiate the academic curriculum with the student development members on their teams, the most successful colleges are those where the faculty listen closely to them, and heed their advice. Further, faculty have to think holistically about the college as a community of learners if the project is to be successful. Even those who enter into the First-Year Program espousing no interest in students' lives or development outside the classroom, realize quickly that there is tremendous promise and peril in working in a living/learning program. The ideal is stated in the program's goals:

> The major goal of the First-Year Program is to promote the integration of academic and social experience. First-Year Program colleges, when successful, develop into communities of learners who value intellectual collaboration and critical reflection. Conversations begun in the classroom on theories, ideas, beliefs, and values are continued in the residence halls, examined, evaluated, measured against students' experience, and picked up again when class reconvenes. In these colleges collaboration and cooperation on readings, papers, and projects help students discover one another as colearners, as different persons with different strengths and interests who have come to this institution to engage in a common project. Thus, the goal of living and learning together is to help students understand how critical intellectual inquiry can directly inform their experience, both subjectively, in their individual reflection on their identity, beliefs, and values, and socially, in the choices they make in how they live together. (First-Year Program Living/Learning Component, 1994)

Faculty seek to achieve this goal by assigning collaborative projects to be done outside of class. Students are asked to read one another's drafts, to plan presentations together, and to cooperate in preparing for exams. In these ways, locating First-Year Program colleges in residential communities has promoted the academic goals of the program, and enabled faculty to think in new ways about how students can learn together.

There is, of course, a dark side to living/learning programs, which confront faculty with issues of gender, substance abuse, and racism, issues faculty are more comfortable with in theory, as large, abstract problems of modern society. In a living/learning program these issues and others can emerge in ways that make palpable their complexity, their intractability, and their capacity to inhibit growth, development, and learning, not just in those intimately involved, but in the larger communities. It is quite different to confront these issues in lived experience, with all of their immediacy, urgency, and reality, than through texts and data. A frequent first reaction of faculty when confronted with these issues is to recoil, to treat them as incursions, to insist that the student development members of the college team make them go away. Quickly, though, faculty realize that the anticommunal, antidemocratic social ills prompted by differences of race, gender, and class are also profoundly disruptive of teaching and learning. The tensions that arise, the differences in power that are exercised, cannot be bracketed in a living/learning community to allow for a rarefied academic space. These social relations in part construct every person's position within the workings of the course; they condition what students and faculty can bring to the collaborative learning process and what they can take away.

What this means is that team teaching in a living/learning community demands that faculty bring all of their critical acumen to bear on the development of the college as a whole, on its members individually as well as on the social and political dynamics of the community. This kind of faculty development can be transformative; it gives faculty intimate access to student culture, and thus affords a deep understanding of who it is we are teaching. It also brings home the point that knowers are whole persons, and that ability to know, to participate in the construction of knowledge, is not some simple quality, intelligence, that can be plotted on a hierarchical continuum. Each person's position in a learning community, what one can contribute, what one can take away, is conditioned by all of the social benefits and burdens one brings to the situation. Working out specific pedagogical implications of this insight, with one's team members, is a long-term project. It is not for the faint of heart. It is not for the teacher who wants a casual, distanced relationship with her or his profession. But the rewards for those who make the commitment to this kind of teaching, to be this kind of teacher, are ample.

The First-Year Program was initially intended as the first of a series of major curriculum reforms to unfold over a number of years. In 1990, the Association of American Colleges Cultural Legacies Project offered a way to think about sophomore and senior curricular initiatives for students. A number of faculty joined the Cultural Legacies reading seminar out of an intellectual interest in the subject matter, but also out of a desire to continue changing institutional culture. While some of the participants had been in the First-Year Program, a number had not. That seminar became the basis for the Cultural Encounters Project, the second program we will analyze. Whereas faculty development was an offshoot of the First-Year Program, it was the central focus of Cultural Encounters. As part of the initial three-year grant, funded by FIPSE and Mellon, participating faculty committed to two years of reading seminars, month-long field study in Kenya and India over two consecutive summers, and to developing one new course. In return they were paid a substantial stipend.[3] This degree of commitment was viewed as extensive, since time for scholarly research at a liberal arts college is already limited mostly to vacation time. Junior faculty who signed on felt they were taking a considerable risk with their careers.

The goal of Cultural Encounters was to create a new intellectual paradigm for the study of cultural interactions globally, both historically and at present. It would be cross-disciplinary and transnational in its approach, eschewing the binary oppositions of the culture wars, incorporating western and nonwestern material in every course, studying self and other dialectically. This paradigm would inform an alternative general education system which would have as its objective preparing students to be global citizens in the 21st century.

As interdisciplinary faculty development initiatives, the First-Year Program and Cultural Encounters manifested important similarities and differences. First of all, the beginning years of both were very rocky. If we were to generalize from these small samples we could say that most faculty enter into interdisciplinary work suspicious of differences and defensive of their own disciplinary assumptions and points of view. Part of this guardedness comes from faculty wanting to feel that they have something to offer the collective enterprise, and that what they have to offer comes from the depth of their scholarly training in their disciplines. Because disciplinary training is so rigidly enforced and reified through the initiation processes of graduate school and tenure, most initiates genuinely believe that theirs is the best and most sufficient approach to knowledge. The guardedness also comes from having to respond to the caricatures of and prejudices toward one's discipline held by one's colleagues, which again are manifestations of internalized disciplinary chauvinism. It is difficult for an economist to hear her colleagues dismiss the discipline as simply being in the service of corporate capitalism. And yet that happened. It is difficult for a literary critic to hear his colleagues dismiss literature as simply appealing to emotions, and persuading readers without data. And yet that happened.

There were eleven disciplines represented among the initial group of seventeen participants. Over the five year history of the endeavor, only five departments and programs have not had participants in the reading seminar (chemistry, physics, education, Canadian studies, environmental studies).

In the early phase of Cultural Encounters, area studies specialists could not imagine what poets could have to contribute, and literary theorists scoffed at the naïve empiricism of social scientists. Feminists felt silenced and nonfeminists thought we talked about nothing but women's issues. Third World specialists felt we put their cultures in an inferior light by reading mythological texts against the philosophical texts of the European Enlightenment. In other words, in the early meetings we all became aware of our own biases, prejudices, and ignorance of other disciplines. But we did not do it well or carefully; there were arguments, and bruised egos, and uncollegial exchanges that several times nearly scuttled the whole project. Complex and multilayered vectors of distrust developed, and people sought alliances on the bases of particular commonalities, at times to avoid feeling completely alienated. Sometimes it seemed that the only thing that kept people coming was that they had made a formal commitment and were being paid a substantial stipend. Again, we find the analogy to intercultural communication and conflict compelling. Nonetheless, participants also felt exhilarated by what they were learning. Being in Cultural Encounters was like starting graduate study over again for many of the faculty involved.

An overnight retreat in January began to create a sense of solidarity as participants found they shared some basic vision of what the Cultural Encounters courses would look like. But it was the field study in Kenya that finally cemented the group's collective identity. It took the shared lived experience of the trip in which we were more human beings than academic specialists to create trust among the members of the seminar. It was disciplinary and area identities which had inhibited that trust and made common discussion exceedingly difficult. This replicated the experience of the first year's planning for the First-Year Program. It was only at the planning retreat in the Adirondacks that the pilot faculty began to trust each other and to feel part of a shared project.

The First-Year Program had a common syllabus for its first four years and during that time faculty debates on what to include were somewhat similar to the debates in Cultural Encounters over readings and ideas. However, the program subsequently shifted to a model in which each college had a different theme, so the interdisciplinary discussion became rooted only in a three-person team. Since these people had a common task to perform, creating a syllabus and teaching a course, their interdisciplinary encounters became quite enthusiastic and productive. Our experience verifies claims that intercultural alliances work best when persons of different backgrounds come together to solve a common problem or to accomplish a task. They are most difficult when they take place in a contextless discussion with no particular goal.

As the years have gone by, the Cultural Encounters seminar has reconstituted itself several times and each time there have been different insights and different conflicts, but each set of conflicts mirrors issues which arise among most groups doing intellectual, interdisciplinary, or political work. The persistence of conflict and struggle, along with the fact that people keep coming back to the group, suggests that growth and transformation are not painless, but they are rewarding. Our biggest success is evidenced in people's identification with both the First-Year Program and Cultural Encounters. A significant number of participants have created new professional identities for themselves out of these efforts. In particular at least nine faculty trained in Eurocentric fields have expanded their teaching and research to new areas, more global in scope and more self-reflective about the points of view being represented.

The most significant change for those already trained in area studies has been increased cross-disciplinary theoretical development. Others have changed their pedagogies to include more self-reflection through writing. A new European studies program which is based on multiculturalism has been created. The European abroad programs have begun to take a more multicultural approach to the nation-states they inhabit.

Given the overwhelmingly positive impact of the project on many individuals and on institutional culture, it is still important to reflect on the conflicts we have had and continue to have. In the second year of Cultural Encounters, the struggles revolved around theory versus empirical knowledge, especially science. We tried having each meeting facilitated by partners, one an expert and one completely ignorant of the topic to be discussed. But we utterly failed at incorporating science satisfactorily into the project. As in the First-Year Program, scientists would not accept learning about science in the guise of history or philosophy of science as "doing science." Admittedly, we the authors of this piece, and the directors of the First-Year Program and Cultural Encounters are humanists, so our account of this impasse is biased. It is our perspective that a number of scientists participating willingly in both initiatives have felt frustrated because they want science to be practiced by those in other disciplines. They feel that we are reading novels and philosophy and ethnographies, so we should practice science too. From our humanist perspectives, they fail to see that we are not writing novels or doing philosophy; we are learning about these areas of expression and analysis. To these scientists, any method of inquiry which is not disciplinary turns the inquiry into "not-science." While this has been a great failure and frustration politically and interpersonally, it has served to illuminate the central role of science per se within western culture, and hence to advance our study of cultural encounters.[4]

The subsequent years of the seminar have brought influxes of new participants. Feminism has remained a very sore point in terms of what can be discussed and how it is discussed, whether attention should be paid to personal feelings or to texts, who feels comfortable in the group and who does not. In 1996–1997, the fifth year of the seminar, this issue caused a near breakdown of the reading seminar. Ironically, the third and fourth years, which were organized by several male faculty with a social science orientation, were the least troubled by internal struggle because the few feminists in the group were willing to go with the flow. In the fifth year, a critical mass of both feminists and people who identify outside the dominant cultural/class identity stood up for their perspectives on how a group studying intercultural issues should conduct its discussions. This conflict has been threatening because everyone there has a strong investment in the Cultural Encounters seminar. As a reading group continues over many years, it is easy to forget that new membership requires constant attention to process and to conscious reflection on goals. No longer does the Cultural Encounters seminar have a stipend or a stated term of commitment; thus it is at great risk for dissolution if the participants cannot find common ground and trust. In addition its very success has spawned competition. In 1996–1997, there were two other interdisciplinary reading seminars going on, so people can now choose which group is most amenable to their styles and interests. This makes life more comfortable within each group, but we face the question of whether grappling with truly incommensurate assumptions and processes is beneficial or inhibiting to intellectual growth.

These are some of the problems which beset the internal dynamics of the seminar, but they now occur among people who share a belief in continuing interdisciplinary and intercultural discourse across differences. A substantial percentage of St. Lawrence's faculty now share a basic attitude that continuing to question one's knowledge and assumptions is important for those who practice the profession of teaching. They share the belief that it is not adequate for us to pass on knowledge we have received in graduate school, that neither the knowledge nor the method of passing on received wisdom is adequate. And they share a belief that getting together with colleagues from across departments to talk about ideas and curricular politics and values is essential to the life of an academic community. Most of these faculty receive their sustenance as St. Lawrence faculty members from faculty seminars and interdisciplinary program boards rather than from departmental homes. And this puts them at odds with what is still the power structure, what controls hiring and tenure and promotion.

St. Lawrence has become a somewhat paradoxical institution in this respect: Interdisciplinary programs receive attention and support from the administration, and many faculty and students are involved in them. Nonetheless, departments retain their entrenched structural power. Senior faculty end up overextended, serving of necessity the department which hired and tenured them, while building interdisciplinary programs as an extra because they believe in them and receive great satisfaction from faculty development projects. The departmental structure has an inertia which maintains it through changes in personnel, but newer programs require immense energy and attention for their survival. A single personnel change, in faculty or the dean's office, can mean renegotiating the basic terms of a program's existence. For example, when the person hired to coordinate the gender studies program assumed the leadership of the First-Year Program, she was replaced in her department by a visiting professor, but it was assumed someone already on the faculty would look after gender studies as a casual addition to her other duties. It turned out, however, that the only tenured members of gender studies were already occupying roles as coordinators of other programs. This is one instance which demonstrates the fragility of interdisciplinary programs versus departments.

Many faculty, especially junior ones, end up caught between what are two different cultures. They receive enthusiastic advice from one set of colleagues about joining interdisciplinary programs, and equally vigorous advice from senior departmental colleagues about building an identity within the department. For those who have no particular desire to work outside the department, this becomes a matter of political strategy, and for some, a matter of high stress. Several faculty hired with the understanding that they would serve in the First-Year Program have found themselves unprepared by graduate training and temperament for the experience. One ended up leaving the institution because of the repercussions, but the others have simply decided to teach exclusively within their departments in the future.

For those who were attracted to St. Lawrence by the excitement of the First-Year Program or Cultural Encounters, conflicts between department and program obligations can be distressing. One new faculty member, hired in part because of her interdisciplinary interests, joined Cultural Encounters enthusiastically only to find that department meetings, departmental search committee meetings, and science colloquia constantly conflicted with Cultural Encounters meetings. She was told formally and informally that missing these to attend Cultural Encounters would prove disastrous to her position in the department. When she expressed great enthusiasm for the First-Year Program and Cultural Encounters, and failed to demonstrate strong commitment to the department per se, she was criticized in a first-year evaluation for showing more enthusiasm for university initiatives than for departmental ones. She decided to leave St. Lawrence after her second year. When one of the most active participants in Cultural Encounters was initially denied tenure, his department chair asked why he should fight for someone who belongs more to Cultural Encounters than to the department. Many suspected that the chair had not presented the strongest possible case for this person because his scholarly values did not adhere strictly enough to the canons of the discipline. But it was unclear whether the chair intended to do this or was unable to perceive the value of extra departmental work. Apparently, the tenure and promotion committee saw rich promise in the candidate's portfolio, and after an appeal in which the candidate was represented by interdisciplinary program coordinators, the committee voted to give the candidate tenure. This case demonstrates that entrenched procedures of decision-making based on older forms of organization can impede colleges from implementing newer forms of learning, teaching, and scholarship. New faculty watch what happens to their colleagues and act accordingly to protect themselves.

Recently, one impassioned speaker in a faculty meeting spoke of the department as home, and of those invested in interdisciplinary work as prodigal sons and daughters. Our point is that the tension and the conflict are structural; departments and interdisciplinary programs find themselves positioned competitively against one another. Chairs and coordinators are politically invested with the duty to protect and nurture the programs under their direction. While some departments have redesigned their majors to work in coordination with interdisciplinary programs, others, especially in the sciences, have major requirements which do not allow this flexibility. The result is that the chairs of these departments perceive the involvement of their faculty in interdisciplinary programs as threatening, as a loss to the department which threatens the integrity of the major. One solution to this impasse is resources: If a school can afford enough faculty to retain strong majors, traditionally conceived, and develop rich interdisciplinary programs, departments and programs do not find themselves structurally in competition. This, of course, is not a solution available to most institutions. The alternative is much more difficult as it calls for a willingness on the part of all concerned to remain in conversation with one another and to abandon defensiveness in favor of negotiating mutually beneficial arrangements.

Despite such tensions, interdisciplinary faculty development projects continue to flourish. A four-year grant in intercultural studies from the Christian Johnson Endeavor Foundation, though controversial on campus, has involved sixty out of a total of 155 faculty members over the past three years. It has sponsored a seminar on connections between US and global diversity in January 1996, a seminar and field study in Caribbean culture in June 1996, reading seminars in environmental issues in 1996–1997, faculty travel to areas of ecological interest (Nepal, Ecuador, Ghana) in January 1997, a summer course in Bosnia in 1996, a January course in Asia in 1997, and there are continuing plans for next year. Other evolving faculty development groups are working on indigenous studies and developing an intercultural studies major.

The recent proliferation of faculty development seminars and workshops suggests that just as the First-Year Program unintentionally became an effective faculty development project, so too Cultural Encounters had the unanticipated effect of institutionalizing the whole notion of faculty development seminars at St. Lawrence. A majority of faculty now expect to participate in seminars and workshops which will add new dimensions to their teaching and scholarship, outside the parameters of their disciplines. Interdisciplinary faculty development has become a central part of St. Lawrence faculty life. There have been regular summer institutes on writing across the curriculum, a seminar on feminist theory, seminars on service-learning and on instructional technology.

If a university administration wants to support and nurture interdisciplinary programs and scholarship, there are several key practices which can help. The most important lesson we draw from the St. Lawrence experience is that the best way to promote institutional change is to provide faculty with the opportunity to work together on substantive intellectual projects across disciplines. This strategy lies at the opposite end of the spectrum from institutional change brought about by visionary deans or presidents.

The second lesson is the necessity of implementing procedural changes which balance the power between interdisciplinary programs and traditional departments. St. Lawrence has done some of them with great success, but it is a long way from others which have worked well at other colleges. First, we include language about our interdisciplinary programs in all faculty job advertisements. This has worked differently at different times. Some departmental positions have been tied to participation in the First-Year Programs. In other cases, the ads just describe the program. In still others, the ads state an expectation that applicants will participate in one interdisciplinary program. Such statements and ads attract candidates who find the prospect of interdisciplinary work inviting and probably deter those who do not. In addition, every search committee has a member from outside the department in which the hire is taking place and the dean tries to steer candidates into conversations with faculty in relevant interdisciplinary programs. The administration also tries to make it clear that participation in extra departmental programs will be recognized as a contribution to the university. In the years when we have had merit pay, there has sometimes been provision for the First-Year Program to nominate persons for merit as well as departments.

We have moved toward a stronger role for the First-Year Program and other interdisciplinary programs in mid-probationary and tenure reviews. Whereas in the past only the department chair appeared before the tenure committee, there is now formal representation by the associate dean of the first year or a comparable program head. And interdisciplinary programs write their own reviews of candidates for the mid-probationary review. Nonetheless, all faculty are still tenured in departments, even when their primary job is interdisciplinary, such as director of the writing program or coordinator of gender studies. This situation pressures such faculty to pay allegiance to the department which will tenure them, and draws their energies away from the interdisciplinary programs which need them. The administration is open to changing this practice, however, and hopes to add tenured members to a number of interdisciplinary programs. Other traditional colleges have made the ultimate move of tenuring faculty in the university as a whole, not in departments. This, more than anything, would mitigate against the hegemony of disciplines and departments, but St. Lawrence is a long way from such a change.

We have chronicled in some detail the pains and struggles associated with interdisciplinary work because we believe they are rooted in the training most faculty continue to receive in graduate school and in much of the external reward system of academia. Nonetheless, the faculty culture at St. Lawrence is radically different than it was ten years ago. For a sizable portion of the faculty, affiliation and identity derive from interdisciplinary programs such as area studies and gender studies, as well as the First-Year Program and Cultural Encounters. A majority of faculty expect to work with people from other disciplines and to drive their teaching and thinking by attention to the big questions which are taken for granted within each discipline. They expect to form new coalitions around new projects and themes: They are open to different ways of thinking.

References

Cornwell, G. H., & Stoddard, E. (1997). Residential colleges: Laboratories for teaching through difference. In R. Guarasci & G. H. Cornwell (Eds.), *Democratic education in an age of difference: Redefining citizenship in higher education.* San Francisco, CA: Jossey-Bass.

Crimmel, H. H. (1993). *The liberal arts college and the ideal of liberal education: The case for radical reform.* Lanham, MD: University Press of America.

Foucault, M. (1997). *Discipline and punish: The birth of the prison.* (A. Sheridan, Trans.). New York, NY: Pantheon Books.

Hill, P. (1991). *Evaluation report on the freshman program* (Internal Document). Canton, NY: St. Lawrence University.

(1994). First-Year Program Living/Learning Component: Statement of Philosophy and Goals [On-line]. Available: http://www.stlawu.edu/fyp:http/resgoal.htm.

Williams, R. (1976). *Keywords: A vocabulary of culture and society.* New York, NY: Oxford University Press.

Endnotes

1. For a different analysis of institutional transformation at St. Lawrence see Crimmel.

2. For further analysis of the living/learning aspects of St. Lawrence's First-Year Program, see our 1997 essay, "Residential Colleges: Laboratories for Teaching Through Difference."

3. Both the First-Year Program and Cultural Encounters compensated faculty amply for their commitment to reeducating themselves. Teaching in the First-Year Program constitutes a one-course overload

and faculty can bank that for a three-year term in the program and then receive a semester's leave at full pay. In the early years of the program they also received a substantial planning stipend for each year they taught in the program. Now each faculty member receives a planning stipend for his or her first year. In Cultural Encounters, faculty received a yearly stipend and two month-long field trips.

4. Nonetheless we have not given up. We are currently participating in a faculty development seminar on women and science under the aegis of AAC&U, and the group seems to be making more progress toward truly intercultural communication, but it is very difficult.

10

VOICES IN SEMINAR: IDEOLOGIES AND IDENTITIES

Susan Fiksdal
The Evergreen State College

One of the hallmarks of a good education should be a full awareness of the multiplicity of voices in a group discussion. This awareness should include knowledge of the power of conversation and the power of collaboration. The most effective pedagogy that helps students and faculty alike to actually hear those voices, interact with them, and collaborate with them, is the seminar. By hearing voices, I do not mean simply listening to other people speaking; instead, I am referring to the difficult task of hearing another person as a fundamental and yet elusive requirement for collaboration. In the sixties, we said, "I hear you" as an empathetic response. In the nineties we are increasingly aware of the difficulty of truly understanding the other.

If we take this perspective of the past 30 years, I believe we have become increasingly knowledgeable of the ways in which diversity affects our educational system, particularly in regards to race and ethnicity. In fact, the notion of diversity itself has deepened and broadened from the acknowledgement of presence that occurred in the sixties to the recognition of complex interrelationships and societal effects that we see today. Still, learning to hear other voices is not easy. It is not easy because of the historical, social, economic, cultural, and linguistic factors that work to silence some voices. Consider, for example, how well you know your students' ethnicities and the ways in which you tailor your teaching methods to those differences. Or, consider how well you understand teaching and learning practices in Native American communities. As educators in higher education, we have been trained in particular disciplines, not in appropriate pedagogies. For that reason, it seems to me that the center of teaching and learning ought to be learning to hear other voices given the current and past social practices in our country and particular geographic regions.

Learning to hear other voices can take place in seminars because they provide a particular place for students to create and reflect upon links between ideas and concepts raised in other venues such as lectures, workshops, films, field trips, and labs. It is during these conversations that multiple perspectives can emerge and engage the faculty and students in colearning that may not be possible in other venues. As small group conversations, seminars provide the collaborative experience students need to grapple with big ideas in a group setting rather than in the largely individual process of writing or the competitive arena of lecture hall discussions.

Conversations in seminars create a context for discovery in the presence of others that is very powerful—many of us have been in conversations in which a collective "ah ha" emerges. On the other hand, seminars can be boring, barren, and even hurtful. To explore seminar as a pedagogy critical for hearing new perspectives and making new connections between ideas and themes, we will examine the seminar as it is used at The Evergreen State College. Using a sociolinguistic and ideological approach to conversation, we will explore some of the reasons why seminar conversations can be powerful and/or hurtful. Finally, we will examine strategies for successful seminars.

One Definition of Seminars

The Evergreen seminar varies in structure, setting, and relative success, but after conducting two studies assessing seminars at the college, I can give the following definition of its use. It is a space to discuss a text (in its largest sense of a written piece, a moving or fixed image, or a common experience) in order to work collaboratively toward a better understanding of it than an individual perspective can provide. Faculty and students alike speak of gaining different perspectives as the satisfying result of a good seminar.

The role of the faculty member can be as facilitator or as a member of the group if students are facilitating. The facilitator helps organize the conversation by either suggesting a structure or eliciting one from the group, and then maintaining the flow of the conversation through questions or observations. It is the students, however, who have primary responsibility in the seminar both to generate conversation topics, and to develop their understanding of those topics. This mode of teaching, then, decenters the authority of the faculty member, placing authority with the students. Finally, because the function of the seminar is to engage students in their individual and collective views of the text, face to face interaction is most appropriate. The group sits in a circle, so the number of participants is necessarily limited to around twenty.

Clearly, the Evergreen seminar is not the same as the seminar in graduate level courses in which students bring prepared texts to present to their professor and other students for their critique (although this is one form a seminar can take). It is also not a discussion in the usual sense of that word in academic settings. Discussions in classes usually have a leader, and that leader is usually the faculty member who stands in front of the class (or who moves in a prescribed space while students remain fixed in their seats), and to whom all comments are truly directed (even if ostensibly some comments respond to other students'). As leader, the faculty member can suddenly shift the conversation, and, in fact, many see the skillful manipulation of the topic in discussions as evidence of their own good teaching. The fact that students are facing the front of the room where the faculty member's space is defined rather than towards each other suggests the directionality of the questions and comments—to and from the professor. In the seminar, by forming a circle with the furniture in the room, students and faculty change their physical perspectives of each other, and this change can facilitate conceptual shifts necessary to really hear each other.

The seminar at Evergreen is an essential part of our learning communities. One of our primary modes of teaching and learning is within full-time interdisciplinary programs. These are team-taught by two or more faculty members and they focus on a theme, question, or problem. A typical week in a program is comprised of a lecture and/or film followed by workshops and/or labs and seminars. The weekly seminar in interdisciplinary programs functions to provide space for students to struggle with their own ideas about the text, its relationship to other texts in the class, and the themes and questions central to the program's content.

Because they are collaborative experiences, seminars fit within the constructivist framework in which meanings are created within the group (Spivey, 1997). This framework is, in fact, highlighted in a seminar although it may not be explicitly discussed: The answer to a question does not receive an answer from an authority and the absence of this voice is palpable. In a constructivist framework, speakers negotiate the meaning of a text by first querying the text itself. It becomes obvious to any group working on a text that there is no one certain meaning dictated by the text; instead, its context within the author's and published world becomes apparent as does the world of the readers. In addition, even though some individuals may contribute particular ideas, the group contextualizes those ideas within the conversation and elaborates them in ways the original contributor did not imagine.

When seminar members focus on hearing each other, they can collaborate to create or build upon ideas. These ideas are then owned collectively rather than by individuals. This experience, which admittedly does not occur in every seminar despite everyone's best intentions, is often called the "ah ha" experience at Evergreen. A narrative world develops from the group—the group constructs a particular understanding, and that particularity is novel and it belongs to that space and time created by the seminar. This point is worth underscoring, because our narrative worlds are often so well established that we cannot easily create new ones. The most revered narratives in academe are the published text and the text (lectures, curriculum) created by the professor. The seminar provides an opportunity to create a new narrative, and to do so collaboratively.

A Sociolinguisic Approach to Voice

As a sociolinguist who investigates conversations, I undertook a large research project at Evergreen from 1990–1993 that involved video taping 21 seminar conversations and asking students and faculty to comment on the video taped seminar in individual playback sessions. My question was, Is there a common notion of the seminar at Evergreen given its 20–year history as an alternative institution? In the course of that project I came to see two very different perceptions of the seminar based on whether the speaker was part of the dominant culture, or from its margins. Two comments from colleagues describing their experience of seminar encapsulate the perspectives and their respective ideologies:

1) The seminar is an arena for serious warfare.
2) Hearing your own voice is essential to claim it. You don't take yourself seriously until you hear yourself in public.

These comments reveal the power of conversation: Conversation in seminars can open the way for students to take responsibility for their own learning—to engage with a text or experience it on their own terms, to gain a voice. At the same time, that conversation occurs in a social, economic, and political context where race, class, and gender are socially constructed moment by moment. Each person's identity, too, is socially constructed in the course of the conversation. The problem for the facilitator (usually the faculty member) is that seminar conversation takes place in real time and it can be difficult to pay attention to group process and ideas at the same time. In addition, unless we as faculty members come from a marginalized position in our culture, we may not recognize the efforts of marginalized students to grapple with ideas and hear each other. Or, we may choose to select a student and ask, "Mary, you're" [here select any number of possible labels—African American, Chinese, Native American], "what do you think about this question?" This sort of directed question implies that one student can or would like to speak for everyone we label in the same way.

In addition to the notion of conversation as creating identity within a diverse group, our students have varied experiences with academic discourse and analysis. Some are quite comfortable with it; others see the seminar as the venue for bringing in debate techniques; and others feel squeezed out of the conversation. Knowing which topics are appropriate, when to introduce personal experience, and how to analyze different genres of text depends not only on students' academic experiences, but also their class background.

One reason we may not immediately recognize the complexity of seminar conversation is the underlying assumption that conversation is something we all do and therefore we are simply asking for students to add the elements of academic content and critical thinking to what they already do routinely—talk. We think of conversation as an exchange of ideas, a time to build upon each other's ideas, or a time to meet a common goal. The notion of conversation itself becomes simplified as we focus on the importance of creating and elaborating upon ideas, the real content of the conversation in a seminar in the view of many teachers. However, the metaphors implied by exchanging, constructing, or traveling are part of the conversation just as the ideas are. Stated otherwise, the process is just as integral to the conversation as is the content of the ideas expressed. Erving Goffman (1981) pointed out that most often what we are trying to do in conversation is to save face (ours and others'), not convey information (See also Fiksdal, 1990). In addition, we might add, our discourse constitutes our identities even as we are trying to reach particular goals, and our style of discourse varies just as our identities do.

Given the social reality of the seminar in which talk constitutes identities, in practice, all sorts of activities are occurring as we work together. As teachers and facilitators we need to be aware of the expectations we create for finding a voice in seminar conversations: Do we expect to hear coherent, rational conversations? Do we expect a particular level of academic discourse? Are we willing for tensions to arise and the very real feelings those tensions create in our students? And, finally, do we accept that a student's conversational style may be very different from our own and do we value it?

Voice, then, is intricately related to ideology, identity, and conversational practices. It is not only essential that we recognize our own conversational style in academic seminars and the ways in which it may influence the construction of meaning, we need to accept that some of us and some of our students will be uncomfortable with the various conversational styles we encounter. However, if some voices are silenced, we may not only discourage particular points of view from being discussed, we may be discouraging learning. Indeed, it may be the finding of one's voice that enables students to recognize they are fully engaged in the questions and material they are studying. In the research I have done on seminars (Fiksdal 1991, 1993), faculty raising the notion of voice seem to refer to at least two, complementary meanings: using one's voice literally to give an opinion or observation; and recognizing one's voice metaphorically as a collection of perspectives the student has developed as a result of her own experiences. In other words, voicing an opinion in itself has some value because the student contributes to the conversation and demonstrates engagement in it. Clearly, understanding one's own stance is essential before further intellectual development can occur within the college experience or in lifelong learning.

Gilligan (1982), in her research on human development and morality, describes voice as a way of talking that reveals the language people use, a world they see and in which they act. Her research points out that the socialized perspective of students is gendered: Women consider relationships and intimacy as primary while men consider independence and autonomy as primary. Because gender relations are fundamental to our socialization, sociolinguists have also examined conversation to analyze the ways in which speakers construct identity.

At least one aspect of talk may stand in the way of students (or faculty) truly hearing each other. This is conversational style. Deborah Tannen is one of the better known spokespersons on conversational style and gender as a result of her popular trade book, *You Just Don't Understand* (1990) and her academic work on gender (1994). She finds that men and women use language to achieve different ends as a result of their gendered socialization: Men use language to give information and establish independence while women use language to make connections and establish and maintain relationships. Gender is not a determiner of conversational style; instead, we routinely use language to express who we are. For this reason we may also express class, ethnicity, age, and geographical region (among other variants). However, because gender influences so much of our socialization, it is a dominant force in our experiences.

Speaking in one's own voice means using a particular conversational style that may not be shared by others in the group. For example, one colleague in my study described an ideal seminar as one in which students showed respect for each other by taking turns in speaking and not interrupting (see Fiksdal 1991). This may seem quite logical to some speakers, and my colleague clearly thought it important enough to include it in a list of general rules for the seminar, an etiquette that fostered serious inquiry. But conversational analysts have found that a preference for not interrupting is just one conversational style. Another, which some women use, calls for overlapping another speaker to show solidarity. To understand this point, we will turn to an example drawn from one of my own seminars that was videotaped, and examine a short transcribed segment demonstrating two women holding the floor at the same time. It is almost as if these two women know what each will say, because by lines 12 and 13 they both say "our country" at the same time.

The transcription shows three female speakers, A, K, and L, all students. They are in the middle of a heated conversation about Latino gangs in Los Angeles (the topic of the text). To read the transcription, please note that underlined syllables are stressed; a line (|) at the beginning of two speakers' words indicate they are speaking at the same time; (.) means a very short pause; and = means that the speaker continues with no pause. A makes a point in lines 1 and 2, and is subsequently overlapped in her articulation of the point by K in line 2, and by L in line 9. In effect, L creates refrains and a coda for A.

EXAMPLE OF OVERLAPPING SPEECH

1) A: Maybe we should be saying assimilate into <u>this</u> country instead of <u>our</u> country.

2) K. | Right excuse me.

3) A: | I mean that's a big part of the problem is that there's so much talk about our

4) country. This (.) is (.) their and this is

5) L: = This is every | one's

6) A: | This is a country

7) L: For everyone

8) A: and the people in it (.) that I mean that's that's that's one of the | biggest

9) L: | yeah

10) A: problems here.

11) L: = Is that we yeah | you know

12) A: | Is that we keep saying | <u>our</u> country.

13) L: | our country.

14) L: Whose country is it you know?

In our playback of the videotaped seminar, I asked A what she was thinking when L joined her explanation of our country. Because she was somewhat tongue tied, as can be noted in lines 4 and 8 with her repetitions and micropauses, A said she welcomed L's help. L mentioned she was showing support for A, and agreement. Her extended agreement included the *yeah* in line 9, but also the repetition in line 12 and final question as well. In this case, even though the conversation was passionate, showing respect did not mean waiting for another speaker to finish her thought, as the idealized version mentioned above would have required. Instead, sharing the floor was considered useful by A and necessary by L.

Overlapping another speaker is explained by Tannen (1984) as showing agreement and solidarity, and as a feature of a particular conversational style—New York Jewish style. Some women in academic conversations use overlap a great deal to show agreement (Edelsky, 1981). My students have shown that it also occurs in some large families, and certainly in those with Italian origins in research they have done. Tannen points out that speakers in her study who did not use overlap in their conversational style (and were overlapped by other speakers who do use it) reported being offended by the overlapping, and that practice tended to silence them.

Overlapping can be confused with interruption, but they are two different practices. Tannen differentiates them, pointing out that to show solidarity or rapport a speaker stays on the same topic using overlaps; interruptions change the topic and may grant the floor to the interrupter. My colleague, then, may have wanted to say that if the interruption disrupts the topic under discussion, it should be banned.

Developing a voice in an atmosphere of respect is essential, it seems to me, but just as important is a sense of equality of each member. A seminar group can declare equality, even develop its own rules for maintaining that value. However, some students will feel unheard or undervalued just as they might in our larger society. Clearly, attending to conversational voice is one variable which may affect equality. Others are addressed in research on pedagogy.

One area of research that concerns itself with this issue is radical (feminist or critical) pedagogy. Feminist pedagogy as outlined by Shrewsbury (1993) is based on democratic principles with power shared by faculty and students. Power is viewed in the Freirian sense of a creative energy rather than a dominant structure (Freire, 1970). The classroom becomes a liberatory environment in which there is continual engagement in reflective practice with the goal of moving beyond sexism, racism, classism, and homophobia as well as other destructive hatreds. In this liberatory environment, teachers encourage students to critically analyze their own and others' contributions in the discussions, and question assumptions underlying these contributions. One of the essential features of a feminist pedagogy is empowering students to speak.

For critical theorists such as Giroux, the notion of voice is crucial because it is through talk that faculty not only build or construct notions of education that replicate the dominant modes of power, but we also reproduce them (Giroux, 1981). If we choose the seminar as one of the times in which we will encourage intellectual development or finding of voice, we as faculty must analyze our own interpretations inherited by the education we ourselves received. How much do our own expectations for intellectual development interact with our assessments of student learning? Aronwitz and Giroux (1991) argue for developing a politics and pedagogy of voice as part of a theory of curriculum. Placing voice within this framework as politics and pedagogy allows us to see that it is possible to question the authority of a text and the authority of academic discourse (including received notions of critical thinking) from subjective, personal perspectives in order to highlight the moment by moment construction of meaning in a seminar.

In my own experience of a difficult seminar conversation focussed on a text about gangs in Los Angeles barrios, students began arguing about whether or not Latino gangs could be called racist. Some students argued it was only the dominant white Eurocentric culture that could be called racist, others countered that any inappropriate action based on ethnic difference could be termed racist. The conversation quickly moved from the text to personal experience with ethnic or racially organized gangs, and the assumption was that the we of the seminar excluded anyone in this sort of gang. In the example of overlapping speech from this seminar that I cited, two students raised awareness of this notion of "we" by talking about our country. The last line in that segment was a question, Whose country is it, you know? It seems to me that this question is at the heart of curricular decisions about texts, design of interdisciplinary programs, courses, and seminar conversations. And if we do not continually remember that this question lies at the center of our work, and actively bring it to the surface of our conversations, we may easily fall into the trap of thinking each of us has one voice, and who and what helped form that voice doesn't really matter.

Pedagogical Strategies to Develop Voice

As I have tried to show, using seminars as a pedagogy to help students find their voice(s) is not self-evident. The process and the structure of the seminar contribute just as much to collaborative work as the content of the text being discussed. Yet, faculty members in higher education do not routinely discuss issues of seminar pedagogy as essential to their work. They conceive of their work as developing critical thinking about the content of seminar: interpretation of the text, its relationship with other texts, and with the thematic content in the class. It does not take more than one actual seminar experience, however, to convince one of the need to consider how to make that experience consistently rich and exciting.

One of the best ways to create the atmosphere of collaborative work is to propose that the seminar group work together at the first meeting to make a covenant for individuals to follow. Ideally, as the seminar conversations develop over time, the group would reexamine the covenant from time to time to ensure that it allowed for the kind of critical analysis of seminar processes essential to understanding the construction of social relationships through talk.

Besides the covenant, there are at least five aspects of the seminar that need to be considered in creating the kind of atmosphere conducive to exploration, collaboration, and recognition of conversational style: text choice, preparation for seminar, seminar goals, facilitation, and assessment.

Text Choice

Choosing a text that is rich enough for seminar conversations is essential. By rich, I mean complex, multilayered, perhaps controversial, and open to interpretation. If students do not have the background to critique the text, then even if it is all of the above, they will have no grounding for developing their own ideas or perspective. For example, if you show only one film in a class with no direction on viewing or "reading" a film, students may not watch it with a critical eye. Similarly, if students have only one example of a particular textual genre, they may not be able to fully engage with that text.

If the text is too long, some students will probably not read carefully or even finish the text. Asking students to focus on particular chapters or selections for the seminar may lead to close reading and consequently better conversations. Keep in mind that one of the most common critiques of an edited volume in published book reviews is that the chapters are uneven. This critique implies that not all authors approach the topic with the same rigor and that the approaches might be too dissimilar to draw overall conclusions. It may be that selecting chapters from an edited volume will serve your purposes better than using the entire volume.

Selecting chapters or essays (or a poem) that discuss a topic from different perspectives will allow you to use a jigsaw seminar. In this type of seminar, students read one of two texts or more, each of which forms a piece of a puzzle or aspects of a question. In seminar, students first discuss the text they read with others who read the same text. Next, they discuss both the texts in small groups with half the students having read one text and half the other. The students report on what they read and then move to a discussion of the themes that seem similar. The facilitator floats from group to group. If time allows, the group can come together at the end to discuss the themes and perspectives they developed.

Finally, it is essential to bring texts (in the broadest sense) from the margins, not just the center of the dominant theories that you want to explore. This approach may mean examining texts outside a particular discipline, outside an accepted viewpoint, or outside a received cultural perspective. One way of doing this work is to propose a standard or canonical text for seminar, and assign a group of students to explore published critiques in book reviews and journal articles, report on them, and then facilitate the discussion by preparing questions relating these critiques to the standard text. I like to ask students to work for a time in small groups, even pairs if appropriate, for part of the seminar period. Working in small groups helps students who are developing a voice explore ideas in tentative or loosely structured ways. Ask that one student in the small groups act as a recorder so that ideas from the small groups find their way into the larger group conversations.

Keep in mind one rule of thumb: If you have closely studied a particular text and it lies close to your intellectual and/or emotional core, you will need to actively work to open your mind to hear the voices students raise and support the collaborative work of the seminar. In such a scenario, I often try to record observations of my colearners in writing as a way of focusing my attention on the moment by moment process and actively hearing the conversation.

Preparation for Seminar

If students are well prepared for seminar, they are more likely to base their conversation on a critical reading of the text rather than a quick or shallow evaluation of it. Ideally, students can refer to a section of the text which inspired a particular thought. Solid preparation will also help them separate ideas from the person contributing the ideas in seminar conversations. The best preparation is a careful reading of the text (or viewing of the film, exhibit). Be sure to provide students with the context they need before the seminar; for example, explain why you chose the text and what questions it raised for you. Most faculty members agree that writing about the text or experience is good preparation for seminar; that writing can be a short seminar essay, part of a seminar journal, or a summary. Students could turn in that writing as a ticket to the first seminar on a particular text or event or share it with a study partner. Alternatively, students could spend the first ten minutes of a seminar writing in order to center their thoughts and prepare for seminar.

It is important to provide students the opportunity to write because writing provides another form of thinking through ideas. Some students may prefer this approach because they need more time to formulate their ideas or because they prefer independent work. At any rate, this alternative for thoughtful discussion of the material is useful for some students for whom talking is not the way they learn most effectively.

Finally, in considering how to help students prepare for seminar, you can model various strategies you use yourself. For example, in an interdisciplinary program we are always working with a range of themes, so as I read any text, whether a novel, an historical account, a poem, or an essay, I try to identify themes as I read and note the place in the text where I made that identification. I often show students the last page of a book where I have listed themes and subthemes with groupings of page numbers, as one way of making sense of the text. I make no pretense that I have an authoritative edge as I do this work; in fact, I sometimes find myself musing that some of my listings appear rather mysterious when I reread the page I have referenced. What is important is to talk about developing a strategy that works. A colleague, for example, asks students to highlight the text sparingly as they read, and after each section or chapter, to stop and write about those highlighted sections in a seminar notebook. This work clarifies for the student both what they are highlighting and why.

Seminar Goals

Goals are important in any group interaction. Johnson and Johnson (1994), leading researchers on group interaction, state that the first and most obvious point to a group discussion must be an elaboration of the goal. In my study of seminars as they are practiced at Evergreen, however, I rarely found a facilitator or faculty member stating the goal of a particular seminar at the beginning of that seminar. Often the stated goal of seminars is codified in a syllabus or covenant, but those indications are quite general. In my study of seminars at Evergreen, I asked over 60 students what their goal was before viewing the playback of their seminar, and I heard answers ranging from "try to say something" to "build a web of understanding that goes beyond our previous discussions." Faculty members always had a ready answer to this question of goals while students often hesitated; interestingly, the goals participants in the study gave never matched each other even when they were in the same seminar. If students' contributions to the conversation focus only on their personal goals, the seminar may not satisfy anyone. Indeed, it has been my experience to hear wildly different evaluations of a particular seminar that I facilitated. Now, I believe one of the reasons for these differences is due to a lack of an explicitly stated, common goal.

If the seminar group decides each time what its goals will be, the common ground the group creates will provide its direction or structure. In addition, students are more likely to learn facilitation, and mediation skills modeled by the faculty member if they share a common goal. Typical goals for a seminar might be to first understand the author's argument in an essay (or the dominant themes in a novel) and find evidence or examples in the text. The second seminar could continue this conversation or move on to explore the relationship of the text to the thematic content of the course or the implications of the argument in students' lives.

One of the most important aspects of interpretation is how the text relates to the personal experience of the student. Some faculty members take this perspective as a beginning and very useful starting point, and ask students to begin with statements like *I feel.* Whether this is a beginning, intermediate, or end point, it is important not to ignore subjective feelings in favor of abstract reasoning. Valuing as many ways of interpretation as possible will create a richer conversation. Some ways to do this are to ask students to role play some parts of the text or to ask everyone to draw for five minutes, and then collectively roam the room looking at the drawings.

Seminar Facilitation

In my study of seminars, students cited two faculty facilitation practices some had experienced that were particularly problematic: turning the seminar over to the students with no direction; and using the seminar for mini lectures. In the first case, students told of faculty who said, "The seminar is yours, I'll sit back and listen," leaving all organization and facilitation up to the students. This practice of laissez faire does not work in students' opinion because they need help in learning to facilitate, and because the faculty member is also the evaluator, and they deserve to know what the expectations are for that evaluation of seminar participation. In the second case, students told of faculty who stopped the seminar saying, "I need to give you some background on this point," proceeding to talk for 30 minutes or more. As experienced speakers, faculty need to recognize that what may seem a short monologue to us may seem like an hour to students. We are practiced at being articulate and giving what we perceive as careful, reasoned explanations. But is this a good practice for seminars?

If the general goal of seminar is to help students become responsible for the text, find a voice, work collaboratively, and create links between the text and the course themes, we need to give them the space to do that in seminar; furthermore, modeling good facilitation is an important goal for the faculty member. It is effective to use phrases underscoring the importance of process; for example, you might say, "Your point seems to connect well with what Theresa was saying earlier" or "Before we go on, can anyone paraphrase what Jordan was saying?"

When the conversation becomes too heated or even hurtful in the facilitator's point of view, a useful approach is for the facilitator to describe what is going on; for example, you might say, "It seems that we have outlined two points of view, and they are . . ." "What we may want to do next is . . . ." I have also stopped the seminar in order to create a space in the conversation. Sometimes students need to have time to separate out a number of issues by writing; other times I have asked that they leave the seminar room and research definitions for the terms they are using in the library.

Gaining a voice begins with speaking, yet that realization alone can frighten students into silence for an entire term. At Evergreen, some facilitators use the round robin as one method of wrapping up seminar: we take turns saying something at the end about either the content or the process, allowing people to pass if they wish. If this practice becomes routine, students will hear themselves and others in each seminar. You can also begin seminar with this technique, allowing each student to raise the question or observation they had uppermost in their minds when they came into the room.

Assessment

Assessment is one of the most difficult aspects of the seminar. Some students are very quiet in every seminar, perhaps silent. Have they gained a voice? Are they engaged in the seminar? If you are using performance, writing, or drawing as a complementary part of the seminar conversation, you will have a way to characterize the students' learning. Probably the most difficult aspect of assessment is watching for a student's own development of voice. Keeping careful notes during seminar of what students actually say can be helpful. Just as useful is making sure the student has many ways to contribute to the conversation, whether you have structured the conversation in small groups for a short time or given a particular role to a quiet student such as summarizer or recorder.

It is essential to share what you expect students to learn with those students. If you hope to empower students through the seminar, you no doubt expect students to make changes in the paradigms they routinely use. If you are attentive to process, you expect students to gain skills in facilitation, summarizing, mediation, probing, deepening, and questioning. If you consider socialization, you may want students to learn academic discourse and to become familiar with authority and the ways it is expressed.

Whatever your perspective on voice, you should communicate your expectations to your students and give them ways to measure their progress. For example, students could assess their own interaction at the end of each seminar. If you choose this method, you could bring the covenant back into focus and brainstorm with students to make a list of questions or criteria that students then use to reflect on their own conversational style and interactions. Or, students could assess their neighbor's interaction on a series of small scales, passing that assessment to that person for comments before handing it in to you. Using students' self-assessments as a valued source for your final assessments will reinforce the major point of this chapter—hearing a multiplicity of voices is not easy. We must consider every aspect of our teaching and learning to allow those voices to be raised.

Conclusion

Although I have been using the term voice in the singular, it is important to realize that just as we construct identity in talk, we construct the related notion of voice. This constructed notion of voice carries with it the issues of class, ethnicity, race, sexual orientation, and gender that are always present in conversations just as they are present in the wider macrocosm of everyday life. And this notion of developing a voice is not an orderly one. In a telling sentence, bell hooks (1994) writes, "Professors cannot empower students to embrace diversities of experience, standpoint, behavior, or style if our training has disempowered us, socialized us to cope effectively only with a single mode of interaction based on middle-class values" (p. 187). She sees much of middle class socialization as keeping order and, consequently, maintaining a dominant ideology. If keeping order means not interrupting, not introducing personal experience, not exploring the emotional value of an argument, not moving off the topic occasionally, then I am not interested in order as a value underlying conversation in seminar. More important than order, I believe, is allowing a variety of perspectives to flow from individuals to be analyzed by the group.

Clearly, the issues I have raised about seminar should be addressed in any introduction to the seminar as pedagogy to new groups of faculty. At Evergreen we offer summer institutes during which faculty seminar together on a text in order to experience the seminar with colleagues—a highly satisfying experience—and also discuss their experiences and/or worries about seminars. We invite experienced and new faculty to take part in these institutes so that we hear a wide variety of experiences. In addition, we provide a variety of writings on seminars so that faculty will have resources throughout the year. Each of us has a particular teaching style, so not all approaches to seminar will be comfortable to us. Trying a few approaches helps determine which is most comfortable. Then, the important point to remember is that you should convey your approach to the students. They will appreciate hearing your point of view.

References

Aronwitz, S., & Giroux, H. A. (1991). *Postmodern education: Politics, culture, and social criticism.* Minneapolis, MN: University of Minnesota Press.

Edelsky, C. (1981). Who's got the floor? *Language in Society, 10* (3), 383–421.

Fiksdal, S. (1990). *The right time and pace: A microanalysis of crosscultural gatekeeping interviews.* Norwood, NJ. Ablex.

Fiksdal, S. (1991). *Seminar talk.* Unpublished manuscript, The Evergreen State College, Olympia, WA.

Fiksdal, S. (1993). *Getting the floor.* Unpublished manuscript, The Evergreen State College, Olympia, WA.

Freire, P. (1970). *Pedagogy of the oppressed.* New York, NY: Seabury.

Gilligan, C. (1982). *In a different voice.* Cambridge, MA: Harvard University Press.

Giroux, H. A. (1981). *Ideology, culture and the process of schooling.* Philadelphia, PA: Temple University Press.

Goffman, E. (1981). *Forms of talk.* Philadelphia, PA: University of Pennsylvania Press.

hooks, b. (1994). *Teaching to transgress: Education as the practice of freedom.* New York, NY: Routledge.

Johnson, D. W., & Johnson, F. P. (1994). *Joining together: Group theory and group skills.* Boston, MA: Allyn & Bacon.

Shrewsbury, C. (1993). What is feminist pedagogy? *Women's Studies Quarterly, 21,* 8–16.

Spivey, N. N. (1997). *The constructivist metaphor.* New York, NY: Academic Press.

Tannen, D. (1984). *Conversational style: Analyzing talk among friends.* Norwood, NJ: Ablex.

Tannen, D. (1990). *You just don't understand: Women and men in conversation.* New York, NY: William Morrow.

Tannen, D. (1994). *Gender and discourse.* New York, NY: Oxford University Press.

SECTION II

Part Two
Rethinking Teaching and Learning

11

POWERFUL PEDAGOGIES

William H. Newell
Miami University (Ohio)

Since the 1960s, faculty in experimental colleges have been pioneers in the development and implementation of interdisciplinary curriculum and a variety of pedagogical strategies such as collaborative learning, experiential learning, learning communities, living/learning, multicultural learning, service-learning, and study abroad, without paying much attention to why they were chosen nor to the educational consequences of combining them. They appealed to faculty and students responded well to them. That was sufficient rationale. Nor have experimental colleges paid much attention to the contribution of each strategy to the overall educational impact of their institutions, the assessment movement notwithstanding. It is the contention of this chapter that there is an underlying logic to why experimental colleges have been attracted to these strategies. Once that logic is recognized, it becomes evident why experimental colleges have such a powerful impact on students. With that understanding comes a reconceptualization of these strategies that should lead to their more effective implementation by faculty in experimental and more traditional institutions alike.

INTEGRATIVE LEARNING

The central insight of this chapter is that the curricular strategy of interdisciplinary study and the pedagogical strategies of learning communities, collaborative learning, living/learning, experiential learning such as service-learning and study abroad, and multicultural learning can all be productively thought of as forms of integrative learning. Their essential commonalty is that they all draw from multiple perspectives on a complex phenomenon for insights which they then integrate into a richer, more comprehensive understanding of that phenomenon. The phenomenon is typically perceived as a real world problem or issue, and often expressed in the form of a question.

These educational strategies share a common concern for learning from diverse perspectives. The perspectives can emanate from academic disciplines, cultures, subcultures, or individual life experiences, and the learning can take place in the classroom, breakout groups, the residence hall, field sites, other communities, or even foreign countries. Insights from these different perspectives must somehow be integrated. In short, then, these strategies are all examples of integrative learning.

The difference between them is that the curricular approach of interdisciplinary study draws its perspectives solely from academic disciplines, while the various integrative pedagogies draw from additional sources of alternative perspective such as the lived experience of self and others. Certainly each of these pedagogies is more than that as well—this is no reductionist argument—but we learn something very important about them when we recognize their common grounding (with each other and with interdisciplinary study) in the integrative approach.

Taken separately, these integrative curricular and pedagogical strategies offer a powerful complement to traditional disciplinary education. They provide synthesis that complements disciplinary analysis, breadth to accompany its depth, and real world personal application to go with its abstract theory. In short, they offer educational balance. Students who experience integrative as well as disciplinary education should be more fully educated and should be better able to make use of what they have learned. That outcome alone justifies the use of any one of these integrative strategies. This chapter, though, is devoted to exploring what happens educationally when integrative strategies are combined.

Combining Integrative Strategies

The first step is to realize that all these strategies are mutually compatible. A single course in a living/learning community can draw on several disciplines (interdisciplinary study), cultures (multicultural learning), and field experiences (service-learning), utilizing collaborative as well as more traditional learning formats. Indeed, one of the distinctive features of experimental colleges has been their use of several of these strategies in combination. It might even be argued that the merger of multiple integrative strategies has been the chief identifying characteristic of experimental colleges. Certainly they all contribute to the generally progressive student-centered approach of experimental colleges.

The pioneering faculty and students who shaped experimental colleges were attracted, I suspect, to these particular educational innovations because they embodied liberal values shared by those pioneers, values that balance conservative individualism and radical communitarianism. Pedagogies such as service-learning, collaborative learning, and learning communities all connect the individual to the group. Students are liberated to express their individuality through participation in a community that values diversity.

Those educational innovations also responded to the tenor of the times. Think of the experimental colleges created in the 1960s as forums for addressing and narrowing fissures that were widening within both society and polity. Even today, experimental colleges are concerned with promoting community as well as developing the individual potential of their students. Thus, it was no accident that experimental colleges gravitated more to integrative innovations than to those that focus, for example, on technology, efficiency, or other imports from the corporate world.

The next step is to realize that integrative strategies are mutually reinforcing—synergistic, if you will. Much of the impressive but poorly documented educational impact of experimental colleges comes, I believe, from the interaction effects among the integrative strategies they employ. Whereas faculty and administrators think of these strategies as distinct, students experience them as an undifferentiated whole. While experimental college faculty see themselves as pedagogically eclectic, reaching into diverse domains such as student affairs, developmental psychology, and community service for educational innovations, their students simply experience the resulting education as consistent.

Assessing Combinations of Integrative Strategies

The multiplicative power of diverse integrative strategies explains both the powerful educational impact of experimental colleges and the difficulty in assessing that impact. Instead of getting different messages about diversity in class and in the residence halls, on campus and off, through formal interactions and informal, students in experimental colleges are confronted with a consistent message in the various parts of their collegiate life, namely that diversity of perspectives is unsettling but essential because a better appreciation of complex real world issues can emerge from integrating what is learned from those perspectives. When messages are conflicting, they tend to cancel out each other; when they are consistent, they are mutually reinforcing, validating, and supporting. The greater the number of settings in which the message is the same, the more its effect is multiplied.

Thus, it is possible that even if an experimental college offers courses of only average academic quality, uses each new teaching technique less effectively than it might, and runs residential programs featuring discord as well as a sense of community, it will still produce graduates who have obviously undergone a profoundly transformative educational experience. Modest but mutually reinforcing inputs can produce spectacular outputs. The whole educational experience is much greater than the sum of its curricular and pedagogical parts. Partial support for this contention comes from research by the National Center on Postsecondary Teaching, Learning, and Assessment (1995) which finds that "it is the interaction of factors, not single solutions and strategies, that leads to improved undergraduate teaching and learning" (p. v). Pascarella and Terenzini (1991) conclude from their review of research literature on higher education that "A majority of important changes that occur during college are probably the cumulative result of a set of interrelated experiences sustained over an extended period of time" (p. 610).

This multiplicative effect of diverse integrative innovations also explains why it is so difficult to capture in statistics most of the educational impact of experimental colleges. Multivariate statistical measures such as regression analysis and analysis of variance are designed to measure the impact of individual independent variables, holding all other variables constant. When the variables being measured are actually interdependent, e.g., when they are correlated with one another, the assumptions of the statistical model are violated. In fact, most inferential statistics are inappropriate for measuring the impact of interrelated variables; the greater the multicolinearity (i.e., the correlation of supposedly independent variables), the less useful the statistical measure. Small wonder, then, that while people involved in experimental colleges are convinced of their educational effectiveness, conventional assessment instruments are lucky to pick up any of that effect.

Recent assessment innovations such as portfolios are much more promising because readers who know what to look for can pick up indications of those interaction effects (e.g., references in academic papers to experiences in residence halls or field sites). Interviews can probe those interactions further. In general, experimental colleges must learn to combine qualitative and quantitative evidence to assess their educational impact effectively.

The Impact of Combining Integrative Studies

The educational benefits of this integrative strategy can be quite powerful. Students should become even better at skills such as critical thinking, synthesis, contextual thinking, and reflexive thinking. They should develop even more fully traits such as tolerance of ambiguity, sensitivity to bias, creativity, and openness of mind. More students should be able to achieve, in all facets of their lives, the developmental goal of shifting from concrete, either/or, authority-based thinking, through simple relativism, to a more critical relativism with commitment. In short, experimental colleges can become even more educationally potent by making conscious use of their distinctive feature of multifaceted integrative learning.

Integrative learning derives its educational power from confronting the tension between conflicting perspectives, much as it derives its understanding from the resolution of that tension. The tension results from threats to perceptual frameworks that provide deep meanings. Caple (1995) points out that "to change or remove the perceptual guidelines can result in a sense of loss, abandonment and chaos. This process can be painful and strongly resisted until a new order with a sense of security is developed" (p. xi). That new order can be thought of as an integration of insights from conflicting perspectives.

Because the conflicting perspectives are based on assumptions, values, and beliefs that have different significance for the individuals holding them, depending on the kind of integrative learning, the strength and nature of the tension will vary as well. Thus the educational impact of confronting that tension will vary. Perspectives originating in a discipline have less significance for the student than perspectives originating in socioeconomic status, the larger culture, or the student down the hall. Challenges to one's idiosyncratic beliefs or to a disciplinary major newly acquired are less threatening than challenges to the outlook of one's race or gender. Most threatening of all are the threats to the entire system of meaning of one's culture.

The social contexts of integrative learning also affect the nature of the conflict. In particular, the role of status and power varies with the kind of perspectives involved, influencing the kind of integrative strategies available. When perspectives come from disciplines, where students have the least personal investment, dispassionate reason can play the dominant role in integration. Even though some disciplines enjoy higher status than others in the academy (e.g., physics more than French), such differences are not foregrounded for students. Interdisciplinary studies, as a result, can rely heavily on purely intellectual processes in the reconciliation of disciplinary conflict.

While feminist scholarship has brought numerous gender differences to light, nonfeminist faculty may be slow to see their implications for integrative pedagogies such as collaborative learning. The result is that males may dominate peer discussions, for example, by virtue of their gender not the validity of their arguments. Since the scholarship on class and cultural differences is even less prominent in the thinking of white, middle class faculty and staff who control most academic institutions, those power differences can have an even more insidious effect on the adjudication of differences in perspective.

Consequently, we can expect students to respond to integration differently in the various pedagogies. They may respond with intellectual curiosity to the integrative opportunity of interdisciplinary study, with more initial resistance followed by accommodation to the integrative challenge of collaborative learning, with more difficulty yet to the integrative demands of living/learning and service-learning (depending on the diversity of perspectives involved), and with intransigence to the integrative threat of multicultural learning. Majority students may respond differently than those with nondominant race, class, or gender. The differences in responses may reflect the epistemological distance between perspectives, the tenacity with which they are held, the power relationships behind the conflict in perspectives, and the race, class, and gender of the students.

The challenges to integrative teaching may likewise vary. The greater the student resistance, the more important the emotional content of their response. That's because more of their identity is bound up in their response. Thus, integrative pedagogy must be alert to the noncognitive, nonintellectual dimensions of learning. Teachers must try to facilitate the creation of common ground by forging connections among those holding divergent perspectives and by providing emotional support for students going through the process.

The strategy for constructing that common ground is to build on the noncontested dimensions of their relationships. This is no easy task when faculty or staff have their hands full, just to keep anger and conflict that come out of perceived personal threat from cycling out of control. The more of students' very being that is challenged by integrative learning (because it threatens their cognitive, social, racial, gender, or cultural identity), the greater the possibility for change but also the greater the possibility for students to reject the threatening perspective and intensify their hold on beliefs under attack. The risk of seeking integrative change is that it can backfire and result in further polarization.

On the other hand, the risk of not recognizing the integrative nature of these pedagogies is that they may end up producing no change at all in students. If we set up encounters with contrasting perspectives but permit students to avoid dealing with the differences—if they need not integrate what they learn from those encounters—the process can have little educational impact. In the absence of explicit connections with classroom work, for example, Clements (1995) points out Haberman and Post's finding that " . . . even when using field experiences, college students perceive their experiences selectively, ignoring information that is inconsistent with their previously held ideas" (p. 116).

Residence hall staff and faculty in living/learning programs need to do more than identify and connect explicitly the issues raised in each setting; they must get students to confront the implications of those issues. Faculty teaching multicultural courses must get beyond celebration of difference to addressing questions of how we can live with those differences in a multicultural society. Directors, faculty, and staff of experiential learning programs need to go beyond promoting discussion of how the classroom connects to students' personal experience; they need to focus attention on the consequences for personal values and future behavior. Faculty teaching interdisciplinary courses or utilizing collaborative learning need to help students develop strategies for integrating insights from the perspectives of disciplines or peers. As faculty and staff become increasingly self-conscious about the need for integration, the more impact each pedagogical strategy is likely to have and thus the greater the synergistic effect of combining strategies.

Once faculty realize the common integrative thread running through what they formerly thought of as distinct educational strategies, they can enhance the mutual reinforcement of those strategies by making explicit and emphasizing the commonalties of those strategies. The next sections of this chapter are devoted to the separate integrative pedagogies. They probe the integrative nature of each pedagogy and its implications for effective use in experimental and more traditional institutions alike.

Interdisciplinary Study

Julie Klein and I recently set out a definition of interdisciplinary study which I believe represents an emerging consensus. We defined it as "a process of answering a question, solving a problem, or addressing a topic that is too broad or complex to be dealt with adequately by a single discipline or profession" (1997, p. 393). Whether the motivation is liberal education, professional training, problem solving, radical critique, faculty development, response to financial exigency, or the production of new knowledge, interdisciplinary study "draws on disciplinary perspectives and integrates their insights through construction of a more comprehensive perspective" (p. 394).

Central to that definition is the recognition that disciplines are grounded in different perspectives—different assumptions about the world, different epistemologies, even different values. When disciplines are brought in by an interdisciplinarian to help understand a single complex phenomenon, they stand in different places, if you will, reflecting their different assumptions about the world, and they look through distinctive lenses at different aspects of that phenomenon, reflecting their different values and the strengths of their distinctive intellectual tools. The task of the interdisciplinarian is to draw upon the partial, reductionist insights of relevant disciplines to construct a more complex understanding of the phenomenon as a whole.

When faculty fully appreciate the importance of the integrative aspect of interdisciplinary study and its synergy with integrative pedagogies, they can focus class discussions directly on the contrasting perspectives of disciplines, cultures, subcultures, and individual students, and the insights gained from each of them. They can select course readings with an eye to how well they bring out the perspective of each discipline. They can help students probe the assumptions and values underlying each perspective. And they can offer students strategies for integration instead of simply assigning an integrative final paper in which students are expected to achieve synthesis on their own.

Learning Communities

One alternative to individual interdisciplinary courses are learning communities which combine existing disciplinary courses into an interdisciplinary course cluster (such as the Federated Learning Communities at SUNY Stony-Brook) or coordinated studies program (such as at The Evergreen State College) on a specified theme. The coordination can be accomplished via a faculty master learner (at FLC), a one-credit proseminar led by an upper-division peer advisor (at various Freshman Interest Groups), or through weekly coordinating meetings of the faculty involved (at LaGuardia Community College) (Gabelnick, MacGregor, Matthews, & Smith, 1990). Matthews, Smith, MacGregor, and Gabelnick (1997) report that learning communities provide curricular coherence by "juxtapos[ing] diverse perspectives and diverse disciplines, often creating rich social, cultural, and intellectual linkages" (p. 462). The general education impact comes, they tell us, from "[t]he social and intellectual experience of learning together for a whole term" that leads individuals to "the development of multiple perspectives" (p. 463).

Appreciation of the importance of the integrative potential of learning communities could lead faculty to focus the themes which now tend to define each learning community on specific problems or issues. Integration can only occur when disciplinary perspectives have the same focus so that the disciplines illuminate different aspects of the same reality. When disciplines are allowed to probe related but separate questions within an overall theme, students see more comprehensively but they lose the impetus to integrate.

Collaborative Learning

Collaborative learning grows out of desires for active learning and for a less competitive learning environment. Collaborative learning is an umbrella term for a variety of strategies including working in groups, problem-centered instruction, peer feedback approaches and many others. Different types of collaborative learning are found in different disciplines. Drawing on Barbara Leigh Smith and Jean T. MacGregor's article, "What is Collaborative Learning?" (1992), one discovers that, as with interdisciplinary study, collaborative learning begins with and is driven by a question or a problem. Like interdisciplinary study, collaborative learning strategies "bring multiple perspectives" (p. 10) to that question or problem that "build connections" (p. 11) among the new material they contribute. Students, then, "need to attach this new material to, or integrate it with, what they already know—or use it to reorganize what they thought they knew. They are creating something new with the information and ideas" (p. 10). They accomplish this intellectual integration through "an intellectual synergy of many minds coming to bear on a problem" (p. 10). The key to this process is "perspective-taking" (p. 15). In short, collaborative learning is an integrative pedagogy analogous to interdisciplinary study that is distinguished by its reliance on perspectives contributed by students instead of disciplines.

Collaborative learning projects fulfill their integrative potential when they become self-conscious about the collaborative process. Faculty need to shift attention back and forth between product and process, asking not only what a group decided but how they arrived at the decision. The perspectives of individuals, much like the perspectives of disciplines in an interdisciplinary course, should be both validated and probed. Students should be given the opportunity to explain why they took the position they did. The self-reflexive gaze that strong-sense critical thinking promotes (Paul, 1987) should be encouraged as students explore the values and assumptions that led them to take a particular stance.

Living/Learning

When living/learning communities are effective, they integrate the curricular and cocurricular. Schroeder and Mable (1994) argue that residence halls must "integrate students' intellectual and social lives" by becoming what they call "purposeful and intentional educational environments" (p. 17). To that end, they advocate "cross-departmental/divisional project teams" to generate new approaches to "improving student learning" (p. 17). They see these approaches as supporting the "academic mission of the institution" but also as "enhancing an appreciation of cultural and racial diversity" (p. 17). Pascarella, Terenzini, and Blimling (1994) report that the educational impact of residence halls is determined by students' level of "integration into the various cultural, social, and extracurricular systems of an institution" (p. 26). They find that living/learning centers which bring about a "closer integration of the students' living environment with his or her academic or learning environment" (p. 32) lead to greater cognitive growth and academic achievement and to a more satisfying social environment and more personal growth. Indeed, they conclude that living in college residence halls "is perhaps the 'single most consistent within-college determinant of impact'" (p. 39). The source of the tremendous impact of residence halls in general, and living/learning centers in particular, seems to be their integration of the social and academic dimensions of students' lives, and there is some evidence that it grows out of interaction with racial and cultural diversity. What that diversity contributes exactly has not been determined as yet. My contention is that it contributes alternative perspectives—from other students, not from disciplines—which students must confront and reconcile (integrate, if you will) in order to live together.

Student affairs personnel have long recognized the integrative potential of residence halls. When faculty as well come to realize how it can reinforce (and challenge) classroom learning, they can take steps to fulfill that potential. Faculty can make a point of become more informed about what takes place in residence halls, using incidents there to illuminate and test issues debated in class. Conversely, student affairs personnel need to acquaint themselves with the intellectual substance of core courses taken by students in the residence hall. As we make the educational barriers between living and learning more permeable for students, the staff of different departments need to allow the barriers between them to become more permeable as well.

Experiential Learning

Experiential learning is another umbrella term, covering service-learning, field work, study abroad, and a host of other "learning activities that engage the learner directly in the phenomena being studied" (Cantor, 1995, p. 1). Cantor points out (after Mossier) that effective experiential education leads students to "integrate prior knowledge from the classroom with new information gained in the real world" (p. 23). I would argue that outcome reflects another cognitive development Cantor identifies, namely that students learn through experiential education to "consider various perspectives in problem solving" (p. 23). As Cross (1994) puts it, experiential learning helps "students develop broader perspectives through comparison" (p. 7).

If we begin to think of experiential learning as involving contrasting perspectives from the classroom and from another real world setting, not just the application of theory to practice through active learning, then its full potential can be realized. To probe the multifaceted concept of experiential learning, let's examine more closely two exemplars, study abroad and service-learning.

Study Abroad

At the heart of study abroad is the intercultural experience of what Martin (1994) calls the international sojourner. Building on the general systems model of Young Yen Kim (1988), Martin argues that successful adaptation involves not only the standard pragmatic concerns of psychological health and functional fitness, but an underlying sense of intercultural identity as well. At a pragmatic level, the mechanism underlying this adaptation is social communication between sojourner and hosts. Kim sees intercultural identity as "an inclusive viewpoint that represents more than one cultural perspective—either the home culture or the host culture, but at the same time, transcends both groups" (p. 144). This "broader perspective" comes from "increased cognitive complexity" which, in turn, results from confronting the "adversarial nature of the cross-cultural adaptation process" (p. 144). In short, the intercultural identity a sojourner develops during study abroad is a result of a form of integrative education. Because the study abroad experience is often quite unconnected to the formal courses taken, integrative education is still typically examined by scholars using what Roger Harrison and Richard Hopkins called, in their classic 1967 article, an experiential model as opposed to a university model.

When colleges and universities come to recognize that study abroad is specifically integrative, not just broadly educational, more emphasis can be placed on connecting their experiences abroad with their academic life back on campus. Courses abroad taught by faculty from the home campus should address the implications of the conversation between locals that a student overheard on the bus as well as assigned readings, and debriefing opportunities on campus should focus on more than reverse culture shock. Staff can validate and help students explore the challenges of study abroad to their world view.

Service-Learning

Service-learning grows out of concerns for developing civic responsibility that lie at the heart of American democracy. Drawing on Lori Varlotta's (1997) recent review of service-learning theory, we find what distinguishes service-learning from community service is its integration into academic courses, the development of links between experience and theory. Those links should be mutually enriching: theory learned in the classroom should inform personal experiences at the field site, and those experiences should be used in turn to critically reexamine the theory. On the other hand, what distinguishes service-learning from other forms of experiential learning is the service, which can bring the university service-learner into contact with people from different racial, ethnic, or socioeconomic strata within society, people who see the world differently.

If service-learning experiences are left as disconnected observations, as mere data to be explained by theory or to serve as empirical tests of that theory, then much of the promise of service-learning will go unfulfilled. At its best, service-learning affords the student access to a new perspective, one drawn from a different, often less privileged group in society. The integration of service-learning experiences into a new perspective is best facilitated by conversations with the people being served, so the student can learn how the world looks from their perspective. Otherwise, field observations tend to be framed by the perspective of the student's own socioeconomic location in society.

The new perspective gained through service-learning then presents an opportunity for integrative education. It can be contrasted with the disciplinary perspective of the course, affording different insights into the topic that reveal more of its complexity. If different students in the class are participating in service-learning projects at different field sites, working with different groups, then more than one service-learning perspective may emerge that can be contrasted with the academic perspective of the course. The same would hold true for an interdisciplinary course with a service-learning dimension.

A faculty or staff member setting up service-learning experiences can make better use of their integrative potential by increasing the amount of time in the field devoted to discussion between server and servee. They can also foreground class discussion devoted to connections between theory and experience.

Multicultural Learning

Multicultural learning has its roots in concerns for preserving, celebrating, and empowering the diversity of human cultures, especially those of minority groups within American society. In her work on multicultural learning, Jane Fried (1995) argues that cultures provide a paradigm or frame of reference through which individuals see and interpret the world and out which they construct their own lenses. Grant Cornwell and Eve Stoddard (1994) accept that each cultural tradition brings a different perspective to the curriculum, but they argue that multicultural learning does not live up to its educational potential when it merely celebrates diversity, studying each cultural tradition as separate, static, and morally neutral instead of bringing out their dynamic interactions, power differentials, and competing moral claims. Students need to see diversity not simply as difference but also as "common human needs across cultures or interdependence among groups who identify themselves as different" (p. 42).

Cornwell and Stoddard advocate an approach to multicultural learning, what they call interculturalism, that combines interdisciplinary study and multiculturalism: "One needs knowledge from multiple disciplines and multiple cultures to begin to understand the dynamics of cultural identity, cultural interaction, cultural critique" (p. 44). In short, they present multicultural learning as a kind of integrative pedagogy, not just dependent on interdisciplinary study but analogous to it. Cultures afford perspectives whose insights must be integrated (with each other as well as with those coming out of disciplinary perspectives) in order to understand the cultural complexity of our society.

Integration comes from identifying commonalties as well as differences, then building on those commonalties to mitigate the conflict between cultures. Multicultural learning provides the awareness of one's own perspective which Fried (1995) points out is a prerequisite for that integration: "lenses function unconsciously unless they are challenged or a contrasting view appears. Among people who share them, lenses are taken for granted" (p. 25).

Appreciation of the integrative challenge of multicultural learning should lead faculty to shift the focus of discussions of other cultures and subcultures from celebration of diversity to critical examination of the distinctive contributions of each to a richer understanding of the complexity of the world around us.

What's Next?

As much as interdisciplinary study did in the 1980s, the various integrative pedagogies are shifting in the 1990s from the radical fringe to the liberal mainstream (Newell, 1998). Over half of all colleges and universities in the United States now offer an interdisciplinary component to their required liberal education program (Edwards, 1996). SUNY Stony Brook's original course clusters are now emulated by dozens of institutions nationwide and, thanks to Evergreen's Washington Center for Improving the Quality of Undergraduate Education, learning communities have spread from The Evergreen State College throughout higher education. The work of Vince Tinto and his colleagues (1994) to assess the impact of learning communities and collaborative learning has further fueled national interest. Collaborative learning strategies are now embraced by most of the disciplines and professions; indeed, it would be surprising to find a single college or university where more than one faculty member does not utilize collaborative learning. The economics of contemporary higher education makes a year of study abroad comparable to the cost of a year on campus. In response to societal pressures to reestablish community, Campus Compact and the Corporation for National Service have spread service-learning throughout the institutions of higher education, while the American Association for Higher Education has helped its spread to every discipline. Multicultural learning has been driven by the increasingly diverse cultural composition of the nation. Living/learning, on the other hand, is found in a dwindling number of institutions, perhaps because it runs up against the changing demographics of higher education. Older students with families and jobs barely have time for classes, much less the after-class life of a living/learning community. In short, the mainstreaming of most integrative pedagogies is well under way, thanks to several separate trends in the larger society as well as distinctively educational trends.

So far, however, that mainstream has kept the various integrative pedagogies quite separate. Each integrative strategy tends to be advocated by a different office, and faculty and administrators alike tend to place them in different mental compartments. While a few faculty at each institution are predisposed to try every innovation that comes along, most faculty open to curricular or pedagogical innovation tend to focus on a single integrative strategy at a time. When faculty at mainstream institutions become aware of the synergistic effect of multiple integrative pedagogies, they are now in a position to combine several of them, and dramatically reduce the gap in educational outcomes between experimental colleges and the rest of higher education.

Where would that leave experimental colleges? While they could still claim with justification that they offer a larger package of integrative pedagogies to a higher proportion of their students, the continuing mainstreaming of the integrative strategies they pioneered inevitably reduces the distinctiveness of experimental colleges. They become different in degree not kind. In the crass terms that increasingly drive higher education, their market niche is eroded. Put differently, how can experimental colleges retain their function as vital experimental laboratories when the rest of higher education keeps adopting their successful experiments?

My proposal is that experimental colleges continue to experiment. Instead of refining ever more carefully the curriculum and pedagogies that were innovative and experimental two or three decades ago, becoming merely quaint enclaves disconnected from the mainstream, they should expand their repertoire. Since the hallmark of experimental college innovations has been their integration of insights from diverse perspectives, we should embrace new sources of diversity as they emerge and incorporate them into the educational process. The source of new perspectives is unlikely to dry up, since new ones are uncovered every time old ones become accepted into the mainstream of society. Experimental colleges should continue to thrive as a distinctive leading edge in higher education, even as the initially threatening perspectives they embrace eventually become widely accepted.

John Dewey believed education should prepare students to critique the culture as well as learn from it. Experimental colleges can still serve that function for the rest of higher education by continuing to embrace new perspectives as they emerge as well as perspectives that are now more widely accepted, integrating their insights into an ever-richer understanding of our complex world.

References

Cantor, J. A. (1995). *Experiential learning in higher education: Linking classroom and community* (ASHE-ERIC Higher Education Report No. 7). Washington, DC: The George Washington University, Graduate School of Education and Human Development.

Caple, R. (1995). Foreword. *Shifting paradigms in student affairs: Culture, context, teaching, and learning.* By Jane Fried & Associates. Lanham, MD: University Press of America for the American College Personnel Association.

Clements, A. D. (1995, February). Experiential-learning activities in undergraduate developmental psychology. *Teaching of Psychology, 22* (2), 115–118.

Cornwell, G. H., Stoddard, E. W. (1994, Fall). Things fall together: A critique of multicultural curricular reform. *Liberal Education, 80* (4), 40–51.

Cross, K. (1994). The coming of age of experiential education: Part II. *NSEE Quarterly, 19* (4), 7.

Edwards, A. F., Jr. (1996). *Interdisciplinary undergraduate programs: A directory.* Acton, MA: Coply.

Fried, J. (1995). Telescopes and kaleidoscopes: Lenses that focus our vision. In J. Fried & Associates (Eds.), *Shifting paradigms in student affairs: Culture, context, teaching, and learning* (pp. 21–38). Lanham, MD: University Press of America for the American College Personnel Association.

Gabelnick, F., MacGregor, J., Matthews, R., & Smith, B. (1990). *Learning communities: Creating connections among disciplines, faculty, and students.* New Directions for Teaching and Learning, No. 41. San Francisco, CA: Jossey-Bass.

Harrison, R., & Hopkins, R. (1967). The design of cross-cultural training: An alternative to the university model. *Journal of Applied Behavioral Sciences, 3* (4), 431–461.

Kim, Y. Y. (1988). *Communication and cross-cultural adaptation.* Philadelphia, PA: Multilingual Matters.

Klein, J. T., & Newell, W. H. (1997). Advancing interdisciplinary studies. In J. Gaff & J. Ratcliff (Eds.), *Handbook of the undergraduate curriculum* (pp. 393–415). San Francisco, CA: Jossey-Bass.

Martin, J. N. (1994). Intercultural communication: A unifying concept for international education. In G. Althen (Ed.), *Learning across cultures* (revised ed.) (pp. 9–30). Washington, DC: NAFSA, Association of International Educators.

Matthews, R. S., Smith, B. L., MacGregor, J., & Gabelnick, F. (1997). Creating learning communities. In J. Gaff & J. Ratcliff (Eds.), *Handbook of the undergraduate curriculum* (pp. 459–462). San Francisco, CA: Jossey-Bass.

National Center for Postsecondary Teaching, Learning, and Assessment. (1995). *Realizing the potential: Improving postsecondary teaching, learning, and assessment.* Washington, DC: Office of Educational Research and Development, US Department of Education.

Newell, W. H. (1998, March). Interdisciplinary studies are alive and well. *AIS Newsletter, 10 (1), 1, 6–8. Reprinted in AAHE Bulletin, 40* (8), 10–12, (1988, April); also reprinted in *The National Honors Report, 9* (2), 5–6, (Summer, 1988).

Pascarella, E. T., & Terenzini, P. T. (1991). *How college affects students: Findings and insights from twenty years of research.* San Francisco, CA: Jossey-Bass.

Pascarella, E. T., Terenzini, P. T., & Blimling, G. S. (1994). The impact of residential life on students. In C. C. Schroeder & P. Mable (Eds.), *Realizing the educational potential of residence halls* (pp. 22–52). San Francisco, CA: Jossey-Bass.

Paul, R. W. (1987). Critical thinking and the critical person. In D. Perkins, J. Lochhead, & J. Bishop (Eds.), *Thinking: The second annual conference* (pp. 373–403). Hillsdale, NJ: Lawrence Erlbaum.

Schroeder, C. C., & Mable, P. (1994). Residence halls and the college experience. In C. C. Schroeder & P. Mable (Eds.), *Realizing the Educational Potential of Residence Halls* (pp. 16–17). San Francisco, CA: Jossey-Bass.

Smith, B. L., & MacGregor, J. T. (1992). What is collaborative learning? In A. Goodsell, M. Maher, & V. Tinto, with B. L. Smith and J. MacGregor (Eds.), *Collaborative learning: A sourcebook for higher education* (pp. 10–21). University Park, PA: National Center on Postsecondary Teaching, Learning, and Assessment.

Tinto, V., Goodsell-Love, A., & Russo, P. (1994). *Building learning communities for new college students.* University Park, PA: The Pennsylvania State University, NCTLA.

Varlotta, L. (1997, Summer). A critique of service-learning's definitions, continuums, and paradigms: A move towards a discourse-praxis community. *Educational Foundations, 2* (3), 53–85.

12

Should the Teacher Know the Answer? Two Ways to Organize Interdisciplinary Study Around Inquiry[1]

Donald L. Finkel
The Evergreen State College

My dear man, I said, how could one answer, when . . . he does not know and does not profess to know . . . ?

—Plato, 1974

In Plato's early (Socratic) dialogs, Socrates is notorious for professing ignorance with respect to the philosophical questions he and his interlocutors examine in conversation. Indeed, in Book I of the *Republic,* just prior to the quotation above, the sophist Thrasymachus lambastes Socrates in public for this habit: "You know very well that it is much easier to ask questions than to answer them. Give an answer yourself and tell us what you say justice is" (Plato, 1974, p. 11).

Readers and scholars have argued for centuries whether or not Socrates' profession of ignorance is sincere. One reading of Socrates' approach to philosophy (and education) assumes that it is not. In this reading, Socratic education requires the teacher to guide the student on an inquiry to which the teacher already knows the answer. His knowledge of the answer allows him to formulate the right questions, to provide the right tasks, and in general to structure an effective journey of discovery for his students. Without a knowledge of the answer to the question that provokes the inquiry, the teacher would have no basis for teaching.

Another reading stresses Socrates' repeated insistence that he is not a teacher, and takes him at his word when he professes ignorance. In this reading, Socratic education requires the teacher to organize a genuinely mutual inquiry for student and teacher alike. In this case, the question provides the motive for inquiry, and a shared interest in the question provides the indispensable common ground for student and teacher to inquire together.

It is not my purpose in this chapter to argue for one reading of Plato's dialogs over another, nor will I argue that one of the two methods of teaching "Socratically" is superior to the other. Rather, I shall formulate them as two worthy and entirely distinct approaches to organizing interdisciplinary study around inquiry.

But before we can connect Socratic education to interdisciplinary teaching, we need to understand the concept that links them: inquiry. Organizing study around inquiry is but one of several ways to go about interdisciplinary teaching. Before contrasting the two Socratic approaches to inquiry, we must establish the place of inquiry-centered study within interdisciplinary teaching. Let's begin by examining four different ways that experienced teachers and administrators actually conceive of interdisciplinary teaching.

Four Conceptions of Interdisciplinary Teaching

Imagine that you are in conversation with a colleague; he is a traditional academic who has become convinced of the value of interdisciplinary teaching, but he can't imagine concretely—in terms of the nuts and bolts of teaching—how to go about actually teaching in this fashion. You have done quite a bit of interdisciplinary teaching yourself. You are convinced it provides powerful learning in students and you want to promote this kind of teaching among your colleagues. How would you explain to your colleague how you go about designing and organizing an interdisciplinary course?

Sixteen college faculty and administrators who fit the description of "you" in the above paragraph chose to attend a session entitled "Different Ways to Organize Interdisciplinary Study" at the Conference on Interdisciplinary Education at The Evergreen State College that became the occasion for this book. This session was one of eight concurrent sessions on a Friday morning, so we can assume that those sixteen were interested in the question conveyed by the session's title.

These teachers and administrators were drawn to a session whose title contained the phrase "interdisciplinary study" because they expected to meet like-minded teachers following approaches similar to theirs, and because they hoped to find colleagues with whom to discuss their own teaching practices. The first thing that faced them when the session began was a written version of the question in the paragraph above. I asked them to take 15 minutes to write out an answer to that question and, securing their permission to use their responses, I collected them at the session's end. The participants' written responses to this question, and to the two additional questions on which they wrote,[2] divided naturally into four distinct categories. Each is described below. These conceptions should not be taken to describe the participants' formal definitions of interdisciplinary teaching; rather, they describe what the teachers actually practice under this rubric. Of the 16 participants, six considered interdisciplinary teaching as teaching organized around unifying themes, whose purpose was to help students make connections between separate academic disciplines. They described what they did by emphasizing the topics that required more than one discipline to understand, the perspectives that individual disciplines had to offer on a theme, and the connections between disciplines they hoped students would appreciate. Of the six, four said they found that the term "interdisciplinary" best described their approach (and a fifth opted for "multidisciplinary"), and four said that team teaching was required for interdisciplinary teaching (although one of these hedged).

These participants conceived interdisciplinary education as resting on a disciplinary foundation. They self-consciously chose themes and topics that would link the disciplines that provided this foundation. They did not appear to aim at provoking students into genuine inquiry. One teacher specified a question he finds helpful in starting to design an interdisciplinary course: "What are some shared concepts, vocabulary, approaches and assumptions of *the disciplines feeding into the course?"* (emphasis added). A chemistry professor wrote, "One way we organize interdisciplinary teaching in the sciences is to discuss themes that are common to all areas." A literature teacher said, "I find it useful to ask my colleague to identify a topic or theme which she/he would find it valuable to have more than a single disciplinary perspective on, perhaps a large social or political topic, or a disciplinary approach which might be criticized from another perspective."

In marked contrast to this theme-based approach was the major competing point of view in this pool of responses. Of the remaining ten, six participants considered interdisciplinary teaching to be inquiry-centered teaching. These described the design of their teaching by emphasizing problems, interesting questions, processes, problem solving, and student inquiry. Of the six, only one said she found the term "interdisciplinary" a good label for what she did, and only one felt that team teaching was required.

These last two results reflect the fact that this group of teachers does not see interdisciplinary teaching as resting on a disciplinary foundation, nor do they see its primary aim as getting students to locate connections between preexisting disciplines. Rather, they see education as flowing out of a classroom inquiry into a problem or question. Disciplinary skills and perspectives are brought in only as means to the end of making progress on the problem, not as ends in themselves. Thus, one teacher wrote, "Posing the large question helps to 'open up' the topic and helps us to imagine the disciplinary skills and perspectives we'll need in order to address it." Another said, "It seems to me that real 'problem solving' or 'question-based research' frequently leads to using diverse angles of approach—so I pick a topic that no one discipline 'owns' and look at what they all have to say about it."

This approach puts the students' acts of knowing above the teachers' acts of teaching, and in some cases clearly involves the teacher as partner-in-inquiry with her students. As the first-quoted teacher above put it, "Posing the large question also keeps the focus on the learning rather than the teaching—on what we (faculty and students) want to know rather than on what faculty want to teach." Another teacher advised her imaginary colleague to "leave room for inquiry led by students into areas that you might or might not have thought of." Finally, one teacher explicitly made her own question the starting point of her interdisciplinary teaching: "I find myself drawn in my own thinking and research to topics or *questions* that I can't seem to figure out—so I roam around all the resources I can find that might help me figure it out, wherever I might find them" (her emphasis). Such a question, and the resources she finds to address it, become the foundation of her course.

The remaining four participants split into two further categories. Since these were represented by only two people each in this group, I will discuss them only briefly.

Two teachers conceived of interdisciplinary teaching as the organizing of learning communities for students. These teachers emphasized the collaborative learning of students and the importance of creating a context of community in the course. Neither of them thought that team teaching was required to do this, and neither found the term "interdisciplinary" a good adjective for his approach.

The remaining two teachers took a more individual approach with respect to their goals for students. Their objective was for students to achieve a personal integration that represented a distinct achievement. Such an achieved perspective on a problem or issue might be different for each student, but for each it would be personally meaningful. One teacher spoke of the way different disciplines influence students' "world views" and the other emphasized the need for her students to formulate and integrate "their own perspectives" on the themes and issues of the course. Both these teachers found the term "interdisciplinary" apt for what they did, but only one thought it required team teaching.

Thus, from among 16 faculty and administrators interested and involved in interdisciplinary teaching, we find four distinct ways of conceiving interdisciplinary pedagogy. Each rests on a different foundation: the first on several disciplines that illuminate a common theme, the second on group inquiry into a problem of common interest, the third on the learning community in which study takes place, and the fourth on students' need to find an individually meaningful perspective from which to make sense of their world.

Clearly, each of these approaches represents a significant alternative to traditional single-discipline teaching whose aim is coverage. Clearly, in the hands of an enthusiastic and experienced teacher or team of teachers, each approach can result in exciting courses that provoke significant learning in students. I have no wish to disparage any of them. But I do want to argue that one of them is the most powerful. I would recommend inquiry-centered teaching to all faculty and administrators who wish to promote interdisciplinary study for one simple reason: within its framework the other three approaches can be easily subsumed; all their objectives can be accomplished in the process of organizing interdisciplinary study around inquiry.

Interdisciplinary Study as Inquiry-Centered

What exactly is an inquiry-centered course? Here is one description:

> Inquiry-centered courses are not labeled with the traditional subject-matter names: British Victorian Literature, American History, Micro-Economics. Their object is not to *cover* some amount of material conventionally designated by course titles. They do not aim to *cover* anything, and therefore the teacher is freed from that universal strait-jacket: the demand for *coverage*—the need to get to a certain "place" by a certain date.
>
> Instead, these courses are defined as an inquiry into a *problem* and are titled accordingly. Students learn those parts of traditional subjects they can use to tackle the problem, and no more. In a course called *Political Ecology* students learn large chunks of economics and biology as they wrestle with the problem of reconciling economic prosperity and environmental protection. In *Health: Individual and Community,* they master parts of biology, psychology, anthropology, and sociology in their attempt to discover whether or not there are new ways to conceive of health care.
>
> Such a shift changes everything. To teach such a course the teacher must first have a problem—one that will interest students, and that also interests him. Once he has the problem he can then launch the investigation. It is from the investigation, the attempt to solve the problem, that learning will flow. (Finkel, 2000, pp. 7–8)

Inquiry-centered teaching not only uses inquiry as a basis for organizing teaching and learning, but it also teaches inquiry. That is perhaps its primary justification. By organizing study around inquiry, a teacher engages her students in critical thinking about a problem or question. In addition to learning whatever they must learn to confront the specific question, the students will learn how to use the resources around and within them to solve any problem. These resources include first, their own minds, second, the minds of their fellow inquirers in the class, and third, whatever external resources they end up drawing on (assigned books, library, internet, field trips, labs, the teacher, etc.).

Most (but not all) inquiry-centered courses will be interdisciplinary. Most problems can be fruitfully approached with the tools, resources, and perspectives of more than one academic discipline. Therefore, inquiry-based courses that are interdisciplinary will meet the objectives of teachers who conceive of interdisciplinary teaching as theme-based. But there will be a kind of figure-ground reversal. The point will not be: Look at the interesting connection between psychology and biology. Rather, it will be: Look how psychology and biology together bear in interesting ways on the question of health. Disciplinary connections and perspectives are not sought as ends in themselves, but rather as tools for making sense of a problem. But they are still part of what is learned. Disciplinary learning inevitably goes on in an inquiry-centered course, but not as the primary focus.

There is no better way to organize an inquiry-centered course than as a learning community. While it would be possible to organize a course such that each student pursued his own inquiry as an isolated individual, such an approach squanders much of what is available in a group to advance an inquiry. Seminar discussions, group presentations, study groups, having students read and respond to each others' written work, collaborative research projects: The list of ways to exploit the potential of the group in inquiry-centered learning is almost endless. Through self-conscious use of such means, a teacher creates a learning community dedicated to the investigation of a problem of common interest.

But organizing a course as a learning community in no way precludes the objective held by the fourth group of teachers at the session on interdisciplinary study: having each student achieve his own personal integration or perspective on the subject matter. To pursue a problem together does not necessitate finding a single solution on which all agree. Indeed, in one of my own most successful courses organized as a learning community, "In Search of Socrates," the explicit objective is for each student to come to his own interpretation of Socrates. In the initial handout, I quote a well known Socratic scholar who wrote, "in spite of the application of the most scientific methods, in the end we must all have to some extent our own Socrates, who will not be precisely like anyone else's"

(Guthrie, 1971, p. 4). But in trying to come to our own personal interpretation of Socrates, we work together in this course as a community of inquiry from first to last. We work together on *the same problem* and we *work together* on the same problem. But in the end, we each come to our own conclusion—one that is personally meaningful to us, that is, one that reflects the way each of us individually made meaning of the material we studied together.

Inquiry-centered interdisciplinary teaching is also powerful, then, not only because it promotes inquiry, but also because it so readily fulfills the objectives of the other three approaches to interdisciplinary teaching at the same time. To me it seems the most profound approach to interdisciplinary study.

Two Ways to Organize an Inquiry

If you decide to pursue the path of inquiry-centered teaching, you will be walking in the footsteps of Socrates. "Let us inquire together" was his constant refrain. Socrates insisted he was not a teacher because he claimed he had no knowledge worth imparting and because he never accepted payment for his company in conversation. But many of his admirers felt otherwise and identified themselves as his students. They felt they learned something valuable by conversing with him. From their point of view, organizing a mutual inquiry was a powerful form of teaching.

We may agree up to this point, but we are still faced with the question which with we started. The teacher will organize an inquiry for her students, but should the teacher know the answer?

My purpose here is not to answer this question; rather, it is to argue that how any individual teacher answers it for any one course she teaches makes a big difference. I think the question must be faced when planning an inquiry-centered course. How a teacher (or teaching team) answers it will affect many details of instructional planning, and more important, the overall ethos of the course. A yes answer places the teacher in one kind of relationship with her students, a no in quite a different kind. Let us start with the affirmative answer.

If the Teacher Knows the Answer

To say the teacher knows the answer is shorthand for saying that she has a clear conception of what she wants the students to understand by the course's end. To have such a clear conception, she must already understand what it is she is aiming to get her students to understand. This may not be the answer to the question around which the inquiry-centered course is organized—it may not be the complete answer, the true answer, the definitive answer, or the only answer. But it is an answer, and it is an answer about which the teacher must have considerable conviction, else why would she waste all her time and all her students' time trying to get them to achieve it?

An example of such a course from my own teaching experience is one called "Development: The Aim of Education."[3] When I first conceived, planned, and taught this course, I taught it alone.[4] This was a course for students interested in education—for any reason at all. The course inquiry was centered around the following question: What does it mean to take development as the aim of education? I broke this question down into three subsidiary questions:

1) What does development mean?
2) What are the concrete implications and practical consequences of taking development to be the aim of education?
3) What is the value of taking development to be the aim of education?

At the center of this inquiry was my attempt to get my students to develop a sophisticated grasp of the concept of development as it is used in developmental psychology. The course was interdisciplinary in that it combined developmental psychology, social psychology, and philosophy of education. It also included a teaching practicum. My strategy was to provide several instances of developmental theory (i.e., cognitive development, moral development, personality development, and small group development) and a number of concrete cases of development (from novels, short stories, and their own personal experience in a laboratory group) so that the students could slowly and gradually generalize from them a well-articulated, well-differentiated overall conception of development. This conception was honed and tested in their teaching practicum.

As is obvious, I designed this course based on my own understanding of the concept of development and my own answers to the three subsidiary questions listed above, answers on which I have based my teaching career. As also should be obvious, I could not have designed this particular course without such answers. To plan and teach "Development: The Aim of Education," it was necessary that I thought I knew the answer to the question around which the course was organized. It was also necessary that I believed, as I did, that the conception of development[5] I was teaching was vital to grasp for anyone aiming at a career in education.

The advantage in organizing a course this way is that the teacher has a clear aim, and this aim informs virtually every decision she has to make. Moreover, the aim is conceptual; it is not a process aim; it is substantive. I had an idea in my mind that I wanted students to have in theirs by the end of the course. I knew I could not transfer it to them directly by telling it to them.[6] So I had to organize a learning environment with such a structure, and with such content, that by interacting together in it my students could eventually develop this conceptual understanding for themselves. Designing such an environment is a complex affair. Having a clear, conceptual aim goes a long way toward helping a teacher figure out how to do it.

My conceptual aim informed every decision I made: what readings to assign, what class activities to organize, what to say in response to any given student question at any given moment, what kind of comments to put on student essays, what kind of exams to give, how to guide a class discussion, when to step in and say something, when to keep my mouth shut, and on and on.

This conceptual aim also gave me a clear way to evaluate my own work as a teacher. At the course's end, I could ask myself, drawing on whatever evidence was at hand: How well or how poorly did each student grasp this conception of development? How well or how poorly did each student see its implications in practice? How well or how poorly could each student use the concept in solving concrete intellectual or practical problems? I was not systematic in asking or answering these questions, but they focused my thinking in evaluating my course and in reflecting on what I would do differently the next time I taught it. (And if I had wanted to be systematic, I would have known how to proceed.)

Finally, holding this conceptual aim affected my pedagogical position with respect to my students. It placed me outside their inquiry, as a guide. Even though I wasn't telling it to them, it was obvious from the way I ran the course that I thought I knew the answer to our inquiry. This left me in a fairly traditional role with respect to my students. As is usually the case with teachers, I embodied for my students someone who already knew what they were striving to learn. I represented an end point to their inquiry (at least, a temporary one). My presence as one who knows the answer helped keep the students focused on the conceptual aim, and suggested that attaining it was possible. It also gave them confidence in the value of all the class activities and assignments I imposed on them.

If the Teacher Doesn't Know the Answer

To say the teacher doesn't know the answer means exactly that. But there are many things he must know. Above all, he must have a clear conception of the question which frames the inquiry. And he must genuinely be interested in it himself. Unless the teacher wishes to pursue this inquiry himself, it will probably not work for him to organize an inquiry-centered course around that question. The teacher's explicit or implicit posture in this kind of course is to invite students to join him in an activity in which that he is already engaged.[7]

The teacher must also know how to organize an inquiry into the question. Although he may not know the answer to the question provoking the inquiry, he must already have spent some time pursuing this inquiry on his own or with colleagues, so that he can have an informed judgment about how to proceed with students. This experience will let him know what books to assign, what activities to pursue, what subsidiary questions to ask, what papers to assign—in sum, how to organize his course.

The best example of such a course from my own teaching experience is one called "In Search of Socrates." Like "Development: The Aim of Education," I conceived, planned, and taught this course alone. Unlike "Development," this course lasted for only one quarter. The course inquiry centered around a problem that is best expressed as a series of overlapping and interrelated questions:

- What was Socrates trying to do?
- Why did he carry on philosophical conversations in the frustrating manner depicted in Plato's early dialogs?
- Why does no one apparently ever learn anything from these conversations?
- Why did Socrates live his life the way he did?
- Why did he die the way he did?
- Was he a great teacher, as history has taken him to be?
- Or was he no teacher at all, as he, himself, repeatedly insisted?

The course was designed for anyone interested in the figure of Socrates. It was based primarily on an intensive reading of almost all of Plato's early (i.e., Socratic) dialogs, but also included texts by Aristophanes and Xenophon, the only two of Socrates' contemporaries other than Plato whose writings about him have survived, as well as a few interpretations of Socrates by later critics (including Nietzsche). Our study combined the methods of literature and philosophy.

When I designed this course, I knew I did not know the answers to the questions listed above, but I was keenly interested in pursuing answers to them. I had studied enough of the materials about Socrates to have confidence in my ability to organize an inquiry about him.

Moreover, in this case, the task was fairly simple. Because I had all my students' academic time at my disposal for ten weeks, and because there remains only a small body of primary texts on Socrates, I was able to have them read virtually all of it,[8] and at a fairly leisurely pace. We were thus in the enviable position of having in front of us (admittedly in translation) most of what specialized scholars examine in confronting the same question. And since no one has solved the problem of Socrates to everyone's satisfaction, we stood as good a chance as anyone of making a breakthrough. I told my students that their inexperience, freshness, and naiveté with respect to the material might be just what was needed, and I meant it. Thus, the idiosyncratic features of this particular inquiry, in conjunction with the utterly engaging and perplexing nature of the Platonic dialogs, allowed me immediately to create an ethos of intellectual excitement in this course.

I had as much conviction about the importance of studying Socrates as I did about the value of studying development. In this case, however, my conviction did not stem from thinking I had a fully worked out answer to the question we were examining. It wasn't the answer that I had to assess in order to see the value. It was the process itself. I knew that studying Socratic texts led students to examine their own lives, to learn how to assess logical arguments, to discover the relationship between character and education, to develop dramatic and literary sensitivity, to think about moral and epistemological questions of the first order, and to learn about inquiry by finding themselves in the midst of it. I didn't have to know the answers to the Socratic paradoxes in order to be convinced of the value of confronting them. The teacher's conviction in this approach to inquiry-centered teaching is just as important as in the first mode; it just derives from a different source.

Not knowing the answer to the inquiry myself, my aim in teaching this course could not have been to stimulate the students to develop a particular interpretation of Socrates. Nonetheless, I was guided by a clear aim: that they each succeed in developing some particular interpretation of Socrates, one well grounded in the texts, one they could argue for persuasively, one that connected to their own experience of themselves and the world, one that would have an impact on their future lives—in sum, one they could call their own. I assumed such an interpretation would be different for each student, and, of course, for any particular student, I could not presume to know its shape. Nevertheless, this aim was as clear as the one I had in "Development: The Aim of Education." One might call it a process aim, since I wanted each student to go through a process, but the term would be misleading, since the aim required the completion of a product—a final interpretation expressed in a written essay. To the students this aim couldn't have felt more substantive.

My challenge in helping my students attain this aim was quite similar to my previous one in "Development": I had to organize a learning environment that would provoke my students into developing their own understanding of Socrates. Since I was working on the same project, and was quite a few steps ahead of them, I had a pretty clear notion of how to constitute such an environment. Its most distinctive feature was that I never gave a single lecture or formal presentation during the whole course. Our work consisted of reading texts in common, discussing them together, writing about them, reading each others' writing, and writing back to the authors of those essays. My conceptual aim informed all my decisions, the same ones I mentioned in discussing "Development." Most important, my conceptual aim helped me determine a useful sequence for reading the dialogs[9] and it helped me formulate the five formal essay assignments. Each of these assignments built on the previous ones, and the first four led up to the fifth essay that asked the students finally to formally respond to the question around which the course inquiry was organized.

As before, my conceptual aim gave me a clear way of evaluating my work as a teacher. After reading the collection of final essays, I could ask myself how well I had succeeded in achieving my aim: How many students had succeeded in constructing an intelligent, meaningful, persuasive interpretation of Socrates? How many had succeeded in finding a Socrates that mattered to them, that would have some lasting impact on their lives? In response to questions like these, a teacher doesn't end up with a quantitative answer, but rather strong impressions and an overall conviction that he uses to revise and shape his teaching the next time around.[10]

Finally, not knowing the answer affected my pedagogical position with respect to my students. Rather than placing me outside the inquiry, it placed me squarely within it: my students and I were all in the same boat. Yes, I had more experience with the texts, more historical background, more knowledge of the scholarly commentaries, but I didn't think I knew the answer to the question we were investigating. This crucial factor made us equals despite all our differences. It also kept the students' attention off me and on Socrates. It allowed me to suggest ideas and interpretations in discussions without their being taken as the right answers. Their final essays left no doubt of my students' ability to retain their critical judgment vis-a-vis my ideas and interpretations.

Still, I did function as something of a model for them—not as an embodiment of one who knows, but rather, one striving to know. They saw and felt me working along with them trying to make sense of our problem; I put so much energy into the project, they could be confident that it was worth their while to do the same. Since I did not claim to have succeeded, they didn't need to feel discouraged in the face of their own confusion. What mattered was to stay engaged in the inquiry and to make some progress. When the difficulty of the inquiry is so universally acknowledged, each step in understanding, each insight, is all the more precious. And such moments happened for every student.

Two Sources of Intellectual Stimulation

Every teacher needs intellectual stimulation from her work. Both the approaches to inquiry-centered teaching I have described provide intellectual stimulation for the teacher, but the sources differ. In the Socrates program, my students and I received our intellectual challenges and rewards from the same sources: the puzzles, paradoxes, perplexities, and wisdom contained within the Socratic texts and the deeply interesting figure of Socrates as Plato presents him. These lay at the center of our inquiry. But the process of inquiry itself, along with the members of our community of inquiry, also engaged and animated us. The surprise at a bright new idea spoken in seminar or encountered on the pages of an essay, the thrill of unraveling a knot of meaning during a discussion, the excitement that comes from discovering a link between today's text and one discussed two weeks ago, all such pleasures gratify the teacher just as they do the group of students. In sum, the pleasures of teaching this way are the pleasures of collaborative inquiry itself.

In a course like "Development" the teacher cannot share so directly in the excitement and rewards of group inquiry, because she stands outside it. True, she will be pleased to observe the struggles and victories of her students, she will share vicariously in them, but her direct participation in the process is muted at best. She must look elsewhere for her primary source of intellectual stimulation.

She need not look hard, for she cannot avoid it. With this approach the source of intellectual challenge lies in the teacher's reconstructing the subject matter she understands so that she can design an inquiry for her students that will lead them also to understand it. She must turn the products of her understanding back into the processes that led to them, and then organize her course activities so that her students are induced to go through those processes.

Such a project is rigorous and challenging. It requires taking your subject matter apart and putting it back together again. It requires undoing your own seamless edifice of knowledge, locating the seams and hinges that hold the construction together, and then finding ways to help students build their own construction, piece by piece until it is whole. Their construction may end up looking something like yours, but they must build it themselves.

This project is, if anything, more daunting than that of pursuing the inquiry along with your students. It is certainly as challenging, and, when successful, as gratifying. The passage below suggests something of its flavor.

> The imperative to rethink one's subject matter, whatever else it may entail, implies that the teacher must impose some kind of unity on the subject

> matter of his course. The notions of personal synthesis or individual construction necessarily imply some form of unity—precisely because they are the products of an individual mind, and not a committee or a crowd. The personal synthesis is, in fact, the teacher's organized *response* to his subject matter; it constitutes the very essence of his *responsibility* as a teacher. To assimilate the diverse facts, events, experiences, and questions of a subject to one point of view, to make this diversity organized and coherent, that is what is meant by understanding a subject. And despite all the brilliant scholars in one's field, there is no way to sidestep the job of doing this work for yourself. (Finkel, 1989)[11]

Whether she knows the answer or not, either way the teacher faces a stimulating challenge in teaching her course. Either way she learns something.

A Personal Shift

In my own teaching life, each of these two approaches to organizing interdisciplinary teaching around inquiry has proved gratifying and successful. On intellectual grounds, I have no reasons for preferring one over the other, and I will not argue that one is superior to the other. However, the 22 years I have spent teaching at Evergreen have seen me slowly shift from one approach to the other. I first taught "Development: The Aim of Education" in 1978, whereas "In Search of Socrates" was first offered in 1993. Over the years I seem to have shifted the way I have chosen to teach. The shift has been gradual, and, to me, imperceptible while it was happening. Only recently did it strike me that the ground I like to stand on when I teach is quite different from what it was when I came to Evergreen in 1976.

Why did I change? The first reason is that after a while, I got tired of teaching what I knew so well. What I taught continued to excite students, but after a while it stopped exciting me. The second reason is perhaps more interesting.

The vast majority of my teaching at Evergreen has been done with colleagues. Year after year I have worked in teams of two, three, four, or even five colleagues from different disciplines teaching coordinated studies programs—full-time, usually year-long, interdisciplinary courses of study organized around themes, questions, or problems. Year after year, I have had to read new books assigned by my colleagues, lead discussions of them alone in my seminars, and struggle along with my students to understand them. Even when I taught in programs that were not systematically or self-consciously organized as inquiry, I had to engage in inquiry with both colleagues and students about individual questions, the meaning of individual books, the connections among series of books and assortments of ideas. From the beginning I liked this work, and its spell took hold of me over the years.

My teaching work here is so collaborative that, as part of a teaching team, I never start planning by asking myself, "What do I want to do?" The question is always: "What do we want to do?" And so it is only in those rare instances when circumstances lead me to teach alone that I squarely face the former question. Between 1982 and 1993 I never taught alone. And so in 1992, when I had to decide what to teach by myself the following year, and consequently asked myself: "What do I want to do," I found myself answering it in a profoundly different way than I had in 1977.

It took quite a few years after that for me to realize that I was now answering this question differently and to reflect on that difference. It was interdisciplinary teaching itself—interdisciplinary team teaching—that had slowly led me to understand that there is more than one way to organize interdisciplinary teaching around inquiry. It was the kind of collegial teaching in coordinated studies that is a way of life at Evergreen that first gave me the taste for inquiry-centered teaching, a taste that became a deep-seated appetite, and finally led me to value inquiry-centered study over interdisciplinary teaching. I have come to see that inquiry-centered teaching can be pursued fruitfully even without a team of colleagues, and even, on occasion, when the inquiry isn't interdisciplinary. Regardless of such variations, what seems to have become more constant over the years is my unwillingness to organize an inquiry for students and leave myself out of it.

Either Way

Socrates may or may not have thought he knew the meaning of such ethical concepts as justice, courage, and virtue, but either way he was convinced of the importance of mutual inquiry into their meaning. As he says to Meno at a key moment in his dialog with him:

> I do not insist that my argument is right in all other respects, but I would contend at all costs both in word and deed as far as I could that we will be better men, braver and less idle, if we believe that one must search for the things that one does not know . . . . (Plato, 1976, p. 86b)

If you become convinced of the value of inquiry-centered teaching, you need not decide whether or not Socrates knew the answer. You need only decide whether to organize an inquiry for your students around a question whose answer you understand well, or whether to join your students investigating a question that puzzles and interests you deeply.

Either way you can provide an invigorating education for your students. But, for any one course, you would do well to be clear which endeavor you are choosing.

References

Dewey, J. (1916). *Democracy and education.* New York, NY: Macmillan.

Finkel, D. L. (1989). To teach is to reconstruct. In E. O. y Miranda (Ed.), *Proceedings of far western philosophy of education society, 1989* (pp. 129–135). Alberta, Canada: University of Calgary.

Finkel, D. L. (2000). *Teaching with your mouth shut.* Portsmouth, NH: Heinemann.

Guthrie, W. K. C. (1971). *Socrates.* Cambridge, MA: Cambridge University Press.

Plato. (1974). *Republic.* (G. M. A. Grube, Trans.). Indianapolis, IN: Hackett.

Plato. (1976). *Meno.* (G. M. A. Grube, Trans.). Indianapolis, IN: Hackett.

Endnotes

1. I am grateful to Norman Chonacky, Virginia Darney, Susan Finkel, and Nancy Koppelman for their constructive comments on drafts of this chapter. I would also like to thank the 16 participants in the session discussed in this chapter for their enthusiastic participation and their willingness to let me use their written views.
2. The exact written questions were:

   Please answer the following three questions in writing. We will discuss them during the second hour.

   1. (15 minutes) Imagine that you are in conversation with a colleague; he is a traditional academic who has become convinced of the value of interdisciplinary teaching, but he can't imagine concretely—in terms of the nuts and bolts of teaching—how to go about actually teaching in this fashion. Explain to him how you go about (or would go about) designing and organizing an interdisciplinary course.
   2. (5 minutes) Does interdisciplinary teaching as you conceive it require team teaching? Explain.
   3. (10 minutes) Is the kind of teaching on which your response to questions 1 and 2 are based best described by the term "interdisciplinary"? If so, explain why. If not, is there a more precise term to

describe it? Consider the following possibilities: "adisciplinary," "antidisciplinary," "predisciplinary," "subdisciplinary," "superdisciplinary," "multidisciplinary." Invent your own term if you prefer. Explain why the term you selected fits your approach.

3. Since this course was taught at Evergreen, it was a full-time course of study (equivalent to four normal courses and the only course a student takes for the duration)—what Evergreen calls an academic program. This particular academic program lasted for three academic quarters (one full academic year).

4. Although most of my teaching career has been devoted to team teaching, for the sake of clarity and simplicity, I have taken as my two examples, courses that I have taught alone. Team teaching complicates the issue of whether or not the teacher knows the answer, but it does not make it go away. The third time I taught "Development: The Aim of Education," I did so with a teaching colleague, but we stuck pretty close to my original course design. As a result of a summer project we had engaged in previously, he understood—and shared—the conception of development that was at the center of the course. In addition, our weekly faculty seminars allowed us to attain a common understanding, both of the course materials and of the specific instructional objectives around which we were making weekly decisions in planning the daily details of the course.

5. The conception of development I am speaking of is grounded philosophically in the work of John Dewey, most fully elaborated in *Democracy and Education.* However, it was well understood, though not explicitly articulated, by Jean-Jacques Rousseau in his remarkable classic, *Emile, or On Education.* This conception lies at the heart of Jean Piaget's massive contribution to developmental psychology. It is well described and contrasted with other educational frameworks by Lawrence Kohlberg and Rochelle Mayer in their essay, "Development as the Aim of Education" (*Harvard Educational Review, 42* (4), 449–496, November, 1972), from which I drew the course title.

6. ". . . no thought, no idea, can possibly be conveyed as an idea from one person to another. When it is told, it is, to the one to whom it is told, another given fact, not an idea. The communication may stimulate the other person to realize the question for himself and to think out a like idea, or it may smother his intellectual interest and suppress his dawning effort at thought. But what he *directly* gets cannot be an idea. Only by wrestling with the conditions of the problem at first hand, seeking and finding his own way out, does he think." This bold claim lies at the center of Dewey's *Democracy and Education,* p. 159.

7. If he has teaching colleagues also interested in the inquiry, all the better. Then the teaching team will offer the invitation to the students to join them. This arrangement has the virtue of making more visible to the students the process of inquiry, since they can watch their teachers engage in certain aspects of it. But it has the drawback of making it harder for the students to join in the inquiry, at least at first, since they begin as outsiders to a group already engaged in the process and clearly more proficient at doing so than they will feel themselves to be.

8. We read ten of the 12 Socratic dialogs (all but the *Lysis* and *Charmides*), plus famous excerpts about Socrates from Plato's middle dialogs (e.g., the allegory of the Cave, the metaphor of Socrates as a midwife), Aristophanes' comic satire of Socrates, *The Clouds,* and Xenophon's accounts of Socrates in his *Memorabilia* and *Apology.*

9. Although scholars agree on the group of dialogs called "early," there is no agreement at all on the order in which the early dialogs were written. Thus, I could not fall back on chronology as an ordering device. I had to sequence the readings solely on pedagogical grounds.

10. As I write in June of 1998, I have just completed teaching this course for the third time.

11. As the word "responsibility" in the cited passage suggests, and the final paragraph in the essay (cited below) states, at the time I wrote this chapter, I felt that teachers did have a responsibility to reconstruct their understanding of their subject matter before teaching it:

    > The pedagogical reconstruction of subject matter is the teacher's first responsibility. It shows the students in a multitude of subtle and indirect ways that the teacher is not asking them to do anything that she is not willing to do herself. It sets the proper example. And it creates a spirit of mutual inquiry that does no injustice to the necessary and avowed differences between teacher and students. This spirit is really the only one appropriate for a college classroom in a democratic society (Finkel, 1989).

    I have since changed my mind, because inquiry-centered teaching for which the teacher does not know the answer retains the virtues stated in the above paragraph; it just realizes them in a different, more direct, form.

13

JENNY'S PAINTING: MULTIPLE FORMS OF COMMUNICATION IN THE CLASSROOM

Mark Pedelty
University of Minnesota

Print is not dead yet, nor will it ever be,
but nevertheless, our language-dominated culture
has moved perceptibly toward the iconic.

—Dondis, 1973

Anna lives her life between the speakers, in front of the TV, and on the stage, wearing the ad and dreaming in color. She moves in synch and sings in tune to a world of sound, image, movement, and touch. In the college classroom, however, Anna mostly just reads and writes. It is an experience disarticulated from her world of fun. She is more often bored than inspired, and has, therefore, turned college into an instrumental issue: get the degree, get a job, and try to have a life on the side. Like most adult Americans, Anna is learning how to divide her mind and life, to split her world of work (academe) from the disciplines of fun (popular culture).

Anna's fairly universal condition poses any number of issues for college instructors. How do we integrate multiple media and popular culture into the curriculum without simply surrendering to the world of superficial, commercialized pastiche many students experience outside the classroom? How do we avoid the acritical applications of mass media currently sweeping over much of American education, such as the "Channel 1" (p. 2) cable service (Barry, 1997)? How do we teach students to critically analyze and contextualize the world of images and sounds that surrounds us without taking undo time away from the classical texts and questions which have traditionally formed the core of academic exploration? Finally, how do we integrate multiple modes of student expression and exposition—oral, aural, visual, kinesthetic—into courses traditionally designed for writing?

This chapter is primarily concerned with the latter problem, the inclusion of multiple forms of exposition in the interdisciplinary curriculum, including public speaking, artistic representation, dance, theater, and music. The issues of popular culture and course content will be considered as well, however, since these are closely linked to the problem of implementing nonwritten forms of communication, expression, and assessment in traditional classroom settings.

This discussion develops in four parts. First, I will argue for the importance of integrating multiple forms of communication into the curriculum. I will argue that the multisensory, multimedia world which our students inhabit obligates us to consider integrating oral, aural, and visual modes of literacy into interdisciplinary courses. Related problems involving mass media and audiovisual course materials will be dealt with in the second section. In the third section, I will describe what I believe to be the major ideological, cultural, and logistical sources of resistance to the use of nonwritten forms. In the fourth section, I will describe a few experimental methods for integrating nonwritten forms of communication into the curriculum, describing several successful and unsuccessful cases. I will conclude by dealing with the question of assessment, suggesting ways to teach and assess multiple forms of communication in curricula traditionally designed for expository writing.[1]

WHY INTEGRATE MULTIPLE FORMS OF COMMUNICATION INTO THE CURRICULUM?

I first became aware of the need for multimedia integration while teaching "Anthropological Theory" at the University of Minnesota, Morris, a course that would seem particularly ill-suited to visual or aural communication. A student whom I will call Jenny was having great difficulties comprehending and expressing her understanding of the texts we were reading. Jenny was having particularly acute problems with Nancy Scheper-Hughes' *Death Without Weeping* (1992), a 614 page tome whose theoretical complications and emotional weight would stretch any reader. Looking for an interlocutor between the student and the difficult text in consideration, I asked Jenny to describe her other talents, major, life goals, etc., and discovered that she is a very talented painter.

I asked Jenny to examine the process of critical assessment and representation that goes into her work as a painter. We discussed the similarities between artistic representation and anthropological critique. Weeks later, I received an invitation to a critique session in the art department. When the moment arrived, I was seated in front of a series of paintings, including one six-by-four piece entitled *Death Without Weeping.* The painting is a representation of a thin woman, a mother who is either pregnant or postnatal, hunched over, perched atop a thin projection hanging precariously over an abyss. This woman's body is fighting gravity, being pulled down, slowly, or perhaps rising, awkwardly.

Words do not suffice. And, that is the point. In her version of *Death Without Weeping* Jenny had captured the book's "structure of feeling" (Williams, 1977, p. 128) and a key aspect of Scheper-Hughes' theoretical intent (particularly the Gramscian concept of hegemony) in a way that she could not in writing. Using the painting and her artistic skills as interlocutors between text and concept, course and life project, Jenny was able to articulate her understanding of the text in a much more profound way than would have been possible were she simply forced to write about the book.

The key to success in Jenny's case was not my pedagogical intervention, but the competence of the student and the extent to which she was able to use that which she already knew in order to gain a greater understanding of that which she did not yet fully comprehend. To simply force her into writing, period, would be to lose the opportunity to allow Jenny's outside skills and interests to complement her learning and, in turn, to have the course enrich her life project of painting. This connection between life, passion, and course allowed the course to expand beyond the classroom walls for Jenny. Whereas, as college instructors, we are often competing with experiences and interests in the noncurricular lives of students, we must also remain cognizant of the potential for turning those passions into allies.

At the very least, we must be conscious of the nonclassroom environment, a world in which students spend well over 90% of their time during the academic year. We have, in our seats, musicians and kineticists of all sorts: singers, players, dancers, actors, and so on. We often ignore those aspects of their lives, however, by simply teaching writing in isolation from students' other competencies and joys. Thus we often fail to find the interlocutors—students' pleasures, talents, and preferences—which might allow us to communicate (literally, to "make common") that which we hope to teach them.

With the loss of these communicative interlocutors, we also loose an opportunity to learn from students. For example, I cannot paint trim, let alone a complex and moving work like Jenny's *Death Without Weeping.* I learned a great deal from the experience, and accidentally empowered Jenny as she went from "C-student-with-poor-writing-skills" to "painter-with-thoughts-on-theory" who was then able to learn from teaching others—including myself and her peers—in a more equalized exchange. She was able to speak in the classroom using visual language, her favored form of literacy and intelligence.

In addition to the more direct benefits, it is believed that the inclusion of multiple modes of communication can lead to increased student retention, as students like Jenny find greater articulation with and in their academic coursework. For example, greater attention to oral literacy, or orality (Olson, 1991), may help those who need to greatly improve speaking skills or, conversely, those who are particularly talented at oral communication, but much less capable when using written expression alone (Morreale, Shockley-Zalabak, & Whitney, 1993). Both groups of students may be failing due to an inability to communicate effectively with their instructors, and perhaps even with peers. Explicit attention to oral communication will improve the first group's oral skills, while empowering the second by providing a better channel of expression and course performance. Furthermore, multiple methods of communication may lead to a better understanding and appreciation of student diversity. As new methods of communication are introduced, the capacity for cross-cultural exchange increases (Hughes, 1994).

There are other compelling reasons to offer nonwritten options in the interdisciplinary course. As was mentioned above, students use a great range of communicative methods outside the classroom. They will need each of these, particularly oral skills, in their working lives. Many, if not "most college students are not provided sufficient structured practice with competent evaluation to refine and reinforce their oral communication competence in courses across the curriculum and, therefore, graduate with inadequate oral communication competence" (Cronin & Grice, 1993, p. 1). Given the academy's extreme emphasis on writing to the exclusion of other forms of communication, we might forget that writing itself developed from oral and pictorial traditions, and that there has almost always been a "priority of orality over literacy in human experience" (Havelock, 1986, p. 26). The modern electronic infrastructure is reintroducing, if not prioritizing, oral, aural, and visual modes of communication once again (Havelock, 1986). If we produce students who are unable to effect such communicative integration, we are producing citizens who are only partly literate in the contemporary world.

Mass Media and Audiovisual Materials in the College Curriculum

> The language of vision determines, perhaps even more subtly and thoroughly than verbal language, the structure of our consciousness. To see in limited modes of vision is not to see at all. (Barry, 1997, p. 107)

The general lack of attention to nonwritten communicative skills in academia is further evidence of academe's often distant relationship to other worlds and cultures, including that of popular culture. Our students enter with multiple communicative interests and skills, and will need each of these at least as much or more than writing in their future lives and employment (Welty, 1994). Yet, the academy continues to equate literacy with writing alone.[2] Like Benjamin Barber (1995), we often see books as "democracies' indispensable currency and a faltering bulwark against the new world of images and pictures flashed across screens at a speed that thwarts all deliberation" (p. 118). Following Barber's logic, academics often hold a very dim view of the mass media, looking at electronic media, particularly television, phonograms, and film, as the enemies of education. And, in many ways, they are. The corporate mass media are perhaps the primary vehicles for socializing consumers into capitalist culture. Mass media are, in the main, responsible for producing messages which are antithetical to the stated goals of liberal arts education. At the very least, academic topics are excluded from the great majority of market-driven media.

It is rarely on such grounds, however, that academics reject the mass media. Acculturated within a specific type of literacy which we have falsely universalized as an "indispensable currency," we view with great confusion and suspicion the popular media's visual and recombinant (e.g., MTV's sound and video bytes) form of communication. Our students, however, and indeed many of "us," understand this new language and recognize that the integrated and recombinant audio-visual-textual media forms are not intrinsically inferior, but instead represent forms of communication which entail both advantages and disadvantages relative to the once-dominant print media. Visual communication and images have their own history and linguistic structures which, while distinct, should not lead to Barber's conclusion that they are intrinsically inferior forms of communication (Barry, 1997).

Barber's comment represents the common academic tendency to equate print media with intellect and, conversely, to reject oral and visual communication as emotive, superficial, and less capable of serious consideration. This overwhelming predilection for print demonstrates the social conservatism of academe, operating under the ideology of the Enlightenment print era, the *Guttenberg Galaxy,* in a newer world whose social and technological modes of interaction have become based as much on oral and visual signs as printed text (McLuhan, 1969; Scholes & Willis, 1991). In sum, we are using the cultural schematics of the last century to limit our students' potential in the next.

In order to understand this ideological dichotomy between serious and superficial means of communication, it is useful to deconstruct the larger system of binary oppositions to which this particular schism belongs. In reductively distinguishing between print versus other forms of communication, academe enacts other cultural oppositions—high versus low, authentic versus decadent, elite versus popular—replicating rather than critically examining the dominant system of cultural distinction (Bourdieu, 1984).

This reductive worldview is not only enacted in the restrictive choice of assessment methods and expressive forms (written versus oral, visual, etc.), but also in the related choices concerning curricular content. At the end of the 20th century, written materials continue to dominate the curriculum to the near exclusion of other media.

This is not to say we should abandon or marginalize books for the sake of multimedia materials. There are some very sound reasons for the continued curricular emphasis on the written text. Written works have been able to retain much greater autonomy from the corporate disciplines that have largely patterned the content of electronic media, especially television. The parameters of permissible discourse are much more limited in much of the popular mass media (Herman & Chomsky, 1988; Schiller, 1989). Not only are critical political viewpoints largely excluded due to corporate and market forces, but most scholarly content is also outside the bounds of audiovisual production and broadcasting. Relative to the thousands of excellent analytical pieces in print concerning Latin America, to use my own area of research as an example, the number of useful documentary and fictional films is extremely limited. Even those films that do exist, generally are produced for much wider appeal, due to the per-unit cost of the medium. Therefore, fairly good documentaries like *Panama Deception* adopt the melodramatic narratives of the popular genres in order to reach wider audiences, somewhat limiting their academic utility as tools for use in social analysis. Books and journal articles written for academic, or even wider, distribution are much less effected by the same mass-market disciplines.

Partly due to the factors cited above, books and other written materials remain the central media for academic analysis, and probably will for some time. Audio and visual texts, therefore, are generally restricted to use as teaching aids, and will continue to be until the means of media production are more accessible and acceptable to academic researchers and instructors.

Given the current range of available materials, this selective hierarchy of books over other media is fairly understandable. It is helpful, however, when making content decisions to keep in mind the difference between media as objects for and objects of study. Granted, aside from the occasional course-related documentary or artfully drawn film, written materials often remain the best objects for the study of society. It is when the same distinction is made between legitimate objects of study that we end up reducing the potential for more complete forms of social analysis in the social science and humanities classroom. For example, few would argue that the globally-popular genre of soap opera should serve as an object for the study of society. There are few profound truths communicated via authorship, direction, or dramatic interpretation in the soap text. Yet, as an object of study, soaps provide a lens into the centuries-old serial form and melodramatic narrative (Martin-Barbero, 1987), women's discourse (Brown, 1994; Brunsdon, 1995; Harvey, 1995), cross-cultural, transnational, and global cultural patterns (Allen, 1995; Baldwin, 1995; Kreutzner & Seiter, 1991; Rogers & Antola, 1985), the political economy of mass media, in particular, and consumer capitalism, as its generative context (Flitterman, 1983; Joyrich, 1988; Mattelart, 1986; Willis, 1991).

Yet, and here is the irony and tragedy that links the issue of popular culture as content and multiple modes of communication as a teaching method: Academe tends to disallow those genres and associated texts that are the most socially effective and culturally penetrant, even as objects of study. The irony being that popular culture texts are too socially important—in the extent of their viewership, influence on behavior, articulation with dominant cultural discourses, and the mobilization of capital—to be considered in an educational context, even if that context is a forum ostensibly dedicated to the integrated study of society.

Mexican sociologist scholar Carlos Monsivais offers the following thoughts on the place of one multisensory medium, film, in the potential range of forces which motivate human behavior in the 20th century:

> However you choose to define popular culture (community practices, the catalogue of rituals and tastes, the methods of resistance against the powers that be, the transformation into folklore of the realities of class, race and gender, the assimilation and re-elaboration of the messages of the culture industry, or simply something directed at a large number of people), what is clear is that in the invention or preservation of customs, the cinema is the most powerful influence. (1993, p. 144)

While an argument could also be made for the equally dominant role of television and other media, the fact remains that to simply ignore such texts is to avoid discussion of a significant mirror and maker of social reality.

In addition to ignoring key realms and fonts of social reality, the neglect of popular culture texts (or their segregation to marginal communication curricula) results in the loss of a key interlocutor between teacher and student, between the instructor's print culture and the students' multimediated one. Their inclusion, conversely, allows us to begin a potentially fruitful dialog concerning the relative merits and qualities of each text and medium and—to return to the central topic—provides a forum of experimentation which might lead to new and better ways to use nonwritten forms of expression in the college classroom.

Unfortunately, thrown out along with the bathwater of mass media materials go the nascent forms of oral, aural, kinesthetic, and visual modes of communication associated with them. As demonstrated by the title and content of Dietrich Scheunemann's *Orality, Literacy and Modern Media* (1996), the consideration of oral literacy, or orality, and visual literacy, often calls forth their association with modern mass media. Yet, it is crucial to disentangle and better understand this association between nonwritten texts (media) and nonwritten forms of communication (method) if each is to be critically examined and used well in the college classroom.

Academic, Cultural, and Philosophical Obstacles

I have already mentioned the most profound obstacle to the creative implementation of nonprint media and their associated forms of expression: the simplistic high/low distinction which patterns much of academic content, performance, and culture. This ideological distinction between that which is academic (high) versus popular (low) culture is itself patterned philosophically upon a Cartesian template which separates the world of perception into aspects of mind versus body, intellect versus emotion, and reason versus its many irrational oppositions. In application to modes of communication, writing is viewed as the more controlled, thus cerebral, method of communicating, while oral, and particularly visual, modes are placed in the category of emotional, if not corporeal expression, suitable perhaps to creative performance in the artistic sense, but not for the purposes of serious analytical and academic performance.

Applying this traditional Western model of mind versus body, intellect versus emotion (and quite often its corollary constructs of masculine versus feminine), we privilege writing, coded as the carrier of intellect, while reductively dismissing visual and oral media, marked as they are with the stigmata of emotion. Placing them in order of development, and perhaps causation, David Olson (1991) argues that this view of reason, objectivity, and "[m]odern scientific epistemology" (p. 161) is actually a by product of literacy itself. While such a claim might be overly simplistic, the positivistic pretense which privileges writing to the exclusion of other forms of communication often leads us to reduce, almost by design, our capacity to engage and educate the more fully integrated emotive/rational beings who enter our classes. Either overtly or unwittingly believing in the truth value of simplistic high/low distinctions, we reductionistically proffer writing at the overwhelming expense of forms of expression which might not only open up new avenues of communication and discussion, but which might in fact improve our students' writing skills.

Ironically, this reductive emphasis on writing to the exclusion of other forms of communication ultimately supports the commercial mass media's monopoly of the senses. Mass media is the more affective, and thus effective, form of mass education, partly as a result of its holistic integration of visual, oral, aural, and kinesthetic aesthetics. The traditional response of academe has generally been to ignore these less intellectual senses. While we often proclaim the need for students to develop more critical ways of thinking, we are often the purveyors of the same sort of dichotomous thinking we criticize, in this case positing a reductionist set of academic practices, reading and writing, in opposition to the integrated, multisensorial environment of vision, sound, and movement which dominates cultural life outside the classroom and other disciplined work spaces in modern society.

However, an equally strong reaction is often returned from the other side of the teacher-student dialectic. Students often demonstrate an equally strong tendency to reject academic, especially written, materials and methods. If scholarship is posited as the high in contradistinction to the popular culture's low, then the divide is too often read dialectically by students as a distinction between effete (read empty and rhetorical) versus engaged (or fun) ways of understanding and experiencing the world. Many fail to take films, music, or other forms of nonwritten discourse seriously, because they also happen to be fun. The result of including such materials and discursive options may be the devolution of class time into playtime. I have certainly had to combat that trend whenever opening up the classroom to alternative media and means of expression. Conversely, the reading and exposition of written texts, culturally coded as a serious, intellectual endeavor, automatically carries with it the sort of cultural capital which will keep it from slipping into popular pastiche, if one can get the students to do it at all.

In short, school is experienced as work and popular culture as fun. One of the best expressions of this bifurcated life and mindset is found in Jules Henry's *Culture Against Man* (1963).

> Fun in America is an adaptive radiation, for it is the expression of the American's determination to stay alive. It is an underground escape from the spiritual Andersonville in which technological drivenness has imprisoned us. In fun the American saves part of his Self from the system that consumes him. Fun, in its rather unique American form, is grim resolve. When the foreigner observes how grimly we seem to go about our fun, he is right; we are as determined about the pursuit of fun as a desert-wandering traveler is about the search for water, and for the same reason. (p. 43)

We replicate this ideological system of work versus fun, intellect versus emotions, function versus pleasure in our academic coursework, by reductively removing that which has the taint of popularity, commercial connections, or mass production, including most of the methods of communication that accompany them. Just as we make a reductive attempt to expunge the study of popular texts from the curriculum, we often view visual, oral, aural, and kinesthetic modes of communication as greatly inferior to the work of writing. We see the lives and minds of our students colonized by popular, commercial forms, and take as our duty the presentation of more elevated ones. To their fun we posit our work.

In doing so we fall into the culturalist biases (Martin-Barbero, 1987) which reject all that would appear to contain elements of popular entertainment, even if many of the texts we attempt to substitute in their place were once both popular and entertaining (e.g., Shakespeare was once primarily offered for popular entertainment value). As in the Sony commercial that has an entire class of students replace their live presence before a droning professor with Sony portable tape recorders, we live out the critique engendered by popular culture by making noncommercialized spaces boring, pointless, effete, and unrelated to the cultural lives of our students, just as commercial culture would have it.

The blame can be equally shared with students, however. For each case where a student uses her outside artistic knowledge and skills (as in Jenny's case) or popular culture interests (such as a young rock musician who is moved to study ethnomusicology) successfully to enrich their learning and critical thinking skills, I have experienced at least as many students whose outside interests and modes of communication are used as a means to block their academic exploration of academic theory and material, students whose dedication to the more fun realms of communication—song, dance, cinema—is instead used in dismissive opposition to the central goals of academic exposition. "All that stuff is just (academic) bullshit," goes the line, a reductive position implicitly arguing for the primacy of more popular or sensual modes of exposition. This is perhaps the students' favored form of reductive essentialism, an argument that popular culture, art, and alternative modes of communication are able to simply explain themselves without need of expositional prose or argumentation of any sort. This is a form of extreme relativism, often identified with the postmodern (Gitlin, 1989; Sacks, 1996), which places the work of explication and any other type of expression on the same flat plane, reducing the power of both art and argument in the process.

Rather than indicate the futility of the attempt, however, such cases simply demonstrate the necessity of breaking the dichotomous thinking that takes place both among both students (the popular), and we who instruct them (the academic). In other words, perhaps we should not view this problem as a matter of art/academe versus popular culture (e.g., Shakespeare versus soap operas), or written versus multisensory modes of expression, but rather as a challenge to find ways to rigorously study and effectively teach both, while searching for new forms of expression, performance, and assessment which will get us beyond our rigid segregation of the senses.

Methods for Integrating Multiple Forms of Communication into the Curriculum

The above argument might uncover certain obstacles to the integration of nonprint forms of media and communication into the curriculum, when and to the extent that such forms intersect with issues of popular culture; but, admittedly, the argument fails to explain the extreme lack of the high arts—those which are not painted with the damning stigmata of popular culture. For example, why don't we do more to bring painting, music, dance, and the other plastic and performing arts into our classrooms? These are hardly the sorts of materials and practices which draw the damning glance of oversight committees, colleagues, and congresses. So why don't we use these arts more actively to enliven learning throughout the curriculum?

The answer to that question, while lying partly in the Cartesian argument made earlier, probably has more to do with our own talent and training limitations, and the serious logistical difficulties such additional forms of integration often entail. The beginning of this section is concerned with the latter issue, logistics. Then I will move on to matters of talent and training, demonstrating ways in which a nonspecialist might integrate the nonprint arts into his or her classes.

Oral communication is the most common and most accessible form of nonprint communication used in college courses. Disciplinary communication specialists often promote communication across the curriculum, or CAC, as a means of integrating oral modes into the curriculum (Morreale et al., 1993). Piloted at several small universities and colleges, these programs involve either full scale consultancy and direct student and faculty training on an ongoing basis by communication scholars, or less direct involvement via faculty training, audio-visual materials, and center-based instruction.

Such programs are a good idea. CAC is an additional curricular expense, however, and one which, in the current political economic climate, will not be initiated by most academic institutions. This is particularly true in the case of interdisciplinary studies, given the more limited scale and expanded mission of such programs. Therefore, I will aim this discussion more directly at the individual interdisciplinary instructors who, like me, are trying to find ways to expand the repertoire of communicational skills incorporated into their courses.

To deal with the problem of methodological integration, it would help to once again return to related questions of course content. One of the best ways to deal with the unreflective segregation of high and low cultural forms is to critically juxtapose them, perhaps as in Carlos Fuentes' play *Ceremonias del Alba* (Ceremonies of the Dawn) concerning the Conquest compared with a *telenovela* representation of colonial New Spain, or the intentional art film *Danzón* with the *cabaretera* (cabaret) films to which it draws critical reference. This allows students to appreciate the qualities of each via comparative critique, while becoming more textually aware and media savvy. The popular serves as an interlocutor into the artful, so that both popular and classic might be better understood, critiqued and appreciated on their own terms and in proper social context. This might allow students and teachers alike to find ways of thinking between and beyond the poles of absolute segregation, on one side, and extreme relativism on the other.

The same method can be applied to the question of written versus nonwritten forms. I often have students draw comparisons between written and nonwritten versions of the same or similar works. For example, to enhance their understanding of the text *MacBeth,* particularly its semiotic elasticity and differences between written and audiovisual modes of exposition, my coteachers, Terry Perlin, Andy Garrison, and I presented key scenes from three film versions of the play. Film became a form of entrée into the written text, while providing new avenues for discussion. Neither the written nor film texts alone would probably have engendered as much creative thought and learning.

The same can be said of multiple modes of communication in the classroom. It is best to integrate oral and written skills in order to cross-fertilize and improve both. K-12 teachers have known this for decades, using oral methods to improve writing. Unfortunately, oral methods and testing have largely been limited in higher education to speech, theater, and language departments (Underhill, 1987). Visual methods have found an equally limited home, largely in the professional and applied arts, including medicine (Berg, 1983).

For those of us who have centered our curricular performance around writing for so long, it is probably best to require a written component to all projects. That way we can use a familiar assessment tool to initiate critique of forms we are less comfortable with. Conversely, students who are more comfortable with nonwritten forms of communication are able to use their other talents as a means to improve writing skills. This may take the form of a process paper (i.e., describing the development of a nonwritten work) or complementary exposition (putting the argument of the nonwritten work into explicit, written prose). I prefer a combination of both. Process writing helps students discover the often unreflective aspects of audio, visual, and/or kinesthetic creation and criticism.

Expository writing helps students to develop and translate the messages of nonwritten work into the language of traditional academic argumentation, with an explicit thesis, evidence, and conclusions placed in a coherent and logical framework. Of course, this is much less of an issue with oral exposition than image-based presentations, whether visual or aural. Oral exposition, like written work, is already verbal, whereas image-oriented forms of communication need a great deal of translation to be made comprehensible in terms of verbal argumentation. Yet, fair assessment usually requires such translation.

Naturally, there should be a substantial reduction in the page length requirements for students completing visual, oral, musical, or multimedia components. As is true of interdisciplinary studies in general, some verticality, in this case page length, has to be exchanged for horizontal integration, in this case modes of performance.

It is best to continually focus on course objectives, placing all methods in service of the same goals. This was true, for example, in Jenny's case, where the mode of communication was modified, but the goal of developing insight into the conceptual content of the course was not. For most interdisciplinary courses, logistical and temporal limitations demand that nonwritten communication, like writing itself, be put immediately to task as methods for discovery and exposition, rather than viewed as ends in and of themselves (art students may balk at that suggestion). Teaching speaking skills is in itself a laudable goal, for example, but given schedule constraints this end often must be merged with and even placed in secondary service to other course objectives. As is true of much of interdisciplinary training, it is hoped that integration will have equal or greater benefits than more segmented and specialized forms of liberal arts education. While a student in a disciplinary liberal arts program would experience one concentrated speech course during her college career, her interdisciplinary counterpart would complete several courses integrating various aspects of oral communication. In the interdisciplinary curriculum, therefore, there is the danger of pastiche and lack of focused concentration on oral skills. Yet, in the interdisciplinary context oral communication would be integrated more completely and holistically into the rest of the curriculum, providing greater potential for creative integration, assimilation, and application of oral skills. The proposition of using multiple modes of exposition in the classroom, therefore, rests on the same theoretical foundation as interdisciplinary studies itself: that basic skills and subject areas need not be concentrated into their own courses in order to be effectively learned. The validity of that proposal cannot be assessed until more communicative integration is actually attempted throughout the interdisciplinary studies curriculum.

I will now briefly illustrate a few fairly successful cases, and a few less so that I have experienced, in order to provide examples of communicative integration. One example comes from a physical anthropology course that I taught before entering an explicitly interdisciplinary program. The students taking the class included a mix of science students looking for a liberal arts breadth requirement, nonscience students looking for a science not overly weighted toward mathematical performance, and a few residuals who where, as opposed to many of the others, proactively motivated and interested in the subject. Early on I was finding that the first group, the scientists, were most comfortable with the course. As one trained in science largely on the side of my more central cultural and archaeological anthropological training, I was probably overcompensating for my own prior inadequacies, focusing perhaps too directly on in-depth explanations of genetics, population dynamics, and mathematical modeling than were called for in an introductory course, having just learned and relearned many of these subjects myself. The nonscience students felt that they were out of their element, and some started falling noticeably behind.

Therefore, I started to design class periods which would allow them breathing space, and a means to incorporate their own skills and interests more directly into their learning. Foremost among these were oral debates, on ethical, social, and cultural issues, where the various skills of all students could be brought to the fore in arguing individual and collective positions. The debate concerning the use of primates as lab animals, for example, was designed as a three-way discussion. Those with a definite yes or no position would move to the right or left and those who needed convincing would move toward the middle. In a class of about 80 students, only six took sides to start, evenly split between yes and no positions. The middle group, in addition to making up their minds, was put in charge of challenging each side, forcing each to nuance their arguments and position, until at the end a decision would be made by the group via majority vote. Those in the middle who made up their mind before the conclusion of the debate and wished to become advocates of a position, could move into a positional camp at any time during the debate.

Only those who were comfortable with their rhetorical skills chose positions to start the debate. Others would look to these communication leaders as models for fashioning their own arguments. Some students chose to illustrate their arguments on the board or overhead, finding words inadequate to express their conceptual concerns. In addition to the oral and visual elements of the debate, the vote-with-your-feet format provided a kinesthetic dimension, engaging not just a floating mind, but the whole student body in the argument. Of course, the positive outcome of this series of debates was largely unintentional, more of a byproduct than result of design. Most importantly, it was the possibility of multiple presentational modes that allowed the florescence of communication, creativity, and learning to take place. Having found arenas of communication and performance suited to those being left behind, I attempted to use similar methods, the new spark of interest, and their increased sense of control to teach them the less accessible material.

A more recent example involved the use of dramatic interpretation. I cotaught a course concerning the psychological and sociological study of violence with the colleagues whom I mentioned earlier. Dr. Garrison suggested that we use two complementary texts in one segment of the course, James Gilligan's sociopsychological study *Violence* and, as introduced earlier, Shakespeare's *MacBeth.* We had the students enact select scenes each week, taking turns playing the roles of those who would introduce, perform or analyze the scene and subject in question. My students watched several different film versions of the scenes they enacted as well, to get a sense of separation between text and interpretation.

This experience lent credence to Maryann Feola's claim concerning the efficacy of dramatic methods for teaching critical textual analysis:

> Dramatic literature, filled with personal conflict, emotion and moving language has the potential to transform students in developmental reading courses into more responsive readers. While reading drama, students become intimately involved with a character's life. The journey into someone else's beliefs, frustrations, and responses provides students with an opportunity to explore their own. (1996, p. 624)

Once again, the cross-fertilization between fiction and nonfiction, cerebral and corporal, oral and written modes of communication allowed students to develop more profound understandings of each. While, admittedly, some students conceived of the acting as playtime—either due to inhibition, disinterest, or both—the engagement of all senses in the activity produced learning outcomes that simply would not have been possible without the inclusion of film and dramatic performance.

Similarly, group discussion of a creative text can be fostered by breaking up a class into groups of three and four, allowing each group to choose a visual illustrator, facilitator-leader, and discussant to deal with individual scenes or chapters. The groups are given explicit instructions to create visual representations which incorporate and illustrate issues and concepts in the text. The group-as-a-whole discussion which follows is then a tour through the various illustrations, a physical retracing of the day's assigned chapters via visual media (e.g., chalk on board, paint on paper, computer LCD, and erasable overhead markers on the windows). The act of visually representing conceptual problems leads to fascinating new insights into the written texts. One of several memorable examples that comes to mind was produced by students who were illustrating the concept of diasporic identities and *indigenismo* in the lives of Frida Kahlo and Diego Rivera. The illustrations involved surrealist, Kahlo-esque montages of relevant historical figures in liminal conditions and transnational spaces. The associated discussion was a breakthrough moment wherein students began to seriously debate the text and relevant theoretical constructs.

Finally, a less successful case of integration is worth considering. I have been involved in several courses now where an oral presentation is used in place of the final exam. Objecting to tests as superficial tools of training and assessment, I have generally advocated semester-long research projects wherein several shorter papers are then combined into a single long work by semesters' end. The results are then presented during a final exam period, becoming a "(Course Topic) Conference" where students share their projects in oral, and sometimes, visual form.

The written results of the semester long projects have been astounding. Yet, the presentations have often not lived up to their promise. The ongoing diagnosis (and I would appreciate feedback on this issue) is that: 1) I have not had my students practice their presentations adequately beforehand as the semester and projects develop, 2) have not provided adequate training and feedback, 3) have not adequately described the criteria via which the oral presentation would be assessed, and 4) have undervalued the presentations in terms of grade percentage. Each of the first three problems have been progressively reduced over successive attempts. I continue to struggle with the latter point, however. Given the lack of oral training and emphasis in the curriculum as a whole, I am reticent to assign a significant percentage of the grade to what amounts to an oral test. Given the high anxiety already encouraged by oral performance, I have only assigned five percentage points to the final presentation. Short of the preferable nongraded environment, I find the two goals of giving serious attention to oral communication, on the one hand, versus the need to reduce barriers (e.g., anxiety) to student performance, on the other, to be incompatible. It is here that direct, individualized work with the more anxious students has become key, and where the CAC plan of communication training centers, emphasizing anxiety-reduction, would be of great benefit to the nonspecialist instructor (Morreale et al., 1993).

The most successful cases I have experienced, however, have not involved course-wide requirements, but rather assignments which offer the option of nonwritten components, as was true in Jenny's case. Usually when the alternative communication option is offered, I find that several students will jump at the chance to incorporate their personal skills and interests in ways which significantly improve their performance. It is particularly important that all of the students receive a handout with very clear, coherent, and consistent assessment criteria well in advance when options for nonprint performance are offered. This allows them to understand the basic structure and goals of the assignment, thus guiding their creative work and, at the same time, freeing them from concerns that their chosen mode of performance may not be what the teacher is looking for.

For much of what I have discussed, and particularly regarding assessment, it is helpful to turn to expert colleagues as resources. The art faculty, for example, was invaluable in my work with Jenny. I am simply not equipped to provide that sort of training, and was greatly aided by colleagues in the art department when it came time to assess the visual part of her project as well. While semiotic analysis can be applied as easily, if not more so, to visual forms such as Jenny's painting, "visual semiotics presents itself as an altogether new scientific discipline" (Saint-Martin, 1987, p. 1) that most scholars and teachers are much less familiar with than print critique and technique.[3]

There are certain key traditional components of our work as professorial instructors, however, which should give us all the ability to lead by example, particularly in the case of oral argumentation. Carefully prepared and well performed lectures are invaluable in this regard. If we want our students to develop competent oral communication skills, as applied to academic scholarship and critical inquiry, we must provide the example. Self-reflexive and public explication of our own lecture preparation and performance processes takes us even further toward this goal of teaching by example. When students, in turn, start to present effective oral presentations, the lecture ceases to be the much maligned method of one-way presentation/regurgitation, and instead becomes a form of reciprocal exchange. This sort of exchange, although apparently on the wane, is an indispensable complement to less formal seminar style discussions. In short, one of the best ways to teach oral and rhetorical skills is to demonstrate them.

How Should we Assess Nonwritten Forms of Communication?

The problem of teaching and assessment continue to loom large. Just as I have struggled with the question of integrating multiple forms of communication, I continue to look for ways to aid and assess the students' use of them. How do we who are trained to assess written explication assess multiple forms of communication without falling into the sort of pedagogical dilettantism for which interdisciplinary studies is so often critiqued? Given that education is "mainly concerned with literacy," and that as a result, "few educated people think easily or confidently in visual terms, apart from artists and some scientists and mathematicians," how are we to start thinking in ways which creatively incorporate and fairly assess visual, not to mention oral, aural, and kinesthetic modes of expression (Chaplin, 1994, p. 244)?

Once again, my solution is preliminary and incomplete. My own answer has been not to create a completely new set of criteria, but rather to have core criteria for all projects, related more to the expositional and pedagogical goal of the course than the medium of expression. As with all assignments, an assessment form clearly listing the key criteria is given out beforehand, in addition to an assignment guide, so that students will be aware of the goals of the project and the criteria by which it will then be assessed. Ideally, this material is included in the syllabus. While leading to gargantuan syllabi, this provides the student with an integrated set of assignment expectations, aids, and parameters from the start, reducing anxiety and providing the opportunity for experimentation with project design and alternative methods of communication to start early.

Additionally, and so as not to separate the academic core from other forms of visual, aural, or kinesthetic competence, I always require some form of written exposition to accompany the project. Furthermore. I do not provide the visual, oral, or kinesthetic options for all, or even most assignments. Written texts are still by far the best method for accomplishing our educational goals. It is what most of us know best.

The basic assessment criteria designed to assess written projects, including argumentation (thesis, evidence, logical development, transitions, and conclusions), successful inclusion of course concepts, and critical insight, can be usefully applied to multimedia texts, as long as the particular merits and disadvantages of each form of expression are taken into consideration. Certain forms of expression will naturally allow for greater articulation of particular aspects of the object/topic at hand, and demonstrate less capacity for others. The visual arts, for example, are often better vehicles for communicating certain aspects of social theory (e.g., dialectics, affect) than writing, and often provide a stronger emotive dimension, as mentioned earlier. Yet, admittedly, the visual arts often lack explicit temporal and causative detail, both of which can be more effectively communicated via writing. A news photo, for example, while having great emotional impact, may serve to either strongly support or subvert a given ideological position, depending on the written caption that accompanies it (Pedelty, 1995). As Elizabeth Chaplin explains: "image always conspires with its frame, or—in the context of a book—with frame, caption and verbal text, to produce an argument" (1994, p. 244).

If there is a major distinction in quality to be made, it is that "[p]ictures represent the world, words describe it" (Espe, 1990, p. 24). Granted, images can describe, but they must often first be framed, organized, and serialized to do so, by which time they are transformed into a form of proto writing, as found in Aztec codices and other picture writing or glyph forms. Short of that sort of processing, however, imagery remains a distinct form of exposition better understood as representation than explanation per se. It is important to judge a student project, visual or otherwise, with the qualities and limitations of the medium in mind.

The conspiracy of writing and image described by Chaplin is useful to keep in mind as well. It is not so much a matter of writing versus other forms of communication. Effectively written arguments always evoke imagery, via simile, metaphor, or other visual evocation, whether those images and transfers of meaning are implied or explicit, illustrated on the page or brought forth in the imagination of the reader. So too, oral, visual, and kinesthetic expression will almost always require some form of written, expository complement, albeit appropriately reduced in length. In the case of Jenny's incredibly expressive *Death Without Weeping*, for example, brief spoken and written explanations were also required to accompany her visual exposition. One of the dangers, otherwise, is that the student's nonverbal submission might become a giant Rorschach test onto which the teacher will read all manner of things, whether they are part of the student's intentional design or not.

Conclusion

To conclude, I will now admit to a great deal of ambivalence. In a world increasingly dominated by postmodern pastiche, our more traditional objective of developing in-depth written arguments and fully articulated ideas is a laudable, if seemingly impossible, goal. Yet, not only is the reductive reliance on expository writing alone inadequate, but even counterproductive as it fits too neatly into the ideological model through which the popular culture has coded all things academic as boring relative to that which cultural industries serve up as fun and engaging. Out there in real life students gain cultural competence by learning to watch, listen, and move in response to multimedia texts. In the academy, they are disciplined into texts which, almost quixotically, aim to produce the internalized forms of imagination and fascination that are part of a passing print world and print literacy (McLuhan, 1969; Anderson, 1983). I am not advocating surrender to mass or popular cultures, but instead a reasoned and self-reflexive consideration of the surrounding cultural environment and recognition of the potential benefits of incorporating alternative methods of communication.

Hopefully this work will engender further discussion concerning the appropriate placement, use and assessment of nonwritten forms of communication in the interdisciplinary curriculum. Given the cultural context within which we teach, there is not only the opportunity, but an absolute requirement that other skills be incorporated into our courses. The interdisciplinary environment, however, particularly in a residential setting, provides a prime setting for communicative integration and "a major opportunity to integrate the classroom experience directly with students' cocurricular life" (Welty, 1994, p. 79). The ways of thinking facilitated by this integration and the communication skills gained will benefit our students greatly as they move on to negotiate other cultural and institutional environments in a world no longer dominated by print media.

References

Allen, R. C. (Ed.). (1995). *To be continued: Soap operas around the world.* New York, NY: Routledge.

Anderson, B. (1983). *Imagined communities: Reflections on the origin and spread of nationalism* (revised ed.). New York, NY: Routledge.

Baldwin, K. (1995). Montezumas' revenge: Reading Los Ricos Tambien Lloran in Russia. In R. C. Allen (Ed.), *To be continued: Soap operas around the world* (pp. 285–300). New York, NY: Routledge.

Barber, B. (1995). *Jihad vs. McWorld.* New York, NY: Times Books.

Barry, A. M. (1997). *Visual intelligence: Perception, image and manipulation in visual communication.* Albany, NY: State University of New York Press.

Berg, G. (Ed.). (1983). *The visual arts and medical education.* Carbondale, IL: Southern Illinois University Press.

Bourdieu, P. (1984). *Distinction: A social critique of the judgment of taste.* Cambridge, MA: Harvard University Press.

Brown, M. E. (1994). *Soap opera and women's talk: The pleasure of resistance.* Thousand Oaks, CA: Sage.

Brunsdon, C. (1995). The role of soap opera in the development of feminist television scholarship. In R. C. Allen (Ed.), *To be continued: Soap operas around the world* (pp. 49–65). New York, NY: Routledge.

Cassata, M., & Skill, T. (1982). *Life on daytime television: Tuning in American serial drama.* Norwood, NJ: Ablex.

Chaplin, E. (1994). *Sociology and visual representation.* New York, NY: Routledge.

Cronin, M. W., & Grice, G. L. (1993). A comparative analysis of training models versus consulting/training models for implementing oral communication across the curriculum. *Communication Education, 42,* 1–9.

Dondis, D. A. (1973). *A primer in visual literacy.* Cambridge, MA: MIT Press.

Douglas, S. J. (1994). *Where the girls are: Growing up female with the mass media.* New York, NY: Times Books.

Espe, H. (1990). The communicative potential of pictures: Eleven theses. In K. Landwehr (Ed.), *Ecological perception research, visual communication, and aesthetics* (pp.23–28). New York, NY: Springer-Verlag.

Feola, M. (1996). Using drama to develop college students' transaction with text. *Journal of Adolescent and Adult Literacy, 38* (8), 624–628.

Flitterman, S. (1983). The real soap operas: TV commercials. In E. A. Kaplan (Ed.), *Regarding television* (pp. 84–96). Frederick, MD: University Publications of America.

Gitlin, T. (1989). Postmodernism: Roots and politics. In I. Angus & S. Jhally (Eds.), *Cultural politics in contemporary America* (pp. 347–360). New York, NY: Routledge.

Harvey, P. (1995). Interpreting Oshin: War, history and women in Japan. In L. Skov, & B. Moeran (Eds.), *Women, media, and consumption in Japan* (pp. 75–110). Honolulu, HI: University of Hawaii.

Havelock, E. (1986). *The muse learns to write: Reflections on orality and literacy from antiquity to present.* New Haven, CT: Yale.

Henry, J. (1963). *Culture against man.* New York, NY: Vintage.

Herman, E. S., & Chomsky, N. (1988). *Manufacturing consent: The political economy of the mass media.* New York, NY: Pantheon.

Hughes, M. (1994). Helping students understand and appreciate diversity. In C. Schroeder & P. Mable (Eds.), *Realizing the educational potential of residence halls* (pp. 190–217). San Francisco, CA: Jossey-Bass.

Joyrich, L. (1988). All that television allows: TV melodrama, postmodernism and consumer culture. *Camera Obscura, 16,* 129–153.

Kreutzner, G., & Seiter, E. (1991). Not all "soaps" are created equal: Towards a crosscultural criticism of television serials. *Screen, 32,* 154–172.

Martin-Barbero, J. (1987). *Communication, culture and hegemony: From media to mediations.* Newbury Park, CA: Sage.

Mattelart, M. (1986). *Women, media, and crisis: Femininity and disorder.* London, England: Comedia.

Mattelart, A. (1991). *Advertising international: The privatisation of public space* (M. Chanan, Trans.). New York, NY: Routledge.

McLuhan, M. (1969). *The Guttenberg galaxy: The making of typographic man.* Toronto, Canada: The New American Library of Canada.

Monsivais, C. (1993). Mexican cinema: Of myths and demystifications. In J. King, A. Lopez, & M. Alvarado (Eds.), *Mediating two worlds: Cinematic encounters in the Americas* (pp. 139–146). London, England: BFI.

Morgan, J., & Welton, P. (1986). *See what I mean: An introduction to visual communication.* Baltimore, MD: Edward Arnold.

Morreale, S., Shockley-Zalabak, P., & Whitney, P. (1993). The center for excellence in oral communication: Integrating communication across the curriculum. *Communication Education, 42,* 10–21.

Murphy, Y., & Murphy, R. (1985). *Women of the forest.* New York, NY: Columbia.

Olson, D. (1991). Literacy and objectivity. In D. Olson & N. Torrance (Eds.), *Literacy and orality* (pp. 149–164). New York, NY: Cambridge University Press.

Pedelty, M. (1995). *War stories: The culture of foreign correspondents.* New York, NY: Routledge.

Quinones, S. (1997, April 12). Mexican telenovelas scramble to keep up with changes in society. *Houston Chronicle,* p. 22A.

Rapping, E. (1994). *Media-tions: Forays into the culture and gender wars.* Boston, MA: South End Press.

Rogers, E. M., & Antola, L. (1985). Telenovelas: A Latin American success story. *Journal of Communication, 35* (35), 24–35.

Sacks, P. (1996.) *Generation X goes to college.* Chicago, IL: Open Court.

Saint-Martin, F. (1987). *Semiotics of visual language.* Bloomington, IN: Indiana University Press.

Scheper-Hughes, N. (1992). *Death without weeping: The violence of everyday life in Brazil.* Berkeley, CA: University of California.

Scheunemann, D. (Ed.). (1996). *Orality, literacy, and modern media.* Columbia, SC: Camden House.

Schiller, H. I. (1989). *Culture, Inc.: The corporate takeover of public expression.* London, England: Oxford University Press.

Scholes, R., & Willis, B. (1991). Linguistics, literacy, and the intensionality of Marshall McLuhanis' western man. In D. Olson & N. Torrance (Eds.), *Literacy and orality* (pp. 215–235). New York, NY: Cambridge University Press.

Schroeder, C., & Mable, P. (1994). *Realizing the educational potential of residence halls.* San Francisco, CA: Jossey-Bass.

Underhill, N. (1987). *Testing spoken language: A handbook of oral testing techniques.* New York, NY: Cambridge University Press.

Welty, J. (1994). Achieving curricular objectives through residence halls. In C. Schroeder & P. Mable (Eds.), *Realizing the educational potential of residence halls* (pp. 70–92). San Francisco, CA: Jossey-Bass.

Williams, R. (1977). *Marxism and literature.* New York, NY: Oxford University Press.

Willis, S. (1991). *A primer for daily life.* New York, NY: Routledge.

ENDNOTES

1. I recognize that this work falls somewhere between pedagogical reflection and editorial advocacy. I may too freely use terms like "we" and "our" when critiquing academic tendencies, and perhaps should have substituted "I." In order to remain safely between the poles presented by positivistic prose (and passive sentence structure) and the sort of navel-gazing narcissism found in much of the postmodern literature, however, I will imagine and write about this as a fairly common problem faced by others as they grapple with similar pedagogical issues and obstacles. It should be clear by the conclusion, however, that this chapter is as much or more of a reflection of my own ambivalence and efforts toward including alternative modes of communication in the curriculum, as it is advocacy thereof.

2. We are very fortunate at Miami University's Western College Program to have the services of the Windate Writing Center, an innovative institution working under the guidance of Carolyn Haynes which offers an alternative to more narrowly-focused traditional writing programs. Where additional support is needed for nonwritten forms of communication, it is probably preferable to extend additional resources and support to such writing centers, rather than inventing an additional oral communication center.

3. Morgan and Welton provide a particularly useful introduction to the analysis of visual forms in *See What I Mean* (1986), which is recommended as an assessment tool.

14

Student-Active Science in Interdisciplinary Studies: Problems and Solutions

Janet F. Ott
The Evergreen State College

Nothing in education is so astonishing as the amount of ignorance it accumulates in the form of inert facts.

—Adams, 1918

Much of what happens in most classes is a waste of everyone's time. It is neither teaching nor learning. It is stenography.

—Felder & Brent, 1996

Reform in college science teaching has called for a radical departure from lecturing off old yellowed notes used for so many years. Studies have shown that students learn better when they are doing, not listening—engaged in the material, not passively accepting the information, when learning collaboratively, and when the material is presented in context (Basili & Sanford, 1991; National Research Council, 1996; Narum, 1997). The first idea has led to a call for more student-active learning in our teaching, and the second has led to the idea of teaching interdisciplinarily (National Research Council, 1996; Narum, 1997).

Student-active teaching in the sciences ranges from conventional laboratories to problem-based or real world question-based teaching, to small group work of all kinds. The use of interdisciplinary themes within a field helps students see many of the aspects of an issue, rather than attempting to piece it all together for themselves outside their disparate classes. For instance, imagine a student is learning about genetics. One can use the example of sickle cell anemia. Rather than just hearing about single point mutations theoretically, students are more likely to understand and remember the concept if they are aware of the geographic as well as racial nature of this disease, and its adaptability due to its protection against malaria in the heterozygous form—having only one copy of the sickle cell allele rather than two, which is far more serious. Evolutionary and medical explanations help the student remember and understand the genetics.

Or if one is learning calculus, one is far more likely to remember the formulas used and when to use them if the calculus is taught within a context where it is often applied, such as in physics. If a student is given a large problem, with increasingly difficult questions to answer that actually utilize and ask them to figure out how to dock a shuttle with a space station, then those formulae begin to have value to the student. If one adds the historical impetus of Newton and Leibnitz and the race and back biting that went into the development of calculus, then students can grasp that calculus isn't just esoterica, but a real and necessary tool. If the developed formulae are then applied to the historical questions of orbiting planets, and the need to know where each planet is in space and time, then those seemingly obscure and irritating formulae begin to take real shape and are held not only in memory, but in the imagination of the student, and she can begin to utilize them in her own world with orbiting space stations and docking shuttles.

Tradition has brought most of our schools to the idea of teaching each of our disciplines separately. This has grown out of ideas of teaching that are so old that we have long since forgotten the reasons for it, except that most schools find it easier to organize that way. It has become so ingrained that we don't see it as either a choice or as socially constructed. But we are finding that these singular issue classes and the (often broad) survey courses at the introductory level are not the best way to learn material (Allen, 1997; Dees, 1991; Ebert-May, Brewer, & Allred, 1997; Jones & Brickner, 1996; Valentino, 1988). It may be the easiest way to teach and an efficient mode of information transmission (from the faculty point of view), but our students are not retaining information as well as they might. Nor are we attracting or retaining students with such courses as well as we might (Malcom, 1993; Tobias, 1990). Many schools at all levels are starting to use integrated studies as a way to increase our students' retention of information. At The Evergreen State College, we handle much of our material by crossing two or more disciplines in one course or program for one term or all year.

Knowing that many colleges do not, and more importantly, cannot, for various reasons, use interdisciplinary teaching in the way that Evergreen does, I address some of the ways student-active science can be used in both interdisciplinary and traditional courses.

Problems with Student-Active Science and Interdisciplinary Teaching

There are many reasons that science faculty in particular give for not doing student-active science or interdisciplinary teaching.

Coverage

Coverage is the strongest argument science faculty give for not doing either student-active science or interdisciplinary teaching, especially in classes for majors. But in reality, we don't cover our fields as it is. Survey courses in biology, physics, or inorganic chemistry are notorious for having 1,000 page texts that we cannot possibly get through in the time allotted, so we pick and choose even when teaching conventionally (lecturing). Advanced topic texts themselves tend to cover far more than can be adequately managed in a quarter, or even a semester. We already are forced to make choices about what topics we will cover in any given school term, and we often base our choices on what the faculty who teach the next level insist that we cover. Lecturing may be the most efficient way to convey these large amounts of information in a short time, but if the students do not remember it or cannot transfer the concept to another field, to what purpose is it done?

In courses for nonmajors, we have often used watered down survey courses. Students take them because they have to get their general education requirements, but in few of them are we engaging nonmajors in the joy that is doing science. Nor are we answering the call to increase scientific literacy in our students if we only give them facts, but never engage them in how to find facts, how to organize those facts, or how to analyze those facts, and then make inferences, conclusions or, possibly more importantly, recommendations based on those analyses (AAAS, 1990).

We need to remember what our goals are in teaching. Is it to make sure we have covered the material—said the words, had the ideas on an exam, made sure our colleagues will not come back at us the following year for not having taught topics used in their courses? Or is it to have the students understand the work, comprehend those ideas, and realize the usefulness and purpose in learning the skills we believe to be important in their future? If the first, then the old way is fine; if the second, then we need to revisit our teaching methods because we have lost, and continue to lose, a lot of potential students. In the 1980s, the National Commission on Excellence in Education (1983) showed that students dropped out of the sciences during the first two undergraduate years, and questions of why we were losing them arose (Seymour & Hewitt, 1997). This was especially true of women and people of color (Malcom, 1993; Stewart, 1994; Tobias, 1990). Looking at curriculum, especially the general education requirements, the realization took hold that survey courses for nonmajors turned them off. The need to revamp these courses in hopes of being a pump rather than a filter—bringing students into the sciences, rather than weeding them out—emerged (Narum, 1997; NSF, 1996). Too much coverage seemed to be turning students off to science, not turning them on.

Many faculty might think that losing students is not a bad idea, thinking that only the best and the brightest should be allowed through the system, and that only those inherently interested in science should be the students we are concerned with, or that our filter courses are useful in bringing forward only those that deserve to be there and our nonmajor courses are not the ones we should be spending our time revamping. Science is now a rather select society, and there are those among us who believe it should remain so. It takes a really good mind to do science, and those who do it need to be indoctrinated in our way of doing things. But I would argue that we may be losing some very good scientists, who have yet to discover their potential, or even know yet that they might like science. I had a student who came to college to be a psychologist, but in the freshman program we taught, she got entranced with development. She taught herself math skills from pre-algebra to precalculus in a year, along with a full-time load, finished several science programs, was begged to come to graduate school where she had done a summer internship, but said she needed a break from school and went to work. She's now a project manager (where the only other project managers are PhDs in the sciences) at Immunex in Seattle. She would not have discovered that she enjoyed science in science classes taught as we have conventionally taught them, and I would hate to have lost her to another field. There is no basis for the thinking that only those that survive coverage courses are the students who will make fine scientists except for tradition.

Students were also leaving majors classes. Faculty wondered why, when we so clearly love doing science and showed enthusiasm for it, we were losing students? The intense weeding out classes, used for exactly that purpose, have, in many places and times, done too good a job. And in part, the massive amounts of material caused some students to cave. At Washington State University, faculty in the introductory biology class, traditionally a weedout class, changed their teaching style to more interactive collaboration. As a preliminary analysis, they asked students to identify the most important concept that they had learned in the first two weeks. Most answered with abstractions only, but more importantly, they reported that the amount of information given in courses and labs was overwhelming (Brown, Kardong, & Kiene, 1996). The use of the new method increased both lecture/lab linkages, and increased retention to 98% (Brown et al., 1996). This alone ought to give us pause and find out how we can inspire students to stay to learn the work we enjoy.

It Doesn't Work

That student-active science and interdisciplinary studies are unsuccessful is the second biggest reason we hear for not using them. Faculty will become aware of a new student-active teaching method, use it once or twice, find it did not go well, and then give it up (Felder & Brent, 1996; Schmier, 1997). Even if they try it for several weeks, they often give up on it before students have become effective at this new way of learning, and revert back to their personal tried and true lecture notes. Sometimes it's a matter of funding. Faculty at the Conference for Student-Active Science at Hampshire College stated that a grant may allow faculty to get new materials, some help, or new equipment, but when the funding runs out, they haven't put the maintenance factor into the implementation, and without the added funding or help, it seems to be too much work. The reality is that this type of teaching takes practice for the faculty as well as the students (Felder & Brent, 1996): students have to unlearn modes of learning and faculty need to learn modes of teaching. When a student asks a question, it has become second nature to answer it, rather than direct them to answer it on their own. For students, finding the answers themselves takes more work and effort than they first bargained for. Since this mode is student-active, they often balk at first, which brings us to a third reason for resistance.

Student Resistance

Until students get used to these new modes (whichever ones the faculty might be attempting), they are often opposed to them (Felder & Brent, 1996). Precisely because it is student-active, students begin to resent the fact that faculty aren't up there lecturing at them, providing them with the right answers, giving them ideas about what will be on the exams, or supplying them with the most important material they will need to get to the graduate school or job of their choice. They start whining and complaining that we are not doing our jobs, that this isn't helping, and that they aren't learning anything. Some interesting arguments come from students who have already had interdisciplinary or alternative education. Some of them will say that wasn't how they had done it, so this is the wrong way. In our program this past year, we heard every single one of these arguments. It takes time to break down the resistance, and more time to get their engagement and motivation in gear, but once that happens, look out. It is then that the interesting work begins.

Felder and Brent (1996) have some wonderful ideas about how to break down resistance, and to help the students move out of the received knowledge mode of Perry (1970) and Belenky (Belenky, Clinchy, Goldberger, & Tarule, 1986) into a more constructed knowledge. In brief, they argue that students are going through a grieving process, and that one needs to provide structure and guidance.

Control Issues

Faculty control issues also come into play here. These are of two types: the control a faculty has in directing the flow of learning, and that more insidious type, that internal control, the sense of being in charge, of knowing it all. The first often takes a notion of needing to keep everyone quiet and writing down your every word, as if when they are doing this, we are in control. The second is the far more entrapping, and comes from our own sense of inadequacy. A colleague of mine commented that when he retires, he wants to say, "well, now you're rid of me, someone who's play-acted at being a professor all these years." He feels a fake and is often sure that others feel that way about him. I know he's not alone. This comes from the idea that the information we know comes from some unknown source, that we are the fonts of knowledge and must know everything about our field. But of course we don't and shouldn't be expected to. If we realize that our job is to get our students to be able to do what we do—learn things for ourselves—then we should begin to think of ourselves more as guides than as fonts of knowledge, not the encyclopedia, but the reference librarian, teaching where and how to find information, guiding them in how to analyze and sort that information, and coming to learn what is important to remember and what can always be looked up.

Yes, student-active work does get rather noisy at times, but many of us who have taken up this type of teaching have come to feel that unless the students are talking with one another, not much learning is taking place. Students learn best what they learn for themselves and among their peers, teaching each other, not what we spout at them. There is this feeling among faculty that if they are not talking, then they are not teaching. Some deans feel that way too. For example, one dean came to visit a faculty member while she was doing small group work. He walked around watching the students talk with one another, search for answers in several reference books, then sidled up to her and whispered "I'll come back when you're teaching" (J. Moore, personal communication, Summer 1994). That story, and I'm sure many of you have heard similar ones, has become a rallying call for many of us.

Are we committed to our students learning, or to having our say? If we are more interested in hearing our own voice than in having our students learn more effectively, then we should keep lecturing. If we believe that we never really learn something until we begin to teach it, and also realize that students need the chance to begin the process of truly learning how to learn, then we realize that the structure, guidance, and expertise (control) we provide comes in the creation of the workshops, open-ended questions, and small group activities rather than in the perfect lecture (Finkel & Monk, 1983). Teaching becomes more a management issue, and invisible rather than overt management—guiding, encouraging, setting parameters, and analyzing student products.

Rationale for Using Interdisciplinary Teaching and Student-Active Teaching

Several years ago now, our planning group (Evergreen has no departments) started at the beginning in designing curriculum. We asked a series of questions that helped us think about exactly what we were attempting to do with our students: Who are the students we are serving? The answers fell into a couple of groups. The majors, the students who might be interested in science but do not know it yet, and the dabblers—those intrigued by the ideas but have no interest in the rigors involved in becoming a science major. Since having no distribution requirements, the general education students do not fall into any category. Then we asked what each of these groups needed to know coming in to any particular program (a set of courses tied together thematically), and what we expected them to get out of these programs. In other words, we thought seriously about our goals.

This idea of asking who our students are and whether or not we are serving them well is a useful starting point for thinking about reform. In many colleges, getting a new course listed can take years, much less thinking about radically changing an entire curriculum. Several colleges have begun the process of looking at their requirements, their courses for general education requirements, and how well they are meeting the needs of students in both the requirements and the courses themselves (Ramaley, 1997). What do we want our students to learn in these courses? And more importantly, why? Asking good questions (of ourselves or of our students) requires being open to new answers. We expect it of our students, believing that shaking their foundations is part of our work with them, and helping them discover that right and wrong, as well as right and left, change with time and culture. Knowledge isn't just the accumulation of facts, but the construction of our own reality with those facts. Since we expect this openness in the face of new answers to old questions, we should expect it of ourselves, and question our own authorities—both the ones set by tradition, as well as the ones set by administration. Hence the value of considering curriculum as changeable.

Our world is increasingly explained scientifically. The difficult problems we face in the coming years—issues of pollution, of genetic engineering, of whether or not to keep people alive at both ends of the lifespan—will take scientific literacy, if not full comprehension, to understand enough to engage in these difficult discussions. Are survey courses the best way to get our nonmajor students to think critically about these issues? Is memorizing the intricacies of the nitrogen cycles without giving the context the way to engage our students in thinking about global warming? If scientific literacy is an important consideration from the point of having students be able to think about these issues in an intelligent manner, rather than just be able to have short-term memory retention for the exam, then our modes of teaching have not been the best way to serve our students. Thus, many of us are looking at new and, hopefully, better methods.

There are many ways to add student-active methods to one's class. The following are several examples, with references of how to get more detail about any of them or about other ideas.

Solutions

Cutting Back

One way to break out of our concept-driven coverage (which chapters to cover in which order) is to pick and choose the concepts to be covered from our texts even more carefully, choosing only the essentials of our field and teaching the students how to learn them, not just by lecturing at them, but by giving them the guidance about how to learn in the same way that we do, in order to give those lectures. Thus, we become references and guides rather than the fonts of knowledge students are used to. Using student-active techniques, and putting the material in some context, we get them to think more deeply about these topics, and they begin to do the synthesis that comes easily to us after years of practice. We need to let them know exactly what topics we haven't covered and why we chose what we did and left out what we didn't. If we assume their intelligence, we assume an ability to fill in the gaps once they learn how to learn. If we do not or cannot assume their intelligence, then coverage is not going to help anyway. When one teaches in a student-active way, we may use fewer examples, but we cover them in depth, and the students have a far better grasp of how to get information than they do if they are acting as vessels that we pour information into. A wider range of students grasps more of the concept, since we are generally approaching the issue from several different angles, not just auditorially in lecture or visually by having them read a text. We use methods that use their kinesthetic sense, their problem solving mode of learning, and often, because they may be presenting the material they have covered to colleagues, they learn as we do, by teaching.

To give an example, I regularly teach physiology interdisciplinarily with a chemist. I always cover neurophysiology and kidneys, because these are two topics that are just too complex for students to grasp without lots of help from the faculty. These topics get the most minilecture, explanations, and workshops of all the topics, for the reasons given above. When covering respiration, circulation, or digestion, much of the information is self-taught and taught in groups to one another, since these are somewhat easier to grasp, especially if one has really drummed in the concepts of membrane transport, diffusion, and acid-base chemistry. The topics we let go are such things as development and hormones, since in many ways, they have already been touched on in covering the other topics, and in addition, they can be read and understood easily with the background they now have. Different faculty may choose different reasons for their choices, but the idea is that the student is now capable of learning this material on their own, and of determining when they might need to do so.

Although fewer topics may be covered in a year of physiology, physics, or chemistry, the ability to comprehend, synthesize, problem solve, and transfer the concepts are techniques that they will carry far further than memorization of any particular detail of one topic (M. O'Brien and others, personal communication, Summer 1998). Several faculty have said that they need to at least mention a topic so that their colleagues at the upper levels do not accuse them of slacking. But just because a topic gets mentioned does not mean that there is retention or understanding, even if the student does well on the exam. I went to graduate school not remembering that I had covered counter-current flow in two classes, much less that I had notes and had gotten As on both exams. One professor at Harvard began using student-active teaching in physics when he found that his students did not know how to answer simple basic questions, such as "why do the seasons change?," even though this class's grades on the exams were quite good (Derek Bok Center, 1993).

Mini Reforms

There are many student-active techniques designed to help students understand the material that take little time or effort on the faculty's part. One is the minute exam. In the middle of a lecture ask a question involving the main idea or concept of the lecture. Give the students a minute or two to answer, having them write on a 3 x 5 card. Ask them also to give their confidence level in their answer (how sure they are of their answer) using a rating system such as one to five. Then have the students turn to their neighbor, explain their answers, discuss them, change the answers if necessary, and rate these answers with their confidence. This gives immediate feedback to the faculty as to effectiveness of the lecture. Many have reported that the conversation the students have with one another greatly increases both the correctness of the answer, as well as the confidence.

Another quick method of feedback done at the end of the lecture asks students to write down the three main points of the lecture and any questions that they had about it. Again, having the students turn to a neighbor, they check to see if they have the same three main points, and if they can help answer their neighbor's questions. One can expand this by opening it up to further discussion with more neighbors. Again, this gives immediate feedback as to whether or not we are getting across what we think we are, and it helps the students articulate both what they've learned and what they've missed.

We can use the same methods with exams or homework by having students check their answers with their neighbors after the exam or when the homework is due. We've used this method with take-home exams because we give a lot of quantitative reasoning questions. We've found that the students have difficulty beginning the question, but often can get it once they have a starting point. We give them some time when we hand out the exam to discuss strategies for tackling the problems or where to find information (rarely are our exams directly from our texts). This has increased their ability to struggle through tough complex questions and decreased their frustration level.

Some faculty have found the use of study groups or work groups very useful. A group of three to four that works on labs, homework, and research projects together helps build cooperative effort rather than competition. I've heard it taken so far as to have exams be based on the lowest performance of a group member. In other words, though taken individually, each member gets the grade of the member whose grade is lowest. This forces them to make sure that each knows as much as possible. It can make for some stressful situations; on the other hand, it is defensible as a real world working situation.

Poster Sessions

The use of posters in the classroom is wonderfully versatile and really engages the students. For many students here at Evergreen, their display of posters and the poster session itself is the highlight of the quarter, or of the year.

This past year, my colleague Jim Neitzel and I used posters in the first quarter of our "Vital Stuff" program. In groups of two to five, we had the students choose a food item, research that food item, create a poster that covered the history and cultural use of that food, some aspect of the biology and chemistry of the food (either the production or use), and something about the ecology (area found or impact of production). We had just read Visser's *Much Depends on Dinner* (1988) and Nabhan's *Gathering the Desert* (1997), books looking at food items from a cultural, historical, and to some degree scientific way, and wanted them to think more expansively than science students usually do. The posters were some of the best we have seen undergraduates do, and, in our opinion, there were a couple of reasons for this.

First, we allowed them to choose their own food item. These were within limits (narcotics were not allowed), but fairly broad, and ranged from tea, coffee, and wine, to pigs, shitake mushrooms, and breastmilk. Allowing students choices within projects, but with firm limits, has made an enormous difference in the quality of their work. Second, we had a practice session a couple of days before the session itself. They were to bring all material to the class with the poster board and lay it out as it was to be on the poster. Then they had to have three other groups give feedback on it and they had to give feedback to three groups. This did several things. For one, the last minute things were mostly completed a couple of days beforehand, or at least they saw all that needed to be done in the next days. They saw their classmates' posters in mid-completion and it upped the ante in terms of quality. They saw things that "they would never do" and how font, readability, color coding of information, the amount of information, and graphs and visuals made for good (or bad) posters. They learned how to write concisely and with clarity when other students would indicate "too much" or "I don't get it." Some of this must seem obvious but we often don't have our students do a practice run, and this was one of the best experiences we had for the year. The revised versions of these posters were fabulous and very professionally done. Their obvious pride continued to grow as the posters were used several times in the course of the year for a Native American food production conference, and again for the student science show.

The versatile poster session, done well, masters many of our goals for students. Writing skills, presentation skills, quantitative reasoning (in the presentation of graphical material), content understanding, and synthesis are all addressed in this one fun project. It is a miniature of our own work in coverage, figuring out what's most important to put on the poster, and what of the mass of material they have gathered just has to be let go. They feel like the expert about their topic. Rarely do they have more to say than room or time to say it about something important. There is the aspect of the public practice of science, defending your work in a public forum. There is the issue of theme—addressing one and sticking to it. The layout and the choice of the key concepts involves judgment. There is the issue of scientific literacy—learning to communicate difficult concepts to lay readers.

Problem-Based Projects

Again, this is a wonderfully versatile idea used in many ways and on many levels. One can use it for simple small groups or even diads during class, for homework in groups, for term projects, or for the entire course (see the Portland example below). At its best, a problem-based approach uses complex real world problems to tackle. Unlike canned labs or problems at the end of the chapter, these are important issues and students sense that they are not just doing time but doing real work that could be used in the future. These can range from those delightful year-long projects that create a real product to thought experiments such as the medical school models where beginning students are given neurological symptoms and asked to determine where and what the problem is. Like the poster session, the advantages are that they get the student engaged, in part because they are working on something real, not the usual busy work that they so react against.

Deborah E. Allen, at Delaware, has brought problem-based learning to the introductory biology classroom. She says "While our content-driven lectures allowed for efficient delivery of content material, they seemed to do little to help our students reach the deeper level of understanding needed to connect the information they received to the conceptual framework of our disciplines, or to apply it to novel situations" (Allen, 1997, p. 259). Deborah used multistage problems gathered from sources such as *Discover, Science News,* and the science pages of *The New York Times.* She has developed problems on finding biological solutions to global warming, on in vitro fertilization, and AIDS. If one of our goals is to have our students to be informed citizens that can add intelligently to the difficult conversations that we will have to have in the future on these issues as well as issues of overpopulation, pollution, and genetic manipulation, then we would be far better served by teaching them to think for themselves about difficult issues than to memorize a set of facts to be forgotten immediately after the tests.

Portland State University takes problem-based learning several steps further. They base their nonmajor (science in the liberal arts-SLA) curriculum for general education requirements on science-in-the-making—doing, rather than talking about science. Their gateway class, "Natural Science Inquiry," sets the tone for the rest of the curriculum. There, in two two-hour blocks/week, they spend the first week getting acquainted and introduce elements of collaborative inquiry. The second week they do a cold read on a challenging scientific article, reading and reflecting on a piece of scientific literature. They then respond to such questions as 1) Summarize your understanding of the article, 2) Make a list of works, terms, and symbols you do not understand. What is your reaction to this list?, and 3) What is the significance of this study? To whom is it significant? and so on. They use this article as an assessment tool by having the students read it again at the end of the ten-week quarter and respond to a similar set of questions. In the second week they also look at a "rich data set" and do some analysis. The example given is a set of weather data for a day in the Portland area. The students, in groups, then analyze the data using Excel, and make predictions about the weather for the day. The faculty often do not know the weather for the day's data given, and thus, cannot be relied on to give the right answer when all is completed, precisely as it is in the real world. The last four or five weeks of the term is devoted to a major project that may carry over (and generally does) from term to term. It is largely student driven and the faculty act more as guides and resources than instructors. For instance, the fall of 1994 students gathered together, analyzed, and summarized data on urban environmental quality from a variety of local, state, and federal documents. In the winter, students further honed this information, and created a booklet entitled *Portland Today.* Updated by another set of students, *Portland Today* is a guide to public understanding of environmental problems. I saw the original and the update, and the students have created an increasingly readable, usable, and very professional piece of real world literature for practical purposes. It is this sort of project that gets students involved and hooked into science.

For those with concerns that the students are not getting the skills they need by faculty directed, content driven material, this quotation from Jill Hamer, student in "Rates of Change" should put these qualms to rest:

> Never in a million years would I have tried to work on a physics or math course book if I had not taken the SLA courses first. The book is based on the units we did during the course. We do the assignments, discuss what we understood, what was helpful, what we learned. We're working on a teacher's guideline which gives examples of common mistakes, points out potential difficulties to watch for, and ways to work them out. It's more work that I thought it would be, but it's fun.
>
> You don't need to be a math major to do something like this. It is a matter of common sense, working it out, knowing how to 'think scientifically' like they taught us . . . Isn't it amazing that after two terms of SLA I have the confidence to help write a book for a course I would never before have imagined taking.

The work at Portland State is part of a large reform measure, one that affects several schools at once. But the reforms are the kind spoken of in many places. Their work is a useful model for nonmajors and majors' curricula alike.

Ann P. McNeal and Charlene D'Avanzo's book *Student-Active Science: Models of Innovation in College Science Teaching* (1997), offers an expansion of these and other uses of problem-based learning.

Thematic Courses

To give an example, this year I taught a program titled "Vital Stuff: The Biology and Chemistry of Food" with my chemist colleague, James

Neitzel. We had the students for ten of their 16 credits each quarter for the whole year. Our intent was to integrate physiology, biochemistry, and microbiology around the theme and issues of food. Our students were juniors and seniors. Inorganic chemistry and precalculus level math were prerequisites. They were taking organic simultaneously or had had it. Many had had either some biology and/or some physics before entering. The class credits were equivalent to classes in microbiology, cell biology, anatomy and physiology, and biochemistry, all with lab. In addition, credits were given in history and culture of food, and credits appropriate to their projects.

We started with water, since most food has a high percentage of water, and water is such a basic issue in both chemistry and biology. We tested water from sources the students chose, and tested water content in food the students brought in. We covered some microbiology as it pertains to food issues, especially spoilage and food and water-borne microbes. They grew bacteria, did gram-staining, and learned the basics of microbial taxonomy. We began teaching physiology with neurobiology to get to sensory systems, since sight, smell, taste, and touch are such a major part of food consumption. We then did the digestive system, for obvious reasons. Since they were taking organic chemistry simultaneously (or had taken it before), we began discussing topics of biochemistry as they came up with the physiology topics. So as we got to digestion, we brought in metabolism, metabolic rates, acid-base chemistry, and numerous other biochemical topics. Because it tied together, it made much more sense to them. Further, as a small group project, they followed a fat, protein, or carbohydrate molecule through the system. This forced them to think much more globally than they normally would, and to incorporate physiology, metabolic issues, biochemical reactions, as well as nutritional considerations into their thinking. Some groups expanded on this by bringing in medical conditions such as starvation, protein deprivation, or extreme exertion such as mountain climbing or pregnancy into the work. They then reported their work to their colleagues. Besides our poster project (noted above), we had them write on a famine and report on it in a paper as if it were a short news article. This was in conjunction with our seminar, which at the time of that project was exploring the Irish potato famine. The major projects of the year were a combination of lab and library research projects, which started in winter and went through the spring. These were student-originated and ranged from testing a homeopathic caffeine remedy to isolating and studying the antioxidant and antibacterial properties of berberine from Oregon Grape. Our seminar was all about food in one way or another, and began with Visser's *Much Depends on Dinner* (1988), Nabhan's *Gathering the Desert* (1997), and had several weeks each covering the meat industry, the Irish potato famine, and women's relationship to food and cooking. Short stories and scientific works on food-related topics rounded out the year. We also had several films on food and cooking.

To be sure, though we did not cover every physiology, biochemistry, and microbiology topic, we explored 80–90% of the material we would have taught in the typical way. The students, by the end of the year, were doing a fine job of presenting the material themselves, and proved that they were absolutely capable of learning the material that we had not covered by themselves. We made sure that the topics that are the most difficult to understand in the field (such as neurons and kidney function or enzyme kinetics) were ones covered so that they thoroughly understood them.

Understanding that most faculty cannot teach in such an all-encompassing manner, I still thought it instructive to give an example of thematic teaching, because Jim and I are both convinced that even in a regular class in any of the topics covered, one could use the theme of food, or any number of other themes, and increase the students' interest greatly. For example, in a traditional anatomy and physiology class, food could be used as a theme. Every system is part of processing food, or needs food to do its work, and can be tied in in that way. In a biochemistry class, food is the basis for many, if not most of the processes that go on, and can be easily tied to food. One can add in controversies in either class with articles from current journals about nutritional issues, and an occasional seminar or discussion group can be part of understanding a topic more deeply.

It is the controversy that often helps the comprehension. This is the difference between a topic and a theme. A theme has a edge to it. It has meaning in the context of the real world that the students live in. A good theme gets students so hooked that it is generative; it becomes demanding on both the students and the faculty to follow leads that develop within the class. It feeds back to both the students and the faculty and greatly increases the enjoyment and engagement of all involved. In short, a good theme develops and sustains excitement about the material and learning it. Just as in good writing, where a writer might stay on topic the whole way through but the paper is a bust because there is no theme, no question, nothing to argue for and against, and nothing to engage the reader, teaching a series of facts and concepts without a unifying theme becomes a process of stenography and rote memorization.

If part of our pleasure in doing science is that we enjoy long-term and sustained discussion and work around an absorbing issue, then the Portland and Evergreen ideas answer that desire in students who rarely get the chance to experience this sort of ongoing enterprise. As Joseph Tussman said many years ago: "The student presents himself to the teacher in fragments and not even the advising system can put him together again . . . to pursue one thread is to drop another . . . [the student] seldom experiences the delight of sustained conversations" (Tussman, 1969, p. 47). Disparate courses pull the student apart. Coordinated studies, linked classes, and federated learning communities allow students to make connections, to work more fully with one another, and to have a richer, more complete learning experience.

Resources

I offer the previous ideas in hopes of exciting faculty to the possibilities of both student-active science, as well as teaching interdisciplinarily. The following resources have many more ideas. As Barbara Smith, provost of Evergreen and former director of the Washington Center for Improving the Quality of Higher Education has said: "When people feel empowered to take charge and change educational structures, they discover lots of solutions to old problems. As one faculty member put it, 'For the first time, I think teachers and administrators recognize that it is in their power to shape college education. I don't think most of us had seen it quite that way before. So much of it seemed precast, dictated, inherited, and assumed'" (Smith, 1991, p. 48). It is time to question our assumptions.

There are many useful resources for changing teaching styles toward more student-active, problem-based, and context-based learning. McNeal and D'Avanzo's book *Student-Active Science: Models of Innovation in College Science Teaching* has many ideas for setting up student-active methods in math and the sciences. Further, their list of sources is very useful. For setting up any sort of learning community or asking about interdisciplinary studies, the Washington Center for Improving the Quality of Higher Education, a statewide public service initiative at The Evergreen State College has enormous resources. Learncom@listserv.temple.edu, a listserve at Temple University, discusses issues of learning communities, and the conversations are often about the difficult issues of setting up learning communities and related educational and bureaucratic issues. Finally, information on Project Kaleidoscope, which works to revitalize undergraduate science teaching, can be found at their web site: http://www.pkal.org/.

References

AAAS. (1990). *Science for all Americans: Project 2061.* New York, NY: Oxford University Press.

Adams, H. B. (1918). *The education of Henry Adams: An autobiography.* New York, NY: Houghton Mifflin.

Allen, D. E. (1997). Bringing problem-based learning to the introductory biology classroom. In A. P. McNeal & C. D'Avanzo (Eds.), *Student-*

active science: Models of innovation in college science teaching (pp. 259–278). Fort Worth, TX: Harcourt Brace.

Basili, P. A., & Sanford, J. P. (1991). Conceptual change strategies and cooperative group work in chemistry. *Journal of Research in Science Teaching, 28,* 293–304.

Belenky, M. F., Clinchy, B. M., Goldberger, N. R., & Tarule, J. M. (1986). *Women's ways of knowing: The development of self, voice, and mind.* New York, NY: Basic Books.

Bonsangue, M. (1991, January). *Achievement effects of collaborative learning in introductory statistics: A time series residual analysis.* Paper presented at the Joint Annual Meeting of the Mathematical Association of America/The American Mathematical Society, San Francisco, CA.

Brown, G. R., Kardong, K., & Kiene, T. (1996, February). Interactive collaboration in Biosci. *Washington Assessment Group (WAG) Newsletter, 5* (2), 10–12.

Dees, R. L. (1991). The role of cooperative learning in increasing problem-solving ability in a college remedial course. *Journal for Research in Mathematics Education, 22,* 409–421.

Derek Bok Center (Producer). (1993). Thinking together: Collaborative learning in science [videotape]. Boston, MA: The Derek Bok Center, Harvard University.

Ebert-May, D., Brewer, C., & Allred, S. (1997). Innovation in large lectures: Teaching for active learning. *BioScience, 47* (9), 601–607.

Felder, R., & Brent, R. (1996). Navigating the bumpy road to student-centered instruction. *College Teaching, 44* (2), 43–47.

Finkel, D., & Monk, G. S. (1983). Teachers and learning groups: Dissolution of the Atlas complex. In C. Bouton & R. Y. Garth (Eds.), *Learning in groups* (pp. 83–97). New Directions for Teaching and Learning, No. 14. San Francisco, CA: Jossey-Bass.

Jones, J. D., & Brickner, D. (1996, June). *Implementation of cooperative learning in a large-enrollment basic-mechanics course.* Paper presented at the American Society for Engineering Education Annual Conference, Washington, DC.

Malcom, S. M. (1993). Letting nurture take its course. In D. C. Fort (Ed.), *A hand up: Women mentoring women in science* (pp. 181–193). Washington, DC: Association for Women in Science.

McNeal, A. P., & D'Avanzo, C. (Eds.). (1997). *Student-active science: Models of innovation in college science teaching.* Fort Worth, TX: Harcourt Brace.

Nabhan, G. P. (1997). *Gathering the desert.* Tucson, AZ: University of Arizona Press.

Narum, J. L. (1997). Some lessons learned. In A. P. McNeal & C. D'Avanzo (Eds.), *Student-active science: Models of innovation in college science teaching* (pp. 3–18). Fort Worth, TX: Harcourt Brace.

National Commission on Excellence in Education. (1983). *A nation at risk: The imperative for educational reform.* Washington, DC: US Government Printing Office.

National Research Council. (1996). *From analysis to action: Undergraduate education in science, mathematics, engineering, and technology* (Report of a Convocation). Washington, DC: Center for Science, Mathematics, and Engineering Education, National Research Council.

National Science Foundation. (1996). *Shaping the future: New expectations for undergraduate education in science, mathematics, engineering, and technology.* Executive summary of its review of undergraduate education by the advisory committee to the National Science Foundation directorate for education and human resources. Arlington, VA: Author.

Perry, W. G., Jr. (1970). *Forms of intellectual and ethical development in the college years.* New York, NY: Holt, Rinehart, and Winston.

Ramaley, J. A. (1997). Creating a supportive environment for major curricular changes. In A. P. McNeal & C. D'Avanzo (Eds.), *Student-active science: Models of innovation in college science teaching* (pp. 121–135). Fort Worth, TX: Harcourt Brace.

Schmier, L. (1997). *Learncom listserve at Temple University* [On-line]. Available: learncom@listserv.temple.edu

Smith, B. L. (1991, March/April).Taking structure seriously: The learning community model. *Liberal Education, 77* (2),42–48.

Seymour, E., & Hewitt, N. M. (1997). *Talking about leaving: Why undergraduates leave the sciences.* Boulder, CO: Westview.

Stewart, J. L. (1994, September). Why so few women? *Council on Undergraduate Research Quarterly,* 13–24.

Tobias, S. (1990). They're not dumb. They're different. A new 'tier of talent' for science. *Change, 22,* 110–30.

Tussman, J. (1969). *Experiment at Berkeley.* New York, NY: Oxford University Press.

Valentino, V. R. (1988). A study of achievement, anxiety, and attitude towards mathematics in college algebra students using small group interaction methods. (Doctoral dissertation, West Virginia University, 1988). *Dissertation Abstracts International, 50* (02), 379A.

Visser, M. (1988). *Much depends on dinner.* New York, NY: Macmillan.

15

Increasing Access in the Sciences Through Interdisciplinary Feminist Perspectives

Gary L. Bornzin
Fairhaven College
Western Washington University

Science education in grade schools and high schools has received a great deal of attention in recent years, and one of the big improvements for many students has been increased emphasis on experiential learning— hands-on work, field work, learning science by doing science. Yet many students, men and women, still arrive at college disliking science, convinced that science is alien to them, to their values and interests, and moreover that they are no good at it. Understandably they dread their science requirements.

One approach to addressing this problem is to offer students college-level classes which attempt again to pique their interest by involving them more profoundly in a highly reflective, preferably collaborative process of doing science and achieving the satisfaction of participating in the discovery of relationships, the careful, systematic gathering of data, and the interpretation and communication of results. A number of diverse models using this basic approach have recently been collected in a useful and inspiring book *Student-Active Science: Models of Innovation in College Science Teaching*, edited by Ann P. McNeal and Charlene D'Avanzo

(1997). My experience has been that such an approach is most effective when students are persuaded of the relevance of the work they are doing, and especially when they are offered the opportunity for participating in the class enterprise in ways commonly regarded as outside the realm of real science—e.g., viewing the project through the eyes of an artist, poet, musician, historian, social activist, ethicist, or journalist. By making room to teach the links between science and other disciplines, we are serving science students by broadening their outlook and stimulating their creativity, and are serving nonscience students by including and honoring the diverse interests, perspectives, and skills which they bring.

To complement the approach of learning science by doing science, introducing students to an interdisciplinary feminist critique of science engages many students who have otherwise been alienated from science. This approach enables students to see science as a human adventure, alive and relevant, controversial and fallible. Many students are relieved and delighted to find they are not alone in their critique of science—that their personal difficulties with science might be less a problem with themselves and more a problem with science and how it is conceived, practiced, and taught. With their vague sense of unease validated, articulated, and defined, students frequently discover a latent curiosity and enjoyment in reapproaching science in a new way, and grow in confidence and competence when encountering scientific material.

I have been teaching a class called "Feminist Perspectives in the Sciences" at Fairhaven College for the past ten years. Fairhaven College is a division of Western Washington University which features interdisciplinary approaches to learning. This particular course is one of several options in our upper-division science core, taken primarily by liberal arts majors plus a few science majors. The intention of the class is to enable students to approach science in new, unconventional ways, to see science from different perspectives, and thereby to better appreciate its strengths, limitations, and possibilities for greater inclusiveness. Students are also introduced to an extensive and fascinating literature rarely encountered in other science classes or women's studies classes. Many students who have felt alienated from science in previous classes discover the possibility of a new, more comfortable and lasting relationship with science, while finding support for a more sophisticated critique of science in today's culture.

While most universities are unlikely to create space for a new course mixing science and feminism, I have met many faculty, women and men, who, with support, would like to include ideas and material from such a course in their more traditional courses in science or women studies. I offer here an assortment of ideas which I hope will prove both provocative and helpful.

The sections of this chapter roughly parallel the segments of the course: evoking the students' own critique of science and their understanding of feminism, introducing the literature, discussing typical student projects, and citing typical student responses.

An Approach Which Respects Students

Early in the quarter, before the students engage any of the reading, I ask them to write down what they think science is and what they like and dislike about it. The quality, richness, and depth of their collective critique, based on the seemingly simplistic question of likes and dislikes, always amazes me—and them. The passion of their dislikes amazes me too. To many of them, science appears as a cold, narrow-minded, inhuman, dogmatic, oppressive, arrogant, elitist, greed-motivated, irresponsible, out of control, destructive, and poorly taught tool of wealth and power! One student called science "a dense, steaming locomotive, rip-roaring down the track." They are fascinated by some of its discoveries and admire some of its practitioners; but they are angry that science seems to have betrayed its potential.

One consistent observation seems to be that the abuses in science and of science arise from its inhumanity—its narrow-minded devotion to a particular exclusive methodology and its intentional lack of human feeling, of empathy. They contend that we humans couldn't do the things we do to other people and to the earth—war, genocide, ecocide, rape—if we had any empathy, any feeling for what we are doing to them. Scientists cut up frogs; science promotes nonfeeling.

Their complaints anticipate those of many feminist critics of science, whom they haven't yet read at this point in the course (Palmer, 1983, 1987). Their complaints also echo those of many women students who, despite an early attraction to science, feel compelled to turn away from it later in their education (Alper, 1993; Brush, 1991; Tobias, 1990).

After we discuss science, I ask the students to write down what they know about feminism, still without having done any reading for the class. What does feminism mean to them? How has it been represented in their experience or in the things they have read or studied? After some superficial answers, several students typically start asking and answering larger questions, such as what perspectives, approaches, and values do feminists bring to bear in looking at things, in critiquing them, in seeking change? What assumptions or changes of emphasis do feminists tend to make when looking at history, or literature, or social institutions—or science? And, perhaps most interesting, what has been the pattern of my own personal experience as a woman or as a man which reflects larger social issues of oppression, power, privilege, and patriarchy? Recognizing that there are many different kinds of feminists with many different priorities, agendas, and perspectives, can we nevertheless talk about some of the attributes common to most of these perspectives? And what do we see when we look at science with these perspectives?

Attributes of a "Feminist Perspective" as Defined by Students

This section discusses various attributes, emphases, or values which students associate with feminism, and which they have suggested over the years I have facilitated this course. Interestingly, the students seem both willing and able to reach consensus around the importance of these values and the sense that they are largely undervalued throughout our culture and especially in science. I wish to emphasize that the ideas of this section are not simply what students understand feminism to be according to prior reading but also how they define, defend, and use feminism for themselves according to their personal experience and insight. The distinctive quality of this list is that most of these attributes of *a* feminist perspective have been reconstructed and reshaped year after year through students interacting with one another and building on each other's ideas in a largely consensual process, with minimal direction or prompting from me. I do remind them that they are constructing a feminist perspective, one among many, and that not all feminists would necessarily agree with their choice of attributes (Jones, 1989; Merchant, 1990). More than once students have responded, "Let's not limit ourselves to what feminism is, let's figure out what it ought to be." As the citations in this section are intended to show, most of their ideas do indeed find support from at least some feminist writers.

The heart of a feminist perspective must be that it derives insight from women's experience (Collins, 1989). The predominant pattern of women's experience throughout history, in our culture and in most other cultures, has been subordination to male authority and serving the role of mother/caregiver, with occasional women (usually heroic) challenging male domains.[1] A feminist perspective is shaped then by the struggle to emerge from a long history of patriarchal oppression. It therefore emphasizes equality; seeks liberation and full human potential for all people; challenges existing power, wealth, and authority relationships; challenges sexism, racism, classism, and paternalism (Gray, 1981, 1982).

A feminist perspective honors individual experience in general as a valid way of knowing, along with intuition, feelings and emotion (Belenky, Clinchy, Goldberger, & Tarule, 1986),[2] the mystical and the paradoxical (Starhawk, 1982), giving less credibility to authority which is strongly associated historically with male authority. A feminist perspective particularly attends to the individual, the exception, the anomaly, the minority opinion (Collins, 1989; Keller, 1983; Warren, 1990). It celebrates diversity and is comfortable with plurality (Cole, 1985). It insists upon personal responsibility while seeking to extend to everyone the ability to respond, the empowerment of having and making choices.

Honoring individual experience and intuition challenges the assumption of universal truth, that anyone can speak for all, as men have so often claimed to do. Hence, a feminist perspective assumes biases in every statement, and it assumes perspective dependency. Every statement comes from a point of view; no statement is value-free. Another way of saying this is that empathic knowledge and contextual knowledge are as valuable as objective knowledge; or even stronger, that there is no such thing as objectivity in the sense of having a point of view that is so emotionally removed and rationally pure as to be without bias (Keller, 1985).[3] The challenge in science should not be to try somehow to transcend bias, but rather to try to be as open and honest as possible in discerning and acknowledging biases (Harding, 1991).

Many students suggest that a feminist perspective emphasizes relationship, interrelationship (reciprocal), interconnectedness, heterarchy instead of hierarchy (Shepherd, 1993), systemic cooperation (Shepherd, 1993), networking, synergy, and nonviolence (Kelly, 1994). These qualities resonate with systems thinking (Capra, 1982, 1996)—wholistic, nondualistic, qualitative, pattern-sensitive, process-oriented—emphasizing connections among body, mind, and spirit, human connections with earth/nature—a profoundly ecological mindset which values diversity and adaptability over quantitative efficiency, which recognizes that you can't do only one thing, and that spillovers and byproducts always occur (Diamond & Orenstein, 1990; Plant, 1989; Spretnak & Capra, 1984).

Some students suggest that a feminist-ecological perspective may also derive from women's traditionally domestic role, as the word ecology derives from the Greek word *oikos* for home. Caregivers, male or female, frequently develop a deep concern for children, for future generations, for sustainability, for life, for creativity (Merchant, 1990; Spretnak, 1986, 1997). A sense of the importance of the ordinary, the everyday, the practical, the life sustaining nitty-gritty may also find its way into such a perspective (Diamond & Orenstein, 1990). It considers theory incomplete without practice.

Finally, to make explicit what has been implicit above, a feminist perspective, in its impatience with the existing order, will readily question anything and everything: it revalues, redefines (e.g., power, anger, conflict, human nature, language, history—and science), calls attention to new things, and proposes alternatives.

Nothing in this list is new, nor the exclusive province of women. Yet this perspective is clearly not the dominant one of our culture, certainly not the academic culture, and especially not the culture of science.

Invariably, someone will question using the word feminist. Some male students associate feminism with male-bashing. Why not call it a holistic perspective, an ecological perspective, a complementary perspective, an alternative perspective, or a new paradigm? While the word feminist may push a lot of buttons and carry a lot of unwanted baggage, it represents the only perspective which highlights the gross underrepresentation of women in science. The persistent lack of women in science is not an inconsequential historical accident but a key challenge to the acclaimed universality of science. Can any field which either excludes women or fails to attract or retain women be complete, open, and value-neutral? A feminist critique of science—examining the gender biases in the conception, theories, practice, and teaching of science—provides an inclusive framework for other critiques of science from philosophical (Feyerabend, 1993; Kuhn, 1970) and social perspectives (Harding, 1993).

Looking at science through various feminist perspectives inevitably and naturally draws upon multiple disciplines and enables students to see how addressing real world issues commonly requires crossing disciplinary boundaries. Moreover, insofar as feminist perspectives emphasize relationship over object and multiplicity over singularity, they are predisposed toward seeing the world in interdisciplinary and multidisciplinary terms. To critique science from a feminist perspective could include and enable, for example, a study of the history of women in science; biographies of women in science today; the socioeconomic situation of women in science today; the sociopolitical culture of the science community; race, class, and gender issues in science; social critiques of science; philosophical critiques of science; and science, ethics, and public policy (e.g., cloning, genetic engineering, environmental issues). Most of these issues are rarely addressed in science courses which tend to glorify science and ignore its human side; nor are they commonly addressed in history, sociology, or political science classes, which tend to ignore science, preferring to leave it to the scientists. Without exposure to a comprehensive interdisciplinary epistemology such as feminism, our students risk remaining blind to academia's blind spots.

Exploring the Literature

Once the students have considered their own experience and shared their perceptions of science and feminism, and recognized how broad and diverse those perceptions are, we begin reading other writers who have dealt with these issues. My favorite article for introducing students to the far-reaching consequences of seeing and working with a new perspective, a new paradigm, and a new epistemology, is Parker Palmer's "Community, Conflict, and Ways of Knowing: Ways to Deepen Our Educational Agenda" (1989). This four-page article contains an excellent account of the epistemology of objectivism which Palmer contends dominates higher education and shapes our ethics. According to Palmer the approach of objectivism is 1) objective—distancing the knower from the world to attempt to keep knowledge from contamination by subjective prejudice and bias, 2) analytic—chopping things into pieces, and 3) experimental—manipulating the pieces for convenience.

Palmer's warning is that an objectivist epistemology leads insidiously to an ethic which objectifies the "other" and contributes to the breakdown of community. Objectivism, he says, destroys "an inward capacity for relatedness" and "must be countered if the academy is to make a contribution to the reweaving of community" (p. 24). Fortunately, he sees promising new epistemologies emerging "in fringe areas of the academy's work" (p. 24)—such as feminist thought, African American scholarship, Native American studies, ecological studies, and the philosophies of the new physics and scientists like David Bohm (1980) and Barbara McClintock (Keller, 1985). Many students confirm that Palmer accurately represents their complaints about science, discussed earlier.

A related article by Patricia Hill Collins, "The Social Construction of Black Feminist Thought" (1989), contrasts an Afrocentric feminist epistemology to positivism, which, like Palmer's objectivism, is presented as the dominant epistemology of academia. In addition to distancing the researcher from the object of study and attempting to exclude emotions, ethics, and values from the research process, positivism involves using adversarial debates as the preferred method of ascertaining truth.

In contrast, Collins develops the contours of an Afrocentric feminist epistemology, in summary consisting of four principles:

1) uses concrete experience (life "wisdom") as a criterion of meaning ("I'm talking about myself . . . about what I have lived")
2) uses dialog in assessing knowledge claims—connected, participatory
3) uses the ethic of caring—emphasizing individual uniqueness, appropriateness of emotions in intellectual dialog, and developing the capacity for empathy
4) uses an ethic of personal accountability, assessing the character, values, and ethics of the speaker.

Several African American women science students have told me that Collins's analysis reflected their experience and helped them to better understand their own frustrations with science. If Collins speaks for many African American women, this mismatch of preferred epistemologies is surely part of the reason why so few African American women feel welcome in science.

If science is our means for understanding and knowing the natural and physical world, is positivism, or objectivism, the only epistemology by which this may be accomplished? Or can science be strengthened, our knowledge become more true and complete, less dominating and more compassionate, if it makes room to include Afrocentric feminist epistemology, if it acknowledges its biases and opens itself to a healthier balance which honors a feminist perspective in its midst? This is the question many feminists are raising, and the answer they are creating is yes.

Having seen the far-reaching significance of feminist challenges to science, students are ready for an overview of the issues and the literature. My favorite review article is by Sue Rosser (1987) who provides helpful categories for organizing the diverse work of recent feminist writers: 1) teaching and curriculum transformation, 2) history of women in science, 3) current status of women in science, 4) feminist critique of the practice and results of science, 5) feminine science, and 6) feminist theory or philosophy of science. I encourage students to focus their supplementary readings and work in one of these areas as preparation for selecting their project topic. Each quarter several students may also choose to study and report on some new development in science, such as Chaos Theory (Gleick, 1987), Complexity Theory (Casti, 1994), Fuzzy Logic (McNeill, 1993), new physics (Capra, 1982), new biology (Augros & Stanciu, 1988), or ecofeminism (Diamond & Orenstein, 1990; Plant, 1989)—whether or not women are prominent in these areas—as long as they can show how the new ideas are challenging established masculine-biased assumptions (Shepherd, 1993).[4]

Although there are many excellent books and articles covering particular aspects of feminism and science,[5] finding an appropriate, comprehensive text has been difficult. In 1993, the textbook I had dreamed of finding was finally published: *Lifting the Veil: The Feminine Face of Science,* by Linda Jean Shepherd (1993). It is written with great sensitivity, insight, clarity, and conviction. Shepherd advocates for greater gender balance in the ways science is conceived, practiced, and taught. Specifically, she imagines a more inclusive science—inclusive not only of women and people of color, but also inclusive of certain qualities customarily associated with women and customarily undervalued in Western science. Each chapter features one of these qualities: feeling, receptivity, multiplicity, nurturing, cooperation, intuition, relatedness, and social responsibility. Shepherd also manages to address to some degree all six of Rosser's categories of feminist science scholarship. Her writing style is engaging and readable. Endnotes, bibliography, and commentary within her text are exceptionally illuminating guides to the literature, and facilitate further research by students. Moreover, students like the book, and read it—even the most skeptical males.

Shepherd exposes male bias in science not in an accusatory way but simply by proposing a positive and appealing alternative—"more creative, more productive, more relevant, and more humane" (p. 50)—noticing how a more feminine, inclusive science is emerging already in a thousand different ways, and unveiling the places where it has all along been present but unseen. Her book seems to take into account, as if by design, most of the complaints about science voiced by my students. No wonder they find in this book and this course a new face of science to which they can relate.

Student Projects

With the inspiration of Shepherd's text and a few other resources, students are generally eager to begin their particular projects, done singly or in small teams, which they summarize in a paper and report to the class. They support one another through small interest groups.

The interdisciplinary nature of this course is always manifest in the diversity of student projects, which range from historical and philosophical to environmental and ethical. Some opt for the familiar form of a book report. Several students typically do biographies of women scientists, past or present. Students may interview women scientists on campus. One student compiled a survey of attitudes among men and women science students on campus. Several reports typically deal with some frontier of science, whether or not women are particularly active in the area, as long as they can show how the area relates to issues discussed in class. Another popular topic is the medical system, past or present, and its effects on women—something the women have experienced first hand. Ethical controversies with a science base—cloning and genetic engineering, euthanasia, loss of natural biodiversity, global warming, sustainable agriculture—always generate interest. Someone may look at biases in science textbooks used on campus. Someone may investigate feminist teaching style as defined by others, and then offer their own framework. Education majors have been inspired to research and create more inclusive, female-friendly curricula. Some students may design their own experiment with feminist perspectives in mind, and try it out with the class. Because of the interdisciplinary nature of such projects, they would typically not find a home elsewhere on campus.

Because students are researching and presenting a topic of their own choice (with faculty consultation!), their motivation and enthusiasm at this stage is especially high. Since students have participated to some extent in one another's process of developing a project, they take considerable interest in the final reports. Moreover, they seem to have an uncanny knack for choosing topics which their peers also find interesting, and for communicating their own infectious enthusiasm.

Response to the Course

Many science teachers might object to a course such as this, saying that it doesn't teach students science, it teaches about science. Exactly. It sees science not as an accumulation of facts and techniques but as a very human enterprise. It asks how science is done and how scientists see, more than what science has learned. It explicitly looks at science in our everyday lives more than at science in the lab. It does not replace but complements conventional scientific information with a perspective rarely offered elsewhere.

It begins with somewhat different objectives than a conventional science course. The objectives are:

- to build confidence in approaching science and appreciating its methods, concepts, and imagery
- to build confidence in knowledgeably critiquing science, asking penetrating questions, recognizing unstated assumptions, biases, and subjectivity—to not shy away from technical discussions
- to nurture a motivation for lifelong learning
- to celebrate certain qualities of good science which are valuable assets in any field, such as open-mindedness, flexible-mindedness, careful observation, curiosity, imagination, creativity, and perseverance.

Student response has been consistently gratifying. Many report seeing science in a whole new light, or actually enjoying science for the first time in years. One student wrote:

> Previous to this class the word "science" always retained a kind of a cold, clinical feeling . . . . Through this class I rediscovered the intuitive part of science that I had enjoyed so much [when I was younger].

Another wrote:

> The ideas here are not new to me—the application to science, however, is an aha! No wonder I put off my science requirements for 14 years: the context was missing.

That feeling of discovery and relief is expressed by many students. Science teachers who have loved science all their lives may find it hard to understand. One student expressed the feeling especially well:

> I have had a fear of science all of my life. All through my schooling I was socialized to believe that because I failed at science and math I was less

> intellectual than my male classmates . . . . This class . . . has enabled me to discover other women writers that speak in my dialect . . . . I have realized it isn't that I am inadequate to science, it is that science has excluded me. [The text] introduced me to a refreshing new perspective, one that includes me, and my feminine traits. At last, a critique of science that I not only understand but live. [This class] has empowered me to create my own perspective of an all-inclusive science.

Some students say they finally understand why people become scientists. Some discover popular science journals like *Discover* and *New Scientist,* and intend to continue reading them. Students enjoy being able to make connections with other courses they have taken, seeing how science as a human enterprise is not all that different from their other interests:

> The value of an interdisciplinary approach to learning has never been more apparent to me than it was in this class.

Some science majors, women especially, express great relief and affirmation in learning that they are not alone in their struggles with the way science is generally taught. Science majors and nonmajors are more confident and articulate in the integrity of their critique of science. As citizens engaged in political debates, they will no longer be intimidated by the "objective scientific facts" but will be able to question assumptions and biases and make appropriate use of scientific evidence. Students learn to see multidimensionally by looking from diverse perspectives:

> Science had, prior to this course, seemed far too much of an unassailable institution. In viewing it from more diverse perspectives and realizing that all scientific 'truth' is constructed knowledge, I have gained a more intimate and personal appreciation for science. I now have a 'way into' science, or a way of approaching it so it does not seem so dark and forbidding as it once did.

For some students, this approach changes their lives:

> This class was a welcome source of inspiration and creativity. The topic urged me to look into myself and find the feminine qualities that I had devalued for too long. I was surprised to find that I had been deeply affected by the mass devaluing of the feminine. Previously, I had never been in touch with this side of myself. Consequently, I began to see things from a slightly new perspective that gradually became a profoundly new perspective. A door seemingly was opened for me and I finally found where most of my feelings and creativity had been stored for so many years.

Teaching this class has had a transformative effect on me as well. As my own understanding of feminism and my critique of science and technology have deepened, I have at times despaired over the mess we humans are making of this world: war, oppression, intolerable inequity, cavalier annihilation of cultures, of species, of whole ecosystems. Science first serves its rich and powerful patrons and amplifies their destructive power. But I am reminded each time I teach this class that science also helps us heal and nurture. Through books like Shepherd's I am more aware that changes are already happening. I see the far-reaching transformative power of the feminist vision, and rediscover with the students the hope and potential of a new science in a new society made whole with a balance and respect of both masculine and feminine.

References

Alper, J. (1993). The pipeline is leaking women all the way along. *Science, 260,* 409–411.

Augros, R., & Stanciu, G. (1988). *The new biology: Discovering the wisdom in nature.* Boston, MA: Shambhala.

Belenky, M. F., Clinchy, B. M., Goldberger, N. R., & Tarule, J. M. (1986). *Women's ways of knowing: The development of self, voice, and mind.* New York, NY: Basic Books.

Bohm, D. (1980). *Wholeness and the implicate order.* London, England: Routledge & Kegan Paul.

Brush, S. G. (1991). Women in science and engineering. *American Scientist, 79,* 404–418.

Capra, F. (1982). *The turning point: Science, society, and the rising culture.* Toronto, Canada: Bantam.

Capra, F. (1996). *The web of life: A new scientific understanding of living systems.* New York, NY: Anchor/Doubleday.

Casti, J. L. (1994). *Complexification: Explaining a paradoxical world through the science of surprise.* New York, NY: HarperCollins.

Cole, J. (1985, April). *Male science is singular and explanatory; feminist science is plural and exploratory.* Symposium on Gender and Science, Lewis and Clark College, Portland, OR.

Collins, P. H. (1989). The social construction of black feminist thought. *Signs: Journal of Women in Culture and Society, 14* (4), 745–773.

Diamond, I., & Orenstein, G. S. (Eds.). (1990). *Reweaving the world: The emergence of ecofeminism.* San Francisco, CA: Sierra Club Books.

Einstein, A. (1938). *The evolution of physics.* New York, NY: Simon and Schuster.

Feyerabend, P. (1993). *Against method.* New York, NY: Verso.

Gleick, J. (1987). *Chaos: Making a new science.* New York, NY: Viking.

Gray, E. D. (1981). *Green paradise lost.* Wellesley, MA: Roundtable.

Gray, E. D. (1982). *Patriarchy as a conceptual trap.* Wellesley, MA: Roundtable.

Harding, S. (1991). *Whose science? Whose knowledge?: Thinking from women's lives.* Ithaca, NY: Cornell University Press.

Harding, S. (Ed.). (1993). *The racial economy of science: Toward a democratic future.* Bloomington, IN: Indiana University Press.

Jones, K. B. (1989). Feminist theory. In H. Tierney (Ed.), *Women's studies encyclopedia, Volume I: Views from the sciences* (pp. 139–142). New York, NY: Greenwood Press.

Keller, E. F. (1983). *A feeling for the organism.* San Francisco, CA: W. H. Freeman.

Keller, E. F. (1985). *Reflections on gender and science.* New York, NY: Yale University Press.

Kelly, P. (1994). *Thinking green: Essays on environmentalism, feminism, and nonviolence.* Berkeley, CA: Parallax.

Kuhn, T. (1970). *The structure of scientific revolutions.* Chicago, IL: University of Chicago Press.

McNeal, A. P., & D'Avanzo, C. (Eds.). (1997). *Student-active science: Models of innovation in college science teaching.* Fort Worth, TX: Harcourt Brace.

McNeill, D. (1993). *Fuzzy logic.* New York, NY: Simon & Schuster.

Merchant, C. (1990). Ecofeminism and feminist theory. In I. Diamond & G. F. Orenstein (Eds.), *Reweaving the world: The emergence of ecofeminism* (pp. 100–105). San Francisco, CA: Sierra Club Books.

Palmer, P. J. (1983). *To know as we are known.* San Francisco, CA: Harper & Row.

Palmer, P. J. (1987, September/October). Community, conflict, and ways of knowing: Ways to deepen our educational agenda. *Change, 19* (5), 20–25.

Plant, J. (Ed.). (1989). *Healing the wounds: The promise of ecofeminism.* Philadelphia, PA: New Society.

Rosser, S. V. (1987, Fall). Feminist scholarship in the sciences: Where are we now and when can we expect a theoretical breakthrough? *Hypatia, 2* (3), 5–17.

Shepherd, L. J. (1993). *Lifting the veil: The feminine face of science.* Boston, MA: Shambhala.

Spretnak, C. (1986). *The spiritual dimension of green politics.* Santa Fe, NM: Bear.

Spretnak, C. (1997). *The resurgence of the real: Body, nature, and place in a hypermodern world.* Reading, MA: Addison-Wesley.

Spretnak, C., & Capra, F. (1984). *Green politics: The global promise.* New York, NY: Dutton.

Starhawk. (1982). *Dreaming the dark: Magic, sex, and politics.* Boston, MA: Beacon.

Tobias, S. (1990). *They're not dumb, they're different: Stalking the second tier.* Tucson, AZ: Research Corporation.

Warren, K. J. (1990, Summer). The power and the promise of ecological feminism. *Environmental Ethics, 12,* 125–146.

ENDNOTES

1. There are enough exceptions to this cultural pattern, however, to support the argument of most feminists that gender role differences are culturally constructed and not biologically innate. If culturally constructed, they can be changed.

2. Liberal feminists have largely avoided associating feminism with qualities such as feeling and intuition, which our culture customarily associates with women. One good reason for doing so is to resist the cultural constructs of gender stereotyping which customarily values stereotypical male qualities, such as thinking and analytical reasoning, while devaluing stereotypical female qualities, such as feeling and intuition. To achieve equality in a male-dominated world, one naturally disassociates oneself from weaknesses as judged by that world, such as feeling and intuition.

   More recently, some feminists are asserting the need to recognize and revalue qualities such as feeling and intuition, empathy and nurturing, in a world sorely out of balance and in need of these qualities customarily associated with women. Students generally say yes to both: that gender stereotyping is invalid and detrimental, but that certain culturally undervalued qualities, culturally associated with women though not essential to their sex, need to be honored and revalued to achieve a healthier, more balanced world.

The text I am currently using for this class, *Lifting the Veil: The Feminine Face of Science* by Linda Jean Shepherd (Boston: Shambhala, 1993), takes this integrated view. An entire chapter is devoted to "Feeling: Research Motivated by Love" and another to "Intuition: Another Way of Knowing." Shepherd's chapter notes and bibliography offer additional references for concepts discussed in each chapter.

3. In her Introduction, Keller quotes physicist Steven Weinberg: "The laws of nature are as impersonal and free of human values as the rules of arithmetic" (p. 6). Compare this with Albert Einstein: "Physical concepts are free creations of the human mind, and are not, however it may seem, uniquely determined by the external world." (p. 31)

4. Shepherd presents a convincing case that Chaos Theory represents a movement toward a more feminine science (note especially, pp. 90–95).

5. With great restraint, I have here limited my recommendations in each area to a few enduring favorites which have proven popular with students as well.

History/Women in Science

Alic, M. (1986). *Hypatia's heritage: A history of women in science from antiquity through the nineteenth century.* Boston, MA: Beacon.

Keller, E. F. (1983). *A feeling for the organism: The life and times of Barbara McClintock.* San Francisco, CA: W. H. Freeman.

McGrayne, S. B. (1993). *Nobel prize women in science: Their lives, struggles, and momentous discoveries.* Secaucus, NJ: Carol Publishing Group.

Montgomery, S. (1991). *Walking with the great apes: Jane Goodall, Dian Fossey, Biruté Galdikas.* Boston, MA: Houghton Mifflin.

Practice and Impact on Women

Benditt, J. (1992, March 13).Women in science: First annual survey. *Science, 255,* 1365–1388

Benditt, J. (1993, April 16). Gender and the culture of science: Women in science '93. *Science, 260,* 383–430.

Bleier, R. (1984). *Science and gender: A critique of biology and its theories on women.* New York, NY: Pergamon.

Hubbard, R. (1990). *The politics of women's biology.* New Brunswick, NJ: Rutgers University Press.

Theory and Philosophy

Haraway, D. (1989). *Primate visions: Gender, race, and nature in the world of modern science.* New York, NY: Routledge.

Keller, E. F. (1985). *Reflections on gender and science.* New York, NY: Yale University Press.

Merchant, C. (1980). *The death of nature: Women, ecology, and the scientific revolution.* San Francisco, CA: Harper & Row.

Wertheim, M. (1995). *Pythagoras' trousers: God, physics, and the gender wars.* New York, NY: Times/Random House.

Education

Rosser, S. V. (1990). *Female-friendly science: Applying women's studies methods and theories to attract students.* New York, NY: Pergamon.

Tobias, S. (1990). *They're not dumb, they're different: Stalking the second tier.* Tucson, AZ: Research Corporation.

16

Building an Organization that Reflects Interdisciplinarity

Anne G. Scott and Celestino Fernández
Arizona International College of the University of Arizona

Creating a new institution of higher learning presents many unique and wonderful opportunities, as well as exceptional challenges. What professor or academic administrator has not dreamed of having the opportunity to start a new college? Initially, the idea of starting from scratch and building on the knowledge gained from existing institutions can be very appealing. But during such a process it becomes clear that there are many reasons why institutions are organized the way that they are in terms of both structure and culture, and that it is very difficult to try to break out of the traditional mold, particularly since all of those involved in the planning and development of a new institution were educated, trained, and worked in traditional institutions.

Although being involved in the initial years of a new institution is a truly exceptional opportunity to develop innovative curricula, personnel policies, and structures, as well as to foster a more cooperative and engaging culture for students, faculty, staff, and administrators, the challenges of trying to break out of the traditional mold and patterns, while enjoyable and interesting, are often daunting. There were many times along the way that those of us directly involved in the development of a new college or university have thought about the adage "be careful what you wish for, it may come true," and the Chinese proverb "may you live in interesting times." Well, our wish came true and we certainly have lived in interesting times, and although overall it has been an enjoyable ride, it has been a wild one as well.

Arizona International College (AIC) of the University of Arizona is a new institution with a distinct mission and clearly articulated goals. Planning for Arizona International College began in 1990 when the Arizona Board of Regents (ABOR) saw the need to plan for very dramatic enrollment growth that was expected to occur between the years 1995 and 2010. The number of new students enrolling in four-year institutions was expected to increase by 55,000, an increase of well over 50% in just fifteen years.

Because Arizona had only three large, comprehensive, public universities, two of which enroll over 33,000 students each (placing them among the twenty-five largest institutions of higher education in the United States), and community colleges, a state-wide commission advised the Regents to begin planning immediately for the development of two additional campuses. The new institutions were to be located in the two most densely populated areas of the state, Phoenix and Tucson.

Because of the problems associated with large comprehensive universities—course availability, access to professors, extensive use of teaching assistants in lower division courses, impersonality of a large bureaucracy, etc.—the state-wide commission recommended, and the ABOR decided, that AIC should be a different type of institution. First and foremost, AIC was to focus exclusively on undergraduate education, interdisciplinary liberal arts education. Secondly, AIC was to be much smaller than the existing institutions, serving no more than 5,000 students at full growth. Thirdly, although AIC was to begin under the auspices and wing of the University of Arizona, it was to have its own mission and objectives, and eventually become fully independent.

Overview

The goal of Arizona International College is to offer students educational opportunities that will prepare them for life and work in an increasingly competitive, dynamic, and global society. Faculty work closely with students to create educational experiences that are tailored to each student's strengths and weaknesses, interests, and goals—keeping in mind current trends in technology, the job market, and graduate program requirements. Learning is fostered through a challenging learning environment; one that offers small classes, strong faculty-student interactions, a comprehensive assessment program that ensures a value-added, outcomes-oriented education, service-learning, career internships, the development of a global perspective, and a capstone project.

The focus of Arizona International College's academic program is on delivering a practical, liberal arts education. Practical education means that students will be purposefully challenged to apply their liberal arts knowledge by learning a specific set of skills and competencies, and experiencing real life situations, thus preparing them for productive careers and lifelong learning. An interdisciplinary approach is seen as the best way to foster this learning. As major employers and others have noted, students' education needs to be broader and more holistic than what the more narrowly defined, discipline-based structure can provide. During the beginning stages in the planning of the academic program, two issues were predominant: 1) to create an interdisciplinary four-year academic program, and 2) to ensure that this interdisciplinarity is maintained and does not get diluted or revert back to a discipline-based model. This last point implies that the structure and organization of the institution somehow needs to foster interdisciplinarity.

These two issues are particularly challenging in today's climate—one in which diminishing resources for education has become the norm and one that will need to endure increasing public scrutiny for accountability. Many of the approaches traditionally used to foster interdisciplinarity (e.g., team teaching) are very costly and not feasible in the traditional sense. In order to create a new interdisciplinary institution, careful planning and creative thinking were required, particularly in the structuring of the academic program and the institution itself. This chapter will describe the approach taken at Arizona International College during its planning and throughout its first two and one-half years of operation, focusing on some of the structural changes that have been implemented and on some of the major challenges encountered along the way.

STRUCTURE OF THE ACADEMIC PROGRAM

Creating an academic structure that fosters interdisciplinarity is critical to the success of holistic, integrated teaching and learning. As the chapter by Joseph Comprone indicates, it is not sufficient to create an interdisciplinary curriculum and have the academic programs housed in traditional departments and colleges. We know from the experiences at other institutions (e.g., The University of California, Santa Cruz) that unless the disciplines are removed from the institution, faculty will revert back to their discipline in part because that is where they are intellectually comfortable, receive their rewards, identity, and recognition.

The organizational approach used at Arizona International College is the concept of an interdisciplinary academic house, which replaces the traditional discipline-based department and college. Academic houses are not residence halls, they are simply the academic units (departments) around which the institution is organized. Each house is comprised of about ten faculty and 250 students. Students within a house take their first two years' course work within their house. After their core courses are completed they take courses throughout the institution depending on their area of study. The curriculum in each academic house is organized around a major theme such as civic responsibility, sustainable development, international business, technology and society, etc. Faculty within a house represent each of the six areas of study offered at the institution (i.e., humanities, natural science and quantitative methods, language and culture, fine and performing arts, social sciences, and liberal studies). These faculty meet on a regular basis to discuss academic, curriculum, advising, policy, and other types of issues. They also serve as each other's peer reviewers—as opposed to having peer reviewers from across the campus within their own traditional discipline. This does not mean that faculty never work with members from their own field, but it does ensure that they all do work closely with faculty from disparate fields, which is rarely done in a discipline-based institution, particularly in large universities. It also means that faculty are being judged and their development plans are determined on criteria outside those specific to their individual discipline.

Within the house structure, the grouping of several disparate courses that students take as a block or cluster can help foster an interdisciplinary approach. At Arizona International College, the idea for cluster classes came about as a method for approximating team teaching without the high faculty costs. Each cluster of three courses from different academic areas of study (for example, natural science, composition, social sciences, humanities) revolve around a common theme. During the 1997–1998 academic year, one of the themes was the human brain. The total number of units for the cluster (in this case 11) is scheduled as a solid block of 15 hours of classroom time (the four additional hours are divided between class breaks and optional workshop time). In this way, faculty are free to schedule their courses depending upon the demands of the subject matter on a weekly basis. For example, the humanities professor may wish to show a two-hour film in one sitting, as opposed to scheduling it over two class periods, and therefore can block a time period of sufficient length to do so. This humanities professor would need to trade time with another professor, say the professor of science, who would make up the time in the future, say the following week. This flexibility is conducive to creative course delivery and material and helps to foster communication and cooperation among faculty from different areas of study.

More importantly, the cluster concept places various different disciplines together and forces the integration of these diverse areas of study. This structure serves to open up the area of study (or theme) since faculty from each of the involved disciplines need to approach the course theme from their own perspective and still work together with the other faculty to create a whole, fully integrated learning experience for students. Theoretically, this structure fosters communication and cooperation between faculty from different disciplines on a daily basis. By integrating (not simply linking) the courses together, the students learn that not only can learning quantitative methods help them to analyze data collected as part of a science project, but that interpreting results from a survey conducted as part of a humanities or social science course can provide insights to that area of study as well. In other words, students are learning to apply skills, methods, and knowledge gained in one area of study to that of another.

Another advantage to this approach is that it can help bring a fresh perspective to what might otherwise be familiar territory to an individual faculty member. Professors from a particular discipline often become interested and involved in other disciplines, which helps to bring new perspectives and approaches into the classroom and can help invigorate an area of study. In addition, because the theme and composition of the clusters is always changing, it means that the material is not likely to get stale, as is very likely to occur when the same course is taught over and over again by the same professor in a traditional setting.

The curriculum created for Arizona International College reflects its interdisciplinary nature. The first stage of the academic program is the core, which is taken by all students. It consists of 60 units of course work and provides a broad and intensive foundation across the generally recognized four areas of human knowledge and understanding—sciences and mathematics, social sciences, humanities, and fine arts. Each of the required courses is interdisciplinary, beginning with the course "Becoming a Fully Educated Person," which provides the philosophical rationale and operational basis for Arizona International College. This course also provides some practical skills such as technology and self-knowledge on learning styles, for example, that will help students in their other courses. Similarly, other courses offer a much broader spectrum of knowledge than do most discipline-specific courses taught at traditional institutions. The emphasis on skills and competencies that cut across disciplines helps to ensure that the focus remains on these as opposed to focusing on specific, narrow knowledge in a given discipline.

Although students focus their academic program after the first two years to a major area of study, these areas are very broadly based. The six areas offered by Arizona International College are fine and performing arts, humanities, language and culture, natural sciences and quantitative methods, social sciences, and liberal studies.

Having in place a structure that fosters interdisciplinarity is particularly important when there are stringent budget constraints. If an institution could count on using only full-time faculty who were hired specifically on the strength of their interdisciplinary teaching skills, then the implementation of the curriculum would be relatively straight forward. However, public institutions seldom have this luxury and it is often necessary to rely heavily on other options such as faculty from other institutions, visiting faculty, adjunct faculty, and administrators who were not trained or hired for their interdisciplinary skills. These outsiders will have an easier time filling the correct niche in the institution when the objectives of the curriculum are more clearly defined. At Arizona International College, these faculty are usually linked with full-time faculty during their teaching (by being part of a cluster), making them more effective at delivering an interdisciplinary approach.

Although the foregoing description of AIC's academic program reads as if the program was 1) straight-forward and easy to develop, 2) easy to implement, and 3) working smoothly and exceptionally well, none of these have been the case. In fact, we have encountered major problems every step of the way. Let us provide some examples.

During the development period, when a group of faculty members (individuals who had demonstrated a commitment to undergraduate teaching and interdisciplinarity) were asked to develop the academic framework and plan for the entire institution, they spent endless time debating the pros of a traditional curriculum and academic structure. These were folks who supposedly understood interdisciplinarity and its importance in the undergraduate curriculum. Also, when asked on several occasions to describe the academic and cocurricular experience that students would have at AIC, in other words, what the academic programs would do and be like for students, this same group of faculty invariably would end up talking much more about what the experience and programs would be like for faculty rather than for students.

During the implementation stage, we encountered great obstacles and resistance in several places, particularly among some very negative, bitter faculty (a few of this type seem to be found in every institution of higher education) at the University of Arizona, the mother institution of AIC. Some of these individuals were found in every formal body we worked with, e.g., the university-wide general education committee, undergraduate council, and faculty senate. These particular faculty members, along with other negative types randomly found throughout the university, took every opportunity to clamor through the media and create barriers along AIC's curriculum path and in other areas as well, even though the Arizona Board of Regents had already approved our academic and curriculum plan. On one occasion, the University of Arizona's Faculty Senate voted neither to approve nor reject but simply to "receive" AIC's academic and curriculum plan after two hours of contentious debate, the kind of debate that tends to be more monologue than dialog. Afterward, several people came congratulating us, although no one seemed to know exactly what this formal action meant since the senate had not voted to "receive" anything in anyone's recent memory.

Numerous problems internal to Arizona International College were also encountered throughout the development and implementation phases. Even when one takes special care to recruit only professors who are fully committed to interdisciplinarity, things do not usually work out as anticipated. In fact, it seems that more often things can go wrong than right—faculty members each have their own specific ideas about how everything should operate (of course, every professor believes his/her ideas are the best and should be completely adopted by everyone else and the entire organization), all the way from academic policies to the size and color of paper clips. Other troublesome areas include faculty who do not get along and are uncooperative with others, including peers, faculty, and administrators who are often moving at different speeds (and sometimes in different directions), people who do not show up for meetings that were scheduled to meet their idiosyncrasies and then complain because some (any) action was taken and they were not consulted, and the list goes on and on and on . . . . It suffices to say that although theoretically AIC's academic program and curriculum are sound and innovative, the process of developing and implementing them has not been easy or straight-forward. On the contrary, like any real personal or institutional change, it has been extremely challenging.

Organizational Structure

Just as an interdisciplinary model using a house structure breaks down traditional boundaries of academic disciplines, the organizational structure can help create a different type of culture and atmosphere. The more traditional a structure is the more likely it is that individuals within the institution will revert back to a more standard way of thinking and working. Because traditional structures make some sense and are comfortable for most people coming from institutions with such structures (the overwhelming majority of institutions), it can be difficult to break out of a highly traditional way of thinking about how work is conducted and normal things are accomplished in an organization.

One technique used at Arizona International College to counter these forces is that of teams. Teams are used to accomplish a wide variety of tasks and organizational planning across the institution. All of these teams are made up of representatives from various constituencies, such as faculty, administrators, staff, and students. Teams tend to have about five to ten members and are much more action-oriented and outcomes-focused than are the traditional committees utilized by most institutions. Team members are expected to participate not only by attending and talking in meetings but also by carrying out specific assignments that come directly out of team meetings. For example, the educational technology team was completely responsible for the creation of the institution's new web site. The team had specific tasks that it needed to accomplish within a specific timetable and budget.

By having teams handle various important responsibilities across the campus, two objectives are met: 1) the organization is allowed to remain relatively flat and therefore is more cost efficient, and 2) it ensures that all groups on campus are represented in all major areas of decision-making. This approach also helps to break down the natural barriers of a discipline-based structure and the traditional barriers between groups of people on campus, particularly faculty and administrators.

Having a team structure eliminates the need for several administrative positions found at traditional institutions because many tasks are accomplished by groups. People involved in these various aspects of the institution are more involved in the entire institution, which, ideally, means they have a broader perspective and understanding of the learning community as opposed to being narrowly focused on teaching their individual courses.

Faculty Composition

Hiring the right faculty is always an important issue for any institution. But hiring for a new institution with a unique mission is key to being able to accomplish the learning goals established by that institution. For Arizona International College, this task is more problematic and perhaps quite apparent. Although quite a few faculty candidates have either received their PhDs from interdisciplinary programs or have vitas that reflect interdisciplinary backgrounds (either through multiple degrees or professional experiences), virtually none of them come from a truly interdisciplinary institution. Most candidates come from traditional discipline-based colleges and universities—even if they have been working in an interdisciplinary program within that type of institution. This distinction makes an important difference because, in the end, these faculty are all coming from more or less traditional schools with more or less traditional structures, which often makes it very difficult to work in an entirely new and different structure that revolves around interdisciplinarity.

One issue that has become evident at our institution is that faculty often have significantly different perspectives on what interdisciplinarity means. Their definitions (a faculty assessment was undertaken at the beginning of the first school year in order to establish a baseline for a FIPSE-sponsored project on faculty evaluation and development) range from "taking a given topic and approaching it from one or more disciplines," to "a mastery of each discipline before they can be combined," to "the way to connect different disciplines and identify a common area of research." In order to address this discrepancy and to ensure that Arizona International College delivers a consistent academic program, it is necessary to have all faculty participate in discussions, workshops, and regular meetings on interdisciplinary teaching. Follow-up meetings among faculty began early during the first year of AIC's operation and continue taking place to ensure long-term incorporation of these concepts into the classroom.

Because most traditional institutions do not value interdisciplinarity and because AIC, like most new colleges and universities, is experiencing political and budgetary insecurities, faculty have been reluctant to let go of disciplinary ties, partly because of their fear of job security and partly because it is more familiar and safe ground to them. However, unless faculty fully embrace an interdisciplinary approach and shift their focus from their often narrow research and teaching interests to student learning, the academic program will not be successful.

We fully recognize that newly hired faculty will have varying levels of experience and expertise in several areas that have been identified by Arizona International College as being critical for effective teaching and mentoring in an interdisciplinary environment. Thus, new faculty are assessed as soon as they begin work as to strengths and weaknesses and appropriate programs are developed for them by their peer faculty mentors. Part of this development usually includes the viewing of videos of workshops previously given to existing faculty along with relevant readings and mentoring by senior faculty. It is clear that maintaining a level of interdisciplinarity will take sincere commitment and active participation on a regular and ongoing basis.

Reward and Recognition System

To further break down the traditional structure, faculty rewards and recognition are tied to student learning/outcomes, which are defined as being interdisciplinary in nature. When outcomes are based more on skills and competencies, as opposed to focusing only on substantive knowledge within a narrow discipline, students need to be exposed and assessed on skills across disciplines. This broader focus will help students learn how to generalize to other areas what they have learned in one area, which is how the skills are defined and tested. For example, critical thinking skills are very difficult to teach effectively within a narrow substantive area. When taught this way, students tend to learn to use those skills only in the subject area in which they were taught and do not do well when asked to apply those skills to other areas. Obviously, if students are only taught within a narrow range of discipline-based courses, they will do poorly in a skills-based assessment program.

At Arizona International College we are in the process of developing a system that links faculty rewards to student outcomes (with the support of a recent FIPSE grant). Part of this endeavor is predicated on having a comprehensive student assessment program (see next section) that focuses on clearly defined interdisciplinary learning outcomes. Linking faculty performance to these outcomes is not a straightforward undertaking because outcomes are not linked to specific courses but, rather, cut across all courses.

One key component to tying faculty evaluations to student outcomes is having strong faculty-student relationships. Faculty are assigned specific students to advise as students enter the institution. Academic advising at Arizona International College is intended to be more comprehensive than at most institutions because it involves not only a discussion of available courses but also the creation of a specific learning contract. This learning contract is begun during a student's first year in college and involves input from his/her baseline assessments, own objectives and self-assessments, and extensive collaboration with their faculty advisor. These contracts are revisited at least yearly and faculty are held accountable for their students' learning as measured by the regular assessment of students. If a student is deficient in a particular area then it is the faculty member's responsibility, in part, to provide options to their advisee for raising the deficiency to an appropriate standard (such as additional coursework, outside study, independent study, etc.). Of course, a faculty member is not to blame if the student does not follow the advice provided, but the student portfolio and learning contract provide evidence of the advisor's focus on the student's learning outcomes. These contracts and portfolios are reviewed periodically by faculty committees as part of the major progress reviews.

Another more broad-based approach being taken is to determine which of the learning outcomes is being targeted in each faculty member's individual classes. Each of the learning outcomes is very specifically defined. For example, in the case of technology it is defined as consisting of very specific tasks, including word processing, database management, spreadsheet applications, web site, Internet, and presentation graphics. Within these skills, specific examples are identified that students need to demonstrate that they know how to do before they can truly be deemed proficient in that skill (e.g., for word processing, students need to be able to create footnotes within a document, create outlines, change formatting, use a spell/grammar checker, and insert a table and/or graphics). Without this level of specificity it is too easy for most faculty to respond affirmatively to the question of whether they are providing students with comprehensive experiences in the classroom. Similarly, all of the skills and competencies are reduced to this level of specificity. This exercise serves several purposes, including the assurance that the courses as a whole are covering all of the intended outcomes and the determination of which outcomes are accountable by each of the faculty. It also serves to remind faculty of the relevant learning outcomes.

Evaluation/Assessment

At Arizona International College assessment is an integral part of the academic program. Partly, this is because the institution is new, innovative, and nontraditional (in a conservative political environment), but also because the targeted outcomes are not discipline specific. Instead, the targeted outcomes are various skills and competencies that cut across the different disciplines. These skills and competencies include communications, critical thinking and problem solving, quantitative and analytical thinking, technological competency, global and multicultural perspective, and moral discernment.

Because of this focus on skills and competencies, it is not sufficient that students obtain passing grades in their required courses. Seat time and the accumulation of credits is not enough. Rather, Arizona International College's goal is that students be proficient at skills and competencies that cut across the disciplines. It is certainly possible for students at most institutions to obtain a baccalaureate degree without really being able to write well or do basic quantitative reasoning. Some students are adept at finding ways of beating the system—usually by finding the easiest courses and majors. Having a comprehensive assessment program in place will help identify (catch) students who are deficient in the identified skills, skills that are critical to their future success.

The assessment approach taken at Arizona International College is to assess students on the specified skills and competencies at four major time points during their college career. Assessments take place when students are first enrolled at Arizona International College (in order to establish a baseline), mid-way through the core requirements (qualifying exam), a candidacy exam near completion of the degree, and a final capstone project.

An important component of the assessment program is that all of the learning outcomes are clearly defined and agreed upon by the faculty, which means not only that faculty and students are fully informed of the learning objectives but that they remain focused on them. This is an important point because otherwise it is easy to slip into teaching from the perspective of the subject matter only (which is usually discipline specific). Being reminded of the targeted outcomes helps keep faculty focused on incorporating those skills and competencies into their curriculum and at the same time it also provides a common language and goals. In addition, these outcomes are revisited regularly to ensure that they are still relevant and to determine how students are progressing through the academic program.

Conclusion

As noted earlier, creating Arizona International College has been an exceptionally challenging experience. At every step of the way we have inadvertently stepped on someone's toes and have encountered resistance, in some cases rather fierce resistance.

The pressures against innovation in American higher education are phenomenal, particularly when it involves establishing a new institution that is organized without a discipline-based academic program and organizational structure (not to mention, without tenure for faculty members—this is a topic for an entire separate chapter or book!). Even though the University of Phoenix is serving a need for higher education for a particular sector and even though it has been highly successful, the traditional institutions resist it because it is different (e.g., it is a for-profit university and it employs mostly part-time faculty). Western Governors University is also encountering resistance among traditional faculty and institutions because it, too, is nontraditional (e.g., it is an entirely distance education and outcomes-based educational model).

Undoubtedly, at one time or another, every professor and administrator has experienced, to some degree, resistance to change at their respective institutions of higher education. Such resistance is common with even the introduction of new courses and it quickly escalates, and often becomes prolonged for years, when someone attempts to modify the general education or core curriculum. It is not uncommon for it to take years to make even the most minor changes in an institution's general education program. *The Chronicle of Higher Education* and many other journals and magazines that report on higher education routinely cover issues involving resistance to change in the curriculum, personnel policies, structure, etc.

Creating a different structure in any institution, even a new one, is a difficult venture. Maintaining this new structure, given the many forceful pressures from the traditional higher education model, is even more difficult. Although we at Arizona International College have worked hard to institute a new approach and create a new structure, only time will tell whether we are successful in this endeavor, successful at keeping the pressures at bay, successful at keeping the malcontents quiet, successful in staying out of the abyss created through hundreds of years of tradition.

EPILOGUE

Arizona International College is a very young institution; it was only in its third year of operation at the time this book chapter was written. Yet, it has undergone some dramatic changes: a change in location and the loss of its initial leader.

AIC was moved after its second year of operation from its original site, a former IBM plant located about eighteen miles southeast of the University of Arizona, to the edge of the campus of the University of Arizona. When the college was initially sited, the IBM location was selected by the Arizona Board of Regents as a temporary location from a list of four possible alternatives. The selection was somewhat contentious and it was viewed by the media and others as being political. And although the former IBM site was selected as a temporary location, many people believed it would eventually end up being the permanent site.

The state legislature, however, failed to allocate the resources necessary to continue the development of AIC, particularly costs associated with infrastructure such as renovation of additional classrooms and science and technology laboratories, library equipment, and other purchases necessary to any basic college or university. Members of the legislature had been lobbied by some of the University of Arizona faculty who complained that the cost of education at AIC was higher than the main campus. There was also pressure from the other state universities because they did not want to see another player at the table (nothing unusual here, just the normal turf battles common in higher education).

Although the few but very vocal faculty members who lobbied the legislature were basing their case on fiscal conservatism, that was nothing but a smoke screen. (When have faculty been fiscally conservative?) The real issue, the one that got them initially upset and which they would not let go of had to do with the fact that AIC did not offer tenure. All faculty appointments were on a contractual basis, ranging from one to five years. One University of Arizona faculty member shouted in a faculty senate meeting that "there is no such thing as a university and cannot be without tenure." AIC's provost was routinely criticized for retaining his tenure at the University of Arizona while leading an institution without tenure, never mind that the University of Arizona, like almost every college and university in the United States employs faculty under different conditions of service, including part-time and full-time nontenure eligible lecturers. Interestingly enough, the past provost (a Mexican American) is still being criticized by the University of Arizona's chairman of the faculty for this same issue, yet AIC's current leader (who is white and now carries the title of dean) who also retained his tenure has not once been criticized for this. In fact, no one has ever raised the issue publicly. (The current chairman of the faculty is also white and from the same department as AIC's dean.)

In any event, when the legislature did not provide the necessary resources, a decision had to be made regarding the future of AIC. A small group, including the incoming president of the University of Arizona, decided to relocate AIC to the main campus. There AIC could share the University's infrastructure, e.g., library, classrooms, laboratories, residence halls, etc., although AIC would continue to operate its own academic program with its own students, faculty, and personnel policies.

Some of the political turmoil also had to do with AIC's initially low enrollment in the context of a declining enrollment at the University of Arizona. AIC was expected to open in fall 1996 with well over 100 students and to grow slowly for the first four or so years; however, for a variety of reasons including the negative publicity, the newness of the institution, the location, and its innovative program and structure, only 48 students enrolled for the first semester. The second year, fall 1997, 106 students registered. During the spring 1997 legislative session, AIC again encountered a major obstacle that resulted in much negative publicity. The staff of the Joint Legislative Committee recommended that AIC's budget contain a footnote stating that if it did not achieve an enrollment of 300 students by October 1, 1997, AIC would be closed. Such an unreasonable footnote was never included in the final budget bill; however, the damage had already been done. What parents would want to sent their daughter or son to a college that might close within the same semester that she/he initially enrolled?

The fact that the legislature did not provide the resources necessary to develop Arizona International College had little to do with fiscal issues and a great deal to do with politics. During the same years that the legislature denied AIC's budget request, it was providing large allocations to the other new institution in the state, ASU East, as well as increases to another offshoot of Arizona State University—ASU West, which was not experiencing any growth and which was already operating at a higher per student cost than the other public universities in Arizona.

In addition to the tenure issue, the political problems regarding the initial location, and the overall innovativeness of the academic program, Arizona lacks any tradition of liberal arts colleges. In a conservative state like Arizona, some people cannot get beyond the word liberal in liberal arts. One member of the Board of Regents called the curriculum "touchy feely." This was an individual who, although invited to the campus on several occasions, never once visited. Had he done so and taken the time to review the program, visited classes, spoken to students and faculty, he would have had a very different opinion; or at the very least, he would have had an informed opinion.

Arizona International College continues to operate and is likely to do well in the future. Every demographic projection reaffirms that Arizona will continue to grow at a rapid pace; the University of Arizona's enrollment increased by 500 new students during fall 1998, for example. As time passes and the other universities also experience growth, they are less likely to attack AIC for taking "their" students. Also, as time passes, it is likely that AIC's organizational structure and academic program will become more like those of every other college and university. The pressures to normalize are great, and the rut made by tradition is now a large abyss from which few, if any, ever escape.

17

The Academic Department in a Multidisciplinary Context: An Argument for the Administrative Holding Company Amidst Communities of Learners

Joseph J. Comprone
Arizona State University West

Arizona State University West opened its door on a new campus in 1988. The school had been in existence in a shopping center and on the grounds of an elementary school for about an additional ten years, but the real planning of unit curricula and academic programs began in earnest in the late 1980s and early 1990s. This is where our story begins.

ASU West was, in the parlance of new campuses, "front-loaded." In other words, the Arizona legislature and the University Board of Regents provided the campus from the start with the funds, buildings, and land required to serve 5,000 FTE students and approximately 7,000-student headcount within an eight-year period.

Front-loading created both opportunities and risks. The opportunities focused on the potential for coordinated planning of innovative programs from the start. ASU West took up the challenge of this opportunity by carrying out a massive amount of hiring during those early years. In fact, stories told by arts and sciences faculty include renditions of newly hired assistant professors serving on seven or eight search committees simultaneously, and of meetings at local hotels of newly hired department coordinators in which they divided up the hiring spoils among themselves with only vague ideas of how those hired might fit together into articulated programs.

These challenging opportunities led directly to the risks. Among the most challenging was the risk of hiring a faculty that had only a loose concept of the kind of programs planned for the college. In the face of this developing risk, a small group of founding faculty developed and held on to an interdisciplinary vision of interlinked faculty joined together in pursuit of cooperative goals that larger and more specialized universities could not match. As the college grew, however, this group experienced greater and greater difficulty in holding on to the interdisciplinary vision. Not all founding faculty were hired with the interdisciplinary vision foremost in mind. As the campus grew, students were recruited who often showed little interest in interdisciplinary learning for its own sake. Often, these students found the descriptions of the interdisciplinary programs confusing and unfamiliar. Finally, as the campus grew to its current condition and the enrollment benchmarks established at the beginning proved difficult to accomplish, the goal of enhancing enrollment began to take precedent over all other goals. This goal further eroded the strength of the interdisciplinary movement, given that students were in most cases far more attracted to disciplinary programs and because new faculty were encouraged to be cautious in their selection of courses and intellectual focuses.

Two contrasting examples will make the above dichotomy between disciplinary and interdisciplinary programs more palpable. The psychology program at ASU West is by far the largest in the college of arts and sciences. It is not a coincidence that this program carried the entire curriculum from the thriving main campus psychology program intact to the west campus. Overflow from that campus, the popularity of psychology programs everywhere, and the easy to understand psychology curriculum template all worked together to guarantee the rapid disciplinary growth of the psychology program. More directly, this growth to some degree diminished enrollment in other social science programs.

Contrast this "success" story to the story of the interdisciplinary arts and performance (IAP) program at ASU West. This program got off to an auspicious interdisciplinary start, hiring eight faculty members in a single year with a clearly defined interdisciplinary program consisting of core, matrix, and concentration courses. The curriculum was carefully interlinked and included faculty specialists who were to develop their special courses with an eye toward crossing discipline boundaries. In many instances, the emphasis on performance was to create connections where content could not do so.

Just about the opposite from psychology proved to be the fate of the IAP program. Enrollment never took off because recruiters found it difficult to articulate the value of an interdisciplinary arts degree. Once confronted with greater pressure to enhance enrollment, the IAP faculty had an understandably difficult time transforming its vision into one of greater disciplinarity. Gaps between faculty and their different areas of expertise that might have been filled by cooperative efforts across discipline boundaries were left unfilled because of greater enrollment pressure.

Examples like these are often compounded by another difficulty that occurs because many faculty, when they gather to build curriculum, are naturally inclined to work only from their own backgrounds and training rather than from what they know or need to learn about the institutions within which they work. This often leads to carefully developed and well-informed programs that make little sense, or have little impact on, the local student and community markets. Few institutions have been able to apply a balanced approach to the coordination of faculty knowledge and potential student and community interests and needs when producing new or revised programs.

These two departmental cases illustrate a set of dichotomies that evolve whenever traditional departments and interdisciplinary programs attempt to exist side by side. Surprisingly, interdisciplinary faculty members are often the first to be driven back into their special fields and become more isolated from one another when administrative efficiencies are foremost among institutional priorities. Meanwhile, disciplinary faculty, because they are often more comfortable and recognizable in such enrollment-driven environments, are often able to respond positively to these pressures because they are not engaged in forming and attempting to promote new structures and relationships.

Another dichotomy occurs between the need for efficiency and the need for quality. Departments, when under the gun of enrollment, faculty workload scrutiny, and underlying costs often relegate discussions of programmatic quality to the bottom of meeting agendas. This subordination of quality by definition places interdisciplinary programming, which almost always demands fuller and more analytical discussion of program than the more familiar disciplinary categories, at a disadvantage. The result is often a gradual but definite erosion of morale within interdisciplinary faculties.

Learning from the ASU West Experience

Defining the Problem

As I look back over my six years at ASU West, I can now see that a major cause of low faculty morale, high political tension, and an unwillingness to cooperate in the college derived from one structural difficulty. The

College of Arts and Sciences at ASU West, while it struggled to support intellectual and curricular interdisciplinary work, attempted to build programs within a traditional department structure. Although the names of departments seemed on the surface interdisciplinary—i.e., interdisciplinary arts and performance, American studies, integrative studies, life sciences, social and behavioral studies, and women's studies—the actual functioning of departments assumed a faculty coordinated around disciplinary structures. This paradox, or worse yet, this contradictory structure led to planning and decision-making problems in every department, and, of course, in the college as a whole. Two particular areas of conflict stand out as examples.

The first focused on budgeting for new positions across the college. Because it proved easier and more defensible to support position requests in areas where larger enrollment was ensured, and because larger enrollment was often best ensured in familiar disciplinary areas, department faculties began to engage in what I came to see as paradoxical planning in which interdisciplinary curriculum was often superficially camouflaged behind disciplinary majors. History, English, and Spanish brought in the numbers while the interdisciplinary American studies major, arguably one of the department's most creative and innovative degree programs, entertained small enrollments and even less notoriety. In social and behavioral sciences, the interdisciplinary degree by that name, also arguably the most imaginative and intellectually challenging degree in the department, attracted relatively small student numbers while disciplinary majors in psychology and the social sciences attracted much larger numbers and greater notoriety.

This skewed situation did not arise simply out of external pressures for enrollment. A great deal of the problem derived from the kind of administrative processing and categorizing that occurred. First, department meetings were consistently taken up with business, with, in other words, practical discussions and decisions related to requests for new positions, with shaping other kinds of budget requests, and with curricular mechanics. In and of itself, this is to be expected and is necessary. Nonetheless, this kind of emphasis on the pragmatics of academic life leaves almost no time for the kind of intellectual intensity and creativity that must go into forming and nurturing strong interdisciplinary programs.

Second, and perhaps most significant, was the fact that interdisciplinary programs can thrive only when faculty members find it relatively easy to make connections with each other across traditional boundaries. While the college's administrative structure had recognized the need to make collective practical decisions, it had not in any way fostered the making of intellectual and curricular linkages across disciplines. The pioneers of the college of arts and sciences had mistakenly assumed that these mostly interdisciplinary community initiatives would evolve naturally, even as departmental barriers began to grow more formidable because of increasing enrollment and budgetary pressures. The result was an almost complete inability of the college to forge learning communities that possessed identities equal to those of the formally-recognized departments. Also, from the beginning, the college failed to address effectively a central, strategic question: How might external (for example, the need for higher enrollment) and internal (the need for program innovation and coherence) influences be reconciled and integrated in the planning and building of a college on a new campus?

Some Earlier Administrative History

Studies of the histories of university and college departments, when they first came into prominence in the mid-to-late 19th century and as late as the early 20th century in some institutions, suggest that three central developments in American universities of that time fostered the existence of the academic department:

1) American universities were for the first time coming under the direct influence of post-industrialization; departmentalization was a management concept that began, for efficiency's sake, to move from industrial to university life. Head counting and budgetary accounting were simply more efficiently done within smaller, more tightly defined departments than they were under the more loosely federated and intellectually driven faculties of the liberal arts colleges and smaller public universities.

2) On the other side of the earlier university and college coin, the more interdisciplinary faculties in 18th and early 19th century American universities and colleges were usually organized into loosely federated intellectual communities focused on interdisciplinary subjects such as rhetoric, the sciences considered broadly as a learning enterprise, and the more inclusive professional fields such as law and the ministry.

3) By the close of the 19th century, however, Harvard and Johns Hopkins had already begun to reorganize their faculties into departments that represented more specialized bodies of knowledge to meet the more focused needs of an industrial managerial elite and for the sake of internal efficiency.

This somewhat complicated administrative and intellectual history behind the university department has thus created a larger quandary than the recent problems faced by many interdisciplinary programs. Interdisciplinary struggles are actually more usefully seen as part of the larger pattern of specialization and accountability; these struggles are not at their core occurring between faculties, or between administration and faculty, or, for that matter, between disciplines and larger, more eclectic academic entities. In other words, many interdisciplinary initiatives are motivated by productivity and efficiency goals more than they are by intellectual creativity. Yet, these initiatives are often at a distinct disadvantage because the faculty members who lead them do not know or acknowledge that these practical goals are at least equally important.

The Department as Holding Company

Given this very complicated collection of causes and effects, my six years as dean within a college striving to create interdisciplinary programs has convinced me that the solution to the administrative problem is at least conceptually a simple one. Any institution that wishes to acknowledge the inherent complexity and integrated nature of knowledge in contemporary society must first acknowledge that departments are not, and were seldom intended to be, real intellectual or academic entities. They are not places where intellectual problems are solved, where faculty go to engage in true intellectual dialog, or where students or staff members are most often even admitted. Rather, departments function best as loosely connected groups of faculty who make final decisions regarding budget, personnel, and curriculum. But even in the curricular area, where one would most expect straightforward and detailed intellectual engagement, the department often serves only as a place where final decisions are made—often on very practical terms. In most cases, a sound curricular decision depends on loads of hallway and office conversation, and not on the practical and procedural considerations put forward in department meetings.

Once departments are recognized for what they are—as budgetary, personnel and curricular holding companies where final decisions are made based on practical constraints—institutions can proceed both to recognize their administrative importance while not looking to them to accomplish what they were never meant to accomplish. Fewer departments meetings that are more narrowly focused on translating the in-depth intellectual work of faculty, students, and staff into the practical terms of legislators, boards of regents or governors, and central administrations can proceed in the kind of practical atmosphere uncluttered by real intellectual work. But what about the other half of the story? Where, then, does a more inclusive and open dialog focused on real intellectual and interdisciplinary issues occur? And how do decisions evolving from that dialog come to get at least equal support from the institution as do the decisions made in departments?

Learning Communities

It is possible for colleges to create situations in which departments and learning communities coexist within an integrated environment where individuals align themselves with different learning communities within the overall decision-making context of a department structure. In other words, the dean and department chairs must work with faculty leaders in promoting a visibly bicameral structure in which learning communities focused around predetermined academic and curricular themes and content areas carry most of the heavy intellectual work of the department. These communities must work independently from the functional aspects of a department, and administrators must find ways to assure the ongoing productivity and integrity of these groups. Administrators must also do everything they can to separate the functional department meeting from the more process oriented meetings of the community of learners. The functional department meetings ought in most cases to be limited to one or two long meetings each semester, while the community meetings occur more regularly. Budgetary and practical curricular decisions should occur in the functional department meetings only after the learning communities have concluded their more substantive discussions and have reached consensus on recommendations.

If colleges and universities are to foster such creative interaction between the functional and intellectual, however, they must recognize the following:

- that learning communities do not spring naturally out of faculty, student, or staff inherent interests; they must be planned for and supported. This often requires careful initial planning of curriculum with an eye toward the future and toward both the practical and more creative aspects of academic life. It also requires the hiring of faculty with a clear perspective on curriculum in mind so that new faculty members are more easily able to accommodate their special knowledge and skill to the needs of that curriculum.

- that department chairs and deans must provide formal support for the activities of learning communities, and they must build that support into department plans in a formal and consistent way. Effective change in the processing of departmental and disciplinary life cannot occur as long as functional department meetings have all the decision-making power and learning communities are left in an informal and powerless state. The trick here is for faculty leaders to work together no matter what their disciplines to assure that the work of learning communities is supported. This support must include assurances that faculty brought together in functional department meetings will make decisions that are clearly based on the ongoing work of the separate learning communities.

- that structural accommodations must be made to bring together and sustain the dialog of faculties, students, and staff across the usual disciplinary margins if learning communities are to become an everyday part of academic life. This step might include eliminating all department committees with the idea of collecting faculty and students together in learning communities predicated on the common career and intellectual interests of community members. Each learning community would then be encouraged to develop an approach that would encourage intergroup creativity with an eye on efficient communication of the results of the group's work to the functional department or unit as a whole.

- that secure plans must be made to ensure that the intellectual activity (as represented by learning communities) and practical concerns (as addressed by departments) come together in open, timely, and unfragmented dialog, with both the practical and the intellectual perspectives influencing the decisions that are made. Functional department units would be responsible for enunciating current fiscal and political constraints early in each academic year; they would also conduct open meetings focused on decision-making toward the end of each semester. Learning communities would provide the substance for the latter meetings.

Of course, entire articles could easily be devoted to answering the following questions regarding learning communities and their existence within formal academic contexts: What kinds of issues, challenges, and interests usually bring learning communities into existence? Who belongs to learning communities and what are their goals? Exactly how does the work of a learning community come to influence the rest of the system? My purpose in this chapter suggests only that 1) we define learning communities by what they are not (their motives are not managerial or administrative, but intellectual, and practical only in the sense of transforming knowledge into innovative learning structures), and 2) that they include groups usually not included in formal academic decision-making—i.e., all faculty, students, and staff who are interested in a particular perspective on the curriculum. Finally we can add some best examples of learning communities to help shape this beginning definition: undergraduate students, faculty, and staff working together on grant-supported interdisciplinary research; students, faculty, community members, and staff working together on experiential learning and internship projects; students, faculty, staff, and community members working together to flesh out a new ethnic studies minor; and students, local film industry representatives, faculty, and staff working together on formulating a film and media studies minor. All these projects have created in the college of arts and sciences at ASU West communities of learners that might now be sustained through ongoing conversations focused on new interdisciplinary challenges.

Establishing a more pristine world of either total administrative focus or complete interdisciplinary integration, given current external and internal pressures, is not possible in today's colleges and universities. The friction between internal and external pressures is at this point simply too great for such integration to occur. Higher education must learn to live with dichotomies, not fight them—to nurture and tease out the insights that creative tensions can produce rather than hide from their negative possibilities. Creative tension is perhaps in any case superior to the pristine but oversimplified sense of direction that either a wholly internal and discipline driven or entirely external and consumer oriented approach would produce.

18

Alternative Ways of Organizing: The Importance of Organizational Culture

A Case Study of Interdisciplinary Curricula at SUNY Potsdam

Sandra J. Sarkela
SUNY Potsdam

While it is true that organizational change often requires a shift in cultural norms and values, it may also be argued that reference to traditional values within the organization can support innovation. Such is the case at SUNY Potsdam, a small, liberal arts, state supported college that, despite territorial imperatives of traditional disciplinary units and budget constraints that drained resources from one initiative after another, continues to resurrect generation after generation of interdisciplinary initiatives. The purpose of this chapter is to record the history of these initiatives as accurately as possible, and offer an explanation for the persistence of curricular reform throughout the life of this institution.

Scholarship in organizational theory increasingly recognizes the importance of culture in the process of change and innovation. At the same time, though, the power held in the ways of the people has not been adequately acknowledged. This is probably true in part because discovering the ways of the people is not a process that easily conforms to a scientific model of discovery. However, over the past ten years or so, with objectivity in disrepute and a postmodern subjectivity in vogue, the power of language to shape various realities has been recognized as a force worthy of study. Various ethnographic techniques rendering such study more scientific have been developed (see, for example, Eisenberg & Goodall (1993), esp. Chapter 5).

But, it may actually be a simpler task than we realized. Perhaps learning the ways of the people simply requires listening to the stories they tell. It is important, though, not only to hear our people's stories and respond to them informally, but also to recognize and record these stories in an official way. For those stories will reveal the parameters within which real change can be supported and beyond which it is bound to fail.

The SUNY Potsdam story has two parts. The first is the story of its creation as St. Lawrence Academy, a teacher training school, and its subsequent evolution into one of the teachers colleges that formed the State University of New York in 1948. This history is detailed in a book by former Potsdam history professor W. Charles Lahey, entitled *The Potsdam Tradition: A History and a Challenge.* It is also chronicled in college catalogs dating from 1875, and some alumni publications.

The second part of the story begins in 1962 when Potsdam State Teachers College became a liberal arts institution, officially named a State University College of Arts and Sciences. This history is told in college catalogs, various program documents, and a few written statements from various program directors. The rest of this chapter, then, will take a closer look at these two periods in the history of the college, with particular attention to curricular innovation and interdisciplinary study. Our purpose is to reveal how an organization's cultural traditions, revealed in the stories of its people, can support change and innovation.

THE STATE TEACHERS COLLEGE: 1816–1962

The 1997–1999 college catalog explains that "The State University of New York College at Potsdam is one of 64 units of the State University of New York and one of 13 SUNY arts and sciences colleges. Its origin was the St. Lawrence Academy, founded in 1816 by early settlers of the region" (p. 6). In the opening chapter of his book, Lahey writes that

> The initiative for the [St. Lawrence] Academy rested with men in a frontier environment. Frederick Jackson Turner has labeled this phenomenon a rebirth of American institutions. The need for the school rested on an emerging capitalistic, industrial mobility that would utilize science and technology to produce the necessities of life for all Americans. The demand for the Academy depended upon a democratic mobility that had caught sight of the fulfillment of democratic vistas, made possible by this science and technology. Access to this fulfillment depended, in part, on an adequate education. (1996, p. 5)

Three important themes are revealed in this explanation of the college's creation that continue to resonate on the campus today. First is a sense that we were created and continue to survive in a frontier, or wilderness, setting. Second is a belief in the need for educated citizens to maintain our democratic society. Third is pride that this institution, reflecting our democratic society, provides the opportunity of formal education to all Americans.

The college catalog outlines the rest of the college's history, noting that "it continued as Potsdam Normal School in 1867, as Potsdam State Teachers College in 1942, and became part of the largest university system in the United States, the State University of New York in 1948" (p. 6). Not mentioned in this catalog is the fact that SUNY Potsdam did not offer any degrees other than teacher education until 1962 when it became a State University College of Arts and Science. Thus, until 1962 the college offered only two degrees: teacher education for grades one through eight, and music education.

Until 1962, students were required to complete an interdisciplinary, liberal arts curriculum in order to receive their teacher education degrees. In 1900, students could enroll in one of three courses of study: English, scientific, or classical. The English course required algebra, geometry, geology, general history, vocal music, drawing, rhetorical work, physics, astronomy, English literature, chemistry, teaching in schools of practice, and a course of reading and discussion connected with professional work. However, while the curriculum was interdisciplinary in the sense that all students were required to complete a broad, general liberal arts program, there were no courses or programs prior to teaching in schools of practice that attempted to integrate the content of several different disciplines (State Normal and Training School, 1900–1901).

In the 1928–1929 catalog, "The Freshman Forum" was listed for the first time as an extracurricular activity. It was described

> as an institution which, to students entering the school for the first time, is of special interest. Here all freshmen girls come together once each week for what might be termed a freshman chapel program. Here girls are oriented with respect to school life and their profession; here they learn to work together in a variety of ways and to develop certain desirable social and professional attitudes. An effort is made to learn every girl's special aptitudes or skills and to offer an opportunity to use her talent in giving pleasure and stimulation to the rest of her classmates .... Members of the faculty and upper classmen appear there and speak on various topics of school interest. Opportunity is given to discuss matters of social movement. In short, this is an organization which attempts to help every girl to develop a well rounded personality, poised and efficient. (p. 26)

Clearly, this noncurricular program was premised on beliefs related to the interplay between formal education of teachers, and their future role in a democratic society. Also intensely interesting is the fact, not widely acknowledged in college histories, that the student body was largely female. The Freshman Forum continued in this form until 1935, and then reappeared in 1940 as a one-hour, zero-credit course within the teacher education curriculum. There is no additional description, but it appears that it was meant as a discussion session to help students integrate their college experiences. This remained in place until 1962 when the college became a liberal arts institution, rather than purely teacher education. The link between formal and informal learning experiences was not as easily made outside the teacher education curriculum.

At the same time, Helen Hosmer began experimenting with the music education curriculum. Initiated in the late 19th century by Julia Crane, the music education program was the first of its kind. In this curriculum, students were required to develop skills as practicing musicians as the means to becoming successful music teachers. In 1933, according to W. C. Lahey (1996), Hosmer

> set out to demonstrate that a richer education could be obtained outside the existing ground rules . . . . [A]t a meeting of the Crane freshmen, she asked for volunteers to enter an experimental program . . . . There were imaginative innovations in this experiment. Subjects were studied in blocks of time instead of following the regular schedule. This permitted more concentration and study in depth . . . . The highlight of the experiment was one semester of study in Europe. *The New York Times* reported the event as 'A noteworthy step in the training of music teachers . . . . For the first time in the history of teacher training in the United States, a normal school is offering a semester's work in the various centers of Europe'. (pp. 165–170)

Hosmer concluded that the trip, a 24–hour per day educational experience, "stimulated a greater interest in living" (p. 170).

Curricular innovation in the arts continued. After World War II, the teacher education program expanded, and with that expansion one of the most successful and interesting interdisciplinary courses was developed. Eventually, all students preparing to graduate from the college would be required to enroll in what we would now call a two-semester, nine-credit learning community entitled "Expression in the Arts." It was a logical outcome of the school's pioneering commitment to music education, which then extended to both art and literature, and its mission to prepare elementary teachers.

The 1951–1952 college catalog describes the course as follows:

> For freshmen enrolled in the elementary teachers curriculum, the studies and activities of Art 101–102 are coordinated and, insofar as feasible, integrated with the studies and activities in English 101-102 and Music 101-102. The three courses brought thus together are designated by the general name of 'Expression in the Arts' . . . . Experience in observed and creative expression are discussed in such a manner as to enable students to increase their understanding of the interrelationship of the arts and of the role of the arts in human existence. (p. 46)

Lahey writes again, that "an essential feature of the organization of the course was that of scheduling. . . . Block scheduling was the key to the course and cleared the way for a least two serviceable procedures:

1) Combined meetings of two, three, or all six sections for periods of time up to two hours in length . . . .
2) Temporary regrouping of members of the two sections in any one area . . . . Under such a system each department kept its identity while the subject matter of all areas became fused" (pp. 218–219).

The faculty who taught in this program are now retired, but their stories still circulate through invited reminiscences both orally and in writing. In a fall 1995 art department newsletter, former department chair, "Red" Garner, described the evolution of this unique course:

> In the spring of 1947 the ten teachers colleges (now the ten liberal arts colleges) sent representatives from their Art, English and Music departments (Crane) to a conference in Syracuse for consideration of the possibility of coordinating their efforts on an introductory (freshman) course to be known as 'Expression in the Arts.' The offering of such a course was to be optional. Potsdam was the only one of the ten colleges to proceed with 'Expression in the Arts.'
>
> When I arrived at Potsdam in August 1947, . . . I was advised that I would be responsible for the art content of this program. Three faculty were to be involved: Florence Lockerby of the English Department, Bob Weidman from Music and myself. There were three sections of freshmen with thirty to forty students in each section. In addition to regular classes in each subject we scheduled a weekly two-hour seminar in which all students and the three faculty participated. Course content and written assignments were coordinated. As the semester progressed, the need for first-hand experience with major works of art led us to plan a week in New York to occur between semesters. This took place in January 1948. Unfortunately, we could not then require this trip. About one-third of the

> students managed to go. In time, all freshmen took this course, many faculty were involved, the New York week became a requirement and we yearly found ourselves and five hundred freshmen successfully working through remarkable educational experiences. (p. 5)

Garner's colleague, Ben Goldsmith, lends his commentary in the same art department newsletter, stating:

> Worthy of an entire testimonial in its own right must be the program named 'Expression in the Arts.' The hub of the program centered around a week-long stay in New York City where freshman students were immersed in major experiences involving music, art and drama. The material was then used for classroom purposes during the semester. The best plays, musical events and art exhibits were required. Authors, artists and musicians were available for meetings and discussions with our students. Studios were visited. This was education at its best. (p. 6)

Bill Gambling also taught in the program, observing in the newsletter,

> One of my most pleasant memories of those early years (i.e., the 50's) relates to the 'Expression in the Arts' program which involved on-site art experiences in New York City. A day or so before we left for the city, the freshman class assembled and each student was given tickets and last-minute instructions by the faculty. The highlight of the meeting was the remarks by Dr. Patience Haggard of the English Department on conduct becoming ladies and gentlemen. (p. 7)

Surely this is a remarkable venture in interdisciplinary study at a state supported teacher education college. Imagine the entire freshman class assembled weekly to discuss expression in the arts, integrating three courses and three professors, with a school trip to New York City as a fulcrum between semesters. For those who experienced the program as teacher or student, it was a defining concept for both the college and the individuals involved. Like Hosmer's experiment, which was developed in conjunction with students, Expression in the Arts built on the arts using block scheduling to promote integration of courses. In addition, an experiential component involving travel away from our remote, rural location to the cosmopolitan worlds of New York City and Europe was included. In doing so, location became an implicit foil and focal point for study of the arts.

State University College of Arts and Sciences, 1962–Present

In 1962, the college was expanded from a teachers college to the State University College of Arts and Science at Potsdam. This was a time of major growth for the SUNY system as a whole, and Potsdam experienced its share. Budgets were strong, as were enrollments, and many new faculty were hired, particularly to support the new arts and sciences mission of the college. During this period, disciplinary departments built new domains and the long history of interdisciplinary studies was temporarily abandoned. In fact, SUNY Potsdam became the only school to require its education majors to have two majors, one in a discipline and one in education.

Nevertheless, many faculty from the 1950s were important members of the school of arts and sciences. The first interdisciplinary initiative recorded in the college catalogs appeared in 1969. An "Interdisciplinary Humanities Program," described as "experimental" was "authorized from September 1969 to June 1971 for sixty juniors and seniors with a cumulative average of at least 3.0 at the time of registration." The program would be "taught by a committee of five faculty members, one each from philosophy, literature, history and political science, art, and music. The program serves as a high-level synthesis of the knowledge and insights that students have gained in individual courses within the area of the humanities" (p. 44).

It seems that this program did not have a long history, but six years later another, more ambitious interdisciplinary program was announced: The School Within a School. A former director of SWS, Robert Snow, offers the following reflections on its history:

> SWS was an interdisciplinary program for freshmen that brought together science, social science, and the humanities to address major issues of the modern world. The program was historically oriented. From 1977 through 1981 it was a 30 semester hour program. Beginning in the fall of 1982 it was reduced to 20 semester hours (10 each semester). From its inception the SWS program emphasized the reading of original texts wherever possible, substantial writing assignments, team teaching, and strenuous efforts to integrate course materials. From 1978 there was a historian of science on the SWS staff. Beginning in 1981 the program also incorporated materials from the history of technology.
>
> Most years the enrollment ranged from 40–45 students with a maximum of 50. Faculty teaching in the SWS program were initially drawn from the various departments. The SWS teaching format did not change much during its nine year history. Each course had small tutorial sections (6 to 10 students in each) and two lectures a week which were attended by all students and all faculty. There also was a two hour class each Friday which was usually devoted to viewing a film or video which helped to bring together material from the various courses. All faculty and students were expected to attend the Friday class.
>
> From 1977 through the fall of 1982 the SWS program had very strong administrative support from the Dean of Liberal Studies. Near the close of

1983 a new dean was appointed who also supported the program, but it was not his special project. The SWS program was administrated by a Coordinator who also taught in the program.

There were a number of trends which were quite constant throughout the history of the program. These were:

a. Each year the SWS curriculum was refined and the interdisciplinary connections were made stronger and clearer.
b. Almost every year of the program, the College lost teaching positions. By 1982 it was becoming quite difficult for departments to spare faculty members to teach in the SWS program.
c. As the College lost teaching positions, average course enrollments in the departments tended to increase. Since SWS classes were small from the beginning and did not increase over time, there was an increasing gap between the teaching environment for SWS faculty and faculty in departmental programs.
d. The interests of high school graduates matriculating at SUNY Potsdam became increasingly vocational as the SWS program developed. Consequently it became increasingly difficult to interest them in a broad interdisciplinary general education program.
e. In Spring 1986 the New York State budget support for higher education was disappointing. To cope with a budget shortfall, SUNY Potsdam elected to eliminate most of its temporary service positions. For SWS this meant that two of its staff for the coming year lost their jobs. It also meant that the program could not be offered for academic year 1986/87. When the budget outlook did not improve for the next year, it was clear that SWS could not be revived. (personal communication, August 29, 1997)

Conceived in the final wake of SUNY's boom period, SWS could not survive the realities of state budget vagaries. The contrast between the stories of SWS and Expression in the Arts is dramatic: sober reflection on what should have been a model of interdisciplinary education versus the excitement of an entire college community joining in a fully integrated arts education experience.

Another interesting initiative that attempted to integrate ideas was a new version of the Freshman Forum. The 1981–1982 college catalog announced the beginning the Dean's Freshman Seminar. This was an ambitious program that aimed to help students understand and appreciate the breadth and interconnectedness of the liberal arts. The catalog explained that

> This course will be conducted by faculty members from many of the departments of the School of Liberal Studies. These faculty members will also work closely with the twenty or so students in their discussion sec-

> tions as academic advisors for the freshman year. Topics to be covered in the discussion meetings will raise such questions as: how do human beings make choices? . . . what is the value of a liberal arts education? The purpose of these discussions is to bring faculty and students together in a common content to the breadth and freedom of thinking traditionally associated with the life of the mind in liberal education. (p. 7)

Unfortunately, a method of keeping faculty regularly involved as discussion leaders was never devised. Arts and sciences faculty preferred teaching courses in their own disciplines, and the seminar lost its sense of purpose.

Institutional memories don't die quickly, however, and from the remains of the Dean's Freshman Seminar, SWS, and, perhaps even most importantly, the unforgotten excitement of Expression in the Arts, faculty reconstituted themselves into a committee to develop a new general education program. Today, ten years later, it is still referred to as the new general education program.

In a document dated February 1987, given to all faculty, entitled "General Education Program for Potsdam College," the development of the current GEP is described in detail. Three years into the program, a brief statement was added to the beginning of the document. Its tone is optimistic, but reflective of the instability that has plagued the campus and the SUNY system as a whole, the same conditions that forced the end of SWS:

> After considerable study and debate, the Faculty Assembly of Potsdam College approved the proposal for a new general education program at this institution. Students enrolled in the graduating class of 1992 were the first to enter under the new General Education requirements.
>
> During its first three years, the new General Education Program functioned under two different Presidents and one Acting President, as well as four different Academic Vice Presidents. Given the amount of administrative turnover, the General Education Committee and its Committee Chair had to operate fairly autonomously. The General Education Program was allocated a sizable budget which was used for faculty development with emphasis on methods for developing students' critical thinking ability. In addition, money was used to purchase computer equipment and to develop computer skills of General Education Faculty . . . .
>
> The term of the first Chair expired in the summer of 1990. It was at that point that the newly hired Vice President for Academic Affairs appointed a permanent Administrator of General Education . . . . The Academic Vice President also appointed a new General Education Committee Chair. In addition, the General Education budget was eliminated. However, the Academic Vice President allocated money to the new Teaching and Learning Committee which was dedicated to faculty development . . . .

> One feature of the General Education Program which has not been fully realized is its interdisciplinary potential. The structure of the program, while not mandating an interdisciplinary approach to general education, does allow for an interdisciplinary general education curriculum. It lends itself well to the initiative in Coordinated Studies and Learning Communities established by the new Academic Vice President in 1990–91.
>
> It is our hope that the administrative problems of the program will continue to be resolved in order to properly implement the spirit of the original General Education Proposal. (1990, pp. 1–2)

While the new General Education Program is still fraught with problems, it did provide a mechanism for development of learning communities, pairs and clusters of courses that exist within the School of Arts and Sciences and a few that cross school boundaries between arts and sciences and education. A modified coordinated studies program on the theme "The Adirondacks" has succeeded for four years, headed by a former SWS faculty member. Built on a block scheduling concept, available to all interested first-year students, focused on the region, including an element of the arts, this program has seen continued support from the college and community.

Learning communities have survived for seven years, and the number of learning communities is growing as faculty see a need to reconnect with colleagues and disciplines outside their more narrow disciplines and schools. Perhaps the most interesting development has been the rise of learning communities within the School of Education. A recent application for participation in the Washington Center's Learning Community Dissemination Project[1] explains:

> Our School of Education differs from the traditional model because our students are required to complete an academic major in addition to an education major. This has facilitated the creation of Learning Communities that have forged connections between faculty in Education and Arts and Sciences. Further, Potsdam is in a remote rural area of upstate New York. Finding time for students to gain necessary field experiences is facilitated by clusters such as "Teaching Elementary Science," "Teaching Elementary Math," and "Classroom Management."

A recent issue of *Potsdam People,* the alumni newspaper, featured the learning community initiative on the front page. The article concludes with the assertion that SUNY Potsdam is "at the forefront of leading institutions, nationwide, which are willing to experiment, prudently and judiciously, with improving the undergraduate learning experience" (Loucks, 1998, p. 2). It is possible to promote change and innovation by appealing to traditional organizational values.

Preliminary Conclusions

This first look at formal narratives about interdisciplinary curricula at SUNY Potsdam reveals a history of commitment to the arts and teaching. When the college changed from a teacher education college to an arts and sciences college, a change initiated by the SUNY central administration and facilitated by a strong economy, the traditional interdisciplinary curriculum was eliminated. Maintaining interdisciplinary studies in the School of Arts and Sciences has been a struggle carried forth by a segment of committed faculty. This contrasts with the inherent nature of interdisciplinary studies in teacher education curricula, and the unanimous, enthusiastic support present for the two-semester sequence Expression in the Arts.

These stories tell us that interdisciplinary curricula will flourish if they work for students and faculty. A structure imposed without recognition of history and tradition can be propped up with adequate funding, but not with enthusiasm. Furthermore, at our institution, the heritage of education and music is fundamental. Links to that tradition will help any reform effort succeed. In particular, reviewing and paying attention to an organization's stories may offer a key to unlocking traditions which support innovation.

In describing and analyzing an organization's stories, recent work on the function of narrative is helpful. David Lodge (1990) writes that "A narrative cannot be reduced to a proposition, but it must have a point, and it must have some kind of unity . . . Wanting to know what happened next is the basic narrative appetite, and it usually depends on the narration privileging some persons involved in the events over others—we call these privileged persons the hero or heroine. We shall be still more interested in the sequence of events if they are connected by causality" (p. 142).

For SUNY Potsdam, stories of failure emphasize lack of financial resources as the immediate cause of failure, but ultimately a person, typically the president of the college, is held accountable. On the other hand, the successful story, one of survival, might be stated as follows: A gifted person of great vision (the college president or the head of the music program) persuades those people outside the region who do not understand or appreciate the college, of the need to prepare teachers, especially in the arts, through an innovative, integrated curriculum, combined with a lively, rich student life in a remote, beautiful, and nourishing physical location. In addition, faculty persistence and initiative are often credited, but the need for leadership and support from an administrative leader is always present.

Finally, a point that may benefit many colleges considering interdisciplinary studies is to look more carefully at their education schools for models. In liberal arts colleges the framework for curriculum is disciplinary, so interdisciplinary studies must fight the establishment. That is not true for schools of education, particularly elementary education. Perhaps neglect of this tradition is part of a more generalized bias in American history that tends to exclude much reference to women's roles and achievements.

This research suggests a need for a larger study of teacher education programs in the United States, especially curricula developed at the State Normal Schools. Such a study could reveal the extent of interdisciplinary integrated curricula in this important category of American higher education.

References

Arnold, G., & Civian, J. (1997, July/August). The ecology of general education reform. *Change,* 19–23.

Art Department. (1995, Fall). *Art news.* Potsdam, NY: State University of New York College at Potsdam.

Eisenberg, E., & Goodall, H. (1993). *Organizational communication: Balancing creativity and constraint.* New York, NY: St. Martin's.

Kanter, S., Gamson, Z., & London, H. B. (1997). *Revitalizing general education in a time of scarcity.* Boston, MA: Allyn and Bacon.

Klein, J. (1990). *Interdisciplinarity.* Detroit, MI: Wayne State University Press.

Lahey, W. C. (1996). *The Potsdam tradition: A history and a challenge.* New York, NY: Appleton-Century-Crofts.

Lodge, D. (1990). Narration with words. In H. Barlow, C. Blakemore, & M. Weston-Smith (Eds.), *Images and Understanding* (pp. 140–153). Cambridge, MA: Cambridge University Press.

Loucks, P. (1998, Winter). Exploring new teaching strategies to maximize student learning. *Potsdam People,* 1–2.

Potsdam College. (1987, February). *General education program for Potsdam College.* Unpublished document, Potsdam College, Potsdam, NY.

Potsdam College. (1990). *The general education program at Potsdam College, 1988–1991.* Unpublished document, Potsdam College, Potsdam, NY.

Potsdam College of the State University of New York. (1985). *Undergraduate catalog, 1985–1986.* Potsdam, NY: Author.

Potsdam College of the State University of New York. (1986). *Undergraduate catalog, 1986–1988.* Potsdam, NY: Author.

Potsdam College of the State University of New York. (1987). *Undergraduate catalog, 1987–1988.* Potsdam, NY: Author.

Potsdam College of the State University of New York. (1988). *Undergraduate catalog, 1988–1990.* Potsdam, NY: Author.

Potsdam College of the State University of New York. (1990). *Undergraduate catalog, 1990–1992.* Potsdam, NY: Author.

Potsdam College of the State University of New York. (1993). *Undergraduate catalog, 1993–1995.* Potsdam, NY: Author.

Potsdam State Normal School. (1924). *Potsdam State Normal School, Potsdam, New York, catalogue, 1924–25.* Albany, NY: J. B. Lyon.

Potsdam State Normal School. (1925). *Potsdam State Normal School, Potsdam, New York, catalogue, 1925–26.* Albany, NY: J. B. Lyon.

Potsdam State Normal School. (1926). *Potsdam State Normal School, Potsdam, New York, catalogue, 1926–27.* Albany, NY: J. B. Lyon.

Potsdam State Normal School. (1927). *Potsdam State Normal School, Crane department of music, Potsdam, New York, catalogue, 1927–28.* Albany, NY: J. B. Lyons.

Potsdam State Normal School. (1928). *Potsdam State Normal School, Potsdam, New York, department of music.* Albany, NY: J. B. Lyon.

Potsdam State Normal School. (1929). *Potsdam State Normal School, Potsdam, New York, catalogue, 1928–29.* Albany, NY: J. B. Lyon.

Potsdam State Normal School. (1930). *Potsdam State Normal School, Potsdam, New York, catalogue, 1929–30.* Albany, NY: J. B. Lyon.

Potsdam State Normal School. (1932). *Potsdam State Normal School, elementary teachers course, 1932–33.* Potsdam, NY: Burland.

Potsdam State Normal School. (1934). *Potsdam State Normal School catalogue, 1934–35.* Potsdam, NY: Author.

Potsdam State Normal School. (1935). *Potsdam State Normal School catalogue, 1935–36.* Potsdam, NY: Author.

Potsdam State Normal School. (1937). *Potsdam State Normal School, Potsdam, New York, catalogue, 1937–1938.* Potsdam, NY: Author.

Potsdam State Normal School. (1938). *Potsdam State Normal School, Potsdam, New York, catalogue, 1938–1939.* Potsdam, NY: Author.

Potsdam State University. (1976). *Potsdam State University bulletin, 1976–1978.* Potsdam, NY: Author.

Potsdam State University. (1978). *Potsdam State University bulletin, 1978–80.* Potsdam, NY: Author.

Rudolph, F. (1997). *Curriculum.* San Francisco, CA: Jossey-Bass.

State Normal and Training School. (1879). *Annual report of the State Normal and Training School at Potsdam, New York, for the year ending September 30, 1879.* Albany, NY: The Argus Company.

State Normal and Training School. (1879). *Circular and catalogue of the State Normal and Training School, Potsdam, New York, for the year beginning September 1, 1875 and ending July 1, 1879.* Watertown, NY: Book and Job Printing.

State Normal and Training School. (1886). *Circular of the State Normal and Training School, Potsdam, St. Lawrence County, New York, 1885–1886.* Potsdam, NY: Courier and Freeman.

State Normal and Training School. (1890). *State Normal and Training School, Potsdam, New York.* Potsdam, NY: Author.

State Normal and Training School. (1893). *Circular of the State Normal and Training School at Potsdam, New York.* Potsdam, NY: Courier and Freeman.

State Normal and Training School. (1895). *Circular of the State Normal and Training School at Potsdam, New York.* Potsdam, NY: Courier and Freeman.

State Normal and Training School. (1900). *Circular of the State Normal and Training School, Potsdam, New York.* Potsdam, NY: Elliot Fay and Sons.

State Normal and Training School. (1903). *Circular of the State Normal and Training School, Potsdam, New York.* Potsdam, NY: Elliot Fay and Sons.

State Normal and Training School. (1906). *Circular of the State Normal and Training School, 1906–1907.* Potsdam, NY: Herald-Recorder Press.

State Normal and Training School. (1908). *Circular of the State Normal and Training School, 1908–1909.* Potsdam, NY: Elliot Fay and Sons.

State Normal and Training School. (1909). *The State Normal and Training School circular, Potsdam, New York, 1909–1910.* Potsdam, NY: Elliot Fay and Sons.

State Normal and Training School. (1912). *State Normal and Training School, Potsdam, New York.* Potsdam, NY: Author.

State Normal and Training School. (1920). *Announcement, school year 1920–21.* Potsdam, NY: Author.

State Normal and Training School. (1922). *State Normal and Training School, Potsdam, New York, catalogue, 1922–1923.* Potsdam, NY: School Shop.

State Normal and Training School. (1923). *State Normal and Training School, Potsdam, New York, catalogue, 1923–1924.* Potsdam, NY: School Shop.

State Normal School. (1939). *State Normal School, Potsdam, New York, catalogue, 1939–1940.* Potsdam, NY: Author.

State Normal School. (1940). *State Normal School, Potsdam, New York, catalogue, 1940–1941.* Potsdam, NY: Author.

State Normal School. (1942). *State Normal School, Potsdam, New York, catalogue, 1942–1943.* Potsdam, NY: Author.

State Teachers College. (1943). *State Teachers College, Potsdam, New York, general catalog, 1943–1944.* Potsdam, NY: Author.

State Teachers College. (1944). *State Teachers College, Potsdam, New York, general catalog, 1944–1945.* Potsdam, NY: Author.

State Teachers College. (1945). *State Teachers College, Potsdam, New York, general catalog, 1945–1946.* Potsdam, NY: Author.

State Teachers College. (1946). *State Teachers College, Potsdam, New York, general catalog, 1946–1947.* Potsdam, NY: Author.

State Teachers College. (1947). *State Teachers College, Potsdam, New York, general catalog, 1947–1948.* Potsdam, NY: Author.

State Teachers College. (1948). *State Teachers College at Potsdam, New York, general catalog, 1948–1949.* Potsdam, NY: Author.

State Teachers College. (1949). *State Teachers College at Potsdam, New York, general catalog, 1949–1950.* Potsdam, NY: Author.

State University College at Potsdam. (1974). *Undergraduate bulletin, 1974–1976.* Potsdam, NY: Author.

State University College of Arts and Sciences. (1981). *1981–1982 undergraduate catalog, State University College of Arts and Sciences.* Potsdam, NY: Author.

State University College of Arts and Sciences. (1982). *1982–84 Potsdam College undergraduate catalog.* Potsdam, NY: Author.

State University of New York. (1951). *State University of New York, State Teachers College at Potsdam, New York, general catalog, 1951–1952.* Potsdam, NY: Author.

State University of New York. (1952). *State University of New York, State Teachers College at Potsdam, New York, general catalog, 1952–1953.* Potsdam, NY: Author.

State University of New York. (1953). *State University of New York, State University Teachers College, Potsdam, New York, general catalog, 1953–1954*. Potsdam, NY: Author.

State University of New York. (1955). *State University of New York, State University Teachers College, Potsdam, New York, general catalog, 1955–56*. Potsdam, NY: Author.

State University of New York. (1956). *State University of New York, State University Teachers College, Potsdam, New York, general catalog, 1956–57*. Potsdam, NY: Author.

State University of New York. (1958). *State University of New York, State University Teachers College, Potsdam, New York, general catalog, 1958–1959*. Potsdam, NY: Author.

State University of New York. (1959). *State University of New York, State University Teachers College, Potsdam, New York, general catalog, 1959–1960*. Potsdam, NY: Author.

State University of New York. (1960). *State University of New York, College of Education, Potsdam, New York, general catalog, 1960–61*. Potsdam, NY: Author.

State University of New York. (1961). *State University of New York, College of Education, Potsdam, New York, general catalog, 1961–1962*. Potsdam, NY: Author.

State University of New York. (1962). *State University of New York, College of Education, Potsdam, New York, general catalog, 1962–1963*. Potsdam, NY: Author.

State University of New York. (1963). *State University of New York, College at Potsdam, undergraduate bulletin, 1963–1964*. Potsdam, NY: Author.

State University of New York. (1964). *State University of New York, College at Potsdam, undergraduate bulletin, 1964–1965*. Potsdam, NY: Author.

State University of New York. (1965). *State University of New York, College at Potsdam, undergraduate bulletin, 1965–1966*. Potsdam, NY: Author.

State University of New York. (1966). *State University of New York, College at Potsdam, undergraduate bulletin, 1966–1967*. Potsdam, NY: Author.

State University of New York. (1967). *State University of New York, College at Potsdam, undergraduate bulletin, 1967–1968*. Potsdam, NY: Author.

State University of New York. (1968). *State University of New York, College at Potsdam, undergraduate bulletin, 1968–69*. Potsdam, NY: Author.

State University of New York. (1969). *State University of New York, College at Potsdam, undergraduate bulletin, 1969–70.* Potsdam, NY: Author.

State University of New York. (1970). *State University of New York, College at Potsdam, undergraduate bulletin, 1970–71.* Potsdam, NY: Author.

State University of New York. (1971). *State University of New York, College at Potsdam, undergraduate bulletin, 1971–72.* Potsdam, NY: Author.

State University of New York. (1972). *State University of New York, College at Potsdam, undergraduate bulletin, 1972–74.* Potsdam, NY: Author.

State University of New York at Potsdam. (1985). *First quarto-centennial history of the State Normal and Training School, Potsdam, New York, 1869–1894.* Potsdam, NY: Author.

State University of New York at Potsdam. (1995). *1995–1997 undergraduate catalog.* Potsdam, NY: Author.

State University of New York at Potsdam. (1997). *1997–1999 undergraduate catalog.* Potsdam, NY: Author.

State University of New York at Potsdam. (1999). *1999–2001 undergraduate catalog.* Potsdam, NY: Author.

Endnotes

1. The National Learning Communities Dissemination Project (with initial funding from FIPSE (1996–1999) and continued support from the Pew Charitable Trusts (2000–2004)) is a national effort to support learning community approaches to curriculum reform and teaching improvement. It is led by the Washington Center for Improving the Quality of Undergraduate Education at The Evergreen State College. The FIPSE-funded project engaged 19 colleges and universities in strengthening and assessing their learning community efforts, and then produced case studies on lessons learned.

19

Reconceptualizing the Faculty Role: Alternative Models

James R. Chen, Michael V. Fortunato, Alan Mandell, Susan Oaks, and Duncan RyanMann
SUNY Empire State College

There is little doubt that university education has been the focus of intense debate over the last two decades. The goals of college-level learning, the students with whom we work, our definitions of knowledge, the taken for granted forms of teaching and learning, the connections between the academy and noneducational institutions, and even the traditional academic calendar have been scrutinized, critiqued, and sometimes reconfigured. Whether these changes have been the result of pragmatic adjustment to shifting socioeconomic circumstances, or the outcome of thoughtful analysis that has sought to respond to the perceived shortcomings of conventional educational assumptions is, of course, a significant question that we must address. But whether or not we in the academy understand ourselves to have awakened to the need to become more effective participants in the realities of contemporary market-driven life, or to have offered an alternative and imaginative vision that can guide us with the use of new principles and innovative practices, it is clear that our institutions have changed and will continue to change. Indeed, as the Commission for a Nation of Lifelong Learners (1997) recently concluded, "rethinking and reorganizing" our institutions in order to provide more "innovative and more flexible approaches" to learning has become a necessity (p. 21).

Empire State College is one of those colleges that grew out of a tradition of public institutions seeking to respond to a shifting culture, to the expression of new values, and to the needs of those who had either been excluded from (or not been welcomed into) established educational forms—to the necessity for innovation. Over the last 29 years, our mission as an Arts and Science College of the State University of New York has been to provide access to higher education for adult learners who have sought alternatives to the fixed schedule, place, program, and structure of campus-based education. At the heart of ESC's practice has been the individual learner and the belief that with the use of a range of flexible and developing resources, and the guidance and insight of a faculty mentor, students can gain the knowledge and skills and create whole programs of study relevant to their academic, professional, and personal worlds. The examples of the more than 30,000 adults who have completed their associate, baccalaureate, and master's degrees from the more than forty sites of ESC around the State of New York (and in a number of international offices as well) since 1971, reflect the significance of searching for effective and academically meaningful ways to respond to a growing number of students who are demanding access to higher education that is not oblivious to the realities of their lives.

Yet what has been fascinating about the history of our "open university" is that the models with which we began have themselves continued to change. New resources based on faculty research and experience have been created. Even more flexible systems of delivery (particularly those that have been made possible by the development of new technologies) have become the norm. Ongoing changes in the workplace have created new areas of study and new populations of students. Other institutions have developed imaginative programs from which we have been able to learn. The economic implications of a public institution faced with the realities of diminishing state resources has meant a rethinking of our daily practices. An increasingly senior and accomplished teaching faculty have sought new arenas for professional development. And the recognition that any academic institution isolated from the learning needs of individuals or of other public and private institutions not only cannot survive but is not fulfilling its mission as an academically vibrant and effective place of learning, has permeated discussion, both fiscal and academic. All of these factors—some internal some external—have pushed us to reflect on what we do, why we do it, how our once experimental forms can themselves become calcified, and how we must continue to respond to adults who need our services now more than ever.

Within such a context of reflection and change, the role of the faculty has itself continued to evolve. Indeed, one of ESC's major and complex challenges has been to find ways to foster an institutional environment that is open to reconceptualizations of the faculty role within a context of academic integrity and consistency. Our basic goal in this discussion is to elaborate upon an evolving definition of the faculty that begins to take account of this central goal and of the kinds of transformations in society and in the academy noted above. We see it as contributing to what Guskin (1994) claims to be the "monumental undertaking" of "reconstructing the role of faculty member" (p. 16). It is an effort to articulate how faculty as mentor, as resource creator, and as program developer have helped us envision and try out a new kind of expertise that questions old assumptions and offers new and challenging models of professional work.

Faculty as Mentor

A certain privilege has traditionally been associated with the status of the faculty member: access to specialized knowledge, the prerogative to identify what is important to learn, the right to impart that knowledge to those who come to us to gain it, and the authority to judge if another has acquired appropriate learning. In conventional academic settings, the very expertise of the faculty has been framed by a set of boundaries that separated faculty from students. Faculty held the important knowledge, conveyed it to those who cared to know, and developed criteria for and carried out what was determined to be appropriate evaluation.

The presuppositions of such a model have been opened to debate by a range of issues and realities that now characterize our educational landscape. We live in a world where the question of what is important to know is not easily answered and where the amount of knowledge at least theoretically available to us continues to expand at a phenomenal rate: that is, in a world where such authority is fleeting. Even the supposedly clear and meaningful disciplinary conditions that informed so much of our own education and our identities as academic professionals have been thrown into question. No thoughtful faculty person can know enough about what there is to know to make final claims about that knowledge.

Further, the institutions within which we work have dramatically changed. The range of students who enter our classrooms—in terms of ethnicity, race, gender, age, and life experiences—has expanded. It is nearly impossible to prejudge who will sit before us, what they already know, what they want to know, and what tools we might employ to most effectively help them learn. What we had taken for granted before (however appropriately or inappropriately) we cannot assume today.

Institutions have responded to some of these realities in a number of ways. The drive to find a viable market niche and to respond to new clientele has meant more flexible schedules, evening classes, weekend options, distance learning programs, the formal acknowledgment of learning gained outside of accredited academic institutions, and institutional fixtures (from orientations to the library to course guides) that are more user-friendly. Clearly, colleges have become more aware of trying to meet the needs of an increasingly diverse student body—of providing levels of access, particularly through newly devised delivery systems that had not existed before.

Most of these institutional changes have been at the edges of faculty experience. They have not usually touched the more protected arena of faculty privilege. Particularly with the inclusion of a greater number of working adult students, however, faculty have been called upon to expand the range and nature of their interactions with students. On a simple level, it has not been unusual for faculty to have increased the hours they are available to students outside of the classroom. More significantly, because of the experiences, goals, dilemmas, and academic strengths and weaknesses that these so-called nontraditional students have brought to our academic worlds, faculty have found themselves taking on more advisory roles, serving as guides and consultants, and helping their students negotiate their way through formerly alien academic terrain to gain the kinds of skills and competencies that we know they need. The inclusion of such a counseling dimension into the very fabric of many of our lives as academic instructors has also meant a subtle but important shift in the nature of communication between faculty and student. We have learned to listen with new attentiveness and care, knowing that our ability to understand and respond is directly related to our students' success as learners.

But the most powerful shift occurs when the interrelated movement from providing better institutional access to listening and counseling does touch the very core of the conventional faculty role. And it is here that the potential of a new relationship between student and teacher emerges. As Mandell and Herman (1996) have described, such a collaborative stance is at the heart of the role of faculty as mentor. That is, in an institutional context that works for true access (not only for admittance but for the possibility of success), listening becomes a necessary art, and teaching—and the knowledge upon which it is based—becomes an ongoing project of locating and/or creating imaginative learning tools to respond to the academic needs of individual students whose voices we can never disregard. Garrison (1992) describes the emerging dialog this way:

> Only through continuous and critical dialogue between learner and facilitator can a dynamic and optimal balance of control be realized. The balance of control will probably shift depending on the context and the proficiency of the learner. However, through sharing control there is an increased probability of students reaching desired and worthwhile learning goals which, in turn, would result in improved motivation, ability to learn, and self-directedness. (p. 144)

In the last few years, the word mentoring has taken on a rather hierarchical cast. In such contexts (many of them corporate), mentors are experienced guides who know and can offer expert advice, those who have been especially successful and can show others how to succeed. But the notion of faculty as mentor introduced here emphasizes sharing control and meaningful reciprocity. In fact, it is about the deliberate creation of opportunities for common learning. It also is motivated by the quest to follow the lead offered by an individual student's questions, concerns, or idiosyncratic understanding into new areas of academic exploration, even those that stretch and challenge our own sense of what we know. In this way, mentoring accents the importance of our strengths as academic generalists who have learned to work with problems that cut across the disciplines and themes that are inherently interdisciplinary. Mentoring embeds us in a distinctive approach to teaching and learning that deliberately legitimates the questioning of faculty authority and the claims to knowledge upon which that authority rests. By inviting a student to participate in his/her own learning (for example, through faculty and students creating individualized learning contracts as an integral part of the learning process or working together to design an entire curriculum), and by providing room for a student to gain the new skills necessary to work independently, we offer ourselves as engaged interlocutors who demonstrate that we care deeply about dialog and reflection and about the critical examination of pertinent questions, many of which were not our questions at the start.

In effect, through interactions with their students, mentors try to model the very kind of learning they hope their students will continue to pursue. That is, in a quite powerful and palpable way, the ideal of lifelong learning, usually reserved for students, equally pertains to the faculty mentor. We are always in the process of creating new studies with students, tinkering with old plans, searching for and coordinating effective resources, immersing ourselves in a new question, following the lead of an issue that a student has begun to articulate, making connections with a colleague who may offer a suggestive direction. We are, above all, listening, guiding, trying out new learning strategies, and staying alert to what may become yet another opening.

Perhaps like all more democratic experiments, the experience of faculty as mentor is a rather precarious one. Traditional faculty authority has been based on bodies of knowledge and academic structures that reinforce them. To enter a world of mentoring is to practice with the expectation that through serious and honest discourse and negotiation (and a community of other mentors who can provide support, encouragement, and critical scrutiny), plans for individual studies and curricula can be built that are academically rich and that flow from the lives of our students as parents, workers, scholars, members of a community, and citizens. To gain experience in such a faculty role that emphasizes not separation but connection, dialog, and a reweaving of relationships of authority is, in itself, a new kind of privilege.

Faculty as Resource Creator

The role of faculty as mentor thus begins with the individual student, with listening to and learning about that student's interests, background, and skills, encouraging the student's reflections about his/her learning, helping that student make meaningful connections among things learned, and facilitating new and unique learning explorations. How then can such a philosophy be applied to groups of students, many of whom need to work on similar skills and content areas at the same time? The notion of a prepared course or a standardized learning activity seems to run counter to the belief in individualized instruction. The role of faculty as resource creator thus introduces certain tensions—between individual and group student needs, between being content and format experts, and between faculty and administrative roles—as we develop resources on the course, community, and institutional levels.

Those of us who create new resources or remold those we have used in the past do not always strive to cover a standard set of topics in the field of study. The challenge, instead, is to sift through the knowledge and skill areas embedded in those topics, choose what is essential to the student's understanding of the topic, and work at creating a carefully designed guide (a true map of relevant learning activities that does not aim to reproduce a set of faculty lecture notes and the authority they hold) with a structure flexible enough to engage the student as a significant participant in the process of learning.

For example, students taking a course in "Communication Decisions" are asked to choose five communication situations in which they are currently involved as the basis for their work. Course work throughout the term consists of the development and multiple revision of these communications as students learn about the theories that underlie the communications. Toward the end of the study, students are asked to implement the communications and analyze their effectiveness as well as reflect upon the ways in which their understanding of communication has developed. That is, while the course has moved through certain learning activities in a preplanned order (something that an individualized learning contract would lack), students are able to retain control over learning situations and applications.

To engage the student in the learning, faculty who create both print and web course guides often begin by asking for some reflective piece that is intended to move the student to think about the new field of learning as it relates to personal experiences and goals. Throughout the course, students are also encouraged to apply learning to real world situations, and often there are leading questions to help them relate information to their experience and knowledge. And the use of learning journals and other opportunities to pursue particular interests within the context of an overall topic of study allows for a high degree of individualization that is crucial to the resource creator's success and consistent with the spirit and practice of mentoring.

Courses also are structured to foster personal assessment and reflection about learning. Self-test questions and the articulation of criteria for evaluation are typical. Course tutors—hired to aid and respond to a student's learning, not to instruct—use these evaluative criteria in their responses to assignments, thereby helping students internalize a way to assess their own ongoing learning. In these ways, new resources are thus not only designed to enhance knowledge of a specific content area but to facilitate a broader process of learning. Courses try to develop both the instrumental (learning the course content) and the communicative (gaining experience relating course content to one's own learning, assumptions, and understandings), aspects that Mezirow (1994) identifies as crucial to learning in adults.

The role of faculty as resource creator also includes an administrative and training dimension. Faculty have to arrange for experts to review the new course and editors to supervise publication of the course in pilot form. They also have to hire and train tutors (subject matter specialists) who can work with adults as learning facilitators once the course begins. They supervise student and tutor evaluation of the course pilot and then are intimately involved in course evaluation and ongoing revision, drawing upon student questionnaire responses, tutor suggestions, and their own expertise. Even with a created course in hand, there is always room for change: for rethinking assignments, readings, directions, and problems for students to critically examine.

Like faculty mentors, faculty who create courses juggle academic, design, and administrative roles, working within more well-defined procedures and conventions of course creation that make the shift from one role to another relatively seamless. Faculty who create resources on the level of the community deal with more ambiguous situations as they enter increasingly new contexts, particularly with groups of students who come to the institution through employer-sanctioned programs. As some of these new students may not have chosen to pursue guided independent study on their own, faculty who work with these kinds of programs need to develop additional resources and structures to better enable students to succeed.

For example, in one program in which most of the students are located at the same work site, faculty are experimenting with various community resources to help those students who are less capable as independent learners. Experiments range from arranging a process for scheduling meeting rooms so that students can organize their own study groups, to offering a session on "how to navigate your course work," to arranging for workplace volunteers to offer academic support groups and/or tutoring services in certain academic areas.

One final example of the faculty member as resource creator is useful in understanding this role and its interrelated dimensions of mentoring, instructional design, administration, training, and evaluation. Faculty from three different academic programs worked with a professional from ESC's Center for Learning and Technology to create The Writer's Complex, our institution's virtual writing center on the world wide web. The complex contains many "rooms," including research, essay, grammar, and punctuation workshops, a "foyer" that presents information about academic writing, a "file cabinet" with model student papers, a space for faculty to post information and have discussions related to a specific course, a student discussion area, and a mailbox to contact a writing tutor. In creating such a resource, faculty were committed to engaging students in meaningful dialog, not merely posting information for students to print out. As Minock and Shor (1995) state, "one of the pedagogical promises of computer conferencing is the opportunity for students to decenter the authoritarian discourse of the teacher and to assert their own initiatives in creating an extended dialogue" (p. 357). Implementing such a dialog not only involves faculty with students in a mentoring relationship, but for faculty developers, encompasses tasking ranging from designing brochures for the site to coordinating with other faculty in the college, to training and supervising staff, to reviewing data on student use.

Faculty as resource creator thus spans multiple roles: academic, coordinative, administrative, training, and evaluative. Yet, in keeping with a commitment to both access and the belief that students can direct their own learning, faculty as resource creator has its philosophical origins in faculty as mentor. Both seek to build upon Laurent Daloz's assessment in *Effective Teaching and Mentoring* (1986) that "as we learn to see people in the context of their potential for growth, the possibilities for enriching their educational experience expand rapidly" (p. 57).

Faculty as Entrepreneur and Program Developer

The possibilities for enriching educational experience to which Daloz refers can move from the level of the individual student (mentoring) to the level of the group (resource creator) and, from here, to the level of new academic program development. While each level accents a different moment of the faculty role and calls upon distinctive faculty skills and responsibilities, all three seek to respond to broad avenues of academic change, to the desire to respond to the specific learning needs of a particular constituency through the use of new pedagogical models and approaches to the delivery of educational services, and to our institution's mission to offer access and opportunity for educational individualization. Very importantly, too, this third level provides significant opportunity for creating the kinds of "service enclaves" that Singleton, Burack, and Hirsch (1997) argue that all academic institutions need to nourish as they try to transform themselves into "service cultures" (p. 4).

No doubt, program development poses perhaps the most compelling tension in the academic environment: How can institutions maintain their standards while providing sufficient freedom to and incentives for successful entrepreneurship, especially in the development of new programs inclined to deviate from current academic models already regulated by academic policy, for new populations of students? And what are the criteria that the faculty as entrepreneur and program developer can use to guide such work?

Most importantly, program development must ensure consistency with institutional mission. Some colleges primarily serve their communities; others have a disciplinary focus; others of us work in institutions that serve religious aims; still others, like our own, have distinctive pedagogical objectives. Assessing consistency with goals such as these may appear simple, but in practice the gray areas can prove hard to discern. A key aspect of faculty as program developer is to announce and sustain thorough discussion of strategic consonance from the outset. If effective in their jobs, faculty who work in this role must be strong advocates of potential programs (particularly given the likelihood of institutional resistance), but the institution must also offer open-minded and effective constraint on its attempts to develop programs that cannot or should not be delivered by that institution.

In order for program developers to succeed, it is essential that the highest levels of the organization support innovation and the challenges of risk-taking (long recognized by commercial organizations but viewed as anathema to many educational institutions). The realpolitik suggests strongly that more experienced, respected, and senior faculty should lead such development efforts, and that an overall faculty environment be created to support critical reflection on and experimentation with current forms and contents of academic practices.

Fortunately, there are natural incentives for faculty program developers which are not costly to institutions. For example, the promise of control over some of the resources generated by new programs, autonomy and flexibility for programs once developed, the chance to create something new and academically successful, and the opportunity for a faculty member to put his/her imprimatur upon a vital and exciting new program, are all important in determining the likelihood of a program's success or failure. They are also central to the task of articulating the parameters of a new faculty role that, like its commercial counterpart, must balance professional development, risk-taking, accountability, and rewards.

Like the evolving expertise of the mentor and resource creator, the program developer needs to learn many new skills and nourish new ways of wondering about, approaching, playing with, and understanding the ambiguities of new situations, often outside the world of academia that we know best. In effect, faculty need to be aided by a "toolbox" for program development that includes a repertoire of skills.

First is the ability to gain comfort in the language of human resource managers, workforce development professionals, and others who are involved in utilizing the services of higher education institutions. This requires knowledge of and respect for training programs as well as corporate and community goals. Second is the capacity to carry out a legitimate needs assessment of a target population. Indeed, the opportunity for program development lies fundamentally in our ability to identify a target population with specialized learning needs and to assess those needs within a framework for innovative curricular development. (How flooded the academic marketplace is with off-the-shelf courses and curricula simply taught at new times or in new places that lack academic imagination, significant relationship to the students who are expected to learn from them, and meaningful risk.) For example, FORUM, a program targeted at mid-level managers pursuing bachelor's degrees was structured around a series of weekend residencies with extensive student-mentor contact and guided independent studies between residencies. This program's developer designed an interdisciplinary theme study to provide students with a broad understanding of the social and institutional context within which their organizations operate, in addition to developing important critical thinking, writing, oral communication, and teamwork skills. This innovative curricular component engages the entire program faculty, with diverse disciplinary interests in multifaceted facilitator roles, guiding groups of students through research and writing, argument and debate, and group process learning activities.

Another needed skill is insight into the structure of learning and knowledge that can help us assess and build upon what students already know and what they need or desire to know. (Here, for example, our own institution's dedication to the evaluation of college-level experiential learning and to the possibilities inherent in individualized program development nurtured by the mentor and resource developer have allowed us to transcend the inherent constraints of taking for granted the generic freshman curriculum.) Finally, gaining skills in assessing the true cost and burden of new student populations served through new programs, in understanding the fundamental operational and academic limitations on all programs, and in articulating and sustaining outcomes assessment and reporting systems in order to chart the ongoing value of its educational services to its customers, are all part of what becomes the lifelong learning of the faculty program developer.

But perhaps most critical to the work of this faculty person is the responsibility to guide a clear, ongoing, and effective quality assurance and outcomes assessment process. Most clients will not, and our institutions should not, tolerate old-fashioned quality control imposed well after key program features have been developed at great time and expense. Clearly, this requires clarity about institutional goals, academic and operational standards, and the boundaries of potential activity from the outset. At ESC, for example, advisory boards of faculty and administrators at our Verizon Corporate College and our FORUM programs were engaged actively early in the development process. So too, knowledge that the faculty developer is overseeing program development and will do so for the program's first few years allows the kind of reflective attachment to and responsibility for the program that is central to its success.

Indeed, experimenting institutions must develop and maintain flexible systems that articulate principles of academic policy at a high level but require, for their implementation, substantial invention and interpretation as they are applied across diverse, and sometimes incipient, programs. That is, no statutory set of proscriptions can cover the wide variety of existing, changing, and developing programs. This is the "common law" of academic policy that is required of the most innovative institutions of higher learning. It is the complex and judgment-filled terrain upon which the faculty program developer must work. It is one that offers many rewards, particularly the ability to develop and maintain fruitful relationships with groups of individuals, community organizations and corporations and, of course, the possibility of profoundly touching the lives of student populations—of making connections with those who would not otherwise be well served, or served at all, by our institutions.

None of the alternative models introduced in this chapter are entirely new. In fact, they seek to build upon and reinvigorate many of the activities and responsibilities of the traditional faculty member. Yet, by inviting a rethinking of the ways we work, the priorities that inform our actions, and the traditions that have both supported and constrained our understanding of our lives within the academy, our goal has been to offer a useful vantage point from which to approach thoughtfully and critically our assumptions about teaching and learning and about the responsibilities of colleges and universities today. As we hope to have acknowledged, in the current political, economic, and cultural contexts within which we work, there are many complexities, tensions, and significant differences of opinion. Such an environment demands that we reflect upon and rearticulate our commitment to the academic values that we cherish. Our challenge as innovative educators is to use imaginatively that commitment as a foundation for creating meaningful learning opportunities for those already within the academy and for a range of new audiences whose learning needs we need to understand better and with whom we need to communicate more effectively. Certainly, too, it is in this spirit of questioning and change that we must continue our ongoing efforts in reconceptualizing the faculty role.

References

Commission for a Nation of Lifelong Learners. (1997). *A nation learning: Vision for the 21st century.* Albany, NY: Author.

Daloz, L. (1986). *Effective teaching and mentoring.* San Francisco, CA: Jossey-Bass.

Garrison, D. R. (1992). Critical thinking and self-directed learning in adult education: An analysis of responsibility and control issues. *Adult Education Quarterly, 42,* 136–148.

Guskin, A. E. (1994, September/October). Restructuring the role of faculty. *Change,* 16–24.

Mandell, A., & Herman, L. (1996). From teachers to mentors: Acknowledging openings in the faculty role. In R. Mills & A. Tait (Eds.), *Supporting the learner in open and distance learning* (pp. 3–18). London, England: Pitman.

Mezirow, J. (1994). Understanding transformation theory. *Adult Education Quarterly, 44,* 222–232.

Minock, M., & Shor, F. (1995). Crisscrossing Grand Canyon: Bridging the gaps with computer conferencing. *Computers and Composition, 12,* 355–365.

Singleton, S. E., Burack, C. A., & Hirsch, D. J. (1997, April). Faculty service enclaves. *American Association for Higher Education Bulletin, 49,* 3–7.

SECTION III

Taking Stock and Looking Ahead

This final section describes a number of approaches to assessing innovative programs and concludes with a look toward the future. It addresses critical questions about the effectiveness of efforts to reorganize around new approaches to teaching and learning and concludes with a number of chapters that describe the lessons from past attempts to promote interdisciplinary education, collaborative teaching and learning, and new pedagogies, and the similarities and differences between the climate of reform now and in the past. New directions for alternative education in the future are also explored.

Innovative programs and institutions often carry a special burden to demonstrate their effectiveness. This can be a challenge since many of these programs were established with different goals than traditional programs. They therefore require new yardsticks. What this has often meant is that innovative programs must prove they are effective in terms of traditional measures and then also demonstrate their added value. When measures of effectiveness are too narrow, assessing innovative efforts can be a difficult challenge. But many of the nontraditional colleges and programs have led the way in developing new approaches to educational assessment, especially in the classroom. Alverno College, for example, has been the leader in outcomes-based assessment and has widely influenced other institutions across the United States. The Evergreen State College has been a pioneer in student self-evaluation and the development of student and faculty portfolios as a vehicle for developing self-reflection and documenting performance and development. Writing across the curriculum was firmly in place at a number of these institutions long before it appeared on the national landscape. The same can be said about service-learning and a variety of other reform efforts.

In the last 15 years, assessment has become a dominant theme in higher education. Interest comes from many different directions. Thoughtful educators see assessment as integral to understanding student learning and improving teaching. Classroom assessment has become a critical component of many new pedagogical approaches as teachers increasingly recognize that their effectiveness depends upon better understanding their students. At the same time, as goals for student learning have become more complex, assessment has become even more of a challenge.

While many institutions have voluntarily embraced assessment as a means of improving their effectiveness, colleges have also come under pressure from external bodies—including accreditation agencies, higher education coordinating boards, and legislatures—to demonstrate their effectiveness. The multiple audiences for assessment has often created strains in meeting the demands of many masters. By 1998, the assessment movement and the accountabilty movement had become closely intertwined, and more than 40% of the states had some accountability goals in place. At the same time, the national assessment effort has been in place for more than a decade. Thoughtful crititcs are raising difficult questions about the impact of the assessment movement and the next steps. Issues relating to the content of the curriculum are now becoming more pressing in both K-12 and higher education. As Robert Benedetti argues in his chapter, this may represent the next and most difficult discussion.

Arguing that the only appropriate assessment for innovative interdisciplinary programs is an interdisciplinary, innovative approach, Karl L. Schilling recounts the progression of the campus assessment efforts over the last twelve years at Western College at Miami University. Examples and evaluation of various assessment approaches used, ranging from a number of quantitative, standardized approaches to qualitative efforts, are shared. The chapter ends with a plea for the importance of assessment (the "unexamined university is not worth attending") in relation to higher education in general, and for innovative, interdisciplinary programs in particular.

In the chapter "Students on Interdisciplinary Education: How They Learn and What They Learn," John McCann tells how students from different traditional and nontraditional institutions describe their experiences with interdisciplinary education. Students' descriptions often center on how meaningful interdisciplinary learning environments are structured, and the importance of theme-based integrated programs, team teaching, seminars, and student responsibility. Surprisingly, students describe many more dimensions of student learning in interdisciplinary environments than faculty normally describe.

In "Learning to See Academic Culture Through the Eyes of Participants: An Ethnographic Folkloristic Approach to Analyzing and Assessing the Cultures of Alternative Instititutions" Peter Tommerup explores the use of ethnographic/folkloric approaches to assessment. The author spent a year analyzing a nontraditional college, The Evergreen State College, with this approach. In this chapter he describes the culture, structures, and practices of this institution through new eyes. This chapter provides a new way of thinking about assessment.

In "The Interdisciplinary Variable: Then and Now, " Julie Thompson Klein draws upon the other chapters in this volume and the 1997 Evergreen Conference on Interdisciplinary Education (the genesis of this book) to examine historical changes in the notions of interdisciplinarity. She discusses definitions of interdisciplinarity, differences of implementation across time, and summarizes the many institutional examples presented by contributors to this volume.

In "Joining the Conversation: An Essay in Guiding Images for College Teaching and Learning," Robert H. Knapp, Jr. argues that the prevailing guiding images for college teaching and learning need to be rethought. The author contends that contemporary language describing colleges in the language of consumers and businesses is misguided. He goes on to explore the notion of conversation as a more meaningful image of the academy.

In "After the Revolution: New Directions for Alternative Education," Robert Benedetti argues that alternative colleges must now turn their attention to issues of content. These issues, he contends, will be far more difficult and far more important than the current reform agenda around process and pedagogy. The author argues that issues of citizenship, moral character, and the world of work are promising avenues for exploration.

In "Knowledge, Politics, and Interdisciplinary Education," Charles W. Anderson argues that to be coherent, any program of interdisciplinary education must rest on an epistemology, a theory of knowledge. From this, a moral philosophy and a political philosophy, an ideal of personal life and citizenship, will follow. Anderson contends that we should be very self-conscious of these foundational commitments that guide our teaching. This chapter compares classical, culturist, positivist, postmodern, and pluralist approaches to the problems of knowledge and politics, and argues for pragmatic idealism as a foundation for contemporary interdisciplinary education.

20

Interdisciplinary Assessment for Interdisciplinary Programs

Karl L. Schilling
Miami University of Ohio

By their very existence, innovative, interdisciplinary programs are an implicit critique of current educational practices and, as such, are often seen as a threat. When programs/institutions choose to deviate from the norm in educational practice they are often perceived as weird, trendy, irresponsible, lacking rigor, and of questionable quality. Higher education's conservatism has promoted skepticism about alternative ways of structuring intellectual work. As a result, it has been more necessary for innovative programs than for more traditional programs to demonstrate with convincing evidence the quality of their work.

This introduces quite a dilemma. These innovative programs are often structured to achieve different goals than those of their traditional counterparts. Since they have their origins in traditional disciplinary conceptions of knowledge, most available standardized instruments for assessing educational outcomes are probably not well suited to providing the kinds of evidence that will be useful for innovative programs to use with either internal or external audiences. The complex and ambitious goals which have been articulated by innovative programs are not appropriately indexed by one-dimensional assessment approaches. Just as few innovative programs have retained traditional disciplinary structures to achieve the goals they have identified for their students' education, traditional assessment strategies have rarely offered adequate documentation of the impact of interdisciplinary or other innovative curricular structures. Few innovative programs would claim to do the same thing as their traditional colleagues but simply do it better. Rather, they offer different orientations or conceptions of knowing that presume to lead to qualitatively different kinds of performance on the part of students. These different kinds of performance require new approaches to assessment to capture their effectiveness.

Indeed, the multifaceted approaches to development of the kinds of evidence that will prove useful to innovative programs in demonstrating their accomplishments might best be called interdisciplinary assessment. A mix of quantitative and quality measures drawn from various disciplinary traditions and new tools designed specifically to assess new interdisciplinary competencies may be necessary to index effectiveness of new educational approaches. Using an interdisciplinary approach to assessment, which can be closely tied to the goals of innovative, interdisciplinary curricula, not only through the use of a range of approaches, but also in the philosophy which undergirds it, is probably the best means of capturing the ineffable goals that typify such programs/institutions.

The Context: The Western College Program at Miami University

The Western College Program, founded in 1974 as an experimental, innovative residential college within Miami University, combines a two-year interdisciplinary, liberal arts core curriculum (48 semester hours) taken within the Western Program, with a student designed, interdisciplinary, upper-level program of study (32 semester hours) drawn from coursework taken from other departments and programs across the university, and a year-long senior project (ten semester hours) that serves as an interdisciplinary capstone experience. The goal of the program is to create active learners who are able to draw upon a wide range of resources in the quest to answer important questions.

First and second year students are required to live in a residence hall that houses faculty offices, classroom space, administrative offices, and recreational facilities. The residential component makes a significant contribution to the educational experience of students through the strong community of learners that it creates. Because students share common texts, lectures, and ideas (frequently across, as well as within years), they easily are able to engage each other in intellectual conversations that have depth as well as breadth. The core courses are taught in a small seminar format, with emphasis on the active engagement of students with the materials through discussion and the writing of papers. The twenty-four hour a day character of the Western Program provides a powerful educational experience that could not exist without the unique combination of an interdisciplinary core curriculum, seminar/discussion teaching format, and the residential character of the program.

What Did We Do?

My initial approach to assessment reflected my disciplinary training as a psychologist. I was oriented toward hypothesis testing using standardized instruments and statistical analysis. When I was teaching in a psychology department, using scores on the Advanced GRE Test in Psychology to assess the impact the psychology curriculum was having on students made a certain amount of sense. One could make the case for student achievement based on the results of the testing. Seniors scored at levels above national norms in their knowledge of psychology. We concluded that we must have been doing something right.

However, when I moved to the Western College Program, I began to see some of the problems with this approach, 1) there was no GRE or equivalent standardized test which matched the interdisciplinary curriculum at Western, 2) the mastery of specific content was not the primary goal of the curriculum, even if such a test were to exist, and 3) the curriculum was continuously evolving, so a locally developed standardized instrument would have to change so frequently to reflect these alterations in the curriculum that such an approach would be logistically impossible.

However, I did not readily give up on the hope of finding a standardized instrument that might prove suitable. I came across the ACT COMP (and later the ETS Academic Profile, C-Base, and others) which promised to provide information on the development of generic liberal arts skills. Indeed, such instruments initially seemed to offer some promise for measuring "value-added," since students could be tested upon entry to the program and again at exit. However, it quickly became apparent that the use of such tests, developed to serve the needs of a vast variety of liberal arts curricula, had several problems:

1) Selecting from the potential pool of items in any curricular area involved a necessary, but unfortunate, sampling. If, for example, the social science section in a particular year had mostly geography questions and our curriculum had not dealt with geography, scores on this section probably revealed less about the effectiveness of our curriculum than they did about students' high school work or personal interests.

2) Making tests that were generic enough to fit any liberal arts curriculum means that the scores end up reflecting general intelligence as much or more than impact of specific curricula. (Irrespective of the impact of our curriculum, our students would score well on these measures since we admit primarily high ability students. Scores on such measures thus reflect more on our recruitment/admissions process than on our teaching).

3) Test scores that are based on items that aren't tied to the actual goals of the curriculum are of little use in evaluating the impact of the curriculum or in providing information to be used for its improvement.

We also tried other assessment approaches. With its roots in a different area of psychology, clinical/projective testing, the McBer Tests of Thematic Analysis and Analysis of Argument, which served as the basis for most of the results reported in *A New Case for the Liberal Arts* (Winter, McClelland, & Stewart, 1981) seemed to offer an intriguing possibility. However, the testing company discontinued its scoring service and the scoring manual provided inadequate guidance for us to reach a reasonable level of inter-rater reliability. This instrument provided a model for a different approach to assessment of outcomes in liberal education. It provided a less content-based approach that looked at liberal arts thinking skills independent of particular content.

Another approach that we used that is also less content driven and which provides information about intellectual development related to the goals of a liberal arts education is the Measure of Epistemological Reflection (MER). The MER, developed by Marcia Baxter-Magolda (1992), provided a measure of intellectual development based upon the work of William Perry. While it is difficult to tie the results of this and other similar measures to specific courses in the curriculum, it is possible to document change over time which can reasonably be attributed to the total college experience. This seems consonant with the way in which many innovative programs, particularly residential colleges, conceive of their educational impacts. The theory which undergirds the instruments also provides insight into why the desired development might not be occurring. In our early efforts, this was clearly the most useful instrument in terms of providing the kind of information that could be used by the faculty in relation to curricular discussions. Baxter-Magolda has identified particular pedagogical strategies that are effective with students at different levels of cognitive development. Since the scores of Western students showed gains in their level of cognitive development, the program could use the results to support claims of providing a high quality educational experience. We were also able to adapt teaching strategies to match more closely the cognitive developmental needs of our students.

All of the above approaches were used as part of a FIPSE-funded project that used a traditional experimental design to compare two matched groups of students who were enrolled in two different models of liberal education—a disciplinary approach and an interdisciplinary one (Schilling, 1993). However, we quickly discovered the difficulty in bringing this controlled experiment out of the lab and into the world. Trying to keep a matched sample participating over a four-year period proved far more difficult than we had imagined. From the original 50 matched pairs, we ended up in the senior year with only 12 matched pairs and, even more importantly, on several of the instruments, particularly the Academic Profile, our first year students "topped out" on the senior norms (i.e., the average first year Western student scores gave them a 95th percentile ranking using the norms for seniors), making it very difficult to demonstrate gains.

So we began to feel the need to move beyond traditional psychometric measurement models and approaches to develop techniques better suited to the task we were trying to address. We began to break free from discipline-based approaches to explore interdisciplinary approaches that combined techniques and philosophies from a number of different areas. Our model shifted from one in which we were trying to demonstrate impact by controlling variables and standardizing instruments to one that sought to develop pictures or provide materials for stories. Our predominant metaphors shifted. We talked about "listening to the sounds" of the curriculum, much like the NPR Car Guys, Click and Clack, use sounds to diagnose automobile problems (Schilling & Schilling, 1993a). We thought of ourselves as archeologists or cultural anthropologists trying to unearth the artifacts of the curriculum and construct meaning. Or we viewed our task as a diagnostic problem solving endeavor constructing a great CAT scan of the curriculum. By taking many, many slices of the curriculum, as in a CAT scan, a picture of the curriculum as experienced by students begins to emerge. No one slice provides the definitive answer to the question, but a number of different slices together create a picture of what is happening. So, much of our effort shifted to descriptive approaches to assessment (Schilling & Schilling, 1993b) which sought to describe "what is" rather than "how well." Our expanded metaphors invited the use of a variety of approaches to assessment in order to develop "thick descriptions."

We soon discovered the power of description to elicit change. For example, several years ago, Western had a "dumb" senior class that didn't seem to know how to do a senior project. They didn't know how to write an annotated bibliography or literature review, how to integrate citations into an extended argument, etc. As any good faculty will do, we blamed the students. However, shortly after these discussions of our problematic students, we began our first reading of comprehensive student portfolios (students were asked to keep copies of all the work they completed for their classes in the portfolio) in which faculty were asked to identify assignments that asked students to address one of the central issues of the Miami plan for liberal education, e.g., critical thinking, dealing with different perspectives. About an hour into the reading, the room got quiet. Then, a faculty member spoke up, stating that he thought he knew why we had had such a "dumb" senior class the previous year. He observed from the portfolios that it was clear that we had stopped teaching students how to write research papers. They were doing lots of writing and getting lots of feedback on that writing, but they were not writing traditional research papers. This became clear to all who were reading through the student work.

One of the nice things about descriptive assessment is that it provides a picture of "what is" without a value judgment. So what followed the observation by my colleague was a surprisingly nondefensive discussion of what needed to be changed in the curriculum. One possibility was to change the nature of the senior project from a traditional research project to an action project with reflection. Since we weren't asking students to write research papers, maybe we no longer thought they were appropriate for our students and needed to change our capstone experience to reflect our curricular practice. Or perhaps we needed to change our curriculum to provide the appropriate background that would allow students successfully to complete a research thesis. After several thoughtful discussions (it is wonderful to have faculty discussions based on evidence rather than on opinions or anecdotes), we decided to take responsibility as a group for ensuring that our students were systematically introduced to the various components of research writing before their senior year. Students would learn the research paper writing process in a series of steps that would enable them to be able to successfully complete a senior thesis with the tools that we had given them before their senior year.

As we began conceiving of our assessment work as an interdisciplinary activity, we thought about looking at our chosen assessment techniques in terms of their ability to assist us in capturing the student experience. A package of techniques that are rooted in different disciplinary traditions were brought together in order to maximize our ability to get a more holistic understanding of the students' experience and provide the framework from which to develop powerful descriptions that could assist us both in our internal discussions as well as in making our case to external audiences. As part of this descriptive, interdisciplinary approach to assessment, we have used a wide range of instruments which are listed and briefly described below:

Comprehensive Portfolios of Student Work

Students keep copies of all materials that they produce for class (preferably with instructor comments on them) as well as course syllabi and assignment sheets. Periodically (usually at the end of the semesters), portfolios are collected from students willing to share them and copied with any identifying information removed; then the original is returned to the students. While we worked with paper copies, several institutions have started "burning" CD versions of student portfolios.

Advantages:
- Makes the curriculum visible
- Materials can be used in a variety of ways

Disadvantages:
- Time consuming
- Bulky
- Students do not always remember to put things into the portfolio

Structured Interviews

Students are interviewed at the end of the year and asked to reflect on their experience by responding to a wide range of questions designed to capture the students' understanding of their experiences during the past year.

Advantages:
- Reflecting experience is useful to both the student and the institution
- Allows for nuances
- Captures the wide-range of student experience
- Is a powerful experience for faculty interviewers

Disadvantages:
- Difficult to adequately capture and reduce the insights gained into presentable format

Student Free Writing

At summer orientation and at the start of each semester, students are asked to free write for five minutes about the "hopes, dreams, fears, and expectations of the coming semester," or whatever topic is of interest.

Advantages:
- Inexpensive and quick
- Provides powerful insights into students' expectations
- Often gives information that can be used immediately to make changes responsive to student concerns

Disadvantages:
- Captures only a moment in time, which can change quickly

Ethnographic Study

Observations are drawn from a participant/observer who becomes part of the student community.

Advantages:
- Provides a powerful, compelling story that reveals program strengths and weaknesses

Disadvantages:

- Extremely time consuming
- Requires an "outsider"

The Cooperative Institutional Research Profile (CIRP) and the College Student Experiences Questionnaire (CSEQ)

These provide information on who are students are coming in (what they did in high school and what they value and believe—CIRP) and who they are later in their college career (reports on inside and outside the classroom behavior and values—CSEQ).

Advantages:

- These two instruments provide interesting opportunities to see the impact the educational institution is having on student values and behaviors since they can be used in a pre- and post-manner

Alumni Surveys

These provide an opportunity to collect reflection from students after graduation on the strengths and weaknesses of their educational experience. They can collect information in a variety of formats both quantitative and qualitative, behavioral and attitudinal, etc.

Advantages:

- Information that has been reflected upon based on experiences outside of the institution
- No longer in a "power" relationship with the institution, so more direct feedback

Disadvantages:

- Experiences may not connect to current institutional practices
- No opportunity to press for deeper meaning of their answers
- "Halo-nostalgia" effect

What Have we Learned?

We have learned several different things from our assessment efforts. The first set of learnings was about assessment itself; the second, about our students; and the third, about using this information to make a difference.

From our work, we have come to see 1) the advantages and disadvantages of various assessment approaches and instruments, 2) the problems in collecting, analyzing, and reporting results in a manner that allows people not involved in the process to understand the meaning and implications of the results, 3) the importance of adopting a scholarly approach to assessment that is faculty-centered and uses the existing skills of faculty from all areas of inquiry—e.g., not asking literature faculty to do statistical analysis, but rather having them involved in analysis of narratives, etc., and 4) we have learned to take advantage of unobtrusive measures and existing materials that were produced for a purpose other than assessment.

An example of this unobtrusive approach is that every Western student is required to do a senior project and publicly present it. For years we have had faculty members from outside the Western College Program publicly critique the projects. We were able to review these critiques for observations about our students' work: to see if there were common weaknesses and strengths that were frequently identified by these different respondents that may reflect more about our curriculum and teaching than about individual student problems and strengths. Many other observations about assessment approaches and instruments have been shared in previous sections.

The second learnings and, ultimately the more important ones, were about the student experience in the Western Program and Miami University. Through interviews, questionnaires—particularly the Cooperative Institutional Research Profile and the College Student Experiences Questionnaire—freewriting, and portfolios, we have begun to be able to describe the kinds of work Western students do. We understand the proportion and kinds of papers, exams, group work, etc. that are assigned. We have begun to understand the rhythms of their semester—i.e., to know what kinds of assignments or intervention programs to do at what point in the academic year. We have begun to understand how to orient prospective and entering students to the program. The senior project example shared earlier suggests the power of descriptive information to create change. The CIRP and CSEQ provided evidence as to the difference between interdisciplinary students and students enrolled in other university programs, thereby helping Western make the case for attracting a different kind of student to Miami.

The third learnings were about how to use assessment to make a difference. Assessment information helped the Western Program make its case for excellence during financially difficult times. Indeed, using information gathered from our assessment efforts enabled the program to receive two State Program Excellence Awards (state-wide competition that provided $100,000 discretionary fund awards), two Academic Challenge Awards (which enabled us to hire two new tenure-track faculty members, to equip a computer lab, and to hire two visiting scholars each year on an ongoing basis), to make the case for the strengths and importance of the Western Program within the university in terms of the diversity and intellectual vitality of the program, and to develop a strong reservoir of information that assisted us in receiving external grants as well.

Through our assessment efforts we have identified several areas of the curriculum for enhancement. We developed a quantitative reasoning program to help our students better deal with numerical information and shifted the focus of our science instruction into a discovery approach. We were also able to use the work in student portfolios to reflect on the core curriculum in relation to the goals for liberal education specified in the university's liberal education plan. We were able to excerpt from the portfolios powerful examples of student assignments that were directly connected to the liberal education goals to make our case for meeting the university's liberal education requirements through a different curricular format.

While most groups, both inside and outside the university, charged with reviewing outcomes evidence have been very responsive to our interdisciplinary, descriptive approach to assessment, there has been an occasional exception. Some members of review committees are convinced that only numbers are "real" (from Likert scale student-self report instruments and other "objective" measures) indicators of quality and fail to see the value and validity of a close reading of student work. Such skeptics can usually be convinced when they can be persuaded to read the portfolios or interview students for themselves. The power of descriptive material is very convincing when it is experienced first hand.

Conclusion

In order to create a powerful case to demonstrate to the various publics the high quality of the educational experience being provided by innovative, interdisciplinary programs we need to develop an interdisciplinary approach to assessment that brings together a wide range of information gathered through a number of techniques. The hope for one single measure that will make our case is inappropriate for programs that embrace complexity and ambiguity as part of their core identity. Innovative and interdisciplinary programs need to make their case by embracing a wide range of assessment approaches. We need to use an interdisciplinary approach to the development of evidence that will make our case to the public and to internal institutional constituencies and provide us with information that will allow us to continuously improve the quality of the educational experiences we provide our students.

The important realization that different disciplines have different perspectives on what constitutes adequate evidence and how to construct an adequate argument further shaped our work. These varied perspectives add different, and nonredundant, components to our understanding. Reductionistic strategies, which try to provide a metaperspective that subsumes these disciplinary perspectives or reduces them to one perspective, necessarily provide a limited understanding. The rich, variegated perspective of interdisciplinary work can only be adequately captured by a matchingly rich interdisciplinary assessment that draws upon and integrates the results from a variety of assessment approaches.

Just as many of us may repeat to our students the Socratic imperative that the "unexamined life is not worth living," we must come to grips with the institutional corollary to that statement: "the unexamined institution is not worth attending." While much of higher education may be able to remain blissfully and proudly ignorant around issues of the quality of student educational experiences—being content, as faculty, to do unto students what was done unto us—innovative programs can not afford such ignorance, or we do so at our own peril. Developing a compelling institutional story backed by a complex array of information/data is the first step in the process of becoming an examined institution which, through reflection on evidence developed through an interdisciplinary conception of assessment, continues to improve the quality of the educational experience being created for its students.

References

Baxter-Magolda, M. (1992). *Knowing and reasoning in college: Gender-related patterns in students' intellectual development.* San Francisco, CA: Jossey-Bass.

Schilling, K. (1993). Miami University: Assessing models of liberal education—An empirical comparison. In D. Marcus, E. Cobb, & R. Schoenberg (Eds.), *Lessons learned from FIPSE Projects II* (pp. 35–40). Washington, DC: US Government Printing Office.

Schilling, K., & Schilling, K. (1993a, March 24). Professors must respond to calls for accountability. *Chronicle of Higher Education,* back page.

Schilling, K., & Schilling, K. (1993b). Descriptive approaches to assessment: Moving beyond meeting requirements to making a difference. In *A Collection of papers on self-study and institutional improvement* (pp. 171–174). Chicago, IL: North Central Association.

Winter, D., McClelland, D., & Stewart, A. (1981). *A new case for the liberal arts.* San Francisco, CA: Jossey-Bass.

21

Students on Interdisciplinary Education: How They Learn and What They Learn

John McCann
The Evergreen State College

What aspects of interdisciplinary education are visible and meaningful to students? How does the process of interdisciplinary education affect students' lives? As faculty and administrators we devote our lives to teaching and learning, but students' voices are often peripheral to our conversations. This chapter focuses entirely on how students learn through the pedagogical structures we design and on what they learn—in their own words. In researching this chapter and compiling the voices you will hear below, I interviewed students from a number of Puget Sound area interdisciplinary institutions and programs:

- The undergraduate liberal studies and graduate master of education programs at Antioch University in Seattle
- Coordinated studies programs at North Seattle Community College, The Evergreen State College in Tacoma and Olympia, Seattle Central Community College, Bellevue Community College, and Skagit Valley College
- The interdisciplinary program at Fairhaven College of Western Washington University

The students I interviewed participated in panel discussions at the 1997 American Council of Learned Societies (ACLS) and John D. and

Catherine T. MacArthur Foundation sponsored Evergreen Conference on Interdisciplinary Education, and the 1998 Fund for the Improvement of Postsecondary Education (FIPSE) sponsored National Conference on Learning Communities Conference, both held at The Evergreen State College.

These students evaluated their experiences in different ways than we do as teachers. They valued the wholeness and interconnectedness of their experiences. They acknowledged the great degree of responsibility they had for their own education. They expressed a feeling of excitement and joy in the learning process. They spoke of building and then drawing strength from the learning communities they helped make and to which they belonged. They saw their teachers and fellow students as colearners. They saw strong relationships between life, work, and education. And universally, the students I talked with viewed their learning as a truly engaging activity rather than as a passive process of merely receiving information. These perceptions grew from students' participation in interdisciplinary, team-taught programs, in seminar, in design of their own education, in building community, and in colearning with fellow students and teachers. Here is what they had to say.[1]

How They Learn

Interdisciplinary Programs

The students whose voices you hear in this chapter come from differing interdisciplinary programs. Most were learning communities: half to full-time, quarter-long to year-long, interdisciplinary, team-taught programs organized around a central theme. Some were not learning communities, but student-planned interdisciplinary curriculum consisting mostly of courses linked together around a theme. Some were combinations of learning communities and courses.

One student, a middle-aged, married African American man with two children who worked as a counselor at the McNeil Island state prison, comments on a program he took at Evergreen. "Shaping a Nation" was a year-long, half-time program in US history and literature for working adults. It was an evening class which surveyed major themes in US history and culture from the presettlement period to the present. The program required heavy reading and writing and included a community service component.

> Before Evergreen I went to schools that were real traditional. And it was always the same. It was like you went up to a vending machine, stuck in a coin, and out came a biology class. I would get so much information every week. I was expected to know that information for the quizzes, the midterm, and the final. And that was it. There was nothing about how

> biology applied to other areas. Nothing about studying biology in the United States, and the relationships between science, politics, and racism. You never got that. It was just one dimensional. At the end of the quarter you took your final and two weeks later you'd forget the stuff because you'd never use it again. It was a joke. And I didn't like it.
>
> The program at Evergreen was a part of everyday life. I would go into class and we would talk about stuff that was directly relatable to what I was doing. We would talk about history and the construction of this country with all its problems, racism, class conflict, sexism, and then I'd go back to work and see the people I worked with. I could see people act out everything that we talked about in class. I could see people trapped by their class, trapped by their gender. I could see people working out of those things. But it was really neat. I go to school and hear the theory then go to work or go out into the community, and there is the practice. I can see it. I mean, it was real.
>
> For adult students, Evergreen teaches the way we think, the way we interact. If you go into a classroom and just learn biology, or just learn anthropology, or just learn history, it is not natural. When I am out in the world I am learning everything. If I go to a job I have to learn the culture of the job. I learn the politics of the job, the structure. We learn all that stuff together. In a traditional education you don't get that. You study Spanish. You learn the language. You don't learn the culture; you don't learn the history; you don't learn the politics. You don't learn any of that. You just learn the language. But that is not how you live. You need to learn the language, learn the culture, and hang out with the people, and see how the language has affected the people. So what I found at Evergreen was a natural way to learn.

Another student, a young African American man, married, with a young child, teaches at a Catholic high school in Seattle. He attended Antioch University's interdisciplinary master of education program.

> My undergraduate education was very compartmentalized. That's what I thought education was. You take math, sciences, English, and yet, that is not the way we learn naturally. Life is not compartmentalized. So, when I went to Antioch we were sort of in charge of our education and had a large role in developing our classes. We had power over our own education. At Antioch we participated with the teacher in learning. We developed knowledge together, rather than coming into the experience empty and then be handed the information, which was my previous experience of education. From first grade through college, we sat in rows, with teachers in the front of the room. They handed us stuff and we spit it back to them. At Antioch teachers and students roll up their sleeves together, delve into the information, and construct meaning from it.

> I got my undergraduate degree in philosophy. I had to do all the requirements, all the sciences, all the math. I can't help high school students with math to save my life. I passed the courses because that is what I had to do. I focused on the major. I don't teach math now and I don't know science. I don't know mitosis from mycosis. Taking those compartmentalized courses is not me anymore. Now I think just the opposite. If some of that required material had been integrated into some other things I was interested in, and I could have explored that material in a wider context, I would have retained it better. I would be more effective now. I'd maybe have been more likely to pursue some things I didn't pursue.
>
> There is a fear that in using interdisciplinary approaches students might not get the basics. For example, I think it is quite neat that a Catholic education teaches religion because I think a student is supposed to come out of a Catholic education knowing about the church. Some people tell me that with the way I teach students are not going to get the basics. But I think what do I really want them to get out of my class? Should they be able to name the seven sacraments, or whatever? To me the point is, when students leave my class do they have a deeper understanding of something beyond themselves, a deeper sense of morality, for example. Do they have a clue how to live?

In their comments about what interdisciplinary education meant to them, students consistently talked about participating in a form of education that was liberating to them, that constituted a whole rather than separate parts, that imitated the way we learn throughout life. One young woman, an Evergreen student, reflected on her high school career with dissatisfaction, saying she chose Evergreen because, "I just couldn't think in boxes anymore."

Team Teaching

Not all of the students I talked with participated in team-taught programs throughout their entire encounter with interdisciplinary education. All had some experience; most had extensive experience. At Evergreen, for example, most students take most of their credits in team-taught programs, while at most of the community colleges, learning communities form a smaller, but highly significant portion of the curriculum. The exception to this is Skagit Valley College, where learning communities are widespread throughout the curriculum. The students I interviewed who attended Antioch had both taken team-taught programs, but had spent much of their time in courses taught by one instructor. Team teaching helps make interdisciplinarity clear to students; it also provides students with a model of the learning process.

A young woman who recently completed her Evergreen education explains her first experience with interdisciplinary education and team teaching:

> During the first week of my coordinated studies program, I was going crazy. It was very difficult to see the larger picture because I came out of high school thinking in a very compartmentalized way. When I first got to class, each teacher got up and gave a spiel about what his or her piece of the puzzle was in our class, and given my background, it was so easy for me to say, "OK, first we have statistics, then we have history, then we have literature." I just broke it all up again like I had in high school. But then the faculty said, "No way! We are not just four people from different fields who are saving you time from going class to class by teaching you everything in the same room. There is a reason we are all here together." So I realized that there was a reason we were studying statistics when I thought we were going to just study literature. It was all connected. And that made me see the bigger picture and I wanted to go deeper.

A student who took "Shaping a Nation," a year-long, half-time, team-taught program at Evergreen that I planned and taught with my colleague Susan Preciso, had this to say about team teaching:

> I learned a lot from team teaching. You and Susan each brought different things to the program. You know, you brought the history and Susan had the literature. So the program was about how you look at history through literature. And one thing that was really good was that you guys were doing some of the same stuff we were doing. It was almost as if you had to learn with us, to a large extent. So here you guys are, it's like you are out of your element, in a sense, I mean you are reading all these novels and poems that Susan picked. And here's Susan reading all this history that you picked.
>
> Between the both of you, things took on larger dimensions. So as a student I was forced to look at this and I learned from it. I remember sitting there with Susan and watching her struggle with a difficult historical concept. And it was so cool, because I got to see that she had to wrestle with this too. And I remember looking at the story of Huck Finn with the historical background that you gave us when we read *The Peculiar Institution* and the other stuff about slavery and that period. And then reading Huck Finn, it was like, Whoa. All of a sudden the river is much wider and the raft is floating on a lot more. Without team teaching that wouldn't have happened. The different things you both brought to the program made the experience so much more valuable.

A student who participated in several team-taught learning communities at North Seattle Community College before earning his AA degree and transferring to a major research university had these comment about team teaching and the lack of it:

> I thought that team teaching at North Seattle was great, because you could witness these intelligent people speaking to each other, presenting different disciplines, and I learned a lot from the interchanges. It wasn't always utopian. They would argue, and sometimes sort of snap at each other, but the bottom line was like, wow, we're all just working together. When you're getting into ideas, into those areas where nothing is cut and dried, but everything is a matter of degrees of meaning and knowledge, I think that is really very high level stuff. It doesn't get any better than that.
>
> I don't think that in today's world you can take a strictly disciplinary approach. When I wrote my senior thesis at the university, I had to incorporate American history, culture studies, musicology, and anthropology. I couldn't contain my thesis in one particular discipline. When I went to speak to the head of the ethnomusicology department about my project, he would only give me an ethnomusicological framework of looking at it. And when I went to the culture studies people, they would give me a culture studies way of looking at it. It really illustrated for me that people get bogged down in their own disciplines. That's because of the structure. My major at the university was the comparative history of ideas program, which was great, and we had a great seminar on pedagogy. But when I went to speak with people in the education department, I realized that although they talked about the same sorts of ideas about pedagogy, they didn't know anyone in my program. And people in my program, even though we were doing a lot of work on pedagogy, didn't know anyone in the education department. I remember thinking, well, this is ridiculous. There should be interchange. We live in a society where all knowledge is connected and contingent on other knowledge. We are doing a disservice to students by saying there are demarcations between the disciplines.

Seminar

I've always seen the seminar as the most important part of education at Evergreen, where I taught programs for adult students for about four years. Good seminars can be tremendously rewarding and exciting. They are places where hard intellectual work as well as play occur, centered around a particular text, film, or presentation. It's important to view the seminar as interactive, with students and faculty pursuing a common goal of wresting meaning from a text. This is simply because at many conventional colleges and universities, seminar means a professor talking at students for three hours instead of just one. A good seminar is interactive above all, with faculty and students as committed colearners. As Susan Fiksdal's chapter says, seminar should convey a multitude of meanings: respect for students' voices, the pure fun of working together in a common purpose, the hard work of textual analysis, the epiphany that occurs when the group achieves a common insight or an individual voice succeeds in a particularly interesting analysis of the material.

One student contrasts his experience with a coordinated studies program at North Seattle Community College and a program at a research university.

> The program at North Seattle turned me into an active reader, a person who understood how to discuss a text, both what we read and what went on in class. So when I got to the university and took dry classes from experts in their fields, people who had the charisma of a potato, I knew how to interact, how to ask the right questions, how to make the subject interesting for me. The thing about the university is that you can begin as a freshman and go all the way through to graduate as a senior and never say a word.
>
> I know this music teacher at the university and we were walking around and he wanted to drop in on a friend of his. So he and I both walked into one of these big lecture rooms. His friend was giving a lecture and we went over and talked to him for a second. But I was just sort of standing there, face to face with this group of 500 students, who were throwing stuff and moving around. Maybe 20% of the people were focused on the speaker and everybody was doing something else and not focused on the lecture. And that is bad. That is terrible. Right before we left the bell rang and VROOM! I mean it was like that everybody said, "Right, I'm out of here!" There is nothing of value going on there. That is just processing.
>
> So they put their freshmen in these huge 500 seat classrooms, and the lecturer spews forth. The problem is that after two years of that you get these people into an upper division class that has maybe 25 people in it, and you walk into those rooms and everybody is still doing exactly the same thing. They are passively watching the instructor like they would a television.
>
> Much of seminar is the opposite of this. It is community building. And if everybody else in your community is doing their assignments and their reading, and their analysis, their writing and everything, the pressure is on to sort of live up to the norms and values of that particular community. I mean it's just community building. Community Building 101. It seems very basic to me. I am a music teacher and I teach performance ensembles, and it is the same sort of thing when I get a group of kids together. Every single person in the ensemble has to do their part. If one person doesn't do their part, it affects everyone. So you are getting out of competitive

> individualism and into, maybe, competitive communalism. We're not competing against each other, but striving toward the goal of performance. Or, in a seminar, striving toward the goal of understanding this particular book. This text is here and we have all committed ourselves to sitting in a room and trying to get the essence of this text as best we can.

Another student talked about the democracy of seminar, and how the process helped him to find his own voice. His comments also highlight the joy of learning in this way.

> Seminar is a really democratic environment. I mean the whole idea of having seminar where everybody has something to say and it all counts. Everybody gets an equal opportunity to make a great point, or to make a fool of themselves, which I think is so honest. And you don't get to sit there and hide out. Because eventually somebody is going to get you. I think that is the best part of it. I enjoyed seminar. I think I enjoyed seminar because I was able to see my thinking.
>
> If I had an idea about what we read and how that fit into something else, to a larger thought, I could present that. This was a group of people who didn't owe me anything one way or the other, who were going to be critical of that thought. They would either say, "Oh you know, you've got holes here, here, and here," or "Hey that's good and you know maybe it could fit into this, that, or the other." So I was able to see how my thinking was. In a lot environments you don't get to see how you are thinking—whether or not your thinking is clear. Because you don't get the feedback. That was really important to me.
>
> I work with people who almost intentionally try to make you crazy. (He works in a prison for the department of corrections.) The people I work with think killing is fun. But their statements about capital punishment are based on belief, not logic. So arguing with them is meaningless, because it's almost like a religion—that capital punishment is good. After a while—even to myself—my thinking can appear to be wrong, because all the people around me are not engaging in logical argument or discussion, but always reciting an opinion or belief, and not even trying to engage with what I'm saying. This can make you nuts.
>
> At Evergreen people look at how you think. Is the argument sound? Does it make sense? Does it hold together? Does it work? And I think there is a lot of strength in that—I mean a lot of strength that I got out of that. Because my thinking is not always in line with the larger group around me. So you want to be able to go someplace to check your thinking. Evergreen is the place where I got see that my thinking was sound. And you can't ask for a whole lot more than that.
>
> It is almost like school becomes a love affair. You put that kind of energy into it. I was in love with going to school. There was all that

> energy. And it was a little difficult, because when you get home you don't show the same enthusiasm. You know, like when the wife says, "Hey, let's go to the movies," and you're thinking, "Oh man, I got a hot seminar tonight and I know I am right on the mark with my reading and my arguments." Or you've just finished a great seminar, and you are glowing because everything clicked the right way or you got that great insight, and it's not that kind of high when you come home. It's "take out the garbage and where is the checkbook." So it's a transition, and I'd say to myself, "Oh, OK, I am home. Honey, I am home."

Taking Responsibility

The degree to which students take responsibility for their own education varies depending on the institution. Perhaps Evergreen demands the most from students; we have no preplanned majors and very few prerequisite courses. The student is completely responsible (with the aid, if desired, of faculty and academic advisors) for planning his or her own course of study. When the student earns a total of 180 credits, he or she graduates. Evergreen employs narrative evaluations in lieu of grades. Faculty evaluate students; students evaluate faculty and themselves. This freedom and responsibility is a delight for many students, a daunting challenge for others. An Antioch student describes her experience:

> I graduated from Antioch's bachelor of arts completion program. The BA was in liberal studies, so right away you are faced with how to design your degree. That was probably the best thing and the hardest thing about an interdisciplinary education for me, realizing that I could study just about anything that is relevant to me but that I also had to shape it into something that would be meaningful. I found that really a challenge and I was also afraid of that responsibility. That combination of fear and challenge provided a kind of tension which was pretty much what got me through the process. That tension. "I am afraid of this, but I really need it."
>
> Antioch's is a portfolio degree, so you are responsible to document your education and to put out what your intentions are. Now, they may change and you may need to revise them, but that is OK, it is not written in stone. But to be responsible is the main thing, and you are responsible to state what is going on, what your plan is, and you get a lot of support in this. Having to have it out there in black and white, although the plan is changeable, I think is really important. I found that very challenging, because I was always someone who didn't want to get boxed in, but then my faculty would say, "You don't have to, but you do need to state what your intentions are and provide a kind of parameter." So it is the combination of open-endedness and the requirement of educational planning that made it really kind of gel. That was totally one of the most important

things.

There was only one required course and that was about how to get an Antioch degree. That meant my education was wide open. That meant that I had to put together a program that would be meaningful and relevant but that I had the freedom to do it and I had the support. It is the combination of the support and freedom that really makes it kind of a special thing.

The structure of the program was discussion-based with maybe some short lectures. When you get into that you are having a discussion not just with the teacher, but also with the other students. So you become kind of a learning community. Instructors say all the time that they learn a lot from teaching courses. And that kind of acknowledgment is so different from a lot of other places. And I think even something as simple as sitting in circles, or everybody sitting around a couple of tables, as opposed to rows, seems like a small thing, but it is really important. Teachers and students both provide encouragement if you are trying to do independent studies. You get a sense of what being self-directed really is and you also get the support you need to find that direction. You are responsible with your advisor to create the syllabus and do the work, document the work, and evaluate your work. That it is really confidence building.

The self-reflective part of it is very important. It is one thing to be a lifelong learner, but it is also really important to know that you are, and to know what you've learned, and to be able to identify themes. At the end of every quarter, students are required to write narrative evaluations that discuss each learning activity and any connections with other activities, both in this quarter and quarters past, and what you are planning in the future. Did you notice any themes? Did you have trouble areas? The act of writing it helps you realize what themes are there for you. That is a really important part of it. And the mid-quarter evaluations are taken pretty seriously. I have seen instructors change something in the course because of feedback gotten mid-quarter. I don't know any instructor who hasn't taken it pretty seriously. So if there is too much reading, if things are really overwhelming, or if there is a case where a couple of people are dominating the conversation in the class, sometimes that gets noted and the instructor makes adjustments. All that kind of stuff is really important, because it amounts to a kind of a collective self-direction.

What They Learned

Commenting on the student panel which I facilitated at the 1997 American Council of Learned Societies and John D. and Catherine T. MacArthur Foundation sponsored Evergreen Conference on Interdisciplinary Education, Jerry Gaff noted:

> I was in a fascinating session with the student panel. They were talking about what they were learning in different kinds of institutions, and they were talking about a very different kind of learning than what most academics think about.
>
> First, they talked about the importance of personal learning. They found identity and were finding themselves in the kind of alternative institutions that focused on them so much.
>
> Second, they talked about social learning—learning to work with others, discussing, sharing, dealing with differences.
>
> Third, they talked about independent learning—deciding what to study, fashioning their own independent study contracts, setting up their own internships.
>
> Fourth, they talked about what I would call (they didn't use the word) emotional learning. They talked about assuming responsibility for learning. This is something students have to do for themselves. Faculty and institutions can support, encourage, nudge, and help, but it's the students' job. They talked about being excited about an ideal or the joy of learning, or, negatively, overcoming fear or frustrations and difficulties.
>
> Fifth, they talked about spiritual learning—discovering meaning, seeking values.

While the students I interviewed were acutely aware of how they learned, they were not as specific as Gaff in describing what they learned. They did not use Gaff's categories, nor did they self-consciously summarize their learning in that way, although the concepts of personal, social, independent, emotional, and spiritual learning certainly resonate in the comments of students. Rather, the students I interviewed talked more in practical terms of lifelong learning, of how they applied their education to their lives. One student took the lessons he learned into his own high school classroom:

> I was really strongly impacted by the critical pedagogical approach to education that empowers students to be responsible for their own learning. I started trying to implement those principles into my own teaching. When you walk into my classroom, aside from the fact that I am the only adult in the room, I hope it is not immediately obvious that I am the teacher. The students negotiate the curriculum. If there is an assignment they negotiate what it is going to look like and how much time they think they need, and they take turns facilitating the discussion.
>
> I don't have tests any more in my classes. The students do various projects, and gather a portfolio of what they have done over the year. They tell me, this is what I think my grade is based on, and we negotiate that grade together. The kids are so much more productive.

> There's a fear that if you allow democracy to happen and the kids have a say in what is going to be taught, or what they are going to learn, that their education will somehow be watered down, but I found that it actually gets enhanced. This takes a lot of courage on the part of the educator to let this process happen. It is really scary. You think you are giving up things. If I am to empower them, I have got to give up power and that is a scary thing. You are afraid you are going to lose the control which you are supposed to maintain. Antioch gave me the power to do that. Because I saw my own teachers doing that. My big thing right now is to see how I can further transform where I am working.

Another student's experience spoke to Jerry Gaff's comment about social learning:

> My programs gave me a taste of what it's like to work in a real community, in real life. The work world is changing. We work side by side with people, and we need to learn how to operate. And I think that was the biggest benefit of a coordinated studies program—that we learned how to work together, to put our heads together, to put our thoughts together, and how to communicate, dialog, and be innovative together. It gave us the opportunity to apply our learning in a real life situation and I think it is going to do our world a service. It is going to make our whole world better. It is going to start in the classroom, we are going to take it home to our children, our children's children, and it is going to spread. Cause this is the way real life is.

Finally, a student who worked as a drug and alcohol counselor in the prison system told about how his idealism was reawakened and how he applied the critical skills he learned in college to his job situation:

> I think back to when we did our program "Shaping a Nation." I think that program just woke up a lot of dormant bodies. For me, it raised questions like, "What do you do in a system where people are oppressed? What do you do in a system where you are oppressed?" You know, I have spent like the last twenty years making the best of it. So what do you do when you're confronted with this stuff? I mean, what do you do? All of a sudden you get kind of pissed off. I mean, that was the first thing. You know, it is like ehhhh, this is something that needs to be dealt with. So on a personal level I got pissed off, but on a larger level I knew that something had to change. So some of my idealism got reawakened. That meant that I could do pieces of my job better. Basically what I do is work with people to help them get out of the situation they were in. So if I could show folks that, hey look, here you are doing dope, you know, and you don't own the dope, you don't own the dope that comes in. If you start to look at drug use where you live—in predominantly black communities,

> poor white communities—I bet you'll start to think that maybe getting high is not in my best interest but maybe it is in somebody else's best interest. Even if you don't tell people specifically that, even if you kind of lead them to those issues and let them make their own connection, I think you are doing something. Evergreen helped me do that. I mean it woke me up. And I was able to wake people up that I worked with. You know, the inmates. I thought that was important if not so much in practical terms but just in mental health terms. It did something for me. I started to think. It wasn't just go to work, go home, do this, do that. I started to think about what I was doing and what I was going to do, and what roles my kids would play in all of this. So yeah, it woke me up.

A curious thing happened at both the 1997 American Council of Learned Societies and John D. and Catherine T. MacArthur Foundation sponsored Evergreen Conference on Interdisciplinary Education and at a 1998 FIPSE-sponsored National Conference on Learning Communities (also held at Evergreen) during the student panels. At each panel a member of the audience—one a college professor, one a newspaper reporter on higher education for a major Seattle paper—said, and I quote the faculty member, "I am really skeptical. You must be the elite students in your programs, or the programs you are in only attracted elite students." The reporter commented, "I wonder if the deck is stacked here, and you only picked the best students to be on this panel." They said this because the student panelists were confident, articulate, and thoughtful. In fact, these students are not the elite. They are normal people who blossomed in a humane educational environment which respected them as learners, guided them in making connections among themes and disciplines, enabled them to take responsibility for their own education, and helped them find their own confident voices in seminar. How ironic that knowledgeable observers, faced with intelligent, active students, see them as abnormal. As one student replied: "I believe there is creativity in all of us and learning is about students and teachers—all with different learning styles—working together to release this creativity."

ENDNOTES

1. Thanks to participating students: Dawn Rhodes and Mark Smith (Antioch University, Seattle); Michael Martin (North Seattle Community College); Will Bailey, Jennifer Evans, and Jennifer Koogler (The Evergreen State College, Olympia); Lilethia Williams, Tomonari Otake, and Tia Grant (Seattle Central Community College); Sandra Daniels and Lee Springer (The Evergreen State College, Tacoma); George Means (Bellevue Community College); Carolyn Parse and Dan Shephard (Fairhaven College, Western Washington University); and Annie O'Connell (Skagit Valley College). I am grateful to Audrey Streeter for transcribing my interviews.

22

Learning to See Academic Culture Through the Eyes of the Participants: An Ethnographic/Folkloristic Approach to Analyzing and Assessing the Cultures of Alternative Institutions

Peter Tommerup
California School of Professional Psychology

The real voyage of discovery begins not with visiting new places but in seeing familiar landscapes with new eyes.

—Marcel Proust

- What are the animating characteristics of the nontraditional academic culture(s) which we have evolved at our institution? How do these affect the formal and informal teaching and learning that transpires here?
- As we attempt to inquire nonjudgmentally into the ways our institution's culture(s) affects teaching and learning, how can we understand

and manage the biases and blindspots that we inevitably bring to our assessment research by virtue of the fact that we have been socialized into this academic culture ourselves?

These were the kinds of questions that engaged, excited, frustrated, and—at times—stymied the faculty, administrators, and students who made up the assessment study group at The Evergreen State College in the late 1980s. It was then that they, in conjunction with the school's office of institutional research, began to explore how they could develop an in-depth understanding of their institution's academic culture(s) along with the impact these might have on students' educational experiences. How this particular research project unfolded and how its findings contributed to the study group's evolving cultural understanding is an important narrative which constitutes one thread of this chapter. A second focus is to explore how individuals involved with assessment at other institutions can strategically immerse themselves in their own school's academic culture in order to develop a more in-depth understanding of it, on the one hand, as well as discover how it may influence teaching, learning, and other aspects of everyday institutional life, on the other hand. Through the juxtaposition of these two themes, it is hoped the reader will come away with enough knowledge to understand a useful approach to—and possibly begin a program of—cultural inquiry.

On Assessment, Cultural Inquiry, and Ethnography at Evergreen

Inspired by the belief that "Evergreen has something special going for it in the higher education process" (Assessment Study Group, Memo No. 2, undated, p. 1), and sensing that this special quality was somehow grounded in the school's nontraditional academic culture, study group members set off to ascertain which aspects of Evergreen's culture contributed to or detracted from students' educational experience. To gather this information, they initially turned to the narrative self-evaluations that students write in order to assess their own learning. They selected these as a place to start because they had long been considered a central and defining aspect of the school's nontraditional approach. What they hoped to discover in these essays were detailed descriptions of students' experiences of the nontraditional cultural forms and processes that characterize an Evergreen education. Instead, they were stunned to find that students did not explicitly mention this pervasive writing ritual. As far as the study group could determine, students seemed to take many of the unique aspects of their education for granted, including the process and impact of writing self-evaluations. This led study group members to begin questioning some of their own assumptions about certain of

Evergreen's distinctive cultural elements, including whether the tradition of narrative evaluations was of "any more direct value in assessment than say, burning incense or performing magical incantations" over students (Assessment Study Group, Memo No. 1, undated, p. 1).

Hitting a conceptual and methodological snag so early in their assessment research motivated study group participants to pause, reflect, and regroup. It also gave them time to reconsider their approach, and to recognize a significant limitation that might affect any cultural research they would undertake. Essentially, they realized that they were "so involved in this culture" that they would most likely unconsciously "assume important cultural frameworks" in their research in much the same way "as students tend to in their self-evaluations" (Assessment Study Group, Memo No. 3, undated, p. 2). Following this insight, members took a step back from trying to envision and conduct the investigation on their own. Instead, they decided to locate an "impartial external observer" to help them "examine those aspects of the culture which are widely accepted as important, as well as those we are unable to see due to our immersion in the culture" (Assessment Study Group, Memo No. 3, undated, p. 2).

Once the study group decided to engage an outside observer, another concern surfaced: What kinds of disciplinary backgrounds and methodological training would be most appropriate in an outside observer? Bringing in an ethnographer to direct this project had appeal, especially given that students of culture have long utilized an ethnographic approach in researching a variety of milieus (e.g., Fetterman, 1984; Jones, Moore, & Snyder, 1988; Stocking, 1992). Of the various fields they considered that utilize ethnography—e.g., anthropology, education, folklore studies, and sociology—folklore turned out to be of particular interest. This is because the study group became intrigued with the kind of detailed data and in-depth cultural insights that would likely be generated via a focused folkloristic examination of students' stories concerning their participation in and experience of teaching and learning culture(s) at Evergreen (Tommerup, 1993).

Eventually study group participants proposed that an ethnographic study be conducted on their campus, and that an outside ethnographer be located to direct and conduct the study in consultation with this committee. At this point in time, their vision of the project—which was still in flux—could be briefly characterized in the following way:

> Evergreen has earmarked a portion of . . . assessment funding for an ethnographic study. For this pilot study, an ethnographer is spending one academic year observing and describing the academic culture as fully as possible with particular attention to teaching and learning where it happens—within and outside the classroom. (Assessment Study Group, Memo No. 3, undated, p. 2)

Overall, the appeal of such an investigation for study group participants was that it could provide them with a trained outside observer's perspective on what was special and/or unique about Evergreen's culture without the bias which they themselves would bring to it, due to their many years of participation in that same culture. As they noted, "We realized that an (outside) ethnographer might have insights into Evergreen's educational system that we simply couldn't imagine" (Assessment Study Group, Memo No. 1, undated, p. 1).

It was at this point in time that I entered the scene. I responded to the ethnographer position announcement (*Chronicle of Higher Education*, 1990) and was ultimately hired to co-envision the project with the study group, direct it, conduct the research, keep the committee informed of my progress, accumulate data and insights, and in general help them to understand the process of cultural inquiry and its applicability for their evaluation needs. I also contributed to the research design of the project, given their interests—and my background and training—in the interdisciplinary fields of folklore and organizational culture studies (Tommerup, 1993). Because the fruits of our collaboration are relevant to future research of this type, how and why our research proceeded as it did, and what we learned in the process, will be discussed throughout the remainder of this chapter.

Other Applications for an Ethnographic/ Folkloristic Approach to Cultural Inquiry

Although the study group's principal objective was to engage in cultural inquiry so as to better understand and be able to evaluate the processes and impacts of nontraditional teaching and learning at Evergreen, there are many other issues that crop up in administrating, teaching and otherwise participating in alternative institutions that can benefit from an ethnographic/folkloristic approach. Among these are

- planning and instituting important successions, for example, between the founders and the next generation of faculty and administrators
- facilitating understanding and respectful dialog among members of various class, ethnic, occupational, or other subcultures on campus that are experiencing ongoing political conflict
- facilitating or reinforcing a meaningful sense of community and a playful attitude among participants at any level (e.g., within the evolving microculture of a course or coordinated studies program) or even on a campus-wide basis (e.g., at a macrocultural level)
- reinforcing and building on grassroots ways of doing things that are effective and which participants have evolved in their various subcultures

- generating feelings of engagement and commitment among participants in various parts of the institution
- working to make the voices, points of view, and experiences of those who are under represented and/or feel marginalized on campus more clearly heard and understood by the campus community as a whole
- building support for change by linking future visions and/or plans to past traditions that are experienced as meaningful, positive symbols
- developing pedagogical and administrative practices that complement and support deeply held community ideals and assumptions
- developing an orientation system for students and/or faculty that is responsive to incoming participants' needs and is perceived as being supportive insofar as it helps them to understand the nontraditional institutional culture they have just entered as well as how to become productively immersed in it
- developing an image of the institution or program that is both compelling and attractive to interested outsiders (e.g., prospective students and faculty) and that they believe has integrity even after they have become insiders
- empowering individual participants to think and act culturally by learning and modeling this behavior oneself
- encouraging members to apply this cultural frame to many of the things they do, as it will facilitate their becoming more aware of and self-reflective about their own cultural realities, biases, and blindspots—a helpful orientation in a world that is increasingly recognizing itself as being culturally diverse
- obtaining and evaluating feedback on any one of the above programs/projects in order to make it more responsive to members' needs
- overall, working as a builder of community, a skilled user of efficacious symbols (both for oneself and others), and as a force for helping participants to be able to engage in narrating positive cultural experience stories, both for their own developmental benefit as well as for the benefit of others

Underlying this particular ethnographic/folkloristic vision of organizing and organization in alternative institutions are several basic tenets. Identifying them up front may help to provide context for the discussions that follow. These tenets include:

- When formulating or attempting to implement policy, it is important to recognize that there is no single institution; this is an analytic fiction which privileges administrative points of view (Adams & Ingersoll, 1990). Instead, an ethnographic conception of organization would acknowledge that there are multiple realities within an organization, and that there are likely to be multiple perceptions of those realities among the individuals and groups who participate in them.

- A corollary to the above premise is that everyone is involved in cultural creation, recreation and ongoing maintenance all of the time. There are no privileged elites in this collaborative undertaking (Cohen, 1985; May, 1996), only those whose occupational roles formally legitimize their involvement in this area more so than it does others.

- Any action, regardless of whether it was intended to be of a personal or public nature, can be construed by someone as being symbolic of something, whether or not that action was intended to be symbolic in that way by the person who initiated it (Jones, 1987).

- To teach or administrate in a way that is commensurate with the egalitarian and community-oriented value systems of many alternative institutions, it is important to cultivate a culturally receptive mindset. This leads to a better understanding of the everyday folkways (e.g., storytelling, ritualizing, mythologizing, etc.) that participants engage in to constitute and reconstitute their meaningful worlds on campus. This is significant in so far as these traditions can serve as a window through which you can learn to appreciate where community members are coming from and why they see things as they do (Jones, Moore, & Snyder, 1988).

- Regardless of whether one is an administrator or faculty member, it may be helpful to evolve a new professional metaphor (Lakoff & Johnson, 1980; May, 1996) in order to view yourself as also being a facilitator/initiator of cultural creation, participation, and renewal. Developing a culturally receptive mindset can help by making you more knowledgeable about, reflective of, and creatively responsive toward (May, 1996) the campus culture(s) in which you navigate on a daily basis.

- For example, as a cultural participant, you can learn to nurture and positively influence people through imaginative symbolic and expressive means (e.g., by creating nurturing and/or healing rites of passage to help members transition through difficult times; by engaging others in listening to/understanding their own stories of cultural participation/experience; by facilitating collaborative myth-making to develop a compelling future to work toward as a community).

- Individual misunderstandings are generally a misnomer: Misunder standings are likely to have either an implicit or explicit cultural dimension insofar as the individuals involved are grounded in one or more cultural realities; as such, their reasoning and actions reflect the standards, logic and belief systems, and world view(s) of their reference communities. Understanding this may help to bring clarity to otherwise seemingly opaque administrative and ethical dilemmas (May, 1996).

Up to now, this chapter has focused on two topics. One of these concerns how the members of Evergreen's assessment study group laid the groundwork for an in-depth process of cultural inquiry that was grounded in an ethnographic/folkloristic approach during the late 1980s and into the early 1990s. A second issue has been to identify and discuss other useful applications for this kind of cultural inquiry that can benefit administrators and faculty in other alternative institutions.

At this point, this chapter will expand to accommodate a couple of other interrelated themes. These include 1) developing a working understanding of what constitutes ethnography and folklore, and 2) discussing how fieldwork of this sort can be successfully conducted within an alternative institutional setting. In addition, how the Evergreen ethnography project unfolded will also be covered—both because it is a noteworthy story, given that it was a pioneering effort—and because it may serve as a model in certain respects for those interested in doing a similar study at another institution.

Seeing Alternative Institutions with an Ethnographic Eye

> The world is much too clear as seen through the eyes of social scientists. One reason that it looks so clear is that we have managed to avoid the everyday activities and commonplace events that individuals and groups use to constitute and reconstitute their worlds (Schwartzman & Berman, 1994, p. 63).

Contained within the above is an important defining essence of a distinctive epistemological paradigm (Burrell & Morgan, 1979; Jones, 1988). A principal element of this interpretive paradigm is that those who would engage in cultural inquiry—either of their own cultural realities or of those of others—need to learn to "think culturally" (Bate, 1997, p. 1,153). They need to attend, for example, to those aspects of everyday institutional life that are prevalent in students' and faculty members' lives and carry meaning for them. They also need to pay attention to the concrete ways in which participants customarily express themselves, evaluate and communicate their experiences, learn to navigate through the maze of requirements and cultural possibilities that exist within their institutions, and otherwise try to create and maintain meaningful lives.

One place to begin the process of thinking culturally is the theory and practice of ethnography. According to one definition, "ethnography is the work of describing a culture" (Spradley, 1980, p. 3). Another perspective regards it as "the study of groups and people as they go about their everyday lives" (Emerson, Fretz, & Shaw, 1995, p. 1). Still another views it as "the peculiar practice of representing the social reality of others through the analysis of one's own experience in the world of these others" (Van Maanen, 1988, p. ix). For our purposes, a useful synthesis is the use of ethnographic methods to document and analyze participants' folklore and the role it plays in the nontraditional cultures of alternative institutions. However one defines this approach—and there are probably as many definitions as there are ethnographers—the primary goal of any ethnographically informed enterprise is to try to understand a particular way of life from the point(s) of view of those who are living it through their own words and actions.

Moving beyond a conceptual overview, how does one enact this participant-centered vision of social inquiry? The time-honored advice, handed down to generations of aspiring ethnographers by their more experienced elders, is to try "going out and getting close to the activities and everyday experiences of other people" (Emerson, Fretz, & Shaw, 1995, p. 1). One way to do this is through an approach known as participant observation, the central aim of which is to participate "as fully and humanly as possible in another way of life" (Emerson, Fretz, & Shaw, 1995, p. 2). By doing this, the ethnographer is able to learn "what is required to become a member of that world" and "to experience events and meanings in ways that approximate members' experiences" of their milieu (Emerson, Fretz, & Shaw, 1995, p. 2).

Participant observation begins with an initial overview of a particular cultural reality. Referred to as a grand tour (Spradley, 1979), this consists of the ethnographer going out and observing a variety of salient elements in a setting. These can include spaces, actors, activities, objects, acts, events, times, goals, and feelings (Spradley, 1979). With experience, I've found that a good place to begin an ethnographic exploration is to compile an inventory of the settings and activities which seem central to understanding a particular school's nontraditional culture. An example of such an inventory—reflecting my own research at Evergreen—follows:

> The settings to be researched consist of a number of cultural arenas—including subcultures and countercultures—that are central features of the overall campus environment. These include institutional forums that support "academic" teaching and learning (e.g., core programs, upper division seminars) as well as settings in which so-called "nonacademic"

> teaching and learning take place (e.g., offices of academic advising and career development). In addition, student organizations (e.g., women of color coalition, Asian Pacific Island coalition) that generate a less formal kind of teaching and learning culture on campus are of interest, as are the variety of spontaneous, unplanned events in which significant learning and/or teaching may transpire (e.g., informal continuations of seminar discussions outside of class). (Adapted from Tommerup, 1993, p. 68)

Using such a list as a guide, one can strive to discern the lay of the land in a low-key and unobtrusive manner. One way to get one's initial cultural bearings is to ask a great many very open-ended questions. Such questions which assume little cultural knowledge of a setting are also important for established insiders to ask in their own grand tour experience, but for somewhat different reasons. Whereas I as an outsider needed to make "the unfamiliar familiar" (Ely, Anzul, Friedman, Garner, & Steinmetz, 1991, pp. 127–132) to place my self in a receptive mind set in order to get to learn about a new setting and its distinctive ways of doing things, insiders need to make "the familiar unfamiliar" (Ely et al., 1991, pp. 124–127) to distance themselves sufficiently from the taken-for-granted blinders imposed on them by their immersion within their own institution's cultural reality.

Narrowing One's Field of Vision in the Field

Having achieved enough closeness to an institutional reality to be receptive to it, as well as enough distance from it to maintain an appropriately critical and reflexive mindset about it, one can move to the next deeper level of inquiry: the mini tour (Spradley, 1979). In this stage, the questions posed by the researcher to guide her inquiry typically highlight a "much smaller unit of experience" (Spradley, 1979, p. 79). That is to say, they are focused on one selected aspect—or a limited number of aspects—of a particular cultural reality. In my case, moving through the grand tour questions enabled me to conceptualize and articulate more focused ones which, in turn, allowed me to continue to deepen my cultural understanding. This enabled me to more narrowly articulate my next set of questions: What is striking about the pedagogical and administrative practices, interactional routines, patterns of small group culture creation, and ongoing organizational traditions which are important aspects of teaching and learning at Evergreen? In what ways and to what extent are participants affected by their immersion in these symbolic forms and expressive processes (Tommerup, 1993)?

As you come to feel more grounded and focused in a particular cultural reality, it is time to actively pursue those aspects of the setting that seem to hold clues to the cultural puzzle you are attempting to unravel.

Through these kinds of more selective and intensive encounters with particular people and settings—e.g., engaging in serendipitous conversations with individuals about topics of interest, observing participants interacting with one another in a variety of settings, studying the symbolic aspects of particular areas on campus as well as how members express themselves within and otherwise use these settings, and documenting informal grassroots social activities, etc.—I discovered several cultural themes which repeatedly turned up in my inquiry. These included the significant influence that "flexibility, ambiguity, informality, spontaneity and serendipity" exerted on participants' experiences of teaching and learning at Evergreen (Tommerup, 1993, pp. 77–124).

With this kind and quantity of cultural experience under one's belt, continuing to narrow one's focus can be facilitated by engaging in ethnographic interviews. These are often informal (Fetterman, 1989), even if prearranged and tape recorded, and "flow from a situation." They may be done "on the hoof" or at a moment's notice, should an opportunity present itself (Ely et al., 1991, p. 57). Departing from more predefined and rigid forms of social science data gathering, ethnographic interviews are best thought of as a distinctive kind of mutually engaging, somewhat spontaneous, serendipitous, and reciprocal "speech event" (Spradley, 1979, p. 55). They generally consist of the researcher's open-ended questions and the interviewee's sometimes searching and usually detailed responses in her own words. In some respects, the emerging dialog takes on the form of a friendly conversation (Spradley, 1979). This can include a temporary exchange of roles, the sharing of personal experience stories (Stahl, 1983; Tommerup, 1993), and the use of other expressive and symbolic means for generating trust and rapport (e.g., carrying out an informal interview over lunch, dinner, or a cup of coffee). At times, however, the interviewing process may shift to being more highly structured by the investigator, especially if she becomes concerned that the conversation may be straying from her "specific but implicit research agenda" (Fetterman, 1989, p. 48).

In my own interviewing, I try to achieve a balance between establishing rapport and gently nudging the discussion in what feels like a productive direction. In practice, this means that I develop a list of open-ended questions in case I need them, but I try not to become wed to these so that serendipity remains part of the process. In my own work, for example, "the [actual] questions I asked in a given interview emerged, to a great extent, during the course of that interview" (Tommerup, 1993, p. 64). More specifically,

> Though I had a growing set of [cultural] themes and patterns that I was interested in pursuing—and did—I tried to balance this goal with following my interviewees' lead, especially in terms of the nature and

> progression of topics and stories that were explored. In general, I let an interviewee lead when he/she indicated a desire to do so (e.g., if that person felt strongly about a certain topic, wanted to get something off his/her chest, or was exceedingly happy about something that had recently happened to him/her). (Tommerup, 1993, p. 64)

That said, some of the likely questions I prepared, and sometimes drew on to begin an interview or jump start one that was flagging, include:

- How did you decide to come to this institution?
- What was your experience like when you first came to campus?
- Tell me about your first (second, third, etc.) quarter/semester/year here.
- What course of studies/coordinated studies program are you in? How did you choose it? Tell me about your experience in it.
- If lectures are part of your program, what are they like?
- What are seminars like?
- What kinds of potlucks, field trips, retreats, and/or other festive gatherings have you experienced in your program?
- What is social life like here?
- What do you do for fun and recreation?
- What is it like to live in the dorms? Are there any kinds of teaching and learning that occur there on an informal basis?
- Do you belong to any student organizations on campus? How has your participation in this/these affected your learning here?
- Looking back on the settings you've been in and the learning experiences you've had here, can you tell me what seems to have worked well for you, as well as what did not seem to work so well and why?
- How would you compare the kind of teaching and learning you've experienced here with that of other schools you've attended?
- Is there anything else about your experience—or your friends' experiences—here that you think I should consider in my study? (Adapted from Tommerup, 1993, p. 66)

Overall, the values and techniques utilized in ethnographic learning have one overriding objective: to enable a researcher to experience cultural immersion for a long enough period of time so she can develop a deep and detailed impression of the reality under study. That is, an ethnographer's learning centers around trying to discover what it is like to "become the other" (Ely et al., 1991, p. 49) through her own highly attentive experience of—and reflections on—particular people and events as they unfold within a particular setting.

Looking for Culture in all the Right Places

Thus far we've discussed how to see the culture of an alternative institution ethnographically by learning some basic techniques and by developing a culturally receptive mindset. These enable us to look beyond our own cultural blinders and boundaries and begin moving closer to, and eventually entering, the worlds of others. However, along with learning how to see cultural reality, one also needs to know what distinctive characteristics and qualities of culture to look for and where to find them!

One of the most straightforward and efficacious ways for an interested inquirer to gain access to the cultural reality of an institution, as suggested earlier in this chapter, is through the folklore of its members. This is because folklore, unlike the more familiar and abstract culture construct, is as close to hand as the first personal experience story, joke, proverbial saying, or other tradition you hear voiced or see enacted in a day's work. Whereas culture, as it is commonly utilized in institutional and organizational research (Kuh & Whitt, 1988; Tierney, 1988; Schein, 1985), is a macrolevel construct that tends to be more conceptually distant and removed from the tangible aspects of people's everyday lives, folkloric activity is readily observable in participants' own words and actions. It is, to use a term coined by Clifford Geertz (1973), "experience near"; or, as a student of mine has noted, folklore is "much closer to where people live."

If you are going to pay attention to folklore as an interested inquirer, a working definition is needed. To this end, participant folklore in alternative institutions can be conceptualized as consisting of a variety of fundamental forms of traditional symbolic, expressive and aesthetic behavior (Georges, 1983; Georges & Jones, 1995). These forms are recognizable in so far as they are recurring, stand for something, reflect grassroots interpretations, are generally manifested via informal face-to-face interaction, exhibit shared communication, reveal understandings that are perceived to be significant enough to have become traditional, and highlight aesthetic concerns and preferences. Ultimately, the folklore that is generated, communicated, and perpetuated by a community of participants reflects key metaphoric assertions they make about the nature and ethos of the reality they share (Fernandez, 1986; Lakoff & Johnson, 1980).

In an alternative institution, there are myriad forms of traditional symbolic, expressive and aesthetic behavior or folklore. These are likely to include myths about the founding of the institution (e.g., how the decision was made to start a nontraditional institution); campus legends concerning particular people, places, or events that are considered noteworthy enough to circulate in oral tradition (e.g., crises in the group's history, particular features of the campus, etc.); personal experience stories that concern what it's like to participate in the school's culture (e.g., how members discovered the college and became socialized into its way of doing things); the customary interactional routines that are initiated within and between groups of students, faculty, and staff (e.g., as in seminar, committee meetings, etc.); pedagogical practices that have evolved over time (e.g., how to make sure everyone has a chance to speak in seminar); a variety of formal, informal, and spontaneous celebrations (e.g., potlucks, field trips, retreats, etc.); whole school, small group, and personal rites of passage (e.g., birthday parties, farewell events, end of the quarter/semester evaluation proceedings, etc.); graffiti and other grassroots ways of personalizing or claiming space; as well as other verbal and nonverbal customs (e.g., distinctive artistic and introspective "house needed" and "roommate wanted" flyers, a campus "freebox," etc.) that reflect the ethos and world view of participants in a particular institutional context (Tommerup, 1993).

Folklore is also an appropriate microlevel concept to utilize in an ethnography for another reason: It provides a window through which one can understand the values, concerns, goals, joys, and frustrations of cultural participation. In other words, folklore is a vehicle through which one can learn about the microcultures and worldviews of the various communities on campus, as well as of the school as a whole. Because worldview—characterized as a group's "vision of the world" (Malinowski, 1922, p. 517) or perception of "the way things in sheer actuality are" (Geertz, 1973, p. 127)—is typically held unconsciously, a group's taken-for-granted understandings can surface and be expressed implicitly through their folklore. The folklore of a campus community constitutes a kind of "autobiographical ethnography" which provides "a view of the culture from the inside-out rather than from the outside-in" (Dundes, 1980, p. 70). Thus, folklore is a valuable lens through which to view the cultural life of an alternative institution in so far as it is "a people's own description of themselves" as communicated through their words and actions (Dundes, 1980, p. 70).

Seeing and Appreciating an Institution's Culture from the Inside-Out via Participants' Stories

Among the richest veins of traditional symbolic, expressive, and aesthetic behavior I found at Evergreen were participants' self-reflective comments, personal experience stories (Stahl, 1977; Stahl, 1983; Tommerup, 1993), and community-centered rites of passage (van Gennep, 1960; Turner, 1969; Loubier, 1996; Tommerup & Loubier, 1996). How did I discover these? I both physically and psychologically located myself in a position to come across these by immersing myself in the everyday lives of the people I met. Once there, I expressed my interest—and correspondingly elicited their interest and self-reflective feedback—in what they did, why they did it that way, and how they felt about it.

By interviewing and informally hanging out with students and faculty throughout my research, I was able to learn that they viewed certain points of their own immersion into the school's nontraditional culture as especially resonant and transformative. From carefully analyzing transcriptions of their tape-recorded comments and stories, I was able to identify and describe four critical phases of this ongoing immersion process. Using their folklore as a guide to my inquiry, I confirmed that the experience of these phases was widespread. I also paid attention to their insights and information when I labeled these phases: discovery, initiation, participation, and separation (Tommerup, 1993). More specifically, I learned a lot about what led them to come to an alternative institution, how they navigated through it once they were there, what they learned and where they learned it, what they enjoyed about being there, what they found frustrating and would like to have changed, why they stayed, how they felt about the prospect of eventually leaving, and how their participation here often affected them in deeply personal and transformative ways.

One interesting cultural insight that came out of my work, for example, was the discovery of the kind of compelling beliefs, stories, and images—in a word, mythology (Tommerup, 1988)—that members can hold about their institution's nontraditional culture. Many of my interviewees fervently believed in Evergreen's enigmatic customs, practices, and interactional routines (Tommerup, 1993), and in the quality of experience which these may facilitate. The depth of this attachment is echoed in the mantra-like words related to me by one entering student: "You can do anything you want at Evergreen" (Tommerup, 1993, p. 126). Sharing in this belief, a second year student remarked:

> Evergreen is this Mecca. People hear [that] Evergreen is this great place .... [They think] it's going to be so great here. Everything is going to be perfect. You're going to get to do whatever you want. (Tommerup, 1993, p. 127)

Another student comment provides additional insight into the pervasive feeling among many participants that you are comparatively unfettered to pursue your own interests here:

> If you want to do something [at Evergreen], you just do it. It's not like there's a system that you have to beat before you can go ahead and do the things that you want to do. (Tommerup, 1993, p. 132)

The theme of enjoying the freedom to pursue one's own interests within a stimulating and supportive learning environment also surfaced in many students' personal experience stories (Stahl, 1977; Stahl, 1983; Tommerup, 1993). One freshman, reflecting on what led her to decide to come to Evergreen, narrated about her discovery of what she perceived to be Evergreen's "specialness." (Note: this account, and the ones which follow, have been edited as indicated to facilitate a concise presentation):

> I sat in on a seminar [at Evergreen] and that's what clinched it for me. It was just amazing to sit down in a seminar and see the faculty stepping back and not playing the teacher role, but being interested in what the students were saying. I was really excited to hear what the students' thoughts were on this book that they'd been reading. And the students had really well developed ideas and very well-developed questions. They were very analytical. They just had it together and that really impressed me . . . . I was really amazed at the dynamics of this seminar . . . . I figured that either Evergreen was attracting these kinds of people, and these were the kinds of people I wanted to go to school with, or that Evergreen was cultivating these kinds of people, and that's how I wanted to be. That's what clinched [it for] me in coming here. (Tommerup, 1993, p. 134)

The discovery story of a transfer student in her mid thirties reveals a related theme: not wanting to feel that one is being forced into an unyielding and uncomfortable mold as a student by the culture of an institution. Having dropped out of college some 15 years earlier, she had tried a variety of jobs but yearned to complete her education someplace different. Serendipitously, she heard about Evergreen from some friends who were alumnae. Unlike other institutions she had considered, this one sounded special. In her words:

> The thing I noticed about [my friends who graduated from Evergreen], and this is going to sound like a promotional ad, [is that] they are happy with their lives . . . . They feel good about themselves and what they're doing. I've met plenty of professional people who don't feel this way. I don't need that. I was afraid that might happen [to me] if I went somewhere traditional . . . . [Seeing them happy] gave me a good feeling. [It seemed] like Evergreen was someplace you could go and not have [getting] the degree become the ultimate goal . . . . I change so much I

> didn't want to go to school somewhere and think I was going to be something and then get [stuck in] that for the next 20 years. (Tommerup, 1993, p. 144)

Many Evergreen faculty also share in this compelling mythic construction concerning the special cultural qualities of the school and the emancipatory influence they can have on those interested in alternative ways of doing teaching and learning. In his discovery story, for instance, one faculty member recalls:

> I ended up here because everyone who I worked with [at a community college] kept telling me to go to Evergreen and work. I had a tendency to rebel a bit and not confine my teaching to a 50–minute hour, five days a week. I would seminar with my students. I would make them read outside materials, write a lot, do a lot of mathematics. The trade off was that I would not require them to be sitting in a chair five days a week for 50 minutes. If we reached our weekly goals then we did not need to meet anymore.
>
> That drove people nuts in the traditional setting. A lot of people there just kept saying, "That's great you are doing that, the students are learning a lot, but it is just not the way we operate. You ought to look into Evergreen." It was not a threat at all. It was just some very constructive advice that there was a place that was doing what I was doing. I took it as a compliment. In fact, when I applied to Evergreen and was offered the position there, people where I worked were quite disappointed that I was leaving, but they knew it was a good move for me. In fact everyone remarked, "what a good fit it will be for you when you go down there." So, the transition was easy for me because I was pretty much operating as an Evergreener before I came.
>
> It has been the most wonderful experience—to [go from] what appeared to be a rebellious habit of seminars and interdisciplinary work to suddenly [being] around 175 other people doing the same thing. (Tommerup, 1993, p. 147–148)

To summarize, it was through student and faculty experience stories of teaching and learning that I was able to inductively infer a prevalent participant view of institutional socialization and cultural participation at Evergreen. What emerges from a close textual analysis of a representative sampling of these stories is a portrait of engaging, often transformative learning experiences. By studying this in depth, faculty and administrators can find cultural information that would be useful for a variety of applications, including assessment and developing orientation and mentoring programs for students and/or faculty.

Seeing Beyond Individuals' Stories to the Cultural Dimensions of Learning

Through the ethnographic/folkloristic approach I used in researching the cultural dimensions of teaching and learning at Evergreen, I was able to identify an individual learning scenario. This was reflected in the stories and actions of many students, as well as in my own experience on campus. It can be described as an individual attempt at ongoing meaningful identity construction. More specifically, I view it as a recurring pattern of a deep level of engagement in a particular kind of self-initiated and self-managed response to meaningful learning that was prevalent among those I observed and interviewed (Kondo, 1990). Underlying this scenario is the cultural knowledge I acquired that students (and, to some extent, faculty) are

> . . . frequently forced to come to grips with who they are, what they believe, what they are interested in and how they can make a contribution. In other words, they are forced to create for themselves a unique individual and social identity, since selecting a pre-defined one (i.e., a conventional academic major) and then fitting themselves to it (i.e., acquiring the knowledge, methods and outlook deemed essential by the discipline) is not an option here. (Tommerup, 1993, pp. 564–566)

The learning scenario, as I came to understand it, has a cultural and developmental dimension which tends to unfold according to the following pattern:

1) A student is thrust into a teaching and learning milieu (e.g., a program, seminar, group or individual contract) that is at the same time perceived to be supportive, seductive, flexible, and characterized by ambiguity. At a beginning of this sort, a participant is likely to romanticize the teaching and learning process which he/she believes will transpire in this milieu.

2) Because he/she feels both inspired and under pressure to do something meaningful in such a seductive environment, but usually is not told explicitly what that can be or how to go about doing it, the individual student is forced to figure it out, often with the help of friends, faculty, or other mentors.

3) Usually, he/she tries several tacks in this process, none of which may prove to be appropriate. Eventually, he/she becomes frustrated, disappointed and sometimes even disillusioned or disgruntled. At this point, students often see a downside to their educational experience here.

4) This, in turn, is likely to motivate him/her to go through a sorting out process to figure out what direction to try to pursue next. A frequent outcome of such a process is that what really matters to the student becomes more apparent.

5) Next, something interesting and significant often happens: a serendipitous revelation of a possible path. Exploring this path may lead the student to an engaging intellectual passion. At this juncture, participants are likely to articulate a positive outlook on their learning experiences here. This may be expressed via their personal experience narratives (Stahl, 1977; Stahl, 1983) as well as through supportive practices and routines which they initiate for themselves (Jones, 1987), but generally in the supportive community of others who are deemed to be significant.

6) Over time, if the student remains engaged by this passion (i.e., discovers that it continues to be meaningful and to feel transformative), he/she may come to recognize that he/she has developed a unique way of seeing and thinking about some facet of the world. Some participants refer to this distinctive perspective as the development of a voice. (Adapted from Tommerup, 1993, p. 564–566)

Interesting though this analysis may sound, the question could be raised: Of what practical value are these kinds of culturally derived insights? For one thing, becoming aware of such a pattern may help faculty better understand where their students are coming from at any given point in time, as well as how to help facilitate their movement to where they are aspiring to be, or to explain to them why it might be more appropriate for them to consider moving in an altogether different direction. Similarly, this kind of learning profile would likely be helpful to those doing academic advising. Finally, it could be helpful to students insofar as it can inform them of what they may experience in this particular cultural setting. Knowing this, students can immerse themselves in the academic flow with greater confidence and with less anxiety over what the outcome may be.

Conclusion

Now we have come full circle and are at the end of our journey into the whys and wherefores of cultural inquiry. As such, it is an appropriate time to revisit the basic thesis of this chapter: that an ethnographic/folkloristic approach to understanding the culture(s) of an alternative institution can be uniquely helpful to the faculty, administrators, and other participants in that setting. How and why is this the case?

To begin with, an approach that is grounded in ethnographic methods and folkloristic concepts is well positioned to help faculty and administrators to learn to "think culturally" (Bate, 1997, p. 1,153) about their organizations. For one thing, folklore—consisting as it does of informal grassroots traditional symbolic and expressive forms and processes (e.g., tried and true practices and ways of doing things, stories and storytelling, rituals and ritualizing, celebrations and celebrating)—is an especially accessible element of culture to study. It is also significant because it is prevalent: We all help to generate it, participate in it, and generally come to view it as a reasonably appropriate depiction of the way things are in a particular setting. Moreover, participant folklore reveals a participant's eye view of the nature of cultural participation in an institution, the experience of that participation, as well as an informal critique of that experience.

An ethnographic/folkloristic approach can also provide key insights into the collaborative nature of ongoing culture creation, perpetuation, and renewal in alternative institutions. As such, it is especially well suited to the more egalitarian, democratic, and community-centered ideologies of many alternative institutions. For example, according to this perspective, members use the various cultural forms and processes that are part of their everyday institutional lives as resources for generating the master fictions by which they navigate and work within a specific setting. More specifically, it is through the stories participants invent, learn, tell, believe, or disbelieve, the rites they perform, the practices they engage in, the traditions they reenact, and the organizational worldview they adopt and model that they interpret, understand, comment on, respond to, maintain, and/or change their institution's culture(s).

Overall, participants in alternative—as well as in more conventional—institutions can benefit practically from an ethnographic/folkloristic approach in a variety of ways. Such an approach can help them to become more reflective about the various culture(s) within their campus. In turn, this can help to more fully privilege a greater variety of representative voices and points of view from a more inclusive and engaged community of participants. Beyond this, such a perspective can help academic professionals to expand their conception of their work to include a cultural dimension. Regardless of whether one's professional training is in the area of assessment, advising, teaching, fund raising, or more generally steering the course of an institution, an in-depth understanding of culture can help in the course of working with other professionals and with those whom they serve or represent.

In the end, there is a way you can discover for yourself just how useful an ethnographic/folkloristic approach may be: try it out in your own institution!

REFERENCES

Adams, G. B., & Ingersoll, V. H. (1990). Painting over old works: The culture of organization in an age of technical rationality. In B. A. Turner (Ed.), *Organizational symbolism* (pp. 15–31). New York, NY: Walter de Gruyter.

Assessment Study Group. *Memo No. 1.* Unpublished, undated document, The Evergreen State College, Olympia, WA.

Assessment Study Group. *Memo No. 2.* Unpublished, undated document, The Evergreen State College, Olympia, WA.

Assessment Study Group. *Memo No. 3.* Unpublished, undated document, The Evergreen State College, Olympia, WA.

Bate, S. P. (1997). Whatever happened to organizational anthropology? A review of the field of organizational ethnography and anthropological studies. *Human Relations, 50* (9), 1147–1171.

Burrell, G., & Morgan, G. (1979). *Sociological paradigms and organizational analysis: Elements of the sociology of corporate life.* Portsmouth, NH: Heinemann.

Chronicle of Higher Education. (1990, May 2). *36* (33), B46.

Cohen, A. P. (1985). *The symbolic construction of community.* New York, NY: Tavistock.

Dundes, A. (1980). Thinking ahead: A folkloristic reflection of the future orientation in American worldview. In A. Dundes (Ed.), *Interpreting folklore* (pp. 69–85). Bloomington, IN: Indiana University Press.

Ely, M., Anzul, M., Friedman, T., Garner, D., & Steinmetz, D. M. (1991). *Doing qualitative research: Circles within circles.* New York, NY: Falmer.

Emerson, R. M., Fretz, R., & Shaw, L. (1995). *Writing ethnographic fieldnotes.* Chicago, IL: University of Chicago Press.

Fernandez, J. W. (1986). Persuasions and performances: Of the beast in every body and the metaphors of everyman. In J. W. Fernandez (Ed.), *Persuasions and performances: The play of tropes in culture* (pp. 3–27). Bloomington: Indiana University Press.

Fetterman, D. M. (1984). *Ethnography in educational evaluation.* Beverly Hills, CA: Sage.

Fetterman, D. M. (1989). *Ethnography step by step.* Newbury Park, CA: Sage.

Geertz, C. (1973). Ethos, worldview, and the analysis of sacred symbols. In C. Geertz (Ed.), *Interpreting cultures* (pp. 126–141). New York, NY: Basic Books.

Georges, R. A. (1983). Folklore. In D. Lance (Ed.), *Sound archives: A guide to their establishment and development* (pp. 134–144). Milton Keynes, England: International Association of Sound Archives.

Georges, R. A., & Jones, M. O. (1995). *Folkloristics: An introduction.* Bloomington, IN: Indiana University Press.

Jacques, R. (1996). *Manufacturing the employee: Management knowledge from the 19th to 21st centuries.* Thousand Oaks, CA: Sage.

Jones, M. O. (1987). Aesthetics at work: Art and ambiance in an organization. In M. O. Jones (Ed.), *Exploring folk art: Twenty years of thought on craft, work and aesthetics* (pp. 133–157). Ann Arbor, MI: UMI Research.

Jones, M. O. (1988). In search of meaning: Using qualitative methods in research and application. In M. O. Jones, M. D. Moore, & R. C. Snyder (Eds.), *Inside organizations: Understanding the human dimension* (pp. 31–48). Newbury Park, CA: Sage.

Jones, M. O. (1996). *Studying organizational symbolism.* Thousand Oaks, CA: Sage.

Jones, M. O., Moore, M. D., & Snyder, R. C. (Eds.). (1988). *Inside organizations: Understanding the human dimension.* Newbury Park, CA: Sage.

Kondo, D. K. (1990). *Crafting selves: Power, gender, and discourses of identity in a Japanese workplace.* Chicago, IL: University of Chicago Press.

Kuh, G. D., & Whitt, E. J. (1988). *The invisible tapestry: Culture in American colleges and universities.* College Station, TX: Association for the Study of Higher Education.

Lakoff, G., & Johnson, M. (1980). *Metaphors we live by.* Chicago, IL: University of Chicago Press.

Loubier, C. (1996). *The use of rites of intensification during organizational crises.* Unpublished doctoral dissertation, California School of Professional Psychology, Alameda, CA.

Malinowski, B. (1922). *Argonauts of the western Pacific.* New York, NY: Dutton.

May, L. (1996). *The socially responsive self.* Chicago, IL: University of Chicago Press.

Morgan, G. (1986). *Images of organization.* Newbury Park, CA: Sage.

Reason, P. (1994). Three approaches to participative inquiry. In N. K. Denzin & Y. S. Lincoln (Eds.), *Handbook of qualitative research* (pp. 324–339). Thousand Oaks, CA: Sage.

Rosaldo, R. (1986). Ilongot hunting as story and experience. In V. W. Turner & E. M. Bruner (Eds.), *The anthropology of experience* (pp. 97–138). Urbana, IL: University of Illinois Press.

Rosaldo, R. (1993). *Culture and truth: The remaking of social analysis.* Boston, MA: Beacon.

Schein, E. G. (1985). *Organizational culture and leadership.* San Francisco, CA: Jossey-Bass.

Schwartzman, H. B., & Berman, R. H. (1994). Meetings: The neglected routine. In T. Hamada & W. E. Sibley (Eds.), *Anthropological perspectives on organizational culture* (pp. 63–94). New York, NY: University Press of America.

Spradley, J. P. (1979). *The ethnographic interview.* New York, NY: Holt, Rhinehart, & Winston.

Spradley, J. P. (1980). *Participant observation.* New York, NY: Holt, Rhinehart, & Winston.

Stahl, S. K. D. (1977). The personal narrative as folklore. *Journal of the Folklore Institute, 14,* 9–30.

Stahl, S. K. D. (1983). Personal experience stories. In R. M. Dorson (Ed.), *Handbook of American folklore* (pp. 268–276). Bloomington, IN: Indiana University Press.

Stocking, G. W. (1992). *The ethnographer's magic and other essays in the history of anthropology.* Madison, WI: University of Wisconsin Press.

Tierney, W. G. (1988). Organizational culture in higher education: Defining the essentials. *Journal of Higher Education, 59* (1), 2–21.

Tommerup, P. (1988). From trickster to father figure. In M. O. Jones, M. D. Moore, & R. C. Snyder (Eds.), *Inside organizations: Understanding the human dimension* (pp. 319–332). Newbury Park: Sage.

Tommerup, P. (1992). *Teaching and learning at The Evergreen State College: An ethnographic study.* Olympia, WA: The Evergreen State College.

Tommerup, P. (1993). *Adhocratic traditions, experience narratives, and personal transformation: An ethnographic study of the organizational culture and folklore of The Evergreen State College, an innovative liberal arts college.* Unpublished doctoral dissertation, University of California, Los Angeles.

Tommerup, P., & Loubier, C. (1996). *Farewell rites: Managerial tool or community-based process for individual and group passage.* Paper presented at the annual meeting of the Standing Committee for Organizational Symbolism. Los Angeles, CA: University of California, Los Angeles.

Turner, V. W. (1969). *The ritual process.* Ithaca, NY: Cornell University Press.

van Gennep, A. (1960). *The rites of passage* (M. Vizedom, trans.). Chicago, IL: University of Chicago Press.

Van Maanen, J. (1988). *Tales of the field: On writing ethnography.* Chicago, IL: University of Chicago Press.

23

The Interdisciplinary Variable: Then and Now

Julie Thompson Klein
Wayne State University

Some experimental programs persist for a long time, others die. Even when innovations die, though, they may live on in other ways. Len Clark, Paul Lacey, and Nelson Bingham[1] made this observation, and, for me, it struck home. The program I teach in was built on the ashes of a venerable experiment, Monteith College. Reincarnated today as the Interdisciplinary Studies Program (ISP), the Monteith dream persists in an evolving curriculum for adult working students at Wayne State University. When the ISP opened its doors in 1973, the average student was a male blue-collar worker. The majority received veterans benefits, and many had served in the Vietnam war. Today, the program has a broader range of students, many holding white-collar jobs in area corporations and working in the public sector. The average age of undergraduate students is 41, the average age of graduate students is 48. The typical undergraduate is a married African American woman between the ages of 31 and 45. Once a leader in the field of adult education, the ISP now struggles to compete in a crowded market of accelerated degrees and distance learning programs for older, nontraditional students.

The student profile of the ISP was not typical of the classic alternative colleges. Many participants in the Evergreen Conference on Interdisciplinary Education came from these celebrated experiments. Yet, new programs and institutions serving a broader range of students were equally represented. We were, one participant exclaimed, "standing in lived experience." As we explored the legacy of pioneer experiments and the meaning of new structures, a richly layered picture of the concept of interdisciplinarity emerged. This reflection synthesizes insights from the conference and this book.

Defining Interdisciplinarity

The closing plenary of the conference focused on three questions:

- What does interdisciplinary mean now?
- What are the differences between now and the 1960s?
- What about faculty rewards?

As usually happens when there is good discussion, the group spent more time on the first and second questions.

The first question brought the first dictionary citation to mind. The underlying ideas of interdisciplinarity have been traced to ancient philosophy. It is, nonetheless, a 20th century word. The first reported citation appeared in *Webster's Ninth New Collegiate Dictionary and A Supplement to the Oxford English Dictionary.* It refers to a notice about postdoctoral fellowships offered by the Social Science Research Council (SSRC), which appeared in the December 1937 issue of *The Journal of Educational Sociology* (Frank, 1988). In the mid-1920s, interdisciplinary was a kind of bureaucratic shorthand for research involving two or more of the SSRC's seven societies (Frank, 1988). This isn't the earliest association, though. "Activities," James Davis commented one day, "predate words."

Several events circulate through the history of interdisciplinary education. In 1914, the first survey course, "Social and Economic Institutions," was created at Amherst College during Alexander Meiklejohn's presidency. In 1919, a general education core course, "Contemporary Civilization," was adopted at Columbia University. In 1927, Meiklejohn founded an experimental college at the University of Wisconsin and, the following year, reform of undergraduate education was underway at the University of Chicago. In 1937, Stringfellow Barr and Scott Buchanan, who had taught at Chicago, introduced a Great Books curriculum at St. John's College in Annapolis, Maryland. Motivations differed. Columbia's course on "Contemporary Civilization" promoted shared interdisciplinary knowledge, with emphasis on the process of knowing and examination of contemporary problems (Hutcheson, 1997). Great Books and other text-based programs reflected a belief in unitary knowledge. One of the first reasons for interdisciplinary studies in the American university, Charles Anderson recalls, was to demonstrate the belief that there is one truth. Robert Hutchins's rationale for a liberal education program at Chicago was grounded in an Aristotelian conception of knowledge that located the coherence and integration of all fields of inquiry in an epistemological realism. The Aristotelian-Thomistic legacy of this epistemology, he notes, survives in the curriculum of Saint Thomas Aquinas College of San Francisco and in the Great Books program of St. John's of Annapolis and Santa Fe.

Until the 1960s, most American colleges and universities developing programs of interdisciplinary education tended to emulate models at Columbia, Chicago, Wisconsin, and Harvard (Berquist, 1977). Harvard was particularly influential in general education. Its first model, introduced in 1909, called for a system of concentrations or majors and distribution requirements in three fields outside the major. In 1945, the Harvard "Redbook" on *General Education in a Free Society* called for a new core curriculum covering Western civilization, literary texts, scientific principles, and English composition, with additional courses in humanities, social sciences, and natural sciences. To this day, the distribution model of general education and the idea of multidisciplinary breadth of knowledge gained through a survey of disciplines are closely linked.

These weren't the only values associated with interdisciplinarity. Steven Coleman depicts today's advocates of a greater interdisciplinary approach as inheritors of a movement in the 1920s and 1930s to see college as a platform for social change. This movement was influenced by progressive reform and guided by alternative social philosophies and values. Interdisciplinarity was not the only variable. Yet, it was evident in the founding ideals of Antioch, Sarah Lawrence, Bennington, Bard, Goddard, and New College at Columbia University. Donald Tewksbury of Bard College promoted an inverted curriculum designed to move from concentrations to study of other fields and, ultimately, general survey courses that explored interrelations in interdepartmental seminars. The course of experimentation did not always run smoothly. At Antioch, many faculty were skeptical about taking a more interdisciplinary approach. Coleman points to lack of training and skills in order to oversee independent studies and to extend beyond the boundaries of their fields of expertise. These institutions, moreover, did not have a significant impact on mainstream higher education. Yet, they spawned a generation of faculty and students with experience in alternative education, while marking a historical link between the concept of interdisciplinarity and education for social change.

Moving into the watershed era of the 1960s and 70s, Joy Kliewer revisited "six islands of educational difference"—Pitzer College, New College of the University of South Florida, Hampshire College, the University of Wisconsin-Green, the University of California, Santa Cruz, and The Evergreen Sate College. She portrays them as distinctive niches where innovation was nourished, a composite "hidden jewel" in American higher education that offered a "refuge" from mainstream practices. Once again, interdisciplinarity was not the only variable.

Innovative institutions, Kliewer found, are also defined by their commitments to student-centered education, egalitarianism, experiential learning, and an institutional focus on teaching. She also drew a number of lessons about the ideal conditions for innovation. Establishing open and flexible structures, rewarding interdisciplinary teaching, retaining founding faculty and administrators, and recruiting new ones committed to innovation have been key factors.

At Pitzer, faculty formed field groups with similar interests. At New College, there were no disciplinary departments, academic deans, credit or units, and letter grades. At Hampshire, students took basic studies in four interdisciplinary schools, followed by advanced seminars and an independent project or thesis. At Green Bay, the environment and problem-focused education were primary foci of the new university, with the option of a comajor in a disciplinary field. At Santa Cruz, small residential cluster colleges were intended to function as interdisciplinary teaching communities, alongside research-oriented disciplinary units. At Evergreen, a program of coordinated studies and a commitment to a holistic, collaborative model nurtured interactions. Outcomes differed. Interdisciplinarity remains a prominent feature at Hampshire and Evergreen. In contrast, the experimental promise faded at Santa Cruz. At Green Bay, pressures to accommodate disciplinary and professional interests mounted, though the central organizing units are still interdisciplinary departments, and a critical mass of founding faculty and administrators have kept the spirit of innovation alive.

Interdisciplinarity Today

Alternative colleges were not the only sites of interdisciplinary activities. The concept cannot be understood without factoring in the rise of new knowledge fields. This development was not new. In the 1930s and 1940s, American studies and area studies emerged. The process escalated in the 1960s and 1970s. The intellectual landscape changed with the rise of black studies, women's studies, ethnic studies, environmental studies, urban studies, and other interdisciplinary field studies. The process continues in the current expansion of cultural studies and cognitive science. The rise of new hybrid disciplines, such as social psychology and molecular biology, further complexified the academy and the definition of interdisciplinarity. By the 1990s, the only reliable map of interdisciplinarity would be an overlay of transparencies or a hologram.

The answer to the second question in the closing plenary—"What are the differences between now and the 1960s?"—is shaped in no small part by the current plurality of interdisciplinary activities. In compiling the latest directory of undergraduate programs, Alan Edwards, Jr. (1996) found a wide range of examples:

- interdisciplinary institutions, cluster colleges
- majors, programs, courses, study groups
- general education, liberal arts/liberal studies
- honors, adult education
- humanities, social sciences, natural science
- applied science/technology
- peace/justice studies
- religious/religion studies
- urban studies
- film/media studies
- human developmental gerontology
- science, technology, and society
- environmental studies, neuroscience
- American studies, ethnic/cultural/area studies
- women's/gender studies
- international studies, world/global studies
- educational studies/teacher preparation

Despite downsizing and retrenchment, many programs have originated or been substantially revised since the first edition of the directory in 1986. The concept has also diversified. Interdisciplinary fields have developed or expanded dramatically in areas as varied as cognitive science, neuroscience, leadership studies, bioengineering, cultural studies, politics and economics, and teacher education for integrated middle schools. "Interdisciplinary studies," Edwards concluded, "are not only alive and well, but are also growing and evolving in new and exciting directions" (pp. vii, xi-xii).

The popular metaphor of knowledge explosion signals another development. New cross-fertilizations, symbolized by Clifford Geertz's phrase "blurred genres" (1980), are changing the character of modern disciplines. The intellectual scene is replete with examples—in studies of family systems, the child, gender, culture, language and communication, the body, the mind, disease and health, and the evolution of the earth. As a result, the majority of fields today have what Carol Geary Schneider calls a certain "multidisciplinary" thrust, whether deemed "disciplinary" or "interdisciplinary" (1997, p. 238). Citing one of the conference sponsors, the

American Council of Learned Societies, host Barbara Leigh Smith repeated a widely held belief in her opening address. "Boundary issues get very muddy." McNeal and Weaver concurred, describing many disciplinary categories as "incoherent ensembles of diverse subject matters, approaches, and even epistemologies that colleagues frequently have more intellectual affinity with individuals from other disciplines." One of the invited scholars, Jerry Gaff, mentioned the example of biology. At the University of Washington, the biology program is drawn from ten different biologically intensive specializations.

Interdisciplinarity today cannot be understood without factoring in an added imperative at the heart of the Evergreen conference—innovative pedagogy. The team from St. Lawrence University put the matter succinctly. When faculty engage in interdisciplinary teaching, pedagogy becomes "intentional." William Newell places interdisciplinarity within a larger family of forms of "integrative learning" that draw on multiple perspectives and integrate them into a more comprehensive understanding. Interest in integration spans disciplines, cultures, subcultures, and individual life experiences. Since the 1960s, faculty in experimental colleges have been pioneers in developing interdisciplinary curricula, along with strategies of collaborative learning, experiential learning, learning communities, living/learning, multicultural learning, service-learning, and study abroad. The hallmark of experimental colleges, Newell speculates, may well be the integration of insights from diverse perspectives.

Newell was not alone in attributing growing interest in innovative pedagogies in the mainstream to the influence of alternative institutions. In these enclaves of innovation, new pedagogies were cultivated. So were a number of related practices, including narrative evaluation, team teaching, internships, self-paced learning, individualized study, community based education, hands-on experience in the sciences, student portfolios and self-assessment, project-based learning, and greater awareness of links with other disciplines. Two chapters in this volume take up one of the most vital new areas—science education.

Janet Ott focused on student-active science. Problem- and question-based teaching foster interdisciplinary study in areas as varied as the genetics of sickle cell anemia and the learning of calculus through problem solving. In active learning, the older metaphor of coverage of a fixed body of knowledge shifts to engagement and collaboration. The role model of a teacher shifts, in turn, to a guide, not a font of knowledge, encyclopedia, or reference librarian. Gary Bornzin described a course on feminist perspectives on science. Students' projects range from historical and philosophical inquiries to environmental and ethical studies of women scientists, controversies in and the frontiers of science, and the medical system. Feminism is not an isolated epistemology. Bornzin emphasizes its connections with multiple ways of knowing and other epistemologies, including African American studies, Native American studies, ecological studies, and new approaches to science such as chaos theory, complexity theory, fuzzy logic, new physics, new biology, and ecofeminism. Comparably, in a paper included in the conference packet, Ann Filmyr urged proponents of women's studies to enter into coalitions and alliances with other interdisciplinary fields, including environmental studies. The gains are both practical, in political survival, and intellectual, in forging a shared epistemology and social purpose.

Interdisciplinarity does not end at the campus gate. A commitment to bridging the divide between academic and experiential learning was a defining trait of the earlier experimental institutions Coleman described. Integration, though, is not automatic. In focusing on a site of growing interest today, service-learning, Oates and Gaither contrast a simple apprenticeship model, added onto existing disciplinary and professional courses, with a learning community approach that takes a broader and integrative view of problems and possible solutions. The boundaries of liberal education and professional education are crossed in this and other innovative formats. "Boundaries are breaking down," Gene Rice commented one morning, "recreating social work around reflective practice."

Communication, media, and the arts are also important sites of integration. At the Maryland Institute College of Art, a set of three, team-taught interdisciplinary experiences emanated from restructuring of the illustration department, part of a broadening institutional interest in interdisciplinary studies. In describing a general education arts course, Marian Czarnik and Richard Runkel moved beyond the academic predilection for language-based strategies of teaching arts to include experiential approaches in studio arts. Mark Pedelty was equally mindful of the academic bias towards print that has retarded inclusion of oral, aural, visual, and kinesthetic forms of exposition. Students themselves inhabit a multisensory, multimedia world. Pedelty calls for the kind of "communicative integration" in the classroom that is being developed in the expanding research fields of communications, media studies, and cultural studies. Multiple modes of exposition in the classroom, he suggests, rest on the same theoretical foundation as interdisciplinary studies: "Basic skills and competencies need not be segregated one from another and then separately concentrated into whole courses in order to be effectively learned." Wider recognition of visual language and orality may also lead to better understanding and appreciation of student diversity, a goal Czarnik and Runkel link with Howard Gardner's theory of multiple intelligences.

Definition

Even this brief sketch indicates why the word "interdisciplinary" carries an overload of linguistic freight today. Confusion and disagreement on campuses is a common signal of this overload. Some are new to the concept. "I'm still learning the jargon," one participant admitted. Yet, even veterans do not always agree. There is, to begin with, more than one form of interdisciplinarity. Women's studies, cultural studies, and new disciplinary practices that seek to transform existing structures exhibit a "critical interdisciplinarity" that contrasts with the "instrumental interdisciplinarity" of collaborative teamwork to solve economic and technological problems. The latter motivation is particularly strong in biomedicine, engineering, computers, and industrial production. Interdisciplinary general education focused on themes of culture and democracy differs, in turn.

Participants also disagreed about what constitutes a "genuine" interdisciplinary approach. Because a significant number of participants came from places committed to learning communities, collaborative teaching and learning loomed large. One individual uttered dismay that the leader of a session did not do team teaching. "It isn't even interdisciplinary," she charged. Yet, as Davis (1995) points out in his book on the subject, in reality far more team planning occurs than team teaching. Others believe that explicit clarification and contrasting of disciplinary perspectives is a criterion. Yet, McNeal and Weaver reported that at Hampshire, interdisciplinary education, in and of itself, does not appear to be especially interesting to most faculty and administrators. "Adisciplinary," they suggested, might be a better description of education at Hampshire than "interdisciplinary."

In an exercise on definition in one of the concurrent sessions, Donald Finkel found differing assumptions among the sixteen faculty and administrators who attended. Four ways of conceiving interdisciplinary pedagogy emerged:

- study of a common theme
- group inquiry into a problem of common interest
- a learning community
- creation of individually meaningful perspectives whereby students make sense of their worlds.

Six participants defined interdisciplinary teaching as theme-based. The purpose, for them, is to help students make connections between disciplines. Four of them believe "interdisciplinary" is an appropriate label, though a fifth prefers "multidisciplinary." Four of them felt team teaching is required, while one hedged. For this group, interdisciplinarity rests on a disciplinary foundation. In contrast, a second group of six participants defined interdisciplinary teaching as inquiry-based. Only one considered "interdisciplinary" a good label, and only one felt team teaching is required. Education, for them, flows out of classroom inquiry into a problem or question. Students' acts of knowing, moreover, are placed above teachers' acts of teaching. Finkel described this process as a reversal of figure and ground. When addressing the question of health, for instance, the focus is not on how psychology and biology bear on the question, making disciplinary connections and perspectives ends in themselves. They become tools for making sense of a problem. Of the remaining four participants, two conceived of interdisciplinary teaching in terms of learning communities. Neither considered team teaching a requirement or "interdisciplinary" an appropriate adjective. The remaining two had a more individual approach, emphasizing personal integration. Both considered "interdisciplinary" an appropriate label, but only one thought team teaching is required. Of the final two participants, one emphasized the role that different disciplines play in influencing students' worldviews. The other stressed the need for students to formulate and integrate their own perspectives on course themes and issues.

Taking his turn at the question of definition in the closing plenary, Robert Benedetti reminded us that terms dealing with knowledge evolve. Over time, the meaning of interdisciplinary has become diffuse. Exhorting the audience to go beyond interdisciplinarity, Benedetti contended the term masks other questions, especially the purpose of learning. Gaff and Arthur Chickering concurred in a mid-conference plenary. Efforts to create greater coherence and connected learning, Gaff reported, are visible across the entire curriculum—across general education, majors, and interdisciplinary programs. They are further apparent in courses that connect across disciplines and larger societal issues. Nonetheless, it is a time of trends and counter trends. Specialization and integration, fragmentation and coherence are ongoing tensions, not only across higher education but among conference participants themselves.

Like Benedetti, Chickering emphasized that interdisciplinary studies address one of the fundamental issues facing higher education—purpose. They are a way of realizing meaning and purpose in powerful ways. They enable looking at a social issue or problem area through the insights of multiple perspectives. They also address the question of social responsibility and citizenship, thereby engaging democracy. The changing role of content is no less important. Conceptualization of content is shifting from information to be acquired, concepts to be learned, and particular skills to be gained, to knowledge in the service of larger understandings, larger perspectives, and applications to larger social and individual concerns. This change parallels the shift in pedagogy from coverage to engagement. Interdisciplinary studies, Chickering added, typically address complex content, making them powerful vehicles for strengthening generic competencies that are not typically strengthened by conventional pedagogy and assessments.

Institutional Stories

Participants agreed about ideal conditions for innovation. Many, however, came from new and nontraditional structures where ideal conditions are not the norm—in public institutions, in community colleges, and in environments dominated by a counter ethos. The mix of comments testified to this fact, ranging from "We could never do that" to "We never worry about that." Despite local differences, the value of meeting together was clear. "What you're facing," one individual remarked, "is exactly what we're facing." A member of the team from St. Lawrence University put the matter succinctly: "We share common views of knowledge, but we are in very different institutions." As the conversation continued, new questions signaled a turn toward sharing ideas and collaborative problem solving. "How do you do that? "Have you ever tried . . . ?" "Have you read . . . ?" Kathryn Crabbe reminded everyone that we can't always see things where we sit. The differences in "where we sit" were readily apparent in the invitation to join in this working conference.

Organizers envisioned three categories of participants: holistically organized institutions, institutions with major commitments to interdisciplinary studies (IDS), and new alternatives and community colleges.

Category One: Holistically Organized Institutions

- Alverno College
- Antioch University
- The Evergreen State College
- Hampshire College
- Empire State College
- Other institutions classified in this type include New College of University of South Florida, MacMaster, St. Mary's, College of the Atlantic, and Pitzer College

The present is a dialog with the past and the future. Antioch College, a division of Antioch University in Ohio, retains a founding commitment to integrating experiential and theoretical learning that dates to the 1920s. In 1995, faculty introduced a new curriculum reducing the number of traditional majors and introducing eight interdisciplinary majors in arts; history, philosophy, and religious studies; physical sciences; environmental and biological sciences; self, society, and culture; social and global studies; cultural and interdisciplinary studies; and a self-designed major. With the initiation of a new year-round calendar in 1996, team-taught interdisciplinary summer institutes became available. Antioch's Seattle campus offers an MA completion in liberal arts, giving students the option of defining their concentrations in terms of traditional disciplinary fields or interdisciplinary or problem-centered foci. The BA program is portfolio- and degree-process based. Each student negotiates a program of study, and faculty are expected to act as both generalists and representatives of their particular academic disciplines. Changes on both campuses document widening inclusion of new interdisciplinary knowledge fields in the curriculum, greater concern for process-based learning, and an increase in self-designed majors around the country.

Comparable changes have occurred at two institutions with a strong liberal arts tradition. Alverno College, a four-year college for women, has gained a national reputation for ability-based education and outcomes. Interdisciplinary core courses are required of all students in the general education program. In addition, Alverno offers an integrated major in community leadership and development, a minor in integrated arts and humanities, and a global perspectives support area. Hampshire College, which admitted its first students in 1970, is described as "an evolving and thoroughly interdisciplinary education program." McNeal and Weaver highlight the interplay of four variables:

1) a divisional examination system, in which students design much of their educational program

2) organization of faculty into interdisciplinary schools

3) the nature of Hampshire courses

4) opportunities for faculty to develop as teachers and scholars

Until recently, four schools anchored the curriculum: humanities and arts, social science, natural science, and cognitive science and cultural studies. A recent reorganization, to deal in part with the increasing difficulty of combining cognitive science and cultural studies resulted in three core schools: humanities and arts, social science, and natural science, and two clusters: cognitive science and interarts. Of approximately 200 interdisciplinary courses, about one-third are team-taught. Organization into schools fosters "nondisciplinary connections." The school structure was a striking feature of pioneer interdisciplinary experiments of the 1960s and 1970s. In Europe, the new universities of Sussex, Roskilde, and Tromso organized research and learning into similar structures. At Hampshire, students negotiate concentrations with a committee, resulting in a formal contract of roughly two years of question- and theme-based work. The culmination is an extended senior thesis, a defining feature of full-scale interdisciplinary programs.

At Hampshire, an institutional ideology of innovation and participation creates a shared ethos of responsibility and commitment. Yet, the demands of interdisciplinary inquiry also create a familiar workload pressure. The labor-intensive character of Hampshire's educational mission was underestimated in the original design, necessitating changes in teaching load and clearer guidelines and timetables for completion of student work. Crossing of the divide between education and research has been an unforeseen positive outcome. Student-designed projects bring faculty from different areas together in novel and often long-standing collaborations, including coauthored research with students. Co-teaching within and among schools also creates an opportunity to integrate teaching and scholarship. Faculty have the flexibility to teach in areas that are supported by specialized journals and interdisciplinary associations in the areas of feminism, the Third World, race and ethnicity, cultural studies, environment, AIDS, cognitive science, college teaching, and critical heterodox scholarship.

The Evergreen State College, founded in 1971, also retains its founding commitment to being a different kind of public institution. Interdisciplinarity is embodied, philosophically, in a holistic conception of knowledge and, structurally, in coordinated studies. First- and second-year students take core programs of interdisciplinary, team-taught, theme- and problem-based courses that combine seminars, individual instruction, lectures, field trips, and laboratories. Bachelors degrees are offered in arts or in science. Graduate degrees are offered in environmental studies, public administration, and a master of teaching. Students can also take programs in environmental studies; expressive arts; scientific inquiry; language, culture, and text; Native American studies; and social science. Like other institutions, Evergreen has changed. Reflecting on its 25th anniversary, Barbara Leigh Smith analyzed the changes.

As the result of an accreditation review in 1974, the overall curriculum was organized around interdisciplinary specialty areas to create more sequence, coherence, and predictability. A portion of the curriculum was repeated, not created each year, and several career-oriented areas were established, such as management and the public interest. In addition, an evening program for state workers, an upper-division program in the city of Vancouver, and limited part-time studies in Olympia were added. In recent years, further changes have been made, including the addition of a new bachelor of science degree, new graduate programs, state training programs, interinstitutional programs to share resources, and designated career pathways through the curriculum. The college's narrative transcripts have also been simplified and more predictability and continuity established in the curriculum. Translating innovative programs into disciplinary equivalencies is a response to external pressure that all alternative institutions face. Even as the college moved in new directions, though, it remained innovative. A teacher education program is unique in its use of team-taught coordinated studies. Now reclassified from a regional state college to a statewide public liberal arts college, Evergreen remains committed to coordinating interdisciplinary study in conjunction with four other core educational values of personal engagement in learning, linking theory and practice, collaborative work, and teaching across differences.

Category Two: Institutions with Major Commitments to Interdisciplinary Studies

- Earlham College
- Fairhaven College at Western Washington University
- Gallatin School at New York University
- The Hutchins School of Liberal Studies at Sonoma State University
- Western College, Miami University
- St. Lawrence University
- SUNY Potsdam
- University of Wisconsin, Madison
- Watauga College at Appalachian State University
- Other institutions classified in this type include Johnston C. Smith College, University of Hartford, Marlboro College, Eckerd College, New School, and the Interdisciplinary Studies Program at Wayne State University

Longitudinal perspective is equally revealing in category two. Earlham College, a small private liberal arts institution founded in 1847, continues to be shaped by its Quaker heritage. In addition to a typical array of liberal arts disciplinary majors, Earlham now offers a large number of interdisciplinary majors. They include peace and global studies, human development and social relations, Japanese studies, women's studies, African and African American studies, museum studies, management, international studies, and minors in Jewish studies and in legal studies. Reflecting on their experience, Clark, Lacey, and Bingham stress that interdisciplinary efforts must be supported even when their scope and complexity cast doubt on their survival. The long-term character and commitments of the institution at large should be considered. The most successful programs, they found, have been "built deep into the currency of the institution," integrated into the system of requirements or recognized options for majors and minors. These programs also captured the enthusiasm of faculty and students. Earlham has never embraced the all-or-nothing posture of jettisoning departmental structures. As a result, interdisciplinary programs are vulnerable. At the same time, they conclude, there is a openness at Earlham to emerging interdisciplinary activities that might not have occurred if a single, institution-wide model had been chosen.

A significant number of interdisciplinary programs around the country are alternative formats for fulfilling general education requirements. Watauga College, a division of the department of interdisciplinary studies at Appalachian State University, is an alternative, two-year, residential interdisciplinary general education program. The living/learning environment fosters integration of process and content both within and beyond the academic curriculum. In addition to taking ten-hour blocks of courses each semester, first-year students take Watauga Chautaqua, a weekly discussion meeting. Faculty receive tenure consideration with the department, and they have the ability to create courses without being subject to full institutional review. Fairhaven College at Western Washington University is also an alternative general education program. Since its founding in 1967, Fairhaven has evolved into an undergraduate cluster-college learning community that features multidisciplinary study, collaborative teaching and learning, curricular innovation, and a commitment to social responsibility. The core curriculum acquaints students with a broad range of fields and their relationships. Elective seminars are topic-based, and students may take independent studies. A student-designed interdisciplinary concentration, leading to a bachelor of arts, may include coursework from several disciplines as well as independent studies and a senior project.

Watauga and Fairhaven are smaller institutions in relatively rural settings. Larger and metropolitan institutions are also important sites of interdisciplinary study. The University of Wisconsin, Madison, is a major research university with a long history of innovations, spanning the Meilkeljohn Experimental College (1927–1930), integrated liberal studies (1948 to the present), the Bradley learning community (1995 to the present), and the Chadbourne learning community (1997 to the present). The Gallatin School at New York University has evolved from a university without walls to a regular unit featuring self-designed concentrations, internships, and independent studies. The school combines access to a wide array of NYU courses and more focused interdisciplinary courses. Creation of a wider interface within an institution at large is a notable development in the history of interdisciplinary education. New Century College at George Mason University, established in 1995, offers coordinated studies learning communities leading to a BA or a BA degree in integrated studies. Students can develop their own major or follow a specified interdisciplinary track. Experiential learning and annual portfolios are key features of student work. In many cases, an interdisciplinary unit does double duty, serving as a site for a specific program and a platform for further experimentation. At George Mason, degree programs in Social Work, for adult returning students, and in honors were added in 1997. A Center for Field Studies has also become part of the college.

The Hutchins School of Liberal Studies at Sonoma State University is also a lower-division alternative general education program, in addition to offering an upper-division two-track major in liberal studies and a minor in integrative studies. A more recent development, the Hutchins Center for Interdisciplinary Learning, manages a variety of off-campus programs aimed at learning community development. The process of curriculum building is the heart of interdisciplinary learning in the program. The school admitted its first class in 1969. The curriculum, Les Adler recalls, was built from the ground up by a group of interdisciplinary-minded faculty who were committed to the ideals of interdisciplinarity and education as a community process. They organized into teams to create large thematic units. The result was a sequence of integrated courses focused on such topics as "The Human Enigma," "In Search of Self," "Exploring the Unknown," and "Challenge and Response in the Modern World." The seminar is "the crucible" of the Hutchins School. It is an interactive and collaborative exploration of complex topics and materials. Faculty and students are colearners in a process that transforms their relationship. In a separate chapter, Susan Fiksdal presented a sociolinguistic analysis of videotaped seminar conversations in seminars at The Evergreen State College. The pedagogy of voice in the seminar is an important instance of negotiating difference through dialog, a dialog that places authority with the student. Meanings and identities are created within a group, not dictated by the teacher or an assigned body of knowledge.

Although participants agreed that moving away from the cultural norms and values of departmental structure is an ideal condition for innovation, new programs continue to emerge in environments dominated by disciplines and departments. Listening to the "ways of the people" revealed in their institutional stories, Sandra Sarkela urged, provides a deeper picture of the parameters of change. Her story of SUNY Potsdam is an example. Potsdam is a small, liberal arts, state-supported college. Despite obstacles of structure and finance, it continues to resurrect interdisciplinary initiatives. After World War II, teacher education, which was the only degree offered until 1962, expanded. One of the results of this expansion was a two-semester learning community called "Expression in the Arts." It was a logical outcome of the school's commitment to music education. The program promoted broad and general liberal arts education along with understanding of interrelationships among arts and literature. Block scheduling of combined classes fostered integration through temporary regrouping of two courses in a specific area. In addition, the entire first-year class met weekly for discussions of expression in the arts, and a school trip to New York City was a fulcrum between semesters.

The character of the institution changed in 1962, when Potsdam became a liberal arts college. In 1969 a new experimental interdisciplinary humanities program was introduced. Taught to sixty juniors and seniors by a committee of five faculty, the program was a higher-level synthesis of knowledge and insights gained in individual courses. In 1977, a School Within a School (SWS) for first-year students began, bringing together science, social science, and humanities. The school emphasized reading of original texts, historical perspective on issues of the modern world, substantial writing assignments, team teaching, and integration. From 1977–1981, the SWS enjoyed strong support, the curriculum was refined, and interdisciplinary connections were clarified and strengthened. Yet, in 1982, the curriculum was reduced from thirty to twenty semester hours. The interests of high school graduates were also becoming increasingly vocational.

The demise of the School Within a School is not the end of the story. "Institutional memories don't die quickly," Sarkela advises. In 1981–1982, a new Dean's Freshman Seminar arose, committed to cultivating the breadth and interconnectedness of liberal arts. Then, in 1987, a new initiative in general education began. This course of reform did not run smoothly, but the effort provided a mechanism for developing a new interdisciplinary learning communities project. Founded in 1992, the project actively explores connections between subject areas. Paired, clustered, and linked courses foster interdisciplinary learning and a sense of academic community. Among other course clusters, students can participate in an Adirondacks coordinated environmental studies program that integrates five general education courses focused on the region. The project has survived for several years, growing as faculty perceive a need to reconnect with colleagues and other disciplines. The *Potsdam People* newspaper, Sarkela reports, recently referred to the institution as "at the forefront" of experiment, though "prudently and judiciously." The traditional interdisciplinary curriculum was eliminated, but Potsdam has a heritage of education and music that perpetuates an interdisciplinary view of teacher education. Links to that tradition have aided reform efforts through the years, proving that traditional values within an organization can support innovation. At the same time, Potsdam has been responsive to developments nationwide, such as environmental studies, learning communities, and a search for greater connectedness in liberal arts and sciences.

The story of two programs at St. Lawrence University highlights the dynamics of organizational culture. The first-year program (FYP) is a required, university-wide, year-long program of interdisciplinary courses and experiences. New students live in one of twelve FYP residential colleges. Courses meet twice weekly in plenary sessions with forty-five students and three faculty from different disciplines. In addition, they meet twice weekly in smaller seminars overseen by a single faculty member, who also serves as an advisor. Over time, Grant Cornwell and Eve Stoddard report, the FYP has promoted a shift in faculty culture at St. Lawrence. The "fault line" that emerged between those teaching in FYP and those teaching within department bounds was, in significant part, pedagogy. In its early days, the FYP was a rebellious subculture. Its curriculum and pedagogy differed from traditional norms of teaching and learning. The boundaries of content and inquiry and skill development were also challenged, as well as the tradition of solitary teaching and learning. FYP is now securely institutionalized, a gain that is accompanied by a loss. The earlier culture of radical critique has diminished, but the curriculum is a site of sustained and critical reflection on teaching at the university.

The cultural encounters curriculum is an alternative way of satisfying the university's breadth requirement in general education through a core track of international and multicultural courses. In describing the curriculum, Cornwell and Stoddard emphasize parallels between interdisciplinary inquiry and multi- or intercultural encounters. Multicultural learning is a form of interculturalism that works at the intersections of disciplines and cultures, identifying commonalties and differences then building on commonalties to mitigate conflict. Weighing the impact of both programs, they liken campus communities to larger societies. Both have dominant cultures, stratification, alternative, resistant, and emerging cultures. As interdisciplinary studies make their way within existing cultures, new cultures emerge through critical engagement of new questions and practices. Echoing recent scholarship on the nature of interdisciplinary communication, they liken the form of communication that emerges to a Creole language and culture. A new set of discourses and practices draws on particular disciplines and cultures but is not reducible to any one of them. "Creolized disciplines" can be alternative, resistant, or emergent. Women's studies, for instance, can be viewed as an emergent discipline with its own canons, methods, and issues. It is also alternative or resistant to traditional discursive practices of disciplines.

Innovation along the lines of FYP and cultural encounters, Cornwell and Stoddard warn, is "not for the faint of heart." It also moves beyond older notions of interdisciplinarity. "We've transcended interdisciplinarity," they declare. Instead of simply combining existing disciplines and approaches, they are creating new forms of knowledge, education, and institutional structures. The difference is embodied in the new "cross-disciplinary" and "transnational" paradigm for study of cultural interactions. Reminiscent of changes at Hampshire, new professional identities have also emerged. The teaching and research interests of at least nine faculty trained originally in Eurocentric fields have moved into new areas, becoming more self-reflective and global in scope. Among those trained in area studies, an increasingly cross-disciplinary theoretical development is evident. A new European studies program based on multiculturalism has also been created, and European abroad programs have begun to take a more multicultural approach. Additionally, a number of faculty have changed their pedagogies to include more self-reflection through writing.

The internal dynamics of the faculty seminar that nourishes innovation at St. Lawrence are not without dissent, including conflicting views of feminism. Yet, there is a shared commitment to negotiating differences across disciplines and across cultures. A substantial percentage of St. Lawrence faculty now share the view that continuing to question one's own knowledge and assumptions is important for those who practice the profession of teaching. This commitment, though, is enacted in faculty seminars and interdisciplinary program boards, not departments, which retain control over hiring and tenure and promotion. In an annual ritual that occurs nationwide, participation of individual faculty in interdisciplinary programs must be negotiated. This political economy underscores the "fragility" of such programs and the difficult position that junior faculty, especially, are put in when juggling two institutional cultures. The metaphor of department as "home" and interdisciplinary program faculty as "prodigal sons and daughters" is a gripping reminder that a "gain" to the life of an entire institution is often perceived as a "loss" to a department. The need to "balance the power" remains an ongoing challenge. At St. Lawrence, greater public recognition of programs and tying department positions to participation in the FYP in job ads have helped. Putting a member from outside a department on a search committee helps too, as well as a stronger role for interdisciplinary evaluation in mid-probationary and tenure reviews. In the end, Cornwell and Stoddard conclude, the faculty culture at St. Lawrence is "radically different" than it was ten years ago. The affiliation, identity, and faculty development that derive from new interdisciplinary coalitions is a powerful reason.

Category Two: New Alternatives: Interdisciplinary Colleges

- Arizona International University, Tucson
- Arizona State University, West Campus
- Maryland Institute, College of Arts
- University of Washington, Bothell and Tacoma
- In addition, Florida Gulf Coast University and California State University, Monterey Bay are classified in this type

Community Colleges Significantly Organized Around Interdisciplinary Studies

- Lower Columbia College
- North Seattle Community College
- Seattle Central Community College
- Skagit Valley College
- In addition, De Anza College, Delta College, and Los Medanos College are classified in this category

Just as the meaning of interdisciplinarity has changed, our notions of alternative and mainstream have changed At the welcoming banquet, Smith remarked that the historical alternative colleges were conceived as a place "free of distractions." The new kids on the block, though, often work in places full of distractions and serve new and more complicated agendas. California State University, Monterey Bay was founded in 1994 as "the California State University's 21st campus for the 21st century." It is organized around four learning centers and a graduate programs office. The founding principles were interinstitutional collaboration, an international orientation, and a pluralistic community that serves historically underserved populations in innovative ways. Integration is broadly conceived at Monterey, bridging conventional boundaries of sciences and the arts and humanities, liberal studies and professional training, modern learning technology and pedagogy for a liberal education, work and learning, and service and reflection. Representatives from two new institutions in Arizona provided a fuller picture of the challenges of creating new institutions today.

Arizona International Campus of the University of Arizona opened in 1990 with a mandate to prepare students for an increasingly competitive, dynamic, and global society. Creating a new institution, Anne Scott, Celestino Fernandez, and Edwin Clausen recall, presented both opportunities and challenges. The international campus was designed to provide a practical, liberal arts education through small classes, faculty-student interaction, a comprehensive assessment program, service-learning, career internships, and a capstone project. Interdisciplinarity is regarded as the best way of fostering preparation for productive careers and lifelong learning. In lieu of traditional disciplinary-based departments and colleges, an academic house serves as a community for about ten faculty and 150 students for the first two years of core courses. After that, they take courses throughout the institution in particular areas of study. A core program provides broad exposure to four areas of human knowledge. Clustered theme-focused classes approximate team teaching without higher costs typically associated with this arrangement. Course themes include civic responsibility, sustainable development, international business, technology and society. A beginning course, "Becoming a Fully Educated Person," provides a philosophical rationale and operational basis for the curriculum, along with practical skills to help them in other courses. Other courses, likewise, extend a broad spectrum of knowledge and skills and competencies that cut across disciplines.

At Arizona International, as elsewhere, things didn't always work out as planned. A significant number of new hires had PhDs from interdisciplinary programs or vitas that indicated multiple professional experiences. Almost none came from fully interdisciplinary institutions, however, even if they had worked in interdisciplinary programs. Faculty also had different perspectives on what interdisciplinarity means and have been reluctant to let go of disciplinary ties, needing the familiar comfort of a safe ground and job security. Even though team teaching is not done, a team approach is used for accomplishing a variety of tasks and organizational planning. The team approach keeps the organization more flat and cost efficient, ensuring wide representation in decision-making and helping to break down barriers of discipline-based structure. Although the pressures of normalization are great, as Arizona International moves into a plan linking faculty rewards to student outcomes, an imperative that has undermined interdisciplinary programs elsewhere, faculty are working to include interdisciplinary learning outcomes tied to skills and competencies that cut across disciplines. A learning contract, begun during the first year and revisited at least yearly, will ensure extended faculty-student interaction, along with a portfolio.

Arizona State University's West Campus opened in 1988 with the potential for coordinating innovative programs in an interdisciplinary vision of interlinked faculty. In a gripping tale, Joseph Comprone recalls what happened over the past decade. Not all founding faculty were hired with the interdisciplinary mission uppermost in their minds, and, as the campus grew, many of the students being recruited lacked interest in interdisciplinarity. They found program descriptions to be confusing and unfamiliar. Initial enrollment benchmarks were also set too high, resulting in enrollment pressure that eroded the strength of interdisciplinarity. On the surface, the names of five core interdisciplinary departments beckoned greater integration—American studies, interdisciplinary arts and performance, integrative studies, life science, social and behavioral studies, and women's studies. Yet enrollment pressure took precedence over innovation. A discipline-based psychology program grew, but the arts and performance program, for instance, did not. As a result, interdisciplinary development was impeded.

Like Scott, Fernandez, and Clausen, Comprone emphasizes that maintaining interdisciplinarity requires regular and ongoing participation and commitment. Comprone identified two dichotomies that are not unique to Arizona West. When traditional departments and interdisciplinary programs exist side-by-side, interdisciplinary faculty are often the first to be driven back into their special fields and become isolated, especially in a budget crunch. The need for efficiency and the need for quality also conflict. Enrollment, workload, and cost pressures often relegate discussion of programmatic quality to the bottom of the agenda in departmental meetings. Interdisciplinary programming, though, typically demands fuller discussion than familiar disciplinary categories. Attention to the pragmatics of department business left little time for the kind of intellectual intensity and creativity vital to nurturing strong interdisciplinary programs. A paradoxical planning emerged as departments with strong enrollments, better able to argue for new positions, superficially "camouflaged" interdisciplinary curriculum behind disciplinary majors. Interdisciplinary majors with smaller enrollments, such as American studies and social and behavioral sciences, were in less favorable positions because of smaller numbers.

The administrative structure of Arizona State, West acknowledged the need for collective practical decisions, housed in departments. But, it did not foster making intellectual and curricular linkages across disciplines. They don't happen "naturally." They take work, Comprone emphasizes, ongoing work. Many interdisciplinary initiatives, moreover, are motivated by productivity and efficiency, more than intellectual creativity. His six years in the dean's chair convinced him that an institution wanting to acknowledge "the inherent complexity and integrated nature of knowledge in contemporary society"—the new mantra of today's academy—"must acknowledge that departments are budgetary, personnel, and curricular 'holding companies"' where decisions are made based on practical constraints. Departments and learning communities can coexist. Indeed, many interdisciplinary programs today make their way in environments where departments are dominant. It takes, though, a "visibly bicameral structure." Comprone calls for recognition of the "creative tension" of the functional and the intellectual that nurtures creativity and communication on a long-term basis. The pristine world of total administrative focus or complete interdisciplinary integration, one of the hallmark characteristics of earlier alternative institutions, is no longer possible in today's world of higher education, given the friction between internal and external pressures. Learning to live with the dichotomies is the condition of interdisciplinary innovation today.

The University of Washington, Bothell campus is a pivotal example. Established in 1989, Bothell provides upper-division and graduate programs for community college transfer students and area residents. Bothell represents a new articulation between the traditional university and the growing population of students who take their first two years, at lesser cost, in community colleges. Interdisciplinarity has gained heightened visibility in this subcategory of institutions. Representatives of community colleges in Washington state who attended the Evergreen conference fleshed out the picture of interdisciplinarity more fully.

At Lower Columbia College, learning communities were initiated in 1984, as a result of collaboration among faculty and administrators aimed at creating interdisciplinary connections between discrete outcomes in arts and sciences. Integrative studies present a unified theme developed by faculty who team-teach a course accompanied by a writing component. Linked studies couple theme-based studies taught by an individual faculty member with a writing component. A capstone graduation requirement for students intending to transfer to institutions of higher learning is taken after completing communications, quantitative skills, and added credit requirements. Capstone, which may be research or performance based, is the occasion for incorporating and synthesizing material from at least two disciplines. At North Seattle Community College, students take a minimum of ten credits of integrated courses or coordinated studies programs. Higher retention has been a significant outcome of the coordinated studies format. Results indicate greater likelihood of reenrolling in subsequent semesters, higher grades, and greater likelihood of graduation. Seattle Central Community College has a theme-based coordinated studies program modeled after Evergreen. The program has been a cost-effective means of faculty development, since all faculty are in the classroom together, learning from each other and getting wider feedback from students and colleagues. Skagit Valley College also offers collaborative learning in learning communities that merge different fields and disciplines. Two or three faculty are typically assigned to a theme-based learning community. In addition, linked courses connect English writing instruction with a wide range of disciplines. In reflecting on the changes that have occurred, one community college faculty member at the Evergreen conference spoke with conviction about the positive changes. A great deal more needs to be done, though. She singled out the area of assessment, targeted by legislators and the public. She also called for a more equal partnership. While invigorated by sharing stories with faculty from colleges and universities across the country, she lamented that colleges do not necessarily understand what she and her colleagues are dealing with: "We're told what to do, not asked to participate in a dialog."

Revolution or Evolution?

Earlier in this book, Steven Coleman began with a striking epigraph:

> Never before have so many colleges endeavored to initiate programs leading to sound learning or have so many of them earnestly sought information and guidance for their efforts.

Written in 1932 for a yearbook on changes and experiments in liberal arts education, this statement could just as easily have been written today. Whether the current heightened interest in interdisciplinarity and innovation represents the triumph of educational revolution is debatable, however. One participant longed for the romance and excitement of the 1960s. Another opined, more cynically, "I'm still waiting for the revolution."

In a following chapter, Benedetti deems the pedagogical revolution "in full bloom, but not yet made." It is no longer necessary, he judges, to establish the importance of pedagogy or interdisciplinary approaches. Experimental colleges of the 1930s and the 1960s have informed the agendas of influential national educational associations. The challenge now is to extend the elements of experimentation more widely. Invoking the image of a small polity as a model for the university, against the popular competing image of a corporation, he calls for a new bridging of the academy and the world of work through interdisciplinary strategies that were applied, in the past, to fields such as ethnic studies. The lessons of past experiments, though, must not be reduced to mere technologies. Emphasis on method, he cautions, has resulted in neglect of substance, to the detriment of a conception of the unity of institutions that is responsive to social needs.

Benedetti's deliberation on models calls to mind images of interdisciplinarity voiced throughout the conference. Negotiation, mediation, and tension were common terms of reference. Rob Knapp echoed the dialogical thinking of many participants in proposing the metaphor of conversation as a guide for decision-making. Calling to mind Mary Louise Pratt's notion of "contact zones," Knapp portrayed institutions as social spaces where cultures meet, clash, and grapple with each other, moving beyond simply identifying differences to the genuine give-and-take realized in the cultural encounters curriculum at St. Lawrence University. No less than a new epistemology, Jerry Gaff proposed, is needed. Advances in knowledge not foreseen in another era beckon a new model of learning rooted in an alternative theory of knowledge. Interdisciplinarity is at the heart of the new epistemology, not as a solitary variable but as an integrative force intersecting with shared educational principles.

Charles Anderson and Les Adler addressed the question of epistemology in contemplating the educational philosophy of interdisciplinary programs. By their very nature, Anderson contends, these programs are different: "They propose that there are priorities, relationships, among the fields of knowledge." Despite critics' charges that "anything goes," most programs are structured on the basis of a specific, delimited set of disciplinary perspectives that bear on a particular subject. In an environmental studies program, for example, subjects are not simply thrown together helter-skelter. When students are presented with diverse approaches and perspectives, then asked to decide what to make of them, the pragmatic idealism of a relativist epistemology is at work. The purpose of presenting diverse approaches is to create a problematic situation, require introspection, then personal resolution of an enigma. In this regard, Anderson suggests, many interdisciplinary programs, whether orthodox or experimental, can trace their origins at least in part to Dewey. Pragmatism takes a progressive view of knowledge, promoting an open and flexible approach that is experimental and attuned to diverse perspectives and interpretations. Diversity of opinion sets the stage for inquiry, not scuttles it.

Les Adler proposes a new understanding of holism. The university was originally organized as a society of teachers and students gathered to study the meaning of the "whole." The word "whole" is rooted in the Greek *holon;* its Latin translation was *universum.* Belief in a single namable whole no longer informs the academy or society at large. Neither can anyone achieve complete breadth of knowledge or find a specific methodology adequate for doing so. Echoing Gaff's call for a new epistemology, Adler argues that a new universum of knowledge is emerging in the belief that knowledge and education can be rooted in integration, interconnection, and relatedness. Achieving this new epistemology, though, requires rethinking the method and goals of education. Arthur Koestler's notion of "holon" offers a philosophical framework. Koestler combined the Greek word for "whole" with the suffix that suggests a particle or part. A holon has two seemingly contradictory properties of being a whole and part of larger wholes. The university itself, Adler proposes, may be thought of a holon. Autonomous, self-regulating holons—students, courses, departments, divisions, and campuses—exist at each level within the larger system. Each unit is simultaneously in supraordination to its own parts and is a dependent part in subordination to high levels. Hence, each is independent and relational.

Koestler's idea of a "nested" conception points to a different educational vision that shifts the focus to a hierarchical multiplicity of relationships. Education becomes an expanding three-dimensional web. A student's "mastery" of an area of knowledge depends on the ability to integrate, connect, and define a specific area's own patterns and relationship as well as its reciprocal and relational meaning. The image of the student shifts, in kind, to an active pattern-maker at the center of the web, making connections and applying them. This new "aerial" view of knowledge looks across, beyond, and through disciplines to discover and explore fundamental questions and deep connections. Reconceptualizing the teacher's role, a pervasive theme at the Evergreen conference, is part of the process. In describing current developments at Empire State College, founded in 1971 as the "open university" of the SUNY system, James Chen and colleagues called for a new kind of expertise that questions traditional assumptions, offering new models of professional work in the person of an academic generalist who has learned to work with problems that cut across disciplines and themes.

Moving On

The task of making the revolution real requires nothing less than an interdisciplinary collegium. One of the legacies of experimentation, Lauren Raiken reminded conference participants, is a large body of published knowledge. A number of professional groups now produce and disseminate resources, though Jerry Gaff rightly exhorts them to cross their own organizational boundaries, working collaboratively rather than separately. The national commitment that Raiken urges is necessary to reduce the isolation that many conference participants expressed. Connections must be made locally as well. "We're committed deeply in our unit to interdisciplinary education," one participant admitted, "but we don't know what's happening on the rest of our campus." Connections must extend across the K-16 spectrum as well. In a conference session on K-12 education, Mark Pedelty and Carolyn Haynes suggested that people in higher education who want to know about inquiry-based learning and problem-based learning, reciprocal cross-fertilizations of teaching oral and writing communication, and hands-on science education ought to talk to K-12 teachers, who have been doing it for some time.

An academy facing greater pressures to be of service to the larger society must also bridge narrow conceptions of its province. In addition to crossing disciplines, The Evergreen State College crosses the boundaries of theory and practice in five public service centers described by Elliott, Kuckkahn, Lee, and Decker. The Evergreen Center for Educational Improvement helps K-12 educators incorporate values of collaborative learning communities through workshops and planning meetings. A K-12 partnership, the Virtual Science Classroom Project, integrates technology and communication skills into the teaching of ninth-grade science. The Labor Education and Research Center moves beyond the dominant training model of labor education to involve oral history and a variety of disciplines. The New School for Union Organizers provides a forum for discussion of community and labor issues. The Longhouse Education and Cultural Center, a common gathering place for conference participants, is a locus for cross-cultural exchange and education. The center is testimony to Evergreen's involvement with the Native American community. A native economic development arts initiative partners the college and tribes in the area. Interdisciplinary learning occurs in the study of tribal history, in an artist-in-residence program, and in learning about the meaning of designs, natural resource issues, and technical skills.

The focus of both the Kuckkahn, Elliott, Lee, and Decker chapter and Barbara Leigh Smith's chapter on learning communities as a convergence zone for statewide reform is the Washington Center for Improving the Quality of Undergraduate Education. The center is a nationally-imitated model of fostering grassroots partnerships among faculty, staff, and administrators across disciplines, departments, and other educational institutions. The intersectional nature of integration is readily apparent in the confluence of institutional partnerships that promote interdisciplinary programs. Smith's description of multiple sites of revisioning education as community—writing across the curriculum, infusing technology into the curriculum, freshmen interest groups, diversity and cultural pluralism, and assessment—underscores the relational dynamics of interdisciplinary innovation today. Innovation is not a one-shot strategy. It is a complex and holistic way of revisioning institutions.

One of the greatest needs, to reiterate, is crafting a logic of appropriate assessment. Assessment itself, Karl Schilling advocated, must become "interdisciplinary." It is a diagnostic problem solving endeavor aimed at gaining a picture of what is actually happening in a curriculum. Programs that embrace complexity as part of their core identity cannot be served by a single measure or reductionistic strategies. Most interdisciplinary programs are only beginning to formulate assessment plans. At the School of Interdisciplinary Studies at Miami University (Ohio), an instructive change has occurred in thinking about assessment. Efforts began with nationally-normed standardized tests. Over time, Schilling and his colleagues have moved to qualitative measures, such as portfolio analysis, interviews, pre- and post-testing using ACT COMP, and a nationally-normed questionnaire with students' self-reports. Acceptance of the program's courses in the wider university provides an internal measure of validity. Data on graduate-school exams and admissions plus a nationally-normed alumni instrument provide external data. In moving beyond traditional psychometric measurement models and discipline-based approaches, members of the school have incorporated approaches from multiple disciplines and new tools that combine techniques and philosophies, and qualitative and quantitative measures.

"Listening to the sounds" of curriculum, Schilling recounts, produced a more holistic framework, facilitating more powerful descriptions of student learning and valuable feedback for improving the curriculum. Assessment information also enabled the school to make a case for excellence during a time of financial constraint and to secure major grant support. Like Schilling, Peter Tommerup endorses an ethnographic-folkloristic approach. In his account of an assessment study group at Evergreen State, Tommerup stressed the importance of learning "to think culturally" about educational programs. Reminiscent of Sarkela's call to listen to "the ways of the people," Tommerup urged paying attention to the concrete ways in which participants express themselves, evaluate and communicate their experiences, navigate through the maze of requirements and cultural possibilities within their institutions, and try to create and maintain meaningful lives.

John McCann's rich collection of testimonies from students offers a parallel lesson. Beyond what faculty think, we need to know what aspects of interdisciplinary education are visible and meaningful to students. The students in McCann's study were all involved in interdisciplinary theme-based and team-taught programs, most in learning communities or combinations of courses and communities. His data reveal a common valuing of wholeness and interconnectedness, the co-learner partnership with teachers, and active engagement in learning. The dynamic of freedom and responsibility in interdisciplinary learning is not easy. "That was probably the best thing and the hardest thing about an interdisciplinary education for me," one student remarked—"realizing that I could study just about anything that is relevant to me but that I also had to shape it into something that would be meaningful."

Students rarely get the last voice. The Evergreen conference accorded them first and last voice, reminding us that the concept of interdisciplinarity has evolved, however imperfectly, to include them in new ways in an expanding array of sites across the roughly 3,600 post-secondary institutions of the United States. The Evergreen conference is ample proof of the most important lesson of all. We must keep listening.

References

Berquist, W. H. (1977). Curricular practice. In A. W. Chickering, G. H. Quehl, & M. Gee (Eds.), *Developing the college curriculum: A handbook for faculty and administrators* (pp. 77–109). Washington, DC: Council for the Advancement of Small Colleges.

Davis, J. (1995). *Interdisciplinary courses and team teaching: New arrangements for learning.* American Council on Education Series on Higher Education. Phoenix, AZ: Oryx.

Edwards, A., Jr. (1996). *Interdisciplinary undergraduate programs: A directory* (2nd ed.). Acton, MA: Copley.

Frank, R. (1988). "Interdisciplinary": The first half-century. In E. G. Stanley & T. F. Hoad (Eds.), *For Robert Burcheield's sixty-fifth birthday* (pp. 91–101). Cambridge, MA: D. S. Brewer.

Geertz, C. (1980). Blurred genes: The refiguration of social thought. *American Scholar, 42* (2), 165–179.

Hutcheson, P. (1997). Structures and practices. In J. Gaff & J. Ratcliff (Eds.), *Handbook of the undergraduate curriculum* (pp. 100–117). San Francisco, CA: Jossey-Bass.

Schneider, C. G. (1997). The arts and sciences major. In J. Gaff & J. Ratcliff (Eds.), *Handbook of the undergraduate curriculum* (pp. 235–261). San Francisco, CA: Jossey-Bass.

ENDNOTES

1. Most institutional descriptions derive from summaries culled by conference organizers from *International Undergraduate Programs, A Directory* (1996). Most people named in the text of this chapter contributed to this volume. Others participated in the Evergreen Conference on Interdisciplinary Education, but did not author chapters.

24

Joining the Conversation: An Essay in Guiding Images for College Teaching and Learning

Robert H. Knapp, Jr.
The Evergreen State College

I want to spend some time discussing the need for guiding metaphors as part of our mental habits as teachers and learners, and developing one such metaphor—conversation—in directions that may help guide educational decisions.

In this market-oriented society, especially in this era of triumphant capitalism, a natural source of questions and answers about situations of any kind is business. Is someone not happy with you? Think about the problem as if you were in business. Are they like customers? Like suppliers? Like a bank? A large, well-tested set of categories is ready at hand. For higher education in particular, the overarching question of whether colleges or universities are giving value for money suggests itself at once.

I will not unfold the workings of this system of metaphors here. I propose to explore quite a different system, which does some important work I believe the business or market metaphor cannot do. Notice, though, how useful the latter is proving to many people throughout higher education. It mobilizes and organizes thoughts in powerful ways. It generates passions and logics, directs actions and resistances, sets up resonances and dissonances of far-reaching effect (and affect).

Among the sources of energy for market talk in higher education, I think we college teachers, staff, and administrators have to acknowledge bad or unsatisfactory experiences people have had with higher education in their lives, that is, with higher education as we have been practicing it over the past forty years or so. There is disenchantment, and people are resorting to market language as a way of giving form and direction to their dissatisfaction.

If a student goes to college and encounters a string of impersonal regulations, weakly produced lectures or classes, unexplained delays or additional required activities, arbitrary-seeming evaluations, and so on—and we all know this can happen to students—it is not surprising for people to think that no business would dare treat its customers that way, and to consider their possible actions as if they were dealing with a business. Where is the complaint desk? Who handles customer service? Maybe I should take my business elsewhere.

Not only are business categories readily available, but in situations like this, they address legitimate needs. The market metaphor can point toward needed reforms, and can mobilize energy for carrying them out. I believe that many faculty members, and in effect many colleges and universities, have indeed been self-satisfied and willful in relation to their students in important ways over the past years—especially, I would say, in abdicating the need for education to speak to whole lives and not just be a special kind of car people get out of the garage once in a while and drive around in.

Good educational thinking these days needs to address student experience as it has been and should be. The market metaphor cannot, however, do the job reliably. Despite its ability to mobilize attention to undoubted problems, it is flawed and wrongheaded in the direction it points. My goal here is to explore an alternative, so instead of extended discussion, I offer only a one-line critique, based on the following anecdote, from the Santa Fe Community College web page:

> "Higher education has never been accountable before," Rockland Community College president Neal Raisman was quoted in 1995 as having declared. "We tell the public, 'Give us money, and we will guarantee you nothing.' I would never buy a toaster like that!" (Raisman, 1995)

With all due respect to those trying to use market metaphors thoughtfully and in good faith, I think my response must be this: if Neal Raisman has his way, his students are toast.

So much for where the market metaphor is likely to get us. But what can take its place? We in higher education really do need good guiding language. Moments of disorientation, muddle, and conceptual stalemate really do arise often these days. How are we to get a sense of direction?

Two standard moves are to write mission statements and to establish goals. These can both help, but they have intrinsic limitations. I will just indicate the difficulty by quoting the 1996 mission statement of the University of Texas, Austin, and leave further discussion to an appendix.

> The mission of the University is to achieve excellence in the interrelated areas of undergraduate education, graduate education, research, and public service. (p. 1)

There is almost no information in this, and almost no directive force: the categories are so large and amorphous that nothing is settled by announcing them. What is needed for directing education is not a category or pigeonhole, but something that gives the character or tonality or feel of what is desired (or opposed), down to the finest scales. Metaphor does this. A college is a market, a city on a hill, a factory, an ivory tower, a community of scholars. In the end, the strongest evidence of the need for metaphor is that we resort to it all the time. Hence the importance of prospecting for metaphorical systems that take us where we want to go.

Working consciously with language puts us in unholy company, of course—spin doctors, flacks and pitchmen of all kinds, many deconstructors, and of course the well-oiled Disney apparatus. Perhaps even worse, conscious attention to metaphors puts us all too close to the spiritless, sentimental preachers memorialized in the old Beyond the Fringe mock sermon that started, "Life is like a can of sardines—we're always looking for the key."

There's no help for it. As George Lakoff and Mark Johnson among many others have made clear, metaphors are what we live by. They are the living, dancing flowers and foliage of what we say and write, and the branching woody skeleton that holds the flowers to the light, and the roots that anchor the whole tree of language to the planet of lived experience and natural process. As academics, we are no better able to speak in direct, nonassociative ways than any other users of language; however much we try to make crystalline, transparent meanings, we find like everyone else that our words are made of mud and clay and grit, and bring with them unavoidable odors, textures, and colors of the swamps, deserts, forests, and barnyards from which they come.

Since metaphor is so much a part of language at all levels, you would expect to find an active metaphorical life everywhere you find people talking about education, for example on the World Wide Web. You would be right. One Friday in 1997, an hour or so of web work garnered the following:

- Notice of a speech by Alice B. Hayes, President of the University of San Diego: "From her unique perspective as both scientist and leader of a Catholic institution of higher education, she used the leaf as a metaphor for the personal and professional growth of a scientist and expanded it to discuss biological patterns of growth that also apply to the process of living productive lives in society." (UCSD, 1996)
- Notice of a special lecture by Professor Ted Wragg (University of Exeter, UK) on "a curriculum for the twenty-first century": "Illustrating his argument with wit and frequent observations drawn from classrooms, Professor Wragg suggested that a sort of three-dimensional Rubik's Cube was a useful metaphor, or image, for thinking productively about the curriculum of the twenty-first century." (Electronic Precinct, 1996)
- Remarks of Dr. Clara Lovett of the Arizona Task Force on the Western Virtual University concluded as follows: "Governor Symington made reference to the daring feats of the Wright brothers and the significance of Kitty Hawk. The metaphor is exactly right for the WV experiment. We cannot predict how far the concept of a Virtual University will take us. We need to concentrate on making it take off. The future will take care of itself." (Lovett, 1996)
- In some ways most illuminating of all, Chip German of the University of Virginia office of information technologies launched an essay about organizations by ruminating: "Every person struggles daily with the challenges of locking his or her attention on what it is that he or she is supposed to do . . . . I guess that's part of the human condition. But for some people, that struggle is a constant wrestling match with their basic nature. These are the people modern medical science has categorized with attention-deficit disorder (ADD). Because someone close to me has been diagnosed with ADD, I've recently become more familiar with its characteristics . . . . I am struck that it offers a metaphor for thinking about modern organizations, too." (German, 1997)

What guidance are we looking for? Closest to me are those occasions when I and some colleagues need to ask what liberal education is really about. As a faculty member at The Evergreen State College, where we revise the curriculum yearly and have a thriving independent study option, I confront this question very often. A science student asks why I am insisting she take part in a weekly book seminar instead of my using the time to cover some more material which is technically interesting and important. Or another student wonders why the weekly problems aren't more about the real world. Or earlier, in the design phase of this program, two other faculty members and I, the teaching team, are wrestling with how much of which activities to include in each week. What helps us make our choices coherent and comprehensible? And, recognizing that the medium is the message, what helps us choose the right ways to convey our choices to the students?

At other times, the question at hand is not obviously such a philosophical one. Maybe it is about requirements, exam formats, allocation of space, or some other operational matter. At these times, one often forgets that large educational values are in play, and that the framing of the question needs to recognize these.

A current Evergreen issue of this sort concerns math across the curriculum. For years, we have made writing a nearly universal feature of our programs. Regardless of main subject matter, students can expect to find substantive writing of some sort in each program. It might seem that a similar approach would be possible for mathematics or quantitative reasoning, but we have had little or no success in figuring out what to do or how. As a result, too many of our students leave with inadequate exposure to college-level quantitative reasoning. Yet every time a group of Evergreen faculty try to talk about this, they get muddled, talk from widely different starting points, go in circles, and pursue incommensurate goals. We could use help in achieving coherence and direction in this area.

The current environment of disenchantment with higher education, and especially with its cost, present most of us with recurrent instances of this kind of disorientation. Public institutions hear from their legislatures in both rhetorical and material ways that doubts are rampant about whether they deserve state support at usual level, or at all. Private institutions get the same message in the form of a tightening contradiction between what they need to offer to maintain standing—and enrollment—and what they dare ask in tuition to pay for it. Some colleges and universities are currently managing to escape this squeeze, but most are emphatically not. How to respond?

I think these moments of disorientation and muddle are strategically important. They arise because the question at issue refuses to be ignored, yet exceeds the capacity of the people present to manage it. This is uncomfortable. In these moments, we academics, like most people, resort to metaphor and projection more fervently and far less critically than when matters are comfortably settled. What happens next depends crucially on what metaphors we resort to.

Turning from the web to a thoughtful and provocative recent book on directions in higher education, we find in Bill Readings's *The University in Ruins* (1996) a metaphor (the university is a ruin, like the Roman Forum) used for a good deal more than a quick injection of color. As Readings claims in the course of an extended argument about changes in the university's place in individual lives and national politics,

> we need to recognize the university as a *ruined* institution, one that has lost its historical *raison d'être.* At the same time, the university has, in its modern form, shared modernity's paradoxical attraction to the idea of the ruin (e.g., in Romantic fiction, music, and architecture), which means that considerable vigilance is required in disentangling this ruined status from a tradition of metaphysics that seeks to reunify those ruins, either practically or aesthetically. (p. 19)

This metaphor (the university is a ruin) is not one I find helpful, but without working with it very fully, one can perhaps see that it has two qualities needed by a good guiding metaphor. First, it invites us to look for spin-offs, and they are not far. If the university is a ruin, who are the people who are carting off the stones, what use are they making of them, and what constitutes the stones themselves? There is a whole family or cluster of metaphors here, which inform each other. We need this kind of richness if we are to deal adequately with something as complex as education.

Second, the ruin metaphor has internal structures which naturally lead to perspectives and implications not evident on the surface of the summary image. Readings reminds us that ideas of ruins not only evoke feelings of grief and admiration when one contemplates them directly, but also have moved some people to great efforts of restoration, while moving others to great efforts to construct brand-new ruins, like the gloomy towers and so-called "follies" of early 19th century British estates. Might this not be the character of many honors programs, interdisciplinary centers, and study-abroad options? The metaphor of ruin can be unfolded considerably. It contains narratives which can suggest courses of analysis and initiative, in other words, directions for the perplexed.

With these considerations in mind—a need for guiding metaphors which come in clusters and unfold richly—I want to go (finally) to my favorite. It is old and borrowed, not new and blue; it has at least one serious flaw; nevertheless it has proved very helpful to me. It has to do with conversation. Specifically, when I get puzzled about educational choices, a slogan I keep going back to is "joining the conversation."

At the risk of overplaying things, I want to unfold this idea somewhat and indicate the shape of the cluster of images it belongs to. To put it another way, I want to sketch some of what it suggests to me about the character or spirit of what colleges should be striving for. Simultaneously, I will try to demonstrate ways in which a guiding metaphor can be a tool of thinking, not just a means of expression. My apologies go to innumerable prior and present explorers of this idea.[1]

The starting point is the fairly natural one that discourse, dialog, and intellectual give and take are at the heart of what colleges are trying to introduce to students.

Notice that I am not quite saying that college education is conversation: higher education is about *joining* the conversation. Working actively with ideas and powerful expressions of human life, bringing them to bear on pressing issues, discovering in some interactive way what they mean—I think these are what higher education should enable people to do.

So I would start a manifesto like this:

> JOINING THE CONVERSATION: There is a worldwide conversation, a many-voiced, complex, often disorderly, distinctly coevolving interchange of thoughts and actions. It is grounded in the constraints and opportunities of human life, material and spiritual, but it is not determined by these things. It works by its own internal dynamics as much as by external influences. It is carried on by innumerable groups and subgroups, all working simultaneously, often apparently separate from each other, but never really so. It is this college's job to help its students become participants in this conversation, and to do so in a way which supports the widest participation of all people, whether traditionally recognized as voices or not.

"Conversation" may sound too casual a way of naming these central activities, but with the help of an older, more provocative meaning, I find it takes me closer to the full range of their implications than more formal words like "discourse." The older meaning (current up to the 17th century) is this: Conversation is "the action of living or having one's being in a place or among persons" (*Oxford English Dictionary,* 1989).

You've heard of being "conversant" with a subject, which we generally take to mean acquainted with it, knowledgeable about it, knowing something of its ins and outs. The older meaning is much more emphatic, and it calls attention to the communal side of knowledge. Intellectual life involves one's being and the actions of one's living.

This central image suggests a series of others—the start of a cluster. My manifesto might continue as follows:

> ACQUIRING A VOICE, LISTENING IN, CONVERSING: To take a productive part in the world's conversation, students have to become able to express themselves authentically and with authority. That is, they need to learn (or discover) how to write and speak in accord with their inner selves and also with the outer realities that surround them. In this multivalent time, this is an individual, not a collective task: To put it another way, each person needs to work out an individual relation to the multiple calls and identities available to him or her. This is not only true for the classic white, middle-class liberal arts student, but also for students from indigenous cultures, from the working class, from all the backgrounds that have

> generally received labels from society's dominant segments rather than being allowed to characterize themselves.

Some are familiar with this notion of "voice" from literature. An example of a less familiar use is this: A chemistry instructor allocates time in the last weeks of a year-long introductory course for students to research and present small reports on current chemical topics. Unsure how best to define the task, but stimulated by the notion of voice, the instructor chooses the poster session format, in which each student lays out the report's text and graphics on a 24 x 36 poster board and all are displayed in a large room where the class assembles to stroll around, view the reports that interest them, and possibly discuss them with the author during an assigned time period when he or she is stationed by the poster. The student work is done for an audience wider than just the instructor; it is presented in a format widely used in the profession of chemistry; the presentation is in a semi-protected setting where feedback is easy and the stakes are modest—this combination of things tends to move students toward finding language and content that they can stand behind and that make sense in the larger world. One need not have a metaphor to conceive this teaching tactic, but the voice metaphor nudges one in this direction when one might have stayed with a call for conventional short writing in plastic sleeves.

The image called Listening In comes up in a natural way as one tries to unfold the very general idea of conversation, and begins to connect it to the specific teaching/learning activities that occupy a student's week.

> To speak and be heard in the world's conversation, students need to learn the terms and tonalities in which it is carried on. This requires learning to listen well, to take into memory (or even habit) the often unfamiliar and sometime unwelcome patterns in which the world outside the student expresses itself.

Listening In describes what is going on when people are receiving the facts and tonalities of conversations (e.g., the mind/body conversation, or the one about justice) that began before they arrived and that have their own life with or without students' participation. Listening In is what many lectures are for.[2]

(Why capitalize the terms? Even though I am working with images, I think they are definite enough, directive enough, to be treated as things, and not just as turns of phrase. Capitalization is an attempt to resist the dissolving effect of normal usage.)

In addition to simply listening (of course, it's not actually that simple to listen well), there are other conversations whose whole existence and continuance depends on a student's presence and participation. For example, most Evergreen study programs contain, as a central feature, weekly sessions called seminars in which 20–25 students and a faculty member discuss a common reading. These are multilateral sessions: the emphasis is on what students have to say to each other, and the faculty member is as much a facilitator as a leader.

Students can't productively be governed in such conversations by Listening In. Instead, they need to do things organized around the image of Conversing.

> To join a significant conversation significantly, one must bring responsiveness to evolving moods, needs, and openings.

In his fascinating *Finite and Infinite Games* (1989), philosopher James Carse—developing games as his own guiding metaphor—introduces the notion of an infinite game, one where the object of play is to keep the game going. The world's conversation, concerned as it is with the largest issues of human existence, has the same quality. Rather than bring it to a halt in some partially ordered state of finite understanding, I think one's goal has to be to participate in a way that sustains conversation. To do this, one needs to acquire skill in generative responsiveness to other participants, and a certain hospitality in establishing circumstances in which give and take can occur, rather than fight or flight.

Conversing doesn't only happen in seminar. It can also happen in independent study work, in projects, in community service. The Evergreen seminar is a place where it is center stage as a task, challenge, focus of attention, unlike the other study settings mentioned, where other important things are also going on. It can happen that seminars work badly for some students, because of psychological safety, cultural disjunctions, and so on. Commitment to the image of Conversing then urges us on to arrange other settings where Conversing is also the main work.

As a sample of ways a guiding metaphor can continue to unfold itself, I offer the following journal entry from the time when I was composing this chapter: October 3, 1997. I also notice that within the general activity of listening there are several distinctions to be made, according to the role the listener adopts:

> LISTENING AS BEGINNER: This takes in such occasions as lectures, writing conferences, lab demonstrations. I originally thought of it as Listening to Authority, but I like Listening as Beginner better, because the "as" puts the choice of role more squarely in the student's hands; it makes the student an agent, even though he or she is less tutored than the person being listened to, and is primarily absorbing information, values, and atmospherics in the way that person chooses to put them forward. The student takes little overt initiative in this form of listening, though there is a definite use for active internal work on what he or she hears.

Next comes LISTENING AS PEER: this refers to collaborative settings such as seminars and project groups, and to study groups. Much recent testimony indicates that these settings often make the difference between academic success and failure, and even more often between engagement/satisfaction and its absence. (Listening is only part of peer group work; there is more unfolding to do here.) The etiquette of this kind of listening is quite different from that of apprentice/master relation; the whole setting is much less under traditional faculty influence, though faculty who accept its importance may find ways to foster peer listening.

Next comes the kind of listening people do as part of exercising some mastery. I first thought of this in the context of performing a service for someone, and wanted to call it Listening to Client; but again, it seemed better to find a phrasing that gives some clear kind of agency to the listener. As of now, I'm using LISTENING AS AUTHORITY. In this role, the listener (perhaps an advanced student interviewing for a research project or gathering background for a public service activity) already possesses a structure for organizing and using what he or she hears, and is using listening as a way of settling on what specific moves to take.

What I gained from this rumination went beyond a sense that traditional class activities have suitable places in this metaphorical system and thereby it connects with teaching practice, not just lofty ed-rhetoric. I also found a sharper understanding of important distinctions in student roles, and of the possible usefulness of orienting students to them more explicitly.

Moving back to the elaboration of the main metaphor, Joining the Conversation, I found myself thinking about the relation of one course or study setting to another.

NETWORK OF CHOICES AND CHANNELS: Participating in the world's conversation is not just a matter of words, but also of actions. The character of the college comes as much as anything from the nature of the network of choices and channels it establishes for students.

Students define themselves, direct their talents, and nurture their skills by choices they make, large and small. As they enter college, they face a set of major choices—which program, what housing, what and how much employment. Each choice sets the student within a more or less constraining channel. (Even the choice to come to this college, rather than another, or none, is like this.) Within each choice lie further, more detailed choices, and from each choice sprout later arrays of choice.

This item is not directly to do with conversation. The point is not to find a master metaphor that contains all within it, but to be engaged in a process of unfolding which clarifies the nature and connections of the key aspects of teaching and learning.

Other recent writers have used conversation as a guiding metaphor. Their unfoldings head off in a variety of directions. George Allan (1997) is most interested in what constitutes the essence of a college. He uses the centrality of conversation in intellectual life and moral development, and the uncontrollability of true conversation, as cornerstones in his argument that colleges will wither unless they attend to the character of their activities more than to any overarching mission. In Chapter 25 of this volume, Robert Benedetti has suggestions about the kind of community best suited to conversation of the kind I am urging, and concludes that the city or small republic is the right model. Here a second rich metaphorical system would come into play. Parker Palmer (1998) works from thoughts about the psychology of teaching to pose a related question to Benedetti's: What kind of community is best suited to teaching and learning? His ultimate answer, the "community of truth," centers on "an eternal conversation about things that matter, pursued with passion and discipline" (p. 104). Palmer's direction of unfolding the metaphor takes him toward the emotions and values of the participants. A final example is Donald Schön (1983), who seeks to understand the character of work in professions like architecture and psychological counseling. He finds important assistance in the idea that what professionals work with—buildings, the mind, and so on—reacts to them as a conversational partner might. For Schön, the world conversation includes more than other human subjects, it includes physical and even conceptual entities that turn out to respond with surprises, resistances, and independence that is best understood as coming from a subject.

With these images and commentary, you have a sample of how this guiding metaphor might begin to direct choices about teaching and learning. Part of my own interest in the notion of conversation is already clear, I hope—I find it guides me toward sharper understanding of my own teaching practice. Next come some more general remarks about what work the central image of Joining the Conversation does and doesn't do, in relation to my hopes for liberal education.

The guidance offered by the conversation metaphor is undoubtedly slanted toward the liberal arts—and toward a particular way of understanding that term. By imagining that students take up active roles in a world conversation about human material and spiritual life, it helps move teaching and learning away from the idea that liberal arts means vaguely broad, generalized studies, and toward the idea that liberal education is to put people in touch with the profound issues that life presents.

I confess that my personal slogan for the content of the liberal arts is simplistic to the edge of caricature: the liberal arts are about the Big Eternal Questions. Yet I find this slogan unfolds usefully for my teaching, as follows. Human life generates questions about its meaning and potentials; it always has, and still does. These questions come up in new ways in each time and culture, but there are recognizable themes, including the origins of evil and suffering, the nature of allegiance, the nature of the nonhuman world, and many others; these are the Big Eternal Questions. They keep recurring because life keeps confronting us with them and because there are no answers to them, except local and provisional ones. An important part of maturing as a human being is to recognize all this in some fashion, and to work out some stance in relation to it.

If these questions are inescapable, it is natural to ask how others have understood them and dealt with them; if there turn out to be no crib sheets to memorize, it is natural for inquiry to take the form of exchanging what information and insights people have been able to gather—conversation, in short.

By organizing themselves around the idea of Joining the Conversation, colleges can align themselves with the true grain of the liberal arts. The metaphor encourages learning from the past, but finds high significance in the present, the moment in which people recognize the questions that confront them and take their stands. It directs attention to the social processes of knowing as well as to the content of knowledge, and thereby supports the idea that knowledge can be both definite and continually in flux. It encourages interactive teaching and learning, and thereby supports intellectual empowerment of students.

The idea of conversation can also enhance the acquisition of techniques and skills. At least as far back as Michael Polanyi's discussions of "tacit knowing," close observers have noticed the important ways that technical knowledge cannot be reduced to a collection of rules, but seems to have an essential component of judgment based on experience with the sphere in which the knowledge is applied, whether it is the interpretation of X-ray photographs, the conduct of psychological counseling, the design of school buildings, or whatever. Often this is organized through a mentor or a master-apprentice relation; it can be done solo. In any case, it involves some process of give and take between the learner and the situation under study, and observers such as Donald Schön have found it natural to call this process a conversation.

I said earlier that I find one serious flaw. It has to do with conflict. Conversation has an air of politeness about it which does not easily make room for the full range of struggles present in the world, or even in some classrooms. Going straight to an extreme, do I include the jungle war in Vietnam as part of the world conversation? Can a fight be a conversation, in any reasonable sense? Isn't conversation-oriented education likely to shrink its scope to a tweedy civility among intellectual clones?

The answer to the last question is No, because the answer to the one before is Yes. Leaving extreme cases for the moment, let us recognize that much significant fighting is conducted in clearly conversational terms, from labor negotiation to marital conflict across the dinner table. The interchange is not just in words, but also in actions. It is among persons who live or have their being together, in the words of the old definition. In the nature of living among persons, conflict will arise and be part of the conversation.

The presence of violence is not the end of conversation in this wide sense. Police know this. So did most of those engaged in the voting rights movement of the 1960s, on both sides. The Vietnam War did encompass some of what lies outside conversation—impersonal assault, the blind rage of battle, or the radically silencing intent of extreme torture. But Vietnam, in both its Indo-Chinese and domestic US aspects, was far more about interchange of words or actions between parties who could not escape each other, however much they may have wished to. It was an extended negotiation, not only formally but also in multidimensional informal ways. It was a conversation in many senses.

I open this enormous topic only to make room for a fairly small claim. If the scope of the world's conversation can include the words and actions of things like the voting rights movement, then the work of higher education, which I want to call conversational, can certainly include them. There can be disagreements, arguments, even fights in education. There had better be something of this kind, if colleges are to do their job of preparing students to understand the world they inhabit. The conversation they are joining has plenty of conflict in it. Blindness by colleges to this is always a danger, but it is not required by the guiding metaphor.

I connect the question of conflict in conversation with one that at first glance may seem distant, namely participation. The question of who gets admitted to a given conversation, and on what terms, can in fact be hotly contested. Even when it has been answered in a prima facie way by the convening of a group in a classroom, damaging differences in participation can still be present, arising from race, class, gender, and other dimensions of differential power. This is an occasion of conflict, whether acknowledged or not—and whether to acknowledge it may be a further occasion of conflict.

We should think of today's conversations in relation to what Mary Louise Pratt (1991) has called "contact zones": "social spaces where cultures meet, clash, and grapple with each other, often in contexts of highly asymmetrical relations of power, such as colonialism, slavery, or their aftermaths as they are lived out in many parts of the world today."[3] The language calls to mind images of the waterfront districts of trading cities—many languages and customs rubbing shoulders; transient engagements; only a rough and ready social contract at best. Pratt suggests that college teaching these days can and should recognize how incommensurate are the personal histories and modes of understanding that students can bring to their college work. Where once an instructor might teach to a generic imagined student, in effect asking all his real students to place in suspended animation any divergences in purpose or sensibility from the generic image, here is Pratt writing about one of today's offerings, a course on cultural histories in the Americas:

> As the students in the class saw their roots traced back to legacies of both glory and shame all the students experienced face-to-face the ignorance and incomprehension, and occasionally the hostility, of others. [At the same time,] virtually every student was having the experience of seeing the world described with him or her in it. Along with the rage, incomprehension, and pain, there were exhilarating moments of wonder and revelation, mutual understanding, and new wisdom—the joys of the contact zone. (1991)

The prospect of teaching in such a contact zone is likely to awaken the American anxiety about conflict, whether the response is belligerence or denial. What is available to us as college professors of the liberal arts is in fact something exciting: the lively appearance of some of the Big Eternal Questions in the shared, lived experience of our students and ourselves. This kind of teaching is certainly not easy or smooth; nothing magical is achieved by attaching it to a winsome metaphor. What we can hope is that the contact zone idea keeps our eyes as teachers open to some important realities in our work with students and colleagues.

In running as hard as I am with the metaphor of conversation as a guide, there is a final pitfall to look out for: converting the guiding metaphor into a literal prescription. There are certainly modes of teaching, such as Evergreen's seminars, in which literal conversation—talk among a small group of people physically present to each other—is a primary activity, but it would be unpardonable to constrict teaching and learning just to this. Laboratory teams, field project groups, ad hoc acting troupes, lecture audiences asked to compare answers to a quick question, writing support groups—these are only a few of the other ways that the conversational approach can enter college education. The subjects can range across the whole of the arts and sciences, pure and applied. The key is reflective interchange, on terms of increasing equality, about human thoughts and actions that matter. Taking conversation as a guide also does not mean that each educational moment needs to be one of interchange—there is plenty of scope for simply Listening In—or that it needs to address some Big Question overtly—the balancing of chemical equations, French pronunciation, and other want-of-a-nail topics all need their due attention. A guiding metaphor is help we resort to, consciously or unconsciously, in putting all these disparate components of an education into right relation with each other. For me at present, regarding students (or taxpayers) as consumers of my services gives me little constructive help in making educational choices. (Actually, I find the consumer image pernicious, but polemics is not the point here.) The conversation metaphor, on the other hand, gives me direction and leads me on. It even reframes my academic's dismay at how much is incomplete in the thoughts sketched here.

Appendix 1: A Few Guiding Metaphors

Here are some other voices, some speaking about conversation, some about other metaphors of possible help to education:

> Blair Kinsman:
> In another aspect, and one that is of very practical concern to the beginner, science is a conversation. The conversation has been in progress for a long time—in the case of ocean waves [the topic of Kinsman's book], for a very long time. To make the analogy more exact, science resembles the babble at a very large reception. Most of the participants are more or less intoxicated. (Research, for those capable of doing it, is a very powerful stimulant; and it's habit forming.) They act like any bunch of drunks. Some are euphoric, some saturnine, some quarrelsome, and some inspired beyond their usual capacity. Whatever else happens, the conversation cannot proceed systematically or at the level of humdrum sobriety. The participants in the conversation have sorted themselves into groups, subgroups, and sub-subgroups, each dominated by a few brilliant conversationalists who set the subject and tone. Some scientists wander from group to group, while others remain fixed. Some groups talk about similar things, and occasionally scraps of conversation pass from one group to another. The analogy is quite exact, but we will not follow it further. You have arrived in the middle of the party. You have joined a little knot of very excited and exhilarated men who are talking about ocean surface waves—not always with clarity, but always intensely. My job is to catch you up on the conversation and show you how to find your way to the bar.—from the Preface to *Wind Waves* (Dover; New York, 1984 reprint)

> Donald Schön:
> [The way professionals work on problems] resembles the familiar patterns of everyday conversation. In a good conversation—in some respects predictable and in others not—participants pick up and develop themes of talk, each spinning out variations on her repertoire of things to say. Conversation is collective verbal improvisation. At times it falls into conventional routines—the anecdote with side comments and reactions, for example, or the debate—which develop according to a pace and rhythm of interaction which the participants seem, without conscious deliberation,

to work out in common within the framework of an evolving division of labor. At other times, there may be surprises, unexpected turns of phrase or directions of development to which participants invent on-the-spot responses . . . . In such examples, the participants are *making* something. (*The Reflective Practitioner,* pp. 30–31)

Michael Oakeshott:

The identity of a culture and of liberal learning remains obscure until we have some conception of the relationship of its components . . . . Perhaps we may think of these components of a culture as voices, each the expression of a distinct and conditional understanding of the world and a distinct idiom of human self-understanding, and of the culture itself as these voices joined, as such voices could only be joined, in a conversation—an endless unrehearsed intellectual adventure in which, in imagination, we enter into a variety of modes of understanding the world and ourselves and are not disconcerted by the differences or dismayed by the inconclusiveness of it all. And perhaps we may recognize liberal learning as, above all else, an education in imagination, an initiation into the art of this conversation. (*The Voice of Liberal Learning* (T. Fuller, Ed.), pp. 38–39)

James Carse:

"There are at least two kinds of games. One could be called finite, the other infinite . . . . A finite game is played for the purpose of winning, an infinite game for the purpose of continuing the play." (*Finite and Infinite Games,* p. 3)

Harper's Magazine, September 1997 [announcing a feature]:

On the Uses of a Liberal Education:

I. As Lite Entertainment for Bored College Students
By Mark Edmundson at the University of Virginia

II. As a Weapon in the Hands of the Restless Poor
By Earl Shorris on New York's Lower East Side

Paul Goodman:

"This book is a little treatise in anarchist theory. It can be regarded as a footnote to a few sentences of Prince Kropotkin on *The State* (1903)":

With these elements—liberty, organization from simple to complex, production and exchange by guilds, commerce with foreign parts—the towns of the Middle Ages during the first two centuries of their free life became centers of well-being for all the inhabitants, centers of opulence and civilization, such as we have not seen since then . . . To annihilate the independence of cities, to plunder merchants' and artisans' rich guilds, to centralize the foreign trade of cities into its own hands and ruin it, to seize the internal administration of guilds and subject home trade as well as all manufactures, even in the slightest detail, to a swarm of functionaries—such was the State's behavior during the sixteenth and seventeenth centuries.

Looking at our colleges and universities, historically and as they are, by and large one must say of them what Kropotkin said of the towns that gave them birth. (*The Community of Scholars*, p. ii)

APPENDIX 2: MISSION STATEMENTS

The mission statement is a standard move. (Notice in passing that the appeal is partly metaphorical—we are pilots or spies being briefed for our mission.) Mission statements usually help. They record the categories into which effort is to go, and so they narrow the range of uncertainty. Evergreen's statement, for example, is clear about the importance of teaching relative to other faculty activities: "Teaching is the central work of the faculty at both the undergraduate and graduate levels" (The Evergreen State College, 2000, p. 1). When there is direct conflict at Evergreen between teaching and, say, research, it is clear that teaching will take precedence. The mission statement goes on to highlight interdisciplinary and collaborative study, active participation in learning, community-based learning, and a commitment to continual review of programs and services, among other items. The effect of the statement as a whole is to commit the college to certain categories of effort.

There are limits to what this can do. As a somewhat unfair illustration, here is the mission statement of the University of Texas, Austin: "The mission of the University is to achieve excellence in the interrelated areas of undergraduate education, graduate education, research, and public service" (1996, p. 1).

This conveys almost no information. It can't, in a statement of manageable length, because UT Austin has a student body of 50,000, 12 major schools and colleges, over 100 undergraduate majors, and a campus of 360 acres packed with bricks and mortar. It is a very complex place. If the set of categories is small, each must itself contain a great deal of complexity, too much to give clear direction to educational choices of the kinds we faculty need help with.

Actually every educational mission statement sooner or later reveals the same shortcoming. Evergreen is clear that it privileges teaching. But what kind of teaching? Are we after charismatics like Carl Sagan? Sages like Don Juan? Or like Socrates? Activists? Role models? Or do we judge our teaching by its results, not its personal style, and go for effective coaches or empathetic empowerers? Or what? The point is that categories provide boxes that rule out certain things, the things that are clearly outside the box, but sooner or later we have to choose between various things that fit the box, and the mission statement doesn't help with that.

Another move is to establish goals. As a soccer player, I deeply understand the possibility for the existence of simple, clear goals to give direction to actions of extraordinary vigor, variety, and imagination. But . . . here is the sort of thing that tends to happen (UT Austin again):

> In pursuit of this mission, the University has established several goals, including the following: to educate students to their highest potential of intellectual achievement and personal growth; to develop scholars, professionals, artists, and scientists who contribute to the advancement of society nationally and internationally; to conduct research that advances the frontiers of knowledge; to engage in public service; and to support equal opportunity and develop programs that reflect the diversity of American culture in all activities of the University and to support the principle of equal opportunity in society as a whole. (1996, p. 2)

Once again, there is almost no information here.

Additional Reading (a few items)

Barrett, F. J., & Cooperider, D. L. (1991). Generative metaphor intervention: A new approach for working with systems divided by conflict and caught in defensive perception. *Journal of Applied Behavioral Science, 26* (2), 219–239.

Fuller, T. (Ed.). (1989). *The voice of liberal learning: Michael Oakeshott on education.* New Haven, CT: Yale University Press.

Goodman, P. (1964). *The community of scholars.* New York, NY: Vintage.

Kinsman, B. (1984). *Wind waves.* New York, NY: Dover.

Pratt, M. L. (1992). *Imperial eyes: Travel writing and transculturation.* London, England: Routledge.

Schön, D. (1987). *Educating the reflective practitioner.* San Francisco, CA: Jossey-Bass.

Schwartzman, R. (1995, Winter). Are students customers? The metaphoric mismatch between management and education. *Education,* 215–217.

References

Allan, G. (1997). *Rethinking college education.* Lawrence, KS: University Press of Kansas.

Carse, J. P. (1989). *Finite and infinite games.* New York, NY: Ballantine.

Electronic Precinct. (1996). *The cubic curriculum* [On-line]. Available: http://www.merseyworld.com/precinct/Nov96/prec7.html

The Evergreen State College. (2000). *Mission statement* [On-line]. Available: www.evergreen.edu/user/pol_proc/Board1.htm

German, C. (1997). *Keeping focus* [On-line]. Available: http://www.itc.virginia.edu/virginia.edu/spring97/focus/home.html

Lovett, C. (1996). *Remarks of Dr. Clara Lovett* [On-line]. Available: http://www.acpe.asu.edu/VirtualU/virtual/claremar.html

Oxford English Dictionary. (1989). New York, NY: Oxford University Press.

Palmer, P. J. (1998). *The courage to teach.* San Francisco, CA: Jossey-Bass.

Pratt, M. L. (1991). The arts of the contact zone. *Profession, 91,* 33–40.

Raisman, N. (1995). *Quotes to consider* [On-line]. Available: http://inst.santafe.cc.fl.us/~ccflc/QUOT3–11.HTM

Readings, B. (1996). *The university in ruins.* Cambridge, MA: Harvard University Press.

Schön, D. (1983). *The reflective practitioner: How professionals think in action.* New York, NY: Basic Books.

UCSD. (1996). *Burke lecture* [On-line]. Available: http://orpheus.ucsd.edu/burke/hayes96.html

The University of Texas, Austin. (1996, July). *The undergraduate catalog 1996–98.* Austin, TX: University of Texas, Austin.

ENDNOTES

1. I believe the first explicit mention I encountered of the idea of education as conversation was in Donald Schön's *The Reflective Practitioner,* though it must be very old. Plato certainly brings it forward implicitly. Since starting this chapter, I have learned of Michael Oakeshott's influential writing in this area.

2. and fishbowl faculty seminars, obviously, and, not so obviously, what is actually happening in quite a number of one-on-one conferences, disciplinary encounters, and advising sessions, whether the participants realize it or not.

3. Pratt originates this usage in *Imperial Eyes: Travel Writing and Transculturation* (Routledge, London, 1992) and transfers it specifically to college teaching and learning in "The Arts of the Contact Zone," *Profession, 91* (1991). Actually, the phrase was already in active use in geology, ecology, and other fields where metaphorically similar encounters are important.

25

After the Revolution: New Directions for Alternative Education[1]

Robert Benedetti
University of the Pacific

It is dangerous to predict that an era has come to an end, a revolution made and its ideas institutionalized. History often records changes imperfectly made and ideas resisted despite widespread lip service. Our generation knows from personal experience that the commitments of the civil rights revolution appeared more certain to be implemented in 1970 than they do today. Victory is not assured even when the leaders of a society are publicly converted to a new set of operating principles. What plays well at national gatherings is not always enacted in neighborhoods, and the hinterlands can work to undermine what appears to be an elite consensus, particularly in a democratic society.

What I will argue, therefore, must be evaluated with a critical eye because it depends on the institutionalization of a revolution now in full bloom, but not yet complete. Through the leadership of Ernest Boyer, Art Chickering, and others, the lessons of experimental education have been distilled and argued forcefully to the educational establishment. The experiences of both the experimental colleges of the thirties and their echoes in the sixties have not been lost but have informed the agenda for national educational associations in the 1990s, including the American Council for Education, the Association of American Colleges and Universities, the American Association for Higher Education, and the Carnegie Foundation.

The presentation of this agenda is timely because higher education is returning to a focus on teaching, having spent the latter half of this century developing its research capacities. In addition, the distillation offered by Boyer, Chickering, and others is consistent with the triumph of liberalism in American society in the wake of the international failure of socialism. In their reading, experimental education rightly underscored the learning of the individual student. These educators object to barriers often placed in the way of learning by a narrow disciplinary focus and by faculty disdain for pedagogy. The experiments they champion begin with the interest of students in particular issues and move forward by helping students mobilize disciplines and theories to explicate those issues. In addition, instructors who worked in such experimental places were self-conscious in ordering materials to assure that students with different learning styles mastered the subject. Given the cultural diversity of current student populations, such advice is particularly welcome today. It is also consistent with a tendency to envision students as customers and the university as a corporation responding to market pressures.

At association meetings and other gatherings, conscientious faculty, therefore, trade experiences concerning interdisciplinary programs and new pedagogies. The explosion of technology has advanced these conversations because it has made possible the tailoring of curriculum to specific students as well as the interconnection of faculty across the barriers of space and discipline. However, today's conversations no longer need to establish the importance of pedagogy or interdisciplinary approaches; they assume the challenge is to extend experiments already underway that take these elements seriously. More specifically, the dialog focuses on the way different pedagogies work with students from diverse backgrounds, special populations, or large groups. We are now talking the language of tactics and implementation rather than the language of critical discourse and first principles.

I have no reason to question such conversations nor to raise doubts about their importance. What I am suggesting here is that it is time to ponder where we go next. Assume that the process of education has become important to the academy, that pedagogy (including interdisciplinary curricula) is taken as seriously by instructors as the substance of their disciplines, that the outcome we measure is student learning, not the time and energy spent teaching. Indeed, powerful forces are now arrayed in support of these goals, and there are reasons to believe that they will succeed. That this seems to already be the case in K-12 teaching provides an example of a similar institutionalization near completion.

In fact, the public reaction to the success of focusing on student learning in the K-12 system may provide a clue to what higher education will soon need to address. As polls in the popular press reiterate, the general public is not convinced by the triumph of process in primary and secondary education. They are asking questions about the substance of that education. How does student learning support the family, develop the community, prepare students to contribute to the economy, instill ethics applicable to a wide range of social settings? In other words, the debate has moved from how to teach effectively to what ought to be taught. If higher education faces the same evolution, how can we organize ourselves to respond and what are the questions we need to answer?

While I will provide a preliminary discussion of the substantive issues that I believe await us, I want to move first to what I take to be a prior question: How can we organize the academy to make decisions in relation to the content of our curriculum? What metaphor or model of organization might we consult?

While the revolution in process has been long and difficult, I would argue that it is not as intrinsically divisive as issues of substance. Once teaching is recognized as a major responsibility of a faculty member even at a research institution, it seems reasonable to require faculty to master pedagogy. Further, this is a burden that must be borne equally by all faculty. Pedagogy is as useful and necessary for the humanist as for the scientist. Mastery of pedagogy is the mastery of a set of tools; the craftsman can decide in a given situation which to employ. The set of tools need not limit creativity or individuality; in fact, a focus on pedagogy is little more than a request to be self-conscious in the teaching act and to take the reaction of the student into account. Thus, the revolution we are on the edge of making does not violate the autonomy of the academic practitioner except as his or her craft affects another, the student. The parallel to the relationship among citizens within a liberal democratic republic is striking and possibly intentional: Both the citizen and the scholar are understood to have autonomy except to the extent that the actions of one scholar affect the actions of others.

It is not surprising that the current reform agenda, emphasizing process, does not conflict with the tendency to imagine the academy as a corporation whose primary customers are the students. If the students are customers, then improving the service they are provided by increasing the efficiency and effectiveness of teaching should increase profit. Though faculty are considered already to be leaders in their fields, their mastery will not benefit the college or university unless those scholars can translate mastery into learning at the lowest possible cost. Further, to the extent that the institution uses learning outcomes as a way to identify merit, those faculty who apply cost-effective teaching methods and are therefore responsible for attracting and keeping consumers will be appropriately rewarded. Thus, it should be in everyone's self-interest to embrace the new pedagogy.

On the other hand, questions of substance are either divisive or irrelevant, particularly when viewed from a corporate perspective. Rather than decide what is good for the consumer, the market sensitive college or university should let the market dictate what should be taught. While the institution can profit from improving cost effectiveness in the teaching, it cannot beat the market by moving away from popular subjects to those less interesting to the current generation of students unless it expects subsidies from donors or government.

Further, even if matters of substance need to be decided on grounds other than market considerations, many faculties have found such curricular explorations distasteful. The continuing concern over the quality of general education is, in part, the result of the fact that faculty differ dramatically concerning what should be required of all students and fight hard in defense of disciplinary interest. Thus the decision to favor an approach to general education is often a compromise accepted by faculty who care more about disciplinary coverage than educational vision. There is no reason to believe that, in the current climate, other substantive issues would fair better. If faculty are employees and students consumers, self-interest on both sides dictates that substantive issues are best left to consumer choice, and where this is not possible, solved by opportunistic compromise.

Finally, the discussion of matters of substance, as opposed to matters of process, raises questions of academic freedom. Though there is truth to the adage that the medium is the message, it is also the case that widely varying messages can be carried by the same medium. Thus a particular pedagogical tool only limits the instructor slightly where concerns over substance may be anathema because of their scope. The debate over creationism is one example of the problem. Where it may be possible to implement a writing or service-learning focus across the curriculum, the inclusion of a substantive perspective like the Darwinism/Creationism debate across many disciplines appears oppressive.

If, then, substance is to be seriously discussed, what model or metaphor could provide better guidance than the corporate model with its liberal assumptions? Stanley Katz, former executive director of the American Council of Arts and Sciences, has suggested that we reconsider a religious model.[2] Since the academy grew from seminary roots and was nourished by church connections throughout the 19th century, this model has the virtue of historical validation. Further, the college or university as religious institution would be striving constantly toward a consensus on the substance of its core beliefs.

However, religion as a metaphor suggests that a discrete number of canons and ideologies exist that can attract adherents and will be judged worthy of transmission to a new generation. In the diffusion of ideologies we currently are experiencing, the turn to religion as the orienting metaphor would seem to be inviting a dramatic fragmentation of the academy into antagonistic cults each with a tightly held doctrine. It is doubtful academics could rally behind a single or a small number of canons. The same phenomena face K-12 systems as they contemplate vouchers.

On the other hand, the religious metaphor assumes that whatever the variety of ideological alternatives, they have educational philosophies that could provide a grounding for them. In actuality, today's religious and cultural options seem limited in their scope and not sufficiently powerful to provide the substantive guidance necessary. At best, we appear to be at the dawn of a spiritual revival, not at the point of its institutionalization.

Moreover, liberalism triumphed over religious dogma as the controlling myth of the university because of the freedom of thought it promoted. It is clear that many of us would be uncomfortable returning to a system where severe limits were placed on academic inquiry within an institution even in the name of substantive goods we agree upon. In other words, the religious model seems premature and threatening to what many have accepted as a core value, academic freedom.

Instead, I would like to suggest an alternative that has a distinguished history. Thomas Jefferson suggested that we found academic villages. Paul Goodman (1964) viewed the university as a medieval town. Thomas Bender writes that we should envision the university as an urban neighborhood (1997). These metaphors point to a small polity, a republic in miniature, as the appropriate model for the college or university. The metaphor of the small polity is promising because it allows for a degree of community without the sacrifice of freedom. The city has always been, for political theorists, the structure which best balances the common good and individual liberty.

Following the lead of Michael Oakeshott, (Fuller, 1989) I would hazard a guess that education at its heart is a conversation between scholars and students. The scholars belong to traditions, the students would be initiated into those traditions. The parallel with the initiation into the rights of citizenship is obvious. In the university as in the city, the young come of age by joining the conversations of the elders. Through these conversations, the young learn how to assume the responsibilities that full citizenship in the university as city requires.

Oakeshott's sense of conversation is a discussion that engages universals only through the concrete. It avoids ideological systems and overly generalized principles. No clichés here. He is explicit in comparing the general process of education to political education. In both it is critical to maintain discipline, but also to avoid orthodoxy. An appropriate metaphor of the open debates that Oakeshott is seeking could be a town hall meeting of seasoned citizens where the best in them is often exposed on the most trivial of issues. Truth is proximate and decided by the consensus of those discussing, a parallel to the manner in which an academic discipline accepts or rejects theoretical formulations. Thus the metaphor of the city models the learning process itself; in both cases, new ideas emerging from endless discussion are accepted by action of the community. Here the analogy echoes Thomas Bender's call for engagement of the academy in locality and worldliness (1997).

One might argue that there is a "disanalogy" between discussions in cities and those in the academy in that cities hope for a decision on action while a university aims at theoretical agreement.[3] To be sure, theory is a central concern of university dialog. However, a focus on theory alone denies the importance of action in the generation of knowledge. For those of a pragmatic or dialectic persuasion,[4] action is critical for the development of ever better theories. Certainly it would be difficult for academics to come to consensus even on the trivial if the only criteria is logical consistency because principles from which disciplines make deductions are radically different.

Still, even if one accepts that theoretical discussions are primary and that such discussions provide the sine qua non for a university, the university exists in a lived world and depends on actions to maintain its existence. Whatever the implications for theorizing of the actions universities must take, the model of the university as city where all participate in setting action agendas may provide the best protection for all scholars from actions that disturb contemplation and the perspective necessary to pursue free thought.

Over against the dogmatism implied by the metaphor of religion and the individualism implied by the corporate analogy, the small polity suggests an open society, but one that maintains a commitment to the centrality of the community and its survival. The city, like the university, stands for something more than the sum of the self-interest of its citizens or scholars. It strives toward a vision of the common good and truth itself. In other words, it creates a tension between individualism and commonly accepted values, and one that can change with different issues and decisions. The classical philosophers, Plato and Aristotle, are an appropriate touchstone here; it is precisely in the best of cities where the goals of survival and the pursuit of truth merge. I suggest the university should be the best of cities.

More importantly for what I am pursuing here, the use of the small polity as metaphor for the university indicates that there is a reason for and a mechanism by which substantive issues can be addressed in the academic community as a whole. While both cities and universities recognize the importance of individual initiative and activity, they also accept the need to act in a concerted way in response to both their ideals and external threats to their community. Citizens, and I would add scholars, do not have to fight the good fights alone. Through the participatory institutions of small polities, they can come to common understandings and work together to achieve common goals. Scholars, no less than citizens, can decide that certain challenges need to be met and focus energy on them. A professed dogma or the individual fancy of a scholar or citizen is not the only legitimate way for agendas for action to be set. An open vote of a community to which we freely belong can obligate us as well.

Others who are on the edge of using such metaphors have suggested radical reorganizations of the governance of the university so that it has less the hierarchical structure of a corporation or church and more the form of a New England town (Davis & Chandler, 1998; Gamson, 1997). While such experimentation may be useful, it is not necessary for the metaphor to succeed. Towns and cities have been considered free under a variety of governmental organizations. The model perhaps suggests a greater role for students, particularly after they have matured as scholars at a university (viz. become seniors and graduate students). During the 1960s, various experimental colleges and programs attempted to structure governance models which may provide useful examples here. Clearly, a fully articulated freedom of speech for all stakeholders would be the cornerstone of all such ventures.

One might argue that cities are by nature parochial, run by minorities or majorities who lack vision and cosmopolitan understanding. While this is certainly true of cities that have been allowed to stagnate and have insulated themselves from diverse immigrants, the constant flow of students and competition for faculty has often protected the university from myopia. The growth and change of academic disciplines is a testimony to the receptivity of universities to new ideas. Thus, if the metaphor is to work, the vision must be of cities constantly blessed by migrations from afar (Bender, 1997).

More discussion needs to be had for this metaphor to be accepted, but I would suggest that communitarian theorists[5] have something to teach the academy here. Liberal thought has difficulty envisioning a university that is more than a collectivity of individual scholars while communitarians are attempting to preserve a great deal of individual autonomy, but still embrace full-bodied community. The latter compromise better fits the way the university has been through its history. Further, only a university that still understands itself as a community can respond to the substantive challenges that stand before us today.

Towns and cities are not all process and neither should the core of the university be. They take substantive positions and act accordingly. Our stakeholders are waiting for us to do the same. Since the early 1960s, reports on American higher education have argued that colleges and universities should distinguish themselves by their curricula so that the student could have a choice. The success over long periods of church related colleges indicates that the public is interested in choices that have substantive implications as well as those that deal with process.

What are these matters of substance about which college and university polities should decide and among which the public should choose? Here as elsewhere the place to begin to look for the questions to which higher education should be the answer is the lives of the future students themselves. What do they and those who observe them say they need to know? I do not have a definitive answer here, but rather three possible avenues that could bear further pursuit: citizenship, moral character, and the challenges of the world of work in a post-modern society.

CITIZENSHIP

The first issue derives more from observers of our students than from their own voices. Looking out on the society, commentators despair about our democracy. They sense a withdrawal from the public square of all but the most self-interested and narrow-minded actors. The result of giving over policy decisions to the interplay of such individuals is not only a loss of civility but further fragmentation of an already distrustful society. It seems that democracy today, rather than developing a life together, is driving us apart.

Like the Federal period that marked our founding, our own times seem to call for more attention to the political world for the sake of mere survival. We appear called to rebuild communal institutions. If, for example, we do indeed want to have our lives decided by initiatives and referenda, citizens will have to resist media manipulation. The experience of California in this regard is not promising, while the impulse toward direct democracy is appealing to an increasing number (Schrag, 1998). In the same vein, the current trend toward the devolution of decisions to local authorities suggests the need for more of us to become politically literate. Town government demands popular participation if it is to be fiscally responsible and sensitive to minority as well as majority voices. The experiment in town government in New England has survived in part because of the commitment to an educated citizenry alive in that region of the country.

Finally, the disregard for active participation in government that appears implicit in the representative models characteristic of liberalism is under challenge by the new generation of political theorists. They do not believe that citizens can delegate their political responsibilities and still create meaningful communities (Barber, 1984). It may be that the very act of arguing about public policies and attempting to implement the policy finally adopted provides the glue for citizens who come to the public square with very different presuppositions. Following the logic of pragmatism, it would seem that community development occurs where people work together first and share values later. If this is the case, then political life predates social life and increasingly will need to be the first step if we want to pull our diversity into a unity.

Liberal arts colleges have long argued that they provide training for citizenship. Indeed, as elite institutions, they did provide the leadership for our representative institutions. The basis for this claim was the strength of these institutions in the humanities. Since communications skills, analytical thought, empathy, and ethics have been the foundation for democratic participation from its Greek and Roman beginnings, a curriculum grounded in literature, history, and philosophy could be understood as preparing citizens for public life in the city. On the other hand, the humanities have recently had a difficult time holding their own on campus. Their share of the general education is contested, their majors less than a fourth of the total at most colleges and universities. Indeed, it is a sign of the state of these disciplines on our campus that a major classicist and philosopher, Martha Nussbaum (1988), has rushed to their defense in recent days.

One might have thought that political science should have come to the rescue of the humanities here and provided a curriculum which would foster citizenship. Indeed, political theorists have worked in this vineyard successfully and are providing a rich literature describing alternative models for citizenship. This literature deserves greater attention by educators than it has received (Beiner, 1995). On the other hand, political science continues to display a general bias toward the levels of government least accessible to the average student, the national and international arenas. At best most departments aim to train knowledgeable observers of the political game. The literature of the mid-century, which emphasized the degree to which national and supernational politics was dominated by power elites, did little to encourage students to believe that they had a direct role to play in this world. Even the fashionable sociological and Marxist analyses the discipline offered tended to invite quiescence and the occasional revolutionary. What is called for is a revitalization of the study of state and local, namely community, politics where students can come to understand how people similar to themselves play active roles without sacrificing their careers and personal lives.

But if the humanities rebound and political science reevaluates the importance of community politics, our campuses still could not be said to provide all one could imagine as a preparation for citizenship. De Tocqueville (1945) argued that what made American citizens so supportive of democratic institutions was the number of them that actually had experienced democracies at the grassroots in their towns and churches. Unfortunately, the frequency of some of these experiences may have declined. Robert Dahl (1970) argues that the next democratic revolution, the democratization of all the groups and organizations that play socially supportive roles in our society, has yet to be made. In any case, the universities and colleges are not in the lead here. The turmoil of the 1960s did not result in the institutionalization of new governance models at our institutions which provide all stakeholders, and particularly students, the opportunity to participate in decisions that affect them.

Even if one suggests that students need not play a critical role in the academic aspects of campus governance, it is clear that the shared governance they observe has not provided an adequate modeling of democratic citizenship. Faculty have avoided involvement in "administrative" responsibilities, and administrators lionize the concept of "transformational leadership" which even the creator of the term, James MacGregor Burns (1978), fears may lead to dictatorial decision-making.

And before leaving the current state of our institutions, a third point is relevant. Many colleges and universities have correctly become involved with internships and voluntary service activities. However, the conceptualization behind these programs seems to privilege careerism and social action over democratic citizenship. That is, internships often focus on the apprenticeship skills learned on the job. Voluntary service, on the other hand, usually provides experience with the powerless often in their weakest moments. Neither community experience helps students witness the way that citizens make decisions to regulate the market or to change structures so that others no longer need a helping hand. Students see market opportunities and social problems rather than community institutions attempting to moderate them. No wonder that government and many nonprofit organizations have less than favorable images in the eyes of graduates.

What I am arguing then is that the substance of democratic citizenship needs to be explored and curricula prepared that meaningfully advances the skill and understanding of our students as citizens. To my mind, this means more attention to the humanities and urban political science, to campus governance, and to community experiences that expose the challenges and the possibilities of local governance to students. However, whatever the directions that emerge from an expanded discussion, they would require a commitment from the academy to prefer some disciplines and some programs over others because of the contributions they make to citizenship training. As in any game where not all can be winners if solutions are to be effective, political compromises are required. In making these choices, the university should take into account all opinions and the need to hold a community together. Hence the metaphor of the republic in miniature continues to appear attractive.

Moral Character

While I have criticized the use of the church as a metaphor for the university, it does have one clear advantage. The university as church can never neglect moral questions. I would argue with the ancients that the same is true, however, of a republic. The moral fiber of the body politic is its foundation, the basis of its legitimacy, and the force that keeps leaders and followers disciplined toward the common good.

In any case, there is wide agreement that morality has not received the attention that it should have in American education. Rush Kidder (1994) has documented the moral flabbiness of our republic and suggested that we need a refresher course on those ethical principles that seem to pervade most of the world's religious and philosophical traditions. While his answers may not be fully satisfying, it is clear that the problem is significant.

Moral education continues to be on the agenda of church related colleges, but even there it has often been relegated to a particular course or program. The professional schools have led the way in responding to criticism of the use of the tools they teach by instituting courses in ethics. Medicine and business are leading the way with engineering following. Recently, the former president of Union Theological Seminary met with representatives of schools around Columbia University on New York's Westside (H. L. Hendrix, personal communication, early 1990s). He discovered that his was the only institution that did not have a class in professional ethics required for the degrees offered. Still, in most of these cases, the issue is reserved for a single course or project. Students are assumed inoculated if they have Ethics 101.

Clearly, an approach with more chance of success would be to press an "ethics across the curriculum" initiative as was tried for a short time at Rollins College in Winter Park, Florida. However this implies that many faculty in different fields have to become trained in ethical discourse, a requirement that suggests that some matters of substance are particularly important in comparison to others. Further, for many in the sciences and social sciences, it is not clear that ethics can be established as being more than individual preferences. They assume the subject to be trivial at best, anti-intellectual at worse.

One ally in the attempt to stimulate discussions of values on campus seems to have all but disappeared, the chaplaincy. After the attempts in the 1960s for the chapels to become centers for social action, they declined with the changing tastes of students. Only evangelical groups appear to be growing on campuses, and they have resisted the sponsorship of wide ranging value debates. Furthermore, universities have not underwritten the type of robust chapel programs that might encourage individual denominations and faiths to organize. On the other hand, often community resources exist that could be mobilized to build communities of faith on campus and foster interaction between them where such a dialog is a priority. Interestingly, diversity has usually been defined on campus in terms of race and ethnicity but not religion; diversity initiatives have preferenced the building of ethnic organizations and the bridges between them rather than religious grouping and the opportunities for them to interact.

While faculty have been often willing to serve as role models for professional development and occasionally for citizenship in local communities, they have increasingly been less willing to witness to their ethical and moral commitments. It would seem that the debates during their youth (the Vietnam War, Civil Rights Movement, feminism, gay rights, etc.) exhausted the moral vocabulary of many faculty. While not promoting a return to the turbulency of the 1960s, I believe that active town meetings on campus where faculty, staff, students, and members of the community discuss the moral implications of personal and social action help students develop their character. The teach-in was a vehicle for the learning of ethics we might have continued beyond its earliest manifestations.

Finally, the academy has been slow to institutionalize its own ethical codes of good behavior. Too often cheating continues to be tolerated; the balance between open debate and hate speech is unresolved; harassment, sexual and otherwise, remains without clear definition; the relationship of the academy to the surrounding community is often less than supportive; plagiarism continues in our classrooms; the priority that faculty give teaching is uncertain, etc. A more self-conscious evaluation of the professional ethics of universities could become a case study for students looking for ways to develop their own moral codes.

Again, all these initiatives, ethics across the curriculum, a revitalized chaplaincy, teach-ins on moral issues, and institutional codes of ethics go beyond procedural issues and require a debate on matters of substance. They require the academy to take a stand while tolerating dissent and giving dissenters room to fight another day. The parallel to the city remains.

Transitions to the World of Work

The downfall of socialism and the triumph of capitalism has left the academy without energy to mount a thorough critique of the postmodern market and its cultural baggage. We appear nervous about raining on our national parade. What this has meant is that our students enter the work force armed with media clichés about the nature of our society and their roles in it. They know too little about the realities of an information age in which loyalty is little treasured, but overtime is required. One might say we have demoted the sociological imagination at the precise time that our students need it most.

In the name of resisting vocationalism, liberal arts colleges have been slow to focus on the work place. Career centers and internships are being expanded, but the subject of work in America and the world has not been targeted for special attention. I would argue that our students are right to sense that the world they face is a hazardous one. They may understand the dynamics of their specialties, but not of the market and the society to which they respond. The world of work calls out for the kind of interdisciplinary strategies that have been applied to ethnic studies.

Furthermore, this transition to the world of work suggests the need to integrate our curricula across other borders than those between departments. First, the work world is of as much interest to professional schools as to liberal arts units. This topic invites us to bridge these trenches effectively. Second, in order for students to gather the full benefit from whatever is uncovered of a theoretical nature concerning work, these insights need to interact with practical advice. The world of work is a topic over which student affairs professionals, particularly those in career offices, could come together with faculty and struggle to put their programs together much the same as has been attempted in the area of volunteer service. Third, the work world is an evolving one, and to be relevant, any program must be in constant touch with the current marketplace and the society that surrounds it. This implies outreach to the towns that surround our campuses and to our alumni. If we are to understand the destination of our students and their fate, we need to conceptualize neighbors and graduates as coteachers who have curricular insights as well as financial resources to bring to our campuses.

One of the opportunities that a focus on the transition to the world of work provides colleges and universities is a chance to service graduates beyond their diploma. If properly developed, educational institutions can continue to help their alumni prepare for evolving challenges they meet in their society. One clear part of such a mission is continuing education programs to update professional students, but this is just the tip of the iceberg. Graduates could be invited to return for programs that would develop their avocations and leisure time as well as their employment. Such initiatives are not new, but conceptualizing the role of the college as a silent partner in one's career may be. Could a college diploma in the future entitle a graduate to continuing help in navigating life, a sharing in the results of new learning about the world of work much as university medical newsletters have done for our biological health?

What I have tried to do here is a preliminary sketch of where I sense alternative education may gain new direction. The argument is a simple one. We are on the edge of making a pedagogical revolution, including the acceptance of interdisciplinary foci. However, our emphasis on method has resulted in a neglect of substance. This emphasis has been a good fit with the liberalism that has provided the context for much of our public philosophy in America. However, that philosophy has grown shopworn and is currently under reexamination from a number of quarters.

As we try to respond to these critiques, I believe that we will need to confront directly matters of substance. They will be suggested more often by the social demands being placed on our students than by deductions from theoretical models in the academy. Since decisions on matters of substance will, by their very nature, advantage some teacher scholars at the expense of others, these decisions cry out for a legitimate process by which all stakeholders have the opportunity to voice their arguments and strike their compromises. The corporate metaphor does not suggest an appropriate decision-making framework because it emphasizes hierarchical decision systems that respond to market forces; little deliberative democracy here.

On the other hand, conceptualizing the college and university as a republic in miniature, a city, provides a way to begin constructing an open forum which could make the decisions necessary to maintain the unity of these institutions, but at the same time to develop curricula which responds to felt social needs. If we are going to wade into dangerous waters, we will need to be sure that there are guidelines in place to help us resolve any conflicts over direction without lessening our commitments to one another and to the integrity of our institutions.

As examples of the kind of substantive issues we might debate, I offer citizenship, moral character, and the nature of the world of work. There are, of course, other concerns weighing on our students and we should endeavor to learn more about their realities as a bellwether for the future. Indeed, on a similar list I developed ten years ago, only citizenship was included. At that time, I selected the ability to undertake long range planning and the insight to decide what to conserve among those items, natural and historical, which our generation had been given as its inheritance. These concerns remain, I think, but morality and work appear to be larger challenges in the society we serve today.

In some ways, a return to substance is a return to the roots of liberal arts education in this country. Schools were founded in the nineteenth century with the intent of fostering leadership and moral development. We strayed from discussing these goals in order to give students and faculty their individuality and choice. However, there remain some issues that can only be resolved where scholars agree to collective action. I believe we are quickly coming upon those issues and should prepare ourselves to model for our society ways to regenerate conceptions of the common good.

References

Barber, B. (1984). *Strong democracy: Participatory politics for a new age.* Berkeley, CA: University of California Press.

Beiner, R. (Ed.). (1995). *Theorizing citizenship.* Albany, NY: State University of New York Press.

Bender, T. (1997). Locality and worldliness. *The transformation of humanistic studies in the twenty-first century: Opportunities and perils, 40,* 1–10. American Council of Learned Societies Occasional Paper. New York, NY.

Burns, J. M. (1978). *Leadership.* New York, NY: Harper & Row.

Dahl, R. (1970). *After the revolution.* New Haven, CT: Yale.

Davis, W. E., & Chandler, T. J. L. (1998). Beyond Boyer's *Scholarship Reconsidered:* Fundamental change in the university and the socioeconomic systems. *Journal of Higher Education, 69* (1), 23–64.

de Tocqueville, A. (1945). *Democracy in America, Volume I.* New York, NY: Knopf.

Fuller, T. (Ed.). (1989). *The voice of liberal learning: Michael Oakeshott on education.* New Haven, CT: Yale University Press.

Gamson, Z. (1997, January/February). Higher education and rebuilding civic life. *Change,* 10–13.

Goodman, P. (1964). *Compulsory Miseducation and the community of scholars.* New York, NY: Vintage.

Kidder, R. (1994). *Shared values for a troubled world.* San Francisco, CA: Jossey-Bass.

Nussbaum, M. (1988). *Cultivating humanity.* Cambridge, MA: Harvard University Press.

Schrag, P. (1998). *Paradise lost: California's experience, America's future.* New York, NY: The New Press.

ENDNOTES

1. I owe a particular debt to Philip Glotzbach, Vice President for Academic Affairs at the University of Redlands, for his careful reading and helpful suggestions. In addition, Eugene Rice discussed a number of aspects of this chapter with me and suggested readings that have greatly expanded my understanding of trends in higher education. I thank you both for your friendship and critical gifts.
2. Mr. Katz made these remarks at a national meeting of the American Association of Colleges and Universities several years ago which I attended.

3. I owe Philip Glotzbach for calling these issues to my attention.

4. The work of John Dewey in the past, and Richard Rorty in the present, come particularly to mind in this regard.

5. Amitai Etzioni is usually identified as the leader of the communitarian theorists, but a more inclusive list is the editorial board of the journal, *The Responsible Community: Rights and Responsibilities.*

26

Knowledge, Politics, and Interdisciplinary Education

Charles W. Anderson
University of Wisconsin, Madison

In a free society, we believe that people should think for themselves. Yet we also maintain an institution, the university, whose task it is to prescribe and to teach the better habits of mind, and we invest this institution with powerful sanctions to enforce its teachings.

We don't talk much about this mission. We don't talk much any more about truth, or excellence, or right and wrong. Academics find these topics disturbing. The dominant mood of the academy today is one of skepticism and irony. So we don't really reflect on the powers we have been vested with to shape thought. Rather, we go about our business routinely, teaching familiar doctrines, carrying out expected rituals.

Perhaps it is time for us to wake up. The university should be our most reflective institution. In fact, it has become one of the least self-conscious. The corporations, the military, governments at every level, all have fundamentally rethought their essential purposes in the past generation. They have engaged in deliberate, public, self-conscious reflection. But the universities now are among our most conservative institutions. We hardly discuss their missions and purposes at all.

The Educational Philosophies of Interdisciplinary Programs

The need to be fully self-conscious about educational purpose would seem to be particularly important for interdisciplinary liberal education programs. Such programs must be the most prescriptive of all. They exist, defiantly, to teach that there is a better way of teaching, a better ordering of knowledge, a better way to unlock the powers of the mind.

The mainstream institutions can afford to be more casual about their pedagogy. They can endorse a rough-and-ready intellectual pluralism. There are many different approaches to knowledge. Each has different expectations, procedures, and criteria of meaning and worth. There is no master theory that can define priorities or patterns among these disciplines. You may then study them as you wish. All the university will hold you accountable for are certain distribution requirements and a major, breadth and depth. The university simply teaches the disjointed array of the established disciplines. Beyond this, it does not need a philosophy.

But interdisciplinary programs are different. They propose that there are priorities, relationships, among the fields of knowledge. And they suggest that there are specific things that a liberally educated person should know and know how to do. Those of us who teach in liberal education programs take on an audacious responsibility to prescribe the life of the mind. And most of us do it passionately. But we really do have to be self-conscious and critical about all this: We have to be philosophical all the way down. We really do have to provide a justification for the ways in which we propose to shape the powers of the mind and spirit.

The basing point for any curriculum, I think, must be a theory of knowledge, an epistemology. One starts from some conception, some bold proposition, about the known and the knowable. From this the rest follows. One derives a moral philosophy, a conception of how life is properly lived, and a political philosophy, an ideal of civic responsibility, from the epistemology. I don't believe you can do it, with integrity, the other way around. You can't start with a political program and jury-rig an epistemology. That is pure hypocrisy. Morality and politics follow from epistemology. That is because we want these teachings to follow from our ideals of truth, or, what amounts to the same thing, our doubts and our skepticism.

What then are our options? The first step is for me to lay out a series of potential positions on the problem of knowledge which might serve as starting points for interdisciplinary liberal education programs in this time and place. We can examine these possibilities, perhaps embrace one as our own, perhaps take exception to some or to the entire lot, perhaps point up possibilities missed by the scheme.

However, my point is not just to set up taxonomy. Rather, I am going to suggest that very few will feel comfortable with the obvious alternatives when their full implications are spelled out. I then will go on to argue for a position I shall call pragmatic idealism. I shall try to show how this philosophy captures much of what we have taken to be the fundamental aims of liberal education in America in this century. But I shall also go on to show that this philosophy bears implications for our beliefs in the possibilities of knowledge and the powers of the mind that are far bolder and stronger than what is normally acceptable to the weary skepticism of the contemporary academy. I expect that some will endorse this position as a fair statement of their beliefs and values. I expect that others will turn back, aghast, at this absolute affront to their relativism. At this point, the argument can begin in earnest.

So that is the agenda. At the level of epistemology, I shall distinguish realist, relativist, and idealist positions. Realists believe that it is possible for the mind to contrive ideas that correspond to the actual order of things, both physical and moral. Relativists think that there are no guarantees that any human understanding can capture reality, that our systems of knowledge are at best metaphors, approximations, perspectives. I will use the term idealist to describe those that think ultimate reality is a big idea but also, in a more specifically Aristotelian sense, those who believe that people can be guided, and can correct and improve their performances in light of an ideal of essential purpose, of telos, that they do not know directly from experience, that they perhaps cannot define or articulate. This idealist affirmation, we shall see, has powerful pedagogic implications. It implies that individuals can transcend cultural understanding.

Politically, I shall distinguish liberal, conservative, and democratic implications that follow from the theory of knowledge behind an academic program. Educationally, liberals think that people must learn to think for themselves, autonomously, for most of life's choices concern alternatives where reason or science can prescribe no preferred answers. Conservatives believe that all knowledge is an inherited tradition, that we become human by learning to conform ourselves to the ways of our people. Democrats believe that knowledge is wrought within a community, through criticism, deliberation, and in the end, consensus and consent.

Let me now describe what I take to be the dominant current contending positions for a philosophy on which one might base a program of interdisciplinary liberal education.

CLASSICISM

Let us not forget that one of the first reasons for interdisciplinary studies in the American university was to demonstrate the unity of knowledge, to teach that truth is one. This was, of course, Cardinal Newman's understanding of the purpose of the university but it was also Robert Hutchins's rationale for the liberal education program he founded at the University of Chicago. Many such programs were Aristotelian in conception, and their vision of liberal education was coherent because

Aristotle's teachings are coherent, and integrate all fields of inquiry. Such programs are epistemologically realist in the strong sense, in a sense that in effect anchors one pole of our survey, for we shall find no bolder claims about truth and the educational design that follows from it made in this century. The political and moral teachings of such programs were similarly classical: They would inculcate an understanding of natural right and natural reason, for those that centered on Aristotle, of the way of life that leads to human flourishing, and the public order that permits the best expression of all the diverse human potentialities.

To my knowledge, the only institutions that sustain this philosophy unreservedly are Saint Thomas Aquinas College of San Francisco, which follows strictly in the Aristotelian-Thomistic legacy, and St. John's of Annapolis and Santa Fe, where the Great Books program introduced by Stringfellow Barr and Scott Buchanan in 1937 was intended, explicitly, to demonstrate the integrity of knowledge. I simply do not know if there are other institutions that sustain this commitment. As we shall soon see, such Great Books programs can have other epistemological foundations. Some Bible-based colleges do profess a single source of truth but they cannot make it stick as the core of the curriculum. Scripture simply cannot integrate a curriculum as classical rationalism can. Their treatment of most of the arts and sciences is generally quite conventional.

Conservative Culturism and Multiculturalism

There is a radical and generally unrecognized distinction between the theory of knowledge of the classical Great Books curriculum and its conservative counterpart. In the classical curriculum, the great texts taught the unity of truth. In the more common conception of this program, they are the great works of a particular tradition, of the Western heritage of thought. It may be suggested that this tradition is richer, or more ennobling, than others, or, particularly in the sciences, that it comes closer to the actual order of things. But it is acknowledged that there are alternatives.

There is a striking, sometimes terrifying, relativism at the very core of the thought of some of the strongest protagonists of this conservative conception of integrated education. One teaches the tradition because that is the only way we can find meaning in the world. The individual soul is no source of moral identity. Rather, individuals must enfold themselves in their culture to become selves. All we can know is embedded in these great frameworks and narratives. Thus they must be taught with great reverence and respect. Scrutinize them too closely, approach them with nonchalant, uncaring skepticism, and we fall into barbarism.

But do not ask too persistently if these teachings represent the truth. For the likes of Leo Strauss and Alan Bloom, there is a dreadful secret that the philosopher, the educator, must guard. For once you have penetrated to the heart of Plato, the foundation of it all, one will realize that Plato did not know the truth either. Hence, one must, as educator, ground one's life, and one's teaching, on a noble lie. One must teach the classics as though they were true knowing all along that they are not. This deepest, secret relativism is our only defense against an open, confessed relativism, an education that must end in nihilism, in the admission that we don't have a clue about what is really going on, an education that can only teach that anything goes.

The politics one teaches is a conservative politics of duty and respect. The ways of a people are all that gives life purpose and meaning. Teaching individualism, thinking for oneself, teaching self-definition and self-interest, can only end in license. One lives well by carrying out the customary roles as they are given, and performing them well, according to the standards of the community.

Multiculturalism

Today, the fiercest battles of the academy are waged between the proponents of different versions of culturism. There are those who teach Western culture as our best source of ideals, understanding, sensitivity, and commitment. And there are those who see Western culture as the political tool of the dominant, a vision that debases and discredits alternatives, that justifies the domination of some and the subordination and humiliation of others. For these, the central issue of contemporary education is to give voice to the perspectives of the victims, the neglected.

We think of Western culture and multiculturalism as radical poles, the extreme left and right of the politics of the academy. We do not often recognize that these two educational philosophies seem to share a common conservative epistemology. For the multiculturalists, generally, also take the view that the individual is a product of culture, that who we are, what we think of ourselves, and what we are destined to become depends on the norms, mores, customs, and values we are taught. This is why it is so important to expose cultures of debasement, and to make plausible alternative cultures that give dignity.

The multiculturalist teaches tolerance, for all ways of life have their own validity, none represents the richer understanding by which the others may be judged. This tolerance for diverse ways of life seems consistent with our belief in equal individual rights and equal respect, and we begin to think it liberal. But in fact it is profoundly the opposite. In effect, the multiculturalist must teach that there are ways of thinking and being that are distinctive for African Americans, Hispanics, women. In such a teaching there can really be no place for the large, certain, universal propositions about human rights and human nature that constitute the liberal frame of mind, and that serve the liberal as categoric criteria for judging all cultural conventions, all narratives, all folkways.

As we shall see shortly, one can bring other epistemological commitments to the teaching of multiculturalism. It is not what is taught but the philosophy behind it that matters. What I want to stress at this point is that the relativism behind the teaching of Western culture as an integrating theme for liberal education, as the conservatism that may accompany multicultural approaches, often goes unnoticed.

Positivist Science and Liberal Individualism

Two positions that fit together only in uneasy tension have long formed an underlying epistemology and politics for American higher education.

For much of this century, the dispositions of the scientist have been taken to be the dispositions of mind that should be cultivated by all the arts and sciences. The preferred stance of the educated individual is that of the detached observer: cool, impartial, analytical. The object of inquiry is to reduce nature and human behavior to law-like statement without reference to design or intention. Thus, statements about natural order must be reduced to raw interactions of mindless matter. Similarly, human behavior must be reduced to unconscious cause or interest. Manifest design or purpose does not count. Thus, the scientific explanation of the American Constitution cannot be that James Madison et al. thought it a good idea. The actual cause must lie deeper. In positivist epistemology, such mindless explanations are what count as knowledge, or truth.

This idea of underlying epistemology may still be recognized in many interdisciplinary programs, particularly, I suppose, where the natural sciences and the harder social sciences meet, as in medicine, and sometimes, policy studies.

The overt politics of such programs would seem to be the preparation of experts, those who will apply scientific techniques to the resolution of human problems. And such is indeed often the avowed aim. But today it is hard to sustain such a view unabashedly. The country is increasingly taking a dim view of the pretensions of experts. The legacy of Jeremy Bentham, Auguste Comte, and Karl Marx is not ascendant. We still believe, though with greater hesitation than before, in the social value of scientific analysis. But we do not want to be governed by experts.

There is another political implication to positivism, obvious when you see it though it is seldom discussed. The central epistemological assumption of positivism is that questions of fact can be settled scientifically but not questions of values. Nothing scientific can be said about questions of morals or politics. These must be left to the individual.

Thus does the dominant view of scientific understanding in our time merge with the most important tenets of our liberal public philosophy. For the fundamental grounds of classic liberal political thought, the axiom on which all our doctrines of individual right and individual equality depend, is the proposition, rooted in deepest skepticism, that no one, no elite, no philosophers, no teachers, know enough to tell another how to live. The definition of the meaning of life and its purposes rests entirely with each individual.

The pedagogy that follows should be clear enough. In scientific matters, one is called to a rigorous, objective, and collective intellectual discipline. In politics and moral matters, however, the object is that you learn to "think for yourself." The object of the teacher is to promote individual autonomy. The regimen is familiar. First comes the inculcation of skepticism. One is taught to question, to doubt, received belief: cultural, familial, political, religious. Then one is presented with diverse perspectives, problems, alternatives. One is told to make up one's own mind, for one's own reasons, and that, while there may be better and worse reasons, there are no right and wrong answers. The teaching is familiar. We have all experienced it. Some who read this may believe in it desperately, to the bottom of their souls. Others may believe this is not quite good enough.

For the moment, it is enough to note the incredible, categoric opposition between the potential bases for integrated education presented so far. The classic view that we should teach the unity of truth is not at all the view that we must fix in the mind the wisdom of culture, is not at all the view that we must bring students to question authority, so they can proceed on their own, as autonomous individuals. The cleavages within the academy are deep and fundamental. And there is more to come.

Intellectual Pluralism

The assumption of many who teach in interdisciplinary programs is precisely the reverse of Robert Hutchins's belief that the aim of liberal education is to demonstrate the unity of knowledge. Rather, the position of many educators in such programs is that there are diverse approaches to knowledge, none is sovereign, but that a fair appreciation of the problem must take into account specifiable diverse perspectives.

Such intellectual pluralism would seem to connote a relativist epistemology. Yet, I suspect that behind many interdisciplinary programs there lurks a strong, elusive, but determined streak of realism.

Most interdisciplinary programs do not rest on the assumption that anything goes. Rather, they are structured on the basis of a specific, delimited set of disciplinary perspectives that are deemed to have particular bearing on the subject at hand. Often, the relationship that the student is to see among these disciplines is kept deliberately vague. It hovers, like an Aristotelian essence. Nonetheless, the special quality of these realist interdisciplinary programs is that the student is expected to see *particular* relationships among the teachings. And it is also assumed that some of the conclusions a student might draw from contemplation of these diverse perspectives will simply be wrong.

Consider an orthodox environmental studies program, which might include ecological, evolutionary and microbiology, earth science and climatology, politics, economics, environmental ethics, and environmental law. This is no random selection of subjects thrown together helter-skelter. The intellectual perspectives are certainly diverse, but how each should contribute to a student's appreciation of an environmental problem can be stipulated. In such a program, it is possible to adjudge the solutions proposed by the student, to say that some are better than others, and that some are clearly wrong. The assumptions may conflict with others taught in the university. Thus, the student who reduces all considerations to a utilitarian calculus of gain and loss is right in economics, and wrong in environmental studies. Positivist reduction does not work in such programs. A conception of holistic relationships does.

The classic integrated education scheme of Hutchins may seem poles apart from the pluralist environmental studies program. But how far are such programs—or comparable efforts in other areas and in liberal education generally—from intimating that there might be an implicit unity to knowledge?

There are indeed pluralist approaches to liberal education that rest on a relativist epistemology. The students are presented with a diverse array of approaches and perspectives and asked to decide for themselves what to make of them. The purpose of presenting diverse approaches is to create a problematic situation, to require introspection and, in the end, a personal resolution of an enigma. It is not assumed that the teachers can call some of these resolutions right and others wrong. They may judge them for subtlety, or consistency, or even literary merit, but they do not adjudge the truth value of the products.

The political implications of relativist pluralism must be akin to skeptical, individualist liberalism. The aim is to confront the individual with the need to achieve a personal resolution of a dilemma, without authoritative guidance on how this should be done. But if the politics of relativist pluralism are the same as those of liberal individualism, those of realist pluralism must verge on Aristotelianism.

Postmodernism

Today, the most radical version of relativist pluralism is usually described as postmodernism. Postmodernists are taken to believe that we are living in the waning days of the modern era, which is to say, the age that believed in the objective realism of science and reason. But we have become self-conscious. We know that all our systems of thought and understanding are but human constructs, historically contingent. They do not mirror nature; we could think otherwise.

The pedagogy of postmodernism is derived from literary criticism. The object of analysis is to deconstruct a text, to take it apart, to show how it achieves its effects. This is clearly important to the education of authors and readers. It may be important to liberal education generally.

To reveal that our knowledge is human contrivance is not something we should associate with relativist epistemologies alone. It is absolutely essential to many forms of realism, particularly pragmatism and other approaches that take inquiry to be an unending process of discovery, of the correction and perfection of existing beliefs and practices.

To teach the history of any art or science is to demonstrate how the human artifact was constructed. It is to show the false moves and the pitfalls, the promising openings that were neglected. It is to point up continuing anomalies, puzzles, and outright contradictions in our prevailing modes of understanding. The point of all this is to prepare students to participate in the life of a discipline, a calling, to encourage their curiosity and creativity, to invite them to try to do better than we have done so far.

In radical postmodernism, however, the motives behind the method of deconstruction may be different. Postmodernism becomes associated with a strong, and somewhat peculiar, political position. Following the philosophic guidance of the likes of Michel Foucault and Jacques Derrida, the purpose of deconstruction now is to reveal the ways in which intellectual structures enforce power relations, insinuating the domination of some and the subordination of others.

The political result of all of this would seem to be a kind of Nietzschean anarchism. The object is to disenchant the student, leaving the student free to confront the manifest meaninglessness of the world. (The individual autonomy sought by Nietzscheanism is not at all like liberal individualism. Liberalism rests on the idea that quite explicit principles of right follow from a recognition of the capacity of individuals to decide their own destinies.)

How this political motive came to be associated with deconstruction and critical theory is not at all clear. It is not a necessary entailment. But this has become a widespread, insistent pedagogy in recent years and, for all I know, it may be the implicit guiding theme of some interdisciplinary education programs.

Pragmatism and Idealism

I suspect that many who teach in interdisciplinary education programs will think either the realist or relativist version of intellectual pluralism a shoe that fits rather well. But if so, I want to challenge them with a further possibility. I want to see if they will dare to accept the commitments that go with a philosophy I shall call pragmatic idealism.

Philosophic pragmatism had a great influence on American higher education in this century. Its influence is still apparent in the research traditions and the pedagogy of many disciplines. Many interdisciplinary education programs, orthodox and experimental, can trace their origins, at least in part, to Dewey.

Unfortunately, today, the misunderstanding of the meaning of pragmatism is great and general. Philosophically, pragmatism is anything but the doctrine of raw expediency with which the term is usually associated in the popular media. (So many of the important words have been undermined by the media, including liberal, conservative, morality, practicality, and politics itself, that serious discussion has almost become impossible.) However, even within the academy today, there is considerable confusion about the meaning of pragmatism.

Many would associate pragmatism with a gentle relativism. Pragmatism would seem to suggest an open and flexible approach to liberal education, experimental, attuned to diverse perspectives and interpretations, fallibilist, both communitarian and individual in its idea of inquiry. And all of this is true. However, there are also strong realist and idealist elements in philosophic pragmatism. These cannot be overlooked or brushed aside. They are necessary implications of this philosophic perspective. And they are what I think make this realist and idealist version of pragmatism the most interesting and challenging vision of liberal education available today.

Philosophic pragmatism, in fact, has little enough in common with contemporary skepticism, iconoclasm, and relativism. The great pragmatic philosophers, Peirce, James, and Dewey, were, after all, grappling with the problem of truth. And they taught that the ability of our ideas to work well in practice, to work reliably, time after time, in diverse contexts, was the best assurance that finite minds could have that we might actually be getting at the underlying order of things.

When our ideas don't work out in practice, when they don't fit the way the world actually works, we are puzzled and perplexed. And so we inquire, we explore and correct, we experiment, until we find a new pattern of ideas, of beliefs we can act on, reliably, dependably, until we end in puzzlement once more.

This is, the pragmatists taught, ideally the method of science. But it applies to morality and politics as well: it is ideally the method of democracy. It is when we, as a people, come to sense that our practices are unjust, not rightful, that we become troubled and perplexed, and so we inquire, and criticize, we explore, we look for a better way.

Pragmatism seems to me to be the only 20th century philosophy that takes mind seriously. Most of our disciplines try to explain it away: economics as the endless calculation of gain and loss, psychology as stimulus and response, anthropology as cultural adaptation to the survival needs of the species, and so on. But for pragmatism, humans are essentially inquirers. We are the species that tries to figure out who we are, where we are, and then—most fatefully—what we are expected to do. Pragmatism, I believe, is our last great link to the classic tradition, the tradition that took philosophy seriously.

Pragmatism takes a progressive view of knowledge. Unlike fashionable culturism, or relativist intellectual pluralism, we aren't just spinning our wheels, trading impressions. Rather, if we think together analytically, critically, systematically, trying things out, checking them out, looking for a better way, we might actually learn something, get a better glimpse of our nature and the nature of the world.

Like contemporary relativism, pragmatism is open to diverse viewpoints. But unlike the fashionable contemporary relativisms, pragmatism is not merely tolerant, tolerant because it believes no culture, no practice, no system of belief can be shown to be better than another. Rather, for pragmatism, diversity of opinion necessarily sets the stage for inquiry. In the face of divided opinion, in order to act, in order to go on, we have to ask: Which is the better way? How shall we now proceed?

Politically, pragmatism teaches a daunting view of democracy. The ideal democracy is like an ideal scientific community of inquiry. We come to closer approximations to scientific understanding by seeking consensus through critical deliberation, in a community dedicated to constant scrutiny of its own doctrines and practices. If democracy could operate in the same way, would we not develop laws and policies that might come closer to our intuitive sense of justice, our intimations of our essential purposes?

Central to the political theory of pragmatism then is the remarkable proposition that the habits of mind of the scholar should become the habits of mind of the citizen. To weary, cynical contemporary relativists and culturists, this may seem preposterous. But consider. Is this not precisely the vision of the education of citizens that has animated many of our programs of integrated liberal education through the years?

Is this a worthy vision for liberal education in our time? Not all will readily concur. The culturist will not necessarily accept the idea that if we critically examine our beliefs and practices, individually and collectively, we may be able to transcend them, to achieve an understanding and a way that is closer to an elusive ideal of our purpose and destiny that exists only in our minds.

The relativist pluralists will not readily accept the idea that we can examine our diverse approaches to understanding, and appraise them, not only by their results, but by their worthiness, their correspondence with our ideal sense of what is meaningful and false, excellent and wanting, right and wrong.

The rigorous positivists will dismiss out of hand the notion that we can find intimations of moral order through the explorations of the mind every bit as trustworthy as the patterns we now impute to meaningless matter.

In other words, to adopt the seemingly down-to-earth philosophy of pragmatism as an ideal for integrated liberal education is to accept the view of the powers of the human mind and spirit that was taught by Socrates, Aristotle, Jesus of Nazareth, Thomas Aquinas, Kant, Hegel, Mill, and, most recently, Dewey.

But if you accept that, what becomes of your fashionable skepticism, culturism, postmodernism, relativism? Can this vision actually square with the worldly irony, the iconoclasm, of the contemporary academy?

It is not so much that this vision of pragmatism and idealism goes so very much beyond things that we ordinarily believe about the purposes of education and the life of the mind. It is rather that we are not used to having the fullest implications of these beliefs and convictions made manifest. I do not expect everyone to accept these implications. But I think some will. I think some will affirm that such an ideal does capture their deepest commitments as teachers. And then, we can carry on from here.

INDEX